MARSHALL'S
PRINCIPLES OF ECONOMICS

ALFRED MARSHALL at about the time of the publication
of the first edition of his *Principles of Economics*

ALFRED MARSHALL

PRINCIPLES OF ECONOMICS

NINTH (VARIORUM) EDITION

WITH ANNOTATIONS BY

C. W. GUILLEBAUD

VOLUME II

NOTES

LONDON
MACMILLAN AND CO LIMITED
FOR THE
ROYAL ECONOMIC SOCIETY

NEW YORK
THE MACMILLAN COMPANY
1961

Ninth (Variorum) Edition 1961

Printed in Great Britain at the University Press, Cambridge
(Brooke Crutchley, University Printer)

CONTENTS

v

BOOK II

SOME FUNDAMENTAL NOTIONS

BOOK III

ON WANTS AND THEIR SATISFACTION

BOOK IV

THE AGENTS OF PRODUCTION
LAND, LABOUR, CAPITAL AND
ORGANIZATION

BOOK V

GENERAL RELATIONS OF DEMAND, SUPPLY AND VALUE

BOOK VI

THE DISTRIBUTION OF THE NATIONAL INCOME

CONTENTS

EDITORIAL INTRODUCTION

EDITORIAL INTRODUCTION

1. ALFRED MARSHALL 1842–1924[a]

Alfred Marshall was born at Clapham on 26 July 1842, his father being William Marshall, a cashier at the Bank of England.

On the date of Marshall's birth Ricardo had been dead only nineteen years, Malthus only eight years; while the first edition of John Stuart Mill's *Principles of Political Economy* was published in 1848 when Marshall was six years old. Stanley Jevons was not quite seven years his senior. Marshall was therefore the contemporary, or almost the contemporary, of the most famous English economists of the nineteenth century. The main formative period of his life coincided with the heyday of Victorian England, and in many characteristic respects he was an "eminent Victorian".

At the age of nine Marshall went to Merchant Taylors' School where he remained till he entered St John's College, Cambridge, in 1861, when he was nineteen. At school he had been primarily a classic and was entitled under an old foundation to an entrance scholarship and later a Fellowship in classics at St John's College, Oxford. But he also had great mathematical ability, and despite the opposition of his father, it was as a mathematician that he entered St John's College, Cambridge, thanks to a loan he received from an uncle who had made a fortune sheep-farming in Australia. He was Second Wrangler in the Mathematical Tripos in 1865, the year that Lord Rayleigh was Senior Wrangler. Marshall was at once elected to a Fellowship at St John's College and for a year or two he taught mathematics until he had repaid the debt he owed to his uncle. At the same time he was reading philosophy, especially Kant and Hegel,

---

[a] Having regard to the admirable biographical memoir of Marshall by Lord Keynes, reprinted from the *Economic Journal* of August 1924 in Keynes's *Essays in Biography* (pp. 150–266) and also in the *Memorials of Alfred Marshall* edited by A. C. Pigou (pp. 1–65), I have confined myself to stating in outline the main facts of Marshall's life and career.

and was becoming increasingly interested in questions of human welfare, which led him from metaphysics to ethics and psychology, and finally to his life's study—economics.

There is an excellent characterization of Marshall at this early stage in his career in a study of him by P. T. Homan:

It is possible thus to see what manner of young man it was who ceased his mathematical lectures in 1868 and took up a new lectureship in the Moral Sciences, specially founded for him at St John's College at the instance of the Master, Dr Bateson, where his weight listed the ship sharply to the side of political economy. A brilliant mathematician, a young philosopher carrying a somewhat undigested load of German metaphysics, Utilitarianism and Darwinism; a humanitarian with religious feelings but no creed, eager to lighten the burdens of mankind, but sobered by the barriers revealed to him by the Ricardian Political Economy—one sees the background of the man who was to be to his students sage and pastor as well as scientist; whose objective scientific approach was to give economics a renewed public standing; whose sympathy for social reform was to rout its enemies; whose high gifts were to be as zealously devoted to his intellectual mistress as any artist's to his muse.[a]

For the next nine years Marshall continued at Cambridge, lecturing in logic and economics for the Moral Sciences Tripos, and working out the basis of his system of economic thought.

In 1877 he married Mary Paley, who was one of the first students at Newnham College for women at Cambridge, and who had been his pupil when she was reading for the Moral Sciences Tripos. Under the then prevailing college statutes Marshall was compelled to vacate his Fellowship at St John's College on marriage; and he left Cambridge for Bristol, where he became the first Principal of the University College and Professor of Political Economy.

While still at Bristol Marshall brought out in 1879, in collaboration with his wife, *The Economics of Industry*, a small text-book designed as a manual for use by Cambridge University extension lecturers. In the same year Henry Sidgwick printed with Marshall's permission for private circulation a fragment consisting of four chapters (not consecutive) of a treatise on "The Theory of Foreign Trade, with some

[a] P. T. Homan, *Contemporary Economic Thought*, pp. 197–8.

allied problems relating to the doctrine of Laisser Faire",[a] on which Marshall had been engaged since 1869. The treatise as a whole was never published, but a few fragments of the original manuscript survived and are now preserved in the Marshall Library.

Marshall had not been long at Bristol before his health broke down as a result of a stone in the kidney, and he resigned his post in 1881. After a year of rest in Italy, during which, however, he did important work in economic theory, he was able to return to England. Thanks to his friendship with Benjamin Jowett, the Master of Balliol, he was elected a Fellow of Balliol College, Oxford, in succession to Arnold Toynbee who had just died; and lectured in economics to Indian Civil Service probationers.

On the death of Henry Fawcett in November 1884, Marshall was elected in January 1885 as Professor of Political Economy in the University of Cambridge, a chair which he held for twenty-three years until he retired in 1908 in order to be able to devote the remainder of his life to writing. He was then sixty-six years of age, and he lived for another sixteen years at Balliol Croft, the house which he had had built for himself in the Madingley Road, and where he died on 13 July 1924, within a few days of his eighty-second birthday.

Marshall published the book on which his fame chiefly rests, the *Principles of Economics*, in 1890 at the age of forty-eight and continued to revise it at intervals during the remainder of his life: the eighth and last edition appeared in 1920, only four years before his death. The publication of his other major works, *Industry and Trade* (1919) and *Money Credit and Commerce* (1923) was delayed until his old age; though a good deal of the material contained in them had been written many years earlier.

Much of Marshall's best work, apart from the *Principles*, is to be found in the evidence he gave before such bodies as the Gold and Silver Commission, 1887, the Indian Currency

---

[a] This paper, entitled "The Pure Theory of Foreign Trade. The Pure Theory of Domestic Values", by Alfred Marshall, was reprinted in facsimile by the London School of Economics in 1930 as no. 1 in their series of Reprints of Scarce Tracts in Economics and Politics.

Committee, 1899, the Royal Commission on Local Taxation, etc. This evidence was collected and published after his death in *The Official Papers of Alfred Marshall*, edited by A. C. Pigou, 1926. A selection from his letters and contributions to journals was published in the *Memorials of Alfred Marshall*, edited by A. C. Pigou, 1925, which also contained the Memoir written by Keynes.

Finally, mention should be made of an achievement which Marshall himself ranked high amongst the successes of life. In 1903, nearly at the end of his teaching career, he succeeded in persuading the University of Cambridge to establish a separate Tripos, or Honours School, in Economics and Politics, thereby liberating economics from its subordination to philosophy and academic psychology with which it had previously been joined in the Moral Sciences Tripos.

2. THE BACKGROUND OF THE *PRINCIPLES*

There is a considerable amount of autobiographical material in various of Marshall's writings which throws light on the development of the economic ideas which were subsequently embodied in the *Principles*, and it would seem best to let his own words speak for him.

The following account,[a] taken from Keynes's Memoir, was written by Marshall for a German compilation of portraits and short lives of leading economists:

While still giving private lessons in mathematics,[b] he translated as many as possible of Ricardo's reasonings into mathematics; and he endeavoured to make them more general. Meanwhile he was attracted towards the new views of economics taken by Roscher and other German economists; and by Marx, Lassalle and other Socialists. But it seemed to him that the analytical methods of the historical economists were not always sufficiently thorough to justify their confidence that the causes which they assigned to economic events were the true causes. He thought indeed that the interpretation of the economic past was almost as difficult as the prediction of the future. The Socialists also seemed to him to underrate the difficulty of their problems, and to be too quick to assume that the abolition of private

a *Memorials of Alfred Marshall*, edited by A. C. Pigou, pp. 20–1.
b In 1867.

6

property would purge away the faults and deficiencies of human nature.
...He set himself to get into closer contact with practical business
and with the life of the working classes. On the one side he aimed
at learning the broad features of the technique of every chief industry;
and on the other he sought the society of trade unionists, co-operators
and other working-class leaders. Seeing, however, that direct studies
of life and work would not yield much fruit for many years he decided
to fill the interval by writing a separate monograph or special treatise
on Foreign Trade; for the chief facts relating to it can be obtained
from printed documents. He proposed that this should be the first of a
group of monographs on special economic problems; and he hoped
ultimately to compress these monographs into a general treatise of a
similar scope to Mill's. After writing that larger treatise, but not
before, he thought he might be ready to write a short popular treatise.
He has never changed his opinion that this is the best order of work;
but his plans were overruled, and almost inverted, by the force of
circumstances. He did indeed write the first draft of a monograph on
Foreign Trade; and in 1875 he visited the chief seats of industry in
America with the purpose of studying the problem of Protection in a
new country. But this work was suspended by his marriage; and
while engaged, in conjunction with his wife, in writing a short account
of the Economics of Industry, forcibly simplified for working-class
readers, he contracted an illness so serious that for some time he
appeared unlikely to be able to do any more hard work. A little later
he thought his strength might hold out for recasting his diagrammatic
illustrations of economic problems. Though urged by the late Professor
Walras about 1873 to publish these, he had declined to do so; because
he feared that if separated from all concrete study of actual conditions,
they might seem to claim a more direct bearing on real problems than
they in fact had. He began, therefore, to supply some of the requisite
limitations and conditions, and thus was written the kernel of the
fifth book of his *Principles*. From that kernel the present volume was
extended gradually backwards and forwards, till it reached the form
in which it was published in 1890.

The foregoing summary is amplified in some directions
in a footnote appended to the preface to the first edition:

Many of the diagrams in this book have appeared in print already:
and I may take this opportunity of giving their history. Mr Henry
Cunynghame who was attending my lectures in 1873, seeing me
annoyed by being unable to draw a series of rectangular hyperbolas,
invented a beautiful and original machine for the purpose. It was shown
at the Cambridge Philosophical Society in 1873; and, to explain
its use, I read a paper (briefly reported in the *Proceedings*, Part xv,

pp. 318–19), in which I described the theories of Multiple Positions of Equilibrium and of Monopoly values very nearly as they are given below (Book V, chs. v and viii). In 1875–7 I nearly completed a draft of a treatise on "The Theory of Foreign Trade, with some allied problems relating to the doctrine of Laisser Faire". The first Part of it was intended for general use, while the second Part was technical; nearly all the diagrams that are now in Book V, chs.[a] v, vii and viii were introduced in it, in connection with the problem of the relation of Protection to the Maximum Satisfaction of the community; and there were others relating to Foreign Trade. But in 1877 I turned aside to work at the *Economics of Industry*, and afterwards was overtaken by an illness, which nearly suspended my studies for several years. Meanwhile the MSS. of my first projected treatise were lying idle: and it is to them that Professor Sidgwick refers in the Preface to his *Political Economy*. With my consent he selected four chapters (not consecutive) out of the second Part, and printed them for private circulation. These four chapters contained most of the substance of Book V, chs. v and vii, but not ch. viii of the present work; together with two chapters relating to the equilibrium of foreign trade.[b] They have been sent to many economists in England and on the Continent: it is of them that Jevons speaks in the Preface to the second edition of the "Theory" (p. xlv); and many of the diagrams in them relating to foreign trade have been reproduced with generous acknowledgments by Prof. Pantaleoni in his *Principii di Economia Pura*.

Further light is thrown on the origins and development of Marshall's thought by the following extracts from three letters that he wrote to J. B. Clark.

I note what you say of von Thünen, the great unrecognised, with special pleasure. I cannot recollect whether I formulated the doctrine "normal wage" = "terminal" (I got "marginal" from von Thünen's *Grenze*) productivity of labour before I read von Thünen or not. I think I did so partially at least; for my acquaintance with economics commenced with reading Mill, while I was still earning my living by teaching Mathematics at Cambridge; and translating his doctrines into differential equations as far as they would go; and, as a rule, rejecting those which would not go. On that ground I rejected the wage-doctrine in Book II, which has a wage-fund flavour: and accepted that in Book IV; in which he seemed to me to be true to the best traditions of Ricardo's method (I say nothing in defence of Ricardo's

[a] Book V, chapters v, vii and viii in the 1st ed. correspond to Book V, chapter xii, with Appendix H, and chapters xiii and xiv in vol. i, of the present edition.
[b] The wording of this sentence is somewhat ambiguous. There were only four chapters in all—two on Foreign Trade and two on Domestic Trade.

positive doctrine of wages) and then to have got very close to what I afterwards found to be von Thünen's position. That was chiefly in 1867–8. I fancy I read Cournot in 1868. I know I did not read von Thünen then, probably in 1869 or 70: for I did not know enough German. One side of my own theory of wages has been absolutely fixed ever since, to what by title of priority may be called the von Thünen doctrine. But I thought then, and think still, that it covers only a very small part of the real difficulties of the wages problem.[a]

I may say that my doctrine of quasi-rent, though only gradually developed, took on substance in 1868; when I was very much exercised by McLeod's criticisms—now unjustly forgotten—on the unqualified statement that cost governs value. He said: "Your economist tells you that the wages and profits of people in the iron trade govern the price of iron; but they themselves know better; they know that the price of iron governs their wages and profits". I then started out on a theory of value in which I conceded to McLeod all that he asserted *for short periods*: and in effect, though not in name and not at all clearly, I regarded wages and profits as of the nature of rents for short periods. That went with my translations of all leading economic doctrines into differential equations: and, as far as I can tell, there is no broad difference on *that* side between my position before 1870 and now. But of course in other directions I have changed much. I then believed it was possible to have a coherent though abstract doctrine of economics in which competition was the only dominant force; and I then defined "normal" as that which the undisturbed play of competition would bring about: and now I regard that position as untenable from an abstract as well as from a practical point of view.[b]

I have in earlier years eaten my heart out with doubt and anxiety as to what acknowledgements I should make to others. I fear I am an awful sinner: but I have grown callous. My rule has been to refer in a footnote to anyone whom I know to have said a thing before I have said it in print, even though I may have said it in lectures for many years before I knew that it had ever occurred to him: I just refer, but say nothing about obligations either way; being quite aware that people will suppose me to imply obligations. Instances are Francis Walker and Fleeming Jenkin.

But perhaps in return for your good-natured confidence I may state the reason which has prevented me from making general acknowledgements in any Preface except the first. It is that my main position as to the theory of value and distribution was practically completed in

[a] *Memorials of Alfred Marshall*, pp. 412–13; letter dated 2 July 1900.
[b] *Ibid.* p. 414; letter dated 11 November 1902. See also letter to Edgeworth (p. 809 below).

the years 1867 to 1870; when I translated Mill's version of Ricardo's or Smith's doctrines into mathematics; and that, when Jevons' book appeared, I knew at once how far I agreed with him and how far I did not. In the next four years I worked a good deal at the mathematical theory of monopolies, and at the diagrammatic treatment of Mill's problem of international values (parts of this were printed by Pantaleoni in a kindly way in his *Principii di Economia Pura*).

By this time I had practically completed the whole of the substance of my Mathematical Appendix, the only important exception being the treatment of elasticity (Note III) and Edgeworth's contract curve Note XII *bis*.[a]

Substantially my theory of capital as it exists today is completely outlined in Notes V and XIII–XIV; and my general theory of distribution (except in so far as relates to the element of time) is in like manner contained in Note XXI; to which the preceding notes and especially XIV–XX lead up. I worked that out for the greater part while still teaching mathematics; and while still regarding myself as a mere pupil in the hands of great masters, especially Cournot, von Thünen and Ricardo; and while still extremely ignorant of economic realities. Between 1870 and 1874 I developed the details of my theoretical position; and I am not conscious of any perceptible change since the time when Böhm Bawerk and Wieser were still lads at school or College....

... I scarcely ever read controversies or criticisms. I have not read even a quarter of those which have been written about myself. The books, for instance, which I take to the Alps nearly every summer are almost exclusively concerned with matters of fact; though I try to read or skim any piece of analysis in which a man works to produce knowledge and not to controvert others. Thus I could not make acknowledgements to others properly; and I fall back on the plan already mentioned of referring in silence to any anticipation, of which I am aware, of a suggestion made by myself.

My whole life has been and will be given to presenting in realistic form as much as I can of my Note XXI.[b] If I live to complete my scheme fairly well, people will, I think, realise that it has unity and individuality. And a man who has lost ten of the best years of his life— from 37 to 47—through illness, would, I think, be doubly foolish if he troubled himself to weigh and measure any claims to originality that he has.

One thing alone in American criticism irritates me, though it be not unkindly meant. It is the suggestion that I try to "compromise

a The numbering of the Notes in the Mathematical Appendix, referred to here and throughout this letter, is identical with that in the 8th edition of the *Principles*.

b Note XXI dates from the 1st ed., where it was numbered XX. From the 2nd ed. onwards it was numbered XXI.

between" or "reconcile" divergent schools of thought. Such work seems to me a trumpery. Truth is the only thing worth having: not peace. I have never compromised on any doctrine of any kind. As to the use of terms, that is a matter of mere opportunism and everyone should, I think, not merely compromise but positively yield against his own judgment, if he thinks that by so doing he can facilitate mutual understandings. For that reason I have shifted my use of the word capital, but I have not changed my doctrines as to capital by a hair's breadth: Irving Fisher seems to have misread me in this matter.[a]

There are certain published works of Marshall, antecedent to the *Principles*, to which the attention of students of that book should be drawn. These are, in chronological order:

(1) The review in the *Academy*, 1872, of "Mr Jevons' Theory of Political Economy".[b] Many years later Marshall wrote of this:[c]

That article is the first of the kind I ever wrote, and is particularly crude in form. But it contains the kernel of the theory of distribution which I hold to-day: it is based in the first instance on Adam Smith, Malthus and Ricardo, and in the second on von Thünen as regards substance, and Cournot as regards the form of the thought. On many aspects of economics I have learnt more from Jevons than from any one else. But the obligations which I had to acknowledge in the Preface to my *Principles* were to Cournot and von Thünen and not to Jevons.

(2) The article in the *Fortnightly Review*, April 1786, on "Mr Mills' Theory of Value".[d] This consisted mainly in a defence of Mill against criticisms that had been levied against him by Cairnes.

(3) The four chapters out of a projected treatise on "The Theory of Foreign Trade, with some allied problems on the Doctrines of Laisser Faire" which were printed for private circulation in 1879 by Henry Sidgwick under the title *Pure Theory of Foreign Trade. Pure Theory of Domestic Values*.[e] The two chapters on Domestic Values contained the substance of his long period supply curves.[f]

---

[a] *Memorials*, pp. 416–18; letter dated 24 March 1908.
[b] *Memorials*, pp. 93–9. [c] *Ibid*. p. 100.
[d] *Ibid*. pp. 119–33. [e] See above, p. 7.
[f] Cf. Marshall's footnote, pp. 7–8 above.

(4) Also in 1879 appeared the ªEconomics of Industry by Alfred and Mary Paley Marshall. This had originally been commissioned from Mary Paley to serve as a small introductory text-book on economics in connexion with Cambridge University extension lectures. It ended up by being very much Marshall's own work. It had, however, been no part of his scheme of things to publish his ideas first in an elementary form, and he came to regard this little book with disfavour,ᵇ eventually withdrawing it from circulation after the publication of the *Principles*,ᶜ mainly on the ground that it had attempted the impossible. "You cannot", he used to say, "tell the truth for half a crown." The scope of the book can be seen from the following extract from the Preface which Marshall wrote for its second edition in 1881:

The present volume contains an outline of the theory of Value, Wages and Profits. This theory as it was left by English Economists of the last generation made too great pretensions to finality; and by a natural reaction their work has been severely criticised. But on the whole the progress of inquiry has tended to vindicate it, and to show that while much of it is very incomplete, there is but little in the careful exposition of it given by John Stuart Mill which is not, when properly interpreted, true as far as it goes.

It seems however necessary to go a good way apart from Mill with regard to one important question. He never worked out fully the applications of his own principles to the theory of Distribution: his last utterance on the question in his review of Thornton, left part of it avowedly in an unsatisfactory state; he gave indeed some hints as to the direction in which a solution was to be looked for, but he did not pretend to work it out himself. In this volume an attempt is made to supply the solution, and to show that there is a unity underlying all the different parts of the theory of prices, wages and profits. The remuneration of every kind of work, the interest on capital, and the prices of commodities, are determined in the long run by competition

ª It should be noted that in 1892 Marshall published *Elements of Economics of Industry*, which was a very different book from the *Economics of Industry* of 1879; for apart from a chapter on Trade Unions, it was merely a much abridged version of the *Principles*.

ᵇ Cf. Marshall's own words, p. 7 above.

ᶜ When Marshall sent my father (his brother-in-law) a complimentary copy of the first edition of his *Principles of Economics* in 1890, he insisted on the return for destruction of the copy of *Economics of Industry* which had previously been presented to my father; as the latter was a country parson and no economist, he was dubiously the gainer by the exchange.

12

according to what is fundamentally the same law. This law of Normal Value has many varieties of detail and takes many different forms. But in every form it exhibits value as determined by certain relations of demand and supply; and Cost of Production as taking the chief place among the causes that influence supply. The Second Book begins with a general statement of this law as applied to commodities. This is followed by a discussion of some peculiarities that are found in the laws of supply of unskilled labour, of skilled labour and of business power. The ground is thus cleared for the inquiry how Normal demand and supply determine first the share of the joint produce of capital and industry which goes as interest to capital, and secondly how the share that goes to industry is divided among its different ranks. The volume ends with a discussion of the way in which the Normal action of economic forces is hindered, or even overridden, but never destroyed by friction, by combination or by those passing events which exercise a restless influence on Market values.

The *Economics of Industry* had very considerable merits. Keynes rightly said of it:

It won high praise from competent judges and was, during the whole of its life much the best little text-book available. If we are to have an elementary text-book at all, this one was probably, in relation to its contemporaries and predecessors, the best thing of the kind ever done— much better than the primers of Mrs Fawcett or Jevons or any of its many successors. Moreover, the latter part of Book III on Trade Combinations, Trade Unions, Trade Disputes and Co-operation, was the first satisfactory treatment on modern lines of these important topics.[a]

To a superficial reader the *Economics of Industry* might have seemed to be merely a restatement in brief of Mill, but Edgeworth among others was quick to realize the difference. In the opening paragraph of the "Reminiscences" which he wrote for the *Memorials of Alfred Marshall* he said:

Alfred Marshall first became for me a notable name when Jevons, conversing about mathematical economics, recommended as the latest contribution to that subject the now celebrated Papers on the *Pure Theory of Foreign Trade and Domestic Values*. At the same time Jevons highly praised the then recently published *Economics of Industry*. Eagerly studying these writings I discerned a new power of mathematical reasoning not only in the Papers bristling with curves and symbols, but also in certain portions of the seemingly simple text-book.

[a] *Memorials*, pp. 38–9.

13

With reference to such passages, writing in the year 1881, I characterized the author by a phrase which he himself afterwards acknowledged to be appropriate, "bearing under the garb of literature the armour of mathematics". The phrase might be applied to many passages in the text of the *Principles of Economics*.[a]

(5) The inaugural lecture Marshall gave in 1885 as Professor of Political Economy at Cambridge, and subsequently published under the title *The Present Position of Economics*.[b]

(6) "The Graphic Method of Statistics".[c] This was a paper read at the International Statistical Congress in 1885 and published in the jubilee volume of the *Journal of the Royal Statistical Society* (1885). The last two paragraphs of this paper contain the first reference to Marshall's concept of Elasticity of Demand, and set out the diagrammatic method of measuring the elasticity at any given point on a demand curve, which he subsequently used in the *Principles*.

(7) "Theories and Facts about Wages".[d] In 1885 Marshall read a paper on "Remedies for the Discontinuity of Employment" at the Industrial Remuneration Conference. His article on "Theories and Facts about Wages" was printed as an appendix to his paper in the *Proceedings of the Industrial Remuneration Conference* (1885). In this article, which was written in 1884, he presented in clear outline his theory of Distribution as it appeared in Book VII in the first edition of the *Principles* (Book VI in all the later editions).

(8) "A Fair Rate of Wages".[e] The substance of the preface contributed by Marshall to L. L. Price's *Industrial Peace* (1887). This is one of the best examples of Marshall's power and understanding in the realistic treatment of an economic problem.

For nine years,[f] from 1881 to 1890, Marshall laboured at the preparation of the *Principles*. It is important to bear in mind that when it finally appeared in 1890 he was a man of forty-eight years of age. During the preceding twenty years he had been intensively studying and teaching econo-

<hr/>

a *Memorials*, p. 66. b *Ibid.* pp. 152–74.
c *Ibid.* pp. 175–87. d Reprinted below, pp. 598–614.
e *Memorials*, pp. 212–26.
f Cf. Keynes's Memoir in *Memorials*, pp. 39–40.

mics, while the evidence from his own statements quoted above goes to show that the fundamental bases of his theory had been worked out as long ago as the early 1870's.[a] The *Principles* was thus the product of the full maturity of his mind. The big change which unquestionably took place in the two decades before 1890 was in Marshall's own approach to his subject, which took the form, above all, of the widening of his equipment on the applied side of economics. By a gradual process, in which a visit to the United States in 1875 played a very important part, the young pure theorist, who was used in 1869 "to think in Mathematics more easily than in English", became the most deeply and widely informed exponent of economic affairs since Adam Smith.

3. THE EVOLUTION OF THE *PRINCIPLES*, 1890–1920[b]

In the first edition (1890) the *Principles* was divided into seven books.[c] Books I–IV covered very much the same ground as in all the later editions; though the early chapters in Book I, dealing with the growth of free industry and enterprise and economic science, and with questions of scope and method were transferred later (in the fifth edition) to appendices.

[a] This is certainly true of the theory of value, though with regard to certain aspects of the theory of distribution there is a passage in a letter to Cannan of 7 January 1898 which seems to point to a rather later date: "There remained great lacunae in my theory till about [18]85: when, on my return to Cambridge, I resolved to try to find out what I really did think about Distribution: and I gradually developed (sufficiently to please my complacent self) the doctrines of substitution between prima facie non-competitive industrial groups, of quasi-rents, etc." (*Memorials*, p. 405).

[b] The following is a list of the different editions of the *Principles of Economics* with their dates:
1st ed. 1890: *Principles of Economics*, vol. 1. Pp. xii + 750 (omitting the Index).
2nd ed. 1891: *Principles of Economics*, vol. 1. Pp. xxx + 764 (omitting the Index).
3rd ed. 1895: *Principles of Economics*, vol. 1. Pp. xxxi + 811 (omitting the Index).
4th ed. 1898: *Principles of Economics*, vol. 1. Pp. xxix + 809 (omitting the Index).
5th ed. 1907: *Principles of Economics*, vol. 1. Pp. xxx + 858 (omitting the Index).
6th ed. 1910: *Principles of Economics. An introductory volume*. Pp. xxxii + 858.
7th ed. 1916: *Principles of Economics. An introductory volume*. Pp. xxxii + 858.
8th ed. 1920: *Principles of Economics. An introductory volume*. Pp. xxxiv + 858.
There were thus eight editions over a period of exactly thirty years, or an average of a new edition in slightly less than four years, but only one year separated the 1st ed. from the 2nd, while nine years elapsed between the 4th ed. and the 5th.

[c] The detailed arrangement of the different books and the scope of the chapters in the first four editions can best be seen from an inspection of the tables of contents of these editions, which are printed on pp. 77–130. From the 5th to the 8th editions there were no further changes in the structure of the *Principles*.

Book V, entitled "The Theory of the Equilibrium of Supply and Demand" dealt with value in short and long periods; with joint and composite supply and demand; with the doctrine of maximum satisfaction: and with the theory of monopoly. Book VI, entitled "Cost of Production Further Considered" dealt chiefly with rent and quasi-rent in relation to value; substitution at the margin; and with the distinction between prime and supplementary costs. Of Book VII, entitled "Value or Distribution and Exchange", Marshall said in the introductory chapter to Book VI:

In that Book [Book VII] we are to study the causes by which earnings and interest are normally determined and to bring together into one centre the main issues of the problem of value, or in other words of distribution and exchange.[a]

He expanded this statement in chapter 1 of Book VII as follows:

The supply price of a commodity is the price required to cover its money cost or expenses of production. But whereas we have hitherto gone on the supposition that the undertaker of any industrial enterprise takes for granted the prices which he has to pay for any kind of labour and for the hire of capital, we have now to examine the causes which determine the prices paid for labour and the use of capital, and thus to deal with the problem of value as a whole.[b]

The emphasis placed on the word "value" both in the title of Book VII, and in the passages just quoted was not carried very directly into most of the remainder of the text of that book; though the implications were clear, especially for those who could follow the reasoning of the Mathematical Appendix.[c] Chapter XII, however, entitled "General View of the Theory of Value" represents what is probably the clearest and most direct attempt of Marshall to express in words his theory of value as a whole that is to be found in any of the editions of the *Principles*.[d]

The second edition was called for in 1891, only one year after the publication of the first, and Marshall had not time

---

[a] 1st ed. p. 482. [b] 1st ed. p. 540.

[c] Cf. G. F. Shove, "Marshall's *Principles* in Economic Theory", *Economic Journal* (Dec. 1942), p. 300.

[d] For the portions of this chapter that were deleted from later editions, see below, pp. 546–9.

to undertake more than a somewhat hurried revision of what he had written. The most important change consisted in the amalgamation of the former Books V and VI to make the new Book V under the title "The Theory of the Equilibrium of Supply and Demand", with the subtitle "Including some further study of Cost of Production and with some Considerations bearing on the Doctrine of Maximum Satisfaction". This change, which reduced the number of Books to six, involved a good deal of rewriting of individual chapters. Book VI, which retained the title of the former Book VII —"Value or Distribution and Exchange"—was less extensively altered. The first three chapters containing the Preliminary Survey of Distribution and Exchange were compressed into two and partly rewritten; while chapter xii, which in the first edition (chapter xiii) had been entitled "General View of the Theory of Value", was now called "General View of Distribution", and was revised in some measure. Marshall's own explanations of the changes he made in the new Book V and in Book VI, as given in the Preface to the Second Edition, comprise an important statement of his fundamental position. The chief purpose of the fusion of the old Books V and VI was

to throw further light on the position held by the element of Time in economics, and to show more clearly how Time modifies the reciprocal influence of the earnings of workers and the prices of the goods made by them. For as regards fluctuations in short periods the leading role is held by prices, and a subordinate one by earnings: but as regards the slow adjustments of normal value their parts are interchanged; and the influence which prices exert on earnings is less than that which earnings exert on prices.

It was also in this Preface that Marshall wrote:

To myself personally the chief interest of the volume centres in Book V: it contains more of my life's work than any other part; and it is there, more than anywhere else, that I have tried to deal with unsettled questions of the science.

He said of the alterations in Book VI:

They aim at emphasizing and defining more fully the distinguishing characteristics of the broad problem of Distribution as contrasted with questions relating to the values of particular things; and at showing more clearly how, though the causes that govern demand, and those that govern supply can be studied separately, in the case of any single commodity, yet this cannot be done for the agents of production as a whole. For the demand for the labour of the various grades of workers, and for that "service of waiting" by which capital is accumulated, all comes from the aggregate National Dividend produced by those very agents of production (acting upon the free gifts of nature): and though they are always competing with one another for the field of employment, yet at the same time those agents provide for one another that field of employment.[a]

It was in the second edition also that the Representative Firm made its first formal appearance in the *Principles*; although the concept was already present in the first edition when he said that when seeking the normal supply price under increasing returns, "we must select as representative a business which is managed with normal ability and so as to get its fair share of the economies both *internal* and *external* resulting from industrial organisation".[b] This was, however, the only instance in the first edition of the use of the word "representative" in this connexion[c]; whereas in the second edition the Representative Firm as such was given an important place in the discussion of normal value, especially in Book V, chapter xi, "The Equilibrium of Normal Supply and Demand concluded. Multiple Positions of Equilibrium": and the term was fully described and defined at the end of Book IV, chapter xiii.

Marshall brought out the third edition of the *Principles* in 1895, when his powers as an expositor were probably at their peak. It would seem that from then onwards the further process of polishing, revision, and compression to which the book was subjected, even though this was combined with expansion in certain directions, did a good deal to devitalize it; and robbed it of much of the spontaneity and freshness of expression which characterized it in this and the two earlier editions.

[a] The remainder of the passage in the Preface to the Second Edition, of which this formed part, will be found below, p. 40.

[b] 1st ed. p. 523.

[c] But note the letter to Flux of 7 March 1898: "The chief outcome of my work in this direction [increasing returns], which occupied me a good deal between 1870 and 1890, is in the Representative Firm theory..." (*Memorials*, p. 407). See also below, pp. 69–70.

In the preface Marshall explained that several chapters had been rewritten[a] "chiefly in order to meet the need, which experience has shown to exist, for fuller explanation on certain points". During the five years which had passed since the first publication of the *Principles* a large critical and controversial literature had grown up round it, and it was not until the third edition that Marshall had the opportunity of taking full stock of the criticisms it had received.

He himself picked out two changes as being of chief importance in this edition: the new form of the first two chapters of Book VI, containing the survey of the central problem of distribution and exchange; and the alteration in the definition of capital. Of the former he said:

> In earlier editions the reader was left to import into them [Book VI, chs. I, II] the results of the preceding Books. But I had underrated the difficulty of doing that; as is shown by the fact that able and careful critics both at home and abroad have raised objections to those chapters which had been anticipated in other parts of the volume. It seemed necessary therefore to embody in those central chapters a good deal that had been said before; and to supplement by still further explanation.[b]

Although certain additions and deletions were made later, these two "central chapters" embodying his general theory of value and distribution remain substantially as they were framed in the third edition.

The second change caused Marshall more worry and heart-searching than many a decision of far greater moment. He said in the preface:

> The chapters on Capital and Income have been combined and rewritten...in order to give effect to a long-cherished design from which I have been held back hitherto by the fear of breaking too much with tradition and especially English tradition....Economists remain...free to choose their standard definition of capital with a view to their own convenience; and it seems clear that the discussion of the distribution of the national income or dividend is that to which it is most important that their use of the term should be appropriate;

---

[a] See p. 41. A considerable amount of additional material was added—the 3rd ed. was forty-seven pages longer than the 2nd.

[b] See the full text of this preface below, pp. 41-3 and the notes to Book VI, chs. I and II below.

and this points to the treatment of "capital" and "income" as correlative terms.[a]

In the first two editions he had defined social capital as consisting of "those things made by man, by which the society in question obtains its livelihood; or, in other words, as consisting of those external goods without which production could not be carried on with equal efficiency, but which are not free gifts of nature". In the first edition[b] he added the following sentence after the one just quoted:

It consists firstly of stores of commodities provided for the sustenance of workers of all industrial grades: and secondly of raw materials, of machinery, and all other aids to production.

This latter sentence was deleted from the second edition, but the general sense was retained in a sentence on an earlier page in the same chapter.[c]

When he came to the third edition, however, Marshall defined social capital as made up of "those kinds of wealth (other than the free gifts of nature) which yield income that is generally reckoned as such in common discourse: together with similar things in public ownership, such as government factories".[d]

Among the numerous "minor changes" mentioned in the preface to the third edition was the expansion of Note xiv in the Mathematical Appendix from only two short paragraphs in the second edition and one in the first (where it was numbered xxv) to about six pages embodying the kernel of his theory of value. One important feature of this expansion of Note xiv is the clear statement, expressed in mathematical form, of the pure theory of imperfect competition—the distinction for a firm with an individual market between average revenue and marginal revenue. It may be noted that by the third edition Marshall was becoming sensitive to contemporary criticisms of utilitarian phraseology, and he went through the various pages in which he had used the words "pleasure" and "pain", deleting "pain", and substituting in most (though not in all) cases, for "pleasure" the word "satisfaction", or "benefit", or "gratification".

[a] See below, pp. 42–3.
[b] 1st ed. p. 130.
[c] 2nd ed. pp. 124–5.
[d] 3rd ed. p. 153.

The fourth edition appeared three years later, in 1898. Marshall pointed out in his preface that "the changes have been kept within small compass: and in the hope that they are nearly final the present edition has been made a large one". It was shorter by a few pages than the third, although in actual words it was probably slightly longer, as a number of the more technical sections previously in the text were transferred to Notes in smaller type, which were placed at the end of chapters. Marshall had been growing seriously alarmed by the way in which the book was increasing in length with each successive edition, and he determined in this case that anything new that he added should be offset by equivalent deletions of what he felt to be less essential or redundant matter. Hence a good many paragraphs in the text and footnotes of historical interest, dating from the earlier editions, were omitted. In this edition Marshall paid special attention to his doctrine of quasi-rent. He collected his main study into a single chapter (Book V, ch. ix) entitled "Quasi-rent or Income from an Appliance for Production made by Man, in relation to the Value of its Produce", and it was in this edition that the doctrine was most forthrightly and comprehensively treated.

In the fifth edition, which appeared in 1907, nine years after the fourth, Marshall made very large alterations in the arrangement, added an appreciable amount of new material, and rewrote a number of sections, in particular those dealing with quasi-rent. The whole of chapters ii–vi in Book I of the earlier editions (the Growth of Free Industry and Enterprise and of Economic Science, and Scope and Method), were transferred to the end of the volume in the form of appendices; and a series of long Notes which had been placed at the end of chapters in the fourth or earlier editions were treated in a similar manner. That it was not without considerable regrets that Marshall reconciled himself to the dethronement of the lengthy historical account from the position it had previously occupied at the beginning, may be judged from the defence that he wrote of his policy in this respect in 1898.[a]

[a] In an article entitled "Distribution and Exchange" in the *Economic Journal*, VIII (March 1898), p. 8. See below, pp. 62–3.

One result of the changes was the addition of a good deal of new material to each chapter of Book I and also into Book II, chapter IV on "Income and Capital". A new chapter was added towards the end of Book VI (chapter XIII) entitled "Progress in Relation to the Standard of Life", and Appendix G, "The Incidence of Local Rates with some Suggestions as to Policy", based on evidence he prepared in 1899 for the Royal Commission on Local Taxation, was entirely new. Once again there was a drastic revision of the statement of the theory of rent and quasi-rent. With the exception of the addition of an important footnote in the sixth edition, Marshall made no further alterations in arrangement or treatment of quasi-rent; and some account may be given here of the stages by which the final version was reached.

In the earlier editions Marshall formulated his doctrine of quasi-rent chiefly from the differential standpoint. Thus he said in the first edition:

It will appear that many advantages which are to be regarded as differential, and as affording a quasi-rent, when we are considering the action of economic causes during short periods of time, are to be regarded as not differential, and as yielding profits, when we are studying the broader effects of economic causes through longer periods.[a]

There is no difficulty here so long as it is borne in mind that the differential element under consideration consists of a short period surplus or excess of receipts over prime costs. But Marshall's language in the early editions was often such as almost to invite misconception, especially in the application of the concept to problems of distribution in the short period. There was no part of the *Principles* which underwent more incessant change during the first five editions than the chapters devoted to the exposition of quasi-rent. At the same time it does not appear that there was any real alteration in the content of the doctrine from first to last—it was essentially a matter of successive attempts to meet criticism and to put a difficult and novel conception in as clear a form as possible. In the process of doing this Marshall was led, first, to lay increasing stress on the scarcity aspect of quasi-rent—that is, the scarcity value of specialized equipment,

[a] 1st ed. p. 493.

skilled labour, etc., the supply of which could be regarded as fixed in the short period; and secondly, to increasing use of analogies and illustrations (parables they might almost be termed) as a way of explaining his meaning.

In the first edition the theory of quasi-rent was set out quite briefly in Book VI, chapter iii, entitled "Cost of Production. Limited Sources of Supply. Continued". There were a number of short illustrations: the settler taking up land in a new country; a war which was not expected to last long, but which cut off part of our food supplies; an exceptional demand for a certain kind of fabric caused by a sudden movement of the fashions. Considerable use was also made of the term quasi-rent in Book VII, chapters vi and ix, in dealing with the earnings of specialized skill and with fluctuations of profit. Also in Book VII, in chapter x, entitled "Demand and Supply in Relation to Land. Producer's Surplus", we find the first mention of the parable of a shower of meteoric stones to illustrate the characteristics of both rent and quasi-rent.

In the second edition, where Books V and VI in the first edition were combined to form the new Book V, there was an appreciable expansion of the treatment of quasi-rent in Book V, chapters vii and ix, entitled "On the Value of an Appliance for Production in Relation to that of the Things Produced by it. Rent and Quasi-rent" and "On the Value of. . . . Continued". The meteoric stones illustration was transferred from its original place in Book VII, chapter x, to Book V, chapter viii; otherwise the application of the concept of quasi-rent to problems of distribution (wages and profits) was similar to that in the first edition.

Although there were some interesting changes in detail and additions in the third edition, the general arrangement was the same as in the second. The emphasis previously laid on the term "quasi-rent" in relation to the earnings of labour in Book VI, chapter v, was much diminished.

In the fourth edition, as has already been stated, the whole of the discussion on quasi-rent in Book V was collected in a single chapter (ix); the order was rearranged, and two of the illustrations—the settler taking up land, and the meteoric stones—were placed in a Note on "Illustrations of the General

Principle Discussed in this Chapter", at the end of chapter
ix. A new illustration—the hire of a pony—was introduced
in chapter ix, which was, however, deleted from the subsequent editions.[a]

In the fifth edition there was a very extensive rewriting and
rearrangement of the chapters on rent and quasi-rent. Book V,
chapter viii, entitled "Marginal Costs in Relation to Values.
General Principles", was almost entirely new. It was followed
by chapter ix with the same title "continued", which contained the main theory of quasi-rent in a much altered guise.
The chapter began with a new illustration of a tax upon
printing, and then took up the meteoric stones parable,
which was elaborated so that it ran through the whole of
the rest of the chapter. It is difficult to avoid the conclusion,
that, when explained in this way almost entirely by reference
to an imaginary illustration, the doctrine of quasi-rent was
rendered harder and not easier to grasp than it had been in
the earlier editions, especially the fourth, where it was put
in a more direct form. It may also be noted that, in the fifth
edition, in dealing with distribution in Book VI, especially
in chapter vii on "Profits of Capital and Business Power",
Marshall substituted in a number of sentences the words
"income" or "special earnings", or "gains" for the word
"quasi-rent". Whether Marshall was content with his final
version in the fifth edition it is impossible to say, but at least
he made no further changes in his method of presenting
the doctrine of quasi-rent in the last three editions.

There remains to be mentioned the new long and important preface[b] which Marshall wrote for the fifth edition, and
in which he set out his own attitude towards the "scope and
purpose" of the *Principles*, having noted that "some able
and friendly critics have taken a view of the matter rather
different from my own". Much misdirected criticism has
been levelled at the *Principles* owing to failure to appreciate
the force of his warning that in this volume he was not
attempting to cover more than a part of the field of economics:

Its scope is similar in some respects, though not in all, to that of
volumes on *Foundations* (*Grundlagen*), which Roscher and some other

[a] See below, pp. 480–1.   [b] See below, pp. 45–55.

economists have put at the head of groups of semi-independent volumes on economics. It avoids such special topics as currency and the organisation of markets. And in regard to such matters as the structure of industry, employment, and the problem of wages, it deals mainly with normal conditions. Its motto, *Natura non facit saltum*, does not deny the existence of earthquakes and flashes of lightning. It is designed merely to indicate that those manifestations of nature which occur most frequently, and are so orderly that they can be closely watched and narrowly studied, form the foundations of economic as of all other scientific work; while those which are sudden, infrequent, and difficult of observation are commonly reserved for special examination at a later stage....[a]

The sixth edition (1910) contained for the first time the words *An Introductory Volume*, as a sub-heading to the title *The Principles of Economics*; while the suffix "Volume 1" disappeared from the title-page. Very little new matter was introduced into this edition, and the pagination throughout was virtually identical with that of the fifth edition. It may be noted, however, that it was in the sixth edition that Marshall inserted the famous footnote on what quasi-rent did and did not mean[b] which caused so much perplexity, among others to his critic Davenport.[c] The preface to the sixth edition was also substantially a reprint of that in the fifth, though he added quite an important statement of his views on diminishing returns and on the notion of a margin.[d]

The seventh edition (1916) and the eighth edition (1920) are both almost completely identical with the sixth edition; only a very few alterations were made and there was no change in the pagination. In detail, however, the changes in some cases were of considerable interest, as reflecting Marshall's endeavour to take some account of economic developments which had become more prominent in the twentieth century.[e]

It will thus be seen that the overwhelming majority of the changes which Marshall introduced into the text and

[a] See below, pp. 46–7. [b] Vol. I, page 424 n.
[c] Cf. *The Economics of Alfred Marshall*, by H. J. Davenport, pp. 381–2 n., and "Davenport on the Economics of Alfred Marshall", by C. W. Guillebaud, in *Economic Journal* (March 1937), pp. 33–4.
[d] See below, pp. 59–60.
[e] Cf. the reference to "those great joint-stock companies which often stagnate, but seldom die", which was inserted in the 7th ed., p. 343.

arrangement of the *Principles* took place in the second to the fifth editions. By the fifth edition it had reached what was virtually its final form.

4. THE PRESENT EDITION[a]

Volume I of this edition consists of the text of the eighth edition of Marshall's *Principles* without any alteration apart from the correction of a considerable number of misprints, and the insertion of signs in the text referring to the corresponding editorial notes in Volume II. Volume I has been completely reset in a larger type by the Cambridge University Press, but the pagination is identical with that of the eighth edition as published by Messrs Macmillan and Co. during Marshall's lifetime and reprinted until 1949.[b] The pagination is thus substantially the same as that which has existed since the fifth edition of 1907.

The aims of this second volume are:

(1) In the case of every paragraph or sentence in the eighth edition, to indicate from which edition that paragraph or sentence originated.

(2) To indicate any changes of substance which took place in any paragraph or sentence before it reached the final form in which it was carried into the eighth edition.

It is important, however, with regard to these two aims, that it should be made clear that only those changes are recorded which, in my opinion as editor, are significant in the sense that they represent an addition to, or modification of, the previous wording, which goes beyond a mere matter of the rearrangement of the order of words or sentences on grounds of English style. Where changes of this nature have been made, but the sense of a passage appears otherwise to be completely identical and no change even of emphasis can be detected, then it is recorded as dating "substantially" from the edition in which it first appeared. My editorial bias

[a] In 1934 Maynard Keynes asked me as Marshall's nephew to undertake the task of producing an annotated edition of Marshall's *Principles*. Since then, in the intervals of an otherwise busy life; the writing of three books; and the interruption caused by the war of 1939–45, I have laboured at this work.

[b] By 1949 the old plates of the 8th (1920) edition had become worn out and it was not possible to print more copies from them. The book was reset by Messrs Macmillan and Co. in 1949 with a different pagination.

throughout has, however, been to include too much rather than too little. But the amount of rewriting done by Marshall was very great; and to have taken account of every purely verbal or stylistic change would have involved an enormous inflation of the editorial notes, which would only have distracted attention from those changes which were of substance. When alterations in the marginal summaries to paragraphs merely reflect changes made in the corresponding paragraph, or where they have been abbreviated without alteration of sense, the earlier version is not recorded. But in instances when a new or amended summary seems to throw light on the alteration made in the paragraph, or to have significance in some other way, the change is noted. Marshall experimented with the use of several different kinds of type, capital letters, etc. in the earlier editions, in order to draw attention to technical terms; but his usage in this respect has not been followed in the extracts from these editions which are reproduced in the editorial notes in this volume; and these conform in general to the practice he adopted from the fifth edition onwards.

(3) To reprint material which has appeared in any edition of the *Principles*, but which is not contained in the eighth edition. In some instances this has involved reprinting the whole of a chapter from one of the early editions.

(4) To provide a new and more comprehensive index to the *Principles*; the index to both volumes is placed at the end of Volume ii.

(5) To reprint articles written by Marshall to which he refers in the course of the eighth edition of the *Principles*, and which have not been reprinted in the *Memorials of Alfred Marshall*; as also other of Marshall's writings which have relevance to the subject matter of the *Principles*. Under this head come, *inter alia*, a chapter from Marshall's *Industry and Trade*, and some hitherto unpublished letters to Edgeworth and John Neville Keynes, the originals of which are now in the Marshall Library in Cambridge.

It may be observed that this edition of the *Principles* makes no attempt to reconstruct the form of the first four editions. Their general structure can be seen from the Tables of

Contents of these editions, which are printed below; but a detailed reconstruction would have been quite impracticable in view of the nature and scale of the alterations which Marshall made, and it would have involved an immense amount of needless repetition.

The reader should, however, be warned that a direct comparison of the wording of a number of the much altered chapters, especially in the first two editions, with that of the corresponding chapter in the eighth edition, will show that, while some passages in the earlier editions which appear to have been later deleted are reproduced in the editorial notes to the chapter in question, others are not. The explanation of this is either, that the said passages will in fact be found in another part of the eighth edition of the *Principles*, or that owing to a change of arrangement and context, the appropriate place for the reinstatement of these passages in the editorial notes is in connexion with the text of a different section, or it may be chapter, in the eighth edition.

Some comment may be made here with regard to the significance of the very numerous and extensive changes which Marshall made in the *Principles* from the second to the fifth editions.

It is quite clear from the prefaces to the successive editions that Marshall himself did not claim for them more than that such rewriting and additions as had been made had been undertaken in order "to meet the need which experience has shown to exist for fuller explanation on certain points". Edgeworth, who reviewed the first edition in the *Academy* and the second and third in the *Economic Journal*, found nothing that he could single out as representing a new idea or change of doctrine. In general it may be said that Marshall's major economic theories and doctrines were already crystallized in their final form, in content though not in expression, when he brought out his first edition. The collation of the different editions would not seem to support the view that there was any real evolution or development of his ideas between 1890 and 1920. When new material was introduced in the later editions, for example, the expansion of the Mathematical Appendix in the third edition, it seems as a rule to have been merely a matter of incorporating into the *Principles* results that he had worked out in the twenty years prior to 1890. If it is asked why Marshall should have ceased apparently to develop any further his thought in the range of economic theory covered by the *Principles* from the year 1890 onwards, the most plausible answer would seem to be that as he grew older his mind became increasingly absorbed with the more realistic side of economics and with its ethical aspects, and that he was no longer interested in extending his ideas on the abstract and analytical side. He realized that he had made important advances in economic theory when in 1890 he brought out his *Principles*, and he was content to leave it to others to continue where he had left off. Moreover, to the misfortune of subsequent generations of professional economists he was very desirous that his book should have a wide circulation (as had been the case with Adam Smith's *The Wealth of Nations*) amongst the intelligent and educated lay public, in particular, business men; and he therefore omitted much that he regarded as being of purely theoretical interest.

The amount of material in the earlier editions which was later deleted is very considerable; and the question arises whether Marshall suppressed a passage because it no longer reflected his views on the matter in question or whether there was some other explanation. The vast majority of the deletions appear to fall into three main categories. First, there were expressions of opinion which had given rise, either publicly or privately, to criticism: Edgeworth, above all, was an indefatigable correspondent. If the statement at issue was important for his main position Marshall would usually alter or expand the wording. But often he would merely suppress it, not because he disagreed with it but because he could not afford the space in which to defend and develop it; while he regarded controversy in general as a great waste of time and energy. Secondly, some of the rewriting, for example, in the case of the chapters on quasi-rent, was very thorough; and when Marshall had arrived at a new formulation of his views which seemed less likely to give rise to misunderstanding, he naturally omitted his earlier version. Thirdly, he came to regard the inevitable tendency of his book to grow in length, as a great evil: the first edition was 750 pages, but by the fifth the text and appendices had become 858 pages. Wherever possible, therefore, if he added new material, he endeavoured to off-set it by cutting something else out. For this reason, if for no other, it is very unsafe as a rule to seek to draw positive conclusions from Marshall's deletions.

The foregoing observations represent the personal conclusions of the present editor after many years of study of the text of the eight editions of Marshall's *Principles*; but they have very rarely been obtruded into the editorial notes, which are confined in general to a statement of facts without editorial comment.

In conclusion, I wish to express my gratitude to the Royal Economic Society for financing the publication of this Variorum Edition of Marshall's *Principles*. I am deeply indebted to my printers, the Cambridge University Press, for the immense amount of care and trouble which they have devoted to the printing and preparation of these volumes: the preservation, throughout Volume I, of the pagination of the old eighth edition is itself a typographical feat of no mean order, when account is taken of the fact that both the text and the footnotes are in larger type; while the printing of Volume II gave rise to many difficult problems requiring much skill, ingenuity and patience for their solution. I am also grateful to Mrs W. S. Allen for having undertaken so capably the arduous task of compiling the index to the two volumes.

EDITORIAL NOTES

EDITORIAL NOTES

The following explanations with regard to the technical apparatus of the editorial notes may be of assistance to those who make use of this second volume:

(1) The notes are arranged under the page numbers of vol. I, and are numbered **a. b. c.** etc., so as to distinguish them from Marshall's own footnote references.

(2) A note attached to the first page of each chapter throughout the *Principles* contains a general indication as to origin. In some cases this takes the following form: "Except where otherwise stated the wording of this chapter dates from the...edition"; while in others it runs: "The origin of the wording of this chapter is shown throughout in the editorial notes." In the former case it can be taken for granted that any passage not specifically assigned to a later edition, originated in the earlier edition mentioned in the general indication. It is important when seeking the origin of any particular passage in a chapter, not only to consult the general indication at the beginning of the chapter, but also to look backwards from the passage in order to ascertain whether the paragraph (or section) in which it stands is subject to a specific indication.

(3) The following terms: "So since the...ed." "This sentence dates from the...ed." "This sentence was inserted in the...ed." are used interchangeably and have the same meaning.

(4) It is frequently the case that when a paragraph as a whole is attributed, say, to the first edition, there will be a note in the following terms attached to the first word of one sentence in it: "So since the...ed., where this (and the next sentence) replaced the following sentence (or sentences) dating from the first ed...." In all such cases it should be understood that the words "So since the...ed." relate only to the sentence, or sentences, actually mentioned, and that the remaining sentences of the paragraph are to be taken as dating from the first edition.

(5) When it is stated that a passage dating from one of the earlier editions was deleted from, say, the fourth edition this means, in the absence of any indication to the contrary, that the passage in question did not reappear in any of the editions subsequent to the third.

(6) References in extracts cited from an earlier edition to other chapters and sections in that edition are normally to be taken as applying to the corresponding chapter and section in vol. I of the present edition in the absence of any indication to the contrary. (In the few instances where this is not the case the Tables of Contents of the earlier editions, which are reprinted below, should be consulted.)

(7) Where it is stated that a given passage, paragraph, section or chapter, dates 'substantially' from a certain edition, it is implied that such changes in wording as have been made in later editions are confined to verbal rearrangement without any apparent alterations of sense or meaning (see above, pp. 26–7).

(8) All page references where the word "page" is unabbreviated refer to the text of the eighth edition of the *Principles* as printed in vol. I of the present edition. In all other references the word "page" is abbreviated to read "p.".

TITLE-PAGE

a. So since the 1st edition.

b. So since the 6th edition, where the words "An introductory volume" replaced the words "Vol. 1." dating from the 1st edition.

c. In the first three editions Alfred Marshall was described as Professor of Political Economy in the University of Cambridge; Fellow of St John's College, Cambridge; Sometime Fellow of Balliol College, Oxford. In the 4th edition the designation "Fellow of St John's College, Cambridge" was deleted. In the 6th edition the two remaining designations were deleted.

d. So since the 1st edition.

PREFACE TO THE FIRST EDITION

PAGE V

a. In the 2nd to the 4th editions. the Preface to the First Edition was reprinted almost *in extenso*, except for an alteration in one footnote (see note **d** on p. 37 below). There was in addition a short separate preface to each edition, which preceded the Preface to the First Edition. In the 5th ed. there was a long separate preface which was succeeded by a number of short extracts from the Preface to the First Edition. The same procedure was adopted in the 6th and 7th editions; but in the 8th edition the Preface to the First Edition was again reprinted almost *in extenso*, and the footnote, which had been modified in the 2nd, 3rd and 4th editions, was restored to its initial form as it appeared in the original Preface to the First Edition. It will be observed that in the 8th edition the Preface to the First Edition precedes the separate Preface to the Eighth Edition. The editorial notes indicate the paragraphs which were retained in the 5th, 6th and 7th editions, and the other changes mentioned above.

b. In the 7th ed., but not in the 5th and 6th editions, this paragraph was included in the "Extracts from the Preface to the First Edition".

PAGE vi

a. In the 5th, 6th and 7th editions this sentence and the next four paragraphs were included in the "Extracts from the Preface to the First Edition".

a. In the 5th, 6th and 7th editions the first three sentences of this paragraph were included in the "Extracts from the Preface to the First Edition".

b. The following words inserted in square brackets after the word "led" in the 5th ed., and also retained in the extracts from the Preface to the First Edition in the 6th and 7th editions, were deleted from the 8th edition: "[about the year 1867]". In an undated fragment found amongst Marshall's MSS. after his death there was the following tribute to the influence of Cournot and von Thünen upon his work:

Cournot's work is now easily accessible, mainly through the good efforts of Professor Fisher; and anyone who reads it can imagine the influence which it would exert on a young man, accustomed to think in Mathematics more readily than in English, and bewildered on his sudden entry into the strange land of economics, where many of the cardinal doctrines seemed to be mathematical propositions overlaid by the complex relations of real life; and at the same time distorted and stunted because the older economists had not recognized the mathematical conceptions that were latent in their own. I have long ago forgotten Cournot; and I may be wrong. But my impression is that I did not derive so much of the substance of my opinions from him as from von Thünen. Cournot was a gymnastic master who directed the form of my thought. Von Thünen was a bona fide mathematician, but of less power: his blunder as to the natural wage is not of the same order as Cournot's little slips. But to make up, he was a careful experimenter and student of facts and with a mind at least as fully developed on the inductive as on the deductive side. Above all he was an ardent philanthropist. And I had come into economics out of ethics, intending to stay there only a short while; and to go back as soon as I was in a position to speak with my enemies in the gate, that is, with those men of affairs who dashed cold water on my youthful schemes for regenerating the world by saying "Ah! you would not talk in that way, if you knew anything about business, or even Political Economy." And I loved von Thünen above all my masters. Professor Fisher has cared for Cournot. I would that someone would care for von Thünen. He should not, I think, be translated: but an abstract of his work should be given, with translations of a good deal of his second volume.

The foregoing passage is printed in *The Memorials of Alfred Marshall*, pp. 359–60.

c.   In the 5th, 6th and 7th editions this and the next sentence were included in the "Extracts from the Preface to the First Edition".

d.   Apart from the insertion in the 8th edition of the dates of publication of *Der isolierte Staat*, this is the original version of this footnote as it appeared in the Preface to the First Edition. In the 2nd, 3rd and 4th editions, where the Preface to the First Edition was reprinted *in extenso*, this footnote was reworded as follows:

> The term "marginal" increment is in harmony with von Thünen's methods of thought and was suggested to me by him, though he does not actually use it. It has been for some time commonly used by Austrian economists on the initiation of Prof. Wieser, and it has been adopted by Mr Wicksteed. When Jevons' Theory appeared, I adopted his word "final"; but I have been gradually convinced that "marginal" is the better. (In the first edition this footnote implied wrongly that the phrase, as well as the idea of, Marginal Increment could be traced to von Thünen.)

Marshall returned to the original version when he reprinted the Preface to the First Edition in the 8th edition.

PAGE xi

a.   In the 5th to the 7th editions this sentence was included in the "Extracts from the Preface to the First Edition".

b.   In the 1st ed. there was the following additional, concluding paragraph, and a footnote which was attached to the word "Appendix" at the end of the preceding paragraph in the text:

I have to acknowledge much assistance in preparing this volume for the press. My wife has aided and advised me at every stage of the MSS. and of the proofs, and it owes a very great deal to her suggestions, her care and her judgment. Mr J. N. Keynes, and Mr L. L. Price have read all the proofs and have never returned me any without improving them much: Mr Arthur Berry and Mr A. W. Flux have given me valuable help in connection with the mathematical Appendix; and my father, Mr W. H. B. Hall and Mr C. J. Clay have assisted me on special points.

> Many of the diagrams in this book have appeared in print already: and I may take this opportunity of giving their history. Mr Henry Cunynghame who was attending my lectures in 1873, seeing me annoyed by being unable to draw a series of rectangular hyperbolas, invented a beautiful and original machine for the purpose. It was shown at the Cambridge Philosophical Society in 1873; and,

to explain its use, I read a paper (briefly reported in the *Proceedings*, Part xv, pp. 318–19), in which I described the theories of Multiple Positions of Equilibrium and of Monopoly values very nearly as they are given below (Book V, ch. v and viii). In 1875–7 I nearly completed a draft of a treatise on *The Theory of Foreign Trade, with some allied problems relating to the doctrine of Laisser Faire*. The first Part of it was intended for general use, while the second Part was technical; nearly all the diagrams that are now in Book V, ch. v, vii and viii were introduced in it, in connection with the problem of the relation of Protection to the Maximum Satisfaction of the community; and there were others relating to Foreign Trade. But in 1877 I turned aside to work at the *Economics of Industry*, and afterwards was overtaken by an illness, which nearly suspended my studies for several years. Meanwhile the MSS. of my first projected treatise were lying idle: and it is to them that Professor Sidgwick refers in the Preface to his *Political Economy*. With my consent he selected four chapters (not consecutive) out of the second Part, and printed them for private circulation. These four chapters contained most of the substance of Book V, ch. v and vii, but not ch. viii of the present work; together with two chapters relating to the equilibrium of foreign trade. They have been sent to many economists in England and on the Continent: it is of them that Jevons speaks in the Preface to the Second Edition of his *Theory* (p. xlv); and many of the diagrams in them relating to foreign trade have been reproduced with generous acknowledgments by Prof. Pantaleoni in his *Principii di Economia Pura*.

The paragraph and footnote were retained unaltered in the 2nd to the 4th editions, but they were deleted from the 8th edition where the Preface to the First Edition (with this exception) was again reprinted as a whole. See also pp. 7–8 above.

c. The original Preface to the First Edition was undated. In the 2nd to the 4th editions the Preface to the First Edition was dated "July 1890", and the same date was appended to the "Extracts from the Preface to the First Edition" in the 5th to the 7th editions. In the 8th edition the Preface to the First Edition was dated "September 1890". After consulting their records, Messrs Macmillan state that the correct date for the Preface to the First Edition was July 1890.

PREFACE TO THE EIGHTH EDITION

PAGE xii

a. For the earlier versions of this Preface see the Prefaces to the 5th, 6th and 7th editions printed below (pp. 45–62).

b. When Marshall wrote this sentence in October 1920 he was 78 years old; he died in 1924. The projected third volume on Trade, Finance and the Industrial Future never appeared. But he was able to publish *Money Credit and Commerce* in 1923.

Marshall's few unpublished MSS., which were deposited in the Marshall Library in Cambridge by his literary executor, Professor A. C. Pigou, do not appear to contain any material of importance relating to his views on "the Industrial Future".

a. Although this sentence first made its appearance in the *Principles* in the Preface to the 5th ed. (see pp. 47–8 below) it originated in an article by Marshall in the *Economic Journal* of March 1898 entitled "Distribution and Exchange", to which he refers in the preface to the 5th ed. Extracts from this article, containing the sentence in question, will be found on pp. 312–18 of the *Memorials of Alfred Marshall* (1925) under the title "Mechanical and Biological Analogies in Economics".

EDITORIAL APPENDIX TO THE PREFACES

I. TEXT OF THE PREFACES TO THE SECOND TO SEVENTH EDITIONS

The Prefaces to the 2nd to the 7th editions ran as follows:

PREFACE TO THE SECOND EDITION

THE present edition of Volume I differs from the first only in points of detail and in arrangement.

The most important alteration is the fusion of the old Books V and VI, together with some additional matter, into the present Book V; the chief purpose of the change being to throw further light on the position held by the element of Time in economics, and to show more clearly how Time modifies the reciprocal influence of the earnings of workers and the prices of goods made by them. For as regards fluctuations in short periods the leading role is held by prices, and a subordinate one by earnings: but as regards the slow adjustments of normal value their parts are interchanged; and the influence which prices exert on earnings, is less than that which earnings exert on prices.

Closely connected with this subject are the alterations made in the earlier and later chapters of the present Book VI (the Book VII of the first edition). They aim at emphasising and defining more fully the distinguishing characteristics of the broad problem of Distribution as contrasted with questions relating to the values of particular things; and at showing more clearly how, though the causes that govern demand, and those that govern supply can be studied separately, in the case of any single commodity, yet this cannot be done for the agents of production as a whole. For the demand for the labour of the various grades of workers, and for that "service of waiting" by which capital is accumulated, all comes from the aggregate National Dividend produced by those very agents, of production (acting upon the free gifts of nature): and though they are always competing with one another for the field of employment, yet at the same time those agents provide for one another that field of employment. A rise in the efficiency of any one group of workers may tend to glut the market with their wares: but a general increase in the efficiency of all workers would increase the National Dividend, and raise earnings nearly in proportion. And thus the cost of production of labour cannot be determined as definitely as can that of a commodity; for the "conventional necessaries" of labour, as well as all superfluous comforts and luxuries are not a fixed sum, but depend on the efficiency of labour. The right means therefore to raise wages is to raise, not merely the Standard of Comfort or of wants, but the Standard of Life which includes activities as well as wants.

Another change has reference to the danger that the reaction against the too exclusive study of Supply by the older economists may cause the importance of wants to be over-estimated relatively to that of activities: this point is discussed in Book III, ch. i. In Book III, ch. v, a more careful study is made of the relative attractiveness of present and future pleasures; and finally the account, given in Book I, of the relations in which economics stands to other branches of social sciences has been partly re-written.

To myself personally the chief interest of the Volume centres in Book V: it contains more of my life's work than any other part: and it is there, more than anywhere else, that I have tried to deal with unsettled questions of the science. But for that very reason it may prove unattractive, or even repellent to the general reader; from whose suggestions and co-operation economics has far more to gain than any other science has; and I venture therefore to repeat here the hint given in the text that Book V, ch. vi–xiii, and especially ch. xi, xiii, may be omitted by those whose interest in economics is chiefly from the social and practical side. What use is made of these chapters in Book VI is chiefly confined to the last few Sections of ch. v, viii, ix and xi of that Book.

In preparing this edition I have received help and suggestions from many persons among whom I would especially mention my wife, Dr Keynes, Prof. Edgeworth, Prof. Ashley, Mr Berry and Mr Flux.

12 *June* 1891

PREFACE TO THE THIRD EDITION

In this edition several chapters have been re-written; chiefly in order to meet the need, which experience has shown to exist, for fuller explanation on certain points.

The most important change is in the survey of the central problem of distribution and exchange, which occupies the first two chapters of Book VI (Book VII of the first edition). In earlier editions the reader was left to import into them the results of the preceding Books. But I had underrated the difficulty of doing that; as is shown by the fact that able and careful critics both at home and abroad have raised objections to those chapters which had been anticipated in other parts of the volume. It seemed necessary therefore, to embody in those central chapters a good deal that had been said before; and to supplement by still further explanations.

The first of these chapters, after reproducing a short historical introduction from the earlier editions, discuss one side of the problem of distribution; namely that on which the forces of demand work.

The following chapter deals first with the side of supply, and then with the two sides together. Some economists have treated the causes affecting the supply of the agents of production, as exercising an influence in distribution generally, not co-ordinate with, but only subordinate to that of the forces of demand; and a further attempt is made in this chapter to show that such a treatment, however appropriate to passing movements of distribution, cannot properly be applied to the broad central problem of normal distribution. The chapter ends with a fuller discussion of general wages than had been given in earlier editions; and discusses the relations between different kinds of surpluses.

The fifth and sixth chapters of Book I and the sixth chapter of Book III have been somewhat modified and enlarged in order to make more clear how closely the economist adheres in substance to the methods of inference and judgment of ordinary life; and how thorough are the harmony and the mutual dependence between the analytical and the inductive, or historical, methods of economic study.

The chapters on Capital and Income in Book II have been combined and re-written (see also Book VI, ch. 1, § 10, and ch. 11, § 10) in order to give effect to a long cherished design, from which I have been held back hitherto by the fear of breaking too much with tradition and especially English tradition. I have steadily grown in the conviction that there is, and from the nature of the case there must be, something artificial in every broad distinction between capital in general (or "social" capital, i.e. capital not regarded from the point of view of an individual) and other forms of wealth. For indeed whatever line of division be taken, the attributes assigned to capital are not present in equal degrees in all forms of capital, and they are present in some degree in other forms of wealth: such statements for instance as that capital supports, or aids, or employs labour, are not true without reserve of all things that lie within any line of demarcation that has been proposed for capital; and they are true in a measure of some forms of wealth that lie outside the line. The discussions of ordinary business life give us little guidance, and impose on us no restrictions in the matter: for they refer almost exclusively to capital from the point of view of the individual or "trade-capital": and, when they take a wider scope, they do not draw a firm and clear line between capital and other forms of accumulated wealth. Economists remain therefore free to choose their standard definition of Capital with a view to their own convenience; and it seems clear that the discussion of the distribution of the national income or dividend is that to which it is most important that their use of the term should be appropriate; and this points to the treatment of "capital" and "income" as correlative terms. Of course all wealth is designed to yield what in pure theory may be called "an income" of benefit or gain in some form or other; but the language of the market place refuses to admit so broad a use of the term Income as that. It is, however, tolerably consistent in commonly including a certain number of forms of income, other than money income; and this consensus may well be turned to account. Labour is already defined by nearly all economists so as to include those activities, and those only, which are commonly regarded as the source of income in this broader use of the term: and most if not all economists glide imperceptibly to a closely corresponding use of capital when they come to discuss the problem of distribution. It is now proposed to do this deliberately, and to define capital (from the general point of view) as wealth which yields "income" in forms that are admitted in the broader use of the term in the market place.

The ambiguous term "determine" has been displaced, in spite of its prestige, by "govern" or "indicate" as occasion requires. Technical terms have been dispensed with wherever it was possible to do so without great loss of clearness or brevity.

In preparing this edition I have received very great assistance from my wife, and much from Professor Edgeworth; and helpful suggestions from Profs. Ashley, Mackenzie, Sidgwick and Taussig, and from Mr Bateson and Mr Berry.[a]

[a] Marshall did not date the Preface to his Third Edition.

PREFACE TO THE FOURTH EDITION

THE changes introduced in this edition are slight. A more sparing use is made of technical terms: and discussions which are addressed to academic students rather than to those whose interest in Economics lies mainly on the practical side have been marked off by a change of type, or by an express intimation that they may be omitted without grave injury to the central argument. For instance the main study of quasi-rents is collected into one chapter, and subsequent references to them are marked off as specially addressed to academic students. Some passages which have been found obscure are re-written with further explanations but without change of substance.

The prominence of the phrase "the equilibrium of demand and supply" in Books V and VI has suggested to some readers a mechanical treatment of economic problems. It is true that the analogies offered by mechanics are simpler than those of biology, and are therefore more helpful in the earlier stages of economic analysis. But the chief purpose of the historical introduction as well as of the discussions of the aims and methods of the science in Book I has been to lay stress on the essentially organic character of the larger and broader problems towards which we are working our way. The same purpose may also be detected in much of Book IV, and in parts even of Books V and VI; and it is emphasized by a few new passages in this edition.

The changes have been kept within small compass: and, in the hope that they are nearly final the present edition has been made a large one.

In preparing this edition my first obligations have again been to my wife. But I have received some important suggestions and notes of ambiguities and misprints from several persons. Professor Smart has generously given much time and thought to the matter, and his criticisms have been very helpful. I am under considerable obligations to Professor Flux, Dr Keynes and Mr Cannan; also to Dr Wickett of Toronto and Mr C. E. Edgerton of Ithaca.

BALLIOL CROFT, CAMBRIDGE.
September 1898

PREFACE TO THE FIFTH EDITION

THE appearance of a new edition of this volume affords an opportunity for some explanation of my failure to fulfil the implicit promise, made seventeen years ago, that a second volume completing the treatise would appear within a reasonable time. I had laid my plan on too large a scale; and its scope widened, especially on the realistic side, with every pulse of that Industrial Revolution of the present generation, which has far outdone the changes of a century ago, in both rapidity and breadth of movement.

About twelve years ago I began to despair of completing my scheme in two volumes. Accordingly, I set aside the economic functions of Government (*Wirtschafts-politik*) for a third volume; and rearranged, in ampler space, the materials which I had got together on the modern conditions of industry and trade; of credit and employment. Impressed with the belief that each of these sets of conditions influences and is influenced by the others, I passed backwards and forwards from one to another; and, by successive rewritings, brought a great part of what I had to say into some sort of organic unity. But gradually it became clear that the enlarged space was still too small, and that four thick volumes would be needed for the task. This called a halt: for life is short. In fact a very long consecutive treatise, even if it can be completed, is apt to be heavy to reader as well as writer. References from one volume of it to another are perhaps a greater evil than the repetition in, say, each of two works on International Trade and on Money, of arguments that have been more fully developed in the other.

Accordingly I now propose to bring out as soon as possible an almost independent volume, part of which is already
in print, on *National Industry and Trade*. About one half
of it is occupied with the evolution of the present forms
and conditions of national leadership in industry, with special
reference to the recent changes in the character and functions of giant businesses and of combinations: the second
half applies the conclusions of the first half to the modern
problems of international trade. This may be followed at
no very long interval by a companion volume on *Money,
Credit, and Employment*. And finally it may be possible to
compress these two volumes, together with some discussion
of the functions of Government, into a single volume; which
may supplement the present volume, and form a consecutive
treatise of moderate length. There is little chance that my
life would suffice for this project at my present rate of work:
but I hope ere long to have more command of my time and
my limited strength.

If my plan could have been completed quickly, it might
have been left to explain itself. But as things are, it will be
well to say a little as to the scope and purpose of the present
volume, in addition to what is suggested by the Table of
Contents: and all the more because some able and friendly
critics have taken a view of the matter rather different from
my own.

Its scope is similar in some respects, though not in all, to
that of volumes on *Foundations* (*Grundlagen*), which Roscher
and some other economists have put at the head of groups of
semi-independent volumes on economics. It avoids such
special topics as currency and the organization of markets.
And in regard to such matters as the structure of industry,
employment, and the problem of wages, it deals mainly with
normal conditions. Its motto, *Natura non facit saltum*, does
not deny the existence of earthquakes and flashes of lightning. It is designed merely to indicate that those manifestations of nature which occur most frequently, and are so
orderly that they can be closely watched and narrowly
studied, form the foundations of economic as of all other

scientific work; while those which are sudden, infrequent, and difficult of observation, are commonly reserved for special examination at a later stage. An illustration of this contrast may be taken from the distribution of the study of large businesses between the present and a later volume.

When any branch of industry offers an open field for new firms which rise to the first rank, and perhaps after a time decay, the normal cost of production in it can be estimated with reference to "a representative firm," which enjoys a fair share both of those internal economies which belong to a well organized individual business, and of those general or external economies which arise out of the collective organization of the district as a whole. A study of such a firm belongs properly to a volume on Foundations. So also does a study of the principles on which a firmly established monopoly, in the hands of a Government department or a large railway, regulates its prices with main reference to its own revenue, but with more or less consideration for the well-being of its customers.

But normal action falls into the background, when Trusts are striving for the mastery of a large market; when communities of interest are being made and unmade; and above all when the policy of any particular establishment is likely to be governed, not with a single eye to its own business success, but in subordination to some large stock exchange manœuvre or some campaign for the control of markets. Such matters cannot be fitly discussed in a volume on Foundations: they belong to a volume dealing with some part of the Superstructure[1].

The Mecca of the economist lies in economic biology rather than in economic dynamics. But biological conceptions are more complex than those of dynamics; a volume on Foundations must therefore give a relatively large place to mechanical analogies; and frequent use is made of the term "equilibrium," which suggests something of statical analogy. This fact, combined with the predominant attention paid in the present volume to the normal conditions

---

[1] It is argued in Appendix H that great care is needed in using the term "normal", even with reference to an open market, in regard to industries in which the cost of production per unit is greatly lowered by a moderate increase in output.

of life in the modern age, has suggested the notion that its central idea is "statical," rather than "dynamical." But that suggestion is incorrect in any case; and it is wholly unfounded, if the terms are interpreted as in physical science.

These terms have indeed been used by some economists, partly on Comte's initiative, in a special sense: and confusion may be caused by interpretations of passages in the present volume on the supposition that these terms were used in Comte's sense. He thought it was possible to divide "the Study of Humanity" into two parts: the Statical, which deals with Structure and the laws of Order; and the Dynamical, which deals with the laws of actual development and Progress. But such a division presents great difficulties. For, while a *description* of structure need not concern itself with causes or "forces," an *explanation* of structure must deal with the forces that brought that structure into existence: and therefore it must be in the physical sense of the term "dynamical." The existing structure and order are the outcome of progress in the past.

The present volume deals with the forces of progress, although it does not pursue their influence back beyond modern times. Such a pursuit has been made by Prof. Schmoller in his *Grundriss*, an unsurpassed embodiment of wide knowledge and subtle thought: and both methods of study are needed for the complete work of stripping away the accidental and temporary, and for concentrating attention on the essential and permanent in the action of those forces, which are fashioning progress now, and may be expected to fashion it in the future. They are as indispensable to a perfect knowledge of socio-economic life, as are the geologist's hammer and the physiologist's microscope to a perfect knowledge of physical life. Neither as to physical nor as to economic organisms has the study of distant ages any exclusive right to be called "dynamical"; and the economist, like the physiologist, will often do best to give nearly his whole energy to recent phases of evolution, while welcoming instruction from others as to earlier phases.

Some discussions as to the methods of social sciences have seemed to imply that statics and dynamics are distinct

branches of physics. But of course they are not. The
modern mathematician is familiar with the notion that dynamics include statics. If he can solve a problem dynamically,
he seldom cares to solve it statically also. To get the statical
solution from the dynamical, all that is needed is to make
the relative velocities of the things under study equal to
zero, and thus reduce them to relative rest. But the statical
solution has claims of its own. It is simpler than the dynamical; it may afford useful preparation and training for the
more difficult dynamical solution; and it may be the first
step towards a provisional and partial solution in problems
so complex that a complete dynamical solution is beyond
our attainment[1].

This volume then is concerned throughout with the forces
that cause movement: and its key-note is that of dynamics.
But the forces to be dealt with are so numerous, that it
is best to take a few at a time; and to work out a number of
partial solutions as auxiliaries to our main work. Thus we
begin by isolating the primary relations of supply, demand
and price in regard to a particular commodity: we reduce
to inaction all other forces by the phrase "other things being
equal." We do not suppose that they are inert: but for the
time we ignore their activity. This scientific device is a great
deal older than science: it is the method by which, consciously or unconsciously, sensible men have dealt from time
immemorial with every difficult problem of ordinary life.
The next step is to set more forces free from the hypothetical slumber that had been imposed on them; and to
call into activity, for instance, changes in the demand for
hides when considering the causes that govern the price of
beef [2].

At the end of this second stage the area of the dynamical
problem has become much larger; the area covered by provisional statical assumptions has become much smaller; and
at last is reached the great central problem of the Distribution of the National Dividend among a vast number of

---

[1] This is quoted from an article on "Distribution and Exchange" in the *Economic
Journal* for March 1898.
[2] These two stages are opened out in Chapters III and VI respectively of Book V.

different agents of production. The dynamical principle of "Substitution" is seen ever at work, causing the demand for, and the supply of, any one set of agents of production to be influenced, through indirect channels, by the movements of demand and supply in relation to others, even though situated in far remote fields of industry[1]. Our main concern is with human beings who are impelled, for good and evil, to change and progress. Fragmentary statical hypotheses are useful as temporary auxiliaries to dynamical —or rather biological—conceptions: but the central idea in a volume on the Foundations of economics, as in any other, must be that of living force and movement.

In backward civilizations there are periods of great economic repose. Mill looked forward without dread, and even with some warm hope, to a "Stationary State" in which population would not increase perceptibly; and man's growing power over nature would be applied to making life fuller and more harmonious, rather than to developing larger uses of material comforts and luxuries. And the fiction of a Stationary State, in which the general conditions of production, distribution and consumption remain without great change, has been used as a helpful auxiliary hypothesis by many economists. This State has been made in the past by the forces of progress; but their action is now so far balanced that the general features of social life remain nearly stationary. In the particular Solar System of which this earth forms a part, it happens that the orbits of all planets are stable: one may be a little more elongated now, and another then; but under actual conditions none of the planets can shoot off into distant space. In that sense the State of our solar system is Stationary: but its problems are thoroughly dynamical in the physical sense.

In like manner the problem of the pressure of population, with which Ricardo and Malthus were chiefly concerned, was essentially dynamical even in Comte's use of the term: its whole character was being changed by mechanical inven-

---

[1] The number of actions and reactions thus requiring to be considered is so great that a mere enumeration of the chief of them would fill a large volume; as is indicated in note XXI in the Mathematical Appendix.

tions, the desuetude of the Settlement Laws, and organic social evolution. The occasional use of the term "natural" (or "normal"), and of subsidiary statical hypotheses for special purposes, did not affect the fundamental character of their inquiries.

The Preface to the first edition of this volume stated that one of its chief purposes was to insist that the term "interest" is properly applicable only to "free" or "floating" capital; that the income from investments is of the nature of rent. Thus the rent of land is regarded as not a thing by itself, but a species of a large genus: the features which distinguish it from other incomes of the same genus are of vital importance with reference to long periods; though there are many problems relating to short periods in which land may be conveniently classed with other material agents of production. And this edition develops a little further the argument that from the social point of view and in regard to the actual world, the income derived from any thing the supply of which cannot be practically much enlarged by man's efforts, is not of the same *species* with incomes derived from appliances, such as steam-engines and houses; though it does belong to the same *genus* with them.

This distinction would have been hardly worth making if the volume had been exclusively concerned with the problems of a rigid Stationary State. In such a State for instance there could be no new tax; and therefore there would be no scope for the remark that a heavy special tax on steam-engines would hinder their replacement when worn out, and thus alter the value of things made by steam-engines; while a similar tax on the value of the inherent properties of land would have no such effect. But, in spite of the exceptionally high authority that can be quoted to the contrary, I hold that an exclusive study of purely statical conditions must be unsatisfactory[1].

[1] Prof. J. B. Clark, in his profound and suggestive *Distribution of Wealth*, 1899, "tries completely to isolate the static forces that act in distribution from the dynamic"; while insisting that "actual society is always dynamic, and the part of it that we are most concerned with is highly so" (Preface, p. vi). But we should transgress the boundaries laid down for his treatise, and enter upon "a dynamic social state," if we even took account of the existence of "labour and capital that are shifting their places in the economic system, and thus making some of the

There is indeed a general agreement that the efficiency of every agent of production tends to decline when heavy and increasing calls are made on it: and that this fact bears some analogy to the law of diminishing return from land; though there is room for difference of opinion on the not very important side issue whether the two groups of tendencies should be called by the same name. In the last edition this was indicated in Book V, chapter iv, together with the kindred fact that the line of division between Prime costs (which must be covered by price in order to make any single transaction profitable), and Supplementary costs which need not always be covered by price when trade is slack), is not rigidly fixed: it varies with the duration of the enterprise in question. These hints were designed to prepare the way for, and to be taken continuously with, the parallel discussion of Rents and Quasi-rents in relation to cost and value, which occupied chapters viii–x of Book V. But the continuity was not made sufficiently explicit. And in order to remove this defect chapter iv has been developed a little in the present edition; while chapters viii–x have been rewritten into a group of chapters viii–xi on Marginal costs in relation to values. Advantage was taken in earlier editions of the sharp illustrations which the incidence and shifting of taxes afford of the contrast between immediate and ultimate tendencies of value; and a larger use of them has been made in the present edition:

subgroups larger and others smaller" (p. 58). I on the other hand make no such limitations, except for illustrative hypotheses relating exclusively to short periods, which are to be thrown on one side as soon as their purpose has been filled: I do not base any general conclusion on them. It is therefore not surprising that, while he is adhering strictly to his own limiting rules, his results seem to be in some conflict with mine: but in fact they are generally in a different plane, and therefore cannot be in conflict. He is however constantly impelled to give hints as to the changes which would be introduced by the inclusion of dynamical considerations: and then I almost invariably find myself in agreement with him. I have hitherto avoided any reference to the small apparent differences between us, because I think they are not substantial; and that they will evaporate in time. But I am induced to refer to the matter here by Prof. Ashley's important address at the British Association, which was delivered when the text of this volume was in type. He appeared to overrate the differences of opinion among economists whose lines of work diverge from those in which he is universally acknowledged to be a master. And yet, partly perhaps in consequence of the ambiguity of the term "statical," he appears to class Prof. Clark and me together in regard to the uses of the statical method— the only point on which, so far as I am aware, there is an important difference between us.

especially in the new Appendix G on the incidence of local rates.

The old saying that "rent does not enter into cost of production" is awkwardly expressed and has led to many misunderstandings. Its use has therefore been shunned in these chapters: and much pains have been spent on the endeavour to show that the conception of a margin, like that of other elements in the problem of value, is not absolute. Though marginal costs do not govern price, it is only at the margin that the action of those forces which do govern price can be made to stand out in clear light and thoroughly studied. But the margin that must be studied in reference to long periods and enduring results differs in character as well as in extent from that which must be studied in reference to short periods and to passing fluctuations.

The nature of marginal costs varies indeed, nearly as much as their details do, with the period of time to which the problem in hand refers: and these variations are largely responsible for the well known fact that those effects of an economic cause which are not easily traced are frequently more important than, and in the opposite direction to, those which lie on the surface and attract the eye of the casual observer. This is one of those fundamental difficulties which have underlain and troubled the economic analysis of past times; its full significance is perhaps not yet generally recognized, and much more work may need to be done before it is fully mastered.

The issues thus raised in Book V, chapters VIII–XI, are in a sense central: and it has therefore been impossible to transfer them to Appendices. But they are tedious and heavy to the general reader: and he may if he will pass over them. References are indeed made to them in the discussions of the causes which govern wages in Book VI, especially in chapters I, II, and the almost new chapter XIII on standards of labour and wages. And it is true that if any one desires to probe the doctrines of Owen, Thompson, Proudhon, Rodbertus, and Marx, and even of contemporary socialists, he must make a thorough study of that seemingly simple, but really treacherous, phrase "the whole produce of labour," which has been used with easy confidence throughout a whole century of controversy.

The new analysis is endeavouring gradually and tentatively to bring over into economics, as far as the widely different nature of the material will allow, those methods of the science of small increments (commonly called the differential calculus) to which man owes directly or indirectly the greater part of the control that he has obtained in recent times over physical nature. It is still in its infancy; it has no dogmas, and no standard of orthodoxy. It has not yet had time to obtain a perfectly settled terminology; and some differences as to the best use of terms and other subordinate matters are but a sign of healthy life. In fact however there is a remarkable harmony and agreement on essentials among those who are working constructively by the new method; and especially among such of them as have served an apprenticeship in the simpler and more definite, and therefore more advanced, problems of physics. Ere another generation has passed, its dominion over that limited but important field of economic inquiry to which it is appropriate will probably be no longer in dispute.

Mention has already been made of the facts that Appendix G and the greater part of Book VI, chapter XIII are new: and that Book V, chapters VIII to XI are new in shape. But the most prominent change made in this edition is a mere matter of arrangement; some discussions, which had already been indicated as not essential to the main drift of the volume, having been transferred to Appendices. Partly as a consequence, some new matter has been introduced into each chapter of the present Book I, and into chapter IV of Book II.

My wife has aided and advised me at every stage of successive editions of this volume, and of none more than the present. Throughout each edition a very great deal has been owed to her suggestions, her care, and her judgment. Dr Keynes and Mr Price read through the proofs of the first edition and helped me greatly; and Professor Flux also has done much for me. Among the many others who have helped me on special points, in some cases in regard to more than one edition, I would specially mention Professors Ashley, Edgeworth, Haverfield, Sidgwick and Taussig; Dr Cannan, Mr Berry and Mr Pigou.

BALLIOL CROFT, CAMBRIDGE

August 1907

PREFACE TO THE SIXTH EDITION

THIS edition is practically a reprint of the fifth: a few corrections have been made in it, and some further explanations have been added. But the pagination remains generally unaltered; and a good deal of the last preface is incorporated in the present.

It is now twenty years since the first edition of this volume implied a promise that a second volume, completing the treatise, would appear within a reasonable time. But I had laid my plan on too large a scale; and its scope widened, especially on the realistic side, with every pulse of that Industrial Revolution of the present generation, which has far outdone the changes of a century ago, in both rapidity and breadth of movement.

About fifteen years ago I began to despair of completing my scheme in two volumes. Accordingly, I set aside the Economic Functions of Government (*Wirtschafts-politik*) for a third volume; and rearranged, in ampler space, the materials which I had got together on the modern conditions of industry and trade; of credit and employment. Impressed with the belief that each of these sets of conditions influences and is influenced by the others, I passed backwards and forwards from one to another; and, by successive rewritings, brought a great part of what I had to say into some sort of organic unity. But gradually it became clear that the enlarged space was still too small, and that four thick volumes would be needed for the task. This called a halt: for life is short. In fact a very long consecutive treatise, even if it can be completed, is apt to be heavy to reader as well as writer. References from one volume of it to another are perhaps a greater evil than the repetition in, say, each of two works on International Trade and on Money, of arguments that have been more fully developed in the other.

Accordingly I now propose to bring out as soon as possible an almost independent volume, part of which is already in print, on *National Industry and Trade*. About one half of it is occupied with the evolution of the present forms and conditions of national leadership in industry, with special reference to the recent changes in the character and functions of giant businesses and of combinations: the second half applies the conclusions of the first half to the modern problems of international trade. This may be followed by a companion volume on *Money, Credit, and Employment*: and perhaps by a third, which will treat of the ideal and the practicable in social and economic structure, with some account of taxation and administration.

The scope of the present volume is similar in some respects, though not in all, to that of volumes on *Foundations* (*Grundlagen*), which Roscher and some other economists have put in the forefront of groups of semi-independent volumes on economics. It avoids such special topics as currency and the organization of markets: and in regard to such matters as the structure of industry, employment, and the problem of wages, it deals mainly with normal conditions.

Economic evolution is gradual. Its progress is sometimes arrested or reversed by political catastrophes: but its forward movements are never sudden; for even in the Western world and in Japan it is based on habit, partly conscious, partly unconscious. And though an inventor, or an organizer, or a financier of genius may seem to have modified the economic structure of a people almost at a stroke; yet that part of his influence, which has not been merely superficial and transitory, is found on inquiry to have done little more than bring to a head a broad constructive movement which had long been in preparation. Those manifestations of nature which occur most frequently, and are so orderly that they can be closely watched and narrowly studied, are the basis of economic as of most other scientific work; while those which are spasmodic, infrequent, and difficult of observation, are commonly reserved for special examination at a later stage: and the motto *Natura non facit saltum* is specially appropriate to a volume on Economic Foundations.

An illustration of this contrast may be taken from the distribution of the study of large businesses between the present and a later volume. When any branch of industry offers an open field for new firms which rise to the first rank, and perhaps after a time decay, the normal cost of production in it can be estimated with reference to "a representative firm," which enjoys a fair share both of those internal economies which belong to a well organized individual business, and of those general or external economies which arise out of the collective organization of the district as a whole. A study of such a firm belongs properly to a volume on Foundations. So also does a study of the principles on which a firmly established monopoly, in the hands of a Government department or a large railway, regulates its prices with main reference to its own revenue, but with more or less consideration for the well-being of its customers.

But normal action falls into the background, when Trusts are striving for the mastery of a large market; when communities of interest are being made and unmade; and above all, when the policy of any particular establishment is likely to be governed, not with a single eye to its own business success, but in subordination to some large stock-exchange manœuvre, or some campaign for the control of markets. Such matters cannot be fitly discussed in a volume on Foundations: they belong to a volume dealing with some part of the Superstructure.

The Mecca of the economist lies in economic biology rather than in economic dynamics. But biological conceptions are more complex than those of mechanics; a volume on Foundations must therefore give a relatively large place to mechanical analogies; and frequent use is made of the term "equilibrium," which suggests something of statical analogy. This fact, combined with the predominant attention paid in the present volume to the normal conditions of life in the modern age, has suggested the notion that its central idea is "statical," rather than "dynamical." But in fact it is concerned throughout with the forces that cause movement: and its key-note is that of dynamics, rather than statics.

The forces to be dealt with are however so numerous, that it is best to take a few at a time; and to work out a number of partial solutions as auxiliaries to our main study. Thus we begin by isolating the primary relations of supply, demand and price in regard to a particular commodity. We reduce to inaction all other forces by the phrase "other things being equal": we do not suppose that they are inert, but for the time we ignore their activity. This scientific device is a great deal older than science: it is the method by which, consciously or unconsciously, sensible men have dealt from time immemorial with every difficult problem of ordinary life.

In the second stage more forces are released from the hypothetical slumber that had been imposed on them: changes in the conditions of demand for and supply of particular groups of commodities come into play; and their complex mutual interactions begin to be observed. Gradually the area of the dynamical problem becomes larger; the area covered by provisional statical assumptions becomes smaller; and at last is reached the great central problem of the Distribution of the National Dividend among a vast number of different agents of production. Meanwhile the dynamical principle of "Substitution" is seen ever at work, causing the demand for, and the supply of, any one set of agents of production to be influenced through indirect channels by the movements of demand and supply in relation to other agents, even though situated in far remote fields of industry.

The main concern of economics is thus with human beings who are impelled, for good and evil, to change and progress. Fragmentary statical hypotheses are used as temporary auxiliaries to dynamical—or rather biological—conceptions: but the central idea of economics, even when its Foundations alone are under discussion, must be that of living force and movement.

The Preface to the first edition of this volume stated that one of its chief purposes was to insist that the term "interest" is properly applicable only to "free" or "floating" capital; that the income from investments is of the nature of rent; and that the rent of land is to be regarded not as a thing by itself, but as a species of a large genus: though the features which distinguish it from other species of the same genus are almost as important as those which are common to the whole genus. There have been stages in social history in which the special features of the income yielded by the ownership of land have dominated human relations: and perhaps they may again assert a pre-eminence. But in the present age, the opening out of new countries, aided by low transport charges on land and sea, has almost suspended the tendency to Diminishing Return, in that sense in which the term was used by Malthus and Ricardo, when the English labourers' weekly wages were often less than the price of half a bushel of good wheat. And yet, if the growth of population should continue for very long even at a quarter of its present rate, the aggregate rental values of land for all its uses (assumed to be as free as now from restraint by public authority) may again exceed the aggregate of incomes derived from all other forms of material property; even though that may then embody twenty times as much labour as now.

Increasing stress has been laid in successive editions up to the present on these facts; and also on the correlated fact that in every branch of production and trade there is a margin, up to which an increased application of any agent will be profitable under given conditions; but beyond which its further application will yield a diminishing return unless there be some increase of demand accompanied by an appropriate increase of other agents of production needed to co-operate with it. And a similar increasing stress has been laid on the complementary fact that this notion of a margin is not uniform and absolute: it varies with the conditions of the problem in hand, and in particular with the period of time to which reference is being made. The rules are universal that, (1) marginal costs do not govern price; (2) it is only at the margin that the action of those forces which do govern price can be made to stand out in clear light; and

(3) the margin, which must be studied in reference to long periods and enduring results, differs in character as well as in extent from that which must be studied in reference to short periods and to passing fluctuations.

Variations in the nature of marginal costs are indeed largely responsible for the well known fact that those effects of an economic cause, which are not easily traced, are frequently more important than, and in the opposite direction to, those which lie on the surface and attract the eye of the casual observer. This is one of those fundamental difficulties which have underlain and troubled the economic analysis of past times; its full significance is perhaps not yet generally recognized, and much more work may need to be done before it is fully mastered.

The new analysis is endeavouring gradually and tentatively to bring over into economics, as far as the widely different nature of the material will allow, those methods of the science of small increments (commonly called the differential calculus) to which man owes directly or indirectly the greater part of the control that he has obtained in recent times over physical nature. It is still in its infancy; it has no dogmas, and no standard of orthodoxy. It has not yet had time to obtain a perfectly settled terminology; and some differences as to the best use of terms and other subordinate matters are but a sign of healthy life. In fact however there is a remarkable harmony and agreement on essentials among those who are working constructively by the new method; and especially among such of them as have served an apprenticeship in the simpler and more definite, and therefore more advanced, problems of physics. Ere another generation has passed, its dominion over that limited but important field of economic inquiry to which it is appropriate will probably be no longer in dispute.

My wife has aided and advised me at every stage of successive editions of this volume. Each of them owes a great deal to her suggestions, her care, and her judgment. Dr Keynes and Mr L. L. Price read through the proofs of the first edition and helped me greatly; and Mr A. W. Flux also has done much for me. Among the many others who have helped me on special points, in some cases in regard to more than one edition, I would specially mention Professors Ashley, Cannan, Edgeworth, Haverfield, Pigou and Taussig; Mr Arthur Berry and Mr C. R. Fay; and the late Professor Sidgwick.

BALLIOL CROFT
   6 MADINGLEY ROAD, CAMBRIDGE
     March 1901

PREFACE TO THE SEVENTH EDITION

THIS edition is almost a reprint of the sixth, the only changes being in small matters of detail: and both resemble the fifth edition so closely that the pagination is practically the same in all three.

It is now twenty-six years since the first edition of this volume implied a promise that a second volume, completing the treatise, would appear within a reasonable time. But I had laid my plan on too large a scale; and its scope widened, especially on the realistic side, with every pulse of that Industrial Revolution of the present generation, which has far outdone the changes of a century ago, in both rapidity and breadth of movement. So ere long I was compelled to abandon my hope of completing the work in two volumes. My subsequent plans were changed more than once, partly by the course of events, partly by my other engagements and the decline of my strength: and I am now engaged in writing an independent work, which is to extend to more than one volume, on *Industry and Trade*. It is designed to cover a considerable part of the ground over which I had hoped to travel: but it will be directed mainly to a study of the causes which have brought about the present methods and organization of business: to the influences which they exert on the quality of life; and to the ever widening problems to which they give rise.

The present volume therefore remains a general introduction to the study of economic science; similar in some respects, though not in all, to that of volumes on *Foundations* (*Grundlagen*), which Roscher and some other economists have put in the forefront of groups of semi-independent volumes on economics. It avoids such special topics as currency and the organization of markets: and in regard to such matters as the structure of industry, employment, and the problem of wages, it deals mainly with normal conditions.

... ...

Balliol Croft
6 Madingley Road, Cambridge
25 *June* 1916

The remainder of the Preface to the Seventh Edition was identical with the corresponding part of the Preface to the Sixth Edition.

2. MARSHALL'S VIEW OF THE PROBLEM OF DISTRIBUTION AND EXCHANGE

In 1898 Marshall published an article in the *Economic Journal* (vol. VIII) entitled "Distribution and Exchange", which was a reply to criticisms that had been urged against portions of the *Principles* by Professors Hadley and Irving Fisher.

In the first two sections Marshall dealt with the nature and limitations of the "statical" method in economics, and the substance of these sections has been reproduced in the *Memorials of Alfred Marshall*, edited by A. C. Pigou (1925), pp. 312–18. The third section summarized what in Marshall's view was "the place which the account of distribution and exchange given in my first volume holds in the general system of economics". It was thus in the nature of an additional preface to the *Principles*.

The fourth section was a defence of the definition of Capital which Marshall had adopted in the 3rd ed. of the *Principles*, and is reprinted in this volume in the Editorial Appendix to Book II, chapter IV (see pp. 228–33 below).

The text of section III of Marshall's article in which he discussed his treatment of the basic problems with which he was concerned especially in Books V and VI, ran as follows:

Complaints have been made that my first Book keeps the reader too long from entering on the main work before him. But it is needed from my point of view. The chapters on the Growth of Free Industry and of Economic Science are no doubt long, in spite of their being wholly inadequate if regarded as sketches of economic history. But they have no claim to be so regarded. Their aim is different. It is to emphasise, as the keynote of the treatise, the notion that economic problems are not mechanical, but concerned with organic life and growth. In combination with the following chapters on Scope and Method they claim to offer a view continuous with that of classical tradition, but differing in the stress laid on this element of organic life-growth. They claim to show that the past can afford just guidance for the present and the future only when full account is taken of the changes in man himself, and of his modes of life and thought and work; and to sketch some leading features of those changes which are of most importance for the economist. They insist that, though there is a kernel of man's nature that has scarcely changed, yet many elements of his character, that are most effective for economic uses, are of modern growth. The "strategy" of his economic conflict with nature remains nearly the same from age to age, and the lessons drawn from experiences of it can be handed down usefully from father to son. But the "tactics" of the conflict waged by men somewhat different from us, and under conditions widely different from ours, are of little or no avail. To carry over from one age to another both strategical and tactical lessons, is to incline somewhat towards a mechanical view of economics; to carry over strategical lessons only is characteristic of a biological view.

Book IV is much occupied with organic growth, and its later chapters are designed to prepare the way for the study of the influence of the element of Time in Book V. But this brings me to Professor Hadley's main indictment of my doctrine, and I had better quote that at length. He is good enough to say that my fallacies are not quite so bad as those of some other people's. I can conceive none worse than those which he supposes I have committed. He says:—

"Another instance of the same confusion between quantities and rates is furnished by the 'normal supply curve'; a confusion less glaring than that in the wage-fund, but for this very reason far more dangerous. A *market* supply curve represents a series of relations between quantities of products and costs per unit of product. A normal supply curve represents a series of relations between *rates* of production and cost per unit of product (*not* per unit of time). It is naturally assumed that, barring certain lines of industry, the latter curve has the same general shape as the former, and may be made the basis of the same kind of deductions. Even those writers, like Marshall, who see the essential difference between the two things, usually give a very inadequate study to the extent of the differences. Yet such a study of the most acute and painstaking character is absolutely essential if supply and demand curves are to be made the basis of a theory of distribution; for otherwise the results will often be diametrically opposed to the truth. For an increased *rate* of production involves a totally different set of economic pressures and reactions from those involved in an increasing *quantity* of production at the old rate."[1]

This seems inexact in word, if not in thought. A curve which represents relations between rates of production and costs per unit of product (not per unit of time), is not a scientific curve at all. Reasonings relating to it cannot be fallacious. There can be no reasonings about it, valid or invalid; for it does not exist. An equation between a volume and a weight, or a velocity and an acceleration, is not a wrong equation: it is nonsense. Normal costs cannot possibly have reference either to a unit of amount simply, or to a unit of time simply; they *must* refer to a unit of amount *and* a unit of time, that is, to a unit of amount when production is going on at a certain rate, and a certain number of units of amount are being produced in a unit of time. The terms of my definition of the normal supply curve (or schedule) are that it represents a list of supply prices, "the supply price of the production of each amount of the commodity in a year, or any other unit of time, being written against the amount." And again, "the general drift of the term Normal Supply price is always the same, whether the periods to which it refers are short or long. In every case it has reference to a certain given rate of aggregate production; that

[1] *Economic Journal*, VII, p. 484.

is, to the production of a certain aggregate amount daily or annually."[1]

Next, he seems to imply that I make some confusion between market supply curves and normal supply curves. The fact is, that twenty years ago I abandoned the use of curves for market problems because they were not really wanted; and I found people would not heed the note of warning that the curves for the normal problem relate to rates of production and consumption, and those for market curves to amounts bought and sold.[2]

Later on I found an even stronger objection of the same kind to the use of curves for wages problems; so I ceased to use them also.

Professor Hadley proceeds to settle summarily a much vexed question. He says: "The essential difference between exchange and distribution, which has puzzled so many economists, is that the former deals with funds, and the latter with flows; the former with prices, the latter with rates of wages and interest. Static methods are applicable to the former; Kinetic methods to the latter." In spite of the great authority with which he speaks, I venture to demur to his decision. I hold that in distribution and exchange alike we deal with both stocks and flows; but that, with few exceptions, the more important and difficult problems deal with flows and not with stocks. I hold that the essential distinction between statics and dynamics, if the terms must be used, is not the same as, nor even closely related to that between stocks and flows. In fact the most perfect instances of statical problems are those which deal with "steady flows" of labour, capital and goods, of wages, interest and prices in a stationary country; in which each year is just like the past, in which each generation is like that which went before.

It may be noted, as an incidental confirmation of this

---

[1] *Principles*, V, III, §5, and [a]V, v, §4.

[2] I found also that curves helped rather than hindered in such discussions as those towards the end of my *Principles*, V, II. The contrast between "stocks" of goods dealt with for market problems; flows of goods produced by "stocks" of plant for short normal problems; and secular movements where all is flow is emphasised on [b]p. 450.

---

[a] This reference applies to V, v, §5 in vol. I of the present edition.

[b] This reference applies to pages 378–9 in vol. I of the present edition.

opinoin, that our choicest illustrations of the statical or stationary state relate to agricultural and not to mineral prices. Now the annual output of a farm is a true flow; but the annual output of a mine is not a true flow, it comes out of stock; and, if the mineral veins are not practically unlimited, the exhaustion of the stock will disrupt the statical rest. The statical method is more applicable to the conditions of life in agricultural districts of America than in mineral: because in the former she yields a flow, in the latter a stock. When the stock of petroleum or of silver ore in a place turns out to be but slender, there is no equilibrium and houses are deserted. At last the pressure of population makes farmers settle there, and gather the small but steady flow of the infertile soil, and then first the statical method is applicable. There is much suggestion in the difficulties of the application of the law of diminishing return to the prices of mineral produce, and to the incomes of mine-owners (problems both of exchange and of distribution): for they differ from parallel problems with regard to agricultural land as the fitful oscillation of market price in a day's fish market, when there is a certain stock to be disposed of, differ from those steadier movements of normal value which relate to flows and not to stocks.

Thus I venture to adhere to the opinion that distribution and exchange are fundamentally the same problem, looked at from different points of view. The study of the effects of a new tax, of a bad harvest, of a new invention, of the gradual opening up of a new source of demand or supply, appears as a problem in exchange when the centre of interest is the price of a commodity, say Indian tea: and as a problem in distribution when the centre of interest is in the wages or profits of those who produce or handle the tea. But in substance the two problems are one: no discussion of wages and profits in the tea trade can have any reality if divorced from a study of prices: and *vice versa*. Further, if the harvest is abnormal, a large stock of tea may raise strange market problems in exchange and distribution in regard to the freights earned by the stock of ships, and the wages of the tea porters that happen to be available. But taking one year with another so as to deal with relatively steady flows, in which the machinery of supply can be more smoothly adapted to demand, we have problems in exchange and distribution to which the statical method seems to me more and not less applicable than it is to those connected with stocks.

Let us return from this digression on Professor Hadley's doctrine, and consider how far the statical method is applicable to problems of normal value for periods of varying lengths.

The purpose of the statical method is to fix our attention on some centre, which for the time we regard as either at rest or in steady movement; to consider the tendencies of various elements to mutually adjust themselves relatively to that centre, or perhaps to change the position of that centre. The element of Time is the source of our chief difficulties; and therefore the most important among the many uses of this method is to classify forces with reference to the time which they require for their work; and to impound in *Cæteris Paribus* those forces which are of minor importance relatively to the particular time we have in view. In other words we classify our problems provisionally according to the length of the periods to which they refer.

Thus, to take an illustration which I have worked out in more detail elsewhere,[1] we may classify problems connected with fishing as those which are affected by very quick changes, such as uncertainties of the weather; or by changes of moderate length, such as the increased demand for fish caused by the scarcity of meat during the year or two following a cattle plague; or lastly, we may consider the unprecedented increase during a whole generation of the demand for fish which might result from the rapid growth of a high-strung artisan population making little use of their muscles. The first of these cases is not to our present purpose: let us look at the second and third.

In considering the effects of the cattle plague, we neglect fluctuations due to the weather: they are so quick that they speedily obliterate one another, and are therefore not impor-

[1] *Principles*, V, v.

tant for problems of this class. Again, we neglect or take little account of variations in the numbers who are brought up as seafaring men for the opposite reason: they are too slow to produce much effect in the year or two during which the scarcity of meat lasts. Having impounded these two sets for the time, we give our full attention to such influences as the inducements which good fishing wages will offer to sailors to stay in their fishing homes for a year or two, instead of applying for work on a ship. We consider what old fishing boats, and even vessels that were not specially made for fishing, can be adapted and sent to fish for a year or two. The normal supply price which we are now seeking is the price per unit which will *quickly* call into the fishing trade capital and labour enough to obtain that amount of fish in a day's or week's fishing that has average good fortune; the influence which the price of fish will have upon the capital and labour available in the fishing trade being governed by rather narrow causes such as these.

Next, to consider the influences of the growth of a sedentary artisan population. We now concentrate our chief attention on causes which act slowly but continuously. We put aside fluctuations that come and go in a year or two, very much as in the preceding case we put aside fluctuations from day to day. Our normal supply price now for any amount of fish is the price per unit, which will slowly call into the fishing trade capital and labour enough to obtain that amount of fish in a day's or week's fishing of average good fortune. The governing forces of supply, which we now consider, would not only call sailors back to their fishing homes, but would induce many farm lads in villages neighbouring on the sea to adopt a seafaring life, and they would cause long-headed men to see that there was a trustworthy field for the investment of new capital in building fishing boats of the newest and most expensive patterns, and so on.

So far the relatively short and long period problems go on similar lines. In both use is made of that paramount device, the partial or total isolation for special study of some set of relations. In both opportunity is gained for analysing and comparing similar episodes, and making them throw

68

light upon one another; and for ordering and co-ordinating facts which are suggestive in their similarities, and are still more suggestive in the differences that peer out through their similarities. But there is a broad distinction between the two cases. In the relatively short period problem no great violence is needed for the assumption that the forces not specially under consideration may be taken for the time to be inactive. But violence is required for keeping broad forces in the pound of *Cæteris Paribus* during, say, a whole generation, on the ground that they have only an indirect bearing on the question in hand. For even indirect influences may produce great effects in the course of a generation, if they happen to act cumulatively; and it is not safe to ignore them even provisionally in a practical problem without special study. Thus the uses of the statical method in problems relating to very long periods are dangerous; care and forethought and self-restraint are needed at every step.

But the difficulties and risks of the task reach their highest point in connection with industries which conform to the law of Increasing Return; and it is just in connection with those industries that the most alluring applications of the method are to be found. Long period supply curves in relation to such industries are fascinatingly clear and vivid: but they are made too clear and vivid to be at all near to reality.[1]

Some, though by no means all, of the difficulties of this problem can be avoided by two devices. The first is to estimate the expenses of production with reference to a representative firm. This conception is biological rather than mechanical; and its application in the theory of value is one

---

[1] The great Cournot himself misapplied mathematics here. He ignored the conditions which, in real life, prevent the speedy attainment of monopoly by a single manufacturing firm: and the general drift of his argument is practically misleading. His failure contributed to make me hold back most of my diagrams as to value from formal publication for twenty years; those on monopolies were the last to be developed, and they belong to the early seventies. At about the same time I worked out diagrams relating to international trade, which I have not been able to publish with realistic surroundings even yet. A caution as to the danger of supply curves relating to Increasing Return is given in the first edition of my *Principles*, 1890, pp. 425–9, and this is enlarged in the third edition, [a]V, v, §4 and V, XI.

---

[a] These references apply to V, v, §5 and V, XII and App. H in vol. I of the present edition.

mark of the gradual transition from the mechanical view of the composition of forces, which is suitable to the earlier stages of the theory, to the biological notion of composite organic development, which belongs to its later stages. So I will speak of it in some detail.

Internal economies are those connected with the organisation of an individual firm: they increase as the firm rises to the first rank, and they dwindle as the firm decays. The external economies depend on the general organisation of the trade, on the growth of knowledge and appliances common to the trade, on the development of subsidiary industries, and so on. Now the growth of internal economies is generally more rapid than that of external. The rise and fall of individual firms may be frequent, while a great industry is going through one long oscillation, or even moving steadily forwards; as the leaves of a tree (to repeat an earlier illustration) grow to maturity, reach equilibrium, and decay many times, while the tree itself is steadily growing upwards year by year. For very long periods the oscillation of internal economies may almost be neglected: except in so far as they are indirectly dependent on external; for a large industry offers a better field in most (not in all) ways for large individual firms than a small industry offers. And we may set before our eyes a representative firm, as we might a representative tree in a forest or a representative weaver or carpenter; that is a firm, the equipment of which is representative of the general progress of the trade to which it belongs, and which "has its fair share of those internal and external economies which the aggregate scale of production in that trade will cause to accrue to such a business." By concentrating our attention on such a firm we escape many of the difficulties which attach to problems of very long period equilibrium.

The second device is to take the normal supply price in relation to long periods, not for the narrow margin of a small increase to the aggregate output of the commodity, but for the broader margin of a small increase in the appliances, the persons, and the organisation from the co-operation of which the flow of the commodity proceeds: in other words, we should take it as the supply price of "the processes of production."[1]

It is to be noted that the law of Increasing Return seldom asserts itself in short periods. A sudden increase of demand will generally raise the marginal supply price, even in industries in which the economies of production on a large scale become powerful, when they have had time to assert themselves.[2] And in setting a diminished supply price against an increased amount of the flow of the goods, we mean that a flow of that increased amount will in the course of time be supplied profitably at that lower price to meet a fairly steady corresponding demand. We exclude from view any economies that may result from substantive new inventions; but we include those which may be expected to arise naturally out of adaptations of existing ideas. In making this estimate we look forward to a suitable time. But here is a difficulty. A suitable time to allow for the introduction of the economies appertaining to one increase in the scale of production is not long enough for another and larger increase, so we must fix on some fairly long time ahead, which is likely to be indicated by the special problem in hand, and adjust the whole series of supply prices to it. But after these and other corrections have been made, other difficulties remain behind, chiefly connected with the plastic condition of man and of his appliances and organisation for production. Thus, especially where the tendency to increasing return is strong, the economic pendulum does not swing back along the course by which it came.[3]

[1] *Principles*, [a]V, xi, §3.
[2] *Principles*, V, v.
[3] This is represented by the dotted line in the diagram, *Principles*, [b]V, xi, §3. We could get much nearer to nature if we allowed ourselves a more complex illustration. We might take a series of curves, of which the first allowed for the economies likely to be introduced as the result of each increase in the scale of production during one year, a second curve doing the same for two years, a third for three years, and so on. Cutting them out of cardboard and standing them up side by side, we should obtain a surface, of which the three dimensions represented amount, price, and time respectively. If we had marked on each curve the point corresponding to that amount which, so far as can be foreseen, seems likely to be the normal amount for the year to which that curve related, then these points would

[a] This reference applies to V, v, §6 and App. H, §1 in vol. 1 of the present edition.
[b] This reference applies to App. H, §2 in vol. 1 of the present edition.

In such cases, therefore, it remains legitimate to speak of a position of balance or equilibrium between the forces of progress and decay, which would be attained if the conditions under view were supposed to act uniformly for a long time. But such notions must be taken broadly. The attempt to make them precise over-reaches our strength. If we include in our account nearly all the conditions of real life, the problem is too heavy to be handled; if we select a few, then long-drawn-out and subtle reasonings with regard to them become scientific toys rather than engines for practical work.

For this reason the theoretical backbone of our knowledge of the causes which govern value, on its two sides of distribution and exchange, is put together in my Book V. The word "Theory" applies in the title of that Book alone. It deals with abstractions; and refers to realities for the purpose of illustration only, not of construction. Its aim is not so much the acquisition of knowledge, as of power; power to order and arrange knowledge, especially with reference to the eternal opposition of forces impelling people to do, and forces holding them back. Even where, for some of the many reasons just noted, there is no true oscillation, the best device that has yet been found for studying, analysing, and comparing the chief economic forces at work anywhere, for ordering and co-ordinating facts about them, is to isolate them for the time. When so isolated they will almost always show an equilibrium point; because man's capacities are finite as regards both gratification and work; and however much stronger one may be than the other at first, we have only to conceive a great change in one direction to find the strength of the second overtaking and passing that of the first. And the conception of this equilibrium point helps to give precision to the ideas.

This work is preliminary; it does not lead direct to useful conclusions. But it enables the mind in search for such conclusions, whether as regards the past, the present, or the

form a curve on the surface, and that curve would be a fairly true long period normal supply curve for a commodity obeying the law of Increasing Return. See my *Principles*, b V, xi, § 5; compare also an article by Mr Cunynghame, *Economic Journal*, vol. ii.

b This reference applies to App. H, § 3 in vol. i of the present edition.

future, to strike, as it were, a whole chord at once instead of a single note. In the later stages of our work such preliminary devices should seldom be prominent; their aid should be manifest in the work, but they themselves should not be manifest. Their function is to give increased power to common sense, and common sense is the outcome of the experience of life, our own life and that of our ancestors; it is a biological rather than a dynamical instrument.

Construction begins with Book VI. The business of marketing, whether for labour or goods, does not lie within its field; because these cannot be properly explained without reference to money, credit, speculation, international trade, &c., all of which belong to a later Volume.[1]

But the human element of the problem is carried some way. The keynote of the Book is in the fact that free human beings are not brought up to their work on the same principles as a machine, or horse, or a slave. If they were, there would be very little difference between the distribution and the exchange side of value; for every agent of production would reap a return adequate to cover its own expenses of production with wear and tear, &c.; at all events after allowance had been made for casual failures to adjust supply to demand. But as it is, our growing power over nature yields an ever larger surplus above absolute necessities; and this is not absorbed by an unlimited increase of the population. And there remain therefore the questions: What are the general causes which govern the distribution of this surplus among the people? What part is played by conventional necessaries, *i.e.* the Standard of Comfort? What by the influence of modes and amounts of consumption over efficiency, and the Standard of Life? What by the many-sided action of the principle of substitution, and of the struggle for survival between hand-workers and brain-workers of different classes and grades? What by the power which the

---

[1] Some hold that a realistic description of markets should come early. I think not, on the ground that true description is a very difficult thing; it can be made introductory to analysis only by being made superficial. The outward machinery of the Stock Exchange or the Liverpool cotton market can be explained to a child; but that is not describing the markets. Description and analysis must go, not one before the other, but, as Schmoller says, in alternate steps—right, left; right, left; right, left.

use of capital gives to those in whose hands it is? What part of the general flow is turned to remunerate those who work (including here the undertaking of ventures) and "wait," as contrasted with those who work (and undertake) and consume at once the fruits of their endeavours? An attempt is made to give a broad answer to those and some similar questions.[1]

Meanwhile a general account is given of the broad causes that govern the relative prices of different kinds of effort and sacrifice, that is, of the factors of production of commodities; and thus the exchange side of the general problem of value is advanced together with the distribution side. The discussion relates to flows almost throughout. Land (in an old country) is a stock; the stock of goods or labour of any special kind becomes occasionally important for short period problems. But in the main we are concerned with the prices of flows of goods and labour, of population and capital.

In this last respect the difference between Book VI and the latter part of Book V is not very great. But there is a growing difference in tone. In Book V the theory of oscillations about a point of equilibrium is prominent, but not in Book VI. There we have very little to do with oscillations

[1] It lies beside my main argument; but perhaps I should remark that Professor Hadley seems to have misconceived my position as to the rate of interest. He says (p. 481): "We are told that the interest rate is one which will make the demand and supply of capital equal; and that this is a determinate solution, because an increase of rate tends to increase the supply of capital and to diminish the demand. ...In the first place it is not quite certain that an increase in the rate of interest increases the supply of capital. All that can be said is that the weight of authority favours this view; and when so much is made to depend upon a postulate this is hardly a satisfactory method of establishing it." I think this is a mistake. My reasoning does not turn upon this assumption; it would be unaffected by the supposition that the supply of capital is independent of the rate of interest. Nay, it would be valid even if we amused ourselves by supposing that a rise in the rate of interest diminished the supply of capital; provided we also supposed that it ultimately diminished the demand for capital faster.

He continues:—"In the second place, an increase in the rate of interest does not always appear to diminish the demand for capital.... Before a commercial crisis interest is high, but everybody wants to invest capital; after such a crisis interest is low, but nobody wants to invest capital." Here he seems to mix up two different things. The broad causes which govern interest in general, and with which alone we are concerned in a general discussion of distribution, have little to do with the fluctuations of interest before and after a commercial crisis. The first has only an indirect connection with the machinery of credit. The second turns mainly on fluctuations in the general purchasing power of money caused by a disorganisation of credit following on a great expansion of it. Such questions are expressly deferred to my second Volume. If Professor Hadley thought I had claimed to answer them in my first, he was indeed justified in describing my treatment of interest as slight.

of a mechanical sort about a centre of equilibrium. We discuss demand and supply in their general relations, but ever more and more from a biological point of view. Especially is that the case in the final chapter, which gives a slight partial sketch of the "Influence of Progress on Value." Every page of that chapter is dominated by conceptions of provisional equilibria of opposing forces. An endeavour is made, by their latent aid, to present at once whole chords, instead of single notes. But the equilibria themselves never appear. The chapter aims at being dynamical, if that phrase must be used; but I prefer to regard it as biological. It is, however, of narrow scope. It deals but slightly with the progress of man's economic environment. It scarcely touches the progress of man's nature; and that is, I conceive, the centre of the ultimate aim of economic studies.

The suggestions with which Professor Hadley ends his article are not, as I understand them, inconsistent with the opinions here submitted. The form into which he has thrown them is indeed somewhat paradoxical. But when he comes to convert them, as it is much to be hoped he will, from mere suggestions to solid construction, he will need to limit and condition them; and then perhaps they will appear less unfamiliar than they do now. For instance, something of modern notions as to the dominance of biological, rather than mechanical forces, over the ultimate course of human development seems to be implied in his striking conclusion: "The theoretical solution is found, not at the point of greatest advantage to individuals, but in the conditions producing greatest strength for the community. In other words, it is determined by natural selection, instead of by mercantile competition." The first of these statements reminds me of the unguarded optimism of Bastiat's "Harmonies," which by their exaggeration invited reaction and hindered progress. Further, while holding that natural selection is the strongest and most important of economic forces, I think it is far from being able to "determine" by itself the solution of any great problem. I regard mercantile competition as one of the many agencies through which natural selection works; and not as an alternative to it.

CONTENTS

PAGE xix

a. In its present form this Table of Contents dates substantially from the 5th edition.

PAGE xxxiii

a. The construction of the final clause in this sentence reading: "than he can in the form of any single commodity" is ungrammatical. It would seem to require to be emended on some such lines as the following: "which would not usually be true in the case of any single commodity."

It may be noted that the contrast drawn in this sentence in the Contents between "a given *quantum*" and a "given percentage" of value in the form of money, does not appear in Appendix F, Barter, to which the sentence relates.

EDITORIAL APPENDIX TO
THE CONTENTS

TEXT OF CONTENTS OF THE FIRST TO
THE FOURTH EDITIONS[a]

CONTENTS
OF THE FIRST EDITION

[Italics are used to give references to definitions of technical terms.]

BOOK I

PRELIMINARY SURVEY

Chapter I. Introduction. § 1. Economics is both a study of wealth and a branch of the study of man. The history of the world has been shaped by religious and economic forces. § 2. The question whether poverty is necessary gives its highest interest to economics. § 3. The science is in the main of recent growth. § 4. The fundamental characteristic of modern business is not competition, but *Free industry and enterprise.* § 5. Preliminary account of *Value.* . . . . . . pp. 1–9

Chapter II. The Growth of Free Industry and Enterprise. § 1. Physical causes act most powerfully in the early stages of civilization, which have necessarily taken place in warm climates. In an early civilization movement is slow; but there is movement, and custom is generally a disguised form of slow-moving competition. § 2. Divided ownership strengthens the force of custom and resists changes. The influence of custom on the methods of industry is cumulative. § 3. The Greeks brought Northern energy to bear on Oriental culture. Modern in many respects, they yet regarded industry as belonging to slaves, and their impatience of steady industry was a chief cause of their fall. § 4. The strength of character of the Romans fitted them for business, but they preferred to acquire wealth by the sword, and thus exerted little direct influence on economic science; but the Stoic philosophy and the cosmopolitan experience of the later Roman lawyers led them gradually to enlarge the sphere of contract. § 5. The Teuton slow to learn from those whom he had conquered. Learning kept alive by the Saracen. Civilization moved northwards and westwards, and the old contest between town and country revived. §§ 6, 7. Self-government by the people could exist only in the free towns; which were the precursors of modern industrial civilization. § 8. The influence of Chivalry and of the

---

[a] The lists of Contents of the first four editions are reprinted here, partly in order to show the changes which took place in the structure of the *Principles* before it reached its final form—in the 5th ed.; and partly to enable references and passages reprinted from these earlier editions to be related to the context in which they appeared.

77

Church. The growth of large armies led to the overthrow of the free cities. But the hopes of progress were again raised by the invention of printing, the Reformation, and the discovery of the New World. §9. The first benefit of the maritime discoveries went to the Spanish peninsula. But soon moved further on, to Holland, to France, and to England. pp. 10–30

BOOK II

SOME FUNDAMENTAL NOTIONS

BOOK III

DEMAND OR CONSUMPTION

BOOK IV

PRODUCTION OR SUPPLY

BOOK V

THE THEORY OF EQUILIBRIUM OF DEMAND AND SUPPLY

Chapter I. On Markets. §1. Most economic problems have a kernel relating to the equilibrium of demand and supply. §2. Definition of a *Market*. §3. Limitations of a market with regard to *Space*. General conditions which affect the extent of the market for a thing; suitability for grading and

BOOK VI

COST OF PRODUCTION FURTHER CONSIDERED

BOOK VII

VALUE, OR DISTRIBUTION AND EXCHANGE

CONTENTS
OF THE SECOND EDITION

[Italics are used to give references to definitions of technical terms.]

BOOK I

PRELIMINARY SURVEY

91

BOOK II

SOME FUNDAMENTAL NOTIONS

BOOK III

DEMAND AND CONSUMPTION

BOOK IV

SUPPLY OR PRODUCTION

more capital and labour to be profitably applied. The Law relates to the amount of the produce, not its value. Final statement of the Law. §2. A *Dose* of capital and labour. *Marginal dose, marginal return, margin of cultivation.* The marginal dose is not necessarily the last in time. *Surplus Produce.* Its relation to rent. Ricardo confined his attention to the circumstances of an old country. §3. Every measure of fertility must be relative to place and time. §4. As a rule the poorer soils rise in value relatively to the richer, as the pressure of population increases. §5. Ricardo said that the richest lands were cultivated first; this is true in the sense in which he meant it. But it is apt to be misunderstood; as it was by Carey, who has collected striking instances of new settlers passing by lands which have ultimately become the most valuable. §6. But Ricardo had underrated the indirect advantages which a dense population offer to agriculture, and this has an important bearing on the doctrine of population. §7. The Laws of Return from fisheries, mines and building ground. NOTE on the meaning of the phrase "a Dose of capital and labour." pp. 206–228

BOOK V

THE THEORY OF THE EQUILIBRIUM OF DEMAND AND SUPPLY

BOOK VI

VALUE, OR DISTRIBUTION AND EXCHANGE

Chapter I. Preliminary Survey of Distribution and Exchange. §1. The Physiocrats assumed, in accordance with the peculiar circumstances of their time and country, that wages were at their lowest possible level, and that much the same was true of the interest on Capital. These rigid assumptions were partially relaxed by Adam Smith, and by Malthus. Ricardo's language was loose; but he did not hold the "iron law of wages" commonly attributed to him. §2. The deteriorating effect of low wages has been insisted on by Mill, and more fully by General Walker and other American economists. §§3, 4. Progressive Modifications of the assump-

seen most clearly in the case of independent handicrafts-men; but it can also be traced under the modern system of industry. §6. In estimating the Quasi-rent of the labourer's skill, account must be taken not only of his wear and tear, but also of his fatigue. §7. The extra income earned by natural abilities may be regarded as a rent, when we are considering the sources of the incomes of individuals, but not with reference to the normal earnings of a trade.. . . . . . . pp. 604–614

transport have been greater. §5. Changes in the labour values of corn, meat, house-room, fuel, clothing, water, light, news, and travel. §§6–8. Progress has raised the labour-value of English land, urban and rural, taken together; though it has lowered the value of most kinds of material appliances; and the increase of capital has lowered its proportionate, but not its total income. §§9, 10. Nature and causes of changes in the earnings of different industrial classes. §11. The earnings of exceptional ability. §12. Progress has done more than is generally thought to raise the wages of labour, and has probably lessened rather than increased, the inconstancy of employment of free labour; but very great evils remain. §13. The broader influences of progress. Earnings in relation to the *Standard of Life*, that is of activities as well as of wants. Mischievous ambiguity of the phrase the *Standard of Comfort*. §14. Progress in relation to leisure. The wastefulness of excessive work. §15. In some trades shorter hours combined with double shifts would bring almost unmixed gain. §16. But in many trades shortening the hours of labour would lessen the output. §17. Fallacy of supposing that such a diminution of the hours of work, as did not increase efficiency at least in proportion, could permanently increase the demand for labour or the constancy of employment. §18. Fallacy of supposing that, because one trade can gain by making its labour scarce, therefore all trades can do so. The untrustworthiness of direct appeals to facts and of the arguments *post hoc ergo propter hoc*. §19. General conclusions as to the good and evil of a reduction of the hours of labour.

CONTENTS
OF THE THIRD EDITION

[Italics are used to give references to definitions of technical terms. Asterisks denote Chapters or Sections which consist largely of new matter.]

BOOK I

PRELIMINARY SURVEY

BOOK II

SOME FUNDAMENTAL NOTIONS

BOOK III

DEMAND AND CONSUMPTION

BOOK IV

THE AGENTS OF PRODUCTION

LAND, LABOUR, CAPITAL AND ORGANIZATION

BOOK V

THE THEORY OF THE EQUILIBRIUM OF DEMAND AND SUPPLY

BOOK VI

VALUE, OR DISTRIBUTION AND EXCHANGE

Chapter I.* Preliminary survey of distribution and exchange. §1. The Physiocrats assumed, in accordance with the peculiar circumstances of their time and country, that wages were at their lowest possible level, and that much the same was true of the interest on capital. These rigid assumptions were partially relaxed by Adam Smith, and by Malthus. §§2–5. A series of hypothetical illustrations of the influence of demand in distribution drawn from a society, in which the problem of the relations between capital and labour do not exist. §§6–9. The influence of demand in distribution; the action of the law of substitution being directed by business experts. Marginal uses do not govern value; but, together with value, they are governed by the general conditions of demand and supply. The *net product* of a particular kind of labour; and of capital. The demand for capital in general. §10. The national dividend is taken to include those elements of income which are reckoned as such in ordinary discourse.

pp. 566–589

Chapter II.* Preliminary survey of distribution and exchange, continued. §1. The causes affecting the supply of the agents of production exert a coordinate influence with those affecting demand over distribution. §§2–4. Recapitulation of the causes, discussed in Book IV, which affect the supply of various forms of labour and capital. The irregular influence which an increase in remuneration exerts on the exertion put forth by an individual. The more regular correspondence between normal wages and the growth of the population in numbers and vigour, especially the latter. The general influence exerted on the accumulation of capital and other forms of wealth, by the benefits to be derived from saving. §5. Land may be regarded as a special form of capital in relation both to the influence of demand in distribution, and to the application of the resources of an individual in production: but it stands on a different footing from capital relatively to that normal influence of the forces of supply in distribution, which we are considering in the present chapter. §6. A technical discussion as to consumer's surplus; worker's surplus; saver's surplus; and the temporary producer's surplus or quasi-rent yielded by appliances for production made by man. §7. The mutual relations between the earnings and efficiencies of different groups of workers. §8. We assume throughout no more enterprise, knowledge and freedom of competition than are in fact characteristic of the particular group of workers, employers, &c. at the place and time under discussion. §§9–11. On the relations between labour in general and capital in general. Capital aids labour. And it competes with labour for the field of employment: but this phrase needs to be interpreted carefully. Its general meaning, at all events with regard to normal results, is

114

many trades shortening the hours of labour would lessen the output. §17. Fallacy of supposing that such a diminution of the hours of work, as did not increase efficiency at least in proportion, could permanently increase the demand for labour or the constancy of employment. §18. Fallacy of supposing that, because one trade can gain by making its labour scarce, therefore all trades can do so. The untrustworthiness of direct appeals to facts and of the arguments *post hoc ergo propter hoc.* §19. General conclusions as to the good and evil of a reduction of the hours of labour.

CONTENTS
OF THE FOURTH EDITION

BOOK I

PRELIMINARY SURVEY

BOOK II

SOME FUNDAMENTAL NOTIONS

BOOK III

ON WANTS AND THEIR SATISFACTION

BOOK IV

THE AGENTS OF PRODUCTION

LAND, LABOUR, CAPITAL AND ORGANIZATION

121

BOOK V

THEORY OF THE EQUILIBRIUM OF DEMAND AND SUPPLY

BOOK VI

VALUE, OR DISTRIBUTION AND EXCHANGE

Chapter I. Preliminary survey of distribution and exchange. §1. The drift of the Book as a whole. §2. The Physiocrats assumed, in accordance with the peculiar circumstances of their time and country, that wages were at their lowest possible level, and that much the same was true of the interest on capital. These rigid assumptions were partially relaxed by Adam Smith, and by Malthus. §§3–6. A series of hypothetical illustrations of the influence of demand in distribution drawn from a society, in which the problem of the relations between capital and labour do not exist. §§7, 8. The influence of the principle of substitution in distribution. The net product of a particular kind of labour; and of capital. §9. The demand for capital in general. §10. Marginal uses do not govern value; but, together with value, they are governed by the general conditions of demand and supply. §11. Further study of the national income, or dividend.

Chapter II. Preliminary survey of distribution and exchange, continued. §1. The causes affecting the supply of the agents of production exert a coordinate influence with those affecting demand over distribution. §§2–4. Recapitulation of the causes, discussed in Book IV, which affect the supply of various forms of labour and capital. The irregular influence which an increase in remuneration exerts on the exertion put forth by an individual. The more regular correspondence between normal wages and the growth of the population in numbers and vigour, especially the latter. The general influence exerted on the accumulation of capital and other forms of wealth, by the benefits to be derived from saving. §5. Land may be regarded as a special form of capital in relation both to the influence of demand in distribution, and to the application of the resources of an individual in production: but it stands on a different footing from capital relatively to that normal influence of the forces of supply in distribution, which we are considering in the present chapter. §6. Provisional conclusion of one stage of the argument. §7. The mutual relations between the earnings and efficiencies of different groups of workers. §8. We assume throughout no more enterprise, knowledge and freedom of competition than are in fact characteristic of the particular group of workers, employers, &c. at the place and time under discussion. §9. On the relations between labour in general and capital in general. Capital aids labour. And it competes with labour for the field of employment: but this phrase needs to be interpreted carefully. §§10, 11. The influence exerted on wages by the growth of wealth in other forms than trade capital. The limited sense in which it is true that wages depend on advances made by capital §§12, 13. NOTES on the doctrine of the Wages Fund, and on different kinds of surplus.

Chapter III. Earnings of labour. §1. The scope of chapters III–X. §2. Competition tends to make weekly wages in similar employments not equal, but proportionate to the efficiency of the workers. Time-earnings. Payment by Piecework. Efficiency-earnings. Time-earnings do not tend to equality but efficiency-earnings do. §§3, 4. Real wages and Nominal wages. Allowance must be made for variations in the purchasing power of money, with special reference to the consumption of the grade of labour concerned; and for trade expenses and all incidental advantages and disadvantages. §5. Wages partly paid in kind. The Truck System. §6. Uncertainty of success and irregularity of employment. §7. Supplementary earnings. Family earnings. §8. The attractiveness of a trade does not depend merely on its money-earnings, but its net advantages. Influence of individual and national character. Peculiar conditions of the lowest grade of workers.

Progress has raised the labour-value of English land, urban and rural, taken together; though it has lowered the value of most kinds of material appliances; and the increase of capital has lowered its proportionate, but not its total income. §§9, 10. Nature and causes of changes in the earnings of different industrial classes. §11. The earnings of exceptional ability. §12. Progress has done more than is generally thought to raise the wages of labour, and has probably lessened rather than increased, the inconstancy of employment of free labour; but very great evils remain. §13. The broader influences of progress. Earnings in relation to the Standard of Life, that is of activities as well as of wants. Mischievous ambiguity of the phrase the Standard of Comfort. §14. Progress in relation to leisure. The wastefulness of excessive work. §15. In some trades shorter hours combined with double shifts would bring almost unmixed gain. §16. But in many trades shortening the hours of labour would lessen the output. §17. Fallacy of supposing that such a diminution of the hours of work, as did not increase efficiency at least in proportion, could permanently increase the demand for labour or the constancy of employment. §18. Fallacy of supposing that, because one trade can gain by making its labour scarce, therefore all trades can do so. The untrustworthiness of direct appeals to facts and of the arguments post hoc ergo propter hoc. §19. General conclusions as to the good and evil of a reduction of the hours of labour.

BOOK I

PRELIMINARY SURVEY

CHAPTER I

INTRODUCTION

PAGE I

a. Throughout the first four editions Book I contained chapters on the Growth of Free Industry and Enterprise, the Growth of Economic Science, and the Scope and Method of Economics, which were transferred (with some rearrangement) in the 5th edition to form Appendices A–D. The change in arrangement can best be followed by comparing the Tables of Contents of the first four editions with that of the final (8th) edition. See also the editorial notes to Appendices A–D.

b. So since the 1st edition.

c. Except where otherwise stated, the wording of this chapter dates substantially from the 1st edition.

d. The title of this chapter remained unchanged since the 1st edition.

e. So since the 4th ed. (p. 1), where the present sentence replaced the following sentence dating from the 1st ed. (p. 1):

Political Economy, or *Economics,* is a study of man's actions in the ordinary business of life; it inquires how he gets his income and how he uses it.

Marshall's earlier definition in *The Economics of Industry* by Alfred Marshall and Mary Paley Marshall (1879), p. 5 ran as follows:

Those portions of human conduct which are directed towards the acquirement of material wealth, and those conditions of human well-being which directly depend on material wealth, are called *Economic.* The *Science of Economics* collects, examines, arranges and reasons about the facts which are connected with the economic habits and conditions of well-being in various countries at various times.

See also editorial note **a** to vol. 1, page 43.

PAGE 3

a. In the 5th ed. (p. 3) the word "nineteenth" replaced the word "present" dating from the 1st ed. (p. 3).

PAGE 4

a. The following clause after the word "sake" in the 1st ed. (p. 4) was deleted from the 2nd ed.: "and it is not unnatural that their just contempt for wealth as an end of life should extend itself to the study of wealth, and cause them generally to neglect it."

b. This sentence dates substantially from the 2nd ed. (p. 4).

c. So since the 2nd ed. (p. 4) where the words "it is indeed true ...etc." replaced the words "It may be true...etc." in the 1st ed. (p. 4). In the first three editions the sentence beginning with the words "It may be [is indeed] true...etc." was preceded by the following sentence which was deleted from the 4th ed.: "The ordinary business of life is entirely different in form from what it was even a little while ago."

PAGE 5

a. So since the 3rd ed. (p. 5) where the concluding words of this sentence replaced the following words in the 2nd ed. (p. 5): "the causes that determine the relative values of different things." In the 1st ed. (p. 5) the corresponding words ran as follows: "the causes that determine value."

b. The words "in business" after the word "racing" dating from the 1st ed. (p. 5) were deleted from the 3rd ed.

c. "quite" since the 2nd ed. (p. 5); "fundamentally" in the 1st ed. (p. 5).

PAGE 6

a. So since the 3rd ed. (p. 6) where the opening sentence of this paragraph replaced the following sentences, dating from the 1st ed. (p. 6): "further the term 'competition' not only fails to go to the root of the matter, and thus errs by defect; it also errs by excess. For it has gathered about it evil savour...etc."

PAGE 7

a. So since the 3rd ed. (p. 7). In the 1st and 2nd editions (p. 7) this sentence was in a footnote, with a reference, deleted from the 3rd ed., to "Ochenkowski's *Englands wirtschaftliche Entwicklung im Ausgange des Mittelalters*, pp. 87 and 93–4".

b. The remainder of §4, with the exception of two sentences taken from the 1st ed. (p. 8), was inserted in the 5th ed. (pp. 7–10).

PAGE 8

a. A second edition of the *Economics of Industry* by Alfred and Mary Paley Marshall was published in 1881, and it continued to be reprinted till 1889. After the publication of the first edition of his *Principles of Economics* in 1890, he withdrew copies of the early *Economics of Industry* as far as possible from circulation. In 1892 he brought out a book of a quite different nature, under the title *Elements of Economics of Industry. Being the First Volume of Elements of Economics*, which, apart from a chapter on Trade Unions, was merely an abridgment of his *Principles of Economics* (see also p. 12 above, and note **d** to page 702 of vol. 1 in this edition).

PAGE 9

a. This and the following sentence are taken with only verbal changes from the 1st ed. (p. 8). In the 1st ed. these sentences were preceded by the following words, which were deleted from the 3rd ed.:

There are thus strong reasons for doubting whether the moral character of business in the modern age compares as unfavourably as is sometimes supposed with that of earlier times. At all events, while the controversy on this point is still unsettled, it is best to describe that character by a term that does not imply any moral qualities...etc.

PAGE 10

a. The remainder of this paragraph, except for the last clause, dates from the 3rd ed. (p. 8).

b. So since the 7th ed. (p. 10), where the footnote was added. In its earlier form this clause ran: "will occupy a large share of our attention towards the end of this treatise."

c. In the 1st ed. §5 contained a brief account of the meaning of the word "value", which was transferred in the 5th and later editions to Book II, ch. 11, §6. The present §5 was inserted in the 5th ed., but a good deal of the matter in it dates from the 1st ed.

d. This paragraph dates from the 5th ed. (p. 10).

e. While the last two sentences of this paragraph date from Book I, ch. VIII, §1, p. 91 in the 1st ed., the first three sentences were inserted in the 5th ed. (pp. 10–11) where they replaced the following sentences dating from the 1st ed. (p. 91):

Till not very long ago the *Distribution* and *Exchange* of wealth were governed in the main by conditions which changed but slowly, and by institutions which had the authority of custom and prescription, and which most people were content to take as they found them. Even where there was no slavery and no rigid system of caste, the governing classes seldom took much thought for the material well-being of the great mass of the workers; while the workers had not the habits of mind nor the opportunities of thought and action required for thinking out the problems of their own lives.

The first clause in the first of the sentences just quoted from the 1st ed. was changed in the 4th ed. (p. 110) to read as follows: "Till not very long ago the social and economic conditions of life and work changed but slowly."

f. *Industry and Trade* was published in 1919.

PAGE 11

a. The remainder of §5, which dates substantially from the 1st ed. (pp. 91–3), was there placed in Book I, ch. VIII, §1.

PAGE 12

a. The following clause, dating from the 1st ed. (p. 92), after the word "which", was deleted from the 5th ed.: "weakened as it was by a series of bad harvests."

b. So since the 5th ed. (p. 12) where the first clause of this sentence replaced the following clause dating from the 1st ed. (p. 93): "Some German economists in particular seem to exaggerate its evils."

PAGE 13

a. So since the 5th ed. (p. 13) where this sentence replaced the following sentence dating from the 1st ed. (p. 93):

Some set themselves to collect and arrange facts and statistics relating either to past or to present times; while others occupy themselves chiefly with analysis and reasoning on the basis of those facts which are ready to hand.

BOOK I, CHAPTER II

THE SUBSTANCE OF ECONOMICS

PAGE 14

a. The origin and the wording of this chapter is shown throughout in the editorial notes.

In the 1st edition the subject-matter of this chapter was contained, in its original form, in Book I, chapter v, entitled "Methods of Study", and chapter vi, "Economic Motives". In the 2nd to the 4th editions it was combined in Book I, chapter v, "The Scope of Economics". In the 5th and later editions it was divided between Book I, chapter ii, entitled "The Substance of Economics", and Appendix C "The Scope and Method of Economics".

b. So since the 5th edition.

c. This paragraph and footnote were inserted in the 5th ed. (p. 14).

PAGE 15

a. So since the 5th ed. (p. 15), where this sentence replaced the following sentence dating from the 2nd ed. (p. 73):

The advantage which economics has over other branches of social science appears to arise from the fact that while they deal almost exclusively with *quality* of human motives, it deals with *quantity* as well as quality: for it concerns itself chiefly with just that class of motives which are measurable, and therefore are specially amenable to treatment by scientific machinery.

b. This sentence dates substantially from the 3rd ed. (p. 75).

c. So since the 5th ed. (p. 15), where this sentence replaced the following sentence and footnote dating from the 2nd ed. (p. 73):

An opening is made for the methods and the tests of exact science as soon as the force of a person's motives can be measured by the sum of money, which he will just give up in order to secure a desired satisfaction, or again the sum which is just required to induce him to undergo a certain fatigue.[1]

[1] J. S. Mill had himself indicated the centre of the strength of economics when he says (*Logic*, Book VI, ch. IX, §3) that in economic phenomena "the psychological law mainly concerned is the familiar one that a greater gain is

preferred to a smaller;" and argues that science gets a better hold in economic than in other social phenomena because it deals with motives that can be compared quantitatively and measured one against another.

The reference to Mill in this footnote was placed in the 1st ed. in the text of Book I, ch. VI (p. 78), where the sentence ending with the words "measured one against the other" was succeeded by the following sentence which was deleted from the 2nd ed.: "It is this notion of measurability that he really takes as the basis of his work, though he does not emphasise it."

d. The words between dashes date from the 5th ed. (p. 15).

e. This and the remaining paragraphs of §1 date, except where otherwise stated, from the 3rd ed. (pp. 76–7).

f. The following sentence and footnote after the sentence ending with the word "pleasures" in the 3rd ed. (p. 76) were deleted from the 5th ed.:

On another day he may have neither more nor less money to spare; but his mood may be different, and perhaps there may be several ways in which he can get more pleasure from spending the money than he could have got on the earlier day from any way of spending it.[1]

[1] For simplicity this illustration refers to things consumed in a single use. But most of the material objects of desire are more or less enduring sources of gratification: and of course the desire for such an object is not generally accompanied by a conscious anticipation of the particular pleasures to be derived from its use; among which a prominent place must often be given to the mere pleasure of possession.

Presumably the word "not" in the third line of the foregoing footnote was inserted by mistake and should have been deleted.

PAGE 16

a. So since the 5th ed. (p. 16) where the words "persons under similar conditions" replaced the words "persons who are *prima facie* similar and similarly situated", dating from the 3rd ed. (p. 77).

b. This clause was inserted in the 5th ed. (p. 16) where it replaced the following clause dating from the 3rd ed. (p. 77): "which it is the function of the psychologist to analyse."

c. This and the following five sentences were inserted in the 5th ed. (pp. 16–17).

PAGE 17

a. This paragraph dates from the 3rd ed. (p. 78).

b. The following paragraph in this footnote dating from the 3rd ed. (p. 78 n.) was deleted from the 5th ed.:

Thus T. H. Green (*Prolegomena to Ethics*, pp. 165–6) says: The pleasure to be derived from doing one's duty "cannot be the exciting cause of the desire, any more than the pleasure of satisfying hunger can be the exciting cause of hunger....When the idea of which the realisation is sought is not that of enjoying any pleasure, the fact that self-satisfaction is sought in the effort to realize the idea of the desired object does not make pleasure the object of the desire....The man who calmly faces a life of suffering in the fulfilment of what he conceives to be his mission could not bear to do otherwise. So to live is his good. If he could attain the consciousness of having accomplished, if he could count himself to have apprehended—and probably just in proportion to the elevation of his character he is unable to do so—he would find satisfaction in the consciousness and with it a certain pleasure. But supposing this pleasure to be attained, only the exigencies of a theory could suggest the notion that, as so much pleasure, it makes up for the pleasures foregone and the pains endured in the life through which it has been reached". While to others it appears obvious that the pain of deliberately refusing to do his duty, and so to live "as is his good", is less than the pains which he would endure in so living.

   c. So from the 5th ed. (p. 17). In the 3rd and 4th editions (p. 78 n.) the beginning of the sentence ran: "It is true that this large use of "pain and pleasure" has sometimes served as a bridge by which...etc."

   d. The final paragraph of this footnote which was deleted from the 5th ed. ran as follows in the 3rd and 4th editions (p. 78 n.):

> Reference may also be made to Prof. Mackenzie's interesting discussion of "The relations between Ethics and Economics" in the *International Journal of Ethics*, vol. III, and in his *Introduction to Social Philosophy*; but his position appears to be even more uncompromising than Green's.

PAGE 18

   a. So since the 3rd ed. (p. 79) where this sentence replaced the following sentences dating from the 1st ed. (p. 151):

But even for the same person a shilling may measure a greater pleasure at one time than at another; because money may be more plentiful with him, or because his sensibility to pleasure may be different at different times. And to different persons the same piece of money affords the means of pleasures of very different intensities.

   It may be noted that the substance both of this paragraph in the present ed. (i.e. the paragraph beginning with the words "A shilling may measure a greater pleasure...etc.") and also of the two succeeding paragraphs, was placed in Book III, ch. II, p. 1, pp. 151–2 in the 1st ed. In the 2nd ed. these paragraphs were placed in Book III, ch. VI (pp. 184–6). In the 3rd ed. they were transferred to Book I, ch. V (pp. 79–80), where they remained till the 5th ed. where the order of the chapters of Book I was rearranged, and the paragraphs in question were placed in Book I, ch. II, §2, pp. 18–19. In the 1st ed. (pp. 150–1) these paragraphs were preceded by the following paragraph which, apart from the first sentence, was deleted from the 2nd ed.:

Human wants and desires are countless in number and very various in kind. As we have seen, the highest of them

137

Human
wants and
desires are
various, but
few of them
are alto-
gether in-
capable of
measure-
ment.

cannot generally be weighed in the balance; a virtuous man's desire to follow the path of duty is one against which no inducement can prevail; the economist has to take it as an ultimate fact, which though of vital consequence for his work, is not one on which his special methods of reasoning will throw any additional light. But even when the desire to do one's duty supplies the leading motive to action the necessities of the case may impose a measurable limit on its gratification: the outlay which parents make for the education of their children is prompted by their desire to do right, but yet it is so conditioned and limited by their circumstances, that fairly definite statements can be made as to the prices which parents in different grades are willing to pay for different kinds of education. Nearly all actions of life are governed, at least in part, by desires the force of which can be measured by the sacrifice which people are willing to make in order to secure their gratification: this sacrifice may take many forms, and as has already been observed even the mode in which it is measured may not be the same in other worlds that it is in ours. But in our world it has nearly always consisted of the transfer of some definite material thing which has been agreed upon as the common medium of exchange, and is called "money." The purchasing power of this money may vary from time to time; but in these early stages of our work we assume it to be constant[1].

[1] Corresponding to the movement of the "mean sun" of astronomers. See Book I, ch. i, § 5.

The first sentence of the paragraph reproduced above was retained in the 2nd and all subsequent editions. See Book III, ch. ii, § 1, page 86 in vol. 1 of the present edition.

The reference in the footnote to Book I, ch. i, § 5, in the 1st ed. corresponds to Book II, ch. ii, § 6, page 62 in vol. 1 of the present edition.

b. The words in parentheses "(or other satisfaction)" were inserted in the 3rd ed. (p. 79).

c. In the 3rd ed. (p. 79) the word "benefit" replaced the word "pleasure" dating from the 1st ed. (p. 152).

d. The following footnote attached to the word "use" in the 1st ed. (p. 152 n.) was deleted from the 2nd ed.:

Compare Bentham's *Principles of Morals and Legislation*, ch. vi; also Mr Edgeworth's *New and Old Methods of Ethics*.

e. The words in parentheses "or other satisfaction" after "pleasure" were inserted in the 3rd ed. (p. 79).

f. "satisfaction" from the 3rd ed. "pleasure" in the first two editions.

g. So since the 3rd ed. (p. 79) where this clause replaced the following clause dating from the 1st ed. (p. 152): "the money which people of equal incomes will give to obtain a pleasure or avoid a pain is an extremely accurate measure of the pleasure or pain."

h. "£100 a year" from the 2nd ed. (p. 185). "£200 a year" in the 1st ed. (p. 152).

i. So since the 3rd ed. (pp. 79–80) where the remainder of this sentence replaced the following words dating from the 1st ed. (p. 152):

we may be sure that the loss of pleasure which the tax will cause in Sheffield is almost exactly equal to that which it will cause in Leeds: and similarly anything that increased all the incomes by £1 would give command over almost exactly the same amount of additional pleasure in the two towns.

PAGE 19

a. The remainder of this paragraph was inserted in the 2nd ed. (pp. 185–6).

b. The following sentence in the 2nd ed. (p. 186) was deleted from the 3rd ed.:

But next suppose that instead of falling on families with an income of about £100 a-year, the loss fell in each of the two towns on 600 families with an average income of £50 and on 400 families with an average income of £100; then, although the loss of pleasures to the poorer group would be much greater than to the richer, yet the aggregate loss in Leeds might be taken to be about the same as in Sheffield; because in each place it was distributed in equal proportions among the richer and the poorer.

c. This sentence was inserted in the 3rd ed. (p. 80).

d. The remainder of this paragraph dates substantially from the 3rd ed. (p. 80) though slight changes were made in the wording subsequently. See also editorial note **g** to vol. 1, page 95.

e. So since the 7th ed. (p. 19), where the words "for the cost of a ride by tram or omnibus" replaced the words "for a threepenny omnibus fare" dating from the 5th ed. (p. 18). In the 3rd and 4th editions these words were "for a sixpenny omnibus fare".

f. "benefit" since the 5th ed., "pleasure" in the 3rd and 4th editions.

g. This paragraph was inserted in the 3rd ed. (p. 80).

a. This paragraph dates in its present form from the 3rd ed. (pp. 80–1). In the 1st ed. (pp. 152–3) it ran as follows:

And in fact it happens that by far the greater number of the events with which economics deals affect in about equal proportions all the different classes of society; so that if the money measures of the happiness caused by two events are equal, there is not in general any very great difference between the amounts of the happiness in the two cases. If however it should appear that the class affected in the one case is on the average, say, ten times as rich as in the other, then we shall probably not be far wrong in supposing that the increment of happiness measured by a given sum of money in the one case is, so far at least as its direct results go, about one-tenth as great as in the other.

The second of the foregoing sentences was deleted from the 2nd ed.

b. The first three paragraphs of § 3, together with the footnote on page 20 date from the 3rd ed. (pp. 81–2).

a. The following paragraphs in Book I, ch. VI, § 4 (p. 85), in the 1st ed., dealing with the influence of custom, were deleted from the 2nd ed.:

Custom is an inertia, resisting change.

Lastly, there is a certain class of influences on human action which do not tend to cause change: they play the same part in the moral world that friction does in the mechanical. When several forces are acting on a thing friction throws its strength with perfect impartiality against whichever of them are tending to prevail over the others and to cause movement. So whatever be the social forces that are tending to prevail over others and to cause change, they are opposed by the forces of individual habit, of social custom, of apathy, timidity and ignorance; or to sum up the whole in one word, by the want of free enterprise. Their influence is none the less disturbing because custom and habit have themselves in a great measure been slowly fashioned in the course of long generations by the almost unconscious balancing against one another of the motives for and against different courses of action.

The friction which they exert cannot be measured by itself; because its direction and even its force depend upon the tendency to change by which it is called into action. But it can be often measured indirectly. For instance, when there is a gain to be made by moving from one occupation to another, or by changing one mode of production or one market for buying or selling for another, the resistance of friction has to be overcome: and the amount of the friction can be measured by the amount to which the gain has to rise before the change is made.

b. This paragraph dates from the 1st ed. (pp. 81–2).

c. So since the 3rd ed. (p. 82) where this paragraph replaced the following paragraph dating from the 2nd ed. (p. 74):

Again the unwillingness to postpone enjoyment, and thus to save for future use, is measured by the interest that is got by the possession of accumulated wealth. And, lastly, the desire to obtain anything that is ordinarily bought and sold for money, is for that very reason easily measurable by the price that people are willing to pay for it; though here again allowance must be made for differences in the means of different classes of purchasers.

PAGE 22

a. The first three sentences of this paragraph date from the 2nd ed. (p. 80), and the fourth and concluding sentence with its footnote from the 1st ed. (p. 81).

b. This paragraph dates from the 2nd ed. (p. 76).

c. The following paragraph in the 1st ed. (p. 78) was deleted from the 2nd ed.:

It is sometimes said that economists regard it as "natural" or "normal", and in some sense even right, that man should be governed only by selfish motives; this opinion may however be dismissed at once as a popular error, which finds no support in the teaching or practice of the best economists. But again it is said that the scope of economics is limited to the consideration of those actions which are governed by self-regarding, if not by selfish motives. This view also seems to be mistaken; but there is so much authority for it that it requires to be carefully examined.

d. This paragraph dates substantially from the 1st ed. (p. 80).

e. The first sentence of this footnote was inserted in the 5th ed. (p. 22 n.). The second sentence dates from the 7th ed. (p. 22 n.) where it replaced the following sentence dating from the 5th ed.: "See Appendix C, 3, 4." In the 1st to the 4th editions there was a long footnote at this point, suggesting that public honours might serve as a substitute for money, which was transferred in the 5th and later editions to Appendix D. See editorial note **b** to vol. 1, page 782.

PAGE 23

a. In the 1st ed. (p. 81) the foregoing paragraph in the text was succeeded by the following paragraph and footnote:

Much of the best work of the world has no price, and evades altogether the economic calculus. Any education that a man gives himself or his children comes within its range only in so far as it is given with the purpose of enabling them to earn more money; we can seldom measure the money value of any bodily, mental or spiritual training that is an end in itself, and is not a means of pecuniary gain. Again, some of the work done in science, literature and art has a pecuniary motive; another and a higher part has its chief motive in the desire of fame; but the highest work of all has scarcely any other motive than the love of the work and the wish to do good to the world. The second part is theoretically capable of measurement: but the last, in common with much else that is noblest in human action is as a rule altogether incapable of it.[1]

[1] An instructive argument that non-purchasable, non-measurable pleasures vary at different times and tend to increase with the progress of civilization is to be found in Knies' *Political Economy*, III, 3.

This paragraph was deleted from the 2nd ed., though the footnote was reinstated in the text of Appendix D (vol. 1, page 783) from the 5th ed. onwards.

b. This paragraph dates substantially from the 2nd ed. (p. 77).

c. The following concluding sentence of this paragraph in the

2nd ed. was deleted from the 3rd ed.: "This has always been the practice of economists, though their reasons for it have not been clearly explained."

d. This paragraph dates from the 3rd ed. (p. 86).

e. This footnote was inserted in the 5th ed. (p. 23 n.), though the reference there was wrongly given as Appendix C, 4. This was corrected to Appendix D, 3 in the 7th ed. (p. 23 n.).

PAGE 24

a. This paragraph dates in its present form from the 3rd ed. (p. 86). In the 1st ed. (pp. 82–3) there were the following paragraphs:

In all these kinds of action [*sc.* those mentioned in the second sentence of this paragraph] self-regarding motives are no doubt prominent; but they are not in exclusive possession. For instance, the chief motives of saving capital, of spending money on the education of children, and of buying things for their use, are unselfish; and the actions which are prompted by them occupy a very large place in economics. The reason is that family affection acts with so much uniformity in any given stage of civilization that its effects can be systematically observed, reduced to law and measured.

Those economists who have spoken of their science as concerned chiefly with self-regarding motives, have tacitly included among them a person's desire for the well-being of his family. But this is clearly illogical. The real reason why this desire is included and yet other benevolent and self-sacrificing motives are to a great extent left on one side by economics, is that their action is irregular. The expense which an Englishman with £500 a-year will incur for the education of his children can be told pretty well beforehand. But as the family in England has narrow limits, no good guess could be made of how much he would give to support a destitute second cousin. Still less could it be said how much time he would be willing to spend in visiting the fatherless and widows in their affliction.

In the 2nd ed. the first two sentences of each of the above paragraphs were deleted. The remaining sentences were deleted from the 3rd ed.

b. This paragraph dates substantially from the 1st ed. (p. 83).

c. The following footnote attached to the end of this sentence in the 1st ed. (pp. 83 n.–84 n.) was deleted from the 3rd ed.:

> It may be objected that the higher motives are so different in quality from the lower that the one cannot be weighed against the other. There is some validity in this objection. The pain which it would cause an earnest and good man to do deliberately a wrong action, is so great that no pleasure can compensate for it; it cannot be weighed or measured. But even here it is not the quality of the pain, but its amount, that hinders it from being measured: the pain is practically infinite. People of a less noble nature do however sometimes deliberately act wrongly in order to gain some pleasure: and the pleasure has weighed against and weighed down the pain of wrong-doing. Temptations to do wrong have so much variety in form and manner that their action can seldom be tabulated and reduced to law. But if it happens that the same kind of temptation is presented to a great many people in exactly the same way, it may be measured. For instance in the old days of bribery the pain and shame of voting against one's conscience was measured; and experienced agents could tell how many people in a given district would be induced to incur it for a bribe of 5s. and how many for a bribe of £1. It is not likely that many facts of this kind will ever be ascertained; but if they should, it may be worth while to build up a special branch of economics, a sort of economic pathology, to deal with them.

PAGE 25

a. So since the 3rd ed. (p. 87) where this sentence replaced the following sentence in the 2nd ed. (p. 80):

The earlier English economists paid almost exclusive attention to the motives of individual action.

In the 1st ed. (p. 84) this sentence ran as follows:

Again, it is true that the earlier English economists paid too exclusive attention to the motives of individual action, to the neglect of those which lead to collective action.

b. This and the next sentence date from the 2nd ed. (p. 80).

c. The first four clauses of this sentence date from the 2nd ed. (p. 80), and the remainder of the sentence from the 1st ed. (p. 84).

d. The following sentences at this point in the 1st ed. (p. 84) were deleted from the 2nd ed.:

We shall presently have to consider some of the many forms of collective property. By far the most important is that of knowledge, which generally becomes the property of the world almost as soon as it is obtained. Other forms are roads, bridges, etc.: some people take nearly as great a delight in the beauty of their public buildings as in that of their own houses, in the richness of their public museums as in that of their private collections of pictures; they are glad to tax themselves to enable their government or their town council to carry out various plans for promoting the physical or moral well-being of the nation.

e. This sentence dates substantially from the 1st ed. (pp. 84–5).

f. The following sentences in the 1st ed. (pp. 84–5) were deleted, the second sentence from the 2nd ed., and the first sentence from the 3rd ed. :

Most of the sacrifices which men make for their country are such as cannot be measured: but when many people do the same kind of thing in the same kind of way—, as in the case of compulsory conscription or even volunteer service— the economic calculus has a foothold. The voice of economics is but one among many that must be listened to in the preparation for any public action; but it may do more, as will presently be shown, than it has done towards measuring the advantages of different plans of public enterprise and weighing them against one another.

g. This paragraph was inserted in the 3rd ed. (p. 88).

h. The first three paragraphs of §7 date substantially from the 2nd ed. (pp. 74–5).

PAGE 26

a. Marshall wrote the following account of his own practice when being shown round a factory:

In the years of my apprenticeship to economic studies, between 1867 and 1875, I endeavoured to learn enough of the methods of operation of the greater part of the leading industries of the country, to be able to reconstruct mentally the vital parts of the chief machines used in each, neglecting, of course, all refinements and secondary complications. This endeavour was associated with an attempt to form a rough estimate of the faculties and training needed for working each, and the strain involved therein: and, my guide—if, as generally happened he was the employer or a foreman— would generally answer my enquiries as to the wages which each was receiving. After continuing on this course for some years, I began to ask my guide to allow me to guess the wages. My error did not very often exceed two shillings a week on one side or the other: but when it did, I stopped and asked for an explanation. Sometimes my mistake was due to the fact that the work was easier or more difficult than it appeared to me: sometimes to the fact that the demand for the work was largely seasonal, or liable to variations due to fashion and other causes: sometimes that a high grade operative was being set to rather low grade work, because his proper work was not on hand just then, and was of course being paid the wages of his proper work: sometimes that the work was a blind alley, rather low grade and not leading up to higher work; and so on. These explanations were specially conclusive when I inquired why men were doing work which seemed within the range of women. In almost every such case, it was shown that the work was more difficult, or required more strength or more prompt resource and judgment, than appeared on the surface: or that it extended on occasion into hours that were forbidden to women by law; or—and this was no uncommon occurrence in those industries in which the large majority of the operatives were women—that a man was being paid more highly than a woman would be for the same work, because he seemed to develop the qualities required for a foreman, and the business required a larger number of such men than could find employment in it without some such special arrangements. (*Memorials of Alfred Marshall*, ed. A. C. Pigou, pp. 358–9.)

b. This paragraph dates from the 3rd ed. (p. 89).

PAGE 27

a. This paragraph dates substantially from the 2nd ed. (pp. 75–6).
b. This paragraph dates substantially from the 2nd ed. (p. 81) apart from an alteration in the concluding sentence in the 3rd ed. (see editorial note **a** to vol. 1, page 28).

PAGE 28

a. So since the 3rd ed. (p. 90) where this sentence replaced the following concluding sentence of Book I, ch. v, §7 (p. 81) in the 2nd ed.:

Let us leave it on one side in our scientific studies, but remember that some sort of account of it must be taken by common sense when it comes to apply to practical issues the knowledge obtained and arranged by economics and other sciences.

On the role of common sense as the ultimate arbiter in practical problems, cf. editorial note **e** to vol. 1, page 38 (pp. 157–8 below).

BOOK I, CHAPTER III

ECONOMIC GENERALIZATIONS
OR LAWS

PAGE 29

a. The origin of the wording of this chapter is shown throughout in the editorial notes.

In the 1st edition the corresponding chapter was Book I, ch. VII, entitled "The Nature of Economic Law"; in the 2nd edition it was Book I, ch. VI "Nature of Economic Law. Methods of Study"; in the 3rd and 4th editions the title of Book I, ch. VI became "Methods of Study. The Nature of Economic Law"; in the 5th edition this chapter became Book I, ch. III "Economic Generalizations or Laws". In the first two editions the chapter was very short; in the 3rd and 4th editions it was greatly expanded, but in the 5th edition a good deal of the subject matter was transferred to Appendices C and D.

b. So since the 5th edition.

c. Except for the fourth sentence, this paragraph dates from the 3rd ed. (p. 91).

d. Apart from the last clause, this sentence dates from the 1st ed (p. 77) where it was divided into two sentences.

e. The following footnote attached to the word "place" in the 1st ed. (p. 77) was deleted from the 3rd ed.:

Almost every scientific inquiry into the connection between cause and effect is made up of three rudimentary processes combined and applied so as to suit the special conditions of the problem. The first is to find the same cause working in many different surroundings, and in all producing the same effect; as, for instance, when we observe that so long as the greater part of the English labourers' wages had to be spent in bread, the marriage rate always fell when the price of wheat rose. Another is, having already discovered the effects of all causes, save one, at work in any case, to subtract these from the total effect, and by the method of residues to determine the effect of that one; as, for instance, when we analyze the excess of imports over exports, and, deducting that part which is due to freights and commissions, to the profits on English investments in foreign countries and other causes, determine whether there is any residue which must be accounted for by our borrowing from other countries. (See Giffen's *Essays*.) The third is the simplest, but cannot often be applied. It is, to find two cases which resemble one another in every respect except that a cause is present in one of them but not in the other. Then by holding the cases up to the light, as it were, against one another, the effect of that cause is made to stand out. The best, perhaps the only perfect, illustrations of this method met with in economics have reference to the physical laws which are used by the science, though they are not, properly speaking, economic laws, such as those bearing on the fertility of land: as when Sir John Lawes determines the influence of farmyard manure by cultivating two adjacent plots of similar soil in exactly the same way, except that only one of them is manured.

f. This clause was inserted in the 3rd ed. (p. 91).

g. This paragraph dates from the 3rd ed. (p. 92).

h. The following additional sentence to this footnote was inserted in the 4th ed. (p. 91 n.) but was deleted from the 5th ed.:

> The subject of this chapter is discussed from a slightly different point of view in the course of an article on "Distribution and Exchange" by the present writer in the *Economic Journal* for March 1898.

This discussion is reprinted in *The Memorials of Alfred Marshall* (pp. 312–18).

PAGE 30

a. This paragraph dates, with some subsequent modification, from the 3rd ed. (p. 92).

b. The remainder of this sentence dates in its present form from the 4th ed. (p. 92) where it replaced the following clauses in the 3rd ed. (p. 92): "while others give their chief attention to discovering obscure causal connections between individual facts or classes of facts and to developing the machinery, or organism, of scientific analysis."

c. This sentence was inserted in the 4th ed. (p. 92).

d. At the end of this paragraph in the 3rd ed. (p. 92 n.) there was a long footnote dealing with the controversy over method between Professors Menger and Schmoller. The text of this footnote is reproduced in editorial footnote **f** to Appendix C, page 771 of vol. 1 in the present edition.

e. This section (§ 2) dates from the 5th ed. (pp. 30–1). It was inserted here when the historical chapters dealing with the Growth of Economic Freedom were transferred in that edition to Appendix A.

PAGE 31

a. This section (§ 3) dates from the 5th ed. (pp. 31–3).

b. In the 3rd ed. (p. 105) and the 4th ed. (p. 104) there was the following discussion (deleted from the 5th ed.) of the term "economic laws":

Economic laws correspond to secondary natural laws relating to the action of heterogeneous forces.

This brings us to consider the nature of *Economic Laws*. Some have said that the term is inappropriate, because there are no definite and universal propositions in economics which can compare with the laws of gravitation and of conservation of energy in physics. But the objection would appear to be irrelevant. For though there are no economic laws of that class, there are many which may rank with the secondary laws of those natural sciences, which resemble economics in dealing with the complex action of many heterogeneous and uncertain causes. The laws of biology, for instance, or—to take an example from a purely physical science—the laws of the tides, like those of economics vary much in definiteness, in range of application and in certainty[1].

[1] There is indeed a sense in which all physical laws, including even that of gravitation, are but schemes for holding ascertained uniformities and tendencies in a convenient grip; while they derive their prestige partly from the number and certainty of the facts which they hold within their grip, and partly from the number and cogency of the chains of inductive and deductive reasoning which connect them with other laws.

c. This paragraph dealing with the tides replaced, in the 5th ed., a long footnote on the same subject, dating from the 3rd ed. (p. 97 n.). This footnote is reproduced in editorial note **d** to page 773 of vol. 1 in the present edition.

PAGE 33

a. This paragraph and footnote date substantially from the 3rd ed. (p. 105).

b. In the 3rd and 4th editions (p. 105 n.) this sentence formed part of a footnote and was succeeded by the following paragraph which was deleted from the 5th ed.:

The term Rule (German *Regel*) has been suggested as a substitute for Law: but the objections to it, in English, at all events, seem very great. It seems, however to be the only possible short substitute for Law: and brevity is essential.

c. This paragraph dates substantially from the 2nd ed. (p. 83).

d. So since the 4th ed. (p. 105). In the 1st ed. (p. 87) the following definition was given:

An *Economic Law* is a statement that a certain course of action may be expected under certain conditions from the members of an industrial group: and that action is the *normal* action of the members of that group.

In the 2nd ed. (p. 83) and the 3rd ed. (p. 106) economic laws were defined as in the present text, but without the clause: "or statements of social tendencies". In the 1st ed. (p. 86) the definition of an economic law was preceded by the following paragraphs, of which the first was deleted from the 2nd ed., and the second from the 5th ed.:

The nature of economic law has been in some measure indicated in our inquiry as to the range of economic motive. Those actions that are governed by free enterprise and self-regarding motives are, as we have seen, those which are most easily reduced to law and measured; and reasonings with regard to such actions afford the simplest types of economic theory: but they are not the whole of it. Wherever any motive, whether self-regarding or not self-regarding, whether of public or private interest, whether based on wise judgment or on ignorant prejudices, affects any considerable class of people in the same way, then the action of that motive can often be reduced to some kind of money measure, if not directly, yet at least indirectly by comparison with other motives that can be measured directly; and then it can be brought more or less within the range of economic reasoning.

Economics is a science of human action; and economic laws, properly so-called, are laws of human action. It is true that the term is commonly used to include certain physical laws, which play a part in economic discussions: as, for instance, the law of diminishing return, which economics borrows from the science of agriculture. But we are at present concerned with those laws only which truly belong to economics.

e. This and the following paragraph date from the 2nd ed. (pp. 83–4).

f. In the 3rd ed. (p. 105 n.) this footnote also contained a general reference to J. N. Keynes, *Scope and Method of Political Economy*, and to an article by Professor Ritchie, "What are economic Laws?" in the second volume of the *Economic Review*.

PAGE 34

a. The words "relatively to those conditions" were inserted in the 5th ed. (p. 34).

b. This and the succeeding paragraph date from the 5th ed. (pp. 34–5).

PAGE 35

a. In its present form this paragraph dates substantially from the 3rd ed. (p. 106 n.), where the first two sentences of the paragraph were reworded and the last two were added. In the 1st ed. (p. 87 n.) the first part of this paragraph ran as follows:

It will be noticed that this use of the word Normal is broader than that which is often adopted. Thus is it frequently said that those results only are normal which are due to the undisturbed action of free competition. And if a short and simple account of the term must be given, this is perhaps the best. But the term has often to be applied to conditions in which perfectly free competition does not exist, and can hardly even be supposed to exist. The use of the term now proposed is more in accordance with its etymological meaning, as well as with the ordinary language of everyday life. An objection may be raised that it has not a sufficiently definite and rigid outline: but it will be found that the difficulties arising from this source are not very great; and that the use now proposed will help to bring the doctrines of economics into closer connection with real life.

In some letters from Marshall to John Neville Keynes (the father of John Maynard Keynes), which are now preserved in the Marshall Library, Cambridge, there is the following statement in a letter to Keynes dated 30 January 1902:

Gradually I have been forced to the conclusion that unless the empirical treatment of economics is completely to oust the scientific and analytical to which you and I are almost the only two $\left.\begin{array}{l}\text{elderly} \\ \text{middle aged}\end{array}\right\}$ Economists who are perfectly loyal (I don't count Edgeworth, because he is so extreme) we must throw overboard the most mischievous and untrue statement that, according to the classical economists, "it was only on the assumption of free competition that their principles and terminology could apply, or that, as they held, any economic science was possible".

b. For Marshall's earlier views on the nature of free competition, see the editorial Appendix to Book I, chapter III (pp. 155–6 below).

c. The first, third, fourth and fifth sentences of this paragraph date substantially from the 1st ed. (p. 87). The second sentence was inserted in the 5th ed. (p. 35).

PAGE 36

a. So since the 4th ed. (p. 106) where this sentence replaced the following sentence dating from the 1st ed. (p. 87):

It is one result, a deplorable result of the action of those laws which we have to study.

In the 2nd and 3rd editions the foregoing sentence was followed by a paragraph in square brackets which was deleted from the 5th ed. This paragraph ran as follows:

[The phrase just used—*the action of a law*—is sanctioned by authority, and is convenient on account of its brevity. But it is elliptical: for a law itself does not take action, it merely records action. When we speak of the action of a law, what we mean is *the action of those causes, the results or tendencies of which are described by the law.*]

(2nd ed. pp. 84–5.)

In the 4th ed. (p. 107) these sentences were reworded as follows:

[In earlier editions the elliptical phrase—*the action of a law*—which is sanctioned by authority, was used to mean *the action of those causes, the results or tendencies of which are described by the law*. Perhaps however it is better to use the term "tendency" simply. Some have proposed to use "tendency" instead of "law". But a law is a statement of a tendency.]

b. The remainder of this paragraph dates substantially from the 3rd ed. where it was placed in a footnote (p. 107 n.).

c. The following sentence at this point in the 3rd ed. (p. 107 n.) was deleted from the 5th ed.: "Jonah's prophecy of the fall of Nineveh saved it. (See Venn, *Empirical Logic*, ch. xxv)."

d. This paragraph with the attached footnote was inserted in the 5th ed. (p. 36).

e. The first three sentences in this paragraph date substantially from the 1st ed. (p. 89).

f. The following sentences in the 1st ed. (p. 89) were deleted from the 3rd ed.:

Even in a prediction of an eclipse, there is a suppressed condition that the solar system will not meanwhile have been disturbed by the explosion of one of its members, or the advent of a large external body. Such disturbances are so unlikely that astronomy is justified in taking no account of them; nevertheless it is based on hypothesis. In other sciences disturbing causes are more frequent, and therefore the conditioning clauses more frequent and more prominent.

g. The remainder of this paragraph dates substantially from the 4th ed. (p. 107 n.).

PAGE 37

a. This paragraph dates substantially from the 1st ed. (pp. 89–90).

b. The following clause dating from the 1st ed. (p. 90) after the clause ending with the words "and without their context", was deleted from the 4th ed.: "and they are liable even to be deliberately wrested from their proper meaning for partisan purposes."

c. This paragraph dates substantially from the 1st ed. (p. 90) where the sentences in it were preceded by the following sentences which were deleted from the 5th ed.:

Again, it is sometimes said that law is more universally true and less changeable in the physical world than in the relations with which economics deals. It would perhaps be better to say that an economic law is applicable only to a very narrow range of circumstances, which happen to exist together at one particular place and time, but quickly pass away. When they are gone the law though still true as an abstract proposition, has no longer any practical bearing because the particular set of causes with which it deals are nowhere to be found acting together without important disturbance from other causes.

d. This cross-reference dates from the 5th ed. (p. 37 n.).

e. The two paragraphs of this footnote date from the 3rd ed. (p. 109) where they formed part of the concluding §7 of Book I, ch. vi. The text of §7 in the 3rd ed. (pp. 108–10) ran as follows:

But in all this much turns on the extent to which we are treating economics as an *applied* science. The contrast between pure and applied sciences is not absolute, but one of degree. For instance mechanics is an applied science relatively to geometry; but a pure science relatively to engineering while engineering itself is often spoken of as a pure science by men, who devote their lives to the applied science of railway development. Now in a sense the whole of economics is an applied science; because it always deals more or less with the uncertain and irregular conditions of life as they actually exist.

The distinction between pure and applied science is not absolute but one of degree.

But some parts of it are relatively *pure*, because they are concerned mainly with broad general propositions. For, in order that a proposition may be of broad application it must necessarily contain few details: it cannot adapt itself to particular cases; and if it points to any prediction, that must be governed by a strong conditioning clause in which a very large meaning is given to the phrase "other things being equal." (In logical phrase a proposition can gain in Extension, only by sacrificing Intension.)

And other parts of the science are relatively *applied*, because they deal with narrower questions more in detail; they take more account of local and temporary elements; and they consider economic conditions in fuller and closer relation to other conditions of life. Thus we may have a pure science of credit and an applied science of credit. The applied science of credit will include the science of banking. And even the science of banking itself may be treated in two ways, either as general and relatively *pure*, or as particular and *applied* to special circumstances of individual districts.

There may be but a short step from an applied Science to an Art.

Now in such a matter as banking or taxation, in which the economic element predominates over all others, there may be but a short step from the laws of the applied science in the indicative mood to the precepts of practice, or Art, in the imperative mood. There may be but a short step from the applied science of banking in its more general sense, to broad rules or precepts of the general Art of banking: while the step from a particular local problem of the applied science of banking to the corresponding rule of practice or precept of Art may be shorter still.

But it is best to regard economics only as a Science.

Of course an economist retains the liberty, common to all the world, of expressing his opinion that a certain course of action is the right one under given circumstances; and if the difficulties of the problem are chiefly economic, he may speak with a certain authority. But on the whole, though the matter is one on which opinions differ, it seems best that he should do so rather in his private capacity, than as claiming to speak with the authority of economic science.

In spite of much good authority to the contrary among continental writers, and the earlier English writers, and even some recent English writers, there seems to be a balance of advantage in avoiding the use of the phrase, the Art of Economics or of Political Economy. It seems better to regard the science as pursuing its inquiries with more or less direct reference to certain practical issues, and as pointing the way towards solutions of them, than to make pretension to the authority of an Art, complete and self-contained, and responsible for the entire direction of conduct in certain matters.

The last of the foregoing paragraphs was deleted from the 4th ed., and the remainder (with the exception of the two retained in the present footnote) from the 5th ed. In the 4th ed. (p. 108 n.) the following additional paragraph was inserted but was deleted from the 5th ed.:

> Continental and especially German economists love to classify the various departments of economics. But their schemes differ; and have perhaps too little constructive value to justify the space and time given to them.

EDITORIAL APPENDIX TO
BOOK I, CHAPTER III

In the preface to the second edition of *Economics of Industry* by Alfred Marshall and Mary Paley Marshall (1881, pp. vi–vii) there was the following account of the meaning of free competition:

By an oversight no formal definition of the term *free competition* has been given in the text; and as, the book being stereotyped, there is some difficulty in introducing it at the proper place, it may be given here. A man competes freely when he is pursuing a course, which without entering into any combination with others, he has deliberately selected as that which is likely to be of the greatest material advantage to himself and his family. He is not supposed to be selfish: in fact the normal supply of all grades of industry, except perhaps the lowest, depends on the unselfish sacrifice by parents of their own pleasures for the benefit of their children. But he is supposed to be consulting his own material advantage and that of his family to the comparative neglect of the welfare of others. If every one always found his greatest happiness in trying to do that which was best for others, the world would have no theory of normal values as it is described in this volume: some such communism as that which prevailed among the early Christians would be the basis of economic theory. But in this world, as it is, the chief *active* principle in business is the desire of each man to promote the material interests of himself and his family. Normal results in economics are therefore those which would be brought about in the long run by this active principle, if it had time to overcome—as it necessarily would in sufficient time—custom, inertness, ignorance, and all the other *passive* elements which make up economic friction. It has been urged that as custom is often more powerful than competition, it ought not to be spoken of slightingly as a mere friction. But this is entirely to misapprehend the meaning of the term friction. A friction is not necessarily a small thing, but it is a passive resistance; and an active force, however small it is, acting on a material that is not perfectly rigid, will in the long run overcome any amount of friction. Human nature is never absolutely rigid; and custom never holds its own in opposition to a strong active economic force working for many generations persistently in the same direction.

Normal results are those which competition would bring about *in the long run*. The periods to which they relate must be sufficiently long to give time for the active forces of competition to overcome the passive resistances of ignorance, prejudice, custom, etc. They must be sufficiently long to enable us to neglect temporary fluctuations of supply and demand, the influence of good or bad harvests, etc., and to regard these alternating changes in opposite directions as neutralizing one another. We must be able to see standing up in clear outline the broad effect of the constant action of the forces of competition.

It must however be admitted that there are several difficulties in the way of a precise definition of the period of time to which normal results apply; a great deal must be left to the judgment in each case. In particular it is impossible to lay down general rules as to the time that must be allowed for the spreading of knowledge with regard to new inventions, and to changes in the markets for goods and for labour. Every one has a tendency to seek the most advantageous occupation for himself and for his children, and this active tendency will in the long run overcome the passive resistance of ignorance. But ignorance may act as a drag for a long time, and the advantages of different occupations may vary rapidly. One of the most important of the unwritten chapters of economics is that on the time that elapses between economic causes and their effects in consequence of the slowness with which knowledge diffuses itself.

THE ORDER AND AIMS OF
ECONOMIC STUDIES

PAGE 38

a.   The origin of the wording of this chapter is shown throughout in the editorial notes.

In the 1st edition the corresponding chapter, Book I, chapter VIII, was entitled "Summary and Conclusion"; from the 2nd to the 4th editions it was Book I, chapter VII with the same title. From the 5th edition onwards it became Book I, ch. IV.

b.   So since the 5th ed.

c.   In the first four editions this section contained a summary, two and a half pages in length, of the earlier chapters II–IV, which sketched the growth of economic freedom and of economic science. This summary was moved in part to Book I, ch. I, §5, when these chapters were transferred to Appendices A and B in the 5th ed.

d.   This paragraph dates substantially from the 1st ed. (p. 94).

e.   The following passage dealing with the role of common sense, dating from the 1st ed. (pp. 88–9) was abbreviated in the 2nd ed. (pp. 82–3), from which the footnote was also omitted, and was deleted from the 3rd ed.:

In some parts of the science the province of exact reasoning extends so far, that it can go near to indicating the right solution of practical problems. But in every practical problem it is common sense that is the ultimate arbiter. It is the function of common sense alone to propose a particular aim; to collect from each department of knowledge material adapted, so far as that department can do it, to the special purpose; to combine the various materials; to assign to each its proper place and importance; and finally to decide what course is to be adopted. It is not the function of a science to lay down practical precepts or to prescribe rules of life. The laws of economics, as of other sciences, are couched in the indicative and not in the imperative mood: they are statements as to the effects produced by different causes, singly

The laws of economics are not precepts.

157

or in combination; they are not rules ready for immediate application in practical politics[1].

[1] On this subject there is little difference of opinion among English economists. But many writers in other countries, and especially in France, have not been careful to insist on the purely scientific character of economics; and have enlarged its scope so as to make it include much which we class as principles of practical politics or as utterances of individual publicists. A striking instance of this is found in M. Laveleye's *Les Lois de l'Économie Politique.* Of course an economist retains the liberty, common to all the world, of expressing his opinion that a certain course of action is the right one under given circumstances. And if the difficulties of the problem are chiefly economic, he may speak with a certain authority. But so may a chemist with regard to other problems, and yet no reasonable person regards the laws of chemistry as precepts.

Cf. also Appendix C (vol. 1, pages 778–9).

f. The following sentence after the sentence ending with the words "than would otherwise be possible", dating from the 1st ed. (p. 94), was deleted from the 5th ed.:

Its chief work is connected with the measurement of motives by the price which as a "norma" or general rule, is sufficient to induce a person of a particular class under given conditions to undertake a certain task or undergo a certain sacrifice.

g. This sentence was inserted in the 5th ed. (p. 38).

h. This and the following sentence date substantially from the 1st ed. (p. 94).

i. In the 3rd ed. (p. 114) the words "the law of gravitation" replaced the words "those of physics" dating from the 1st ed. (p. 95).

j. The concluding clause of this sentence was inserted in the 3rd ed. (p. 114).

k. This sentence dates from the 1st ed. (p. 95).

PAGE 39

a. The rest of this paragraph was inserted in the 5th ed. (p. 39).

b. This paragraph dates substantially from the 1st ed. (p. 94).

c. The two paragraphs of this section date substantially from the 1st ed. (pp. 94–5).

PAGE 40

a. So since the 3rd ed. (p. 115) where these two sentences replaced the following sentences dating from the 1st ed. (p. 95): "Economics is then the science which investigates man's action in the ordinary business of life. It pursues the enquiries:—..."

b. So since the 4th ed. (p. 114) where the sentences in this paragraph replaced the following sentences dating from the 1st ed. (pp. 95–6):

How does economic freedom tend, so far as its influence reaches, to arrange the demand for wealth and its production, distribution and exchange? What organization of industry and trade does economic freedom tend to bring about; what forms of division of labour; what arrangements of the money market, of wholesale and retail dealing and what relations between employer and employed? How does it tend to adjust values, that is, the prices of material things whether produced on the spot or brought from a distance, rents of all kinds, interest on capital and the earnings of all forms of work, including that of undertaking and managing business enterprises? How does it affect the course of foreign trade?

c. Apart from the change of two words, noted below, the sentences of this paragraph date from the 1st ed. (p. 96).

d. So since the 4th ed. (p. 114) where the word "desirability" replaced "real utility", dating from the 1st ed.

e. So since the 4th ed. (p. 115) where the word "wellbeing" replaced "happiness", dating from the 1st ed.

f. This paragraph dates from the 1st ed. (p. 96)

PAGE 41

a. This paragraph dates from the 2nd ed. (p. 95) where it replaced the following paragraph dating from the 1st ed. (p. 96):

The practical issues which are a motive in the background to economic inquiries vary from time to time, and from place to place. But the following problems are of special urgency now in our own country:....

b. This and the five succeeding paragraphs date from the 1st ed. (pp. 96–8).

PAGE 42

a. The two last paragraphs of §4 date from the 3rd ed. (p. 118) except for some change, noted below, in the last sentence.

PAGE 43

a. So since the 5th ed. (p. 43), where this sentence replaced the following sentence dating from the 3rd ed. (p. 118):

And it is better described as *Social Economics*, or as *Economics* simply, than as *Political Economy*.

In the 4th ed. (p. 117 n.) the following footnote (deleted from the 5th ed.) was appended to the foregoing sentence:

The science needs to be lightened of every load that is not strictly necessary: and Englishmen generally prefer to avoid that elaborate classification of its various parts for which many schemes have been devised, especially in Germany. They afford good dialectical training: but they occasionally hinder the freedom of constructive work.

It may be noted that Marshall was largely responsible for the replacement in common usage of the older term "Political Economy" by the single word "Economics". His reasons for adopting the latter word were set out in greater detail in *The Economics of Industry* (1879), p. 2: "The nation used to be called 'the Body Politic'. So long as this phrase was in common use, men thought of the interests of the whole nation when they used the word 'Political'; and then 'Political Economy' served well enough as a name for the science. But now 'political interests' generally mean the interests of only some part or parts of the nation; so that it seems best to drop the name 'Political Economy', and to speak simply of *Economic Science*, or more shortly, *Economics*."

b. Both §§5 and 6 were inserted in the 5th ed. (pp. 43–8); but a considerable part of §5 is based on material taken from *A Plea for the Creation of a Curriculum in Economics and Associated Branches of Political Science*, which Marshall issued to the University of Cambridge in 1902, and which is reprinted below in the Editorial Appendix to Book I, ch. IV.

PAGE 46

a. See below (pp. 161–78).

EDITORIAL APPENDIX TO
BOOK I, CHAPTER IV

THE TEXT OF "A PLEA FOR THE CREATION OF
A CURRICULUM IN ECONOMICS AND ASSOCIATED
BRANCHES OF POLITICAL SCIENCE"

In 1902 Marshall circulated to the members of the Senate of the University of Cambridge the following paper in support of his proposal for the formation of a separate Tripos in Economics and Politics:

A PLEA FOR THE CREATION OF A CURRICULUM IN ECONOMICS AND ASSOCIATED BRANCHES OF POLITICAL SCIENCE

1. *Introductory*

EVERY university must consider from time to time whether its scheme of study and teaching is adequate to present needs. This task is relatively light when each candidate for high honours is judged separately. For then each can be allowed to choose almost any branch of study that he likes for his chief examination and for his thesis: a few simple regulations, and those very elastic, suffice to guard against too narrow a specialization. If with the progress of knowledge any particular study grows in breadth and depth and attracts an increasing share of thought, it is offered as their main subject by an increasing number of students: and thus the work of the university in each generation adapts itself almost automatically to the changes in the relative importance of the parts which different branches of knowledge play in the progress of the world. *(margin: Continental universities can make room for growing studies easily.)*

The regulations of a Cambridge curriculum simplify the organization of lectures and lighten the work of examiners. They are helpful to some students and especially to those who are neither very able nor very weak; and they can be modified in detail, on the initiative of the Special Board concerned, without much trouble. But trouble is caused by their lack of elasticity, when a larger adjustment or development is called for by changes in the relative proportions of different branches of knowledge, or in the intimacy and strength of their mutual affinities. And this trouble is at its worst when a curriculum is already full; and a study which claims a large share of thought and work is being compressed by the healthy and vigorous expansion of other studies to which it has no longer any close affinity; but which are rigidly bound in the same three years' curriculum with it. For then the Special Board, however well inclined, can give but little help. That is the position of economics now. *(margin: But Cambridge curricula are inelastic.)*

In foreign countries economics has always been closely associated with history or law, or political science, or some combination of these studies. The first Moral Sciences Examination (1851–1860) included ethics, law, history, and economics; but not mental science or logic. In 1860, however, philosophy and logic were introduced and associated with ethics; while history and political philosophy, jurisprudence and political economy formed an alternative group. In 1867 provision was made elsewhere for law and history; and mental science and logic have since then struck the keynote of the Moral Sciences Tripos.

At present Part I has five papers on psychology, logic, and ethics, treated mainly in relation to individual (not social) problems, and containing some elements of metaphysics. Two papers are allotted to economics. A lad, coming from school to this large and heterogeneous mass of difficult notions entirely strange to him, is bewildered. He scarcely finds himself at all during his first year; and even at the end of his second year he is still so unripe, that he would show to great disadvantage relatively to a man of equal ability, who had allowed time for the abstract notions of mental science and the higher logic to sink into his mind at a Scotch or a provincial university. Consequently scarcely one of those few men who have obtained a first class in Part I in the second year has come to Cambridge straight from school: and that division of Part II in which candidates are allowed to give themselves wholly to economics and political philosophy is practically closed to nearly all candidates for the Moral Sciences Tripos, except those who come to Cambridge with a bias towards the mental or abstract half of the moral sciences. This partial blocking up of the doorway to economic studies against the vast majority of our most promising students might be a little mitigated by alterations in the Tripos regulations. But no sound and realistic study of economics can be compressed into a three years' course together with mental science.

How hard has now become the pressure of this union on economics, is shown by the fact that of those who have passed through Cambridge in the last fifteen years and are now engaged in constructive work in economics, only one has followed the Moral Sciences curriculum; and he having taken his M.A. degree at London in mental and moral science and economics before he entered here as an undergraduate, had plenty of time at his disposal; while several were high wranglers.

But in recent years the regulations of our Historical Board have been increasingly generous towards economics; and thus while the regulations for Part I of the Moral Sciences Tripos are practically prohibitive to students, of the ordinary age, who wish to make a sound study of economics without staying at the University for more than three years, a new route has been opened out for them. Part I of the Historical Tripos taken at the end of the second year can be followed by that division of Part II of the Moral Sciences Tripos, in which a clear field is left to political philosophy and advanced economics. A makeshift combina- tion of Part I of Historical Tripos and Part II of Moral Sciences.

This route is the best at present open. But it contains some curious anomalies; and it is not wholly satisfactory. Much of the first two years of a candidate for the Historical Tripos must be given to the study of mediæval history. If one Board is responsible for the first two years of an economic student's work, and another for the third year, there will be some risk that the regulations of the two Boards will not fit so perfectly that the two parts make a well ordered whole. And again, there may be difficulties as regards the selection of examiners: for there may not be room for more than one economic specialist among the examiners nominated by either Board, and economics is too large a subject for any one person to examine well in the whole of it.

I may add that, had it not been for Professor Sidgwick's untimely death, an appeal to the Senate to allow economics, in conjunction with political science, to be made a main avenue to a degree in honours, would have been set on foot more than a year ago. The matter had been long under discussion: but his decision remained in suspense. In the spring of 1900, however, he said that he thought the time had come for moving. An appeal for a thorough remedy. Professor Sidgwick.

2. *The national interest in the supply of trained economists*

The trained economists in England are few.

The recent creations of a Faculty of Economics and Political Science at London, and of a Faculty of Commerce at Birmingham indicate that England is prepared now to follow the example of other western countries, and take the study of economics seriously. A scheme for a school in economics and politics has been approved by the Board of Studies at Owens College; and movements in a similar direction are already in progress at Oxford and elsewhere.

In the earlier part of the nineteenth century English economics were in the forefront: and even now the sustained unity of England's industrial development gives her economic history during the eighteenth and nineteenth centuries a leading interest for the economists of all nations. But so sternly have her universities restricted the study of economics that the English economist is largely dependent on the work of foreigners for a thorough treatment of many urgent problems. In the United States, in Germany and elsewhere, great numbers of business men and Government officials have studied economics at the universities, and have thus learnt to consider particulars in relation to general principles. They are quick to see how the results of their experience may be serviceable to the public, and to make clear to others what they have learnt from life. But such men are rare in England.

But the need for their work is increasing. For change is rapid;

And yet in England as elsewhere, economic and social considerations are acquiring an ever-increasing influence over thought and action. The Legislature, the Executive, and even the Diplomatic Corps of all countries of the modern world are often occupied with economic issues half their time. None of these issues are quite like those of old days. Many of them are entirely new. And, in spite of the great advance of historical knowledge, the present age has to solve its own economic problems for itself, with less aid from the experience of the past than has been available for any other age. The causes which have made practical economic problems occupy so large a part of the attention of thoughtful men of all classes are mainly the same as those which have moved those problems away from the experience of earlier times. Among the most prominent of them is the rapid extension of international relations.

The increase of wealth and the quickening and cheapening of means of communication has made every country more sensitive to the economic movements of its neighbours; and the term "neighbours" is ever obtaining a wider significance, partly as a result of expansion of empires across the ocean until their frontiers march together in all quarters of the globe. Peace and war have long been governed mainly by the prevailing opinions, true or false, as to national interests and international rivalries in distant fields of commerce, actual and potential. But it is only recently that dependence on distant sources of supply for food and raw produce has made England's continued existence depend on her keeping pace with the forward economic movement of nations against whom she may need to measure her force. In fact England is not, and probably never again will be, completely mistress in her own house. She is not free to weigh the true benefits of a higher culture or a more leisurely life against the material gains of increased economic vigour, without reference to the rate at which the sinews of war are growing elsewhere. *and international economic issues more urgent;*

In the seventeenth century Dutch writers boasted that ten of their countrymen in a Dutch vessel would work as much trade as twenty of any other nation. In the first half of the nineteenth century we could boast that ten of our countrymen could do as much in almost any branch of industry as twenty foreigners, because they were better fed and equipped with better appliances. But as the century wore on, the shackles of political despotism were loosened on the Continent; and when 1871 had seen the close of the wars in Western Europe, there grew up a generation of workers, who turned their increasing command over nature to account in providing the two sources of energy—better food and better education. A great part of our working population was already fairly well fed; and we turned our growing wealth to less good account. Our education has improved very slowly; and our physical energy, though perhaps on the *and the efficiency of English work progresses slowly.*

whole as great as ever, is certainly less relatively to that of other northern nations than it was even half a century ago, while there has perhaps been some decline in our willingness to exert ourselves. We are no longer at the high premium at which we were for those operations in iron works etc. which require exceptional powers of endurance; and in manual skill we have been nearly overtaken by several nations who were far behind us. Our great store of wealth has given us an advantage; and it is increasing as fast as ever. But, after deducting land, it is even now less than ten year's income: and we should quickly be passed by rivals still some way behind us, if their productive energy were a little greater than our own, and their mode of living a little more sparing. Thirty years ago it was expected that the beginning of this century would see the white population of the British Empire greater than that of the German; but this hope has been disappointed. If similar changes continue for long, and go much further, our surplus of revenue over expenditure, available for naval and military use will be less than that of Germany.

Even more urgent is the study of economics in relation to the quality of life. The possibilities of social progress and its perils.

But, urgent as is this study of the causes of "the wealth of nations" in connection with political stability, it is even more urgent in connection with the quality of life. The present age is indeed a very critical one, full of hope but also of anxiety. Economic and social forces capable of being turned to good account were never so strong as now; but they have seldom been so uncertain in their operation. Especially is this true of the rapid growth of the power and inclination of the working classes to use political and semi-political machinery for the regulation of industry. That may be a great good if well guided. But it may work grave injury to them, as well as to the rest of the nation, if guided by unscrupulous and ambitious men, or even by unselfish enthusiasts with narrow range of vision. Such persons have the field too much to themselves. There is need for a larger number of sympathetic students, who have studied working class problems in a scientific spirit; and who, in later years, when their knowledge of life is deeper, and their sense of proportion is more disciplined, will be qualified to go to the root of the urgent social issues of their day, and to lay bare the ultimate as well as the immediate results of plausible proposals for social reform.

For instance, partly under English influence, some Australasian colonies are making bold ventures, which hold out specious promise of greater immediate comfort and ease to the workers. But very little study of these schemes has been made of the same kind, or even by the same order of minds as are applied to judging a new design for a battleship with reference to her stability in bad weather: and yet the risks taken are much graver. Australasia has indeed a large reserve of borrowing power in her vast landed property: and should the proposed short cuts issue in some industrial decadence, the fall may be slight and temporary. But it is already being urged that England should move on similar lines: and a fall for her would be more serious.

We need then to watch more carefully the reciprocal influences which character and earnings, methods of employment and habits of expenditure exert on one another. We need to see how the efficiency of a nation is affected by and affects the confidences and affections which hold together the members of each economic group—the family, employers and employees in the same business, citizens of the same country. We need to analyse the good and evil that are mingled in the individual unselfishness and the class selfishness of professional etiquette and of trade union customs. We need to study how growing wealth and opportunities may best be turned to account for the true wellbeing of the present and coming generations.

3. *The study of economics regarded as a preparation for business and for public responsibilities*

So far the study of economics and politics has been considered in relation to the needs of general students. But something should be added with regard to those who pass through the university on their way to an active career in business, or in public administration.

I do not ask that room should be made here for technical studies. We may do for business men in general something

We should not offer technical preparation for business.

like what our engineering school does for engineers; but we should not attempt more. It may be right that the university of a great city should offer to some classes of business men as direct a training for earning their livelihood as we do to schoolmasters and physicians. But the proper work of the older English universities in relation to business seems to lie in another direction.

Among the many changes in the methods of business of the present age, two stand out clearly; a tendency towards increased specialization in the work of subordinates; and a tendency towards greater breadth and diminished specialization in the work of heads of business, of directors of companies, and of the higher public officials. Other institutions can give a technical training, suitable for the lower ranks of business more easily than we can, and with less harm to themselves. But we are well placed for giving a broad education which will bear directly on the larger management of affairs, and for adding to it that training of personal character which is offered by life at Oxford and Cambridge.

But we should offer a training likely to stimulate mental activity in a business career.

Business men generally recognize the importance of this human training. But they complain that the studies of Oxford and Cambridge almost ignore those questions in which their sons will be most interested in after years; and that they are tempted to lead too easy a life here from the lack of an opportunity of distinguishing themselves by work that is congenial to them. In so far as this is the case, even those who believe that the older studies give the best possible education to students during their university career will probably admit that we are in fault. I myself think that the higher study of economics gives as good a mental training, its breadth and depth being taken together, as any other study: and that, in addition, it develops the human sympathies in an exceptional degree. But even should this not be conceded, economics may yet claim a first place among university studies if account be taken of the mental activities in after-life which may result from a thorough study of it here.

The shafts and galleries of a mine are a scientific museum and laboratory to a colliery manager who has made a thorough study of geology: his mind grows with his work, and he may increase the world's wealth of knowledge. But if the same man had neglected geology, and pursued here other studies, his B.A. degree would not improbably have been the end, instead of the starting point, of the chief intellectual work and interests of his life. As geology is related to mining, so is economics to general business. A Grote, or a Lubbock may harvest rich fields of thought remote from their business; and a Siemens may work in the field of physics with both hands. But yet there remain many business men, whose experiences in later life are likely to be turned to much higher account for themselves and for the world by an early study of economics than by any other training.

Economic training may give a high intellectual tone to business life.

For indeed the survey of business men may be very broad; and it has been well said that States have never been under better rule than when governed by enlightened business men. The Cologne Chamber of Commerce, which is promoting an excellent Handelshochschule, recently declared that "the great merchant ought to accomplish the totality of intellectual work necessary to survey, study, and comprehend the most diverse relations in all parts of the world. His view ought to embrace the civilization of the world. And indeed he ought to follow industrial and commercial legislation in all countries, to know their economic history, their future, and therein forecast the progress of industry and of science[1]."

The business man who is not only a merchant but also an employer of labour, needs to know the real life of the people. His primary relations with his workmen lie in the exchange of pay for labour. But he is likely to fall short even as profit-winner, and he certainly cannot be a good citizen, unless he has thought and cared much about those sides of his work-people's life and character which are, at most, indirectly reflected in the wages bargain. To learn this from personal contact is ever more difficult for the large employer: he is separated from the mass of the workers by too many strata of subordinates. But broad modern economic studies will have prepared him to look at the problems of employ-

The benefit to the large employer of economic studies in a residentiary university.

[1] Quoted in *The Times*, 26 September, 1901.

ment from the point of view of the employee as carefully as from that of the employer. Experience shows that this training helps him to see the drift of the complaints urged by his men, and to make concessions quickly and cordially to such as are reasonable. And especially will this be the case if he has combined with his studies that social training which is afforded by the life of a residentiary university of the Anglo-Saxon type.

For such a life draws out the faculties which are needed in the social relations of those who have to deal with large bodies of men and large public interests. On the river and in the football field the student learns to bear and to forbear, to obey and to command. Constant discussion sharpens his wits; it makes him ready and resourceful; it helps him to enter into the points of view of others, and to explain his own; and it trains his sense of proportion as regards things and movements and persons, and especially as regards himself.

Directors of companies. Municipal Councillors.
Again, directors of joint-stock companies, and members of executive committees of County and City Councils, are called on to decide questions of broad policy in relation to business affairs of which they have not had much specific experience, even if they happen to be established in business on their own account. While leaving even the larger details to salaried officials, it will be their part to bring to bear broad strong well-balanced judgments, insight into character, tact in managing men, and fine intuition as to when to take risks and when not.

Other workers for public well-being.
And nearly the same thing may be said with regard to those who as public officials, as ministers of religion, as the owners of land or cottage property, or in any other private capacity will be largely concerned with "the condition of the people question," with public and private charity, with co-operation and other methods of self-help, with harmonies and discords between different industrial classes, and with the problems of conciliation and arbitration in industrial conflicts which are ever assuming larger proportions. Those who are nearest to these conflicts can seldom be perfectly impartial arbitrators: and there is here a special call for men who have received a sound training in economics and in

political science, and can bring to bear that elasticity of mind and that quickness of sympathy with aspirations and ideals that are not their own, which it is the privilege of a residentiary university to foster.

The petition that provision may be made for a thorough study here of economics and associated branches of political science, is then based mainly on three considerations. One is, that economic issues are growing in urgency and in intricacy, and that economic causes exert an increasing control on the quality of human life. Another is, that such studies offer abundant scope for the training and the exercise of those mental faculties and energies which it is the special province of a university to develop. The third is, that those who are looking forward to a business career or to public life are likely to be preferentially attracted to a residentiary university which offers a good intellectual training and opportunities for distinction in subjects that will bear on their thoughts and actions in after-life. *Summary of the plea for a curriculum in economics and political science.*

It is not suggested that a technical preparation for business should be given here: nor that those looking forward to public life should leave Cambridge provided with ready made opinions on controverted issues of the day. It is suggested merely that economists should be able to obtain here a three years' scientific training of the same character and on the same general lines as that given to physicists, to physiologists or engineers.

I venture to append tentative suggestions for a suitable curriculum. I alone am responsible for them in their present form. But they are based on many discussions that have been held here during the last ten years; and on some study of the more recent developments of economic education in the United States and on the Continent.

4. *Tentative suggestions as to a curriculum in economics and associated branches of political science*

The economist requires a broad knowledge of the history of his own country and of others which are in close contact with it, especially in recent times; of the structure and functions of the modern state; and of the legal form of those *Economics in relation to general history, and political philosophy.*

171

rights and obligations the basis of which lies chiefly in economic conditions.

It may seem at first sight that such a curriculum could most easily be provided by a modification of the Historical Tripos. The Historical Board has been very liberal to economics and politics; it has admitted a multitude of alternatives in their favour, and at some inconvenience to itself; and last year, on the initiative of Mr Dickinson, it considered carefully a plan for a system of alternatives so extensive as almost to constitute an alternative Tripos. But the practical difficulties of such a scheme seemed greater the more closely they were studied.

A thorough study of economics cannot be combined with early general history in a three years' course.

For historical students devote their attention chiefly to the gradual development, the orderly evolution, of certain aspects of social life. They begin with the Middle Ages or earlier; and in their third year work some way into the nineteenth century; but slacking their interest as they reach the events for which state documents are still under seal. On the other hand, students of economics and modern political science need above all things to make an international study of recent and contemporary conditions. They need to give their main attention to that marvellous simultaneity of political, social and economic developments in the modern world, which results from telegraphic and other means of communication; and by which the twentieth century seems likely to be dominated. No doubt the conception of evolution is of vital importance to economic history; and it may be hoped that the Historical Tripos will remain an avenue to the study of economic history and the elements of economics in association with general history. But the economist needs so large an acquaintance with existing conditions and their nearer antecedents that he cannot spare any of his short three years for a detailed study of remote history. He must train his sense of historical evolution, as best he may, in a careful study of recent events aided by some general knowledge of the broader movements of earlier times.

Although economics is based on observation, yet it has an advantage over most physical sciences. For the student starts with a considerable knowledge of the facts on which economics rests. He is acquainted with the main springs of action in the ordinary affairs of life: he can follow illustrations drawn from the more prominent industries and trades and so on; and he should turn this advantage to full account. He should at once set on a course of reasoning and analysis, obtaining from familiar facts the matter on which his mind can work. He should begin to disentangle the interwoven effects of complex causes. He should learn how things, which seem alike and are called by the same name, are often really dissimilar; and how those, which seem dissimilar and are called by different names, are often fundamentally alike. He should seek for the Many in the One, and the One in the Many:—a task in which skill is to be acquired only by long practice: unless indeed the student has rare natural genius, or has mastered some branch of physical science. This task should afford the main exercise to his mind from the very first; and should be supplemented by the less fatiguing work of increasing his knowledge of appropriate facts of all kinds. *The student should begin with analysis of familiar facts.*

Of course only those facts should be studied which are strictly necessary to give reality and a sense of proportion to the student's thought. But the scientific treatment of many economic problems requires a much more thorough knowledge of recent and existing conditions than has hitherto been generally possessed by our ablest students.

This lack has been apparent even in those who have had a large acquaintance with the economic conditions of England in early times. For though there are, no doubt, certain principles which underlie the action of economic forces in all ages; yet modern problems can only be approached by means of a thorough study of the causes and effects of that simultaneity of massive and rapid economic changes which has already been noted as a chief characteristic of the modern age. An attempt to approach them by a study confined almost exclusively to facts anterior to the steam-engine and the telegraph, to cheap printing and the popular diffusion of knowledge, must lack reality. *Existing and recent facts are generally the most important.*

There is then urgent need for a systematic and broad study of existing conditions and their development in recent

The study should be international.

times. The first interest would attach to those relating to Great Britain. Next a preference would be given, other things being equal, to the lessons to be learnt from Britains beyond the seas: but in many directions the experiences of the United States and Western Europe will be more suggestive. One chief weakness of the present study of economics in Cambridge is that it is perforce insular: time does not suffice to make it international.

Economic geography.

It is becoming the fashion to allot a large place to geography in modern economic teaching. That may be carried too far. But much may be gained by a broad, general study of the economic influences which mountains and watersheds, roads, railroads, rivers and seas exert on life and work; and of the geographical distribution of the resources and methods of agriculture, mining, manufactures, and transport. This would prepare the way for an analysis of the interactions of the material and the human elements in the prosperity of cities, of industrial districts and of nations.

A wider study of modern conditions of work and trade.

Passing thus from the material conditions of work to the human, the student should, with a similar use of the international comparative method, make a broad and nontechnical study of the recent development and the present position of:

(*a*) The structure of manufacturing and other industries; the causes and results of the development of machinery, and of man's general command over nature; the expansion of joint-stock companies, the growth and working of trading combinations and monopolies, and of railways, &c.:

(*b*) Organized markets for goods and for credit; monetary and banking systems; stock exchanges; commercial fluctuations:

(*c*) Methods of employment, relations between employers and employees, trade unions, &c.; methods of tenure of land and other real property, and their social results:

(*d*) Earnings, nominal and real, of various industrial classes; and the use made of these earnings; housing, the standard of life, &c.:

(*e*) The course of international trade, and the mutual

interaction of foreign commerce and national industrial character:

(*f*) Systems of taxation, central and local:

(*g*) Regulative influences exerted by public authority and public opinion over the economic conditions of life and work; and over the supply of water, electricity, the means of transport, and other uses of large public rights.

(*h*) Constructive intervention of authority in economic matters; Government undertakings.

On all these subjects there is a much more than adequate stock of solid literature suitable for young students, especially if they are invited to read some books in French and German. In addition there is a vast literature available for the mature student and the teacher: though it is true that their work will lack vitality unless they supplement their reading by direct observation; or—as American economists say—by "field-work."

Lastly, so far as material is accessible, a study should be made of the socio-economic ideals of different nations.

This larger inductive study would be combined with deeper analysis and more thorough construction. The simpler interactions of commingled causes being now taken for granted, attention would be given to the more complex: and thus the study would become truly realistic.

Thus subtler analysis should be applied to larger stores of knowledge.

For nature does not have separate compartments for wages and for profits; for the influence of railway and of banking systems; for the effects of monopolistic combinations, of trade unions, and of international trade competition; for credit fluctuations, and for unemployment and poor relief. The effects of every cause spread in every direction; commingle with other effects, modify them and are modified by them; and become in their turn new causes, reacting on and modifying the conditions by which they were themselves produced.

The more advanced work of the student would thus be given chiefly to the difficulties arising from the breadth of his problems. But part would need to be given to narrower difficulties. Such are for instance some intricate problems relating to currency, to monopoly prices, to railway charges, and the incidence of taxation. Again, some study should be given to valuation and allowance for depreciation, with special reference to goodwill and other things, the values of which are not directly indicated by market competition: for, in consequence of the modern tendency towards the investment of public and semi-public funds in slippery properties of this kind the very difficult questions connected with them are growing in interest and importance.

Statistics, and pure theory and history of doctrine.

Elements of statistical method should be studied early; but mathematical work in statistics should be united with mathematical versions of pure economic theory as an optional subject at the end of the course.

The history of economic doctrine should be another optional subject.

Law in relation to economics.

And lastly, though the question is not free from difficulties, some of which lie outside of my province; and though more than three years are already bespoken; I think that perhaps room should be found for the optional study of the principles of those branches of law, the policy of which is mainly governed by economic considerations. Such are laws relating to contract generally, landlord and tenant, joint-stock companies, bankruptcy, patents, monopolies, combinations in restraint of trade, factory and labour legislation generally.

It is indeed a chief part of the work of the economist to consider the regulative functions of Government as regards such matters. In consequence, the studies of economics and law are associated in the same faculty in the universities of many countries: and where that is not done, as in north Germany, it is customary for students of law to attend some lectures on economics, and *vice versâ*. In fact this appears to be the only western country in which the two studies have been entirely dissociated.

Possible extension of political side of curriculum.

I speak with a view to those students whose interests are mainly economic. I hope that this scheme may be extended by the addition of a few papers on political science, including international law, for the benefit of students who are looking forward to a political career (including diplomacy in its economic relations), who wish to give about half their time to economics, and the other half to recent general history and political science. But I think that those students of politics, whose interests in economics are subordinate, should still be referred to the Historical and the Law Tripos.

7 April 1902   ALFRED MARSHALL

It is with some hesitation that I sketch out a possible grouping of papers on the subjects indicated above between Parts I and II of a Tripos in economic and associated branches of political science. For should this plea find any favour with the Senate, they will probably appoint a Syndicate to report on the matter: and any elaboration of details would be premature until that Syndicate has made considerable progress in its discussion of general principles. The only purpose therefore of this sketch is to indicate the relative proportions which, after some consultation with others specially interested, I should feel inclined to assign to the different subjects in the curriculum.

PART I
MODERN HISTORY, ECONOMIC AND POLITICAL

Papers 1, 2. British Empire, U.S.A., and Continental Europe

The majority of the questions relate to the period subsequent to 1800. A sufficient choice of questions to be allowed to enable the candidate to give his attention mainly to the economic aspects of history.

PRINCIPLES OF ECONOMICS

3. Elements of scientific method, with special reference to economics and statistics. General doctrine of value.
4. Structure of modern industries. Money and credit (i.e. *a* and *b* of p. 174).[a]
5. Conditions of employment. International trade (i.e. *c*, *d*, and *e*, of p. 174).

Papers 4 and 5 to consist in about equal proportions of (i) *questions asking for description and analysis of existing conditions and their proximate antecedents, and* (ii) *questions making a considerable demand on the reasoning faculty.*

6.   POLITICAL SCIENCE
The structure of the modern State (involving a comparison of existing institutions).

7.   ESSAYS

PART II
ECONOMICS

1. Structure of modern industries. Money. Credit.
2. Conditions of employment. International trade.
3. Taxation. Economic functions of Government, central and local. Social ideals (i.e. *f*, *g* and *h* of p. 175).

The general plan of these papers to be on similar lines to those of papers (4) *and* (5) *of Part I; but to require an international study of existing economic conditions and their proximate antecedents, as well as a more thorough analysis of the mutual interactions of different causes.*

4. A paper of questions, of which each candidate is to answer two only.
5. History of economic doctrine, including socialist doctrine.
6. Mathematical treatment of economics and statistics.

7.   ETHICAL ASPECTS OF ECONOMIC PROBLEMS
8.   ELEMENTS OF LAW
in so far as it bears directly on the subjects of papers 1, 2, 3.

9.   ESSAYS
Candidates to take not less than six and not more than eight of the above papers, selected so as to include papers 1–4 and 9.

---

a.   The page references have been altered here to conform to the pagination of this volume.

Part I would be taken at the end of the second year: Part II at the end of the third year; with special provisions for students who had been placed in other Triposes.
I will add a suggestion which is, for the present, quite beyond the range of practical politics. Written examinations are no doubt beneficial in the earlier stages of academic work. But they seem inadequate for its later stages, especially in economics. I could wish therefore that those students in arts whose aims are high should be invited to present a thesis for a second degree to be awarded under regulations somewhat similar to those of the LL.M. degree; except that the verdict of the examiners should be more elastic. If at a distant time any development of this kind is adopted by the Senate, perhaps the German practice may be followed: and the degree be granted (1) simply; or (2) *Cum Laude*; or (3) in very exceptional cases *Summa cum Laude*.

By way of explanation it may be observed that at Cambridge a Tripos consists of a course of study in a particular branch of knowledge (e.g. History, English, Law, Mathematics, Mechanical Sciences, etc.) leading to a first degree with honours. Each Tripos is a self-contained course with clearly demarcated boundaries. Although it is possible for a student to read for a part of one Tripos and a part of another one, the great majority of students take both parts of the same Tripos during their three-year degree course at the University. For each Tripos there is a corresponding Faculty Board which controls the curriculum, teaching, etc. in respect of the subjects covered by the Tripos. Thus it was not until there was a separate Tripos in Economics and Politics that the economists became masters in their own house.

When the new Tripos was just getting under way, Marshall wrote an Introduction to the Syllabus of the Tripos, from which the following extracts are taken:

The Tripos in Economics and associated branches of Political Science was instituted by the University in 1903 in order to give encouragement to a form of liberal education which had already obtained a high place in many of the leading Universities of the Old and New World, and at the same time to make special provision for students who are proposing to devote their lives to the professional study of Economics, and for those who are looking forward to a career in the higher branches of business or in public life.

The Historical Tripos makes provision for the study of Economics in relation to general history from early to recent times: and some students may with advantage combine that Tripos, or a Part of it, with the whole or a Part of the Economics Tripos. But a full three years' work is needed for a thorough study of the economic and social basis of the present phase of civilization. Many of those forces which are most powerful now, were of little strength before the era of popular education, and the welding together of the Western world by cheap and rapid transport of men and goods and the telegraphic transmission of news.

A chief feature of this modern development is, that economic and social history is no longer national, but international. England, favoured by exceptional advantages, was for several generations in advance of other countries, and could almost afford to neglect their experience. The habit of depending solely on her own resources, which she thus acquired, continued after it had lost all justification: and, as meanwhile all other progressive countries were giving much of their energies to learning from her and to learning from one another, she has been grievously handicapped in the race. Suddenly she has awakened to the fact that others, with certainly not greater natural vigour, have so profited by world experience as to advance faster than she has done in many directions, and to reach beyond her in a few. The studies encouraged by the Economics Tripos will help to free England from this great reproach.

Sir Richard Jebb has well defined a liberal education as one which "trains the intelligence, gives elasticity to the faculties of the mind, humanizes the character; and forms, not merely an expert, but an efficient man". The curriculum in Economics and associated studies claims to do this.

To begin with, it exercises the three great faculties, observation, imagination, and reasoning. The student is required to observe closely the conditions of life and labour, and to watch the processes of production and trade around him. His imagination is constantly exercised in tracking those causes and those effects which are remote, or lie below the surface. And severer demands are made on his reason than in most other studies. For indeed in no other studies except Mathematics and the Physical Sciences does there seem to be a more continuous demand for thorough work in tracing the combined effects of many causes acting together in the same problem.

General intelligence and common sense will, of course,

go some way in such matters; they are, in fact, better guides than mere academic training unaided by them, and for simple problems they almost suffice. They put people for instance in the way of looking for the harm to strength of character and to family life that comes from ill-considered aid to the thriftless, even though what is seen on the surface is almost sheer gain.

But greater effort, a larger range of view, a more powerful exercise of the imagination are needed in tracking the true results of, for instance, many plausible schemes for increasing steadiness of employment. For that purpose it is necessary to have learnt how closely connected are changes in credit, in domestic trade, in foreign trade competition, in harvests, in prices; and how all of these affect steadiness of employment for good and for evil. It is necessary to watch how almost every considerable economic change in any part of the Western world affects employment, in some trades at least, in almost every other part. If we deal only with those causes of unemployment which are near at hand, we are likely to make no good cure of the evils we see; and we are likely to cause evils that we do not see. And if we are to look for those causes which are far off and weigh them in the balance, then the work before us is a high discipline for the mind.

In such problems as this it is the purely intellectual, and sometimes even the critical faculties, which are most in demand. But Economic studies call for and develop the faculty of sympathy, and especially that rare sympathy which enables people to put themselves in the place, not only of their comrades, but also of other classes. This sympathy between classes is being developed by studies, which are becoming every day more urgent, of the reciprocal influences which character and earnings, methods of employment and habits of expenditure exert on one another; of the ways in which the efficiency of a nation is strengthened by and strengthens the confidences and affections which hold together the members of each Economic group—the family, employers and employees in the same business, citizens of the same country; of the good and evil that are mingled in the individual unselfishness and the class selfishness of professional etiquette and of trade union customs; and of movements by which our growing wealth and opportunities may best be turned to account for the true well-being of the present and coming generations.

Thus the curriculum attains the broad ideal of a liberal education set forth by Sir Richard Jebb, perhaps as fully as any other academic course, that is compressed into a short three years. But a truly liberal education cannot be completed quickly. Cambridge can do no more for the majority of her students than start their minds on paths by which a liberal education is to be attained in after years. And in this respect a curriculum, which, as Dr Ryle, Bishop of Winchester, said of it, "has the great advantage of lifting what are called 'material' questions into their proper relations with the higher thought of the age and the advance of political science", may claim a high rank.

BOOK II

SOME FUNDAMENTAL
NOTIONS

───────

CHAPTER I

INTRODUCTORY

PAGE 49

a. The title of Book II dates from the 1st edition.

b. Except where otherwise stated the wording of this chapter dates substantially from the 1st edition.

c. In the 1st edition the title of Book II, chapter 1 was "Classification. The Use of Terms". The present title was adopted in the 2nd edition.

d. The whole of §1 dates from the 2nd ed. (pp. 101–2).

PAGE 50

a. The following final sentence of the paragraph in the 1st ed. (p. 101) was deleted from the 2nd ed.:

The continual change and development of economic phenomena renders it impossible to decide once for all, what are the most important purposes which economic classification has to subserve.

b. The following sentence, which came after the sentence ending with the word "growth" in the 1st ed. (p. 102) was deleted from the 2nd ed.:

This is one of many reasons which force us constantly to compromise with regard to the use of terms.

PAGE 51

a. The first two sentences of this paragraph were inserted in the 2nd ed. (p. 103).

b. So since the 3rd ed. (p. 103). In the 1st ed. (p. 102) this sentence ran: "But economics cannot venture to make more than a very sparing use of technical terms."

a. This clause was inserted in the 2nd ed. (p. 103).

b. The following clause at the end of this sentence, and the final sentence of this paragraph in the 1st ed. (p. 103) were deleted from the 2nd ed.: "... he does not get to know what was really in the mind of the writer. Hence have arisen misunderstandings and controversies which have diverted energies from constructive work, have brought the science into disrepute, and are one of the chief causes of its backward state."

c. This sentence was inserted in the 2nd ed. (pp. 103–4).

d. So since the 2nd ed. (p. 104) where the first two sentences of this paragraph replaced the following sentences in the 1st ed. (p. 103):

Other difficulties are caused by the growth of the science. These again are greater in economics than in almost any other science, because most of the chief distinctions marked by economic terms are really only differences in degree. At first sight they have appeared to be differences of kind, having sharp outlines which could be clearly marked out by definitions; at all events if there were no stint to the supply of technical terms.

e. The final sentence of this footnote was inserted in the 2nd ed. (p. 104 n.).

a. The following final sentences of this paragraph in the 1st ed. (pp. 104–5) were deleted from the 2nd ed.:

This can often be managed without any formal interpretation clause. That must, however, be always supplied where there is any danger of misunderstanding: and in a few cases of extreme necessity, special technical terms must be invented. By this means we shall retain simplicity of language, and yet attain a delicate adaptation of definition to the wants of each particular discussion.

b. The following concluding paragraphs of this section in the 1st ed. (p. 105) were deleted from the 2nd ed.:

All these difficulties are illustrated by a group of terms, connected with the notion of wealth: and these we must examine at once, because they will be used a great deal in the coming discussion of demand and supply.

Many of the questions raised in this Second Book are very complex and intricate; they cannot be altogether neglected; but yet they have not a very important bearing on the main problems of economics. The reader who is now first introduced to the subject, is therefore recommended to pass lightly over them, and to return to them at a later stage.

BOOK II, CHAPTER II

WEALTH

PAGE 54

a. Except where otherwise stated the wording of this chapter dates substantially from the 1st edition, though there were considerable changes in the order of many sentences and paragraphs in the later editions.

b. The title of this chapter remained unchanged since the 1st edition.

c. This paragraph dates substantially from the 2nd ed. (p. 106) where it replaced the following paragraph and footnote dating from the 1st ed. (p. 106):

All wealth consists of desirable things, or as we may call them commodities or goods. But many of the goods, or desirable things, which a man has are not reckoned as part of his wealth. We will first roughly classify goods, and then consider which of them are to be regarded as wealth. It will be noticed that here we are looking at goods from the point of view of the individual, and not from the "social" point of view, under which may be included the national and the "cosmopolitan" point of view, or that of mankind at large.[1] This seems to be the best starting point, though there is no substantial difference between the accounts that will ultimately be given of wealth from the individual and from the social points of view.

[1] These terms are used by Prof. Wagner in his excellent account of the fundamental notions of economics, *Volkswirtschaftslehre*, vol. 1, ch. 1, to which the reader may be referred for notices of the chief discussions of definitions by German writers and others. See also Prof. Sidgwick's *Principles of Political Economy*, Book I, ch. III and V.

d. This paragraph dates from the 2nd ed. (p. 106).

e. The following footnote appended to the end of this sentence in the 2nd ed. (p. 106 n.) was deleted from the 4th ed.:

The term *commodity* has also been used for it; but *good* is shorter and in correspondence with the German *Gut*.

f. The following sentence in the 1st ed. (p. 107) was deleted from the 2nd ed.: "Material goods are all external."

g. The remainder of this sentence was inserted in the 7th ed. (p. 54) where it replaced the following words dating from the 1st ed. (p. 107): "ought, strictly speaking to be reckoned under this head."

PAGE 55

a. The remaining sentences of this paragraph were inserted in the 5th ed. (p. 55). In the 1st ed. (p. 107) external personal goods were defined as follows:

A man's external personal goods are benefits he derives from other persons. They include (i) personal services of all kinds; (ii) property in slaves, labour dues, etc.: (iii) his reputation, the organization of his business, and his business connection generally.[1]

[1] To these might be added the pleasures he derives from society, friendship, family affection, etc. But some confusion might be caused by introducing them here.

The same definition (without the footnote) was retained substantially in the 2nd to the 4th editions.

b. This clause was inserted in the 2nd ed. (p. 107), but the footnote appended to it dates from the 1st ed. (p. 108 n.).

c. In the 1st ed. (p. 106) the foregoing quotation from Hermann was in the text, and to the end of it the following footnote was appended:

With these words Hermann begins that masterly analysis of wealth (*Staats-wirtschaftliche Untersuchungen*, ch. III) which is the basis of most modern German work in this direction. The central ideas of his analysis are indeed to be found in earlier writers, English and others. But he was the first to give them the clearness which comes from order and system.

PAGE 56

a. In the 1st ed. (p. 109) the paragraph on free goods was succeeded by the following paragraph, which was deleted from the 5th ed.:

Exchangeable goods are all those transferable goods which are limited in quantity and not free. This distinction is not very important, because there are not many goods which are transferable, but being free, have no exchange value.

b. This section dates substantially from the 2nd ed. (pp. 108–9) where it replaced the following section in the 1st ed. (pp. 109–10):

We may now pass to the question which of a person's goods it is most convenient to regard as constituting his wealth. In the present treatise, when nothing is said to the contrary, a person's *wealth* will be taken to consist of his external goods. The greater part of these are material goods, which, it will be remembered, include not only all useful material things, but all rights and opportunities to hold or use, or derive benefit from material things, or to receive them at a future time. To these have to be added external personal goods, which include business connections, good will, etc., and in some countries property in slaves, labour dues, etc.

It will be found that scarcely any discussions are affected by the question whether the term is used in this sense or in the narrower one which is more common among English economists and which limits it to those of his external goods which are transferable and not free. This narrow sense has its advantages: but it requires us to make a great and often very inconvenient distinction between the point of view of the individual and of society; for many of those things which are free gifts of nature to mankind are not free to the individual. In those very few cases in which the distinction is of any importance, the longer term *exchangeable wealth* will be used to indicate all that part of a person's wealth which consists of those material sources of enjoyment, and of those rights to them which, being transferable and not free, can be appropriated and exchanged.

PAGE 57

a. With the exception of the second paragraph, which was inserted in the 4th ed. (p. 127), this section (§ 2) dates substantially from the 2nd ed. (pp. 109–10) where it replaced the following section in the 1st ed. (pp. 110–11):

While the use of the term "wealth" just adopted is broader than that of some writers, it is narrower than that of others; for they follow on the lines indicated by Adam Smith[1], and include under wealth all personal goods, internal as well as external, which are directly useful in obtaining

[1] Comp. *Wealth of Nations*, Book II, ch. II.

material wealth. Thus they make it include *personal wealth*; which they take to consist of all those energies, faculties, and habits which directly contribute to making people industrially efficient, together with their business connections and associations of every kind. These things have a claim to be regarded as economic, not only on account of their importance as factors in the production of wealth, but because their value is as a rule capable of some sort of indirect measurement[1].

This use of the term wealth has been generally adopted by French economists; and now many German and some English writers are tending in the same direction. There are many purposes for which it is highly convenient; and nothing seems to be gained by debarring ourselves, as some English and American economists wish, from ever having recourse to it. But since in the ordinary business of life the term wealth is generally taken in a narrower sense, it will not be used in this treatise to include internal personal wealth unless an express indication to that effect is supplied in the context.

Here we see a good illustration of the general rule that the analysis of economic notions is a question of scientific truth, as to which there is little disagreement among those who have carefully studied the matter; but that the question how broadly any term should be used is one merely of practical convenience, about which opinions may fairly differ. Every one is bound to make his use of the term clear; but no one can rightly accuse others of error because they use it in a broader or a narrower sense than seems best to his own judgment.

[1] Many curious, but practically unimportant, subtleties are met with in developing the definition of personal wealth; for instance, in so far as a person uses his faculties to do things for his own enjoyment, the benefit that he derives from them, though certainly part of his well-being, is perhaps best excluded from the estimate of his wealth. But the line of partition here is very thin. For instance the faculties of an opera-singer are part of his wealth in so far as he uses them for hire, but are only elements of his well-being and not of his wealth in so far as he uses them to sing in private for his own pleasure. When however a dressmaker makes a dress for herself, her dress-making faculties are to be regarded as wealth in the broad use of that term.

This footnote was retained in the 2nd and 3rd editions, but was deleted from the 4th ed.

PAGE 58

a. This paragraph was inserted in the 4th ed. (p. 127).
b. This paragraph was inserted in the 2nd ed. (p. 110).
c. This footnote dates from the 3rd ed. (p. 128 n.).

PAGE 59

a. This paragraph was inserted in the 2nd ed. (p. 111) where it replaced the following paragraph dating from the 1st ed. (p. 111):

We may now pass to the social point of view. *Social wealth*, to borrow a phrase that is used on the Continent, is the sum total of the wealth of the individuals composing that social group which is under discussion. To take a particular case of such a group:—*National wealth* is the sum total of the wealth of the individuals composing the nation; and the boundary line round it may be drawn on any of the plans proposed for individual wealth. For some purposes an estimate of it is made directly and independently: for others it is more convenient to follow the arrangement adopted in the case of individual wealth, and to regard it as the aggregate of that. The fundamental notion of wealth from either point of view, we may repeat, is the same: the difference is chiefly one of arrangement.

b. This paragraph was inserted in the 2nd ed. (p. 111).
c. The following paragraph in the 1st ed. (p. 113) was deleted from the 2nd ed.:

Secondly, there are many goods which are sometimes ignored in estimating individual wealth (though they are really part of it), because they are free to all; but which must be made prominent in an estimate of national wealth. It is obvious that a road, or a bridge, or a canal, that is open to the public toll free is not in any sense whatever a less important element of national wealth than it would be if it were in private hands and made to yield a direct money revenue; and that it must therefore be always counted in as part of the national wealth.

PAGE 60

a. The following final paragraphs of this footnote in the 1st ed. (pp. 112 n.–13 n.) were deleted from the 2nd ed., with the exception of the first sentence:

188

There are similar difficulties as to how far money is to be reckoned as part of national wealth. Inconvertible paper currency, issued by the authority of government, is an order on the general wealth of the community: convertible notes by whomsoever issued are direct liens on the property of those who issue them. Thus, when reckoning the wealth of the country, we must count in all the precious metals in it, of whatever form they are. But we must not count in the paper currency: for that must be classed with mortgages, adding as much to the debtor as to the creditor side of the national balance, except indeed in so far as they add to the efficiency of its business organization, which is an important part of the country's wealth. Something may be reckoned for them under this head; the Scotch system of £1 notes has added much to the country's wealth. Of course there are some who think that the cost of a metallic currency is not compensated for by the security and other advantages which it affords. But since those nations which have a metallic currency could displace it if they chose by a paper currency, we are justified in assuming for the present that it is worth what it costs.

When we get at national wealth not directly, but as the aggregate of individual wealth, we count the gold and silver coin in the possession of each person as it stands. Notes issued by government and by private bodies are treated on the same plan as consols and railway debentures respectively: that is they are reckoned on both sides of the account: on the one side as part of the wealth of the individuals who hold them, and on the other as deductions from the wealth of the nation or the private bodies who issued them.

PAGE 61

a. See also editorial note **c** to page 54 of vol. I in the present edition.

b. The following footnote, dating substantially from the 1st ed. (p. 114 n.), was deleted from the 5th ed.:

> Here again special reference may be made to Wagner's *Volkswirtschaftslehre*; which throws much light on the connection between the economic concept of wealth and the juridical concept of rights in private property.

c. The following paragraph in the 1st ed. (pp. 114–15), with which the chapter concluded, was omitted from the 2nd ed.:

The main purpose of this chapter has been to inquire what classes of things are to be included under the term wealth: and the question what value is to be ascribed to any element has been discussed only incidentally; as for instance where we had to reject from the inventory of wealth part of the value of a thing on the ground that it had been already counted, or for some other reason. For this purpose private property has been counted at its exchange value. But the value of public property cannot always be so measured. No direct estimate can be formed of the value which the Thames has for England. As we shall see presently the exchange value of a thing is a very imperfect measure of the total real benefits which it confers: it is an imperfect measure even with regard to commodities in the hands of private consumers; a still more imperfect measure with regard to railways, and useless with regard to such elements of national wealth as rivers and seas.

d. The first three paragraphs of this section, together with the first sentences of the fourth paragraph, which date substantially from the 1st ed. (pp. 8–9) where they constituted §5 at the end of Book I, ch. I, were transferred to their present position at the end of Book II, ch. II, in the 4th ed.

e. This sentence was inserted in the 5th ed. (p. 61).

f. So since the 4th ed. (p. 8). In the first three editions the quotation from Adam Smith continued with the following sentence: "The one may be called value in use, the other value in exchange." Marshall then went on as follows:

In the place of "value in use" we now speak of "utility": while instead of "value in exchange" we often say "exchange-value" or simply "value". "Value" by itself always means value in exchange.

PAGE 62

a. This and the next sentence, dating in their present form from the 1st ed. (Book I, ch. I, §5, p. 9), were altered in the 4th ed. (Book II, ch. II, §6, p. 130), where a new sentence was added, while part of the present sentences was transferred to a footnote with some re-wording. The relevant passages ran as follows:

A given sum of money will buy sometimes more, sometimes less of this or that thing: but if one such change about balances another, the general purchasing power of money is said to be steady.... The price of every thing rises and falls from time to time and place to place; and with every such change the purchasing power of money changes so far as that thing goes. So long as man's command over nature remains stationary, we may set off one rise of price against another fall; we may say that the purchasing power of money is constant, if the rises in price have been about equal to the falls, and have affected commodities about equally important.

In the 5th and subsequent editions Marshall reverted to the wording of the 1st ed. In the first three editions the second sentence in the text of page 62 ending with the words "has remained stationary" was succeeded by the following two sentences and paragraph, which were deleted from the 4th ed.:

It is true that this way of speaking is vague, because we have not considered how to compare the importance of different things. This is a difficulty which we shall have to deal with later on: but meanwhile we may accept the phrase in the vague but quite intelligible usage that it has in ordinary discourse.

Throughout the earlier stages of our work it will be best to speak of the exchange value of a thing at any place and time as measured by its price, that is, the amount of money for which it will exchange then and there, and to assume that there is no change in the general purchasing power of money.

It may be noted that in the 1st ed. the statement of the assumption of constant purchasing power of money was repeated in Book III, ch. II, §1, p. 151. See editorial note **a** to page 18 of vol. I in the present edition (p. 138 above), where this is reproduced.

b. The remainder of this paragraph dates substantially from the 4th ed. (Book II, ch. II, §6, p. 130).

c. The words "as representative" were inserted in the 5th ed. (p. 62).

d. This sentence dates from the 4th ed. (p. 131 n.) where it formed the concluding paragraph of the footnote referring to Cournot.

e. So since the 8th ed. (page 62) where this sentence replaced the following sentence dating from the 4th ed.:

This difficulty will not affect our work in the present volume, but will occupy us much in the next.

f. In the 1st ed. (p. 9 n.) the following sentence, which was deleted from the 5th ed., preceded the reference to Cournot in this footnote:

In this case we are only following the practice of the ordinary business of life which invariably starts by considering one change at a time and assuming for a while that "other things are equal".

PRODUCTION, CONSUMPTION, LABOUR, NECESSARIES

PAGE 63

a. Except where otherwise stated the wording of this chapter dates substantially from the 1st edition.

In the 1st edition Book II, chapter III was entitled "Productive" and was followed by chapter IV entitled "Necessaries". In the 2nd edition the two chapters were combined as Book II, chapter III under the title "Production. Consumption. Labour. Necessaries".

b. So since the 2nd ed.

c. This clause was inserted in the 2nd ed. (p. 114).

d. So since the 5th ed. (p. 63) where this sentence replaced the following sentence dating from the 1st ed. (p. 116):

It is true that if there are more traders than are necessary, there is a waste.

e. So since the 5th ed. (p. 63 n.). In the 1st ed. (p. 116 n.) this footnote ran as follows:

> As James Mill has said, "The distinction between what is done by labour and what is done by nature is not always observed. Labour produces its effects only by consistency with the laws of nature. It is found that the agency of man can be traced to very simple elements. He does nothing but produce motion. He can move things towards one another, and he can separate them from one another. The properties of matter perform the rest." (*Elements of Political Economy*, ch. 1.)

In the 3rd ed. (p. 132 n.) the quotation from Bacon was added at the end of this footnote, while in the 5th ed. (p. 63 n.) the extract from James Mill was deleted.

PAGE 64

a. This paragraph, together with the footnote attached to it, was inserted in the 2nd ed. (p. 115).

b. So since the 4th ed. (pp. 133–4). In the 1st ed. (p. 109) where this paragraph was placed in Book II, ch. II, §1, this paragraph ran as follows:

Lastly, goods may be divided into *goods of the first order*, which satisfy wants directly, such as food, clothes, etc.; *goods of the second order*, which satisfy wants, not directly, but indirectly by contributing towards the production of goods of the first order, such as flour mills; while under the head of *goods of the third order* we may arrange all things that are used for making goods of the second order, such as the machinery for making milling machinery, and we may carry the analysis further if necessary. Goods of the first order are sometimes described as *consumption* or *consumers' goods*; those of the second and higher orders being called *production* or *producers' goods*.

In the 3rd ed. (pp. 133–4) this paragraph assumed substantially its present form, the only changes made in the 4th ed. being the insertion of the first two clauses of the first sentence of the paragraph and the deletion of the following final sentence of the paragraph in the 3rd ed.:

The line of division between the two classes is however vague, is drawn in different places by different writers; and the terms can seldom be used safely without explanation.

c. This footnote was inserted in the 3rd ed. (p. 133 n.).

d. So since the 3rd ed. (p. 134 n.) where this footnote (with one additional sentence) replaced the following footnote dating from the 1st ed. (p. 109 n.):

The latter classification [i.e. the distinction between consumers' goods and producers' goods] seems to have been first indicated by Say (*Cours de l'Economie Politique*, Part I, ch. XII). It has been developed with great care and sagacity by Hermann and other writers. The division of goods into successive orders is due to Prof. Carl Menger (*Volkswirtschaftslehre*, ch. I, §2) and is used a good deal by Austrian economists. Of course a good may belong to several orders at the same time. For instance, a railway train may be carrying people on a pleasure excursion, and so far is a good of the first order; if it happens to be carrying also some tins of biscuits, some milling machinery and some machinery that is used for making milling machinery, it is at the same time a good of the second, third and fourth orders. But subtleties of this kind are of little use. There is not even any precise agreement as to the line of division between consumption and production goods. Such things as wheat are commonly ranked with the former, though speaking strictly they are raw materials and ought to be ranked as production goods.

PAGE 65

a. The following final sentence of this footnote in the 3rd ed. was deleted from the 4th ed.: "But such subtleties are of little use."

b. So since the 2nd ed. (p. 116 n.) where these clauses replaced the following clause in the 1st ed. (p. 117 n.): "while a rich man working in like manner may be almost indifferent to the result of what he does."

a. The words "transitory and" between the words "providing" and "unnecessary", dating from the 1st ed. (p. 118) were deleted from the 7th ed.

b. The following paragraph in the 1st ed. (pp. 118–19) was amended in the 2nd ed. but deleted from the 4th ed.:

There seems to be a way of escaping from most of these ambiguities and confusions. It would indeed be unsafe to invent a number of new terms to correspond to the various uses of "productive". But recollecting that it is a transitive adjective, we can avoid all difficulties by the simple plan of considering what is the implied substantive which it governs, and supplying that substantive explicitly. When it means *productive of necessaries* (to anticipate the use of a term which we are just about to define), let us write in the phrase at length and the ambiguity disappears; when it means *productive of capital* in any form, let us say so; when it means *productive of accumulated wealth* in any form, let us say so.

In the 2nd ed. (p. 118) and the 3rd ed. (p. 136) the last sentence of the paragraph just quoted, ran as follows:

When it means *productive of accumulated wealth* in any form, let us write in the phrase at length and the ambiguity disappears; when it means *productive of capital* either in general or only in the particular form of *wage capital* (to anticipate the use of terms which we are just about to define), let us say so.

c. This paragraph dates in its present form from the 4th ed. (p. 136). The first sentence is a slight rearrangement of the text of the three first editions, but the word "durable" was substituted in the 4th ed. for the word "lasting" in the earlier editions.

a. So since the 4th ed. (p. 136) where this paragraph replaced the following paragraph dating from the 2nd ed. (pp. 118–19):

Productive consumption is commonly defined as the use of wealth in the production of further wealth. But this definition is ambiguous. For it is sometimes taken to include everything that is actually consumed by people engaged in productive work, even though it may not conduce at all to their efficiency as workers. But *productive consumption*, strictly so called, must be taken to include only such consumption by productive workers as is necessary for their work; under which head may be reckoned the necessary consumption of children who will hereafter be productive workers as well as that of adults during sickness.

b. This paragraph was inserted in the 2nd ed. (p. 119).

c. This footnote dates from the 2nd ed. (p. 119 n.).

PAGE 68

a. The words "and 'decency'", and the footnote appended to the end of this sentence were inserted in the 8th ed. (page 68).

b. This sentence dates from the 2nd ed. (p. 120) except for the word "apparently" in the second clause, which was inserted in the 3rd ed. (p. 138 n.).

c. The remainder of this footnote dates from the 4th ed. (p. 138 n.).

PAGE 69

a. So since the 3rd ed. (p. 139) where this sentence replaced the following sentence dating from the 2nd ed. (p. 121):

All consumption up to this limit is economical, and any stinting of it is wasteful.

b. This sentence was inserted in the 2nd ed. (p. 121).

c. The first sentence of this footnote in its present form dates from the 2nd ed. (p. 121 n.), where the following concluding sentences of this footnote in the 1st ed. (pp. 122 n.–3 n.), after the sentence ending with the word "outlay", were deleted:

On the other hand when the earnings of an industrial class are already a fair measure of the services that they render to the community, any further increase of their income involves a real burden to the community when it ceases to bring with it proportionate increase of their efficiency. This fact is very important, as will appear hereafter.

PAGE 70

a. The following additional sentences in the 1st ed. (pp. 123–4) were deleted from the 2nd ed.:

But of course if it were the habit of the country that the family should do for themselves, proper time being allowed for it, things which the English labourer generally pays to have done for him (such as baking their own bread, or making their own clothes), his necessary wages would be diminished by a corresponding sum.

The strict necessaries of the unskilled labourer who has to do sustained and exceptionally exhausting work, include a large supply of animal food. Those of the skilled labourer include generally a good deal of animal food, more education and more recreation than those of the unskilled labourer, and his conventional necessaries are considerably greater, particularly in the direction of dress. Again it is necessary for the efficiency of the highest ranks of industry, including the professional classes, that they should have food of the most easily digestible kinds, house-room sufficient for quiet, some travel and change of scene, books and other implements for their work, and a very expensive education. All these are necessaries strictly so called: the consumption of them is productive: to abstain from consuming them is wasteful. In addition to these there are many conventional necessaries, which in the present state of society, no individual can dispense with, without a risk of losing social influence, and perhaps indirectly impairing his efficiency. But society as a whole could, if so minded, dispense with a great part of them without injuring its efficiency. And perhaps more than half of the consumption of the upper classes of society in England is wholly unnecessary.

b. This footnote dates from the 3rd ed. (p. 140 n.).

c. This clause was inserted in the 4th ed. (p. 140 n.).

d. Marshall never revised the estimates in this paragraph, which date from 1890, when the 1st edition was published.

BOOK II, CHAPTER IV

INCOME, CAPITAL

PAGE 71

a. The origin of the wording of this chapter is shown throughout in the editorial notes.

In the 1st edition Book II, chapter v, and in the 2nd edition Book II, chapter iv, was entitled "Capital" and there was appended to this chapter a lengthy "Historical Note on Definitions of the Term Capital" (see the Editorial Appendix to Appendix E). The succeeding chapter (Book II, ch. VI in the 1st edition, and Book II, ch. V in the 2nd edition) was entitled "Income".

In the 3rd edition chapters IV and V were amalgamated to form chapter IV, entitled "Capital. Income.". At the same time the Historical Note was deleted, though the greater part of its subject matter was distributed in footnotes to Book II, chapter IV. Marshall's reasons for making this change and for the accompanying modifications in his definitions of capital are set out in the Preface to the Third Edition (see above pp. 41–3). Cf. also the letter from Marshall to Cannan in the Editorial Appendix to this chapter, pp. 226–8 below, and the extract from Marshall's article on "Distribution and Exchange" in the *Economic Journal*, vol. VIII (1898), which is reproduced in the Editorial Appendix to this chapter, pp. 229–33 below.

The 4th edition saw a considerable rewording and rearrangement of this chapter (again entitled "Capital. Income."); and a "Note on some Definitions of Capital" was again placed at the end of the chapter. In the 5th edition this chapter assumed substantially its present form. Appendix E, entitled "Definitions of Capital" was there added, much of the subject-matter being taken from the Note appended to ch. IV in the 4th ed. In the Editorial Appendix to this chapter the whole of §§ 1–3 of Book II, chapter V in the 1st edition is reproduced, and these sections with the comments on them should be read in conjunction with the editorial notes to Book II, chapter IV in the present edition.

b.   So since the 5th edition.

c.   The first three paragraphs of this section date, substantially in their present form, from the 3rd ed. (pp. 143–4).

d.   The words "no distinction is made between capital and other forms of wealth", which had been inserted in the 3rd ed. (p. 143) between the words "primitive community" and the words "each family" in the first sentence of this paragraph, were deleted from the 5th ed.

PAGE 72

a.   In the 3rd ed. (p. 144 n.) a footnote was attached to the word "business". The footnote consisted of two sentences, the first of which was identical with the last sentence in the fourth paragraph of Book II, ch. V, §1 in the 1st ed. (see below, p. 217). The second sentence ran as follows:

M. Gide has used the term *lucrative capital* to denote that part of trade capital which "does not really serve to produce new wealth; but merely yields an income to its owner".

197

The footnote as a whole was deleted from the 4th ed.

b. The following footnote was attached to the word "capital" in the 3rd ed. (pp. 144 n.–5 n.):

> When we come to discuss the intricacies of the modern money market we shall have to consider the limitations under which coined money, bank notes, bank deposits, bank credit accounts, etc. may properly be regarded as capital, firstly from the point of view of the individual, and secondly from that of the community.

This footnote was deleted from the 5th ed.

c. This paragraph dates from the 5th ed. (p. 72).

d. This paragraph dates substantially from the 2nd ed. (Book II, ch. v, §1, p. 134), where it was preceded by the following opening paragraph of the chapter:

The terms Wealth and Income are closely connected. The former, in our standard use of it includes all stores of *material exchangeable goods*, and all such business connections as are a direct means of obtaining *material goods*. And in our standard use the term *gross income* may accordingly be defined as that stream of *economic goods*, which flows in (or *comes in*) during a certain time of (i) new elements of *wealth*, (ii) benefits derived from the use of *wealth*, and (iii) such passing enjoyments as from their fleeting nature cannot be included in the stock of wealth, but yet have a market value or are commonly acquired by money payments.

In the 1st ed. §1 of Book II, ch. vi ran as follows:

Total Real income.   A person's total income during, say, a year, consists of all the new economic goods which come to him during the year. If in order to obtain some of them he had to part with other goods, his *total real income* is found by deducting the value of the latter from that of the former; or in other words, by deducting from his gross income "the outgoings that belong to its production"[1].

Money income.   But for some of the practical purposes of life it is customary to consider only his *money income*; that is those elements of his total real income which come to him in the form of money. To these are however sometimes added those elements which he can easily convert into money, or which save him some pecuniary expense; for instance, if a man lives in his own house, or farms his own land, the estimated rent of

[1] See a report of a Committee of the British Association, 1878.

the house or of the farm is ordinarily reckoned as part of his income. But no account is commonly taken of the benefit he derives from the use of his furniture; so that if he had been in the habit of hiring a piano, and determined to sell a railway share and buy the piano instead of hiring it, his money income would be diminished by the dividend from the share, although it is probable that his total real income would be increased by the change.

Again, anything which a person does for which he is paid directly or indirectly in money, helps to swell his money income, while no services that he performs for himself are reckoned as adding to his nominal income, though they may be a very important part of his total real income. A man who digs in his own garden or repairs his own house, is earning income just as would the gardener or carpenter whom he might hire to do the work. The factory woman who hires others to tend her children and to do some of her household work, often finds that by staying at home she would increase the real income of the family, even while diminishing its money income by the amount of her wages. In the same way that real earnings are in the factory districts often less than they appear to be, they are generally more than they appear to be where agricultural populations make in the winter evenings cloth or other things for their own use, as was done to a great extent in mediæval times, and as is done even now in some parts of the world. On the other hand the caste system of the Hindoo makes him pay for having things done for him, which labourers in most parts of the world do for themselves; his income is less than it appears to be by what he pays for having himself shaved and for the washing of the clothes of himself and his family[1]. But when we are comparing people whose habits of life are in most respects the same, it is seldom worth while to take any special account of the minor services which each performs for himself.

It would be a great convenience if there were two words available: one to represent a person's total income and

Elements of real income which do not appear in the form of money are in some danger of being overlooked.

---

[1] In a pamphlet published in 1767 on the typical budget of a London clerk with £50 a year, who is supposed to live on the meanest food and clean his own boots, we find entered a weekly item of 6d. for "Shaving, and Combing a Wig twice".

another his money income, i.e. that part of his total income which comes to him in the form of money. For scientific purposes it would be best that the word income when occurring alone should always mean total real income. But as this plan is inconsistent with general usage we must, whenever there is any danger of misunderstanding, say distinctly whether the term is to be taken in its narrower or its broader use. We shall have to revert again to this class of difficulties, especially in our inquiry as to the causes which determine earnings in different occupations.

In the 2nd ed. (Book II, ch. v, §1, pp. 134–5), apart from the rewording of the paragraph which in the present edition constitutes the first paragraph of §2 of Book II, ch. IV, and apart from the insertion of the paragraph preceding it which is quoted above (see p. 198), the subject-matter of the paragraphs just quoted from Book II, ch. VI, §1 of the 1st ed. was substantially retained, though with some abbreviation. All these paragraphs were deleted from the 3rd ed. except the first paragraph, part of the third, and the fourth paragraphs. The first paragraph (reworded) and part of the third paragraph were retained in all the later editions (see pages 72–3 in vol. I of the present edition), while the fourth paragraph was deleted from the 4th ed. In the 1st ed. (Book II, ch. VI, §3, p. 141) there was also the following definition of the *net income* of an individual, which was deleted from the 2nd ed.:

Net income of an indi- vidual, The term *net income* is however often used in a very narrow sense in which the net income of any individual business is that which remains from the gross produce after deducting all the necessary outgoings, that is the wages, price of raw material, interest, depreciation and insurance on capital, and other expenses, which the undertaker is compelled to pay. The price of the necessaries of his own efficiency might logically be deducted also, but as this would be contrary to custom it must be taken not to be done unless special mention is made of it.

e.   As will be seen from the editorial note to the preceding paragraph in the text, this paragraph dates substantially from the 1st ed. (pp. 139–40).

f.   So since the 4th ed. (p. 149) where this sentence replaced the following clause at the end of the preceding sentence in the 3rd ed. (p. 155): "though they may be a very important part of his total real income if they are of a kind which people commonly pay for having done for them."

a. This paragraph dates substantially from the 1st ed. (p. 279), where it was placed in Book IV, ch. VI, §8. It may be noted that, though the marginal summary to this paragraph refers to a "Provisional definition of *net advantages*", no other definition was formally given of net advantages, and that the only subsequent treatment of the significance of this concept was in Book VII, ch. IV, §8 in the 1st ed. and in Book VI, ch. III, §8 in the second and all later editions (pages 556–8 in vol. 1 of the present edition).

b. An earlier definition of the term "net advantages" is to be found in the following passage in the *Economics of Industry* by Alfred Marshall and Mary Paley Marshall (1st ed. 1879, p. 103):

If equal wages were offered in ships going to the Mediterranean and the North Sea, the former would be full and the latter empty; so higher wages are offered on the latter ships to counter balance the disadvantage of the ungenial climate to which they sail. Carters who work underground in mines are paid more than carters who work above ground; and again, a night porter gets higher wages than a day porter. If a trade has any disadvantages, such as unhealthiness, dirtiness, etc., higher wages will be necessary to induce men to seek the trade than would have been required in the absence of the disadvantage, and the necessary addition to wages may be called the money value of this disadvantage. In the same way if a trade offers any exceptional personal advantage, such as a good social position, lower wages will attract men to it than would be necessary in a trade similar in other respects, but without the advantage: and this difference of wages is the measure or money value of the advantage.

If the wages and the money equivalents of the other special advantages of a trade be added together into one sum, and the money value of its special disadvantages be subtracted from the sum, the balance that remains may be called the *net advantages of the trade*.

c. This paragraph dates from the 5th ed. (p. 73). In the 1st ed. (p. 142) the paragraph on interest of capital ran as follows:

The benefits which the owner of wealth derives from it may be called the *usance of wealth*. They include as a special

Corresponding to *interest* of capital is *usance* of wealth.

case the money income which is derived from capital and is called *interest*; and this is most easily measured when it takes the form of a payment made by a borrower for the use of a loan for, say, a year; it is then expressed as the ratio which that payment bears to the loan.

In the 2nd ed. (p. 136) this paragraph ran as follows:

Usance of wealth corresponds to *interest* of capital.

Another convenient term is the *usance of wealth*. It consists of the benefits which a person derives from the ownership of wealth whether he uses it as capital or not. Thus it includes the benefits which he gets from the use of his own piano, equally with those which a piano dealer would win by letting out a piano on hire. Thus it includes, as a special case, the money income which is derived from capital. This income is most easily measured when it takes the form of a payment made by a borrower for the use of a loan for, say, a year; it is then expressed as the ratio which that payment bears to the loan, and is called *interest*.

This paragraph was retained unchanged until the 4th ed. (p. 149), where the first part of the second sentence ran as follows: "It *means the whole income* of benefits of every kind which a person derives from the ownership of wealth...etc." The fourth sentence was deleted, while the following sentence was added at the end of the paragraph after the word "*interest*": "But this term is also used more broadly to represent the money equivalent of the whole income which is derived from capital." In the 5th and subsequent editions there was no mention here of the term the "usance of wealth". But see also editorial note **a** to page 77 of vol. 1, in the present edition.

d. This paragraph was inserted in the 6th ed. (p. 73).

e. In the 3rd ed. (p. 599 n.) the substance of the first sentence of this footnote was inserted and placed in Book VI, ch. 11, §4. See editorial note **b** to page 592 of vol. 1 in the present edition. The second sentence was inserted in the 5th ed. (p. 73 n.) where there was the following additional sentence (deleted from the 7th ed.) which came after the end of the second sentence:

There are difficulties in the way of this suggestion: but after some modification and development, it may perhaps ultimately be of good service.

In the 3rd ed. (p. 154 n.) there was a further reference to Prof. Clark's use of the term "pure capital", in a footnote (deleted from the 5th ed.) to the paragraph in Book II, ch. IV, §10, dealing with the distinction made by Mill between fixed and circulating capital. See editorial note **g** to page 75 n. of vol. 1 in the present edition.

a. The first three sentences of this paragraph date substantially from the 1st ed. (p. 142), while the last two sentences date from the 5th ed. (p. 74).

b. The words in parentheses were added in the 4th ed. (p. 150).

c. This paragraph was inserted in the 5th ed. (p. 74). In the 1st ed. (pp. 142–3) the paragraph on rent ran as follows:

The income derived from the ownership of land is commonly called *rent*, and the term is stretched so as to include that derived from letting houses, and even such things as boats, pianos, and sewing machines. In a much narrower use the term has been applied specially to the annual income derived from those free gifts of nature which have been appropriated. But this use again has been gradually extended until it includes the income derived from things of all kinds of which the supply is limited and cannot be increased by man's action. This we may take to be now established as the scientific use of the term, though it is not free from difficulties, as we shall see hereafter; and we cannot dispense entirely with the use of the term in its broader popular sense.[1]

[1] Further difficulties connected with the use of these terms may be deferred for the present. One of them arises from the fact that in some cases earnings of management and interest on capital together fall short of full profits by the equivalent of the trouble and risks involved in borrowing and lending. Others are connected with the effects on the real rate of interest paid which are due to a change in the purchasing power of money between the date at which the loan was contracted and the date at which it is repaid; and others again are connected with the increase in the nominal value of land and other sources of income which are due to a fall in the rate of interest.

In the 2nd ed. (p. 136) it ran as follows:

The income derived from the ownership of land and other free gifts of nature is commonly called *rent*; and the term is sometimes stretched, so as to include the income derived from houses and other things the supply of which is limited and cannot quickly be increased.

The footnote in the 1st ed. was deleted from the 2nd ed. In the 3rd ed. (p. 156) an additional clause was inserted after the word "increased" which ran as follows: "and we shall need to stretch it yet further." No further change of substance was made in this paragraph in the 4th ed.

PAGE 75

a. This paragraph dates in its present form from the 5th ed. (p. 75).

b. So since the 2nd ed. (p. 127). For the definition of *consumption capital* in the 1st ed., see the Editorial Appendix to this chapter (p. 221).

c. Except for the words "or *instrumental capital*" which were inserted in the 4th ed. (p. 146) this paragraph dates from the 2nd ed. (p. 127). For the definition of *auxiliary capital* in the 1st ed., see the Editorial Appendix to this chapter, p. 222.

d. This paragraph dates from the 4th ed. (p. 146).

e. This paragraph dates from the 1st ed. (p. 134), where it was succeeded by the following paragraphs:

Specialized capital.

Sometimes again we have to distinguish certain kinds of capital as *specialized* because having been designed for use in one trade they cannot easily be diverted to another.

A caution against a source of confusion.

Mill and others have used fixed capital sometimes in the sense that we have retained for it, sometimes in the senses that we have given to specialized and to auxiliary capital. But there is much fixed capital which is not specialized, such as buildings and some kinds of machinery which are adapted to many different trades: while some materials of manufacture and other kinds of circulating capital are specialized. Again much fixed capital is also consumption capital, as for instance workmen's cottages.

Personal capital.

Almost all modern definitions of capital include, as ours have done, business goodwill and similar external personal goods which have exchange value: but many writers go further and include Personal capital. We have already defined Personal wealth[1] to consist firstly of those energies, faculties and habits which directly contribute to making people industrially efficient, and secondly of their business connections and associations of every kind. The first group consists of internal goods and the second of external goods; but both are productive; and therefore if they are to be reckoned as wealth at all, they are also to be reckoned as capital. Thus Personal wealth and Personal capital are convertible; and it seems best to follow here the same course as in the case of wealth, and for the same reasons. That is, it is best to assume

[1] Book II, ch. II, §3.

that the term "capital" when taken alone includes none but external goods; but yet to raise no objection to an occasional broad use of the term, in which it is explicitly stated to include Personal capital.

The first and third of the foregoing paragraphs were deleted from the 5th ed., and the second paragraph from the 4th ed.

f. The whole of this section (§4) dates from the 5th ed. (pp. 75–8) except for part of one sentence in the fourth paragraph of the section (see page 77 in vol. I of this edition).

g. The three sentences of this footnote date from the 1st ed. (p. 137) where they were placed in the "Historical Note on Definitions of the Term Capital". They were transferred to this place in the 3rd ed. (p. 154 n.) where they were succeeded by the following paragraph:

> The notion of the fixedness of capital is like to, and yet different from, the mediæval notion of capital as the *caput* or head of a loan. (See Ashley's *History*, Book II, ch. VI: but also Hewins' review of it in the *Economic Review*, vol. III, pp. 396 etc.) The caput is a fixed stock of "pure capital", in J. B. Clark's phrase; for goods may "circulate" through it, as water does through a reservoir that is kept at a constant height.

This latter paragraph was deleted from the 5th ed.

PAGE 77

a. So since the 7th ed. (p. 77) where the first part of this sentence replaced the following sentence dating from the 5th ed. (p. 77):

But a broad term is wanted to include the whole income of benefits of every sort which a person derives from the ownership of property however he applies it: and the term the *usance* of property may serve this purpose. It includes for instance the benefits...etc.

b. In its earliest version in the 3rd ed. (p. 153) this paragraph ran as follows:

The ordinary practice of life, as exemplified in the rules of the income tax commissioners, is governed by the same considerations as that of economists in this matter. For the purposes of both, it is expedient to count in everything which is commonly regarded as a means of income and treated in a business fashion; even though it may happen, like a dwelling-house inhabited by its owner, to yield its income of comfort directly: and this partly because of its intrinsic importance, and partly because the real income accruing from it can easily be separated off and estimated.

There was no substantial change in the foregoing paragraph in the 4th ed. It assumed its present form in the 5th ed. (p. 77).

c. In the 4th ed. (p. 145) this reference to Jevons, which was there placed in a different context, ran as follows:

All wealth is designed to yield what in pure theory may be called "an income" of benefit or gain in some form or other; and it was reasonable for Jevons and others, when addressing mathematical readers, to argue that goods in the hands of consumers are capital yielding income. The language of the market-place, while refusing to admit so broad a use of the term Income as that, commonly includes a certain number of forms of income, other than money income.

The two sentences just quoted (apart from the reference to Jevons) were taken from the Preface to the Third Edition (p. vii). See above, p. 43, and Marshall's letter to Cannan in the Editorial Appendix to this chapter, pp. 226–8 below).

PAGE 78

a. This section (§5) dates in its present form from the 5th ed. (pp. 78–9), but the individual paragraphs do not differ substantially from their form in the 4th ed. (pp. 142 and 144–6). In the 3rd ed. (Book II, ch. iv, §2, pp. 142–3), after a discussion of the fundamental attributes of capital (productiveness and prospectiveness), there were the following paragraphs:

Differences between capital and other forms of wealth are mainly differences of degree.

The task of finding a good definition of capital is however not so easy as would appear from the fact that these two attributes of productiveness and prospectiveness belong to it in all its various uses. For they belong also in some degree to every form of accumulated wealth. They both belong for instance to cooking utensils and to clothes; and yet when these things are being used by their owners for their own purposes, they are counted as capital only by those who draw no distinction between wealth and capital. To make any consistent distinction between them, we must emphasize differences of degree. Similar differences of degree will be found in the various uses of the term Income; and this suggests a solution of our difficulty.

For Adam Smith said that a person's capital is *that part* Capital
of his stock from which he expects to derive an income; and in yields
income.
fact each use of the term capital has corresponded more or
less closely to one of the uses of the term Income. The significations of the two terms have varied in breadth together:
in almost every use, capital has been that part of a man's
stock from which he expects to derive an income.

In ordinary life capital is commonly regarded from the
point of view of the individual; and economists are much
bound by the customs of the market-place in their uses of
the term *Individual capital*. But they have a freer hand in
dealing with *Social capital*, that is capital regarded from the
point of view of the nation, or the world, or indeed any
social group[1]. We will begin with the former and work up
to the latter; having regard throughout to the relativity of
capital and income.

[1] Compare the discussion of individual and social wealth in ch. II.

In a letter from Marshall to Cannan dated 7 January 1898 (see
Editorial Appendix to Book II, ch. IV, below, pp. 227–8), Marshall
draws Cannan's attention to "what I say (about capital) on top of
p. 143 and on pp. 152–3". The reference to "the top of page 143"
is to the first of the foregoing paragraphs in the 3rd ed. (Book II,
ch. IV, §2). The reference to "pp. 152–3" is to the following paragraphs in the 3rd ed. (Book II, ch. IV, §9, pp. 152–3) in which
Marshall summed up his definitions of capital:

Thus we finally arrive at the conclusion fore-shadowed at No one
the beginning of this chapter. There are several more or definition
convenient
less precise definitions of capital, which are useful for certain for all
special purposes: and there may be something to be said purposes.
for inventing separate terms for each of them. But there is
no one rigid definition which is universally available. Something must be left for explanation by the context.
Standard
use of
Whenever capital is being discussed from the individual individual
point of view, it will be taken in this treatise to mean trade
capital.
Social
capital unless the contrary is explicitly stated. capital may
But we shall be much occupied in considering the way in be defined
as wealth
which the three agents of production, land (that is, natural which
yields
agents), labour and capital, contribute to producing the income as
national income (or the National Dividend, as it will be called commonly
understood.

207

later on); and the way in which this is distributed between the three agents.

Now there is a tacit, but thorough agreement among all writers on economics, to treat this income in its broad outlines only, and not to trouble about petty details. So far as scientific considerations go, we should be quite at liberty to count as part of that income all the income of benefit that everyone derives from the use of his own clothes, furniture, &c. If we did that, we should need to count everyone to this extent as a capitalist; and to credit him under this head with the share of the total national income which corresponds to the use value of his own goods. But in ordinary life no one ever thinks of doing this[1].

It will be found that except in this problem of Distribution it is important practically seldom to define clearly the limits of social capital: and that even in this problem, a precise definition is needed chiefly for the purpose of securing that we do not count in some parts of the true national income twice and others not at all.

[1] As has been already intimated however the application of mathematical phrases to the problem of Distribution tends towards doing it.

The first of the foregoing paragraphs quoted from Book II, ch. IV, §9 is the paragraph referred to by Marshall in his letter to Cannan, where he said: "Fisher puts a strange interpretation on the first para. of p. 152" (see below, p. 228).

In the 4th ed. (p. 144) the second paragraph in this section (page 78, lines 15–23 in vol. I of the present edition) beginning "By far the most important use of the term Capital...etc.", was preceded by the following paragraphs which were deleted from the 5th ed.:

When we pass to the social point of view we are at liberty to lay more exclusive stress on purely economic considerations. But experience shows that there is great difficulty in making good use of this liberty.

The chief difference relates to land, and other free gifts of nature. The balance of usage and convenience is in favour of reckoning rights to land as part of individual capital. But when regarding capital from the social point of view it is best to put under separate heads those of the nation's resources which were made by men, and those which were not;

and to separate the capital which is the result of labour and saving from those things which nature has given freely.[1]

Some simplification of accounts also suggests itself at once. For instance, mortgages and other debts between persons of the same nation (or other social group) can be omitted; since the entries made for them on the creditor and debtor side of the national capital would cancel one another.[2]

So much is common ground to nearly all writers on economics. But here opinions diverge; and there is no general agreement as to the proper definition of capital from the social point of view. The following is a statement of the way in which the term will be used in this treatise.

By far the most important use of the term Capital...etc.

---

[1] This separation is not indeed always easy. See IV, II; V, VIII and IX; VI, X and XI.

[2] Rodbertus emphasized the distinction between individual rights in capital in a historic-juristic sense (*Kapital im historisch-rechtlichen Sinne, Kapital-vermögen, Kapital-besitz*) and the social view of pure capital. And this distinction has been developed by Knies, Neumann, Wagner and others.

The foregoing paragraphs just quoted from the 4th ed. date in turn substantially from the 3rd ed. (pp. 146–7). The references in Marshall's footnote attached to the end of the second of the above paragraphs, apply to Book IV, ch. II; Book V, ch. VIII, IX, X; Book VI, ch. X, XI, in vol. I of the present edition.

b. In the 3rd ed. (p. 153) this paragraph ran as follows:

In all discussions of Distribution therefore, in the present treatise, capital (regarded from the social point of view) will be taken to consist of those kinds of wealth (other than the free gifts of nature) which yield income that is generally reckoned as such in common discourse: together with similar things in public ownership, such as government factories.

c. The first two clauses of this sentence date from the 4th ed. (pp. 145–6).

PAGE 79

a. The remainder of this sentence dates substantially from the Preface to the Third Edition (p. vii). See above pp. 42–3 and Marshall's letter to Cannan, pp. 227–8 below. The transfer was made in the 4th ed. (p. 146).

b. This sentence was inserted in the 5th ed. (p. 79) where it replaced the following concluding sentence of this paragraph in the 4th ed. (p. 146):

In fact many economists glide imperceptibly to this closely corresponding use of Capital when they come to discuss the problem of distribution; and it will be found that nearly every broad proposition, which is commonly made as to the relations between national or social well-being and national or social capital, is true of capital thus defined.

The first clause of the foregoing sentence is taken from the Preface to the Third Edition (p. vii).

c. This sentence dates from the 1st ed. (pp. 140–1), where it was succeeded by the following sentences:

But to reckon it directly is for most purposes simplest and best. Everything that is produced in the course of a year, every service rendered, every fresh utility brought about is a part of the national income. Of course the value of things consumed in the process of production must be deducted from the gross produce, in order to find the net produce. For instance deductions must be made for the value of raw material used, and for the depreciation of fixed capital; but interest on borrowed capital, and wages of hired labour may be counted on the understanding that the services to which they correspond are not entered as separate items.[1]

... ...

The term net produce or income of any social group (when not otherwise specially explained) may be taken to be that which remains from the gross produce after replacing material capital and supplying all that is necessary to sustain the numbers and efficiency of the population, or rather of those classes of them that are engaged in production. It may be reckoned for any length of time, but practically the estimate is of little value unless it covers a period sufficiently long to allow for the accidents of trade and the fluctuations of prosperity.

[1] Thus if A hires B as a private secretary, we must count A's full income as well as B's salary to get the national income; for the payment A makes to B is for those services which he elects to take as part of his income. But if A makes an allowance to his son C, C's income is not to be counted unless a corresponding amount is deducted from A's. For C renders no services to A for it; A simply transfers part of his income to C. This practice is followed in income tax assessments.

In the 1st ed. an additional paragraph was inserted (between the two paragraphs quoted above) which defined "*net income*" of an individual. This paragraph will be found above in the last ten lines of editorial note **d** to vol. 1, page 72 (p. 200 above).

In the 2nd ed. (pp. 136–7) the second of the foregoing paragraphs in the 1st ed. was deleted, and the last two sentences of the first paragraph were replaced by the following paragraph:

Thus it includes the benefit derived from the advice of a physician, the pleasure got from hearing a professional singer, and the enjoyment of all other services which one person may be hired to perform for another. It includes the services rendered not only by the omnibus driver, but also by the coachman who drives a private carriage. It includes the services of the domestic servant who makes or mends or cleans a carpet or a dress, as well as the results of the work of the upholsterer, the milliner, and the dyer.

This latter paragraph was deleted from the 4th ed.

d. This and the following sentence date from the 2nd ed. (p. 137).

e. The remainder of this paragraph was inserted in the 7th ed. (p. 79).

f. This sentence dates from the 2nd ed. (p. 137).

g. The remainder of this paragraph dates from the 5th ed. (p.79) except for the insertion in the 8th edition (page 79) of the word "great" between the word "no" and the word "statistical" in the last clause of the first sentence.

h. This footnote was inserted here in the 5th ed. (p. 79 n.). For references in the first four editions to Jevons's "dictum" see the Editorial Appendix to Appendix E (p. 785 below).

PAGE 80

a. This paragraph dates from the 2nd ed. (p. 137).

b. This paragraph was inserted in the 7th ed. (p. 80).

c. This sentence dates from the 1st ed. (p. 143), except that the last line there ran as follows: "money value of its accumulated wealth." In the 2nd ed. (p. 138) the word "accumulated" was deleted; and in the 4th ed. (p. 151) the words "stock of" were inserted before the word "wealth".

d. The remainder of this section (§7) dates from the 1st ed. (pp. 143–4).

a. In the 1st ed. (pp. 143–4 n.) the following footnote was attached to the word "permanently" at the end of this paragraph:

> All estimates of a nation's richness based on a mere money measure are necessarily misleading, chiefly for the reasons which have been indicated in the chapter on wealth and the present chapter. But since they are frequently made, it may be well to point out that even if we agree for any special purpose to regard the richness of a nation as represented by its money income the question which of two nations is richer than another is still ambiguous. Is the richness of a nation to be measured by the aggregate money income of its inhabitants or by their average income? If the former, India is richer than Holland; if the latter, Holland is far richer than India. The latter is generally the more important measure for the purposes of the student of social science, the former for those of the diplomatist. If, however, we are considering a nation's power of bearing a long continued financial strain of war, we may measure its richness roughly by the excess of the sum total of the incomes of its inhabitants over what is required to supply them with the necessaries of life. A rough notion of the economic strength of a nation, for the purpose of comparison with that of others, may be got by multiplying the aggregate income of its inhabitants by their average income.
>
> The addition that an immigrant makes to the riches of a country may on the same plan be estimated as the excess of the total discounted value of the income he will earn over that which will be required for his own support. This estimate gives results not very different from that got on the plan of estimating the value of immigrants under middle age at the sum of the expenses of rearing and educating them.

The second paragraph of this footnote was deleted from the 2nd ed. and the last sentence of the first paragraph from the 4th ed. The remainder of the footnote was deleted from the 6th ed.

b. The first two sentences of this paragraph were inserted in the 6th ed. (p. 81), where they replaced the following sentences in the 5th ed. (p. 81):

In conclusion it may be remarked that though there is no clear and consistent tradition as to the verbal definition of capital; there is a clear tradition that we should use the term Wealth in preference to Capital when our attention is directed to the relations in which the stock of useful things stands to general well being, to methods of consumption, and to pleasures of possession: and that we should use the term Capital when our attention is directed to those attributes of productiveness and prospectiveness, which attach to all the stored up fruits of human effort, but are more prominent in some than in others. We should speak of Capital when considering things as agents of production; and we should speak of Wealth when considering them as results of production, as subjects of consumption and as yielding pleasures of possession.

These sentences in turn date substantially from the 4th ed. (p. 148).

c. In the 1st ed., in the chapter on Income (Book II, ch. VI, p. 142) there was the following paragraph, dealing with problems of definition in relation to capital and accumulated wealth, which was deleted from the 2nd ed.:

Much error has been caused by the fact that after defining "capital" more or less narrowly, some economists have glided into treating it as coextensive with accumulated wealth. A striking instance is seen in the important enquiry into the causes which determine the accumulation of wealth, which they have often worded as though it were concerned only with the growth of capital in the more or less narrow sense in which they have defined capital. This inaccuracy has been partly due to the fact that interest is habitually associated with capital; and it has been found convenient to speak of the growth of capital as influenced by the rate of interest. But really the substance of the argument was the influence on the accumulation of wealth exercised by the benefits which the possession of wealth gives, whether the wealth was in those forms which they had classed as capital or not. This then is one of the few cases in which the evils of coining a new economic term seem to be outweighed by its advantages.

d. The two remaining sentences of this paragraph date from the 3rd ed. (p. 142) where they were preceded by the following paragraph:

In almost every use, the conception of capital involves two fundamental attributes, that of "productiveness", and that of "prospectiveness" or the subordination of present desires to future enjoyments: and these two attributes have much in common. For as we saw in the last chapter, that labour is commonly said to be employed productively which provides for wants of the future rather than the present. Similarly with regard to wealth: that also is commonly said to be employed productively, when it is devoted to providing for the future rather than the present. And further these two fundamental notions supplement one another, ranging themselves one on either side of the problem of interest; that is, of the value of the command over ready capital. This point can be touched but lightly now, for indeed to touch it at all is to anticipate: but without some reference to it, no true notion can be had of the inner relations of the fundamental attributes of capital.

The last three sentences in the paragraph just quoted were deleted from the 4th ed., and the first two sentences from the 5th ed.

e. The following concluding sentence at this point in the 3rd ed. (p. 142) was deleted from the 4th ed.:

And, as we shall see, the exchange value of the services rendered by capital is governed in the long run by the pressure of the eagerness of demand against the sluggishness of supply.

In the 3rd ed. a footnote was attached to the word "supply" at the end of this sentence, which was subsequently transferred to the last paragraph of Appendix E (page 790 n. in vol. 1 of the present edition).

f. This paragraph, and the footnote attached to it, date from the 6th ed. (pp. 81–2 n.) where they replaced the following paragraph and footnote dating from the 5th ed. (p. 82):

The return of the sacrifice which is generally made by those who are of a *prospective* temperament, and sacrifice something of present satisfaction in favour of the future, will be discussed in Book III, chapter iv. The conditions under which the results of effort when thus stored up as capital are *productive* of greater benefits than if the efforts were devoted to immediate gratification will be indicated in the latter half of Book IV; and their bearing on the causes governing interest will be discussed in Book V, chapter iv, and Book VI, chapters i and vi. It will be shown that there is no universal rule that the use of roundabout methods of production is more efficient than direct methods: there are many household tasks for which it would be wasteful to provide machinery, though in a large hotel the use of machinery is economical. There are some conditions under which the investment of effort in obtaining machinery and in making costly provision against future wants is economical in the long run, and others in which it is not; and capital is accumulated in proportion to the prospectiveness of man on the one hand, and on the other to the volume of those roundabout methods which are sufficiently productive to remunerate those who make sacrifices in applying them.

These two sides are essential. They are indeed the supply and the demand side of the general doctrine of value in its application to capital; and it seems that no important economist has ever neglected either[1].

[1] There seems to be no good ground for the charges which Professor v. Boehm-Bawerk has brought against the great economists of past time, and most of their followers, of having failed to grasp the true character of the problem of capital (see below, VI, vi, §1). In spite of protests, he repeats, *Recent Literature or Interest,* p. 26, the mistaken statement that the account given of capital in this treatise is a mere "abstinence theory." Some historical notes on Definitions of Capital will be found in Appendix E.

EDITORIAL APPENDIX TO BOOK II, CHAPTER IV

The differences between Marshall's discussion of capital and income in the first two editions and that in the later editions were so considerable that his earlier position can only be shown adequately by reproducing (in addition to the extracts cited in the editorial notes to Book II, chapter IV) §§1–3 of Book II, chapter V in the 1st edition. Attention may, however, be drawn to Marshall's statement in his letter to J. B. Clark of 11 November 1902: "I have shifted my use of the word capital, but I have not changed my doctrines as to capital by a hair's breadth: Irving Fisher seems to have misread me in this matter." (For the context of this sentence, see pp. 10–11 above.)

I. TEXT OF §§1–3 OF BOOK II, CHAPTER V IN THE FIRST EDITION

[a]§1. [b]THE term "capital" has many widely divergent uses both in the language of the market-place and in the writings of economists. There is no other part of economics in which the temptation is so strong to invent a completely new set of technical terms; each of which should have a precise and fixed meaning, while between them they should cover all the various significations which are given to the one term capital in the language of the market-place. But this

The term capital has many different uses. We may not venture to invent a separate term for each of them.

---

a. Except where otherwise stated in the editorial notes, the subject matter of these three sections was substantially retained in the 2nd ed. (Book II, ch. IV), but was deleted from the 3rd ed.

b. This paragraph was retained substantially down to and including the 4th ed.

would throw the science out of touch with real life; and academic exactness of logical form would be obtained at the cost of grave substantial injury. We must therefore take the ordinary usages of the term as the foundation of our account, and add such general explanations, and even in some cases such special interpretation clauses, as are required to give to our use of the term some measure of clearness and precision.

Adam Smith's use of the term.

Adam Smith said that a person's capital is that part of his stock from which he expects to derive an income. This account is consistent with ordinary usage so long as we regard capital from the point of view of the individual; and we will confine ourselves for the present to that, leaving the

Individual capital includes Trade-capital.

discussion of Social capital to a later stage.[d] We may slightly modify Adam Smith's phrase, and say that *Individual capital* is that portion of a person's external goods by which he obtains his livelihood (*Erwerbsmittel*).

The most conspicuous elements of Individual capital are such things as the factory and the business plant of a manufacturer; that is, his machinery, his raw material, any food, clothing and house room that he may hold for use of his employés, and the goodwill of his business, at all events in so far as it is capable of being sold to his successor. [e]Here we include all things which are let out on hire, such as houses, carriages, and sewing machines, all wealth or command over wealth which is let out at interest, whether in money or in any other form; whether lent to help people to establish themselves in business or to indulge in idle and injurious dissipation.

These are instances of things from which their owner expects to derive an income in the special form of money. It is no doubt very convenient that this group of things

---

c. This sentence was retained in the later editions. See page 78 in vol. 1 of the present edition.

d. This and the next sentence were reworded in the 3rd ed. (p. 144), and were retained in that form throughout the later editions. See pages 71–2 in vol. 1 of the present edition.

e. This sentence was deleted from the 2nd ed.

should have a common class name. But they do not con- That part
of capital
stitute the whole of *Individual capital*, and we must not from
apply the term "capital" simply to this use, except where which a
money
there is no danger of misunderstanding. The central notion income is
of this grouping is that the things are used for trade pur- derived may
be called
poses, and this notion ought to be expressed by their name. *Trade-*
We may then define a person's *Trade-capital* to consist of *capital.*
those external goods which he uses in his trade, either
holding them to be sold for money or applying them to
produce things that are to be sold for money. Under this
head are to be reckoned fancy ball dresses that are let out
for hire, but not the house in which a frugal working man
lives if he happens to own it himself; ices in the hands of
a pastry cook, but not the store of wheat for his own use
which a man has grown on his allotment; and not even the
sewing-machine with which his wife makes clothes for
the family.

The habit of regarding as of special importance that part
of a person's income which comes to him in the form of
money is a survival of the prejudices of the Mercantile
System; and in the following chapter and elsewhere we
shall be a good deal occupied with the attempt to free
ourselves from its misleading influence, and to group together things that are substantially of the same kind even
though some of them are, and others are not, clothed
in the form of money payments. Leaving then Trade-
capital for its own special uses, and they are not unimportant, we will go on to complete our account of individual
capital.

To do this we have simply to add to Trade-capital all Elements of
those things which are required to enable a productive individual
capital that
worker to do his work and earn his livelihood, whether are not
they are in his own possession or not, whether he derives included in
Trade-
benefit from them directly and without the intermedia- capital.
tion of money or not. Thus it includes a manufacturer's
store of necessaries for his own living and efficiency
as well as those for the living and efficiency of his work-
people: they are part of the means by which he earns his
livelihood.

The question whether free gifts of nature are to be included may be left open.

ᶠA person's capital is most commonly taken to include land and other free gifts of nature, at all events if he uses them directly or indirectly as a means of earning his livelihood. But even in ordinary conversation the "rent" which he derives from them is sometimes separated from the "interest" or "profits" which he derives from his capital.

For some purposes it is convenient to include them, for others not: the same writer will—whatever his formal definition be—often include them in some parts and exclude them in other parts of his reasonings. On the whole it seems best to be bold, and to do this openly. Thus then the question whether the free gifts of nature which are in any person's ownership are to be counted as part of his capital, is left to be decided by an interpretation clause in the context, wherever there is room for misunderstanding on the point.

We arrive on somewhat surer ground when, leaving the discussion of individual capital, we pass to consider it from the point of view of society.

The scope of the term Social capital.

§2. We have already noticed that national wealth stands in the same relation to cosmopolitan, in which individual wealth does to national; and so with regard to capital. But we may here confine ourselves to the discussion of social capital, of which national and cosmopolitan capital are special instances. We must recollect that as the older term national capital represented not that capital only which is the common property of the nation, but the aggregate of the capital which the nation possesses whether in public or private ownership; so the more modern term social capital indicates the aggregate of the real capital, private as well as public, owned by the members of any society which is under discussion.

For this reason, boundaries of private rights of property

---

f. In the 2nd ed. (p. 125) this sentence, which was there slightly reworded without altering the sense, was preceded by the following sentence:

In many discussions great confusion would be caused by the refusal to count as part of his capital the freehold land on which a manufacturer had built his own mill.

do not much trouble us here. The debts and other obligations from one group of persons to another enter on both the debtor and creditor sides of the account, and destroy one another, as soon as we count up the resources of a nation or other society which includes both groups. Moreover the usages of business life are in this case less troublesome; because while the social view of capital is the more important for the general purposes of economics, it plays a less prominent part in ordinary discourse. Thus we are able to be guided more strictly by purely economic[1] considerations; to exclude without hesitation the free gifts of nature; [g]and to regard social capital as consisting of things made by mankind as resources wherewith to meet future needs.

[h]The first quality of social capital is its "prospectiveness": on that all writers are agreed. The second, which nearly all concur in assigning to it, is that of assisting society in earning its livelihood[2], that is in production: for while an individual

[The capital in the ownership of a nation or other society can be defined on more purely economic lines than that in the ownership of an individual.]

[Two attributes of capital:]

---

1 [i]Compare the account of Wagner's position in the note at the end of this chapter.

2 [i]Compare the quotation from Boehm-Bawerk in the note at the end of the chapter.

---

g. This final clause was deleted from the 2nd ed. (p. 126) where its place was taken by the following sentence to which a footnote was attached:

This is the only important difference which there is between our uses of the term Capital from the individual and the social point of view.[1]

> 1 No real difficulty arises from the fact that when wealth is lent to a Government or a person who uses it unproductively, the lender counts that wealth as part of his capital; while yet it does not appear in the inventory of social capital. For negative capital to the amount of the loan may be charged to the account of the borrower: and this course is habitually adopted by those who attempt to express in mathematical form doctrines relating to the quantity of capital.

The foregoing footnote in the 2nd ed. comprises the last two sentences of a footnote in the 1st ed. (p. 132 n.) which was there attached to the end of the last paragraph in Book II, ch. v, §3 (see p. 223 below).

h. This and the next paragraph were placed in the 2nd ed. in §1 of Book II, ch. iv, i.e. as part of the discussion of *individual capital*.

The version of the attributes of capital in the 2nd ed. (p. 125) ran as follows:

Thus the conception of capital involves two fundamental attributes, that of "productiveness" and that of "prospec-

[Prospectiveness as an attribute of capital.]

may obtain his livelihood from others by a course which does not add anything to the production of wealth, a self-contained nation or other social group can add to its means of livelihood only by an excess of production over consumption.

Its pro-
spectiveness.

The histories of the terms "productive labour" and "Capital" are closely allied: productive labour and capital have always been regarded as devoted to providing enjoyment and the sources of enjoyment for the future rather than for the present. Some enjoyment is indeed derived from the consumption of the necessaries of life which are included under capital; but they are counted as capital because of the work for the future which they enable people to do, and not on account of the present pleasure which they afford. Thus capital is said to be the result of saving, of a sacrifice of present enjoyments for the sake of future: and it is chiefly for this reason that economists exclude from capital in its pure economic sense those free gifts of nature which have not been made by man; though they include the value of the improvements which man has added to the natural resources of the land.

Its produc-
tiveness.

[j] While then all economists regard prospectiveness as an essential attribute of capital, the majority of them insist also on its productiveness; and call nothing capital of which it can be said that, if it were taken away, the world's work would go on with equal efficiency. Skill and other kinds of internal wealth which contribute directly to the production of material wealth are omitted; but business organizations are counted

---

tiveness", or the subordination of present desires to future enjoyments: and these two attributes have much in common. For indeed the histories of the terms *productive labour* and capital are closely allied: productive labour and capital..., etc.

i, i. The reference in these two footnotes to "the note at the end of this chapter" applies to the "Historical Note on Definitions of the Term 'Capital'", which will be found in the Editorial Appendix to Appendix E. See pp. 781–9 below. Both of these footnotes were deleted from the 2nd ed.

j. This and the next paragraph were deleted from the 2nd ed.

in at the value of what they add to the efficiency of production[1].

Though the matter is one on which opinions may fairly differ, it seems on the whole best to adopt this position, and to combine the two notions of prospectiveness and productiveness in our standard definition.

Social capital may thus be defined as consisting of those things made by man, by which the society in question obtains its livelihood; or, in other words, as consisting of those external goods without which production could not be carried on with equal efficiency; but which are not free gifts of nature. It consists firstly of stores of commodities provided for the sustenance of workers of all industrial grades: and secondly of raw materials, of machinery, and all other aids to production.

_{Definition of *Social capital.*}

[k]The first group may be called *Consumption capital.* It consists exclusively of such goods as food, clothing, houseroom, &c. which are in a form to satisfy wants directly. That is, it consists of *goods of the first order*[2], or *consumption goods;* [l]but it does not include the whole of them. For those goods which are destined to be consumed without adding to the efficiency of production, are not to be regarded as capital, when they are in the hands of consumers. The food, &c. which is required for children who are growing up to be workers, is to be included here.

_{Consumption capital.}

---

[1] [m]The relation in which capital stands to money and credit may be treated generally on the plan indicated above, Book II, ch. II, §4. But it involves some difficult problems which will require our careful attention at a later stage.

[2] [n]See above, ch. II, §I.

---

k. This paragraph was replaced in the 2nd ed. (p. 127) by the following paragraph: "*Consumption capital* consists of goods in a form to satisfy wants directly; that is, goods which afford a direct sustenance to the workers, such as food, clothes, house-room, etc." This definition of consumption capital was retained unaltered in the later editions.

l. The remainder of this paragraph was deleted from the 2nd ed.

m. This footnote was deleted from the 2nd ed. The reference to Book II, ch. II, §4, applies to a part of a footnote which was deleted from the 2nd ed. See editorial note **a** to page 60 of vol. I in the present edition.

n. This reference applies to Book II, ch. III, §I, page 64 in vol. I of the present edition.

Auxiliary capital.   °The second group may be called *Auxiliary capital.* It consists of all *production goods,* or in other words of all *goods of the second and higher orders.* Since raw materials and machinery are always counted as production capital even though they be devoted to making superfluities, this concession seems to require us to go further in conformity with usage, and to include also stocks of luxuries in the hands of traders.ᴾ

We must include the necessaries of the higher as well as of the lower grades of industry.   That part of consumption capital which goes into the hands of hired labourers may be regarded as wage-capital from the social point of view. But it must be recollected that wage-capital, so defined, and auxiliary capital do not constitute the whole of social capital; there remain the necessaries of the higher classes of industry. On the other hand we ought not, strictly speaking, to include under wage-capital the luxuries as well as the necessaries of the wage-receivers; so long, that is, as we are regarding capital from the social point of view. Much error has arisen from the assumption, into which some writers have glided from a careless use of the term wage-capital, that the necessary consumption of the lower classes of industry stands in a different relation to national capital and national production from the necessary consumption of other workers[1]. This is, for practical purposes, the most important correction which it

[1]q Of course there is a fringe of debateable ground at the margin of each definition. A factory is auxiliary capital simply; a weaver's cottage in which he plies his trade is partly auxiliary and partly consumption capital. The private dwelling-house of a rich man engaged in business is consumption capital to the extent of that accommodation which directly contributes to the health and efficiency of himself and his family: but beyond that, it is not capital at all, in the use of the term which we are adopting.

---

o.   In the 2nd ed. (p. 127) the first two sentences of this paragraph ran as follows:

Auxiliary Capital is so called because it consists of all the goods that aid labour in production. Under this head come tools, machines, factories, railways, docks, ships, etc.; and raw materials of all kinds.[1]

[1] Thus *Auxiliary* capital consists of all *Production Goods,* or in other words of all goods of the second and higher Orders; while *Consumption* capital consists of *Goods of the first Order* or *Consumption Goods,* but it does not include the whole

seems requisite to introduce into the ordinary definitions of capital.

[r]It is scarcely requisite to remark that, as in the case of wealth, there are many things, such as roads, bridges, and the organization of the State, which are part of capital, and are important when capital is regarded from the point of view of the nation; but which it is not necessary to mention when comparing one person's capital with that of his neighbour; and which therefore often drop out of view in estimating individual capital.

Our definitions of Social and Individual capital are in general harmony.

When our standard definitions of individual and social capital are compared, it will appear that they are in general harmony with one another; though usage does not allow us to make them absolutely coincident.[1]

---

1 [s]No great trouble or confusion is caused by the fact that the value of lands without allowing for improvements, and of other free gifts of nature is generally excluded from social capital and more often included in individual capital. More difficulty might have arisen from the habit of reckoning a trader's stock of superfluities as part of his capital, if we had adhered to what appears at first sight the natural course of excluding them from social capital. But the universal habit of including under social capital all raw materials and machinery, even if they are used solely in making superfluities, has brought about the result that less logical inconsistency is involved by including traders' stocks of superfluities in social capital than by excluding them. Nor does any real difficulty arise from the fact that when wealth is lent to a government or a person who uses it unproductively, the lender counts that wealth as part of his capital; while yet it does not appear in the inventory of social capital. For negative capital to the amount of the loan may be charged to the account of the borrower: and this course is habitually adopted by those who attempt to express in mathematical form doctrines relating to the quantity of capital.

---

of them. For those goods which are destined to be consumed without adding to the efficiency of production, are not to be regarded as capital, when they are in the hands of consumers.

This footnote was deleted from the 3rd ed. But the definition of *Auxiliary capital* in the text of the 2nd ed. was retained in all the subsequent editions.

p. The following additional clause after the word "traders" was inserted in the 2nd ed. (p. 127) "on the ground that the process of production is not fully completed and that of consumption has not yet begun."

q. This footnote was retained in the 2nd and 3rd editions, but was finally deleted from the 4th ed. See Marshall's letter to Cannan, p. 228 below, and editorial note **d** to page 788 (p. 780 below).

r. The remainder of this section was deleted from the 2nd ed.

s. The first three sentences of this footnote were deleted from the 2nd ed. For the last two sentences see editorial note **g** (p. 219 above).

§3. ᵗBut while the majority of writers adopt the course which has been followed in our standard definitions of capital, others extend its limits, so as to include not only all things which are destined to promote production, but all things which are capable of being so used. Thus for instance they include all the stock of grain in a country without inquiring whether it is to be used in feeding people who work or people who live idly; whether in feeding cart-horses or race-horses. In short they include what is potentially capital according to our definition as well as what is actually capital. This broad use of the term has its advantages; but on the whole it seems best to take the narrower as our standard use, and to have recourse to the phrase *Potential Capital* when we want to refer to the broader use of things.

ᵘSome writers go even further; and laying stress almost exclusively on the notion of "prospectiveness" include under capital all external goods which are made by man and "saved" to become the sources of future enjoyment.

This divergence as to the use of the term capital is due, as has been already remarked, to the fact that economists may not venture to invent for themselves a technical terminology independent of the ordinary language of business. Thinkers who are agreed on all substantial points, continue to differ as to what is the least injurious method of effecting a compromise between scientific consistency and popular usage; and as to what arrangement of the few terms at their disposal will best eke out their resources. The divergence has been a great stumbling-block to many readers of economics; so great a variation in the use of so prominent a term appears necessarily to land the science in confusion. But in fact the difficulty is much less serious than it seems at first sight.

For whether a writer takes a broader or a narrower view

Some writers extend the meaning of the term so as to include what we may call *Potential* Capital

and some even make it almost co-extensive with stored-up wealth. This divergence in the use of the term is to be regretted.

---

t. This paragraph was deleted from the 2nd ed.

u. This paragraph and the next two paragraphs were transferred in the 2nd ed. (pp. 130 and 131–2) to the "Historical Note on Definitions of the Term Capital". See the Editorial Appendix to Appendix E, pp. 783–4 and 786–7 below.

of capital, he finds that the various elements of which it is composed differ more or less from one another in the way in which they enter into the different problems with which he has successively to deal. He is compelled therefore to supplement his standard definition by an explanation of the bearing of each several element of capital on the point at issue. These special analyses are substantially the same in the works of all careful writers on economics, however divergent may be their standard definitions of capital; the reader is thus brought to very much the same conclusion by whatever route he travels; though it may sometimes require a little trouble to discern the unity in substance that underlies the differences in the words which are used by different schools of economists to express their doctrines relating to capital[1]. But it causes less confusion than might have been expected.

[1] v For instance, whatever definition of capital we take, it will be found to be true that a general increase of capital augments the demand for labour and raises wages: and whatever definition we take it is not true that all kinds of capital act with equal force in this direction, or that it is possible to say how great an effect any given increase in the total amount of capital will have in raising wages, without specially inquiring as to the particular form which the increase has taken. This inquiry is the really important part of the work: it has to be made in very much the same manner and it comes to the same result, whatever be the definition of capital with which we have started. Similar remarks apply to the investigation of the causes which determine the rate of interest on capital, and its aggregate amount.

If we were free to construct a terminology with sole reference to the needs of economic science, it might perhaps be best to invent other terms for other uses which the term capital is now made to subserve, and to devote that term exclusively to representing the amount of labour combined with abstinence that is invested in any particular source of enjoyment made by man. For this conception is capable of being developed, from a purely abstract point of view, with logical consistency, and mathematical exactness of quantitative measurement. To this point we shall return in the historical note at the end of the chapter and elsewhere.

2. LETTER OF 7 JANUARY 1898 FROM ALFRED MARSHALL TO EDWIN CANNAN

In January 1898, the year in which the 4th edition of Marshall's *Principles* was published, Marshall wrote a letter to Cannan in reply to objections urged by the latter to the definitions of capital in the 3rd edition

---

v. The first paragraph of this footnote was placed in the 2nd ed. (p. 132) in the "Historical Note to Definitions of the Term Capital". See the Editorial Appendix to Appendix E (p. 787 below). The second paragraph was deleted from the 2nd ed.

(published in 1895). The letter, which has been printed in the *Memorials of Alfred Marshall* edited by A. C. Pigou (pp. 404–6), ran as follows:

Balliol Croft, Cambridge.

7. 1. 1898.

My dear Cannan,

I have been looking again at the letter you were so very good as to write to me in December; and I have been re-reading part of Fisher's articles.[a] Is this a correct survey of the situation?:

You and Fisher hold that wealth is a stock and a flow: but capital is only a stock.

I take wealth to be a stock only.

So far it would appear that the difference between us is only as to the use of the word "wealth". I can see no advantage in your use; but the matter does not strike me as important, so far.

But I think there is something of more importance behind. I take it that we are all agreed that "capital" from the individual point of view, must be used in the common business way; more or less on the lines of what I have called trade-capital; and that it has no scientific justification: that therefore the discussion is all about "capital in general" or "capital from the social point of view".

Assuming that, I want to adhere to the line of division between "Land", or "Free goods", and "Capital". I can't be sure that you and Fisher do.

You see the position taken up in my Ed. III only comes to this, that I have openly adopted as my *standard* definition one which corresponds to what has been *de facto* my main use of the term ever since about 1869, when I used to think in Mathematics more easily than in English. I then adopted the doctrine of the national dividend, its division into the

---

a.   The articles by Irving Fisher here referred to were: "What is Capital?" *Economic Journal*, VI (1896), pp. 509–34; "Senses of Capital", *ibid.* VII (1897), pp. 199–213; "The Role of Capital in Economic Theory", *ibid.* VII, pp. 511–37.

shares of land, labour and capital, governed by the equi-
valence of differential coefficients of cost of production on
the one hand (or disutility), and utility on the other (I did
not use those words then). There remained great lacunae
in my theory till about '85; when on my return to Cambridge,
I resolved to try to find out what I really did think about
Distribution: and I gradually developed (sufficiently to
please my complacent self) the doctrines of substitution
between prima facie non-competitive industrial groups, of
quasi-rents, etc. But all this, though vital to my special views,
did not affect my use of "capital". That was throughout
the stock of things, other than land, which are instrumental
in satisfying human wants. (In my first version of distribution in 1879, I did not speak of the National Dividend;
because I wanted to get rent out of the way first: and
Earnings-and-interest Fund was National Dividend after
deducting Rent.)

I did not openly define capital in that way; because I did
not dare to set myself in opposition to English tradition.
But in practice I nearly always used the term in that way,
except when I was talking of trade-capital.

Now I have dotted my i's and crossed my t's; and my
position is:

Capital (in general) is a stock.

Wealth is a stock.

But (i) Capital does not include "free goods": this is a
matter of principle.

(ii) Capital does not include those trifles, the income from
which is neglected by ordinary people and income tax col-
lectors. This is a mere matter of convenience; it corresponds
to writing £M437 instead of £437,495,821:14:8$\frac{3}{4}$.

(iii) Though in England (not perhaps in France) wealth
and capital consist for the greater part of the same goods,
yet when we use the term "capital" we are always thinking
of the "productiveness" and "prospectiveness" which mainly
affect the demand for and the supply of wealth,...

Now as to inconsistencies between my Preface and
Book II, ch. IV. Is not what I say about capital in the Preface contained in what I say on top of p. 143 and on

pp. 152–3[b]? (of course I shall not reprint that Preface, so I propose to copy a part of it in at the end of p. 153 together with a paragraph to the same effect as p. 5 of this letter).

Fisher puts a strange interpretation on the first ¶ of p. 152[c]. I don't want it: and I want space. So I shall omit it.

The first line of §6[d] may be clearer as "some writers have thought it specially important", and I admit that [e]the last line of first ¶ of Note 2 on p. 150 is now incorrect. I did not notice it. Of course I shall strike it out.

Is there any other change needed to make me consistent with myself? I cannot alter my definition of wealth to make it include income: for I see only evil in that change. But outside of that, is there anything I can do to free me from reproach in your eyes? You were good in December. Goodness brings its own punishment, in this abominable infliction on you.

Pardon! Yours humbly,

ALFRED MARSHALL.

3. CAPITAL AND INCOME AS A STOCK
AND A FLOW

The following 14 paragraphs comprise the fourth section of an article on *Distribution and Exchange* published by Marshall in the *Economic Journal* for March 1898, in which section he explained his

---

b. For the relevant passages in the Preface to the Third Edition see pp. 42–3 above. The references to "the top of p. 143" and to "pp. 152–3" relate also to the 3rd ed., and the paragraphs in question will be found in editorial note **a** to vol. 1, Book II, ch. IV, page 78 (see pp. 207–8 above).

c. See p. 208 above. Fisher's "strange interpretation" will be found in his article "What is Capital", *Economic Journal*, VI (1896), p. 527.

d. In the 3rd ed. the first line and a half of Book II, ch. IV, §6 ran as follows: "For some purposes it is important to insist on the notion of prospectiveness." See editorial note **b** to Appendix E (p. 779 below).

e. See editorial note **q** (pp. 222–3 above), and editorial note **d** to page 788 (p. 780 below).

reasons for the modification of his definitions of capital in the 3rd edition:

[a] Much of what has been said already has a bearing on Professor Fisher's interesting discussion of capital and interest regarded as a stock and a flow of economic goods. If I understand his position rightly, the difference between us is very small and is mainly one of words.

The chapters on capital in successive editions of my *Principles* have shown changes, which must have been almost as disagreeable to any reader who endeavoured to keep pace with them as to myself. The following short statement is in effect an explanation of and an apology for this lack of decision.

Jevons' famous discussion: "Are articles in the consumers' hands capital?" seems to put, as strongly as it can be put, the case in favour of including under capital either all economic goods, or at all events all that are not the free gifts of nature. And indeed, when one approaches the problem of distribution from the mathematical point of view, there is practically no choice. For following the old tradition which classes as Land, Labour, and Capital the things whose combined agency affords the material means for satisfying human wants, and throwing that tradition into precise mathematical shape, one is impelled to think of Labour as including the work of the employer, and of Capital as including commodities in consumers' hands (so far as one takes any account of their existence at all). In the far-off years, when I used to think naturally in the mathematical language, I jotted down a hundred and one mathematical versions of my central doctrine of distribution; and then invariably thought of capital as the whole stock of goods, and of interest as the whole of the usance or benefits derived from the use of all that stock.

The question whether the same plan should be followed in writing for the general reader is not one of principle; it

---

a. This refers to the third section of Marshall's article, the text of which is reproduced in the Editorial Appendix to the Prefaces (see pp. 62–75 above).

is a question of convenience, on which opinions may well differ. A generation hence the general reader may be more compliant with academical tones of thought than he is now. But as things are, I have concluded, not without doubt, that it is best to follow the example of the tax gatherer, and to omit from a general view of the income derived from land, capital, and labour such details as the benefits which a person reaps from the use of his own clothes, furniture, etc. And if this course be adopted, it follows that these commodities will be omitted from a general view of capital. (A man living in his own house pays rent to himself! Distribution and Exchange are coextensive.)

Land might perhaps be reasonably treated as a form of capital in general discussions of distribution written for a new country—where what little land was occupied at all was mainly in the hands of first settlers. But in an old country it seems essential to bring into the first prominence those characteristics of land which are not shared by other forms of capital; at all events, when one is discussing the affairs of the nation as a whole and not those of individual traders.

The use of capital thus indicated has been practically my dominant use from the publication in 1879 of *Economics of Industry* to the present time. But, in order to keep as close to English tradition as I could, I introduced into my formal definitions references to the dependence of employment for labour on that wealth which was used as capital. None of these definitions were satisfactory; and in my *Principles* I gave notice that the definition of capital was provisional, and that when occasion required I should depart from it, with the aid of an interpretation clause expressed or implied.

At last, however, I changed my opinion as to the effects of a diversion of wealth from use as Capital, in the older sense of the term, to other uses. I had taken for granted that such diversion would tend to diminish the richness of the field for the employment of labour. But on further consideration I concluded that wealth in the form of houses or private carriages helped to give employment to labour as much as when in the form of hotels or cabs, or any capital that did not contribute to the production of goods or services to be consumed by labourers. So my last scruples vanished, and in 1895 I accommodated my formal definition to what had all along been in practice my dominant use of the term.

We seem to be all agreed as to the necessity of conserving the ordinary business use of capital, that is "trade-capital", when considering the affairs of individual traders; and that suggests that we should be as conservative as possible in our use of Capital from the social point of view. For, indeed, though one side of the question may be taken to have been decided by the long series of failures of many attempts by many men to draw a clear and logical dividing line between two parts of the stock of things made by man, and to label one part as capital from the social point of view; there re-mains another side. These failures do not tell decisively against the retention of the term to suggest certain qualities which are more or less common to the whole stock of things made by man, but which we would bear specially in mind in dealing with certain problems. Continuity of tradition is important everywhere; it is nowhere more important than in our use of terms; while in our use of terms it is even more important as regards the tone or flavour which they connote, than as regards the boundaries marked out by their formal definitions. And there is a complete continuity of tradition in favour of dwelling on the attributes of "prospectiveness" and "productiveness" in all general uses of the term capital.

The term Wealth, by which of course I mean the whole stock of economic goods, has indeed been associated with those notions also, but not in so marked a degree. On the other hand, it has been used in preference to Capital, when attention has been directed rather to the relations in which the stock of useful things stands to general well-being; and there seems much to be gained and nothing to be lost by remaining faithful to this tradition. Even if it should ulti-mately be thought best when speaking from the social point of view to treat Capital and Wealth as conterminous, it may still be advisable to speak of Capital when we are considering things as agents of production, and to speak of Wealth when we are considering them as the results of production, as the subjects of consumption, and as yielding the pleasures of possession. Citizens, Taxpayers and Ratepayers are nearly the same sets of people, and they might be exactly the same sets; but it would still be convenient to use now one of these terms, and now another, to suggest this or that notion, this or that point of view.

It is true that the terms "productive" and "prospective", or "telescopic" are slippery; but their faults are on the side of formal classification and enumeration, rather than of suggestion. Further experience may possibly show that even this little piece of conservatism involves more trouble than it is worth; but I submit that at present the balance of probability inclines slightly in the opposite direction and that a breach with tradition as regards notions should be deferred so long as there remains any considerable doubt as to its wisdom. If one is in doubt whether the landscape would be improved by cutting down an old oak, the oak should be left yet a little while.

Professor Fisher seems to use "fund" and "stock" as synonymous. He refers to the contrast so lucidly made by Professor Newcomb between fund in the sense of "stock" and "flow", and says that I "was quick to see its importance". I am not sure that he means that I have recently changed my views on this subject; but, if so, he is mistaken. The general notion of distribution in the *Economics of Industry* published by my wife and myself in 1879 is the same as in my *Principles*. There are changes: for I was unwilling at that time to write upon distribution at all, because I did not then see my way clearly as to some parts of it. But I had settled the main outlines of the problem to my own satisfaction very early, under the good guidance of von Thünen. And the chapter on distribution in our little book proceeds on his plan of marching off to the margin of cultivation (*die Grenze*) of his "Isolated State", where there was lordless (*herrenlos*) land, and to get rid of rent before starting on the general problem of distribution: so that the whole annual produce might be taken as divided between labourer and capitalist. Von Thünen worked out his theory with several curious subtleties, and some perversities but he gave a good lead by suggesting symmetrical relations between labour and capital; the earnings of each being defined by the last profitable application of each at the margin.

Following this lead, our little book discussed rent before distribution, and said: "We may regard the amount which remains after deducting rent and taxes from the net annual income of the country as a given fund, and call it the Wages and Profits Fund.... The problem of distribution consists of an enquiry into the way in which this fund is divided up." This term was chosen in order to direct attention to the most important divergence of the newer from the older doctrines: viz., that instead of treating capital as hiring labour, modern doctrines treated them as mutually finding employment and remuneration for one another.

I hold that a fund is not necessarily a stock; it may be an income or a flow, as when one says: "The charitable funds at the disposal of certain trustees have risen from one to ten thousand a year, in consequence of the growth of the town near which the property is situated." I found, however, that some students did take it to mean a stock; and I was struck by the assumption of Professor Newcomb that a fund *must* be a stock. So in my *Principles* I emphasized the fact that "the National Dividend is a continuous stream, always flowing, and not a reservoir or a store, or, in the narrow sense, a fund of capital.... In Professor Newcomb's words, it is a flow, and not a fund." This was a mere rejection of a word which had been found misleading; it was not a new departure.

Perhaps I attach rather less importance to some of Professor Fisher's points than he does. But that is the way of the world. I concur in his conclusion that whatever we do with the *word* capital, we cannot solve problems of capital by classifying wealth. I may perhaps venture to offer my tribute of admiration to his work. It well supports the hope that in the coming generation America will take a leading position in economic thought, as well as in economic practice.

BOOK III

ON WANTS AND THEIR
SATISFACTION

CHAPTER I

INTRODUCTORY

PAGE 83

a. So since the 4th edition, where the present title of Book III replaced the following title dating from the 1st edition: "Demand or Consumption."

b. Except where otherwise stated the wording of this chapter dates substantially from the 1st edition.

c. The title of this chapter remained unchanged since the 1st edition.

d. So since the 4th ed. (p. 158), where this sentence replaced the following sentence dating from the 2nd ed. (p. 141):

But first of all come "*Demand* or *Consumption*", i.e. the theory of *Wants*; and "*Production*" or *Supply*, i.e. the theory of the *Efforts* and *Sacrifices* devoted to the satisfaction of wants.

PAGE 84

a. The following clause and sentence after the word "neglected" in the 1st ed. (p. 148) were deleted from the 2nd ed.: "the prominent place which consumption has received in the programme of the science has not been justified by any attempt to examine it carefully.[1] Nor has this neglect been altogether accidental.

> [1] James Mill indeed called a large part of his 'Elements of Political Economy' by the title 'Consumption', but it is really occupied almost exclusively with an inquiry into the principles of Taxation."

In the 2nd and 3rd editions the foregoing footnote was retained but attached to the word "neglected". The footnote was deleted from the 4th ed.

PAGE 85

a. This paragraph was inserted in the 2nd ed. (p. 143).

234

BOOK III, CHAPTER II

WANTS IN RELATION TO
ACTIVITIES

PAGE 86

a. This chapter was inserted in the 2nd edition (Book III, ch. II). Except where otherwise stated the wording of this chapter dates substantially from the 2nd edition.

b. So since the 2nd edition.

c. The first clause of this sentence dates from the 1st ed. (p. 150), where it constituted the opening sentence of Book III, ch. II entitled "The Law of Demand". The second clause was inserted in the 4th ed. (p. 161).

d. This sentence was inserted in the 3rd ed. (p. 162).

PAGE 89

a. This clause dates from the 3rd ed. (pp. 164–5) where it replaced the following clause in the 2nd ed. (p. 146): "This is one of the most marked characteristics of our age;".

PAGE 91

a. Parts of this footnote date from the 1st ed. (Book III, ch. II, § 1, p. 150) where it ran as follows:

> Hermann (*Staatswirtschaftliche Untersuchungen*, ch. II) classified wants as "absolute and relative, higher and lower, urgent and capable of postponement, positive and negative, direct and indirect, general and particular, constant and interrupted, permanent and temporary, ordinary and extraordinary, present and future, individual and collective, private and public". And even this long list of divisions might be extended. The adult reader may perhaps be left to think out the details of such classifications for himself. But this opportunity may be taken of noticing that Hearn's *Plutology* is an admirable example of the way in which analytical work of this kind may be made to afford a training of a very high order for the young, and to give them an intelligent acquaintance with the economic conditions of life, without forcing upon them any particular solution of those more difficult problems on which they are not yet able to form an independent judgment.

b. So since the 8th edition (page 91 n.). In the 2nd ed. (p. 149 n.) this sentence ran as follows: "And at about the same time as Jevons' *Theory* appeared, Prof. Carl Menger initiated the splendid studies of wants and utilities by the Austrian school of economists." In the 3rd ed. (p. 167 n.) the word "splendid" was replaced by the words "subtle and interesting", and the sentence remained in this form until the 8th edition where it was reworded in its present form.

BOOK III, CHAPTER III

GRADATION OF CONSUMERS' DEMAND

PAGE 92

a. The origin of the wording of this chapter is shown throughout in the editorial notes.

b. Book III, ch. III (in the 1st edition Book III, ch. II) was entitled "The Law of Demand" until the 4th edition when the title became "Gradations of Demand". The present title was adopted in the 5th edition.

c. This paragraph was inserted in the 5th ed. (p. 92).

d. In the 5th ed. this paragraph with its footnote replaced the following paragraph dating from the 4th ed. (p. 167):

Utility and *Want* are taken as correlative terms. The utility of a thing to a person at a time is measured by the extent to which it satisfies his wants. And wants are here reckoned quantitatively, that is, with regard to their volume and intensity; they are not reckoned qualitatively according to any ethical or prudential standard. Judged by such a standard solid food may be more useful than alcohol of equal price, and warm underclothing than a new evening dress. But if a person prefers the alcohol or the evening dress, then it satisfies the greater want for him; it has the greater utility for him. No doubt this use of utility might mislead those not accustomed to it; but this seldom occurs in practice. But the term has much authority on its side. Substitutes which have been proposed for it, such as *ophelimity* (Prof. Pareto's term), agreeability, enjoyability, desirability, etc., are not faultless: and it seems best for the present to adhere to *utility* in spite of its faults.

The following extracts from the first four editions indicate the changes in Marshall's definitions of the term utility:

First edition

Thus then the desirability or *utility* of a thing to a person is commonly measured by the money price that he will pay for it (Book III, ch. II, §1, p. 151).

We may now turn to consider how far the price which is actually paid for a thing by a person represents the pleasure that arises from its possession, or in other words the "utility" of wealth (Book III, ch. IV, §1, p. 175).

The *marginal utility* to a person of ten lbs of tea is "the difference between the happiness which he gets from buying 9 lbs and 10 lbs." While the *total utility* of tea is "the whole benefit that he gets from the tea" (Book III, ch. II, §4, p. 154 and p. 155).

Second edition

"The pleasure giving power or *utility*" of the marginal increment of a commodity to a person "may be called the *marginal utility* of the commodity to him". While the *total utility* is "the total pleasure affording power of the commodity to him" (Book III, ch. III, §1, p. 150).

Third edition

The utility of a thing is "the benefit that arises from its possession" (Book III, ch. VI, §1, p. 200).

"The benefit-giving power or *utility*", of the marginal increment of a commodity to a person may be called the "*marginal utility* of the commodity to him". While the *total utility* is "the total benefit or satisfaction yielded to him" by the commodity (Book III, ch. III, §1, p. 168). See also below the editorial notes **c** to page 93, **b** to page 95, and **c** to page 124 in vol. 1 of the present edition.

Fourth edition

Marginal and total utility were defined (p. 168) as in the present edition (page 93) where the total utility of a thing to a person is "the total pleasure or other benefit it yields him".

e. The following extracts from a letter from Marshall to A. C. Pigou dated 19 March 1903 have some bearing on the subject-matter of this footnote, which was inserted in the 5th ed., pp. 92n–3n.:

I have just been reading your article in *E.J.* March 1903. . . . Well! Am I right in supposing that your main argument is this:

Though we may pass from the utility curve of an individual to the demand curve of a nation (or other group) as regards bread or milk or any other commodity which is valued only for its direct benefit to us, yet we cannot do that for commodities which we value partly because they impart social distinction. For a large change in the supply all round of such a commodity alters the conditions which we have assumed to be practically constant when making out the curve for an individual.

So far as I can see I concur in this: and think something of the sort ought to have been said by me. But of course I have always insisted that the demand price of a group is not any approximate measure of satisfaction, save on the assumption that people of different incomes and also of different sensibilities are evenly distributed throughout the group. And next it may be said that the continued references to the effect of changes in fashion include in the purview such changes as alter the distinction-giving power of a thing. . . .

Next is your second chief point that, since some moving forces are not associated with great pleasure, possibly not even with great satisfaction, therefore the consumers' surplus shown by the curve may diverge far (even in a society where all are about equally well off) from being a measure of aggregate pleasure or even aggregate satisfaction? If so, I again quite agree. I must some time consider whether I have sufficiently emphasized the fact that the schedule deals with satisfaction only in so far as that arises out of the number and excellence of the things which a man has, and not out of the quality of the man himself. . . . (*Memorials*, p. 433.)

a. This sentence dates from the 1st ed. (p. 155) where it was preceded by the following sentence which was deleted from the 5th ed.:

It is an almost universal law that each several want is limited, and that with every increase in the amount of a thing which a man has, the eagerness of his desire to obtain more of it diminishes; until it yields place to the desire for some other thing, of which perhaps he hardly thought, so long as his more urgent wants were still unsatisfied.

The only alteration in the sentence just quoted, prior to its deletion, was the replacement in the 2nd ed. (p. 150) of the first clause by the following clause: "We have seen that each several want is limited."

b. The first clause of this sentence dates in its present from from the 4th ed. (p. 167). In the 1st ed. (p. 155) this was a separate sentence running as follows: "This important fact may go by the name of the law of the diminution of marginal or final utility." In the 2nd ed. (p. 150) and the 3rd ed. (p. 168) this sentence ran: "This familiar and fundamental law of human nature may pass by the name of the *law of satiable wants or the law of diminishing utility.*"

c. So since the 4th ed. (p. 168) where the rest of this sentence and the succeeding paragraph replaced the following paragraphs dating from the 3rd ed. (pp. 168–9):

The *total utility* of a commodity to a person (that is, the *total utility.* total benefit or satisfaction yielded to him by it) increases with every increment in his stock of it, but not as fast as his stock increases. If his stock of it increases at a uniform rate the benefit derived from it increases at a diminishing rate.

In other words, the additional benefit which a person derives from a given increment of his stock of anything, diminishes with every increase in the stock that he already has.

The increment of the commodity which he is only just induced to acquire (whether by his direct labour or by purchase) may be called its *marginal increment*; because he is *marginal increment.* on the margin of doubt whether it is worth his while to incur the outlay required to obtain it. And the benefit-giving power, or utility, of that increment to him may be called the *marginal utility* of the commodity to him. It is the marginal *marginal utility.* increment of the total utility of his whole stock of the commodity. And thus the law may be worded:—

The marginal utility of a commodity to anyone diminishes with every increase in the amount of it he already has.

The wording of the above paragraphs in the 2nd ed. (p. 150) was identical with that of the 3rd ed. except that in the 2nd ed. the word "pleasure" was used in place of the words "benefit or satisfaction" in the second line of the first paragraph, and that throughout the rest of the three paragraphs the word "pleasure" was used in each case in place of the word "benefit".

d. This paragraph was inserted in the 2nd ed. (p. 151).

e. The first paragraph of this footnote dates from the 2nd ed. (p. 151 n.).

f. This paragraph dates in its present form from the 8th edition (page 93 n.). In the 1st ed. (p. 155 n.) it was a separate footnote and ran as follows:

> Jevons adopted the latter of these terms [final]. But the former [marginal] seems preferable on account of the close relation in which, as we shall see presently, marginal utility stands to marginal cost of production. The term marginal is in correspondence with the German term *Grenz-nutz*.

In the 2nd and 3rd editions this footnote was deleted, but in the 4th ed. (p. 168 n.) and in the 5th, 6th and 7th editions (p. 93 n.) it was reinstated in the following form:

> The term *marginal utility* (*Grenz-Nutzen*) was first used in this connection by the Austrian Professor Wieser. It has been adopted by Professor Wicksteed. It corresponds to Jevons's term *Final*.

Cf. also the footnote in vol. 1 to page x of the Preface to the First Edition and editorial note **d** to that page (p. 37 above).

PAGE 94

a. The first three sentences of this paragraph date from the 2nd ed. (p. 151) where they replaced the following sentences in the 1st ed. (p. 155):

This law has indeed some apparent exceptions: the more pictures or books a man has the stronger is his taste for them likely to become, and the more is he likely to spend on them: avarice and ambition are often insatiable; the virtue of cleanliness and the vice of drunkenness alike grow on what they feed upon.

b. The last two sentences of this paragraph date substantially from the 1st ed. (p. 155).

c. This paragraph, except for its last two sentences, dates substantially from the 1st ed. (pp. 154–5).

d. The words "which is in constant demand" were inserted in the 2nd ed. (p. 151).

e. "satisfaction" in the 5th ed. (p. 94), "pleasure" in the first four editions.

f. This footnote was inserted in the 2nd ed. (p. 151 n.).

PAGE 95

a. So since the 2nd ed. (p. 152), where the words "or final", after the word "marginal" in the 1st ed. (p. 155), were deleted.

b. The following additional sentence at this point in the 1st ed. (p. 155) was deleted from the 2nd ed.:

The relation in which this stands to the whole benefit that he gets from the tea, or its *total utility*, will be considered further on.

c. The remainder of this paragraph dates from the 2nd ed. (p. 152).

d. This paragraph dates substantially from the 4th ed. (pp. 169–70), where it replaced the following paragraph dating from the 2nd ed. (p. 152):

An increase in the amount of a thing that a person has will, other things being equal (i.e. the purchasing power of money, and the amount of money at his command being equal) diminish his *marginal demand* price for it.

e. This paragraph was inserted in the 4th ed. (p. 170).

f. This paragraph dates substantially from the 1st ed. (pp. 155–6).

g. This and the next sentence date from the 4th ed. (p. 170) in their present form. In the 2nd ed. (pp. 152–3) the beginning sentences of this paragraph ran as follows:

But of course a greater utility will be required to induce him to buy a thing if he is poor than if he is rich. A shilling is the measure of less pleasure to a rich man, than to a poor one. A rich man in doubt whether to spend a shilling on a single cigar, is weighing against one another smaller pleasures than a poor man, who is doubting whether to spend a shilling on a supply of tobacco that will last him for a month. The clerk with £100 a-year will walk into business in a much heavier rain than the clerk with £300 a year; for a sixpenny omnibus fare measures a greater utility to the poorer man than to the richer. If the poorer man spends the money, he will suffer more from the want of it afterwards than the richer would.

In the 3rd ed. (p. 170) these sentences ran as follows:

Of course a greater utility will be required to induce him to buy a thing if he is poor than if he is rich. We have seen[1] how a shilling is the measure of less benefit to a rich man, than to a poor one; how a rich man in doubt whether to spend a shilling on a single cigar, is weighing against one another smaller benefits than a poor man, who is doubting whether to spend a shilling on a supply of tobacco that will last him for a month; and how the clerk with £100 a year will walk into business in a heavier rain than the clerk with £300 a year.

¹ Above, p. 80.

The reference to p. 80 applies to page 19 in vol. 1 of the present edition.

Although it was not until the 2nd edition that Marshall made use in the *Principles* of the examples of the rich man's cigar and of the clerk in doubt whether to walk or ride in the rain, the whole of this paragraph in the text is closely derived from the following paragraph in *The Economics of Industry* (1879), p. 70:

The utility of a commodity to any one depends on the amount of it he has at the time, and the opportunity he has or expects to have of getting it, or other things that will serve as substitutes for it. But further, the price which he is willing to pay for a thing depends not only on its utility to him but also on *his means*; that is, the amount of money or general purchasing power at his disposal. A greater utility will be required to induce him to buy it if he is poor than if he is rich. A shilling is the measure of less pleasure to a rich man, than to a poor one. A rich man in doubt whether to spend a shilling on a single cigar, is weighing against one another smaller pleasures than a poor man, who is doubting whether to spend a shilling on a supply of tobacco that will last him for a month. The clerk with £100 a year will walk into business in a much heavier rain than the clerk with £300 a year; for a sixpenny omnibus fare measures a greater utility to the poorer man than to the richer. If the poorer man spends the money, he will suffer more from the want of it afterwards than the richer would. The utility, or satisfaction, or value in use that is measured in the poorer man's mind by sixpence is greater than that measured in it in the rich man's mind. If the richer man rides a hundred times in the year and the poorer man twenty times, then the utility of the hundredth ride which the richer man is only just induced to take is measured to him by sixpence; and the utility of the twentieth ride which the poorer man is only just induced to take is measured to him by sixpence. For each of them the Final Utility is measured by sixpence; but this Final Utility is greater in the case of the poorer man than in that of the richer.

h. The remainder of this paragraph dates substantially from the 2nd ed. (p. 153).

i. "pleasure" in the 2nd ed., "benefit" since the 3rd ed. (p. 171).

j. From the 2nd to the 4th editions, the poorer man's ride cost sixpence, but from the 5th ed. (p. 95) twopence.

k. The cross-reference in this footnote dates from the 3rd ed. (p. 170 n.).

PAGE 96

a. This paragraph with its footnote dates substantially from the 1st ed. (p. 156).

b. "benefit" from the 4th ed. (p. 170), "pleasure" in the first three editions.

c. Except where otherwise stated the wording of this section dates substantially from the 1st ed. (pp. 156–8), though the arrangement of the sentences was changed somewhat in the second to the fifth editions.

d. "list" from the 3rd ed. (p. 171), "schedule" in the previous editions.

e. So since the 5th ed. (p. 96). In the previous editions this number was "18".

f. So since the 4th ed. (pp. 171–2) where the remainder of this paragraph replaced the following sentences dating from the 1st ed. (p. 157–8):

We see then that a person's demand for a thing is indeterminate so long as nothing is said as to the price at which the thing is to be had. There is no use in trying to measure his demand as some writers have done merely by the "amount he is willing to buy" or merely by the "intensity of his eagerness to buy a certain amount." Nothing is gained by representing a notion, which is really complex, as though it were simple. Wherever precision is required, we must speak of a person's demand for a thing as represented by the schedule of the prices at which he is willing to buy different amounts of it.

a. The following additional sentence at this point in the 1st ed. (p. 157) was deleted from the 2nd ed.:

This is enough for most practical purposes, for we seldom want to know all about a person's demand for a thing.

b. The word "general" was inserted before the word "increase" in the 5th ed. (p. 97).

c. "list" from the 3rd ed. (p. 173), "schedule" in the previous editions.

d. This clause was inserted in the 3rd ed. (p. 173).

e. This article has been reprinted in the *Memorials of Alfred Marshall*, edited by A. C. Pigou, pp. 119–33.

a. So since the 2nd ed. (p. 155) where this paragraph replaced the following paragraph in the 1st ed. (p. 159):

In a commodity like tea, which can be purchased in small quantities, every variation in price is likely to affect the amount consumed by an individual. But there are many commodities—such as hats—the demand for which on the part of any single individual cannot vary continuously with every small change in price, but can change only by great leaps. A small fall in the price of hats will not affect the action of everyone, but it will induce a few persons, who were in doubt whether to get a new hat or not, to decide in favour of doing so.

b. This paragraph dates substantially from the 2nd ed. (p. 156).

c. This sentence was inserted in the 2nd ed. (p. 156).

d. The remainder of this paragraph dates from the 1st ed. (p. 159), except for the second main clause of the first sentence which was inserted in the 2nd ed. (p. 156).

a. "list" since the 3rd ed. (p. 174), "schedule" in the first two editions.

b. This paragraph dates substantially from the 1st ed. (p. 159).

c. So since the 4th ed. (p. 174).

In the 1st ed. (pp. 159–60) this paragraph ran as follows:

There is then one law and only one law which is common *The law of* to all demand schedules, viz. that the greater the amount to *diminution of marginal* be sold the smaller will be the price at which it will find *demand-* purchasers; or in other words, as the numbers in the left *price.* hand columns increase, those in the right hand column diminish. Subject to this one condition, demand schedules have every variety of form.

In the 2nd ed. (p. 157) this paragraph was altered to read as in the text of the present edition, except that the first line ran as follows: "There is one *law of demand* which is common to all demand schedules." Also in the 2nd ed. in the fifth line of the paragraph the word "exact" was used instead of the word "uniform". In the 3rd ed. (p. 175) the only change from the 2nd ed. was in the first line, which ran: "There is then one *law of demand* which is common to all demands."

d. This footnote dates from the 1st ed. (p. 159 n.).

e. The first paragraph of this footnote dates from the 1st ed. (p. 160 n.).

f. This paragraph was inserted in the 8th edition (page 99 n.).

PAGE 100

a. So since the 4th ed. (p. 174) where this paragraph replaced the following paragraph dating from the 2nd ed. (p. 157):

The price will measure the *marginal utility of the* commodity to each purchaser: but as the purchasers are likely to be some rich and others poor, we cannot speak of price as measuring *marginal utility* in general but only with particular reference to some individual purchaser.

b. So since the 4th ed. (p. 174) where this sentence (with the italicizing of the last eight words) replaced the following sentence dating from the 1st ed. (p. 160):

It must be remembered that the demand schedule gives the prices at which various quantities of a thing can be sold in a market during a given time and under given conditions.

c. So since the 2nd ed. (p. 157) where this sentence replaced the following sentences in the 1st ed. (p. 160):

If the conditions vary in any respect the figures of the schedule will probably require to be changed. One condition which is specially important to watch is the price of rival commodities, that is, of commodities which can be used as substitutes for it.

The following opening sentence of a footnote attached to the word "rival" in the foregoing sentence in the 1st ed. (p. 160 n.) was deleted from the 2nd ed.

Or to use Jevons' phrase (*Theory of Political Economy*, ch. iv), commodities that are nearly "equivalent".

See also editorial note **h** to vol. 1, page 100.

d. This sentence dates substantially from the 1st ed. (p. 160).

e. This sentence was inserted in the 3rd ed. (p. 176).

f. This paragraph was inserted in the 2nd ed. (p. 158), where it replaced the following concluding paragraphs of this chapter in the 1st ed. (pp. 160–1):

Consumer's demand and trader's demand.

We have so far been looking at demand chiefly from the point of view of the ultimate consumer. But, as we shall see more clearly hereafter, the same law applies to the trade demand for things which are to be sold again or are to be used in making other things that are to be sold. An apparent objection arises from the facts that when a thing is falling in price dealers often contract their purchases in the fear of a further fall; that when the price is rising they often buy largely in the hope of securing the benefit of a further rise; and that speculative purchases of this kind have a very great effect on the temporary fluctuations of prices. But this is not really an exception to the rule: it only illustrates the way in which the expectation of a fall in price will often diminish people's eagerness to buy a thing at the present price; they will prefer to wait till the price has come down. Apparent exceptions of this kind are a source of difficulty in the theory of market disturbances: but they have no real bearing on the relation between demand and price in a steady market; and looking only at normal and average results we find that the cheaper a thing can be sold, the larger will be the purchases of it by private consumers; and therefore traders will buy the more of it, in the long run, the cheaper they can get it.

Later on we shall have to examine the lagging behind of that increased consumption of anything which is sure, other things being equal, to result from a fall in its wholesale price. This lagging behind has many curious effects, some of which are of great practical importance. But at the present stage we may neglect them; and assume that changes in the demand price of a thing will follow instantly on changes in the amount of it offered for sale; and that the demand price for any particular amount which is being offered for sale will always be that price which is set against that amount in the demand schedule representing the normal relations of the market[1].

[1] Discussions kindred to those in the present chapter are to be found in Jevons, *Theory*, ch. II, III; Menger, *Volkswirtschaftslehre*, ch. II, and Böhm-Bawerk, *Grundzüge*, II, iv.

g. This sentence was inserted in the 3rd ed. (p. 176 n.).

h. The remainder of this paragraph dates from the 1st ed. (p. 160 n.) where these sentences were preceded by the reference to Jevons quoted above in editorial note **c** to vol. 1, page 100.

i. This paragraph dates from the 2nd ed. (p. 158 n.).

PAGE 101

a. The first paragraph of this footnote dates from the 2nd ed. (pp. 158–9 n.), with the exception of the last sentence which was inserted in the 7th ed. (p. 101 n.).

b. So since the 4th ed. (p. 176 n.) where this paragraph replaced the following paragraph dating from the 2nd ed. (p. 159 n.).

> Dr Carl Menger's *Grundsätze der Volkswirtschaftslehre*, though not making use of mathematical language is distinctly mathematical in tone, and appears to be in some respects, though not in all, further advanced than Jevons' work, and it is better balanced. A mathematical tone is even more clearly pronounced, though the use of mathematical formulae is still avoided, in the writings of Profs. Böhm-Bawerk, Wieser, and other members of the brilliant Austrian School as well as those of Profs. Clark, Giddings, Patten, Greene and other Americans. Among the many recent writers on mathematical aspects of economics, special reference may be made to Prof. Walras, who was almost as early in the field as Jevons and Menger, to Profs. Pantaleoni, Pareto, Edgeworth and Wicksteed, to Drs Auspitz, Lieben, Launhardt, and Fisher.

In the 1st ed. (p. 149 n.) the following footnote on the application of mathematical methods to problems of demand was appended to the final sentence of Book III, ch. 1:

> Jevons (*Theory of Political Economy*, 1871) has done more than any one else to foster the growth of a widely-spread interest in this aspect of economic science; though unknown to himself he had been anticipated in many of his best thoughts by Cournot (*Recherches sur les Principes Mathématiques de la Théorie des Richesses*, 1838), and by Gossen (*Entwicklung der Gesetze des menschlichen Verkehrs*, 1854). In the same year, 1871, in which Jevons' *Theory* appeared, Dr Karl Menger published the first part of his *Grundsätze der Volkswirtschaftslehre*, which, though not making use of mathematical language, is distinctly mathematical in tone, and appears to be in some respects, though not in all, further advanced than Jevons' work. A mathematical tone is even more clearly pronounced, though the use of mathematical formulæ is still avoided, in Dr Böhm-Bawerk's *Grundzüge des wirtschaftlichen Güterwerts* (1886), which may

247

be regarded as a continuation of the works of Jevons and Menger, but especially the latter. M. Walras has published from 1874 downwards a series of interesting economic inquiries, in which a free use is made of mathematical formulæ, and his example has been followed by Dr Launhardt and others. A bibliography of mathematical writings on economics is appended to the second edition of Jevons' *Theory*.

BOOK III, CHAPTER IV

THE ELASTICITY OF WANTS

PAGE 102

a. Except where otherwise stated the wording of this chapter dates substantially from the 1st edition.

b. Book III, ch. IV (in the 1st edition Book III, ch. III) was originally entitled "Elasticity of Demand". In the 2nd and 3rd editions the title became "Law of Demand continued. Elasticity of Demand". The present title was adopted from the 4th edition.

c. This and the following sentence were inserted in the 5th ed. (p. 102).

d. The words in parentheses were inserted in the 7th ed. (p. 102).

e. The words in parentheses were inserted in the 7th ed. (p. 102 n.).

f. This sentence and the first sentence of the succeeding paragraph were contained in the two concluding paragraphs of a Paper on "The Graphic Method of Statistics" read at the International Statistical Congress, 1885, and reprinted in the *Memorials of Alfred Marshall* (p. 187). In the article referred to there was the following additional sentence after the sentence ending with the clause "and so on":

I believe that inductions with regard to the elasticity of demand, and deductions based on them, have a great part to play in economic science.

PAGE 103

a. So since the 3rd ed. (p. 179) where this paragraph replaced the following paragraph dating from the 1st ed. (p. 163):

When the price of a thing is very high relatively to any class, they will buy but little of it; and even a very considerable fall in the price will cause no great increase in their consumption, i.e. the elasticity of their demand will be small.

But if the price goes on falling they will begin to consume the thing more freely, taking it into ordinary use; and the elasticity of their demand will increase. At last a price is likely to be reached so low that they have got all that they want—a satiety price; and then they will not be induced to increase their consumption much by any further fall: the elasticity of their demand will again have become small. That is to say, the elasticity of their demand is small when the price of a thing is *very high* relatively to their means and again when it is *very low*: while the elasticity is much greater for prices intermediate between what we may call the *high* level and the *low* level.

b. So since the 2nd ed. (p. 161 n.) where the remaining clauses of this sentence replaced the following clause in the 1st ed. (p. 163 n.):

and therefore *the elasticity increases wherever the angle TPM increases relatively to the angle OPM.*

PAGE 104

a. The following paragraph dating from the 1st ed. (p. 164), was deleted from the 3rd ed.:

This rule that the elasticity is great for medium prices and small for those which are very high or very low is seen most clearly when we select for observation a set of people, who, though sufficiently numerous to prevent individual peculiarities from obtruding themselves, are yet economically homogeneous; i.e., have nearly the same wants and nearly the same means of gratifying them. When we add together the demands of several such sets so as to get the aggregate demand of a larger group, as for instance that of the whole body of the rich, or the whole body of the middle classes, or the whole body of the working classes; our rule does not show itself with so clear an outline, and but faint traces of it remain when we add together the demands of these three groups so as to get the aggregate demand of the whole community.

PAGE 105

a. So since the 2nd ed. (p. 164), where the words "their own personal consumption" replaced the words "their consumption" in the 1st ed. (p. 166).

b. The following footnote in the 1st ed. (p. 166 n.) was deleted from the 2nd ed.:

> With regard to this group of commodities it is important to remark that the demand of the rich is not here taken to include the demand for the food, etc., which they give to their servants.

c. The following concluding paragraph of this footnote, dating from the 1st ed. (p. 165 n.), was deleted from the 3rd ed.:

> Looking either at the schedules, or at the curves, we see that the greatest elasticity of demand is somewhere about the price of $5d$. for the rich, and $3d$. for the middle class, while for the poor it is about $2d$.; for the whole market it is somewhere about $3d$. At the price of $1\frac{1}{2}d$. the demands of the rich and middle classes have lost nearly all their elasticity. But the demand of the poor shows signs of remaining elastic even for much lower prices; and since its influence preponderates here, a considerable elasticity is shown by the total demand curve for the lower prices.

d. This and the next sentence were inserted in the 2nd ed. (p. 164 n.).

PAGE 106

a. This sentence dates from the 2nd ed. (pp. 164–5) except for the replacement of the opening words, in the 2nd ed., "And in fact much of the demand" by the words "Part of the demand", in the 3rd ed. (p. 182).

b. This footnote was inserted in the 3rd ed. (p. 182 n.).

c. So since the 7th ed. (p. 106 n.) where the first two sentences of this footnote replaced the following sentence dating from the 1st ed. (p. 167 n.): "This is the famous estimate quoted by Gregory King."

PAGE 107

a. The following additional sentence and paragraph in the 1st ed. (p. 167) were deleted from the 2nd ed.:

But such cases illustrate the theory of market variations of prices rather than that of normal demand.

Wheat and other cheap vegetable foods are the only things of which nearly the whole consumption can be regarded as necessary. Some part of the consumption of water, clothing and house-room is indeed strictly necessary, but there is much of it which could be dispensed with.

b. The following footnote attached to the end of this sentence in the 1st ed. (p. 168 n.) was omitted from the 2nd ed.:

> See Sir J. Strachey's, *Finances of India*, ch. XIII.

c. The remainder of this sentence was inserted in the 2nd ed. (p. 166).

d. In the 1st ed. (p. 168) this sentence was preceded by the following sentences, which were deleted from the 2nd ed.:

Clothing falls generally under two heads: some kinds are desired not only for their direct uses, but also as a means of asserting social position. They are to be classed with house-room; the demand for them is insatiable.

e. This and the succeeding paragraph with the attached footnote were inserted in the 3rd ed. (pp. 183–4).

f. This footnote was inserted in the 7th ed. (p. 107 n.).

PAGE 109

a. This paragraph was inserted in the 5th ed. (p. 109).

b. This paragraph was inserted in the 2nd ed. (p. 166).

PAGE 110

a. This paper is reprinted in the *Memorials of Alfred Marshall*, edited by A. C. Pigou, pp. 175–87.

b. This footnote was inserted in the 3rd ed. (p. 186 n.).

PAGE 112

a. The following footnote attached to the word "supply" in the 1st ed. (p. 173 n.) was deleted from the 2nd ed.:

Unless indeed there is an excited speculation, with perhaps a "corner" in the market for it; and then the movements of its price obey no rule.

b. This sentence was inserted in the 2nd ed. (p. 169).

c. This sentence dates from the 4th ed. (p. 187) where it replaced the following sentence dating substantially from the 1st ed. (p. 168).

A demand schedule is supposed to present a series of prices at which different amounts of a commodity can find purchasers during a given time in a market; . . .

d. So since the 2nd ed. (p. 169) when this and the next sentences replaced the following sentences dating from the 1st ed. (pp. 168–9):

Theoretically a *market* is a district, small or large, in which there are many buyers and many sellers all so keenly on the alert and so well acquainted with one another's affairs that the price of a commodity is always practically the same for the whole of the district. But the facts seldom correspond exactly to this description. Those who buy for their own consumption, and not for the purposes of trade, are not always on the look out for every change in the market: they have other things to think about.

251

e. The following additional clause in this sentence in the 1st ed. (p. 169) was deleted from the 2nd ed.:

and it is very difficult to ascertain the amounts even of imported commodities that are being consumed in any artificially defined area, such for instance as the Staffordshire Potteries, or a straggling large town.

PAGE 113

a. In the 1st ed. (pp. 173–4) part of the subject matter of this Note was in the text at the end of this chapter and part in a footnote. It was rearranged and expanded as a "Note on Statistics of Consumption" in the 2nd ed. (pp. 170–4). Except where otherwise stated the wording dates from the 1st ed.

b. This paragraph dates from the 2nd ed. (p. 170) where it replaced the following paragraph in the 1st ed. (p. 173):

Since the difficulties of deducing accurate laws of demand from statistical tables relating to general consumption are so great; since so many of those which at first sight promise to be useful turn out, at all events in the present state of our knowledge, to be useless, it may be worth while to try another route. There is one which at all events avoids most of the difficulties that have just been considered.[1]

[1] Compare Jevons' *Theory of Political Economy*, pp. 11, 12.

c. The following clause and parenthesis after the word "commodities" in the 2nd ed. was deleted from the 3rd ed.:

and much good work has been done in digesting them (as for instance in Dr Scherzer's *Das wirtschaftliche Leben der Völker* and in the late Neumann–Spallart's periodical *Uebersichten der Weltwirtschaft*).

d. This sentence was inserted in the 4th ed. (p. 188).

e. The clause "or the manager of a co-operative store", after the word "shopkeeper" was inserted in the 4th ed.

f. The following reference in the 1st ed. (p. 169 n.) was deleted from the 2nd ed.:

See Lecky's *England in the Eighteenth Century*, vol. III, ch. XII.

PAGE 114

a. The following sentences after the sentence ending with the word "consumption", dating from the 1st ed. (p. 174 n.) were deleted from the 4th ed.:

Such a shopkeeper's book affords good opportunities for the application of "the Method of Difference." It may be hoped that, as the knowledge of economic science is diffused, local statistical societies will do important work in this and similar directions. Above all this may be hoped from the great co-operative stores.

PAGE 115

a. This paragraph was inserted in the 2nd ed. (p. 172).

b. The following sentences in the 2nd ed. after the sentence ending with the word "England" were deleted from the 3rd ed.:

In particular, working men's budgets have often been collected and compared; as, for instance, by her Majesty's consuls, in the *Reports on the condition of the Industrial Classes*, 1872; and by those of the United States, see Young's *Labour in Europe and America;* and the reports of various American Labour Bureaux, especially that of the United States Commissioner of Labour for 1886, and an abstract of many continental inquiries is presented in a very convenient form in Dr Gruber's *Die Haushaltung der arbeitenden Klassen*.

c. The first paragraph of this footnote with the table, and the succeeding paragraph, date substantially from the 2nd ed. (pp. 173–4).

d. In the 2nd ed. Engel's table was succeeded by the following paragraph and table, which were deleted from the 3rd ed.:

The only systematic inquiry which can at present be quoted for England, is that made by Mr Burnett, the able Labour Correspondent of the Board of Trade. In 1887 he sent out 730 inquiries to selected workmen, and in response he received 34 fairly complete returns, from which the following table was compiled:

TABLE SHOWING SUMMARY OF AVERAGE PROPORTIONS OF EXPENDITURE TO INCOME BY GROUPS ARRANGED IN ORDER OF AMOUNTS

Heads of Expenditure, &c.	Groups of Incomes in Order of Amount									
	28*l.* to 40*l.*	40*l.* to 50*l.*	50*l.* to 60*l.*	60*l.* to 70*l.*	70*l.* to 80*l.*	80*l.* to 90*l.*	90*l.* to 100*l.*	100*l.* to 110*l.*	125*l.*	150*l.*
No. of families in group	4	2	7	3	3	5	4	4	1	1
No. of persons in group	23	8	26	19	19	27	26	19	9	4
	l.	*l.*	*l.*	*l.*	*l.*	*l.*	*l.*	*l.*	*l.*	*l.*
Average yearly income	30·9	43·4	53·2	65·7	75·3	83·3	93·5	104·9	125	150
Rent, taxes, and water	17·7	19·4	13·1	11·7	15·5	12·6	12·0	13·6	11·6	23·7
Fuel and light	4·0	8·2	3·5	7·2	6·1	5·3	5·2	4·1	5·2	5·2
Bread and flour	34·6	12·0	12·7	13·4	12·7	10·7	14·4	7·0	8·3	6·1
Butchers' meat	16·6	9·7	14·8	11·2	9·2	12·0	14·9	9·9	13·1	6·9
Groceries, &c.	56·3	34·6	35·8	33·5	34·2	28·4	37·4	25·8	22·6	21·8
Clothing	2·2	13·5	10·3	9·1	14·6	9·2	9·7	10·5	16·0	8·7
Education, recreation	5·0	4·5	4·4	4·0	3·1	5·1	3·6	6·9	8·2	5·6
Providence	4·5	9·0	4·3	3·0	4·5	3·7	2·8	4·6	3·5	4·3
Medicine, &c.	2·1	1·4	0·9	2·5	1·8	1·9	3·4	1·1	1·2	0·7
Sundries	—	2·5	1·8	2·3	5·5	2·7	2·3	3·7	5·8	2·7
Surplus	7·0	—	4·7	13·6	4·5	9·8	4·4	12·9	4·1	14·4
Deficit	38·8	14·8	6·0	7·7	5·0	—	6·3	—	—	—

e. The following additional sentence and clause after the sentence ending with the word "eye", dating from the 2nd ed. (p. 174), were deleted from the 3rd ed.:

> And in this particular case there is the further evil that the total number of returns is small, and the average results therefore rest on narrow bases. But the Report contains much instructive information; and those who have special opportunities of observing the methods of living of any industrial classes may find it convenient as a basis for registering their own observations: for this border-ground between the provinces...etc.

It may be noted that the reference in the first sentence to "this particular case", applies to Mr Burnett's table; while the Report mentioned in the second sentence is also that of Mr Burnett.

f. This and the next sentence date from the 3rd ed. (p. 192 n.).

PAGE 116

a. This sentence was inserted in the 5th ed. (p. 116 n.).

b. This paragraph dates from the 3rd ed. (p. 192 n.).

c. The following additional references dating from the 3rd ed. (p. 192 n.) were deleted from the 5th ed.:

> See also an article on wages and prices in the *Companion* to the *British Almanack* for 1834, *Workmen's Budgets in Manchester*, in the *Statistical Journal*, 1841–2; Tuckett's *Labouring Population*, 1846; Sargant's *Economy of the Working Classes* in 1857; Reports by her Majesty's Consuls *On the Condition of the Working Classes in Foreign Countries*, 1872; the inquiry for the Board of Trade in 1887; *Workmen's Budgets* by Mr Higgs in *Statistical Journal* 1893; Reports of Subcommissioners on Agriculture to the Labour Commission 1893, 4; some articles in Vols. v and vi of the *Bulletin de l'Institut Internationale de Statistique*, in the former of which a compendious view is given of the results of M. le Play's monumental *Les Ouvriers Européens*; while an abstract of many continental inquiries is presented in a convenient form in Dr Gruber's *Die Haushaltung der arbeitenden Klassen*. Much work has been done in the same direction in the United States; see Young's *Labour in Europe and America*; and the reports of various American Labour Bureaux, especially those of the United States Commissioner of Labour for 1886, and 1891; and Prof. Falkner's introduction to the *Report on Wholesale Prices*, &c. to the Senate in 1893.
>
> Part of the work is now being taken over by the younger sciences of anthropology and demography; and there is much to be gleaned from the *Descriptive Sociology* of various nations compiled under the direction of Herbert Spencer; which, though too ambitious, may be of service to the economist if used with care. See also Lavollée, *Classes ouvrières en Europe;* Barbaret, *Le Travail en France;* Symons, *Arts and Artisans at Home and Abroad;* Mayhew, *London Labour;* and Charles Booth, *Life and Labour in London* and *Condition of the Aged Poor.*

CHOICES BETWEEN DIFFERENT
USES OF THE SAME THING
IMMEDIATE AND DEFERRED USES

PAGE 117

a. This chapter was inserted in the 2nd edition. In the 1st edition the only discussion of the choice between different uses of the same thing was contained in a single brief section (Book III, ch. II, §3, pp. 153–4), to which reference is made below.

Except where otherwise stated the wording of this chapter dates substantially from the 2nd edition.

b. The title of this chapter remained unchanged since the 2nd edition.

PAGE 118

a. So since the 4th ed. (p. 193 n.), where this reference replaced the following additional clause, dating from the 2nd ed. (p. 176 n.), after the sentence ending with the word "supply": "where one particular form of it—the Law of Substitution—will occupy us a great deal."

PAGE 120

a. In the 3rd ed. (p. 196) the word "benefit" or "benefits" replaced the word "pleasure" or "pleasures" in lines 1, 2, 9, 12 and 21, of this paragraph in the 2nd ed. (p. 178).

b. So since the 3rd ed. (p. 196), where the words "or similar benefits" replaced the words "pleasures of equal amount" in the 2nd ed. (p. 178).

c. The words "and other satisfactions" were inserted in the 3rd ed. (p. 196).

d. This sentence dates from the 1st ed. (Book III, ch. II, §3, p. 153); it was succeeded by the following sentences and footnote which were omitted from the 2nd ed.:

Thus the savage can hardly be induced to take the smallest trouble to fence in crops which a few months later might save him from the pains of extreme hunger; the ignorant navvy will often spend the earnings of a prosperous time in ways that give him no pleasure to be compared to what he will suffer when his work is slack and he has no fund to fall back on. And at the opposite extreme the miser goes without ordinary comforts in order to accumulate wealth which he will never bring himself freely to enjoy. But the great body of sensible people in a civilized country estimate a future pleasure at a lower, though not a much lower, value than if it were present: they *discount the future* at a moderate rate.[1]

[1] If a person would just pay 9*s*. for the certainty of a gratification a year hence, which if it were present he would value at 10*s*. then he may be said to discount future pleasures at the rate of ten per cent. a year: if he would only give 8*s*. for it, then he discounts the future at twenty per cent., and so on.

    e.   This paragraph dates from the 1st ed. (p. 153).

    f.   This paragraph was inserted in the 3rd ed. (pp. 196–7).

PAGE 121

    a.   "benefits" in the 3rd ed. (p. 197), "pleasures" in the 2nd ed. (p. 178).

    b.   See editorial note **a** to page 231 of vol. 1 in the present edition.

PAGE 122

    a.   In the 3rd ed. (p. 198) the word "benefits" replaced the word "pleasures" in lines 2, 12 and 15, of this paragraph in the 2nd ed. (p. 179).

    b.   So since the 3rd ed. (p. 198), where the words "capacity for deriving benefit from the things which money will buy", replaced the words "capacity for enjoying the things which money will buy".

    c.   This paragraph dates substantially from the 1st ed. (p. 154 n.) where it was a separate footnote attached to the end of the following paragraph in the text (pp. 153–4) which was deleted from the 2nd ed.:

The uncertainty of an anticipated pleasure as affecting its "discounted" value.

As Bentham says, we must consider the "duration" and "intensity" of a pleasure and its "propinquity" or the nearness of the time at which it is expected; and further we must take account of the "certainty" with which it is anticipated. The less that certainty is, the less is the value of the pleasure, and with every diminution of the certainty the value of the pleasure diminishes in like proportion. Every commodity that is not consumed in a single use, is the probable source of many pleasures, more or less remote; and its value to a purchaser is the aggregate of the value to him of all these pleasures, allowance being made for their uncertainty and for their distance.

d. This parenthesis was inserted in the 2nd ed. (p. 180 n.).

e. In the 8th edition, "p. 209"; emended in vol. 1 of the present edition to give the correct reference.

PAGE 123

a. In the 2nd ed. (p. 180 n.) this footnote replaced the following footnote dating from the 1st ed. (Book III, ch. 11, §3, p. 154 n.):

> It must be understood however that the separate measurement of each element of a pleasure is in practice done roughly by a sort of instinct. The only measurement with which science can directly deal is that afforded by what a person is willing to sacrifice (whether money, or some other commodity, or his own labour) in order to obtain the aggregate of pleasure anticipated from the possession of the thing itself. But see note I in the Appendix.

The reference to "Note I in the Appendix" refers to Note V in the Mathematical Appendix in the 2nd and later editions.

BOOK III, CHAPTER VI

VALUE AND UTILITY

PAGE 124

a. Except where otherwise stated, the wording of §§1–3 and 5–6 of this chapter dates substantially from the 1st edition (Book III, ch. IV).

It should be noted that throughout the first three editions the term "Consumers' Rent" was used. From the 4th edition onwards this became "consumer's surplus".

b. So since the 3rd edition, where the present title replaced the following title dating from the 1st edition: "The Measurement of the Utility of Wealth."

c. So since the 2nd ed. (p. 181) where the first sentence of this paragraph replaced the following sentence dating from the 1st ed. (p. 175):

We may now turn to consider how far the price which is actually paid for a thing represents the pleasure that arises from its possession, or in other words the "utility" of wealth.

d. "satisfaction" from the 3rd ed., "pleasure" in the first two editions.

e. "satisfaction" from the 3rd ed., "gratification" in the first two editions.

f. So since the 5th ed. (p. 124). In the first three editions, where this formed the last clause of the preceding sentence, it ran as follows: "and, for reasons which will appear later on, may be called *Consumers' Rent.*" In the 4th ed. (p. 199) this clause became a separate sentence which ran as follows: "It has some analogies to a rent: but is perhaps best called simply *consumer's surplus.*"

In the 1st ed. (p. 175 n.) there was the following footnote attached to the term "*Consumers' Rent*", which was deleted from the 2nd ed.:

The following account of Consumers' Rent is reproduced with slight alterations from some papers printed for private circulation in 1879. See Preface.

The reference here is to the *Pure Theory of Domestic Values,* pp. 20–4.

g. This paragraph and the footnote attached to the end of it were inserted here in the 3rd ed. (pp. 200–1), but the footnote dates substantially from the 1st ed. (Book VII, ch. IX, §6, p. 656 n.).

PAGE 125

a. This paragraph and the first sentence of the next paragraph date substantially from the 1st ed. (p. 175) except that the commodity chosen there for illustration was coal, and that the corresponding amounts purchased and prices were: one ton annually at £10, two tons at £7, three tons at £5, four tons at £3, five tons at £2, six tons at £1. 10s., and seven tons at the assumed actual price of £1 per ton. The commodity was changed from coal to tea in the 3rd ed. (p. 201). The succeeding paragraphs in the 1st ed. (p. 176), which were deleted from the 3rd ed., ran as follows:

The fact that he would just be induced to purchase one ton if the price were £10, proves that the total enjoyment or satisfaction which he derives from that ton is as great as that which he could obtain by spending £10 on other things. In other words, the satisfaction derived from, or the value in use to him of, a single ton a year, is economically measured by £10; and therefore his power of purchasing one ton of coals for £1 gives him a surplus satisfaction, of which the economic measure is £9; that is to say, it gives him a Consumers' Rent of £9.

Again if the price were £7 a ton, he would just be induced to purchase a second ton; so that the value in use to him of a second ton is measured by £7. The Consumers' Rent that he derives from his power of purchasing this ton for £1 is therefore £6: and so on. Thus the whole Consumers' Rent which he derives from the power of purchasing coal at £1 a ton is $£9 + 6 + 4 + 2 + 1 + \frac{1}{2}$, i.e. $£22\frac{1}{2}$.

We may put the same thing in another way. The economic measure of the total value in use, or, as Jevons says, of the *total utility* of the coal, is the sum of the prices that he would be just willing to give for each successive ton: i.e. $£10 + 7 + 5 + 3 + 2 + 1\frac{1}{2} + 1$, i.e. £29. 10s. His Consumers' Rent is the excess of this sum over the £7 which are the value in exchange or market price of the coal: it thus measures the surplus or excess of the total utility to him of the seven tons of coal which he purchases, over the utility of the commodities which he could have obtained by expending in other ways the £7 which are the value in exchange of those seven tons.

(Those other commodities would be just beyond the margin of his previous purchases, commodities which he had just not thought it worth while to buy at their current prices; and therefore they would not yield him any Consumers' Rent.)

The wording of the paragraph and sentence in the text (Vol. 1, page 125) to which this editorial note relates, as well as the first three of the four paragraphs just quoted from the 1st ed., date substantially from *The Pure Theory of Domestic Values* (1879), pp. 21–2.

b. Except where otherwise stated the wording of the rest of this and of the remaining paragraphs and footnotes of §2, dates substantially from the 3rd ed. (pp. 201–3).

c. The last clause of this sentence was inserted in the 5th ed. (p. 125).

d. So since the 3rd ed. (p. 201 n.) where the first two sentences of this footnote replaced the following sentences dating from the 1st ed. (p. 656 n.):

"Opportunity" is the best translation for some purposes, as "Industrial Environment" is for others, of the German word *Konjunktur*. That term is thus explained by Prof. Wagner (*Volkswirtschaftslehre*, 1, 76). By *Konjunktur* we understand ...etc.

In the 1st ed. (Book VII, ch. IX, §6, p. 656 n.) and the 2nd ed. (Book VI, ch. VIII, §10, pp. 660–1 n.) this footnote was attached to a discussion of the factors influencing the earnings of businesses.

PAGE 126

a. This sentence was inserted in the 5th ed. (p. 126).

b. The first sentence of this paragraph was inserted in the 5th ed. (p. 126 n.).

PAGE 127

a. So since the 5th ed. (p. 127) where the words "at those prices" replaced the word "therefore" dating from the 3rd ed. (p. 203).

b. So since the 5th ed. (p. 127 n.) where this wording of the first sentence of this footnote replaced the following wording in the 4th ed. (p. 202 n.):

> Prof. Nicholson (*Principles of Political Economy*, vol. I and *Economic Journal*, vol. IV), having misconceived the nature of consumers' rent, raised several objections to it, which have been answered by Prof. Edgeworth in the same Journal.

The original version of this sentence in the 3rd ed. (p. 203 n.) ran as follows:

> Prof. Nicholson (*Principles of Political Economy*, vol. I and *Economic Journal*, vol. IV), apparently under some misapprehension as to the drift of the doctrine of consumers' rent, has raised several objections to it, which have been answered by Prof. Edgeworth in the same Journal.

PAGE 128

a. In connection with the subject matter of this section (§ 3) of Book III, ch. VI, it may be recorded that in 1889, when the proofs of the 1st edition of Marshall's *Principles* were being read by John Neville Keynes (the father of John Maynard Keynes), some correspondence took place between them over the meaning and interpretation of certain passages. In reply to a comment by Keynes on the doctrine of consumer's rent (as it was then entitled) Marshall wrote to him on 26 November 1889:

I regard Consumer's Rent as a sum of money not as an amount of utility.

I hold that Jevons' great error was that of applying to utility propositions that are only true of price. It was here that he thought himself most profound: and it is because I think he was wrong in this one point in which he differed from his predecessors Von Thünen and Cournot that I consider his claims to greatness do not to any considerable extent rest on his Theory of Political Economy.

I can see no connection between the loss of Consumer's Rent and the loss of Total Utility resulting from a tax, unless it is known whether the commodity taxed is one consumed by the rich, by the poor, or by all classes alike.

and on 2 December 1889 he wrote again:

I hope I did not imply that you confused hedonics and economics. I did not at all mean to. What I meant is that

the very fact that my protest against Jevons' systematic confusion between the two has been (deliberately) a silent one,
makes me very anxious that my consumer's Rent should not
be sewn up into his Total Utility. I had that prominently
in mind when writing on the burden of a tax. I wanted to
make clear that economic statistics have nothing to do with
Utility but only with its rough money measure.

I considered for a long time whether I would discuss the
difficulty you sense about the change of consumer's rent
derived from other things consequent on a diminished
purchase of coals. Perhaps I shall in consequence of the
difficulties having struck you insert a line or two in the
Mathematical Appendix to say: If he spends less on coals,
the marginal utility for other purchases will be affected to
an *infinitesimal* degree—infinitesimal because the whole of
this class of reasoning is strictly valid only on the assumption
that the purchases under discussion are small relatively to
the purchaser's whole wealth.

Marshall did in fact include a paragraph (the fourth) in his Mathematical Note VI in the 1st ed. (pp. 740–1) dealing with the point
raised in the second paragraph of his letter of 2 Dec. 1889 to J. N.
Keynes. See vol. 1, page 842 and the editorial notes to Mathematical
Note VI (p. 832 below).

The originals of the foregoing letters are in the Marshall Library
in Cambridge.

b. So since the 3rd ed. (pp. 203–5 n.); but the wording of this
paragraph and footnote in the first two editions was substantially the
same as that in the present edition, down to the last sentence but two
of the footnote; except that the commodity selected for illustration
in the earlier editions was coal, and that the units were tons instead
of pounds. The wording in the first two editions, in turn, was taken
substantially from *The Pure Theory of Domestic Values* (pp. 23–5).

It may be noted here that the paragraph in *The Pure Theory of
Domestic Values*, which was taken over into the *Principles* as footnote 1
on page 128, and which ended with the sentence whose concluding
words were "when the price is *AH*.", was succeeded in *The Pure
Theory of Domestic Values* by the following paragraph and footnote:

It has already been remarked that it will seldom be possible
to obtain the data necessary for drawing the demand curve
accurately through any large portion of its length. If *A* is the

point on the curve corresponding to the amount that is wont to be sold in the market, data may be obtained sufficient for drawing the curve with tolerable correctness for some distance on either side of A; but it will scarcely ever occur that the curve can be drawn with any approach to accuracy right up to D. It happens that the practical application of this as of other portions of the theory of domestic values require a knowledge of the demand curve only in the neighbourhood of A. At all events in the present discussion we shall not be much concerned to ascertain accurately the whole area $DCAD$; it will be sufficient for most of our purposes to know the changes in the magnitude of this area that would be occasioned by moving A through small distances along the curve in either direction. Nevertheless it will be convenient to assume, as in the pure theory we are at liberty to do, that the curve is completely drawn for us.[1]

[1] The mathematician will notice that if $y = f(x)$ be the equation to DD' and (a, b) the coordinates of A; the consumers' rent is

$$\int_0^a f(x)\, dx - ab.$$

The foregoing paragraph, which in the 1st ed. (p. 178 n.) also formed part of the footnote beginning with the words "Let us consider then the demand curve DD'..." was deleted from the 3rd ed. The mathematical footnote to the paragraph was not included in the 1st ed.

PAGE 129

a. This paragraph and the first sentence of the next paragraph were inserted in the 3rd ed. (p. 205).

b. The remainder of this paragraph was inserted in the 6th ed. (p. 129) where it replaced the following sentences dating from the 3rd ed. (pp. 205–6):

This line of argument implies that we cannot trust the marginal utility of a commodity to indicate its total utility: on the ground that though, when a person spends sixpence on a quarter of a pound of tea instead of on a stone of salt, he does so because he prefers the tea; and he would not prefer the tea if he did not know that he could easily get whatever salt he needed for his more urgent requirements. And if an attempt were made to give this vague saying greater definiteness, the ordinary course would be to estimate first the price that he would pay for a small quantity of tea, rather than go without it; and next what he would pay for further supplies, if it became a little more plentiful; and next what he would pay for further supplies, and so on: and the whole would be added up. And then the like would be done for salt, and the two would be compared. The process would be the same as in our analysis; but it would remain vague; or if an attempt were made to be definite and exact, there would be much waste of labour in the absence of appropriate phrases and machinery.

 c. The last three sentences of this footnote date from the 2nd ed. (p. 184 n.), where they were succeeded by the following paragraph which was deleted from the 4th ed.:

> The notion of an exact measurement of consumers' rent was published by Dupuit in 1844. But his work was forgotten; and the first to publish a clear analysis of the relation of total to marginal (or final) utility in the English language was Jevons in 1871, when he had not read Dupuit. The notion of consumers' rent was suggested to the present writer by a study of the mathematical aspects of demand and utility under the influence of Cournot, von Thünen and Bentham.

PAGE 130

 a. The first clause of this sentence dates from the 4th ed. (p. 205).

 b. The remainder of this paragraph, with the attached footnote, was inserted in the 3rd ed. (p. 206).

 c. This paragraph dates substantially from the 3rd ed. (pp. 206–7). The corresponding paragraphs in the 1st ed. (pp. 178–9) ran as follows:

Next to take account of the fact that the rich value at a shilling a much smaller gratification than the poor could afford to pay a shilling for. A poor woman who could manage to buy only one pound of tea in a year if she had to pay 10*s.* for it, will derive a vast surplus satisfaction from buying several pounds at 2*s.* a pound. But a much smaller surplus satisfaction is afforded by a change in the consumption of a rich man that has an equal money measure. Suppose for instance that he would buy only one bundle of asparagus at the price of 10*s.*: but that, the price falls to 2*s.*, and he purchases several bundles. He gets from the low price of asparagus a surplus satisfaction indeed, but a much smaller one; and yet these two satisfactions have the same economic measures, the Consumers' Rents in the two cases are equal.

This fact diminishes the practical usefulness of estimates of Consumers' Rent to some extent, but not nearly so much as at first sight appears. For, as has already been pointed out, we may suppose utilities which have the same money power to be fairly equal, provided the prices, which we are considering, are those paid in two markets where the average wealth of the purchasers is equal, (as well of course as the general purchasing power of money). We must however always be careful not to regard the total utilities of things as fairly represented by their money measures when one of the things is consumed chiefly by the rich and the other chiefly by the poor. The neglect of this precaution led economists of the last generation to untrue conclusions, which were unfortunately of such a kind as to seem to imply a want of sympathy with the sufferings of the poor. But of this more hereafter.

In a copy of the first edition of the *Principles* used by Marshall in the preparation of the second edition, the words "the Consumers' Rents in the two cases are equal", in the final clause of the first of the foregoing paragraphs, are queried and there is the following comment in Marshall's handwriting in the margin: "Is this true? cf. curves p. 165." The reference there is to the demand curves on page 104 in vol. 1 of the present edition.

The foregoing paragraphs in the 1st ed. were replaced by the following paragraph in the 2nd ed. (p. 186):

Nevertheless we must constantly bear in mind that the Surplus Satisfaction which a poor person derives from a fall in the price of things bought by him is very much greater than that which a rich man derives from an equal aggregate fall in the price of things which he buys; and that the total utilities of two things are not fairly represented for the purposes of comparison by their money measures when one of the things is consumed chiefly by the rich and the other chiefly by the poor. The neglect of this precaution led economists of the last generation to untrue conclusions, which were unfortunately of such a kind as to seem to imply a want of sympathy with the sufferings of the poor.

d. In the 3rd ed. (p. 206 n.) this footnote began with the following sentence which was deleted from the 5th ed.:

The outlines of this notion are given in the following passage from Harris *On Coins* 1757, which was followed closely by Adam Smith; while the analysis was carried further by Ricardo (see below, Note at the end of Book V).

The Note referred to in the last clause of the extract here quoted became Appendix I in the 5th ed.

PAGE 131

a. The first sentence of this paragraph in the 1st ed. (p. 152) was placed in Book III, ch. II, § 2. See also page 20 in Vol. I of the present edition.

b. This sentence dates substantially from the 2nd ed. (p. 186).

c. "Much" since the 3rd ed. (p. 207), "great" in the 2nd ed.

d. This paragraph and footnote date substantially from the 3rd ed. (pp. 207–8 n.).

PAGE 132

a. This section (§ 4) was inserted in the 3rd ed. (pp. 208–9).

b. This sentence dates from the 4th ed. (p. 206 n.).

c. So since the 5th ed. (p. 132 n.). In the 3rd ed. (p. 208 n.) this paragraph ran:

> Prof. Patten has insisted on the latter of them in various writings, and in particular in some suggestive articles in Vol. III of the *Annals of the American Academy*. His own attempt to express the aggregate utility of all forms of wealth is ingenious: but does not appear to take account of all the difficulties of the task.

In the 4th ed. (pp. 206–7 n.) the paragraph was rewritten as in the present edition, except that in the 4th ed. the end of the first sentence ran: "in some very able and suggestive writings."

d. This clause was inserted in the 5th ed. (p. 132 n.).

PAGE 133

a. So since the 3rd ed. (p. 208) where the first sentence of this paragraph replaced the following sentence dating from the 1st ed. (p. 179):

There is another class of corrections which must be made before the money measure of the total utility of wealth can be taken to represent the real happiness which its possession affords.

b. While the first paragraph of this footnote dates from the 3rd ed. (p. 209 n.) the second and third paragraphs date substantially from the 1st ed. (pp. 177 n.–8 n.) where they formed part of a footnote, now on pages 128 n.–9 n. in vol. I of the present edition.

c. So since the 3rd ed. (p. 209 n.) where this paragraph replaced the following paragraph dating from the 1st ed. (p. 178 n.):

There is however difficulty in estimating the total utility of commodities some supply of which is necessary for life; for instance the utility of the food required to keep a man from starvation is indefinitely great. The best plan is perhaps to take that necessary supply for granted, and estimate the total utility only of that part of the commodity which is in excess of this amount. But here it is especially important to recollect that the desire for anything is much dependent on the difficulty of getting substitutes for it. (See Note VI in the Mathematical Appendix.)

PAGE 134

a. The following sentence after the sentence ending with the word "times", dating from the 1st ed. (pp. 179–80), was deleted from the 3rd ed.:

Subject to these corrections then we may regard the aggregate of the money measures of the total utility of wealth as a fair measure of that part of the happiness which is dependent on wealth.

b. This paragraph was inserted in the 3rd ed. (p. 210).

c. This paragraph together with its footnote was inserted in the 2nd ed. (p. 187).

d. "Happiness" in the 2nd ed. "Wellbeing" from the 3rd ed.

PAGE 135

a. In the 1st ed. (p. 180) this paragraph began with the following sentences which were deleted from the 2nd ed.:

An increase of wealth scarcely ever fails to cause an increase of happiness for the time. Independently of the pleasures got from the things that can be bought with the new wealth, there is a satisfaction in the success of which it is generally a sign.

b. "regard" from the 4th ed. (p. 209), "perhaps suppose" in the first three editions.

c. The first paragraph of this footnote was inserted in the 3rd ed. (p. 211 n.).

PAGE 136

a. The remaining sentences of this paragraph date from the 2nd ed. (pp. 188–9) where they replaced the following clause and sentences in the 1st ed. (p. 181), coming at the conclusion of the sentence ending with the word "possible":

though to carry activity, however high, to the verge of exhaustion is a mistake unless it be done in pursuit of some higher aim. But, particularly in a Northern climate, a great deal of hard work is necessary to enable us to escape from hunger, cold and disease, and a great deal more to provide the means of a fairly cultured life.

b. The following footnote, which was attached to the clause ending with the word "futile" in the 1st ed. (p. 181 n.), was deleted from the 2nd ed.:

> Roscher has written much that is interesting on this subject in his *Political Economy* and in his *Ansichten*.

c. So since the 2nd ed. (p. 188 n.). In the 1st ed. (p. 181 n.) this footnote ran as follows:

> See his lecture on *the Gospel of Relaxation*. I have heard a manufacturer, whose general character stood high, express regret at the tendency of his workmen to care less for drink: because when they drank more, they were more eager to earn high wages, and, having less resources, were more fully under his control.

PAGE 137

a. So since the 6th ed. (p. 137) where the following additional words after the word "living", dating from the 1st ed. (p. 182), were omitted: "which will find their place at the end of this treatise."

b. In the 1st ed. (pp. 182–3) this chapter was concluded by the following paragraph:

Finally then while insisting that every one's chief sources of happiness must be within himself; that health of body and mind and spirit, a pure heart and a love towards God and man will make a person happy however poor he is; and that no amount of material wealth will serve to chase away misery from one who is not of a cheerful spirit; we must recollect that poverty causes mental and moral degradation; and this fact will indeed be brought prominently before us in our ensuing inquiry into the causes which determine the efficiency of labour. A moderate income earned by moderate work offers the best opportunity for the growth of those habits of body, mind and spirit in which alone there is true happiness.

In the 2nd ed. (p. 190) this paragraph was retained down to the words "mental and moral degradation". In the 3rd ed. the remainder of the paragraph was deleted.

BOOK IV

THE AGENTS OF PRODUCTION
LAND, LABOUR, CAPITAL
AND ORGANIZATION

CHAPTER I

INTRODUCTORY

PAGE 138

a. So since the 3rd edition. In the 1st edition Book IV was entitled "Production or Supply", which was changed in the 2nd ed. to "Supply or Production".

b. Except where otherwise stated the wording of §1 of this chapter dates substantially from the 3rd edition, and of §2 from the 1st edition.

c. The title of this chapter remained unchanged since the 1st edition.

d. This sentence was inserted in the 4th ed. (p. 213).

e. This sentence and the following sentence were inserted in the 4th ed. (pp. 213–14).

f. The remainder of the footnote was inserted in the 4th ed. (p. 213 n.).

PAGE 139

a. The following footnote attached to the end of this paragraph in the 3rd ed. (p. 215 n.) was deleted from the 5th ed.:

¹ The objections to the English practice are well stated by Wagner (*Harvard Journal of Economics*, vol. V, pp. 332–3); but nothing much is gained by a compact and thorough treatment of population, unless it is on a scale which would make the treatise far too long for English readers. In the present work the simpler aspects of agriculture are treated early; partly on account of their historical connection with the doctrine of population; partly to make way for a gradual development of the notion of industrial organization in the remainder of the Book. In the great treatise edited, and for the greater part written by Wagner, agriculture (*Agrarwesen und Agrarpolitik*) by Buchenberger fills a large volume, the second of the whole treatise. The first volume is given to foundations (*Grundlegung*); the first half of it being occupied with fundamental notions and method; the second with population, industrial organization and the economic aspects of the State.

a. Except where otherwise stated, the text of this section (§ 2) dates from the 1st ed. (pp. 187–90).

b. This paragraph was inserted in the 3rd ed. (p. 216).

c. In the 3rd ed. (p. 216) the word "sacrifice" replaced the word "abstinence" dating from the 1st ed. (p. 187).

d. The remainder of this paragraph and the succeeding paragraph were inserted in the 3rd ed. (p. 216).

e. The following clause at the end of this sentence in the 1st ed. (p. 187) was deleted from the 3rd ed.: "and such work has for the greater part no measure."

f. The first paragraph of this footnote dates from the 3rd ed. (p. 217), apart from the last sentence which was inserted in the 5th ed. (pp. 140–1 n.). In the 4th ed. (p. 216 n.) the words "or rent" in the 3rd ed., which had been added after the word "surplus" in lines 3 and 8 of this paragraph, were deleted. The second paragraph was inserted in the 5th ed. (p. 141 n.) where there was the following concluding sentence which was deleted from the 6th ed.: "Much will need to be said on this subject especially in connection with Trade Unions in another volume."

a. The following clause after the word "money" in the 1st ed. (p. 187) was deleted from the 3rd ed.: "or command over commodities in general."

b. So since the 5th ed., where this clause replaced the following clause dating from the 1st ed. (p. 187): "but he will probably prefer to store up his strength till he can get paid for his work." In the first three editions this clause was succeeded by the following sentence which was deleted from the 4th ed.:

In most occupations even that part of the work which affords the worker more pleasure than pain, must as a rule be paid for at the same rate as the rest; the price of the whole therefore is determined by that part of the labour which is most unwillingly given, and which the worker is on the verge of refusing to give; or as we may say by the *marginal disutility* of labour.

c. In its present form this sentence dates from the 4th ed. (p. 216).

d. This clause was inserted in the 7th ed. (p. 141) where it replaced the following clause dating from the 1st ed. (p. 188): "so it is with regard to the supply of labour."

e. The second sentence of this footnote was inserted in the 3rd ed. (p. 217 n.).

PAGE 142

a. So since the 5th ed. (p. 142) where the last two sentences of this paragraph replaced the following sentences dating from the 3rd ed. (p. 218):

One reason of this is that with every increase in the hours of labour beyond a certain limit the need for relaxation and the craving for it increase, at all events among those who are in a healthy condition. The marginal disutility of labour increases; partly because, as the time left for rest and other activities diminishes, the marginal utility of free time increases.

b. This clause was added in the 3rd ed. (p. 218).

c. The word "available" was inserted in the 3rd ed.

d. This and the concluding paragraph of this section date substantially from the 3rd ed. (pp. 218–19).

In the 1st ed. (pp. 189–90) the following paragraphs succeeded the two paragraphs dealing with supply price:

This instance [sc. the supply schedule for a commodity] will serve fairly well to indicate the general drift of the inquiry before us; but it does not closely correspond to the actual conditions of life.

As a matter of fact the supply of commodities is not so simply determined: the total efficiency of production depends on many conditions, which we have to consider in the present Book. The first of these is the aid which nature gives to man: which we shall find to be such that though she scarcely ever ceases to respond to his increased efforts, she often affords them only a diminishing rate of return. Next we have to discuss the growth of numbers and the average strength and industrial skill of each class of workers: and to consider them in relation to the causes which determine the supply prices of different kinds and amounts of industrial efficiency. Next after looking at the growth of wealth in general, and in particular those parts of it which aid and support future production, we must examine the causes and the effects of industrial organization: for the collective efficiency of production depends on its organization almost as much as it does on the numbers of those who work, or on their individual efficiency.

Having thus taken a broad survey of the factors of production, we shall be prepared to consider how the supply price of any given amount of a commodity (that is the price at which that amount will be forthcoming under normal conditions), is governed by the supply prices of the several factors that contributed to its production. We shall then be ready for discussing in the following Books the general theory of the relations of demand and supply, and the applications of this theory to the chief practical problems of Distribution and Exchange.

In the 2nd ed. (pp. 195–6) the only alterations of substance in the paragraphs just quoted were that the following sentence was inserted after the third sentence of the second paragraph:

Next, we shall have to revert to that weighing of future pleasures against present, which we have already looked at from the side of demand; and to consider more closely how the marginal disutility of waiting increases generally though not universally, with the amount of that waiting: and this will bring us to a study of the causes that govern the accumulation of wealth in general, and in particular those parts of it which aid and support future production.

and that the final paragraph was rewritten as follows:

This is as far as it will be advisable to go in the study of supply, till we have considered the general theory of the relations of demand and supply. Afterwards we shall revert to some difficult points relating to cost of production.

The foregoing paragraphs were deleted from the 3rd ed.

e. In the 4th ed. (p. 218) the word "work" replaced the word "labour" in the 3rd ed.

PAGE 143

a. In the 4th ed. the word "work" replaced the word "labour" in the 3rd ed.

b. The last two sentences of this paragraph and the first sentence of the succeeding paragraph were inserted in the 4th ed. (p. 218)

c. The following footnote, appended to the word "irregular" in the 4th ed. (p. 218 n.), was deleted from the 5th ed.:

> In the previous edition the word "labour" was used in this discussion instead of "work". And, as unfortunately the supply of labour has later on been used to mean the supply of labourers, this passage has been misunderstood; and has been taken to imply that economic considerations alone control the rate of growth of population. (See e.g. *Annals of American Academy*, VII, p. 100.) That would of course be false. See below ch. IV, V.

d. The following footnote, appended to the word "problems" in the 3rd ed. (p. 219 n.) was deleted from the 4th ed.:

> It may be observed, however, that this income of labour, together with a similar income of capital, varying as it does with changes in opportunity or conjuncture, will be called hereafter a Quasi-rent; and that it is of a different nature from that permanent surplus discussed earlier in this section and corresponds rather to the income derived from land in a new country, which sometimes gives the settler a better reward than he had expected.

BOOK IV, CHAPTER II

THE FERTILITY OF LAND

PAGE 144

a. Except where otherwise stated the wording of this chapter dates substantially from the 1st edition.

b. The title of this chapter remained unchanged since the 1st edition.

c. In the first three editions Marshall misquoted Ricardo's phrase to read: "the original or indestructible properties of the soil." He inserted the correct version of the phrase in the 4th ed. (p. 220 n.).

PAGE 146

a. The remainder of this paragraph dates from the 5th ed. (p. 147) In the 1st ed. (pp. 193–4) the text of the paragraph ran as follows:

Chemically the soil must have the inorganic elements that the plant wants in a form palatable to it. The greater part of the bulk of the plant is made up of so-called "organic compounds"; that is, compounds of carbon chiefly with oxygen, hydrogen and nitrogen[1]; and of these it obtains by

[1] They are called organic, not because they really are organized, but because they are found in vegetable and animal organisms; and because at one time chemists thought that none of them could be made except as a process of organic growth. But Liebig showed that it was a mistake to suppose that plants can absorb organized matter. It must become unorganized before it can be plant food.

far the greater part from air and water. Only a small fraction (somewhere about a twentieth on an average) of its dry bulk consists of mineral matter that it cannot get except from the soil. And as most soils have given them by nature at least some small quantities of all the mineral substances that are necessary for plant life, they can support some sort of vegetation without human aid. Often however they have but very scanty provision of one or two necessary elements; phosphoric acid, potash and lime being those of which the supplies are most apt to run short. It may indeed happen that the deficient food is one of which some kinds of plants require only a little, and then there may be a fairly good growth of just those plants; but such cases are rare; and the vegetation generally is poor and thin whenever the soil is deficient in one of the mineral constituents of plant life. If however it be well provided in other respects, and in a good condition mechanically, there is an opportunity for man to make a great change with but little labour. He can then turn a barren into a very fertile soil by adding a small quantity of just those things that are needed; using in most cases either lime in some of its many forms, or those artificial manures which modern chemical science has provided in great variety.

Again, these special manures are of the highest importance to supply particular mineral elements of plant food of which the soil is robbed by the animal and vegetable products which are sold away from the land. It is true that the soil itself has often large "dormant" stores of many of these things. They are dormant because they are not in a fit chemical and mechanical condition to be consumed by the plant. To bring them into that condition and make them "active" food, they must be well plied with oxygen and carbonic acid gas. This may be effected by proper tillage, even the subsoil being forced to give up its stores of dormant food, if it has them; and in that case the land may be kept fertile with very little aid from special manures, particularly if it receives a general return of its lost constituents in the form of farmyard manure.[1]

---

[1] Farmyard manure contains everything that plant life wants, but in unequal proportions. It has the advantage of aiding the distribution over the whole of

the soil of small particles of everything that the plant wants: each rootlet in contact with decaying vegetable matter finds ready to it all that it needs; nothing is left out. But the mineral elements form only a small part of farmyard manure. The great bulk of it, exclusive of water, consists of organic compounds. The plant draws its chief supply of these, and can in case of necessity get all, from the atmosphere; though it prefers to obtain some through its roots. The supply of mineral elements in the soil is therefore of primary importance: its supply of nitrogen is the chief chemical factor of its "condition", that is of its readiness to meet any immediate demand on it; while its supplies of phosphoric acid, potash and lime are the chief chemical factors of its permanent fertility. But the organic compounds in farmyard manure and other decaying vegetable matter in the soil are of great use even in this respect; for they work the dormant mineral plant food in the soil up into an active form, and hold stores of it ready for the plant. Certain crops absorb an exceptionally large amount of certain minerals and these may happen not to come back in manure to the particular land from which they are taken; and of course any such special deficiency cannot be made good by farmyard manure without giving the soil more than it wants of some other things. Lime for instance sometimes runs short; and potash is often in great demand on sandy soils, particularly when root crops are grown on them. But the most important case is that of phosphoric acid. Of this the soil has scarcely ever any large quantity; while plants, particularly cereals, require a good deal of it. In fact it is believed that there is very little near the surface of the ground which has not already been many times absorbed into vegetable and thence into animal life; and it has nearly always to be supplied by special manures to land that is required to grow continuous heavy crops, particularly of cereals. Farmyard manure generally contains little of it unless the cattle have been fed largely on grain. Human excrements are rich in it: and are of great assistance in this way to most peasant proprietors; but our modern habit of washing sewage out to sea makes the use of artificial manures much more necessary than it was. There is however at last, after many disappointments, some prospect of a remedy for this waste.

No change was made in either the text or footnotes in the above passages in the 2nd or 3rd editions; but in the 4th ed. (pp. 222–3) they were compressed into little more than a page of text and footnotes.

b. In the 1st ed. (pp. 195 n.–6 n.) there was the following footnote attached to the sentence ending with the word "crop":

The basis of most of the modern English rotations is the Norfolk course, which was adapted by Mr Coke (Lord Leicester) to enable light, and so-called "poor" soils to bear good wheat crops. The first crop on his plan is turnips: they do not require to be sown till May or June; and therefore the winter and spring following the wheat crop, with which the preceding rotation closes, can be spent in tilling, cleaning and manuring. In the spring of the second year barley and clover are sown together: in the third year the clover is consumed: the land can be ploughed up in time for autumn sown wheat, which finds the soil strengthened mechanically by the clover roots and improved chemically by the nitrogen which these venturesome explorers have brought up from the subsoil. On these lines an immense variety of rotations have been adapted to various soils and conditions of farming, many of them extending over six or seven years. (A list of the chief of them is given in the *Memoir of the Agriculture of England and Wales prepared by the Royal Agricultural Society of England for the International Agricultural Congress* 1878. Pp. 316–54.) At present rather more than half the cultivated land of the United Kingdom is in permanent pasture; and of the rest one half is in corn crops, rather less than a quarter in green crops, chiefly roots, and rather more than a quarter in clover and grasses under rotation. In England the permanent pasture is proportionately less and the corn crops are greater than in Ireland and Scotland.

In the 4th ed. (pp. 223 n.–4 n.) the reference in parentheses, and the last two sentences, were omitted, and in their place was put the following sentence:

> The present time is witnessing hopeful attempts to supplement artificial chemical manures by "bacterial manures": that is by artificially propagated bacteria of such kinds as have been found to extract nitrogen from the air and store it up in the root-nodules of leguminous plants.

In the 5th ed. the whole footnote was deleted.

c. In the 1st ed. (p. 196 n.) the remaining sentences of this paragraph were placed in a footnote, which contained the following reference and concluding sentence which were deleted from the 4th ed.:

> (See Mr Scott Burn's *Directory for the Improvement of Landed Property*, p. 239.) As it is, when the subsoil is known to contain important elements which the surface soil has lost, or perhaps has never had, the enterprising owner will stir it deeply so that the air and fresh water may act on it, and after a time brings some of it up to mix with the surface soil.

PAGE 147

a. This sentence dates in its present form from the 5th ed. (p. 147) where it replaced the following clauses dating from the 1st ed. (p. 196):

the inherent, or indestructible, properties of the soil, the free gifts of nature, have been largely modified; partly robbed and partly added to by the work of many generations of men.

b. The following footnote attached to the sentence ending with the word "down" in the 1st ed. (p. 196 n.) was deleted from the 4th ed.:

> See in particular "The Influence of Trees on Climate and Productiveness" in Appendix I to the *Report of the Indian Famine Commission*, 1881.

c. In the 1st ed. (pp. 197 n.–8 n.) there was the following footnote attached to the sentence ending with the word "character":

> There is some interest in the attempt to distinguish that part of the value of land which is the result of man's labour, from that which is due to the original bounty of nature. Part of its value is caused by highways and other general improvements that were made for the general purposes of the country, and are not a special charge on its agriculture. Counting these in, List, Carey, Bastiat and others contend that the expense of bringing land from the state in which man found it to its present condition would exceed the whole value it has now; and hence they argue that all of its value is due to man's labour. Their facts may be disputed; but they are really not relevant to their conclusions. What is wanted for their argument is that the present value of land should not exceed the expense, in so far as it can properly be charged to agricultural account, of bringing the land from the state in which man found it to a condition in which it would be as fertile and generally useful for agricultural purposes as it now is. Many of the changes wrought in it were made to suit agricultural methods that are long since obsolete; and some of them even deduct from, rather than add to, the value of the land. And further the expenses of making the change must be the net expenses after adding indeed interest on the gradual outlay, but also after deducting the aggregate value of the extra produce which has, from first to last,

been attributable to the improvement. The value of land in a well-peopled district is generally much greater than these expenses, and often many times as great. The following table, taken from the above quoted *Memoir of the Royal Agricultural Society*, shews the investments of capital per acre on four typical English farms:

	Total value	Cost of farm buildings and labourers' cottages	Fencing and local roads	Drain-age	Leaving for value of land in its natural condition	Tenants' capital	Rent
	£ s.	£ s.	£ s. d.	£ s.	£ s. d.	£ s. d.	£ s.
Dairy farm	75 0	12 15	2 10 0	5 0	54 15 0	12 0 0	2 10
Mixed arable and pasture	45 0	8 0	2 0 0	0 0	35 0 0	12 0 0	1 10
Ditto upland	30 0	6 7	1 0 0	0 0	22 13 0	10 0 0	1 0
Pasture farm	94 10	7 0	1 13 4	0 0	85 16 8	12 0 0	3 3

But the fall in all agricultural values which had begun before 1878, when the Memoir was written, has continued at an increasing rate since then, and there are many who think that the rise in the value of English land during the past generation is a bare return to the capital invested in permanent improvements; that is, they think there has been no rise in the real value of the original properties of the soil for agricultural purposes. M. Leroy Beaulieu (*Répartition des Richesses*, Ch. II) holds that this has been the case at all events in Belgium and France; and Mr Pell supports a similar opinion with regard to England by some instructive statistical instances (see an Article on *The Making of the Land in England* in Vol. XXIII of the Journal of the Royal Agricultural Society). The values of the farms in the United States were $6,645,000,000 in 1860; they rose to $7,500,000,000 (estimated in gold) in 1870, and to $10,197,000,000 in 1880. But as General Walker points out (*Tenth Census*, vol. VII, p. 23), "it is a familiar feature of paper money inflations that real estate, especially rural real estate, seldom begins to rise so early or continues to rise so long as the prices of commodities." Allowing therefore for only half the premium on gold he gets the value for 1870 at $8,250,000,000: and thus arrives at an increase of about 24% in each of the two decades.

In the 4th ed. (p. 225 n.) the first paragraph of this note was deleted, while the rest of the note disappeared from the 5th ed.

PAGE 148

a. The first sentence of this paragraph dates from the 4th ed. (p. 225).

b. The following footnote attached to the sentence ending with the word "now" in the 1st ed. (p. 198 n.) was deleted from the 4th ed.:

Of course wherever the grass is mown, manure should be returned. It has moreover recently been found that manuring permanent pasture enriches it for a long time to come; for then the richest and finest grasses find within their reach as much food as they can consume, and are thus able to beat out of the field the poorer and coarser sorts.

c. The following footnote attached to the sentence ending with the word "ancestors" in the 1st ed. (p. 199 n.) was deleted from the 4th ed.:

Perhaps it is not unreasonable to hope that in time plants may be obtained every part of which will serve an important purpose. Just as in the Arctic regions every fragment of the reindeer's body is turned to account, so it may become possible to use as food, or for some other important purpose, both root and leaves, both stem and fruit of our plants. At present we eat the root of the potato, but the rest of the plant is useless except as food for other plants: we eat the leaves of the cabbage, but root and stalk are useless. The wood of the beech tree, the wood and the fruit of the pear tree are turned to good account: but their leaves are left to decay. Possibly (as Mr Moore Ede has suggested to me) chemical science may enable us to use as food many of those vegetable materials which we now throw away.

PAGE 149

a. So since the 6th ed. (p. 149) where this paragraph, which in the first five editions had been placed in Book IV, ch. III, § 1, was transferred to form the concluding paragraph of Book IV, ch. II, § 4. The wording of the paragraph dates from the 1st ed. (pp. 202–3).

BOOK IV, CHAPTER III

THE FERTILITY OF LAND, CONTINUED. THE TENDENCY TO DIMINISHING RETURN

PAGE 150

a. Except where otherwise stated the wording of this chapter dates substantially from the 1st edition.

b. The title of this chapter remained unchanged since the 1st edition.

c. So since the 4th ed. (p. 227), where this sentence replaced the following sentence dating from the 1st ed. (p. 200): "*The Law of Diminishing Return* may be provisionally stated thus:"

PAGE 151

a. From the 3rd ed. (p. 230) the word "application" replaced the word "doses", dating from the 1st ed. (p. 201).

b. From the 3rd ed. the words "doses of", dating from the 1st ed. (p. 201), were omitted before "capital and labour".

c. This footnote was inserted in the 5th ed. (p. 151 n.).

PAGE 152

a. So since the 3rd ed. (p. 231) where this clause replaced the following clause dating from the 1st ed. (p. 202): "provided the extra doses applied to each acre gave anything more than three-fourths of the return that he got from the earlier doses."

b. The remainder of this sentence was inserted in the 5th ed. (p. 152).

c. From the 3rd ed. (p. 232) the words "state distinctly" replaced the word "formulate", dating from the 1st ed. (p. 203).

PAGE 153

a. From the 4th ed. (p. 230) the word "tendency" replaced the word "Law" dating from the 1st ed. (p. 203).

b. The remainder of this paragraph was inserted in the 6th ed. (p. 153).

PAGE 155

a. In the 1st ed. the first paragraph of this footnote and the table were placed in Book VII, ch. x, §1, pp. 666 n.–7 n. The second paragraph dates from the 2nd ed. (p. 211 n.).

b. This and the next two sentences were inserted in the 5th ed. (p. 155 n.).

PAGE 156

a. This and the first clause of the next sentence were inserted in the 5th ed. (p. 156).

b. This and the next sentence were inserted in the 3rd ed. (p. 235 n.).

PAGE 157

a. The following concluding sentence of this paragraph in the 1st ed. (p. 207) was deleted from the 2nd ed.:

We may say then that, as a rule, man's share of the produce is least when the law of diminishing return applies most sharply: if he stops off his work soon, it is because the return is rapidly diminishing.

b. So since the 2nd ed. (p. 212 n.) where the words "a larger proportionate price for a paper that would cover the whole of the walls of his room" replaced the words "a larger proportionate price for a carpet that would cover the whole of his room", dating from the 1st ed. (p. 206 n.).

c. The opening clause of this sentence in the 1st ed. (p. 206 n.), "But such cases are rare," was deleted from the 2nd ed.

PAGE 159

a. So since the 4th ed. (p. 236). In the 1st ed. (p. 208) the remainder of this sentence ran as follows: "and the produce due to all further applications of capital and labour conforms, at all events so far as this point is concerned, to the law of diminishing returns." In the 2nd ed. (p. 215) this was altered to run as follows: "and the produce due to further applications of capital and labour conforms to the law of diminishing returns."

PAGE 162

a. The following concluding sentences of this paragraph in the 1st ed. (pp. 212–13) were deleted from the 6th ed.:

For the same reason the depression of English agriculture, through which we are now passing in consequence of American competition, is lowering the value of poor lands relatively to that of rich lands of the same character; and especially it is lowering the values of those lands which return good crops to very high cultivation; but which quickly relapse into a poor condition, unless a great deal of capital and labour is constantly spent on them.

PAGE 163

a. The following sentence in the 1st ed. (p. 213) was deleted from the 5th ed.:

There are strong reasons for holding that he had not overlooked the conditions which were necessary to make the law true; he seems here, as elsewhere, to have made the great error of taking for granted that his readers would supply those conditions which were present in his own mind.

b. So since the 6th ed. (p. 163 n.). In the first four editions this footnote ran as follows:

Had he done this, he would have helped his readers to supply the premises that were present in his own mind: if they do that they will find nothing of importance in his statement of the Law of Diminishing Return, or in his deductions from it, which is not true as far as it goes. As Roscher says (*Political Economy*, Sect. CLV) "In judging Ricardo, it must not be forgotten that it was not his intention to write a text-book on the science of Political Economy, but only to communicate to those versed in it the result of his researches in as brief a manner as possible. Hence he writes so frequently making certain assumptions, and his words are to be extended to other cases only after due consideration, or rather re-written to suit the changed case." The followers of Ricardo have accepted John Stuart Mill's re-statement of the law in which the conditions necessary to make it exact were introduced. Nevertheless these conditions are habitually ignored even now by some critical writers: they persist in putting forward what they call refutations of the law, but what are really either arguments that these conditions ought not to be overlooked or else attacks on inferences or deductions that have been made rightly or wrongly from it. For instance some people have inferred from the Law of Diminishing Return that the English people now would be better off if their numbers did not increase so fast. This doctrine is a fair matter for argument; and some of those who have denied it have thought that they were denying the Law of Diminishing Return. But really they were denying something quite different from it. The truth of the law has, I believe, been questioned by no writer who has interpreted it properly.

In the 5th ed. (p. 164 n.) two changes were made in this footnote as it appeared in the earlier editions: first, the whole of the fifth sentence was compressed into a single clause running as follows: "Nevertheless these conditions are often ignored"; secondly, the last sentence was altered to read as follows:"The truth of the law has probably never been questioned by any one who has interpreted it right."

PAGE 164

a.   This sentence dates from the 4th ed. (p. 242).

b.   So since the 6th ed. (p. 164). In the 4th ed. (p. 242) and the 5th ed. (p. 165) the remainder of this paragraph ran as follows:

On the contrary, many of these cases really afford instructive illustrations of those doctrines when rightly understood; though some of them are to be explained, as has already been said, by the necessity of providing for military safety. By insisting on such facts as these Carey did nothing to invalidate the statement that the returns which a farmer will get by applying extra doses of capital and labour to land already well cultivated will be less than those which he got for the earlier doses, *other things equal*; that is, there being no change in his methods of cultivation, in his markets, or in the other conditions by which he is surrounded.

c.   In its present form this footnote dates from the 6th ed. (pp. 164 n.–5 n.) but the subject matter dates with only slight change from the 1st ed. In the 1st ed. (pp. 215–16) the discussion of Carey and his doctrines was as follows (omitting only matter which is identical with that contained in this footnote in the present edition):

Brought up in Ireland in the tenets of Ricardo, he arrived in America early in this century, and before long was struck by the fact that the soil of New England is nearly the poorest in America; and that whenever he saw ruined houses and the traces of abandoned cultivation he found the soil exceptionally barren. This set him to enquire into the history of the occupation of the earth's surface; and he has collected a great mass of evidence in support of his proposition that the general progress of cultivation has been from lands which would be regarded as poor in an old and settled country, to those which would be regarded as rich....

His facts are drawn chiefly from warm if not tropical regions; and with regard to them his conclusions are perhaps true in the main. But much of the apparent attractiveness of tropical countries is delusive: they would give a very rich return to hard work, but hard work in them is impossible. A cool refreshing breeze is as much a necessary of vigorous life, as food itself. Food can be imported but fresh air cannot; land that offers plenty of food but whose climate destroys energy, is not more productive of the raw material of human well being, than land that supplies less food but has an invigorating climate. Again, the importance of many of Carey's facts diminishes on investigation. The choice of New England by the early settlers was an accident; houses on the hills were often, in early times as they are now, the homes of those who cultivate the rich but unhealthy valleys a few miles off.[1]

It may then be admitted that Carey has proved that soils which an English farmer would regard as poor, are in very many cases cultivated before neighbouring soils which he would regard as rich. The facts on which the Law of Diminishing Return is based lead us *a priori* to expect such cases to occur sometimes. Their occasional occurrence is not inconsistent, as some foreign writers have supposed, with the general tenor of Ricardo's doctrines: on the contrary many of these cases really afford instructive illustrations of those doctrines when rightly understood; though some of them are to be explained, as has already been said, by the necessity of providing for military safety.

[1] Passing down the Missouri Valley to St Louis some years ago, I saw it bearing everywhere crops of unsurpassed richness, but the farmers' houses were on the river bluffs several miles away. It may be said that this explanation may account for the absence of houses in comparatively narrow river valleys, but not in broad rich plains. If, however, we follow the maps which show the distribution of population in the United States at each successive census, we find that broad river valleys, such as those of the Lower Mississippi and the Lower Red River, were as a rule peopled in advance of the neighbouring uplands....

The importance of Carey's facts does not then lie in their bearing on the Law of Diminishing Return. They do not tend to invalidate the statement that the returns which a farmer will get by applying extra doses of capital and labour to land already well cultivated will be less than those which he got for the earlier doses, other things being equal; that is, there being no change in his methods of cultivation, in his markets, or in the other conditions by which he is surrounded.

The practical importance of Carey's doctrine lies in its bearing on the conditions under which the growth of population tends to cause increased pressure on the means of subsistence.

In the 3rd ed. (p. 244 n.) there was the following alteration in the account of Carey's early life:

> He had been brought up in the tenets of Ricardo, by a father who had emigrated from Ireland to America, and he began to write as an advocate of Free Trade; but after a while he was struck by the fact that the soil of New England...etc.

In the same edition the following reference was also given:

> A well balanced account of Mr Carey's position is given by Mr Levermore in the *Political Science Quarterly*, vol. v.

PAGE 165

a. So since the 4th ed. (p. 244), where this sentence replaced the following sentence dating from the 1st ed. (p. 217):

Of the way in which organization promotes production, particularly in manufactures, we shall have to speak hereafter. But we have already seen enough to be sure that even as regards agriculture the law of diminishing return does not apply to the total capital spent in a district as sharply as to that on a single farm.

b. This paragraph was inserted in the 4th ed. (p. 243 n.).

PAGE 166

a. The first sentence of this paragraph dates from the 6th ed. (p. 166) where it replaced the following sentences in the 1st ed. (p. 218):

In the following chapters we shall have much to say about the evil effects of local congestions of population in making it difficult to get fresh air and light, and in some cases fresh water. Again natives of New England who have gone to the fertile plains of the West, would often be willing to barter part of their heavy crops for the pure water which the barren granite soil of their old homes supplied; and even in England there are many places, particularly at the sea side, which are kept poor by the want of drinking water.

b. So since the 6th ed. (p. 166) where the present wording after the clause ending with the word " sea-fisheries", replaced the following wording dating from the 1st ed. (p. 218):

that the schedule of the sea's return to additional capital and labour shows no signs of any appreciable diminution. On the other hand it is contended that modern methods of fishing, especially trawling, destroy much spawn; and that experience shows a falling off in the productiveness of those fisheries that have been very vigorously worked.

c. From the 2nd ed. the original "very" was deleted from before "important".

d. This and the next paragraph date in their present form from the 2nd ed. (pp. 225–6). But the alterations then made in the text of the 1st ed. (pp. 218–20) consisted only of a rearrangement of the order of sentences, with a few unimportant verbal changes.

PAGE 167

a. The following footnote in the 2nd ed. (p. 225 n.), itself a rearrangement of a sentence in the text and a footnote in the 1st ed. (p. 219 n.), was deleted from the 5th ed.:

> For the rate of growth of minerals in the earth is so slow, that it may almost be neglected. It has indeed been asserted that the earth is producing petroleum fast by using for the purpose some of its internal heat. If this were true, it would have a great influence on the future of the world; but there seems to be no good ground for hoping that it is.

PAGE 168

a. In the 2nd ed. (p. 226) this sentence replaced the following sentence dating from the 1st ed. (p. 220):

By building high, by careful ventilation and draining, living room and working room can be got for a great many persons on a single acre.

b. This paragraph dates from the 4th ed. (p. 247).

c. This and the next clause were inserted in the 2nd ed. (p. 226 n.).

PAGE 169

a. So since the 3rd ed. In the first two editions this was entitled: "Note on the Meaning of the Phrase 'A Dose of Capital and Labour'."

b. In its present form this Note (with the exception of the final footnote) dates from the 6th ed. (pp. 169–72). It underwent considerable changes in the 3rd and 6th editions. In the 1st and 2nd editions the Note was concerned only with the interpretation of the phrase "a dose of capital and labour". In the 3rd, 4th and 5th editions the first part of the Note consisted of an account of the authorship of the law of diminishing returns and the second part incorporated the discussion in the earlier editions on the measurement of a dose of capital and labour. In the 6th ed. the whole of the first seven paragraphs of the present Note were inserted as new material, while the account of the development of the law of diminishing returns was omitted This account, dating from the 3rd ed. (pp. 149–50), ran as follows:

There has been a long controversy as to the authorship of the law of diminishing return. As has been already observed, the fundamental idea, which it expresses, has been the common property of every one who has had experience of agriculture, whether arable or pastoral, since the world began. What economists did for the law a century ago, was not to discover it; but to give it definiteness, and to deduce inferences from it; which, if sometimes too hasty, yet contained important elements of suggestive and constructive truth. So far as these inferences go undoubtedly the first place must be assigned to Ricardo: while Mr Cannan has shown that Turgot can claim priority over Anderson, Ricardo and other English writers in the clear statement of the law. In some observations written about 1768 (*Œuvres*, ed. Daire, vol. 1, pp. 420, 1) he says: "Granting that where ordinary good cultivation prevails, the annual advances bring in 250 to the hundred, it is more than probable that if the advances were increased by degrees from this point up to that at which they would bring in nothing, each increment would be less and less fruitful. In this case the fertility of the earth would be like a spring which is forced to bend by being loaded with a number of equal weights in succession.... This comparison is not perfectly exact; but it is sufficient to show how, when the soil approaches near to returning all that it can produce, a very great expense may augment the production very little.... Seed thrown on a soil naturally fertile but totally unprepared would be an advance almost entirely lost. If it were once tilled the produce would be greater; tilling it a second, a third time, might not merely double and triple, but quadruple or decuple the produce, which will thus augment in a much larger proportion than the advances increase, and that up to a certain point, at which the produce will be as great as possible compared with the advances. Past this point if the advances be still increased, the produce will still increase, but less, and always less and less."

Turgot, like practical agriculturalists, implicitly refers to successive applications of capital and labour. He assumes things to be measured by their money prices and implicitly regards a dose of capital and labour as the outlay of the equivalent of a certain sum of money distributed, according to the convenience of the case, between the earnings of labour of different kinds (including that of management), the price of seed and other materials, the cost of repair and replacement of machinery, etc., and lastly, interest on all the capital employed. This assumption may fairly be made when we are confining our attention to one place, and time, and method of cultivation.

c. This footnote was inserted in the 6th ed. (p. 169 n.).

PAGE 171

a. The remainder of this Note, except for the footnote to the end of this paragraph and the concluding paragraph of the Note, dates substantially from the 1st ed. (pp. 221–2).

b. The following sentences at this point in the 1st ed. (p. 221) were deleted from the 6th ed.:

This difficulty is closely connected with that of finding a common standard of purchasing power, which we shall have to discuss later on. But it has some features peculiar to itself.

c. This footnote was inserted in the 7th ed. (p. 171 n.).

PAGE 172

a. The word "interest" was inserted in the 6th ed. (p. 172).
b. This paragraph was inserted in the 6th ed. (p. 172).

BOOK IV, CHAPTER IV

THE GROWTH OF POPULATION

PAGE 173

a. Except where otherwise stated, the wording of this chapter dates substantially from the 1st edition.

b. So since the 3rd edition. In the 1st and 2nd editions this chapter was entitled "The Supply of Labour. The Growth of Numbers".

c. This paragraph was inserted in the 3rd ed. (p. 252).

d. So since the 2nd ed. (p. 229), where the words "sometimes, as for instance at Rome under the Empire, for mean motives", replaced the words "sometimes, as for instance during the decay of the Roman Empire, with the vilest and meanest motives" dating from the 1st ed. (p. 223).

PAGE 174

a. So since the 2nd ed. (p. 230). In the 1st ed. (p. 224) this ran as follows: "and in Western Europe during the Middle Ages there may be observed...etc."

b. So since the 2nd ed. (p. 230). In the 1st ed. (p. 224) this ran as follows:

It flowed generally when plague or war had thinned out the people, or when the fear of war made the recruiting officers anxious; but it seems to have ebbed in England after the Reformation, when the abolition...etc.

c. So since the 2nd ed. (p. 230) where the following words after the word "checked" in the 1st ed. (p. 224) were deleted: "by the licentious habits that grew up with the later Stuarts, and..."

d. So since the 7th ed. (p. 174 n.), where this sentence replaced the following concluding sentence of this footnote, dating from the 1st ed. (p. 224 n.):

> The population of Greece is said to have declined from the seventh century B.C. and that of Rome from the third. (See Zumpt, *Bevölkerung im Altertum* quoted by Rümelin in Schönberg's *Handbuch*. Comp. also Hume's essay on "The Populousness of Ancient Nations".)

PAGE 175

a. This footnote was inserted in the 2nd ed. (p. 250 n.).

b. This sentence dates from the 3rd ed. (p. 254 n.).

c. The quotation from Pitt was inserted in the 3rd ed. Two references in this footnote in the 1st ed. (p. 225 n.) were deleted from the 3rd ed.—the first (Twiss, *Progress of Political Economy*, Lect. VII) referred to the Act of 1806 mentioned in the text; the second (Garnier's article on "Population" in the *Dictionnaire de l'Economie Politique*) referred to the action of Louis XIV.

d.   The following sentence at this point, in the 2nd ed. (p. 231 n.), and the reference to Bertillon inserted in the 4th ed. (p. 253 n.), were deleted from the 6th ed.:

> In 1890 the Académie des Sciences was occupied with similar proposals, of which one may be noted as characteristic of our age: it would give to the father of a family two, three or four votes according to its size. See also Bertillon's *Le problème de la dépopulation*, 1897.

e.   This clause was inserted in the 7th ed. (pp. 175–6 n.). The next sentence dates from the 6th ed. (p. 176 n.).

PAGE 177

a.   In the 8th edition, "Bk. II, ch. IV"; emended in vol. I of the present edition to give the correct reference.

b.   In the 8th edition, "Bk. I, ch. III §§5, 6"; emended in vol. I of the present edition to give the correct reference.

PAGE 178

a.   The following footnote attached to the end of this sentence in the 1st ed. (p. 228 n.) was deleted from the 3rd ed.: "This last check was not made prominent in his first edition."

PAGE 179

a.   The rest of this paragraph and the next paragraph were inserted in the 3rd ed. (p. 259), where they replaced the following sentences dating from the 1st ed. (p. 229):

They will require more careful study when we come to discuss the pressure of population on the means of subsistence; but meanwhile it is important to bear in mind that the prevalent belief as to the effects of an increase of population on general well-being itself exercises a great influence over that increase.

After this rapid glance at the history of the doctrine of population, we may proceed to state it in its modern form.

b.   This footnote dates, in its present form, from the 3rd ed. (pp. 258–9 n.) except that in that edition there was the following clause after the words "many writers" in the sixth sentence of the note: "including even so acute a critic as Mr Cannan (*Production and Distribution*,

1776–1848, p. 143)." This clause was deleted from the 4th ed. There was also in the 3rd ed. the following reference which was deleted from the 5th ed.: "Prof. Ashley has edited in a convenient form leading passages of his first and second editions." This footnote in the 3rd ed. replaced the following footnote dating from the 1st ed. (p. 228 n.):

> First edition 1798, second and more careful edition in 1806. Malthus' results were not all new and were not all true: but his work has the merit of being the first thorough application of the inductive method to social sciences. The chief workers therefore in the modern historical school of economics justly regard him as one of the founders of that school and his work as a solid possession for ever. (Thus Roscher calls it κτῆμα ἐς ἀεί and Rümelin in Schönberg's *Handbuch* calls it "ein festes Eigentum der Wissenschaft".) In his first edition however he used an unfortunate phrase which did not express his real meaning; saying that "population tends to increase in a geometric ratio and subsistence only in an arithmetic." There are many other sentences of his which lend themselves to being misunderstood, and he has always been a favourite butt for the ridicule of shallow thinkers. An excellent account of him is given in Mr Bonar's *Malthus and his Work*.

c. This refers to the statement in the fifth sentence of the footnote from the 1st ed. quoted in the foregoing editorial note **b**.

PAGE 180

a. This footnote was inserted in the 3rd ed. (p. 259 n.) where it contains the following concluding sentences:

> Meanwhile there will probably be great improvements in the arts of agriculture; and, if so, the pressure of population on the means of subsistence may not be much felt even in two hundred years. But if the same rate of increase be continued till the year 2400, the population will then be 1000 for every mile of fairly fertile land: and, so far as we can see now, the diet of such a population must needs be in the main vegetarian.

In the 5th ed. (p. 180 n.) the first of the foregoing sentences was modified by making the last clause read as follows (as in vol. 1 of the present edition): "the pressure of population on the means of subsistence may be held in check for about 200 years, but not longer." From the same (5th) ed., the second of the foregoing sentences was deleted from the footnote.

PAGE 181

a. The following footnote attached to the word "birth-rate" in the 1st ed. (p. 230 n.) was deleted from the 2nd ed.

> Mr F. Galton (*Inquiries into Human Faculty*, pp. 320–1) estimated that in England the probable number of children of women married at the ages of 17, 22, 27 and 32 are respectively 9·0, 7·5, 6·0 and 4·5; that is, that their relative fertilities are as 6, 5, 4 and 3. See also the international statistics at the end of this Chapter. Compare columns 2 and 3, with column 5, after allowing for illegitimate births as shown in column 6.

The international statistics referred to in this footnote are printed below in the editorial note **d** to page 191 in vol. 1 of the present edition.

b. The first sentence of this footnote dates from the 2nd ed. (p. 236 n.) and the remainder of the footnote from the 3rd ed. (p. 260 n.).

PAGE 182

a. This paragraph was inserted in the 2nd ed. (p. 237 n.).

b. The first sentence of this footnote dates from the 7th ed. (p. 182) when it replaced the following sentences dating from the 1st ed. (p. 231 n.): "A typical instance is that of the valley Jachenau in the Bavarian Alps. There the custom is rigidly enforced: and there are scarcely any small cottages in the valley".

c. So since the 2nd ed. (p. 237 n.) where the present clause replaced the following clause in the 1st ed. (p. 231 n.): "but seem to think, so far as I could gather their opinions that the Jachenau purchases its material prosperity at too great a cost." In the 1st ed. the whole paragraph was in the present indicative.

PAGE 184

a. This footnote dates in its present form from the 5th ed. (pp. 184 n.–5 n.), with the exception of one sentence which was deleted from the 7th ed.; but a good deal of the material was put together here from scattered footnotes in the earlier editions.

b. The individual sentences in this paragraph date substantially from the 1st ed. (pp. 232 n., 233 n., 234 n.).

c. This paragraph dates from the 3rd ed. (p. 263 n.).

d. The following paragraph in the 3rd ed. (p. 263 n.) after the sentence ending with the word "districts" was deleted from the 5th ed.:

Miss Brownell (*Annals of American Academy*, vol. v) has shown that the birth-rate is generally highest in those parts of America in which population is scanty; that it decreases generally with an increase of agricultural wealth, and even more generally with an increase of manufacturing wealth, and with an increase in the number of deaths from nervous diseases. There are many exceptions, some of which can be explained away by the race differences, which are so disturbing an element in American statistics. (Possibly also the fashion of describing diseases as nervous may not spread as fast in the rural as in the urban parts of America.) But on the whole the facts seem to support Herbert Spencer's position.

e. This paragraph and the accompanying statistical table date from the 5th ed. (p. 184 n.).

PAGE 185

a. In the 1st ed. (pp. 233–4) this paragraph was succeeded by the following paragraph, which was deleted from the 3rd ed.:

There seems to be less ground for the belief, which was at one time held by many people, that abundance of the necessaries of life diminishes fecundity. No doubt this effect follows from excessive eating and lazy self-indulgent habits of life. But any increase of the necessaries and comforts of life that is likely to fall to the share of the working classes is shown by more recent investigations to be likely to increase the rate of growth of population; provided of course that it is not accompanied by a growing dislike to having a large family.

b. This paragraph dates from the 3rd ed. (p. 264 n.), where it replaced the following sentences dating from the 1st ed. (p. 232 n.).

> The birth-rate in France is known to vary inversely with the predominance of small properties, being lowest in those departments in which the largest proportion of the agricultural population are landowners, and highest in those in which there are fewest peasant proprietors. See Dr Berthillon's statistics quoted by M. Yves-Guyot (*Social Economy*, Bk. IV, Ch. I). The birth-rate in France was 32·3 per 1000 at the beginning of the century, and it has diminished steadily from decade to decade till now it is only 24·6.

The extended paragraph dating from the 3rd ed. (page 185 n. in vol. I of the present edition) was there preceded by the following paragraph, which was deleted from the 7th ed.:

> In Belgium also race differences are disturbing: but the figures arranged by Leroy Beaulieu (*Statistical Journal* for 1891, p. 377) show that the birth-rate is highest in those provinces in which wages and education are lowest.

PAGE 187

a. The first paragraph of this footnote dates from the 7th ed. (p. 187 n.) where it replaced the following paragraph and table dating from the 1st ed. (p. 235 n.):

> There is no certain knowledge to be had as to the density of population in England before the eighteenth century. Prof. Rogers while agreeing with Mr Seebohm that the Black Death of 1349 destroyed one half of the population, is inclined to take considerably lower estimates than Mr Seebohm's for the whole of the Middle Ages and to think that population doubled during the seventeenth century. (*History of Agriculture and Prices*, I, pp. 55 &c., IV, pp. 132 &c., VI, pp. 782 &c.) Nevertheless Mr Seebohm's estimates (*Fortnightly Review*, vol. VII, N. S.) probably give us a fairly trustworthy general view. The figures in square brackets are "merely conjectural."

	Agricultural	Non-agricultural	Total
1086	1½ million	½ million	2 million
1348	3 ,,	1 ,,	4 ,,
1377	1½ ,,	½ ,,	2 ,,
1500	[2¼] ,,	[¾] ,,	[3] ,,
1600	[3] ,,	[1] ,,	[4] ,,
1700	[3½] ,,	[2] ,,	5½ ,,

a. The only changes made in this footnote since the 1st ed. (p. 238 n.) are that the statistics of population in the table were extended in the 3rd ed. (p. 268 n.) to cover the year 1891, and in the 4th ed. (p. 266 n.) to cover the year 1901; also in the 4th ed. the words "but these early figures are untrustworthy" were inserted after the word "Decrease" at the foot of the table, and the following tables and paragraph dating from the 1st ed. (p. 238 n.) were deleted after the sentence ending "excess of births over deaths":

Decade ending	mean annual birthrate per thousand	mean annual deathrate per thousand	average an- nual natural increment per thousand	average an- nual actual increment per thousand	net emigra- tion in thousands
1861	34·15	22·25	12·61	11·93	122
1871	35·24	22·50	13·58	13·19	79
1881	35·35	21·27	15·09	14·36	164

The last column is obtained by comparing the census returns with those of births and deaths; for there is no independent record of the net emigration from England and Wales. The following figures show the gross emigration (ooos omitted) from the United Kingdom in the decades ending with the beginning of the years named

decade ending	emigration	decade ending	emigration
1831	247	1861	2,287
1841	703	1871	1,967
1851	1,685	1881	2,228

It may be noted that there would appear to be two errors of calculation in the table in the footnote on page 189 of vol. 1. The "Increase per cent" for the year 1710 should read 4·3 and not 4·9; while the increase per cent for the year 1901 should read 12·2 and not 11·7.

a. The following opening sentence of this paragraph in the 1st ed. (p. 240 n.) was deleted from the 2nd ed.: "Sweden has long been noted for the excellence of its vital statistics."

b. So since the 2nd ed. (p. 246 n.) where this sentence replaced the following sentences in the 1st ed. (p. 240 n.):

Of course the harvest does not declare itself till part of the year's tale of marriages is made up; so we must look at the harvest of the year preceding as well as the year of any particular marriage rate. Partly for this reason and partly because the inequalities of harvests are to some extent compensated for by the storage of grain these harvest figures do not show a close correspondence with the marriage rate.

a. The following sentences, the first of which dates from the 1st ed. (pp. 239–40) and the second from the 2nd ed. (pp. 245–6) were deleted from the 4th ed.:

The statistics even seem to suggest that this is not a merely casual coincidence; but that the price of bread is now so low that a further fall in its price does not perceptibly affect the marriage rate among the population at large; and that its influence in checking marriages among the agricultural population and those directly dependent on them is sufficient to lower the average marriage-rate for the kingdom: but a longer time must elapse, and more coincidences must be noticed, before the result can be regarded as fairly established. Again it must be remembered that those alternate inflations and contractions of credit which more chiefly govern the fluctuations in the employment, and therefore in the marriage rate of the people tend to raise and lower respectively general prices, and the price of wheat among others, though less than most others.

In the 2nd ed. (p. 245), the words "more rapid" were inserted before the word "influence" on line 5 of this passage.

b. This sentence was inserted in the 6th ed. (p. 191).

c. So since the 6th ed. (p. 191), where the figures for marriage rates given in the earlier editions were adjusted on the basis of each marriage counting for two. In the 5th ed. (p. 191), for example, the marriage rates were stated as follows:

The English marriage rate fell from 8·8 per 1000 in 1873, to 7·1 in 1886; the lowest rate that has occurred since civil registration began. It has since risen to 7·8 in 1891 and fallen to 7·4 in 1893 and risen to 7·9 in 1896.

d. This and the next paragraph assumed their final form in the 5th ed. (pp. 191–2) except for the footnote to the second paragraph which was inserted in the 6th ed. (p. 192). These two paragraphs represent a contraction of a longer discussion with a statistical table in the 1st ed. (pp. 240–3). This was turned into a "Note on International Statistics representing the Growth of Numbers" in the 2nd ed. (pp. 246–9). In the 3rd ed. (pp. 271–3) and the 4th ed. (pp. 269–71) this became a "Note on International Vital Statistics" with a different statistical table. The following paragraphs in the 1st ed. (p. 241) were subsequently deleted:

The marriage-rate is generally highest where the number of early marriages is the greatest; and so also is the fecundity of marriages. But there are some striking exceptions. Thus the number of children to a marriage is exceptionally low in France, and even lower in Massachusetts, though the age of marriage is not particularly high in either of these countries; and it is not very low in Sweden, where very few women marry under twenty.

In France and in Massachusetts the "natural" increase is very small; but there is an excess of immigration over emigration, which raises the actual rate of increase. In all other countries of Europe except France, Saxony and Austria proper, emigration exceeds immigration: the natural rate of increase is greater than the actual.

India differs from Russia in the same way that Russia does from the rest of Europe in having earlier marriages, a higher birth-rate and a higher death-rate. But the death-rate is more nearly equal to the birth-rate in India than in Russia.

It is a remarkable fact that the marriage-rate, the birth-rate, and the death-rate are diminishing in nearly every country of Europe. But the birth-rate in the large population of Russia is increasing rather fast, with the result that the average birth-rate for the whole of Europe is scarcely diminishing at all, though the average marriage-rate and death-rate for all Europe are diminishing rather fast. The "natural" rate of increase is on the average slightly increasing in England and Scotland (but not in Ireland) and in most other parts of Europe, and especially in those inhabited by Slavonic peoples.[1]

[1] The "natural" annual increase for Europe for the years 1865–70 was at the rate of ·9 per cent., and for the years 1878–83 at the rate of 1·15 per cent.

The second and fourth of the foregoing paragraphs were deleted from the 3rd ed., and the first and third paragraphs from the 5th ed.

The accompanying tables and concluding paragraph in the 1st ed. (pp. 242–4) were deleted from the 3rd ed.

The "actual" annual increase during the present generation has been greater than in the two preceding generations for most countries of Europe, but not for Great Britain, nor for France and Spain: and not for the United States.[1]

[1] See columns 12 and 13 of the following Table.

AVERAGES FOR THE YEARS 1865 TO 1883
(WITH A FEW EXCEPTIONS)

Countries	1 Population at last Census, 00,000's omitted	2 Marriages per 100 living	3 Marriages males, percentage of, under 25 years	4 Marriages females, percentage of, under 20 years	5 Births per 100 living	6 Births number to a marriage
Europe	319,6	·83 −	39·3	24·0	3·87 −	4·7
England and Wales	26,0	·81 −	51·3	14·4	3·51 −	4·3
Scotland	3,7	·72 −	42·3	13·4	3·47 −	4·8
Ireland	5,2	·48 −	32·6	13·5	2·64 −	5·5
Sweden	4,6	·65 +	23·3	5·6	3·02 −	4·6
Holland	4,0	·80 −	26·6	—	3·59 −	4·5
Belgium	5,5	·72 −	22·6	6·4	3·15 −	4·4
France	37,4	·78 −	27·0	21·2	2·54 −	3·3
Prussia	27,3	·86 −	—	10·3	3·88 −	4·5
Saxony	3,0	·92 −	34·7	10·7	4·24 −	4·6
Bavaria	5,3	·85 −	18·9	6·4	3·95 +	4·7
Switzerland	2,8	·74 −	26·5	8·8	3·02 −	4·1
Austria Proper	22,1	·84 −	—	18·1	3·84 +	4·5
Hungary	13,7	1·03 −	31·7	36·0	4·30 +	4·2
Spain	16,6	·73	38·4	—	3·39 −	4·6
Italy	28,5	·77 +	26·0	16·9	3·68 −	4·8
Russia (European)	82,9	·94 −	68·5	58·0	4·94 +	5·3
United States	50,2	—	—	—	—	—
Massachusetts	1,8	·94 −	40·0	18·9	2·57 −	2·7

The signs + and − in column 2, indicate that the corresponding figures for the last five years of the period were respectively greater or less than those for the first five years of the period 1865–1883; that is that the marriage-rate was tending to increase or to diminish; and similarly for columns 5 and 8. Of course there are occasional irregularities. Thus in Hungary the death-rate was excessively high in the middle of the period; and we cannot therefore say exactly what is the significance of the fact that the death-rate was a little higher at the beginning than at the end of the period. The figures for Europe do not include those for Turkey; but they do include those for Finland and Poland, though the figures for these countries are kept separate from those for Russia. The figures for Ireland must be received with caution: the number of marriages is certainly understated. In column 6 the births are compared with the marriages in the same year: but as Farr has argued, *Vital Statistics*, p. 98, they should properly be compared with the marriages six years earlier. Also in order properly to measure the fecundity of marriages the illegitimate births (column 7) should be deducted from the total number before dividing out. The figures in column 5 exclude stillborn children, except for the United Kingdom.

Column 11 gives the *natural* rate of increase; it is obtained by deducting column 8 from column 5. The Statistics for France, except in the last column are for the years 1870–1882: those for Russia 1867–1878, and for Switzerland 1870–1883. In all other cases the limits are very nearly 1865 and 1883 for all columns except the last two. The excess or defect of its figures over those in column 12 shew the annual percentage of the excess or defect of the emigration compared with the immigration; except in the cases of France and the United States for which the populations are

AVERAGES FOR THE YEARS 1865 TO 1883
(WITH A FEW EXCEPTIONS)

7	8	9	10	11	12	13
Births illegitimate, percentage of total	Deaths per 100 living	Deaths percentage under one year of age	Deaths percentage under five years of age	Annual excess of births over deaths, percentage to whole population	Annual actual increase per cent. in recent years	Annual actual increase per cent. in earlier years of this century
6·4	2·81 −	21·1	32·3	1·06		
5·3	2·14 −	14·9	24·9	1·37	1·32	1·37
9·2	2·14 −	12·2	23·1	1·33	1·02	1·08
2·6	1·78 +	9·6	16·5	0·86	·69	·18
10·2	1·89 −	13·2	22·2	1·13	·77	·83
3·4	2·46 −	19·3	—	1·13	1·02	·71
7·1	2·24 −	14·8	25·3	0·91	·84	·77
7·4	2·38 −	16·9	25·8	0·16	·25	·49
7·5	2·65 −	21·3	32·4	1·23	·94	1·13
13·2	2·90 −	28·2	—	1·34	1·49	1·39
15·2	3·06 +	30·8	39·3	0·89	·71	·55
4·6	2·31 −	18·3	24·9	0·71	·62	·59
13·4	3·10 −	25·5	39·0	0·74	·77	·64
7·5	3·82 +	—	—	0·48	·48	·03
5·6	2·91 −	—	—	0·48	·33	·66
6·8	2·91 −	21·0	37·8	0·77	·68	·61
2·9	3·57 −	26·7	42·3	1·37	1·29	·84
—	—	—	—	—	2·36	3·01
1·4	1·92 +	16·3	27·9	0·65	1·87	1·80

taken for different areas at the beginning and end of the period. For all other countries they are calculated throughout columns 12 and 13 for the areas which the countries respectively had in 1883. Column 12 is based generally on twenty years' figures beginning about 1860, and column 13 on the preceding 60 years. The chief exception is Russia, for which the periods are 1867–79, and 1851–67. The last two columns are taken direct from Signor Bodio's *Movimento del Stato Civile, Confronti Internazionali,* 1884; the rest are taken from the tables, based on Signor Bodio's work which were published by Sir Rawson Rawson in the *Statistical Journal* for 1885.

The following paragraphs and tables which were inserted in the 3rd ed. (pp. 271–3) were deleted from the 5th ed.:

The adjoining tables show the main movements of population in some of the chief countries of the world. [They are compiled chiefly from figures arranged by Signor Bodio in Movimento del Stato Civile, *Confronti Internazionali,* 1884, and *Bulletin de l'Institut International de Statistique,* vol. VII; while the last three columns are taken mainly from Levasseur's *La Population Française,* III, 240, 1. See also his diagram on p. 248.]

The marriage-rate, the birth-rate and the death-rate are diminishing in almost every country; in spite of the unexpected fact that the percentage of brides who are not over twenty-five years of age is increasing in nearly every country, for which the figures are given. (The exceptions are Great Britain, Russia and Massachusetts. Nearly the same is true of the percentage of bridegrooms not over thirty

Countries	1 Marriages per 1000 living		2 Percentage of bridegrooms not over 25 years		3 Percentage of brides not over 20 years		4 Births per 1000 living		5 Births to a marriage
	1865 to 83	1887 to 91	1865 to 83	1887 to 91	1865 to 83	1887 to 91	1865 to 83	1887 to 91	1865 to 83
Europe	8·3 –	—	39·3	—	24·0	—	38·7 –	—	4·7
England and Wales	8·1 –	7·5	51·3	45·6	14·4	11·1	35·1 –	31·3	4·3
Scotland	7·2 –	6·6	42·3	38·2	13·4	11·6	34·7 –	31·1	4·8
Ireland	4·8 –	4·4	32·6	33·6	13·5	11·8	26·4 –	22·8	5·5
Sweden	6·5 +	6·0	23·3	26·8	5·6	6·4	30·2 –	28·4	4·6
Holland	8·0 –	7·0	26·6	31·0	—	10·?	35·9 –	33·4	4·5
Belgium	7·2 –	7·2	22·6	27·0	6·4	8·?	31·5 –	29·3	4·4
France	7·8 –	7·3	27·0	27·3	21·2	20·5	25·4 –	23·0	3·3
Prussia	8·6 –	8·1	–	–	10·3	8·1	38·8 –	37·2	4·5
Saxony	9·2 –	9·3	34·7	39·0	10·7	7·6	42·4 –	41·8	4·6
Bavaria	8·5 –	7·0	18·9	29·4	6·4	10·7	39·5 +	35·9	4·7
Switzerland	7·4 –	7·1	26·5	27·3	8·8	7·2	30·2 –	27·7	4·1
Austria	8·4 –	7·7	—	—	18·1	17·3	38·4 +	38·0	4·5
Hungary	10·3 –	8·6	31·7	—	36·0	36·7	43·0 +	42·8	4·2
Spain	7·3	5·6	38·4	41·9	—	—	33·9 –	36·3	4·6
Italy	7·7 +	7·7	26·0	—	16·9	23·4	36·8 –	37·6	4·8
Russia	9·4 –	—	68·5	64·1	58·0	56·3	49·4 +	—	5·3
United States	—	—	—	—	—	—	—	—	—
Massachusetts	9·4 –	9·3	40·0	37·5	18·9	16·1	25·7 –	25·8	2·7

years of age; see *Bulletin de Statistique*, vol. VII, p. 16.) The percentage of brides who are not over twenty years of age seems to be on the whole nearly stationary, though it is falling rapidly in some countries, and notably in the United Kingdom: and the same seems to be true of those who are not over twenty-five.

In France and in Massachusetts the "natural" increase is very small; but there is an excess of immigration over emigration, which raises the actual rate of increase. In all other countries of Europe except France, Saxony and Austria proper, emigration exceeds immigration: the natural rate of increase is greater than the actual.

The general mortality is high where the birth-rate is high. For instance, both are high in Russia and Hungary; both are low in Sweden, France and Massachusetts.

In comparing the aggregates of population shown in the last three tables, it must be recollected that the areas of Russia and the United States were much larger in 1890 than in 1801, those of Prussia and the Austrian Empire rather larger: while that of France was much smaller; for in 1801 it had included Belgium, and part of Germany and Italy.

The signs + and – in the first column of division 1 indicate that the corresponding figures for the last five years of the period were respectively greater or less than those for the first five years of the period 1865–1883; that is, that the marriage-rate was tending to increase or to diminish; and similarly for divisions 4 and 6. It will be noted that they generally point in the same direction as the subsequent changes shown by the second columns of those divisions.

e. In the 2nd ed. (p. 246 n.) the first sentence of this footnote ran as follows:

Statistics of exports are among the best indications of commercial prosperity: and in the article already quoted, Dr Ogle has shown a close correspondence

Countries	6 Deaths per 1000 living		7 Deaths percentage under five years of age	8 Annual percentage increase 1860 to 1880		9 Population in millions (partly estimated)		
	1865 to 83	1890		natu-ral	actual	1801	1840	1890
Europe	28·1 −	—	32·3	10·6	—	175·0	250·6	360·9
England and Wales	21·4 −	19·5	24·9	13·7	13·2	8·9	15·7	28·8
Scotland	21·4 −	19·7	23·1	13·3	10·2	1·6	2·6	4·0
Ireland	17·8 +	18·2	16·5	8·6	− 6·9*	?	8·0	4·7
Sweden	18·9 −	17·1	22·2	11·3	7·7	2·8	3·1	4·8
Holland	24·6 −	20·5	—	11·3	10·2	2·0	2·9	4·5
Belgium	22·4 −	20·8	25·3	9·1	8·4	—	4·1	6·1
France	23·8 −	22·8	25·8	1·6	2·5	33·1	34·1	38·5
Prussia	26·5 −	24·2	32·4	12·3	9·4	8·7	15·1	29·9
Saxony	29·0 −	26·9	—	13·4	14·9	—	—	3·5
Bavaria	30·6 +	27·3	39·3	8·9	7·1	—	—	5·6
Switzerland	23·1 −	20·9	24·9	7·1	6·2	1·8	2·2	2·9
Austria	31·0 −	29·4	39·0	7·4	7·7	} 25·8	35·8	41·0
Hungary	38·2 +	32·0	—	4·8	4·8			
Spain	29·1 −	—	—	4·8	3·3	11·0	12·0	17·2
Italy	29·1 −	26·4	37·8	7·7	6·8	—	—	30·2
Russia	35·7 −	—	42·3	13·7	12·9	35·0	54·6	98·6
United States	—	—	—	—	23·6	5·4	17·1	62·6
Massachusetts	19·2 +	—	27·9	6·5	18·7	·4	·7	2·2

* Decrease.

The groups of years for which the figures are collected differ slightly in some cases from those given at the heads of the various columns.

between the marriage-rate and the exports per head, by means of an artifice which is both ingenious and instructive though perhaps not entirely free from objection.

This sentence was reworded in its present form in the 4th ed. (p. 268 n.), except that "most convenient" replaced "best" in the 6th ed. (p. 191 n.), and the rest of the footnote was then added.

PAGE 192

a. So since the 5th ed. (p. 192) where this sentence replaced the following sentence, dating from the 1st ed. (p. 241): "For instance both are high in Russia and Hungary; both are low in Sweden, France and Massachusetts."
b. This and the following sentence were inserted in the 5th ed. (p. 192).
c. This footnote was inserted in the 6th ed. (p. 192 n.).

THE HEALTH AND STRENGTH
OF THE POPULATION

PAGE 193

a. Except where otherwise stated, the wording of this chapter dates substantially from the 1st edition.

b. So since the 3rd edition where the present title of this chapter replaced the following title, dating from the 1st edition: "The Supply of Labour, continued. Health and Strength."

PAGE 194

a. The remainder of this paragraph was inserted in the 2nd ed. (p. 251 n.).

b. So since the 3rd ed. (p. 275 n.) where this sentence replaced the following sentence in the text dating from the 1st ed. (p. 246):

In the war of 1870 the Berlin University Corps, which seemed to be weaker than the average, was found to be able to bear more fatigue than almost any other corps.

PAGE 195

a. The following sentences and footnote after the sentence ending with the word "food" in the 1st ed. (pp. 248–9 n.) were deleted from the 3rd ed.:

It must supply the nitrogenous and other elements that are required to build up growing tissues and to repair the waste of the body. It must also afford heat, some of which can be converted into muscular force; and for this purpose carbonaceous food, when it can be properly digested is the cheapest[1].

[1] The nitrogenous elements are most easily got from animal food. They exist also in vegetable foods; but not in a form that is so easily digested and assimilated. The supply of it is most abundant in beans, peas, lentils &c., and to a less extent in cereals; but in these it is found chiefly in the outer parts of the grain, which are preserved in wholemeal flour, but are thrown away when white flour is made. Vegetable food generally, but especially the cereals, and potatoes give abundant supplies of the carbonaceous or starch elements.

b. In the 1st ed. (p. 247) the subject-matter of this footnote was placed in the text. The following footnote attached to the sentence ending with the clause "and higher in cold winters than in warm", in the 1st ed. was deleted from the 4th ed.:

A high temperature increases the deaths from such diseases as those of the liver and the alimentary canal, but in England it diminishes to a greater extent the deaths from diseases of the lungs and old age. (See an article by Dr Guy, *On Temperature and its relation to mortality, Statistical Journal*, June 1881, also Farr, *Vital Statistics*, pp. 412, &c.) The error of popular opinion on this subject illustrates well the untrustworthiness of those general impressions on which much of our social history is based. Vols. XI and XII of the *Tenth Census of the United States* contain some interesting investigation on the influence of geographical conditions on vital statistics.

c. The following sentences after this sentence in the 1st ed. (p. 247) were deleted from the 3rd ed.:

But in warm climates the autumn is generally the most unhealthy part of the year. In India moisture is more hurtful to health and strength than either heat or cold: while the dry cold of Colorado, Canada and the Alps is often beneficial to those who are well fed, clothed and housed.

PAGE 198

a. The following footnote attached to the word "self-mastery" in the 1st ed. (p. 251 n.) was deleted from the 2nd ed.: "Hegel's subjective freedom. See above Bk. I, ch. II, §4." In vol. I of the present edition this reference would apply to Appendix A, §4.

b. The following additional sentence in the 1st ed. (p. 252) was deleted from the 3rd ed.: "Infant mortality is diminishing, though there remains much room for improvement in this direction."

c. So since the 2nd ed. (p. 257) where this sentence replaced the following sentences and footnote dating from the 1st ed. (pp. 252-3):

But it is generally higher, especially where there are factories. This arises from that survival of mediæval fallacies, to which we have already referred[1], and which leads some people to think and act as though the family income was increased by all that the mother earns when she goes out to work; though a little consideration would often show that the things she can buy with her earnings are of far less importance for the health and happiness of the family than the mere material services she could have rendered them if she had stayed at home, to say nothing of her moral influence in educating the children, in keeping the household in harmony and making it possible for her husband to be cheered and soothed in his evenings at home. This fact is getting to be understood by the better class of artisans and their wives; and there are not now very many mothers with young families at work in English and American factories.

¹ See above, Bk. II, ch. vi. Roscher (*Political Economy*, §242) says that the Jewish population of Prussia has increased faster than the Christian, though its birth-rate has been lower, the chief cause being that Jewish mothers seldom go away from their homes to work.

For the reference in this footnote see p. 199 above.

PAGE 199

a. So since the 7th ed. (p. 199) where this sentence replaced the following sentence dating from the 1st ed. (pp. 253–4):

But by the time their children and children's children have grown up without healthy play, and without fresh air, there is often little trace left of their original vigour.

The following additional sentence also dating from the 1st ed. was deleted from the 3rd ed.:

This is seen in trades that require but little muscular strength; only a very small proportion of those artisans to whom London owes its pre-eminence as a centre of highly skilled work come from parents who were born there; and there are scarcely any whose grandparents were born there.

b. This and the next sentence were inserted in the 7th ed. (pp. 199–200).

c. This footnote dates substantially from the 3rd ed. (pp. 280 n.–1 n.), though the statistical data relating to the years 1901 and 1905 were added in the 5th ed. (p. 199 n.). In the 1st ed. (p. 253 n.) and in the 2nd ed. (p. 257 n.) this footnote ran as follows:

Thus at the beginning of this century the population of London was just under a million, and that of the sixteen next largest towns in England and Wales was about two-thirds of a million: but in 1881 each of these figures had risen to nearly four millions. That is the population of the very large towns has increased more than four-fold, while that of the rural districts has not nearly doubled. A third of the population of England now lives in towns having more than a hundred thousand inhabitants, another third in towns having more than three but not more than a hundred thousand inhabitants, and only a third in rural districts.

Since the beginning of this century, while the population of France has increased only by one-third, that of Paris has increased four-fold (from about six to twenty-four hundred thousand), and that of the nine next largest towns has increased three-fold (from about six to eighteen hundred thousand).

In the United States of America at the beginning of this century only four per cent. of the population lived in cities of eight thousand inhabitants and upwards; but more than twenty-two per cent. in 1880.

In Germany the towns increase at the expense of the country by about one half per cent. of the population every year.

In each of these countries the growth of the town population is in a great measure due to immigration from the country. But especially is this the case in France. In the five years 1876–81, the excess of births over deaths in Paris was but 23,000 while the total increase of population was 280,000: in the 46 towns next in size to Paris the excess of births over deaths was 15,000 and the total increase of population was 838,000. In Lyons and Marseilles, where there are many Italians, though the total population increased by 33,000 and 41,000 respectively, the births actually fell short of the deaths by 3,000 and 2,000 respectively. (See M. Toussaint Loua's paper reproduced in the *Statistical Journal* for December, 1885.)

d. In the 3rd ed. (p. 280 n.) there was the following sentence after the sentence ending with the words "scattered town":

The suburbs of Liverpool are growing so fast at the expense of the city, that its actual increase is less than its excess of births over deaths; those who go out from it exceed in numbers those who emigrate into it, as was shown by Mr Cannan in the *Economic Journal*, vol. IV.

In the 4th ed. (p. 278 n.) the second clause of the foregoing sentence was changed to read as follows: "though indeed the increase in the whole district is less than its excess of births over deaths." This correction was made as a result of a letter from Cannan to Marshall in which Cannan pointed out that the statement Marshall made in this footnote in the 3rd ed., as to the growth of the population of Liverpool, was erroneous. Cf. Cannan's obituary article *Alfred Marshall 1842–1924* in *Economica* (November 1924), pp. 258–9. In the 5th ed. (p. 199 n.) the whole sentence was deleted, and was replaced by the concluding sentence of the first paragraph of this footnote showing the population of Liverpool in 1881, 1891, and 1901.

e. The following paragraph in the 3rd ed. (pp. 280 n.–2 n.) was deleted from the 5th ed.:

We shall presently need to discuss the causes of the growth of great cities especially in English-speaking countries. On the growth of modern cities generally see Longstaff's *Studies in Statistics* and Levasseur's *La Population Française*, Book II.

PAGE 200

a. So since the 7th ed. (p. 200). In the 1st ed. (p. 254) the subject matter of this paragraph ran as follows:

The death rate of large towns gives no just indication of their effect on the health and vigour of the people, chiefly because many of the town influences which lower vigour, do not appreciably affect mortality. Other reasons are that the immigrants into towns are generally picked lives and in the full strength of youth; and that young people whose parents live in the country generally go home to die. The mortality of females in London between the ages of fifteen and thirty-five is for this reason abnormally low.

These sentences were reworded in the 3rd ed. (p. 281) as follows and remained unaltered until they were replaced by the present paragraph in the 7th ed.:

It is sometimes urged that the death-rate in some large towns, and especially in London, is not as high as might have been anticipated if town life is really injurious to health and vigour. But this argument seems untrustworthy, partly because many of the town influences which lower vigour, do not much affect mortality; and partly because the majority of immigrants into the towns are in the full strength of youth, and of more than average energy and courage; while young people whose parents live in the country generally go home when they become seriously ill.

b. The following paragraph which was inserted in the 3rd ed. (pp. 281–2) after the paragraph ending with the words "seriously ill", was deleted from the 7th ed.:

It is not to be concluded from this that the race is degenerating physically, nor even that its nervous strength is on the whole decaying. On the contrary the opposite is plainly true of those boys and girls who are able to enter freely into modern outdoor amusements, and frequently spend holidays in the country, and whose food, clothing and medical care are abundant, and governed by the best modern knowledge. But until quite recently the children of the working classes in large towns have had a bad time: and it is doubtful whether the recent diminution of their hours of labour, the advances of sanitation and medical science, improvement of their food and clothing, of their education and even in some cases their playgrounds quite makes up for the evils inherent in town life.

c. The following clause and sentences which came after the clause ending with the words "and to take their industries with them"; in the 1st ed. (p. 255) were deleted from the 3rd ed.:

while money spent on reducing the cost of living in large towns by building workmen's houses at a loss or in other ways, is likely to do almost as much harm as good, and sometimes even more. If the numbers of the working classes in the large towns are reduced to those whose work must be carried on there, the scarcity of their labour will enable them to command high wages; and therefore if sanitary laws and rules against overcrowding are rigidly enforced, and space enough is secured to provide opportunities of healthy play for their children, those who live in large towns will have a better chance of leaving a healthy progeny behind them; and meanwhile some check will be given to the migration from the country to the towns.

d. The first sentence of this footnote was inserted in the 4th ed. (p. 279 n.).

e. The following reference attached to the word "population" in the 1st ed. (p. 254 n.) was deleted from the 3rd ed.: "Dr Beddoe on the *Progress of Public Health.*"

f. This paragraph was inserted in the 3rd ed. (p. 282 n.). A reference in the 3rd ed. to "an excellent article by Prof. Clifford Allbutt in the *Contemporary Review,* February 1895" was deleted from the 7th ed.

g. This article is reprinted in *The Memorials of Alfred Marshall.* Edited by A. C. Pigou (pp. 142–51).

PAGE 201

a. So since the 3rd ed. (p. 282) where the two opening sentences of this paragraph replaced the following sentence and clause dating from the 1st ed. (p. 255):

In the earlier stages of civilization natural selection and competition caused those who were strongest and most vigorous to leave the largest progeny behind them. It is to this cause, more than any other, that the progress of the human life, as of all other forms of life, is chiefly due; and though in the later stages of civilization the rule has been for the upper classes to marry late, and in consequence to have fewer children than the working classes, this has been compensated for by the fact...etc.

b. The qualification "great" before "danger" in the 1st ed. was deleted from the 3rd ed.

c. So since the 3rd ed. (p. 283). In the 1st ed. (p. 256) and 2nd ed. (pp. 259–60) the rest of this paragraph ran as follows:

The causes are partly selfish and partly unselfish; and the former probably do less harm than the latter; for perhaps it is best for the world that hard and frivolous people should leave but few descendants of their own type. But many people marry late, and have but few children, in consequence of a desire to secure as good a social position as possible for themselves and their children. This desire contains many elements that fall short of the highest ideals of human aims, and in some cases, a few that are distinctly base; but after all it has been one of the chief factors of progress; and those who are affected by it include many of the best and strongest of the race. Such persons with a high sense of duty, are specially likely to be influenced by the doctrine that large families are injurious to the world and that they can do better for a small than for a large family. We must postpone to a later stage the enquiry how far the real demand for labour is capable of being increased, how far the growth of population involves an increased pressure on the means of subsistence. But looking now only at the side of supply, and considering the causes that determine the supply of vigour, we must affirm with Mr Galton that if the doctrine were to be acted on generally by the upper part of the nation including the great part of the more intelligent and capable artisans, but not the lowest classes, it would cause the race to decay.[1]

[1] It has already been noticed that the celibacy of the religious orders probably did not affect the growth of numbers very much: it gave a particular direction to the forces tending to keep that growth in check, but it probably did not add much to their effects. Its main influence was not on the quantity but on the quality of the population. "Whenever a man or woman was possessed of a gentle nature that fitted him or her to deeds of charity, to meditation, to literature or to art, the social condition of the time was such that they had no refuge elsewhere than in the bosom of the Church. But the Church chose to preach and enact celibacy.... She practised those arts which breeders would use who aimed at creating ferocious, churlish and stupid natures. No wonder that club law prevailed for centuries in Europe." Meanwhile by her persecutions of those who were "the most fearless, truthseeking, and intelligent in their modes of thought and therefore the most suitable parents of a high civilisation, she put a strong check, if not a direct stop to their progeny." (*Hereditary Genius*, p. 356).

PAGE 202

a.   The following sentence dating from the 1st ed. (pp. 257–8) was deleted from the 7th ed.:

And though these evils may be reduced within small compass by those parents who are exceptionally good managers; yet example is always more potent than precept, and habits of prudence will not spread among the people, so long as the natural leaders of the people marry early and have larger families than they can expect to bring up well if they should meet with any considerable misfortunes in their own career.

b. The first two sentences of this footnote date in their present form from the 5th ed. (p. 202 n.), where they replaced the following sentences dating from the 1st ed. (p. 257 n.):

> The extent of the infant mortality that arises from preventable causes may be inferred from the facts that while the annual death-rate of children under five years of age is only about two per cent. in the families of peers and is less than three per cent. for the whole of the upper classes, it is between six and seven per cent. for the whole of England. For the upper classes the expectation of life at birth is 53 years, and at ten years of age it is 52 years: but for the whole of England the expectation of life at birth is only 41 years, while at ten years of age, instead of being lower, it rises to 47 years. (See Mr Humphrey's paper in the *Statistical Journal* for June, 1883).

c. This sentence dates from the 3rd ed. (p. 284 n.).

PAGE 203

a. So since the 5th ed. (p. 204), where this clause replaced the following clause and sentences dating from the 1st ed. (p. 259):

and the rest are much better fed and clothed, and with a few exceptions are stronger than they were. The old English Life Table, based on the figures of the years 1838–54, shows one-half of the males dying before they are 45, and of the females before they are 47, while the New Table, based on the figures of 1871–80, raises these ages to 47 and 52 respectively. The death-rate is much lower than it was in the earlier years of life, though higher in the later years: and of the total number of years added to life by the greater longevity, two-thirds fall within the most important period of 25 to 65 years of age.[1]

[1] See Supplement to the 45th Annual Report of the Registrar General; and Mr Humphrey's paper in the *Statistical Journal* for June 1883. On the comparative length of life in different countries, see Dr Bodio's work already referred to, and Dr Perozzo's *Sulla Classificazione per Età*, &c.

INDUSTRIAL TRAINING

a. Except where otherwise stated the wording of this chapter dates substantially from the 1st edition.

b. In the first two editions this chapter was entitled "The Supply of Labour, Continued. Industrial Training". The present title was adopted from the 3rd edition onwards.

a. The following clause after the word "mother" in the 1st ed. (p. 263) was deleted from the 2nd ed.: "when she does not abdicate it for the sake of dearly bought wages or for more selfish purposes."

b. So since the 2nd ed. (p. 266) where the remainder of this sentence replaced the following sentence dating from the 1st ed. (pp. 263–4):

Wherever any high class industry is localised the habits of mind and body required for it are as is said "in the air": and are in a great measure acquired unconsciously.

c. In the 4th ed. (p. 287 n.) the word "retriever" replaced the word "pointer" dating from the 1st ed. (p. 263 n.).

a. So since the 2nd ed. (pp. 266–7) where this sentence replaced the following sentence in the 1st ed. (p. 264):

In school the faculties are educated and the mind is prepared for the serious work of life.

b. So since the 4th ed. (p. 288) where this sentence replaced the following sentences dating from the 1st ed. (p. 264):

But this suggestion seems to overlook the fact that the advance made during school-time is not nearly so important as the power of future advance which a school education gives. Reading and writing afford the means of that wider intercourse which leads to breadth and elasticity of mind, and which is enabling the working man of to-day to be as capable a citizen as was the country gentleman of last century.

c. This sentence was inserted in the 2nd ed. (p. 267), where it was in the text.

d. So since the 5th ed. (p. 208 n.). The following separate footnote dating from the 1st ed. (p. 264 n.) was deleted from the 4th ed.

> It is true that learning to spell does not educate the faculties to any considerable extent, and that the time spent on it is nearly wasted. If spelling and pronunciation could be brought into harmony in the English language, as they are in most other languages, children would, it has been estimated, be able to read fluently a year earlier than they are now.

No reference to the question of spelling reform (always dear to Marshall's heart) was made in the 4th ed.; but it was restored in its present form in the 5th ed.

PAGE 209

a. This sentence was inserted in the 5th ed. (p. 210). The following passages in the 1st ed. (pp. 265–6) were deleted from the 5th ed.:

Continental systems of technical education give habits of order, assiduity and docility, they store the mind with useful information; and the German system, in particular, has produced a race of men who are better fitted in some respects to do the work required of the middle ranks of industry than any that the world has ever seen. Aided by their knowledge of modern languages German clerks, commercial agents and scientific advisers are supplanting others, in England, on the Continent, in South America and elsewhere. Those of them who have natural resource and can turn the advantages of their position to good account, become the heads of firms, and some of the best business of the world is passing into their hands. They also make excellent administrators under government, and that is a chief reason why business under the control of government compares so much more favourably with that under private management in Germany than in England. But the balance of evidence seems to show that the German system, excellent as it is in many ways, is not in all respects well suited for developing that daring energy and restless enterprise which go to the root of the hardest difficulties. For this purpose the existing English system is already superior in some respects; and its deficiencies, though still great, are rapidly being filled up.[1]

[1] On the whole we may say that at present England is very much behind hand as regards the provision for the commercial as well as the technical education

of the proprietors and principal managers of industrial works; but that, chiefly through the influence of the Science and Art Department of South Kensington, elementary (or lower secondary) scientific and technical education covers a wider area in this than in any other country. Unfortunately however these advantages are prevented from being turned to the best account by the still backward condition of our elementary schools. Compare Sir Bernhard Samuelson's Preface to Mr Montague's excellent summary of the Report of the Commission on Technical Education.

b. In the 1st ed. (p. 265 n.) this footnote was attached to a clause in the text ending with the words "eyes and fingers". (See the fourth line from the top of page 209 in vol. 1 of the present edition.)

c. So since the 5th ed. (p. 210 n.) where the following opening sentence of this footnote in the 1st ed. (p. 266 n.) was deleted:

> See the Report 1884 of the Commissioners on Technical Instruction, vol. 1, pp. 506, 514, also the opinions of Sir Lowthian Bell, Prof. Huxley, Dr Siemens and others in vol. III of the Report, also Scott Russell's *Technical Education*. See also the various publications of the National Association for the Promotion of Technical Education.

PAGE 210

a. So since the 7th ed. (p. 210 n.) where this sentence replaced a similar sentence in the 5th ed. (p. 210 n.) referring to "thirty" years ago and not containing the words in parentheses. In the first four editions this sentence ran as follows:

> The present writer introduced this plan several years ago at University College, Bristol, and it has also been adopted in Japan. (See the Report above quoted, vol. III, p. 140.)

The reference to "the Report above quoted" applies to the Report of the Commissioners on Technical Instruction, 1884.

b. The following reference in the 1st ed. (p. 267 n.) was deleted from the 2nd ed.: "An excellent study of apprenticeship in relation to the problem of new countries is contained in the *Report of the New York Bureau of Statistics of Labour* for 1886."

c. The following sentence in the 1st ed. (p. 268) was deleted from the 2nd ed.:

For those who cannot afford to venture on costly experiments themselves may if they will, read the record of every important new departure that is made in their businesses in any part of the world. But of this more hereafter.

PAGE 211

a. The following footnote in the 1st ed. (p. 268 n.) was deleted from the 4th ed.: "The splendid Massachusetts Institute of Technology is under the direction of the economist, General Walker."

b.   The following sentences in the 1st ed. (p. 269) were deleted from the 2nd ed.:

But yet the English retain the first position in the alkali industries, the leading idea in the aniline trade was due to an Englishman, and so are the most important chemico-mechanical inventions in the manufactures of steel. Adding to the above the mechanical inventions of Armstrong, Nasmyth and Lister, and the electrical work of Cooke, Wheatstone, Thomson and others, it is perhaps not too much to say that more than half of the prominent new industrial departures even of recent times are due to our countrymen.

c.   The following sentences in the 1st ed. (p. 269) were deleted from the 2nd ed.:

It may indeed be granted that some advocates of a great extension of general and technical education have injured their cause by exaggerating the direct and immediate benefits which the ordinary workman would derive from it. It is true that at present only a comparatively small number of the ordinary workmen in the country are called on to go beyond their explicit instructions, and to bring a knowledge of mechanics, of chemistry, or of physics to bear on the tasks which they have in hand. And although this number is steadily and rapidly increasing, in consequence of the growing complexity of the appliances of ordinary life, as well as of agricultural and manufacturing industries; yet it must be admitted that the chief benefits which the ordinary workman derives even now from a good education are indirect.

PAGE 213

a.   This paragraph was inserted in the 2nd ed. (p. 273).

b.   The words "frivolities of" before the word "fashion" in the 1st ed. (p. 272) were deleted from the 2nd ed.

PAGE 215

a.   The following opening sentence of this paragraph in the 1st ed. (p. 273) was deleted from the 2nd ed.:

The profession of the designer has not yet risen to the best position which it seems capable of holding even under modern conditions; as is shewn by the fact that Paris, which does not hold altogether the first rank in the highest walks of art, is supreme in the skill required for designing.

b. This and the next sentence were inserted in the 5th ed. (pp. 215–16).

c. The following concluding sentences of this paragraph in the 1st ed. (p. 275) were deleted from the 2nd ed.:

Thus the artistic education of the lower grades of industry is necessary for its own sake, and because it raises the tone of all branches of manufacture by increasing the demand for art products. But its chief economic value is indirect, and arises from its counteracting the tendency of machinery to narrow the sources of supply of artistic genius.

d. The following sentence dating from the 1st ed. (p. 274) was deleted from the 2nd ed., while the succeeding paragraph and sentence were deleted from the 4th ed.:

Meanwhile in England we are giving more attention to artistic design; there are signs that its rapid improvement during the present generation will be continued during the next; and that it will continue to become purer in tone and stronger in conception.

It is probably true, though opinion is still somewhat divided on the subject, that schools of artistic design are not so urgently needed in England, as a more efficient and cheaper system of popular education in art proper. For in this respect, perhaps more than any other, the child of the English workman has less opportunities than his continental rivals, and especially those of France. If we could secure that all who have a natural turn for it should receive a fairly good education in art proper, the applications of art to design and decoration might perhaps be left pretty much to take care of themselves.

The highest branches of art escape many of the disadvantages under which artistic design labours. He who designs a picture executes it with his own hands; there is not in painting nor even in sculpture that divorce between design and technical familiarity with the material, which is so great an obstacle to the progress of our metal and wood work.

e. This and the next sentence were inserted in the 2nd ed. (p. 275 n.).

PAGE 216

a. The following sentences in the 1st ed. (p. 276) were deleted from the 2nd ed.:

A slave owner or a dog trainer expects himself to reap the full pecuniary value of any education he bestows on his charge; and in a primitive society in which the family is held together by strong and lasting bonds of custom, the father derives nearly as much gain in a direct material form from anything that increases the efficiency of his sons, as from anything that increases his own. But in modern life it is otherwise. Those who bear the expense of a child's education do not as a rule reap, in a direct material form, any considerable part of the benefits which will arise from it.

b. The following concluding sentences of this paragraph in the 1st ed. (pp. 274–5) were deleted from the 2nd ed.:

But even as it is, the total supply of genius of a high order among the ranks of our artists is not small. In some directions there is marked originality, as for instance in landscape painting, especially in water colours: while the development of wood engraving is a good example of the growth of new industries which educate the higher artistic faculties of artisans.

PAGE 217

a. The following paragraphs in the 1st ed. (pp. 276–8) were deleted from the 2nd ed.:

But there it is highly developed; the heroic sacrifices which some middle-class parents make for the sake of their children's education are instances of the latent romance of modern life. And as we shall see later on, the income that can be secured by a good education, when it is bestowed on children who have not more than an average share of natural vigour, does not bear a very high ratio to the expenses incurred in it. In other words the pecuniary advantages of a high class education are discounted at a moderate rate of interest; the supply price of ordinary educated ability in the middle and upper ranks, that is the price that is required to call forth a full supply of it, is calculated at a moderate rate of interest on the expenditure that was incurred for it a long time before.

But it is different with the less educated classes. Many of these were made to contribute to the income of their parents at an age much below that up to which the law now compels them to keep their children at school; and their affection, strong though it may be, seldom suggests that they should go far beyond the requirements of the law. Thus in the lower ranks of industry the advantages that are to be got by the child in after years in consequence of the expense incurred by its parents now, are discounted at a high rate of interest: the supply price of educated ability of the lower grades is calculated at a high rate of interest on the expense necessary to obtain it.

In consequence however of the great growth of wealth relatively to population, and of the mental and moral improvement of the age, there is a rapid fall in the rate of interest at which the future benefits to be got by expenditure on education are generally discounted. High as it is for the lower classes, it is not as high as it was; and low as it has been for the upper and middle-classes it is now becoming rapidly lower.

But these obstacles to movement of labour from any one grade to other grades above it, do not hinder movement between two occupations in one grade: they hinder vertical movement, but not horizontal. For indeed the industrial classes may be regarded as so many horizontal strata. All the occupations in any one stratum require on the part of those of ordinary ability about an equally expensive education and equally difficult preparation; so that in the absence of special circumstances the supply price for them all is equal. It is indeed true that when a person has once chosen his occupation he is more likely to move vertically than horizontally; he is more likely to rise to a higher grade in his own line of business than to pass to another line of business in his own grade. But most people stay in that grade in which they are placed by their parents, and that is generally the grade in which the parents themselves are.

b. The sentences in this paragraph and the first three sentences in the succeeding paragraph formed part of a long summary of Book IV, chs. IV, V and VI, in the 1st ed., the deleted portions of which are reproduced in editorial note **b** to page 218 of vol. I in the present edition.

c. At this point in the 1st ed. (p. 279) there was a brief discussion and definition of the term "net advantages" which was deleted from the 2nd ed., where the passage in question were transferred, without any significant change, to Book II, ch. V, §2 (in vol. I of the present edition, Book II, ch. IV, §2).

PAGE 218

a. The remainder of this paragraph dates from the 5th ed. (p. 218).

b. The following summary in the 1st ed. (pp. 279–81) was deleted from the 2nd ed.:

We may now sum up the results of this and the preceding two chapters. A temperate climate keeps the length of a generation fairly long, and generally prevents both birth-rate and death-rate from being very high. It is favourable to vigour and the power of sustained exertion; but it causes a great part of the energies of the people to be spent in providing the necessaries of life: and thus seldom allows much intellectual achievement till after a good deal of material progress has been made.

The habits of the people both as to their marriage and in their marriage, affect birth-rate directly and death-rate indirectly. The chief causes by which these habits are influenced are climate, religious and social sanctions, the excess of their own incomes over what their habits and "standard of comfort" lead them to regard as needful for their subsistence and their expectation of being able to start their children in life easily. Children are hardly any burden when they can add at an early age to the family income, whether in money as in a factory town, or in kind as on the farms of a new country. But when the mode of living is such that parents have to furnish their children with a capital large in proportion to their own means, then every additional child involves a great strain on the resources of the family. Among peasant proprietors this cause combined with the preference which is given to heiresses tends to keep the families gener-

313

ally small. On the other hand the vigour that works its way up into the middle classes in England, assists the prevailing social habits of the class in preventing the families from being very small in spite of the fact that their marriage age is kept late by the great expense of educating a family. The social sanctions, and in some cases the religious sanctions which affect the age of marriage are in a great measure the abstract of the experience of the people as to their power of supporting increased numbers; and these sanctions often out-last the conditions in which they had their origin. But on the whole the average size of families in any place or rank of life is very much under the influence of economic causes, and dependent on the incomes of the people present and prospective. This dependence is however complex, and changes its character with circumstances: a rise in the incomes of any class cannot be relied on to cause an increase in the average size of their families; indeed it may have the opposite effect if it leads them to adopt more artificial modes of living.

But an increase of incomes always acts directly in diminishing the death-rate and increasing the vigour and efficiency of the present and the rising generation. It is true that the increased income may be obtained at the expense of moving into towns and adopting sedentary pursuits; and the want of fresh air and light and joyous play may injure health and vigour. But, other things being equal, an increase of income, except in the case of those who are already rich, increases the bodily and mental strength of those who earn it, and of their children: it lowers the death-rate, it lengthens life, it shortens the time of sickness, and thus it increases the number of people at work, the time during which they are in full work and their efficiency when at work. It is no exception to this rule that when a nominal increase of income is got by a mother's going out to work to the neglect of her children and of her household affairs, the result is to injure their health and vigour; for in substituting less important gains for more important she has really diminished the income of the family.

Again it must always be remembered that the growth of material wealth, the increase of the demand price for labour of all grades, is only one of many causes that affect the supply of labour as regards both numbers and vigour; for its action is modified by changes in knowledge, in the habits of married life, and in the modes of expenditure. Better housekeeping, greater temperance in the use of alcohol and other luxuries, and less desire for social display would enable parents to do better for their families with their present incomes; and again, the labour-supporting power of a given national income would be very much increased by its more even distribution, if this were effected by causes that did not impair security and discourage energy and thrift. In every way the moral and mental strength of the rising generation depends on the character of the mothers of that generation; it is raised by everything that enables women to develop their highest intellectual faculties truly and womanfully. But since moral and mental strength rest in a great measure on a physical basis of nervous strength, it is a scarcely less important condition that the children should be well nurtured; and this requires that the mother should be a skilled housewife and nurse, and that the material resources of the household should not be insufficient.

The decadence of the old apprenticeship system, the growing rapidity of industrial and social change, the increasing use of machinery, and the ever widening range of science and the arts of production, all these causes combine to increase the urgency of improvement in our systems of education both general and technical. This is all the more important because the social and industrial changes of our time are blocking up some of the old paths by which lads of great natural ability might rise to distinction in spite of the poverty of their parents. The poverty of parents is a great obstacle to their giving their children a start in life very different from their own: for independently of the material difficulties in their way, the narrowness of their lives makes it difficult for them to realize vividly the distant future, and to go out of their way to make provision for it.

Speaking generally the rate of interest at which parents discount future benefits for their children is governed by their affection and unselfishness; but this being given it falls with every increase of their material means and of their general enlightenment.

   c. This paragraph was inserted in the 5th ed. (p. 219 n.).

PAGE 219

   a. This paragraph was inserted in the 6th ed. (p. 219).

BOOK IV, CHAPTER VII

THE GROWTH OF WEALTH

PAGE 220

   a. Except where otherwise stated the wording of this chapter dates substantially from the 1st edition.

   b. The title of this chapter remained unaltered from the 1st ed.

   c. This paragraph was inserted in the 4th ed. (p. 300).

PAGE 221

   a. In the 4th ed. (p. 301) the word "some" replaced the word "many", dating from the 1st ed. (p. 285).

PAGE 223

   a. So since the 5th ed. (p. 223) where "fifteen" replaced "ten" dating from the 1st ed. (p. 286).

   b. So since the 5th ed. In the 1st ed. (pp. 286–7) this clause ran as follows:

while a capital of £700,000,000 invested in Railways in England and Wales is (even after deducting the cost of the land and the artificial legal and parliamentary expenses which have been heaped on them) equivalent to the work for more than thirty years of the 140,000 people employed on them.

In the 2nd ed. (p. 283) the figure of "£700,000,000" was changed to £900,000,000"; the words in parentheses were deleted; "more than thirty years" became "perhaps twenty years"; and the figure "140,000" was changed to "400,000". In the 3rd ed. (p. 305)

"£900,000,000" became "£1,000,000,000" and the word "wage-earners" replaced the earlier word "people".

c. The following footnote dating from the 2nd ed. (p. 283 n.) attached to the sentence ending with the word "them" was deleted from the 3rd ed.:

> The number of persons employed on the Railways of the United Kingdom in 1884 is shown by a Parliamentary Return to be 367,793. The numbers given in the Industrial Census of 1881 are much less, and indeed altogether untrustworthy.

PAGE 224

a. The following paragraphs in the 1st ed. (pp. 288–90) were deleted from the 2nd ed.:

Thus we see that till recently land was the only very important kind of wealth from which its owner looked to derive a revenue. He laboured hard to make things, or he stinted his consumption in the present in order to save things, or he engaged in public or private war to appropriate things, which it would be pleasant for him to have, and which would afford him immediate gratification; but the whole auxiliary capital in the world was small if we except the land; and was very small if in addition we except the live stock on it. If a person were in doubt whether he would give up a present pleasure or undergo an extra fatigue in order that he might get a better house, or better clothes, or richer ornaments, he had to weigh in the balance the pleasures of the present against those of the future; and human nature being what it is, he probably seldom preferred the future pleasures to the present unless he expected them to be much greater. But that is all we can say: there was generally no exact money measure of what he gave up on the one hand, and what he obtained in exchange for it on the other. Gradually the habit of making commodities for sale increased, and the amount of auxiliary capital used in production increased too; and with this double change people got into the way of making their calculations as to the gains of saving in an arithmetical form. When a prince wanted to forestall some of his future revenues he borrowed perhaps a thousand ounces of silver and undertook to pay back fifteen hundred at the end of a year: there was however no perfect security that he would fulfil the promise; and perhaps the lender would have been willing to exchange that promise for an absolute certainty of receiving thirteen hundred at the end of the year. In that case the nominal rate of interest would be fifty per cent., and the real rate thirty. This habit once started, the same sort of calculation would be made if the loan were arranged in terms of miscellaneous goods; those lent and those returned would be reduced to a common measure in terms of silver, and the rate of interest calculated out.

This change in the form of the income derived from wealth has been accompanied by the development of an organized market for the loan of capital, or as it is commonly called the money-market. The funds available for loan at any one time are rapidly increasing with the growth of wealth and the prevalence of subtler forms of business organization. But they are even yet small in comparison with the value of land, buildings, and other old-fashioned forms of wealth.

PAGE 225

a.   This footnote was inserted in the 2nd ed. (p. 285 n.).

PAGE 226

a.   In the 5th ed. (p. 226) the words "last century" replaced the words "the century" dating from the 1st ed. (p. 292).
b.   This clause was inserted in the 2nd ed. (p. 286).

PAGE 227

a.   This paragraph with the footnote attached to it was inserted in the 2nd ed. (p. 287).

PAGE 230

a.   In the second edition (pp. 290–3) this section was largely expanded.
Except where otherwise stated the wording of this section (§8) dates from the 2nd ed.

PAGE 231

a.   The remainder of this paragraph dates substantially from the 1st ed. (p. 296) where it was preceded by the following paragraph and sentences which were deleted (except the last sentence) from the 2nd ed.:

There is another point on which the doctrines of the older economists were expressed with too much sharpness. Founding themselves on the just observation that a fall in the rate of interest (or, as they said, of profits) is often an indication of diminishing prosperity[1], and that it always diminishes the reward of saving, they went over-hastily to the conclusion that a considerable fall in that rate would diminish the reward of saving so much that scarcely any one would care to save: they were sure that a high rate of interest (or profits) was essential to a rapid accumulation. This conclusion has not been completely borne out by subsequent experience; and it seems to be founded on a faulty analysis.

It is no doubt true that when a future pleasure (or relief from pain) is preferred to a present, the reason is that the latter is expected to be greater. But this result may be brought about in either of two ways; it may be due to the expectation of an increase in the material source of the pleasure (such as is represented by a high rate of interest); or it may be due simply to the expectation that the need at the later time will be more urgent than at the present. When a person puts away eggs for the winter he does not expect that they will be better flavoured then than now; he expects that they will be scarce, and that therefore their utility will be higher than now.

[1] How untrustworthy an indication it is we shall see later on.

It may be noted that the last sentence beginning with the words "When a person puts away eggs for the winter..." was transferred in the 2nd ed. to a footnote in Book III, ch. v, §4 (p. 179 n.). See page 121 n. in vol. 1 of the present edition.

PAGE 232

a. In the 1st ed. (pp. 615–16) the main substance of this and the succeeding paragraph was contained in Book VII, ch. vii, §4. See the Editorial Appendix to Book VI, ch. vi of vol. 1 in the present edition (p. 644 below).

b. The following footnote in the 3rd ed. (p. 314 n.) was deleted from the 4th ed.:

> A Producer's Surplus or Rent is yielded by those writings which need little or no reward, but are yet rewarded at the market rate, as it is by labour in a like case. See above, p. 217. But we must return to this point.

The reference in this footnote to "p. 217" applies to Book IV, ch. 1, §2, pages 140 n.–141 n., in vol. 1 of the present edition.

c. This footnote dates substantially from the 1st ed. (p. 616 n.).

PAGE 233

a. This sentence was inserted in the 5th ed. (p. 233).

b. This sentence was inserted in the 5th ed. (p. 233).

c. In the 1st ed. (pp. 613–14) the main substance of this paragraph was contained in Book VII, ch. VII, §3. See the editorial appendix to Book VI, ch. VI of vol. I in the present edition, pp. 642–3 below.

d. This sentence dates from the 2nd ed. (Book VI, ch. VI, §1, p. 615 n.).

PAGE 234

a. So since the 2nd ed. (p. 294) where the remainder of this sentence replaced the following clauses in the 1st ed. (p. 297 n.): "the less will be the future usance of the wealth accumulated by each day's work: and this will no doubt tend to prevent them from increasing the size of their cottages."

b. This paragraph was inserted in the 2nd ed. (p. 294).

PAGE 235

a. This paragraph dates from the 2nd ed. (p. 295).

b. This footnote was inserted in the 4th ed. (p. 315 n.).

PAGE 236

a. This paragraph dates substantially from the 2nd ed. (p. 295).

PAGE 237

a. In the 1st ed. (p. 298 n.) this subject was treated in a fairly short footnote, but in the 2nd ed. (pp. 296–8) this was much expanded and became the *Note on the Statistics of the Growth of Wealth* at the end of Book IV, ch. VII. The origins of the subject-matter of this Note are shown throughout in the editorial notes.

b. This paragraph dates substantially from the footnote in the 1st ed. (p. 298 n.) just referred to, except for the omission from the 2nd ed. (p. 296) of the following reference: "(see in particular, General Walker's remarks on *The Statistics of Capital invested in manufactures* in the Report of the Tenth Census, Vol. II)." The remaining sentences of this footnote in the 1st ed. ran as follows:

They indicate that the wealth per head rose from 187 dollars in 1790 to 220 dollars in 1840, and 870 dollars in 1880. Of this last sum about a quarter is set down to the value of agricultural land, about one half to real property of other kinds and fixed capital, while of the remaining quarter about one half is put to the account of household furniture, &c. Relying chiefly on the history of the death duties, M. de Flaix recently estimated that the wealth per head in France had increased about fourfold during the last hundred years. Mr Giffen in a memorable paper on the growth of capital calculated, chiefly on the basis of income tax returns, that the wealth of the United Kingdom rose from £6,013,000,000 in 1865 to £8,548,000,000 in 1875, but much of this rise was merely nominal and due to estimates of profits which were not justified by subsequent events. An instructive history of changes in the relative wealth of different parts of England has been deduced by Prof. Rogers from the assessment "of the several counties for the purposes of taxation".

The first four of the foregoing sentences were deleted from the 2nd ed., while the last sentence was retained in this Note.

c. This and the next paragraph and the first two sentences of the succeeding paragraph, date from the 2nd ed. (pp. 296–7).

PAGE 238

a. The following clause at the end of this sentence, dating from the 2nd ed. (p. 297), was deleted from the 4th ed.: "and the free trade which has enriched the people has checked the rise in the value of that part of the land which is devoted to agriculture."

b. So since the 4th ed. (pp. 317–18) where the remaining sentences of this paragraph replaced the following sentences dating from the 3rd ed. (p. 319):

Thus various causes, of which her free trade policy is the chief, have made the general purchasing power of money rise in England relatively to the continent. Early in this century 25 fr. would buy more, and especially more of the things needed by the working classes, in France than £1 would in England. But now the advantage is the other way: and even if it were true (as Mr Harris argues by methods otherwise open to criticism in the *Statistical Journal*, Vol. 57) that the money wealth of France is rising faster than that of England, it might yet be true that the real wealth of England is rising faster than that of France.

c. The wording of this paragraph dates from the 2nd ed. (p. 297).

d. The following concluding clauses of this sentence after the word "accurate", in the 2nd ed., were deleted from the 3rd ed.: "and the general purchasing power of money remained always the same: and neither of these two conditions is approximately fulfilled."

e. This and the next paragraph date from the 5th ed. (pp. 238–9). In the 2nd ed. there were the following sentences before the statistical table, and before the paragraph immediately after the table, which were deleted from the 3rd ed.:

The following table is compiled chiefly from data collected by Mr Giffen in his excellent *Growth of Capital*; and arranged so as to show the values of land, houses, farmstock and other forms of wealth in different countries, and in England at different times. It must however be premised that the term farm-capital is not always used in the same sense: it is used broadly in England and narrowly in the United States. Also it should be noted that that part of the value of houses &c., which is really the value of the land on which they are built, increases with the density of population, and especially with the growth of large cities. Thus for instance in the United States it is already considerable, and is rapidly growing.

[Table]

There is some interest in comparing the growth of wealth and population in England during the last 300 years and in the United States during the last 100. Making use of Mr Giffen's survey of contemporary estimates, we may take the following pairs of figures as giving approximately the number of millions in the population of England, and the number of £ in the property per head: A.D. 1600, 4½, £22; 1700, 5¾, £60; 1750, 7, £70; 1800, 9, £167; 1850, 18 [£180?]; 1885, 27½, £315. And from the census for the United States, we get similarly A.D. 1790, 3·9, £37; 1800, 5·3, £40; 1810, 7·2, £42; 1820, 9·6, £39; 1830, 12·8, £42; 1840, 17·0, £44; 1850, 23·2, £62; 1860, 31·5, £102; 1870, 38·5, £156; 1880, 50·1, £165. (These estimates of wealth up to 1830 are private; afterwards official.) It may be noted that in 1880 the railways of the United States were a little over £100,000,000 in value, while those of the United Kingdom were somewhat less: and that the value of household furniture, &c., is put at £1,000,000,000 for the former and £700,000,000 for the latter. In 1800 Beeke had estimated furniture, &c. (including plate and jewels, which were relatively more important then than now) at £210,000,000; and in 1812 Colquhoun put them at £250,000,000.

f.   This table dates from the 2nd ed. (p. 298), with the exception of the estimate of Chiozza Money for the United Kingdom for 1905, and of the census figures for the U.S.A. for 1900, both of which were inserted in the 5th ed. (p. 238).

PAGE 239

a. So since the 5th ed. (p. 239) where the word "tentative" replaced the word "instructive" in this sentence, which otherwise dates dating from the 1st ed. (p. 298 n.).

b. The rest of this paragraph dates from the 3rd ed. (p. 320), (except that a reference there to the translation of a paper by de Foville in the *Statistical Journal*, vol. 56, was deleted from the 4th ed.), where it replaced the following reference in the 2nd ed. (p. 298):

> Some interesting details of the growth of wealth in France, collected by M. Neymarck, have recently been published in England in the *Statistical Journal*.

c. This paragraph was inserted in the 8th edition (page 239).

BOOK IV, CHAPTER VIII

INDUSTRIAL ORGANIZATION

PAGE 240

a. Except where otherwise stated the wording of this chapter dates substantially from the 1st edition.

b. The title of this chapter remained unchanged since the 1st edition.

c. The words "and vegetable" were added after "animal" in the 3rd ed. (p. 321); and the last clause of this sentence was also inserted in that edition.

PAGE 241

a. So since the 2nd ed. (p. 300). In the 1st ed. (p. 301) the remainder of this sentence ran as follows: "is as yet but partly thought out and imperfectly established, so far as its minor details go, both in biology and in social science."

b. In the 2nd ed. the following final clause of this sentence in the 1st ed. (p. 301) was deleted: "or, to use a more familiar phrase, that a demand for any economic arrangement will soon create a supply of it."

c. So since the 6th ed. (p. 241) where the following additional references in the earlier editions were deleted: "The writings of Herbert Spencer on this subject. Bagehot's *Physics and Politics*, Hearn's *Plutology*."

a. In the 3rd ed. (p. 323) the following final clause of this sentence dating from the 1st ed. (p. 302) was deleted: "not those which are best fitted to benefit the environment, except in so far as, by benefiting it, they may increase the support which they derive from it."

b. This sentence dates substantially from the 3rd ed. (p. 323) where it replaced the following sentence dating from the 1st ed. (p. 302):

This seems a hard fact: but some of its harshest features are softened down by the principle of heredity; which causes those races to flourish in their environment the members of which render unrequited services to other members.

a. This sentence was inserted in the 3rd ed. (p. 325) where it replaced the following clause at the end of the preceding sentence, dating from the 1st ed. (pp. 303–4): "for it may do so by having merely the parasite power of turning the peculiarities of that race to good account for its own purposes."

b. So since the 3rd ed. (p. 325) where this sentence replaced the following sentence dating from the 1st ed. (p. 304):

But such classes are exceptional: and on the whole heredity softens the harshest features of the struggle for existence among the races of men; and causes those races to survive and predominate in which the best qualities are most strongly developed.

a. So since the 6th ed. (p. 246), where the following sentences dating from the 1st ed. (p. 306) were deleted:

They were not contented with insisting that the new industrial organization was spreading rapidly and obtaining victories over its rivals in every direction, and that this very fact proved that it met a want of the times, and had a good balance of advantages over disadvantages. But they went further and applied the same argument to all its details; not perceiving that the very strength of the system as a whole enabled it to carry along with it many incidents which were in themselves evil. For a while they fascinated the world by their romantic accounts of the flawless proportions of that "natural" organization of industry which had grown from the rudimentary germ of self-interest; each man selecting his daily work with the sole view of getting for it the best pay he could, but with the inevitable result of choosing that in which he could be of most service to others.

b. So since the 6th ed. (p. 246) where the first two sentences of this paragraph replaced the following sentences dating from the 1st ed. (pp. 306–7):

They were right in contending that these were important truths which could not be properly understood without a much more careful study than was given to them by those ready writers who, then as now, attained an easy popularity by indiscriminate attacks on the existing state of society. But their own defence of it, though more intelligent, was almost equally open to the charge of partisan bias.

c. This footnote dates in its present form from the 7th ed. (p. 246 n.) where it replaced the following footnote dating from the 1st ed. (p. 306 n.):

Reference has already been made (Book I, ch. IV, §3) to the inaccurate use of the term *Smithianismus* in Germany.

The reference to Book I, ch. IV, §3 in the 1st ed. relates to Appendix B, §3, page 758 n. in vol. 1 of the present edition.

PAGE 247

a. This sentence was inserted in the 6th ed. (p. 247).

b. So since the 6th ed. (p. 247) where the opening words of this sentence in the text replaced the following words dating from the 1st ed. (p. 307):

Mr Herbert Spencer has done more than any one else to establish the truth and the significance of the law that if any physical or mental exercise...etc.

c. The word "rule" replaced the earlier word "law" from the 6th ed.

d. The following opening clauses of this sentence dating from the 1st ed. (p. 308) were deleted from the 6th ed.:

The physical superiority of the English race over all others that have lived as largely as we are doing a town life, is due to a great extent to the games in which our youth exercises its physical faculties for the sake of exercising them:

e. This paragraph was inserted in the 3rd ed. (p. 329); but the present wording of the opening part of the second sentence was not adopted until the 7th ed. (pp. 247–8) where it took the place of the earlier wording which ran as follows: "But there seems no good reason for doubting that the children of those who have led healthy lives... etc."

f. The following opening sentences of this footnote dating from the 1st ed. (p. 307 n.) were deleted from the 3rd ed.:

> The giraffe whose long neck enables it to survive by feeding on the shoots of trees when the grass is dried up, may possibly lengthen its neck yet further by constantly stretching it, and thus further increase its power of surviving; but this effect is not purposely sought. Again, the tendency for all peculiarities of this sort to increase their rate of growth as time goes on, within certain limits, is allowed to work itself out unopposed (unless by sexual selection) in the animal kingdom. The longer, within certain limits, a giraffe's neck is, and the more exclusively he feeds on the shoots of trees, the more will his chance of survival depend on the length of his neck; and the greater will be the force which the struggle for survival will exert in tending to accelerate that growth (see Note XI in the Mathematical Appendix).

The illustration of the giraffe's neck was retained in Note XI in the Mathematical Appendix until the 3rd ed. where it was deleted. See editorial note **f** to Note XI in the Mathematical Appendix (p. 834 below).

PAGE 248

a. The following footnote attached to the word "case" in the 3rd ed. (p. 329 n.) was deleted from the 4th ed.:

> On these grounds we may admit the embryological doctrines on which Mr Kidd bases so large a part of his doctrine of social evolution, and yet decline to accept his conclusions.

b. This paragraph was inserted in the 6th ed. (pp. 248–9).

c. The remaining sentences of this footnote were inserted in the 7th ed. (p. 248 n.).

PAGE 249

a. The opening words of this sentence from "Progress" to "point of view" were inserted in the 6th ed. (p. 249).

b. The following words in the 1st ed. (p. 308) preceding the word "changes" were deleted from the 4th ed.: "In harmony with the results of our inquiries as to the supply of labour we may conclude that."

c. The following concluding sentences of this chapter in the 1st ed. (p. 309) coming after the sentence ending with the word "distribution" were deleted from the 3rd ed., with the exception of the clause beginning with the words "but a final judgment" which was deleted from the 5th ed.:

Such are the considerations which we must have in our minds when examining the present forms of the organization of industry, and the part which they play in governing the supply of material wealth: but a final judgment as to their good and evil effects must be deferred until we are able to take a broader survey. Many important elements of the problem, in particular those connected with the fluctuations of trade, and the inconstancy of employment, depending as they do upon the influence of foreign competition, and of changes in the money market, lie beyond the sphere of those elementary inquiries as to the methods of production which we are to make in the following chapters.

d. The remainder of this sentence was inserted in the 3rd ed. (p. 330).

e. The following concluding paragraph of this chapter, dating from the 4th ed. (p. 328) was deleted from the 6th ed.:

We may then proceed to study provisionally the present forms of the organization of industry, and the part which they play in governing the supply of material wealth.

BOOK IV, CHAPTER IX

INDUSTRIAL ORGANIZATION, CONTINUED. DIVISION OF LABOUR. THE INFLUENCE OF MACHINERY

PAGE 250

a. Except where otherwise stated, the wording of this chapter dates substantially from the 1st edition.

b. The title of this chapter remained unchanged since the 1st edition.

PAGE 253

a. So since the 3rd ed. (pp. 334 n.–335 n.) where this concluding sentence of the footnote replaced the following sentences dating from the 1st ed. (p. 314 n.):

(See Miss Beatrice Potter's article on "East London Labour" in *The Nineteenth Century* for August, 1888). Very much the same account may be given of the present condition of the boot trade; in very large American boot factories, more than ninety distinct classes of workers are already recognized. (See the *Report of the New York Bureau of Statistics of Labour* for 1886.)

PAGE 255

a. So since the 3rd ed. (p. 336 n.) where the first three sentences of this footnote replaced the following sentences dating from the 1st ed. (p. 315 n.).

For instance, one great inventor is rumoured to have spent £300,000 on experiments relating to textile machinery; and his outlay is said to have been abundantly returned to him. No doubt some of his inventions were of such a kind as can be made only by a man of genius; and however great the need, they must have waited till the right man was found for them. It is said that he charged not unreasonably £1000 as royalty for each of his combing machines, and I have been told by a worsted manufacturer that, being full of work, he found it worth his while to buy an additional machine, and pay this extra charge for it, only six months before the expiry of the patent.

PAGE 257

a. So since the 5th ed. (p. 257) where the last sentence of this footnote replaced the following sentence, dating from the 1st ed. (p. 318 n.): "There is a good account of it by Mr Trowbridge in vol. II of the Report of the tenth census for United States."

PAGE 261

a. The following sentence in the 1st ed. (p. 322) was deleted from the 6th ed.: "When the machinery has been got ready, one man can manage it entirely and it will print off 12,000 copies in an hour."

b. This paragraph was inserted in the 6th ed. (p. 261).

PAGE 262

a. In the 1st ed. (p. 316) this and the next paragraph were placed in §3 of this chapter. They were transferred to §6 in the 2nd ed. (pp. 321–2).

b. The first sentence of this footnote dates in its present form from the 6th ed. (p. 262 n.) where it replaced the following sentences, dating from the 1st ed. (p. 323 n.):

The jack-plane, used for making smooth large boards for floors and other purposes, was the worst enemy of the carpenter. All but specially skilled men were compelled to spend a great part of their time with the jack-plane, and this brought on heart disease, making them as a rule old men by the time they were forty. But now those who become prematurely old through overwork, are to be found almost exclusively among the professional classes, among those engaged in the more anxious kinds of business, and in some agricultural districts in which the rate of wages is still very low and the people are habitually underfed.

NOTES TO BOOK IV CHAPTER IX

a. So since the 5th ed. (p. 263) where this sentence replaced the following sentence dating from the 1st ed. (p. 324):

The social surroundings in the factory and out of it stimulate mental activity; and even those workers in it whose occupations are seemingly the most monotonous have much more intelligence and mental resource than has been shown by the English agricultural labourer whose employment has more variety.

a. The first two clauses of this sentence were inserted in the 2nd ed. (p. 323).

b. In the 1st ed. (p. 324) there was the following clause after the word "machines": "and the English agricultural labourer is following in his steps and is steadily improving his position." In the 2nd ed. (p. 323) this clause became a fresh sentence as follows: "The English agricultural labourer has had many great disadvantages to contend with; but is steadily improving his position." In the 5th ed. (p. 264) the second clause of this sentence was deleted and the remaining sentences of this paragraph were inserted.

a. So since the 2nd ed. (p. 325). In the 1st ed. (pp. 326–7) this paragraph ran as follows:

Many of those economies in the use of specialized skill and machinery which are commonly regarded as within the reach of very large establishments, can be secured in a great measure by the concentration of many small businesses of a similar character in particular localities: or, as is commonly said, by the localization of industry. This subject has such important bearings on much of our future work, that it will be worth while to study it with some care.

a. This paragraph dates from the 2nd ed. (p. 325).

BOOK IV, CHAPTER X

INDUSTRIAL ORGANIZATION, CONTINUED. THE CONCENTRATION OF SPECIALIZED INDUSTRIES IN PARTICULAR LOCALITIES

PAGE 267

a. Except where otherwise stated the wording of this chapter dates substantially from the 1st edition.

b. The title of this chapter remained unchanged since the 1st edition.

c. So since the 4th ed. (p. 346), where the beginning of this sentence replaced the following words dating from the 1st ed. (p. 328): "But the slowness with which customs changed, made it easier for producers...etc."

d. So since the 3rd ed. (p. 348 n.) where this clause replaced the following clause dating from the 1st ed. (p. 328 n.): "and others having travelled by land to the Hanse towns and thence by sea to England."

PAGE 268

a. The words "though perhaps not quite accurately" were inserted in the 3rd ed. (p. 349).

b. This paragraph was inserted in the 3rd ed. (p. 349 n.).

PAGE 269

a. The following footnote attached to the word "chairmaking" in the 1st ed. (p. 330 n.) was deleted from the 2nd ed.:

> A good account of the localized handicrafts in the South Midland agricultural districts is given in the Companion to the British Almanac for 1861.

b. The following footnote in the 1st ed. attached to the word "time" (p. 330 n.) was deleted from the 2nd ed.:

> Smiles' *Life of Nasmyth*, p. 207.

PAGE 270

a. So since the 7th ed. (p. 270), where the present sentence replaced the following sentence dating from the 1st ed. (p. 332):

330

The causes which determine the economic progress of nations will require further study when we come to discuss the problems of international trade.

The following footnote attached to the last word of this sentence in 1st ed. (p. 332 n.) was deleted from the 4th ed.:

> Meanwhile attention may be drawn to an article on "The Migration of Centres of Industrial Energy" by Mr Courtney in the *Fortnightly Review* for December 1878.

PAGE 271

a. This clause was inserted in the 7th ed. (p. 271).

PAGE 272

a. So since the 3rd ed. where this sentence in its present form replaced the following sentence dating from the 1st ed. (p. 333):

These difficulties are still very great, though they are being diminished by the railway, the printing-press and the telegraph.

PAGE 273

a. So since the 3rd ed. (p. 354) where the sentence in the present text replaced the following sentence dating from the 1st ed. (p. 334):

If one of them fails for a time, the others are likely to support it in many ways, chiefly indirect; one of these being that they keep in heart the local shopkeepers, who are thus enabled to continue their assistance longer than they otherwise could, to the work-people in those trades that happen to be depressed.

b. This paragraph and the footnote attached to it were inserted in the 4th ed. (p. 352).

c. This sentence was inserted in the 3rd ed. (p. 354 n.).

PAGE 274

a. The following footnote attached to the word "products" in the 1st ed. (p. 335 n.) was deleted from the 4th ed.:

> The high intelligence of the Cornish men has combined with the comparative poverty of their own mines to make them take the lead in this movement: and they even send to England from distant continents parts of the tin and copper which enter into many of her most valuable exports; and thus in some ways increase the specialization of her industries.

b. The word "this" dating from the 1st ed. (p. 336) was replaced by the words "the last" before "century", in the 5th ed. (p. 275).

PAGE 275

a. The following footnote attached to the word "distribution" dating from the 2nd ed. (p. 334), was deleted from the 5th ed.:

> Dr Ogle has recently shown (*Statistical Journal*, June 1889) that the aggregate rural population of England—i.e. that living in the open country or in villages with less than 5000 inhabitants—has decreased only by 2 per cent. between 1851 and 1881: but of course the decrease has been greater in certain counties. "The decline was brought about by the migration of young people, mainly under twenty-five years of age, from the rural to manufacturing districts, and of young men in greater proportion than women.... The main decrease was among those engaged in agriculture. But a very considerable share of it was borne by the rural handicraftsmen.... There was a considerable increase among those engaged in the transport of goods, among shopkeepers, among domestic and other servants, and also, in the professional class, among those engaged in teaching."

b. This and the next sentence were inserted in the 5th ed. (p. 275).

PAGE 276

a. So since the 5th ed. (p. 276) where the date "1901" replaced the date "1881" in the earlier editions, and where the following footnote dating from the 1st ed. (p. 337 n.) was deleted:

> Mr Booth in his admirable paper *On occupations in the United Kingdom* 1801–1881, published in the *Statistical Journal* for 1886, separates as well as he can the dealers from the manufacturers; and finds that those engaged in manufacture were 32·7 per cent. of those earning independent incomes in 1851 and only 30·7 per cent. in 1881.

b. So since the 5th ed. (p. 276). In the earlier editions the only occupations mentioned were: "education, domestic service, building, dealing and transport by road." The following footnote attached to the end of this sentence in the 1st ed. (pp. 337–8 n.) was deleted from the 5th ed.:

> Of course transport by railway, which is a mechanical industry, occupies more people than it did; for it is only of recent origin. But the shipping industry is of old date; and there we find that recent mechanical improvements have enabled a traffic increased fourfold to be carried without any increase in the number of those who work it. Except in the matter of tramways there has been no considerable improvement in the vehicles used on the roads, and a comparatively slight increase in traffic by road has caused those who work it to increase in numbers faster than those engaged in almost any other manual occupation.

c. The remainder of this paragraph was inserted in the 5th ed. (p. 277).

PAGE 277

a. The following sentence dating from the 5th ed. (p. 277) was deleted from the 7th ed.:

In consequence the number of domestic servants is just now (1891–1901) growing only at about the same rate as the total population.

b. The remaining clauses of this sentence were inserted in the 2nd ed. (p. 336).

c. The first paragraph of this footnote was inserted in the 5th ed. (p. 277 n.).

d. This paragraph was inserted in the 7th ed. (p. 277 n.).

BOOK IV, CHAPTER XI

INDUSTRIAL ORGANIZATION, CONTINUED. PRODUCTION ON A LARGE SCALE

PAGE 278

a. Except where otherwise stated the wording of this chapter dates substantially from the 1st edition.

b. The title of this chapter remained unchanged since the 1st edition.

PAGE 279

a. This clause was inserted in the 6th ed. (p. 279 n.).

PAGE 282

a. This paragraph dates from the 6th ed. (p. 282) where it replaced the following paragraph dating from the 1st ed. (p. 343):

Many of these economies in the matter of buying and selling can be secured by a large trading house, which puts out its work to be done by small manufacturers or by work-people at their own homes. So far therefore they do not tell in the direction of destroying small manufacturers, but rather of limiting the character of the work of business management done by them; as we shall see more fully in the next chapter.

PAGE 284

a. So since the 2nd ed. (p. 343) where the word "great" before "advantages" in the 1st ed. (p. 345) was deleted.

333

b. The rest of this sentence was inserted in the 2nd ed. (p. 343). In the 1st ed. (p. 345) the sentence succeeding the word "workmen" ran as follows:

Again by keeping things himself under lock and key, and in other ways, he can save much of the book-keeping, and nearly all of the cumbrous checks...etc.

c. The first clause of this sentence was inserted in the 2nd ed. (p. 343).

PAGE 285

a. The following concluding paragraph of this section in the 1st ed. (p. 346) was deleted from the 2nd ed.:

On the whole then the small factory can seldom compete on equal terms with a larger establishment which is organized on the ideally best plan. But as a rule a large business is itself only the development of a smaller one which has prospered under good management: after a time the management becomes incompetent, or for some other reason the business is broken up; and again the cycle is renewed by other small businesses pushing their way upwards. But this point must be further considered in the next chapter.

b. §5 in its present form was inserted in the 4th ed. (pp. 364–6), but a good deal of the material was taken from material previously placed in Book V, ch. xi, §2, where in the 2nd and 3rd editions it formed part of the discussion of the working of the law of increasing returns. (See the Editorial Appendix to Book V, ch. xii, below.)

c. The first six sentences of this paragraph date from the 4th ed. (p. 364).

d. The remainder of this paragraph dates substantially from the 2nd ed. (p. 486).

PAGE 286

a. The first three sentences of this paragraph, and the footnote attached to the second sentence, date from the 4th ed. (p. 365).

b. The rest of this paragraph dates substantially from the 2nd ed. (p. 487).

c. The first two sentences of this paragraph date from the 4th ed. (p. 365).

d. The remainder of this paragraph (except for the addition of one clause dates substantially from the 2nd ed. (pp. 487–8).

e. This clause was inserted in the 4th ed. (p. 365).

a. The following additional paragraph at this point in the 2nd ed. (p. 488) was deleted from the 4th ed.:

And even in these industries, to produce for an open market, means generally to produce for sale to middlemen who will sell to others: those producers, who can miss out one in the link of middlemen, will often gain by so doing a good deal more than the additional economies to be got by increasing an already large and well found stock of machinery; and when this is so, a large part of the value of any business will consist of its particular trade connections and external organization, in spite of the fact that the commodities which it produces resemble those made by many other firms.

b. This paragraph dates substantially from the 2nd ed. (p. 488), apart from the last two clauses of the concluding sentence which were inserted in the 4th ed. (p. 366).

c. This paragraph dates from the 4th ed. (p. 366).

a. This sentence was inserted in the 2nd ed. (p. 345).

a. The following sentence dating from the 1st ed. (p. 348) was deleted from the 5th ed.:

On the other hand in some branches of the textile trades, the ease with which large packets of patterns are distributed by manufacturers and warehousemen, is telling perceptibly on the side of the small shopkeepers.

b. The following footnote attached to the word "food" in the 1st ed. (p. 348 n.) was deleted from the 3rd ed.:

But the large business of the Aerated Bread Company and others of a like kind in London is probably the forerunner of many similar movements.

c. The following sentences dating from the 1st ed. (p. 348) were deleted (after some intervening changes) from the 5th ed.:

But on the whole he [the small shopkeeper] is losing ground rapidly. The decay of the small manufacturer appeared to the economists in the first half of the century as one of the chief causes that were changing the character of England's industrial and social life: the decay of the small shopkeeper seems to be a more potent influence just at the present time. And it is noteworthy that those small shopkeepers who are holding their own best, are also as a rule producers on a small scale, and *vice versa*.

In the 2nd ed. (p. 346) the word "rapidly" at the end of the first sentence of the passage just cited was deleted and the following additional sentence was inserted after "ground":

It is not certain that they are positively decreasing in number; but they certainly do not get their share of the rapidly increasing retail business of the country.

d. The remaining sentences of this paragraph date from the 3rd ed. (p. 368 n.).

e. The following clause in the 1st ed. (p. 348) after the word "trade" was deleted from the 6th ed.: "and American experience causes some doubt as to how long cabs will remain in general use."

PAGE 290

a. The following footnote attached to the word "business" in the 1st ed. (p. 349 n.) was deleted from the 5th ed.:

> While the output of coal in this country is increasing, the number of mines is diminishing: but this is partly due to the closing of many of the new mines which were hastily opened some years ago when the price of coal was very high. The contests between the large and small methods of production has led to interesting episodes in the African diamond mines and the American oil regions. The Sutro tunnel and the American oil ducts are good instances of the way in which a provision may be made for the joint use of a number of mines, which no one of them could afford separately; but they also show how this course gives openings for the formation of powerful monopolies.

b. This clause and the following sentence were inserted in the 2nd ed. (p. 348). In the 1st ed. (pp. 349–52) this section was concluded by a discussion covering two-and-a-half pages dealing with the relative advantages of large and small farms. In the 2nd ed. this material was transferred, without much change, to Book VI, ch. x, §8. (See pages 651–3 in vol. 1 of this edition.)

c. The following footnote dating from the 3rd ed. (p. 307 n.) was deleted from the 5th ed.:

> There is much of general interest bearing on the subjects of this and the neighbouring chapters in general economic histories, such as those of Ashley and Cunningham; and in Cooke Taylor's *Factory System*, Jevons' *Coal Question* and Hobson's *Evolution of Modern Capitalism*. A further discussion of the causes which prevent a single large firm from so availing itself of the economies of production on a large scale as to drive out all its rivals, will be found below, Book V, ch. XI, §2.

The reference at the end of the foregoing footnote applies to Book V, ch. XII, §2 in vol. 1 of the present edition.

INDUSTRIAL ORGANIZATION, CONTINUED. BUSINESS MANAGEMENT

a. Except where otherwise stated, the wording of this chapter dates substantially from the 1st edition.

b. The title of this chapter remained unchanged since the 1st edition.

c. The first two sentences of this paragraph were inserted in the 7th ed. (p. 291), while the third sentence dates substantially from the 2nd ed. (p. 349).

d. The following words and sentences after the word "affection", dating from the 1st ed. (p. 353), were deleted from the 7th ed.:

...and the desire to promote the well-being of others. Business management or undertaking has always had many different forms, and their number and variety was never so great as in England now. Relics remain of almost every form that has ever been in use; while new forms are constantly being developed.

a. So since the 2nd ed. (p. 351). In the 1st ed. (p. 354) the opening words of this section ran as follows:

But we have already seen how unsuitable the primitive pattern is for the greater part of the business of the modern world. The task of directing production so that a given effort may be most effective in supplying human wants is so difficult under the complex conditions of modern life, that it has to be broken up...etc.

b. So since the 2nd ed. (p. 351) where this sentence replaced the following sentences in the 1st ed. (p. 355):

The good and the evil effects of the action of speculators such as these are however so complex themselves, and are so intimately interwoven with fluctuations of commercial credit and the changes of the money market that they cannot be conveniently discussed in this place. It is true that there is an element of speculation in almost every kind of business: but in this early stage of our inquiry it is best that we should give our chief attention to those forms of business in which administration counts for most and the subtler forms of speculation for least.

PAGE 295

a. This reference was inserted in the 3rd ed. (p. 375 n.).

PAGE 297

a. So since the 7th ed. (p. 297) where the opening words of the above sentence replaced the following words dating from the first ed. (p. 359):

The ideal manufacturer for instance, if he makes goods not to meet special orders but for the general market, must . . .etc.

PAGE 298

a. The following footnote attached to the word "management" in the 1st ed. (p. 360 n.) was deleted from the 2nd ed.:

This is what German economists call "*Unternehmungsformen*".

PAGE 301

a. The following opening sentence of this paragraph in the 1st ed. (p. 363) was deleted from the 2nd ed.:

But the expansion of old trades and the growth of new trades have long tended to outgrow the capitals that can easily be obtained by private companies.

b. The following clauses in the 1st ed. (p. 364) after the word "concerned" were deleted from the 2nd ed.:

. . .and various plans with which we need not occupy ourselves just now, have been adopted in different countries for enabling the shareholders to limit their risks to their shares.

c. The first sentence of this footnote was inserted in the 2nd ed. (p. 359 n.).

PAGE 302

a. So since the 6th ed. (p. 302). In the 1st ed. (p. 365) the first clause of this sentence ran as follows:

Since the joint stock companies in the United Kingdom have an aggregate income of £100,000,000 and do a tenth of the business of all kinds that is done in the country, . . . etc.

In the 5th ed. (p. 302) the words after "United Kingdom" were altered to read: "have an aggregate gross income of £250,000,000 and do a great part of the business of all kinds. . . etc."

PAGE 304

a. These last two paragraphs of this section (§9) were inserted in the 5th ed. (p. 304).

b. The following footnote dating from the 5th ed. (p. 304 n.), attached to the sentence ending with the word "kind", was deleted from the 7th ed.:

A long discussion of trusts and cartels, originally written for the second volume of this work, has been expanded for a separate study of *National Industries and Trade*, which is now (1907) in the press.

Marshall's *Industry and Trade* was published in 1919.

PAGE 305

a. So since the 2nd ed. (p. 362). In the 1st ed. (p. 366) the first two sentences ran as follows:

The evils of these two methods of business organization are however in a great measure avoided by the system of co-operation, at all events where it appears in its best form. For there a part or the whole of those shareholders who undertake the risks of the business are themselves employed by it; and all the employees, whether they contribute towards the material capital of the business or not, have a share in its profits, and some power of voting at the general meetings at which the broad lines of its policy are laid down, and the officers appointed who are to carry that policy into effect.

b. This paragraph dates in its final form from the 3rd ed. (pp. 384–5). In the 1st ed. (p. 367) this paragraph ran as follows:

But the system has difficulties of its own which have hitherto kept it from succeeding on a large scale except in the business of retailing commodities consumed by working men. Many of these difficulties do not belong properly to it, but are due to the fact that the system itself is not thoroughly carried out; for the greater part of those establishments which call themselves co-operative have not adopted co-operative principles in their entirety. But other difficulties belong strictly to it. For instance in buying and selling on a large scale the officers of a co-operative society are fallible and need assistance and control; and yet the ordinary members have little means of knowing what it would be best to do, and of detecting what is really being done. In some cases they have been served excellently by men of great genius both mentally and morally; men who for the sake of the Co-operative Faith that is in them, have worked with great ability and energy, and with perfect uprightness, being all the time content with lower pay than they could have got as business managers on their own account or for a private firm. But though men of this stamp may be more common among the officers of co-operative societies than in other occupations, they are not very common even there.

In the 2nd ed. (pp. 362–3) the opening words of this first sentence ran: "But unfortunately the system has very great difficulties of its own which have hitherto kept it from...etc." In the second sentence the words "many of these difficulties" were changed to "some of these difficulties". The third sentence ran: "But there are grave difficulties inherent in it."

c. The following paragraphs which came after this sentence in the 1st ed. (p. 368) were deleted from the 2nd ed.:

Some of these difficulties will be diminished by experience, by the diffusion of a better knowledge of the true principles of co-operation, and by that increase of general education which is every day fitting a larger number of the people for entering into the complex problems of business management. Others of the difficulties again will be partially or wholly removed by the increase in the number of co-operative societies, and by their growing tendency to act in alliance, if not in federation, with one another: for by this means they will avoid a considerable part of those speculative risks which are the chief of all the hindrances to the good management of many kinds of business on the co-operative plan.

We shall have to recur frequently to the problems suggested by both branches of the co-operative movement, that which has already achieved success in retail trade, and that which is entering on the more difficult and perilous paths of agriculture and manufacture.

d. This sentence dates from the 3rd ed. (p. 385).

a. The wording of the remaining paragraphs of this section (§ 10) dates substantially from the 2nd ed. (pp. 363–5) except for the first four sentences of this first paragraph and the first clause of the fifth sentence, which date from the 1st ed. (p. 641), where they were placed in Book VII, ch. VIII, § 7. In the 1st ed. these sentences were preceded by the following sentence which was deleted from the 2nd ed.:

Co-operation promises more than any other form of business association to turn to good account the capabilities of the working man for the higher posts of business management.

a. The following sentence after the sentence ending with the word "industry", in the 2nd ed. (p. 364) was deleted from the 5th ed.:

Under the scheme of profit-and-loss-sharing, a small part of the market wages of the employees is held back as a contribution towards any loss that may be shown on the year's working; while they receive a more than proportionate share of the profits in a bad year.

b. So since the 3rd ed. (p. 386) where this sentence replaced the following sentence in the 2nd ed. (p. 364):

Another partially co-operative scheme is that of some Oldham cotton mills which are really joint-stock companies; among their shareholders are many working men who have a special knowledge of the trade, but not many of their own employees.

c. So since the 4th ed. (p. 386) where this sentence replaced the following sentence dating from the 2nd ed. (p. 364):

And another is that of the Productive establishments, such as the Leicester Boot-works, owned by the main body of co-operative stores, through their agents, the Co-operative Wholesale Society; but in which, partly on account of technical difficulties, the workers as such have as yet no share either in the management or in the profits of the works.

d. In the 1st ed. (p. 641) there was the following sentence and footnote concluding the discussion of co-operation there, which were deleted from the 2nd ed.:

The lessons, both economic and ethical, which the history of co-operation has to teach are very important, but we must postpone the study of them.[1]

[1] One cause that makes the lessons of co-operation difficult to be read may be noticed in passing. It is that the successes of the co-operative movement in retail trading are in a great measure due to the exceptional advantages which it has there in the matters of marketing; and on the other hand many of the failures which it has suffered in manufacture are due to the exceptional difficulties which independent co-operative societies have met in their attempts to market their goods. Reference may be made to an Address given by the present writer to the Co-operative Congress at Ipswich in 1889 for some further explanation of the remarks in the text, and for an argument that true co-operation cannot have a fair trial unless the Productive societies federate themselves, at all events for the limited purpose of marketing their goods. See also above, Book IV.

Marshall's address to the Co-operative Congress is reprinted in the *Memorials of Alfred Marshall* (pp. 227–55).

e. This footnote was inserted in the 5th ed. (p. 307).

PAGE 308

a. So since the 6th ed. (p. 308) where this sentence replaced the following sentence dating from the 1st ed. (p. 369):

Much of this capital passes into the hands of bankers and others, people of keen intellect and restless energy; people who have no class prejudices and care nothing for social distinctions; and who would promptly lend it to any one of whose business ability and honesty they were convinced.

PAGE 310

a. This paragraph was inserted in the 6th ed. (pp. 310–11).

PAGE 311

a. So since the 2nd ed. (p. 368 n.) where this clause replaced the following in the 1st ed. (p. 372 n.):

i.e. those earnings which are properly to be ascribed to the business abilities of those who, when employing their own capital, get full profits.

PAGE 313

a. This clause was inserted in the 2nd ed. (p. 370).

b. The concluding paragraph of this chapter was inserted in the 2nd ed. (p. 370).

BOOK IV, CHAPTER XIII

CONCLUSION. CORRELATION OF THE TENDENCIES TO INCREASING AND TO DIMINISHING RETURN

PAGE 314

a. Except where otherwise stated the wording of this chapter dates substantially from the 1st edition.

b. In the first three editions this chapter was entitled "Conclusion. The Law of Increasing in Relation to that of Decreasing Return". In the 4th and 5th editions the title became "Conclusion. The Tendencies to Increasing and to Diminishing Return". The present title was adopted from the 6th edition.

PAGE 315

a. This paragraph was inserted in the 2nd ed. (pp. 372–3).

PAGE 316

a. This and the next sentence were inserted in the 6th ed. (p. 316) where they replaced the following sentences dating from the 2nd ed. (p. 373):

And as with the growth of trees, so it is with the growth of businesses. As each kind of tree has its normal life in which it attains its normal height, so the length of life during which a business of any kind is likely to retain full vigour is limited by the laws of nature combined with the circumstances of place and time, and the character and stage of development of the particular trade in which it lies.

b. So since the 6th ed. (p. 316) where the first clause of this sentence replaced the following clause dating from the 2nd ed. (p. 373):

The laws of nature press upon it by limiting the length of life of its original founders.

In the 1st ed. (pp. 375–6) the corresponding sentence ran as follows:

But the brevity of human life and the still greater brevity of that part of it in which men's best faculties are in full vigour prevent this concentration.

c. So since the 6th ed. (p. 316) where this sentence replaced the following sentence dating from the 2nd ed. (p. 373):

But it is almost sure to have lost much of its elasticity and of its progressive force; the advantages are no longer exclusively on its side in its competition with younger and smaller rivals: and, unless it be in banking, or transport or some other of those exceptional trades, which will require a separate discussion, it can no longer obtain from every increase in its scale of production the means of reducing considerably the price at which it sells its goods or its services.

The sentence just quoted from the 2nd ed. differs from the corresponding sentence in the 1st ed. (p. 376) only by the insertion in the 2nd ed. of the clauses: "and, unless it be in banking, or transport or some other of those exceptional trades, which will require a separate discussion."

The following paragraph, dating from the 1st ed. (p. 376), where it succeeded the sentence just quoted ending with the words "price at which it sells its goods or its services", was deleted from the 6th ed.:

The growth and the decay of the energies of a great business establishment seldom follow twice on exactly the same lines even in the same trade: they vary with the varying incidents of the life and fortune, of the personal friendships and the business and family connections of the individuals concerned; but they also vary much from one trade to another. Thus for instance no single very large business has appeared in agriculture, while in banking and insurance, in the supply of news, and in transport by land and sea, such small businesses as still remain find a constantly increasing difficulty in holding their own. There is no rule of universal application; but the struggle between the solid strength of steady-going firms with large capitals on the one hand, and the quick inventiveness and energy, the suppleness and power of variation of their smaller rivals on the other, seems inclined to issue in the large majority of cases in the victory of the former. We may conclude that as a general rule, subject to important exceptions, an increase in the total volume of any branch of production tends to increase in an even greater proportion the average size of the businesses engaged in it.

PAGE 317

a. The remainder of this paragraph was inserted in the 2nd ed. (p. 375), where it replaced the following sentences in the 1st ed. (pp. 377–8):

Speaking generally, and leaving allowance for special cases to be made separately, we now see that we may neglect the fact that when more of a commodity is wanted, the extra production is very likely to come from some new producer just struggling into business, who works under many disadvantages, and has to be content for a time with little or no profits, but who is satisfied with the fact that he is establishing a connection and taking the first steps towards building up a successful business. For although this extra produce may sometimes be raised at a greater cost of labour and sacrifice than that which went before, even in an industry which derives great economies from production on a large scale, yet the general rule will be the other way; and it will more commonly be got by increasing the output of businesses already established, at a less than proportionate cost of extra labour and sacrifice. The way is thus prepared for the general theory of equilibrium of demand and supply in the next Book: and we may there regard an increase in the aggregate volume of production by any branch of manufacture as likely to be attained generally at a less than proportionate cost of labour and sacrifice.

b. Although the term "representative firm" was not actually employed in the 1st ed., the notion is clearly contained in the following passage in Book V, ch. IV, §5, pp. 413–14 in the 1st ed., which was deleted from the 2nd ed.:

We must select as representative a business which is managed with normal ability; and so as to get its fair share of the economies resulting from industrial organization.

As we shall presently see more clearly, it is important to remember that when endeavouring to observe the normal supply price we must take care to select a business which is managed with normal ability; and by normal ability is of course meant not the ability of the average man, but the ability that is normally to be expected of those in the responsible position of undertakers and managers of a business of the kind in question, whether it be a private or a joint stock or a co-operative business. We shall find that it is necessary to take great care to avoid all ambiguity on this point.

The business which we are observing must also be able to obtain its fair share of benefit from those economies of production both in the internal arrangements of the factory and in its external, which arise out of the aggregate scale of production of the commodity in the district. The relation between the internal and external economies of a factory or other productive establishment was discussed carefully at the end of the last Book, partly with a view to this difficulty; and we may here revert to the conclusion reached there.

We concluded that though many of the economies arising from an increase in the aggregate scale of production of a commodity are not within the reach of a small business; yet the gradual increase in the aggregate production increases the facilities for starting a business on a comparatively large scale, and increases therefore, other things being equal, the economies both internal and external which are within the reach of those who are on the point of applying additional capital and labour to extend yet a little further the total production.

The succeeding sentences in the 1st ed. (pp. 414–15) after the sentence ending with the words "to extend yet a little further the total production" will be found in the editorial note **a** to vol. I, page 378 (pp. 392–3 below).

Attention may also be drawn to the third paragraph of page 396 in Book V, ch. VII, §2, in vol. I of the present edition. In that paragraph, which dates without change from the 1st ed. (Book VI, ch. vi, §2, p. 523), there is a formulation of the representative business, which is practically identical with that of the marginal summary to the paragraph just quoted from Book V, ch. iv, §5 in the 1st ed.

PAGE 318

a. This paragraph was inserted in the 6th ed. (p. 318).

b. This paragraph dates substantially from the 2nd ed. (p. 375).

c. This sentence and the next paragraph were inserted in the 2nd ed. (p. 376).

PAGE 319

a. This paragraph and the footnote attached to it were inserted in the 6th ed. (pp. 319–20).

b. This footnote was inserted in the 5th ed. (pp. 319 n.–20 n.). It was there the first paragraph of a much longer footnote, the remainder of which was deleted from the 6th ed. The excised portion ran as follows in the 5th ed.:

It has been proposed, notably in Professor Carver's able and suggestive *Distribution of Wealth*, that we should abandon the old broad uses of the terms Diminishing and Increasing Return; and should use these terms only when we are considering variations in the net return obtained from an increased employment of any one agent, or group of agents of production, on the supposition that there is no change in the amounts of other agents employed in the same process of production. For instance we may consider the additional return to be obtained by applying more intensive cultivation to the same plot of land: or we may consider the additional return to be obtained by a farmer who takes over an additional piece of land, and applies the same total amount of capital and labour to the increased area of land. The proposed change would be consistent with that use of the term "net marginal product of any agent" of production, which is playing a *rôle* of ever increasing importance in the progress of modern economic science; and thus it would bring some gain in symmetry. (See below, V, iv, §3, 4; and V, viii, especially §§1–3.)

But it would deprive us of an old use of the term which is of great importance; and in which the distribution of the resources of production among different uses is supposed to have been made carefully and well, so far as the knowledge and skill of those engaged in the industry will carry. The older economists applied the law of Diminishing Return in warnings as to the dangers of the growth of a very dense population when unable to import large supplies of food from a distance: and they consistently assumed that the distribution of resources among different uses would be about the best which were at the command of the population in question (see below, V, viii, §3). When discussing the distribution of managing ability, with special reference to the question how far it should be concentrated in agriculture, they found fit phrases in "large and small holdings," or "grande et petite culture."

It has also been proposed to speak of the laws of Diminishing and Increasing Cost of production on a large scale, when special reference is made to those tendencies to Increasing and Diminishing Return, which result from variations in the efficiency of organization. But these terms do not suggest the special uses to which it is suggested to appropriate them. And if specialized terms are to be allotted to those, it would seem advisable that they should afford scope for indicating the fundamental distinction between the "internal" economies and wastes which come with an increase in the size of the individual representative firm; and those "external" economies and wastes which come with an increase in the aggregate volume of a national or a local industry.

a. So since the 6th ed. (p. 320) where this sentence replaced the following sentences dating from the 1st ed. (p. 378):

Our discussion of the character and organization of industry taken as a whole tends to show that an increase in the volume of labour causes in general, other things being equal, a more than proportionate increase in the total efficiency of labour. But we must not forget that other things may not be equal.

b. The words "if their wealth is not consumed in great wars" were inserted in the 6th ed. (p. 320).

c. The words in italics "for the time" were inserted in the 2nd ed. (p. 377).

a. In the 2nd ed. (p. 378) the words in italics "*at the present time*" replaced the word "now" in the 1st ed. (p. 380).

b. The remaining words of this line date in their present form from the 3rd ed. (p. 400 n.). In the 1st ed. (p. 379 n.) these words ran as follows:

American economists from Carey to Henry George no less characteristically use their highest eloquence in splendid descriptions of the growing richness . . . etc.

In the 2nd ed. (p. 378 n.) they ran as follows:

American writers no less characteristically use their highest eloquence in fervid descriptions of the growing richness . . . etc.

BOOK V

GENERAL RELATIONS OF DEMAND, SUPPLY AND VALUE

CHAPTER I

INTRODUCTORY. ON MARKETS

PAGE 323

a. In the 1st edition Book V consisted of nine chapters, and was followed by Book VI, entitled "Cost of Production Further Considered", consisting of six chapters; while the theory of distribution was contained in Book VII. From the 2nd edition onwards Books V and VI were combined in the single Book V, and the theory of distribution was placed in Book VI. For the detailed changes in the scope of Book V in the different editions see the Tables of Contents of the first four editions (pp. 77–130) and of the present edition (vol. 1, pages xxiv–xxvii). It should be noted that the changes in the scope and structure of Book V in the 5th edition were definitive, and that there were no further changes of this nature in the subsequent editions.

b. In the 1st edition Book V was entitled

"THE THEORY OF

THE EQUILIBRIUM OF DEMAND AND SUPPLY

WITH SOME CONSIDERATIONS AS TO ITS BEARING ON THE

DOCTRINE OF MAXIMUM SATISFACTION."

In the 2nd edition, where Books V and VI in the 1st edition were amalgamated to make the new Book V, the title was extended as follows:

"THE THEORY OF

THE EQUILIBRIUM OF DEMAND AND SUPPLY

INCLUDING SOME FURTHER STUDY OF COST OF PRODUCTION, AND

WITH SOME CONSIDERATIONS BEARING ON THE DOCTRINE

OF MAXIMUM SATISFACTION."

349

In the 3rd edition the title became:

"The Equilibrium of Demand and Supply"

and in the 4th edition:

"Theory of the Equilibrium of Demand and Supply"

The present title was adopted from the 5th edition onwards.

c. Except where otherwise stated the wording of this chapter dates substantially from the 1st edition.

d. In the first three editions the title of this chapter was "On Markets". The present title was adopted from the 4th edition.

e. This paragraph was inserted in the 4th ed. (p. 401). In the 1st ed. (p. 383) the opening paragraph of §1 ran as follows:

Most economic problems have a common kernel relating to the equilibrium of demand and supply.

In spite of a great variety in detail nearly all the chief problems of economics agree in this that they have a kernel of the same kind. This kernel is an inquiry as to the balancing of two opposed classes of motives, the one consisting of desires to acquire certain new economic goods, and the other of desires to avoid certain efforts or retain certain immediate enjoyments or other economic goods, the command over which has already been acquired; or in other words it is an inquiry into the balancing of the forces of Demand and Supply, these terms being used in their broadest sense. In the study of this equilibrium there is much that is common ground to many economic problems, the other incidents of which have little in common, or may even belong to widely remote districts of the region of economics. And therefore a great saving of time, as well as some gain in scientific thoroughness is to be attained by treating this common kernel carefully once for all.

The last two sentences of this paragraph were deleted from the 3rd ed. and the first two from the 4th ed.

f. This paragraph was inserted in the 7th ed. (p. 323).

PAGE 324

a. This and the next paragraph were inserted in the 4th ed. (p. 402).

PAGE 328

a. So since the 6th ed. (p. 328) where the opening words of this sentence replaced the following words dating from the 1st ed. (p. 387):

This illustrates well the great law, of which we shall have much to say when we come to consider the influence of foreign trade on economic progress, that the larger the market for a commodity . . . etc.

b. The first sentence of this footnote dates in its present form from the 5th ed. (p. 328 n.). In the 1st ed. (p. 387 n.) it ran as follows:

> In extreme cases the difference between the price at which a dealer is willing to buy and that at which he will sell amounts to from five to twenty per cent. of the selling value of the security.

In the 2nd ed. (p. 387 n.) the words "In extreme cases" were replaced by the words "In the case of shares of very small and little known companies".

c. This footnote was inserted in the 3rd ed. (p. 406 n.).

PAGE 329

a. The remaining clauses of this sentence were inserted in the 2nd ed. (p. 388).

b. So since the 2nd ed. (p. 389), where this paragraph replaced the following paragraph dating from the 1st ed. (pp. 388–9):

Intermediate between the two extremes of world markets and secluded markets are the great majority of markets which the economist and the business man have to study. It is always difficult to know how much influence to assign to the indirect competition between distant markets; the allowance to be made will often depend upon causes which can be detected only by those who have special knowledge of the facts; and in such cases much must be left to the trained instincts of the traders immediately concerned. But some sides of these difficulties are common to a great variety of economic problems, and cannot be evaded by the economist: they take a prominent place in the discussion of local variations of value, and in that particular branch of it which deals with Foreign Trade; but we need not consider them further now.

PAGE 330

a. The words "more or less" were inserted in the 4th ed. (p. 408).

b. So since the 4th ed. (p. 408), where this sentence replaced the following sentence dating from the 1st ed. (p. 389):

This latter distinction will be seen to be one of degree only, and to be not clearly and firmly drawn: and even the

351

former is not perfectly definite, but yet it is definite enough to merit a separate discussion.

c. The first two clauses of this sentence date from the 4th ed. (p. 408) and the last two clauses from the 7th ed. (p. 330). In the first three editions this sentence ran as follows:

Accordingly we shall consider in the next chapter those temporary equilibria of demand and supply, in which the cost of producing the commodity exerts either no influence or merely an indirect influence.

d. The following concluding paragraph and footnote inserted in the 3rd ed. (p. 407) were deleted from the 4th ed.:

At a later stage we shall have to combine the difficulties with regard to time on the side of supply with those on the side of demand, of which something has already been said.[1]

[1] Book III, ch. IV, §§ 5, 6.

BOOK V, CHAPTER II

TEMPORARY EQUILIBRIUM OF DEMAND AND SUPPLY

a. Except where otherwise stated the wording of this chapter dates substantially from the 1st edition.

b. The title of this chapter remained unchanged since the 1st edition.

c. The suggestion that weariness may be due more to monotony than to fatigue was inserted in the 3rd ed. (p. 408).

d. The reference to Book IV, ch. I, §2, was inserted in the 3rd ed. (p. 408 n.).

a. The word "value" was inserted after "equilibrium" in the 3rd ed. (p. 409).

b. So since the 5th ed. (p. 332), where this paragraph in the text replaced the following footnote dating from the 2nd ed. (p. 391 n.):

We may put aside also as of very little practical importance, a class of dealings which have occupied a good deal of space in economic literature. They relate to such things as pictures by the old masters, rare coins and other things, which cannot be "graded" at all; for each of them is unique, and has no direct equivalent or competitor. Anyone who offers to buy such a thing, without any thought of selling it again, has to assure himself only that the pleasure he will derive from its possession is as great as that which he could get by spending its price in any other way; the highest price to which he will go is governed by the utility or pleasure giving power to him of money on the one hand and the object of worth on the other. And therefore the price at which such a thing is sold will depend very much on whether any rich persons with a fancy for that particular thing happen to be present at its sale. If not, it will probably be bought by dealers who reckon on being able to sell it at a profit; and the variations in the price for which the same picture sells at successive auctions, great as they are, would be much greater still if it were not for the steadying influence of professional and semi-professional purchasers. The "equilibrium price" for such sales is very much a matter of accident; but the curious might reap some reward from a minute study of it.

c. So since the 5th ed. (pp. 332–3). In the 1st to the 4th editions the table at the end of the first paragraph of § 2 was placed in a footnote, while both the first and second paragraphs of this section were compressed into a single paragraph as follows:

Let us take an illustration from a corn market in a country town. The amount which each farmer or other seller offers for sale at any price is governed by his own need for money in hand, and by his calculation of the present and future conditions of the market with which he is connected. There are some prices which no seller would accept, some which no one would refuse. There are other intermediate prices which would be accepted for larger or smaller amounts by many or all of the sellers. Let us assume for the sake of simplicity that all the corn in the market is of the same quality. An acute dealer having corn for sale may perhaps, after looking around him, come to the conclusion that if 37*s.* could be got throughout the day, the farmers between them would be willing to sell to the extent of about 1,000 quarters; and that if no more than 36*s.* could be got, several would refuse to sell, or would sell only small quantities, so that only 700 quarters would be brought forward for sale; and that a price of 35*s.* would only induce some 500 quarters to be brought forward. Suppose him further to calculate that millers and others would be willing to buy 900 quarters if they could be got at 35*s.* each, but only 700 if they could not be got for less than 36*s.*, and only 600 if they could not be got for less than 37*s.* He will conclude that a price of

36*s*., if established at once, would equate supply and demand, because the amount offered for sale at that price would equal the amount which could just find purchasers at that price. He will therefore take at once any offer considerably over 36*s*.; and other sellers will do the same.

PAGE 333

a. So since the 5th ed. (p. 333). In the first four editions this figure was 500.

PAGE 334

a. This footnote was inserted in the 3rd ed. (p. 411 n.).

PAGE 335

a. So since the 4th ed. (p. 412), where this sentence replaced the following sentence dating from the 1st ed. (p. 393):

In either case the marginal utility of money to him is not appreciably altered.

b. This sentence was inserted in the 5th ed. (p. 335).

c. In the 1st ed. (pp. 393–4) these paragraphs (apart from two subsequent additions) were in the text. They were transferred to a footnote in the 2nd ed. (pp. 393 n.–4 n.).

d. This sentence was inserted in the 5th ed. (p. 335 n.).

e. This clause was inserted in the 5th ed. (p. 335 n.).

PAGE 336

a. This sentence was inserted in the 5th ed. (p. 336). From the 2nd to the 4th editions the reference to this characteristic of the labour market (which did not appear in the 1st ed.) was contained in a footnote attached to the end of this paragraph which ran as follows:

> The analogy which we are now considering between a labour market and a market for commodities is weakened, as most others of this kind are, by the fact that each seller of labour has only one unit of labour to dispose of.

b. The remainder of this paragraph was inserted in the 5th ed. (p. 336), where the "Note on Barter", which in the earlier editions had been placed at the end of this chapter, was transferred to the end of the volume as Appendix F. The sentences in the present text replaced, from the 5th ed. onwards, the following sentences dating from the 1st ed. (pp. 394–5):

When we do this we are really reverting to the problem of barter, in which the changes in the marginal utilities of both commodities are of course prominent. As we have re-marked, barter, though earlier historically than buying and selling, is really a more complex transaction: and the theory of it is curious rather than important. Some account of it is given in the adjoining Note, chiefly with a view of throwing additional light on the exceptional cases which we have just been considering.

c. The following footnote, attached to the sentence ending with the word "value", which was inserted in the 5th ed. (p. 336 n.), was deleted from the 6th ed.:

> Compare above, III, v, §1, where a few provisional remarks are made as to the influence of money in steadying marginal utilities over a market.

BOOK V, CHAPTER III

EQUILIBRIUM OF NORMAL DEMAND AND SUPPLY

PAGE 337

a. Except where otherwise stated the wording of this chapter dates substantially from the 1st edition.

b. The title of this chapter remained unchanged since the 1st edition.

c. This paragraph was inserted in the 5th ed. (p. 337).

PAGE 339

a. Perhaps the simplest and most direct statement of Marshall's doctrine of real cost is to be found in the following passage taken from *The Economics of Industry* by Alfred and Mary Paley Marshall (1st ed. 1879) p. 97:

> Firstly some confusion has arisen from the use of the term "cost of production" in two senses. It has been used to indicate what are here called the "expenses" as well as what is here called the "cost of production".[1] Thus the law

> [1] Mill used the phrase in these two senses; he himself distinguished clearly between them; and a careful examination of the context will show what sense he meant in each case. But the want of a formal distinction between them has confused many of his readers. See the *Fortnightly Review* for April 1876.

355　　　　　　　　　23-2

of (normal) value has been stated to be that value tends to equal cost of production; this of course does not mean that the value of a thing tends to equal what is called in this book its cost of production, i.e. the efforts and abstinences that have been required for making it. What is meant is that the value of the thing tends to equal the sum of those values which measure the efforts and abstinences required for making it; that is, cost of production is used to denote what we have expressed by the term expenses of production. For an exchange value or price, though it may be equal to a set of exchange values or prices, cannot be equal to a set of things unlike in kind to it. There cannot even be any direct comparison between one set of efforts and abstinences and another. We cannot subtract the labour of a carpenter in making a box from the labour of a watchmaker in making a watch. But we can subtract the exchange measure or price of the work of a carpenter in making a box from the price of the work of a watch maker in making a watch. It may happen that an hour's work by a business manager, or two days' work by a watchmaker, or three days' work by a carpenter, or ten days' work by an agricultural labourer, may all have the same exchange measure, say, a guinea. A guinea may also be the exchange measure of the abstinence or sacrifice involved in the loan of 20 guineas for a year. These various efforts and abstinences, these elements of cost of production, are certainly not equal to one another. But they would all exert an equal influence upon value; because their economic measures, *the expenses which would have to be incurred by anyone who would purchase them* are all equal.

The reference, in the footnote attached to the second sentence in the foregoing passage, to the *Fortnightly Review*, April 1876, is to Marshall's article entitled "Mr Mills' Theory of Value", which was reprinted in the *Memorials of Alfred Marshall*, edited by A. C. Pigou (1925), pp. 118–33. The same article is referred to in the footnote on page 339 in vol. 1 of the present edition.

    b.   "Sums of money" since the 2nd ed. (p. 399); "prices" in the 1st ed. (p. 399).

    c.   This paragraph dates from the 2nd ed. (p. 400 n.); the reference to ch. xii dates from the 6th ed. (p. 339 n.).

a. This sentence was inserted in the 4th ed. (p. 420).

b. So since the 4th ed. (p. 420). In the first three editions this was termed "The law of substitution". In the 2nd ed. (pp. 401–2) the following sentences were inserted after the word "substitution", but were deleted (save for one clause) from the 4th ed.:

In the course of our future work we shall be constantly referring to this law: its applications extend over almost every field of economic inquiry, and indeed include a great part of the results that are often referred to the action of competition. From another point of view the law may be regarded as closely akin to the law of the distribution of a commodity between different uses.

In the 3rd ed. (p. 420) the following footnote was attached to the word "uses" in the second of the above sentences, but was deleted from the 4th ed.:

This general statement of a broad principle is called a law, not very appropriately, but for lack of a better term. Its applications are numerous; and many words would be wasted in bringing it to bear, if it had not a special name. See Book I, ch. VI, §6.

This last reference applies to Book I, ch. III, §§ 3 and 4 in vol. I of the present edition.

c. The word "much" was inserted before "free competition" in the 5th ed. (p. 341). In the earlier editions the words "free competition" were put in italics.

a. So since the 3rd ed. (pp. 420–1), where this paragraph replaced the following paragraph dating from the 1st ed. (p. 402):

In such a market there is a definite demand price for each amount of the commodity, that is a definite price at which each particular amount of the commodity can find purchasers in a unit of time; and in like way there is a definite supply price, that is a definite price which will call forth a supply of each particular amount in a unit of time.

b. The following final clause of this paragraph in the 1st ed. (p. 403) was deleted from the 2nd ed.: "so that the demand and supply schedules remain unchanged throughout the whole period."

c. The wording of this paragraph dates from the 2nd ed. (p. 403) apart from the substitution in the 3rd ed. (p. 421) of "conditions of normal supply" for "law of normal supply".

In the 1st ed. (p. 403) this paragraph ran as follows:

The law of supply is less definite. At all events when the period for which the normal supply price is reckoned is very long, the supply of some of the factors of production of the commodity will probably conform to the law of diminishing, and that of others to the law of increasing return. The net result of adding together the supply prices of the factors may be either that the supply of the commodity on the whole conforms to the law of diminishing return, in which case the supply price for each unit will rise as the amount increases; or that the supply of the commodity on the whole conforms to the law of increasing return, in which case the supply price for each unit will fall as the amount produced increases; or lastly it is even possible that the supply price may alternately rise and fall as the amount produced increases. In every case however it is true that an increase in the amount produced involves an increase in the aggregate expenses of production.

In the 1st ed. there was the following footnote attached to the end of the paragraph just quoted:

This last term involves difficulties which will be noticed in ch. v of the present book, and again in Book VI.

The reference here to "ch. v" relates in vol. 1 of the present edition to Book V, ch. III, §§5–7 and to Appendix H, while the reference to "Book VI" relates to Book V, ch. IV, §§5 and 6 and ch. XII in vol. 1 of the present edition.

d. In the 2nd ed. (p. 403) the following sentences (deleted from the 3rd ed.) were interposed between the sentence ending "slow growth and decay" and the sentence beginning "Let us then call to mind the 'representative firm'....etc.":

We shall find that in consequence the earnings which they get in any particular, short period are to be regarded rather as what we shall call a "quasi-rent" governed by the price got by their produce, than as those representative wages and profits which govern the true normal price of their produce. This difficulty is briefly indicated here merely for the purpose of guarding against the danger, which experience has shown to be a very real one, that the general theory of equilibrium of normal demand and supply may be applied beyond its proper scope.

e. The wording of this paragraph dates from the 2nd ed. (pp. 403–4), apart from an addition (noted below) to the concluding sentence, in the 6th ed.

f. This reference was inserted in the 2nd ed. (p. 403 n.).

PAGE 343

a. The last two clauses of this sentence were inserted in the 6th ed. (p. 343).

b. Although this section (§ 5) dates, in its present form and place (with a few subsequent changes), from the 2nd ed. (pp. 404–6), the wording dates largely from the 1st ed., where the substance of the first paragraph was placed in Book V, ch. iv, § 2 (pp. 407–8), and of the second paragraph in Book V, ch. v, § 1, (pp. 419–20).

c. So since the 2nd ed. (p. 404) where the first sentence of this paragraph replaced the following sentences in the 1st ed. (p. 407):

We may find an illustration of this every-day use of the term "normal" which will help us on our way to a clear notion of a normal supply price. Let us suppose that a person conversant with the woollen trade sets himself to calculate whether a factory could afford to turn out, say, a million yards annually of a certain kind of cloth at a price of 5s. For simplicity it may be taken that the whole process of making the cloth is conducted in the factory and that nothing else is done there.

d. The following footnote in the 1st ed. (p. 408 n.) was deleted from the 2nd ed.:

> We need not trouble ourselves to consider just here whether the ground-rent of the factory must be put into a class by itself: this belongs to a group of questions which will be discussed in Book VI. We are also taking no notice of rates and taxes, for which he would of course have to make his account.

The reference in this footnote to "Book VI" relates to Book V, ch. x in vol. I of the present edition.

e. This clause was inserted in the 5th ed. (p. 343).

f. In the 1st ed. (p. 419) this opening clause ran as follows: "Let us suppose a supply schedule made on just the same plan as our demand schedule:"

g. This reference was inserted in the 2nd ed. (p. 403 n.).

h. This reference was inserted in the 2nd ed. (p. 404 n.).

359

a. The words "flow, or" before the word "(annual)" were inserted in the 4th ed. (p. 423).

b. So since the 2nd ed. (pp. 405–6). In the 1st ed. (p. 420) the remainder of this sentence ran as follows:

but at a later stage in the growth of the volume of production, when it has perhaps become profitable to substitute largely machine work for hand work and steam power for muscular force, the supply price may diminish in consequence of an increase in the volume of production.

In the 1st ed. (p. 420 n.) there was the following footnote attached to the word "production" at the end of the sentence here quoted, which was deleted from the 2nd ed.:

> Some difficulties connected with the aggregate outlay required for producing any given amount of a commodity, will be discussed in the following Book. But if we agree provisionally to regard it as estimated by multiplying the amount produced into its marginal supply price, we may then fairly assume that no economies in production which arise directly out of an increase in the amount produced, that is, no economies which do not require the supply curve to be re-drawn, could have the effect of making the total outlay for a large amount less than for a smaller amount. Thus we get the law that though the supply price may diminish with an increase in the amount produced, its diminution cannot be greater than in proportion to the increase in the amount produced. If a curve be drawn such that the product of the distances of every point of it from Ox and Oy is a constant quantity, such a curve may be called a *constant outlay* curve. Let a series of such curves be drawn (that is, a series of rectangular hyperbolas with Ox and Oy as asymptotes). The one law then which a supply curve is bound to obey is that a point moving along it towards the right can never pass from a larger constant outlay curve to a smaller one: and of course, therefore, no supply curve can cut the same constant outlay curve more than once. The geometrical reasonings of this chapter however assume nothing more than the obvious fact that there cannot be two supply prices per unit for the same amount; that is, that the supply curve cannot cut the same vertical line twice.

c. Although the text of footnote 1 dates without change from the 1st ed. (Book V, ch. v, §1, p. 419 n.), apart from the two concluding sentences which were inserted in the 2nd ed., the diagram in its present form dates from the 2nd ed. (p. 405 n.). In the 1st ed., in place of the curves of supply prices required by the text, Marshall inadvertently put in the series of demand curves shown here.

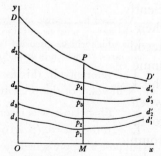

d. This and the next sentence were inserted in the 2nd ed. (p. 405 n.).

a. So since the 6th ed. (p. 345) where this clause replaced the following concluding sentence of this section, dating from the 2nd ed. (p. 406):

And, in order that we may get a clear view of the broad relations between normal demand and supply, let us leave them out of account, and confine our attention in the remainder of this chapter to cases in which the normal supply price either remains constant for different amounts or increases as the amount produced increases.

b. In the 1st ed. (Book V, ch. v, pp. 420–2) the foregoing paragraph and footnotes 1 and 2 on page 346 of vol. 1 in the present edition (in their original form) were succeeded by the following paragraph and section, which were deleted from the 2nd ed.:

The remarks that were made in the course of the preceding chapter on the terms Normal and Market contain all that it is necessary to add here to the account of the demand schedule which was given in the third Book. Attention was then called chiefly to the direct demand of the ultimate consumer: but in the long run the demand of dealers for a finished commodity is completely governed by and implicitly follows the demand of its ultimate consumers. The trade demand for raw materials and other factors of production presents some difficulties of its own, which must be reserved for discussion later on under the head of joint demand.

Normal demand schedule.

§2. In choosing our typical case of the equilibrium of normal demand and supply, we will consider a period sufficiently long to enable the economic forces at work to develop their chief effects; and we will provisionally leave out of account the facts that none of them act instantaneously and some of them act very slowly. Provisional assumptions of this kind are dangerous if made tacitly or unconsciously, but when properly used they are of great service in helping us to break up, and conquer one by one the difficulties of a complex problem.

Let us then again distinctly call to mind that interval between an economic change and the full development of its effects, to which we have already referred as obscuring

Difficulties arising from the lagging of effects behind their causes occur with regard to both demand and supply.

the influence that a fall in the price of a commodity has on the volume of its consumption[1]. And on the side of supply the same lagging of an effect behind its cause makes it very difficult to say what part of the economies which followed any increase in the volume of production are to be attributed to it, and what part are more properly to be ascribed to the mere lapse of time. We know that an increased production cannot instantly create that improved organization of industry which is sure to result from it after a while. Time is required to enable more economical methods to be gradually worked out; and some economies would certainly have been attained through the growth of knowledge, even if there had been no increase in the volume of production. In many practical problems the difficulties arising from this source are very serious, both on the side of demand and on that of supply. Each case must be treated on its own merits; no universal rule is possible.

They are set aside by the convention on which we now proceed.

But let us now agree, as a working arrangement, that the increase of consumption which will result from a fall of price, when people have become familiarized with the change, is to be supposed provisionally to follow immediately on it; allowance being made separately and at a later stage for the gradual growth of this familiarity. In like manner all those economies which will be effected in consequence of an increase in the volume of production, are to be attributed to it as their cause, and to be supposed provisionally to follow immediately on it; allowance for any interval that may have elapsed between the cause and the effect being deferred till the details of the special case are under study, and account is being taken of other disturbing influences. But any economy in production that is the result of an independent invention, is to be placed from the first on a different footing, and regarded as an improvement in the arts of production.

Thus any broad change in fashion, any substantive new invention, any catastrophe such as a great war or pestilence, or the development or dwindling away of a source of supply of the commodity in question, or of a raw material used in it, or of another commodity which is a rival and possible

[1] Book III, ch. II, §8 and ch. III, §6.

substitute for it:—such changes as these may cause the prices set against any given annual (or daily) consumption and production of the commodity to cease to be its normal demand and supply prices for that volume of consumption and production; or, in other words, they may render it necessary to make out a new demand schedule or a new supply schedule, or both of them. But so long as there is no substantive change in the conditions of demand or supply; so long as the only important changes in the price at which purchasers can be found for the commodity, and the price at which producers can afford to supply it, are those changes which are due to an increase or diminution in the volume of the amount of the commodity produced and sold; so long we may regard the demand schedule and the supply schedule as representing the broad outlines of normal demand and normal supply.

The footnote to the first sentence of the second of the paragraphs just quoted refers to Book III, ch. ii, §7 and ch. iii, §5 in vol. 1 of the present edition. It should be noted that the first sentence of the concluding paragraph beginning "Thus any broad change in fashion, any substantive new invention...etc." was retained with only minor verbal changes in later editions and will be found in Book V, ch. xii, §1 (page 462) in vol. 1 of the present edition. See also Book V, ch. xii, §3.

c.   It may be noted that in the 1st ed. (pp. 403–5) the first five paragraphs of this section (§6) were placed in Book V, ch. iii, §5, and that the footnote to the fourth paragraph (page 346 in vol. 1 of the present edition) was placed in Book V, ch. v, §3 (pp. 422 n.–3 n.).

d.   So since the 2nd ed. (p. 406). In the 1st ed. (p. 404) the first part of this sentence ran as follows:

The only equilibria of any practical importance are stable equilibria, that is, are such that if the price is displaced a little from one of them it will tend to return...etc.

PAGE 346

a.   So since the 3rd ed. (p. 425) where this sentence replaced the following sentences dating from the 1st ed. (p. 405):

If the stone is allowed to fall freely it will move back to its equilibrium position, pass through it, return again through it, and after several rhythmical oscillations be gradually reduced to rest by the resistance of the air. The oscillations of the scale of production about its position of equilibrium will be of a somewhat similar kind. If all the general conditions of the market, other than the original disturbance, the effects of which we are tracing, remain unchanged sufficiently long, it will be brought to rest in its position of equilibrium by the friction which its surroundings oppose to its continued movement; and meanwhile the price of the commodity will have been oscillating in like manner about its equilibrium position and will come to rest when the scale of production comes to its position of rest.

b. This and the next sentence were inserted in the 5th ed. (p. 346).

c. This clause was inserted in the 2nd ed. (p. 408 n.).

d. The following paragraphs, which concluded this footnote in the 1st ed. (p. 423 n.), were deleted from the 2nd ed.:

> Though in this chapter we take our typical case of stable equilibrium with reference to long-period normal prices, the above diagram is equally applicable to short-period normal prices; but, as was argued in the last chapter, the supply price will in that case increase, under all ordinary conditions, with an increase in the amount produced: that is the supply curve will generally be inclined positively.
>
> The diagram may also be adapted to represent the oscillations of a market price similar to those described above in chapter II. But the causes which determine supply price for market bargainings are fundamentally different from those that determine normal supply price, whether for long periods or short; and the chief purposes for which the diagram is wanted in the theory of normal value have nothing corresponding to them in the theory of market value.

Marshall's attitude towards market demand and supply curves is reflected in the following extract from a letter from him to John Neville Keynes dated 26 October 1888, when the latter was reading the proofs of the first edition of Marshall's *Principles of Economics*:

I intended to tell you that I acted deliberately in applying the curves only to problems of Normal Values and not to Market Values. Market curves can be drawn: but I should agree with Wicksteed that they could never have a shape that would correspond to the Law of Increasing return. And I don't think they would be of much practical use. I considered whether I would introduce "market" curves, and explain the difference between them and Normal curves: but thought I should only bother the reader.

In a later letter to J. N. Keynes, dated 8 December 1888, Marshall wrote as follows:

I am quite ashamed to ask you to look at MSS. of mine when you ought to be doing your own book. But the case is one in which I do very much want advice: The inclosed was part of the first systematic account of my views on value (I can't fix the date, but I believe it was 1870. I know for certain it was before 1874). In them I have divided markets according to lengths of periods A, B, C, D (for short statement see p. 24, 1) and make the supply curve a horizontal straight line for A, necessarily inclined positively for B and C, and of all sorts of shapes for D. (There is some exaggeration in the D figures as I drew them.)

Substantially I believe the account given in these papers to be right and that given by Wicksteed (as I understand it) to be wrong. I have however a great deal more to say about the D curves some of which is already in slip; and some of which was to have come later, but will now go anyhow into Books IV and V.

In writing the chapter on "Domestic Values" in the appendix to my Treatise on Foreign Trade, I left out about $A:B:C:D$ partly because they do not bear directly on foreign trade problems. And when writing my present Book V, I decided after some doubt to do the same.

But now I am inclined to think that my fear of over-complexity has led me to adopt a course which is likely to be misunderstood; and I am doubtful whether I ought not to bring back the substance of $A:B:C:D$.

Ought I?

There appears to be no record amongst Marshall's papers of the curves to which he refers in this second letter.

The originals of the two letters cited here are in the Marshall Library at Cambridge. Keynes's reply is not extant.

PAGE 347

a. This sentence was inserted here in the 2nd ed. (p. 408).

In the 1st ed. (p. 503) this sentence was placed in Book VI, ch. III, where it ran as follows:

This then points to a limitation of the doctrine that the price at which a thing can be produced represents its real cost of production, that is, the efforts and sacrifices which have been directly and indirectly devoted to its production.

In the 1st ed. this was succeeded by the following sentence:

That doctrine might indeed represent facts accurately enough in a stationary society, in which the habits of life, and the methods and volume of production remained unchanged from one generation to another; provided that people were tolerably free to choose those occupations for their capital and labour which seemed most advantageous.

In the 2nd ed. (p. 408) the word "might" in the first line of this second sentence was changed to "would".

In the 4th ed. (p. 427) the following additional sentence was inserted after the one just quoted: "In that state average value and normal value would be the same thing." Both these latter sentences were deleted from the 6th ed.

b. This sentence dates from the 1st ed. (Book VI, ch. III, §7, pp. 503–4) except for the insertion of the word "rapid" before "change" in the 6th ed. (p. 347). In the 1st ed. it was succeeded by the following sentence which was deleted from the 5th ed.:

It represents only the equilibrium of the forces working at the margins of demand and supply, tending to increase the amount demanded on the one hand, or to diminish the amount supplied at the equilibrium price.

c. The remainder of this paragraph dates from the 2nd ed. (p. 409).

d. The first two sentences of this paragraph date from the 5th ed (p. 348) and the third from the 2nd ed. (p. 409).

e. This paragraph was inserted in the 5th ed. (p. 348).

f. This footnote was inserted in the 6th ed. (p. 347 n.).

PAGE 348

a. The first sentence of this paragraph dates from the 2nd ed. (p. 409).

b. This and the succeeding sentence date from the 4th ed. (p. 427) except that in that edition the references in the first sentence were to "chapters v and xi of this Book" and to the "Note at the end of chapter xiv", in place of the references in the text of the present edition, which date from the 5th ed., where the latter part of Book V was largely rearranged and the Note at the end of ch. xiv became Appendix I. By an oversight in the 5th ed. the reference to ch. xi was retained, although owing to the rearrangement, it should have been altered to ch. xii.

c. This and the next three paragraphs and the first sentence of the fourth paragraph date from the 3rd ed. (pp. 427–8).

a. The remainder of this paragraph dates from the 5th ed. (p. 350).

a. This paragraph dates from the 6th ed. (p. 350).

BOOK V, CHAPTER IV

THE INVESTMENT AND DISTRIBUTION OF RESOURCES

a. Except where otherwise stated the wording of this chapter dates substantially from the 1st edition.

b. In the 1st edition this chapter (Book VI, ch. v there) was entitled "Cost of Production. The Investment of Capital in a Business"; in the 2nd ed. (Book V, ch. IV), "Investment of Capital in a Business. Prime Cost and Total Cost"; in the 3rd and 4th editions, "Investment of Capital for a distant Return. Prime Cost and Total Cost"; in the 5th edition, "The Investment of Resources. The Principle of Substitution". Its present title dates from the 6th edition.

c. This sentence was inserted in the 6th ed. (p. 351). In the 1st ed. §1 (p. 513) began as follows:

THE relations between the cost of production of a commodity, and that of the things used in making it, have been considered in the preceding chapters chiefly with reference to limitations of various kinds in the sources of supply; and we have next to discuss the principles on which the general expenses of carrying on a business are to be shared among its several products.

The true nature of the investment of capital is disguised by the modern methods of doing business, in which the undertaker buys most of the labour required for his work; for he thinks chiefly of the expenses of production and seldom pays much attention to the efforts and sacrifices to which those payments more or less closely correspond, and which constitute the real cost of production. It will be well. . . etc.

In the 2nd ed. (p. 410) the first paragraph just quoted was deleted and § 1 opened with the sentence beginning: "The true nature of the investment of capital. . . etc."

In the 3rd ed. (p. 429) the words "investment of capital" were replaced by the words "investment of resources for a distant return".

In the 5th ed. (p. 351) the following sentences were inserted before the sentence beginning: "The true nature of the investment of resources for a distant return. . . etc.":

THE first difficulty to be cleared up in our study of normal values, is the nature of the motives which govern the investment of resources for a distant return. Incidentally it is to be seen how these motives operate in nearly the same way in all phases of civilisation, and are not peculiar to its modern, or so called "capitalistic" phase. Our illustrations will be equally applicable to Robinson Crusoe and to an enterprising capitalist builder of to-day.

In the 6th ed. (p. 351) the sentence beginning "The true nature of the investment. . . etc.", and the sentences beginning "The first difficulty to be cleared up. . . etc." were deleted and were replaced by the opening sentence in the present text.

PAGE 352

a. So since the 4th ed. (p. 431).

In the first two editions this sentence ran as follows: "Probably the impelling motive would be much stronger than the deterring with regard to some part of the house;"

In the 3rd ed. (p. 430) it ran: "Probably the gain would be much stronger than the 'real' cost with regard to some part of the house; (and from this he would derive a Producers Surplus or Rent)."

b. The following note, attached to the word "capital" was inserted in the 5th ed. (p. 352 n.) but was deleted from the 6th ed.:

Prof. Boehm Bawerk (*Recent Literature on Interest*, p. 37 fn.), seems to suggest that this analysis counts compound interest twice over. It may be well therefore to make an explicit statement on the subject. The balance between efforts and the satisfaction resulting from them may be made up to any day that is found convenient. But whatever day is chosen, one simple rule must be followed:—Every element whether an effort or a satisfaction, which dates from a time anterior to that day must have compound interest for the interval accumulated upon it: and every element which dates from a time posterior to that day must have compound interest for the interval discounted from it. If the day be anterior to the beginning of the enterprise, then every element must be discounted. But if, as is usual in such cases, the day be that when the efforts are finished, and the house is ready for use, the efforts must carry compound interest up to that day, and the satisfactions must all be discounted back to that day.

c. In the first two editions this section was concluded by a sentence, which in the 3rd ed. (p. 430 n.) was placed in a footnote together with a reference to Mathematical Note XIV; while in the 4th ed. (p. 431 n.) a further reference was added to Pareto. The sentence and references, which were deleted from the 6th ed. ran as follows:

> On such a supposition as that made in this Section, we may look upon capital as stored-up effort, the amount of effort and the amount of sacrifice involved in the waiting for the result being measured quantitatively. See Mathematical Note XIV. Comp. also Pareto, *Cours d'Economie Politique*, §§ 720–8.

PAGE 353

a. This sentence was inserted in the 7th ed. (p. 353).

b. "future gratification" from the 6th ed. (p. 353) "distant pleasure" in the first five editions.

c. The remainder of this paragraph and the whole of the next paragraph, with the footnote attached to it, were inserted in the 6th ed. (pp. 353–4).

PAGE 354

a. So since the 4th ed. (pp. 432–3), where this paragraph replaced the following paragraph dating from the 1st ed. (p. 516):

But in fact in nearly every business undertaking the incomings are a constant process as well as the outgoings. And to complete the case we must suppose a balance sheet struck looking backwards and looking forwards. Looking backwards we should add together the net outlays accumulated up to that time, deducting from each element of outlay any incomings that came in at the same time. Looking forwards we should deduct from each future incoming any outlay that would be made at the same time, together with allowance for the undertaker's own remuneration; and regarding the result as the net incoming at that time, we should discount it at compound interest for the period during which it would be deferred. The aggregate of the net incomings so discounted would be balanced against the aggregate of the accumulated outlays: and if the two were just equal, the business would be just remunerative.

b. Although the paragraph to which this footnote is attached dates from the 4th ed., the wording of the footnote dates from the 1st ed. (pp. 516–17).

PAGE 355

a. This paragraph reached its final form in the 6th ed. (p. 355), where the word "alert" was inserted before the words "business man", and where two sentences dating from the 4th ed. were deleted.

In the 1st ed. (p. 517) this paragraph ran as follows:

When at the beginning of a business an estimate is made of the profits likely to be earned in it, all the entries for out-goings and incomings alike are prospective. And at that and every successive stage the mind of the undertaker is ceaselessly striving so to modify his arrangements as to obtain greater results with a given expenditure or equal results with a less expenditure. He is continually comparing the efficiency and the supply prices of different factors of production which may be used in obtaining the same result, so as to hit upon that combination which will give the largest incomings in proportion to any given outlay; or, in other words he is ceaselessly occupied with the law of substitution.

In the 4th ed. (p. 433), where the first sentence of the paragraph (except for the word "alert") was inserted as in the text of vol. 1 of the present edition, the remainder of the paragraph ran as follows:

He is continually comparing the efficiency and the costs of different ways of obtaining his object. He is always look-ing for new suggestions, watching the experiments of others and trying experiments himself; so as to hit upon that com-bination which will yield the largest incomings in proportion to any given outlay; or, in other words, he is ceaselessly occupied with the principle of substitution.

These two sentences were deleted from the 6th ed. It should be noted that in the first three editions Marshall always used the term "the law of substitution", but that from the 4th ed. onwards he changed this to "the principle of substitution".

b. The remainder of this sentence was inserted in the 5th ed. (p. 355).

PAGE 356

a. The words "the outer limit, or" were inserted before the word "margin" in the 4th ed. (p. 434).

b. This clause was inserted in the 7th ed. (p. 356).

c. Apart from some additions to the concluding paragraph in the 6th ed., the whole of this section dates from the 5th ed. (pp. 356–9).

PAGE 357

a. This footnote which was inserted in the 5th ed. (p. 356 n.), refers to Book VI, ch. 1, §7 in the 4th ed. In the 3rd ed., the corresponding reference would be to Book VI, ch. 1, §6; in the 2nd ed. to Book VI, ch. 1, §2; and in the 1st ed. to Book VII, ch. 1, §3. It may be noted that the section referred to (Book VI, ch. 1, §7 in the 4th ed.) deals with the operation of the principle of substitution, but that the actual wording of the greater part of that section was transferred in the 5th and subsequent editions, not to Book V, ch. IV, §4, as might seem from this footnote, but to Book V, ch. VIII, §2.

PAGE 359

a. The word "alert" was inserted before "business man" in the 6th ed. (p. 359).

b. This and the following sentence were inserted in the 6th ed. (p. 359).

c. This sentence was inserted in the 5th ed. (p. 359).

d. So since the 4th ed. (pp. 434–5). In the 1st ed. (Book VI, ch. IV, §1) and the 2nd ed. (Book V, ch. IV, §4) this paragraph ran as follows:

WHEN investing his capital in providing the means of carrying on a business, the undertaker looks to being recouped by the price obtained for its various products; and he expects to be able under normal conditions to charge for each of them a price that will cover not only its (money) *prime cost*; *i.e.* the expenses which he incurs directly and specially for its production, but also a share of the general expenses of the business, which we may call its *supplementary cost*. These two elements together make its (money) *total cost*.

In the 3rd ed. (p. 434) the words "*special, direct,* or" were inserted before "*prime cost*"; the clause following after the words "*prime cost*" in the earlier editions was deleted, and the words "but also bear its proper share" were substituted for the words "but also a share".

e. This paragraph dates from the 4th ed. (p. 435). In the 1st ed. (pp. 519–20) and the 2nd ed. (pp. 415–16) there was the following account of prime cost:

We may follow ordinary usage, and take the term *prime cost* in a narrow sense, which includes nothing but the (money) cost of the raw material used in making the commodity and the wages of that part of the labour spent on it which is paid by the day or the week: the salaries of the upper employees are excluded, partly because the time which they have devoted specially to it cannot always be easily ascertained, and partly because the charges to which the business is put on account of their salaries cannot be adapted quickly to changes in the amount of work there is for them to do.

This is the *prime cost* which a manufacturer has commonly in view when, trade being slack, he is calculating the lowest price at which it would be worth his while to accept an order, irrespectively of any effect that his action might have in spoiling the market for future orders. And in extreme cases he will even be willing to accept a lower price than this. For when he has been for some time short of work, and has already dismissed all save the best of his employees, it would —to say nothing of any less selfish motive—almost answer his purpose to pay the remainder full wages to beat time, so to speak; in order that he may have them at hand when trade revives, and high profits are again to be made.

In the first three editions these paragraphs were succeeded by a discussion of supplementary costs which was transferred in the 4th and later editions to Book V, ch. v, §6.

In the 3rd ed. (p. 434) the first five sentences of the paragraph in the present text beginning "There are great variations in the usage of the term prime cost in business." were substantially in their present form, though with the interpolation, after the third sentence ending with the words: "...changes in the amount of work there is for them to do.", of the following sentences: "Special costs are those incurred for a near return. Supplementary costs are those incurred for a distant return." The next paragraph in the 3rd ed. began: "This is the special cost which a manufacturer has commonly in view...etc." and was the same as in the second of the above paragraphs quoted from the first two editions, except for the substitution of the word "special" for the word "prime" before "cost" in the first line.

PAGE 360

a. The first five paragraphs of this section (§6) were inserted in the 5th ed. (p. 360–2).

b. This quotation and reference were inserted in the 3rd ed. (p. 434 n.) where they were succeeded by the following sentences, which (after being abbreviated in the 5th ed. (p. 360 n.)) were deleted from the 7th ed.:

> Elaborate statistics of the various elements of cost of production in certain trades have been made by the Commissioner of Labour in the United States; and his Report for 1890 contains many suggestive remarks on the subject of this chapter. See also the Report of the Massachusetts Bureau of Labour for the same year.

PAGE 361

a. So since the 7th ed. (pp. 360–1), where this and the next sentence replaced the following sentences dating from the 5th ed. (p. 361):

For instance, foremen and other trusted artisans are seldom dismissed even in slack times: and, on the other hand, the staff in the office can be in a great measure adjusted to variations in the work of the firm by leaving vacancies unfilled and even by weeding out inefficient men during slack times; and by getting extra help or putting out some of the work in busy times. That is, some outgoings for wages are not strictly speaking prime costs in regard to any task; and some outgoings for salaries are to be regarded as more or less special to even small tasks such as that of building a single locomotive.

PAGE 362

a. So since the 6th ed. (pp. 361–2) where this sentence replaced the following sentences dating from the 5th ed. (pp. 361–2):

In the following two chapters the element of time falls into the background and some side issues connected with indirect and joint supply and demand are discussed. After which we return to consider marginal costs in relation to value, with special reference to those variations in the character of those prime and supplementary costs ... etc.

It may be observed that the reference in the first of these sentences to "the following two chapters..." was clearly intended to apply to Book V, chs. VI and VII and not to chs. V and VI.

b. This and the next paragraph were inserted in the 6th ed. (p. 362).

c. In the 7th ed. (p. 362) the following sentences, dating from the 6th ed., after the sentence ending "...he will avoid it", were deleted:

And further—though this is rather a different point—in reckoning up his probable money outgoings and incomings, if he is looking very far ahead, he may find it necessary to make some allowance for probable changes in the purchasing power of money; and even for changes in the money costs of the special kinds of labour which he is buying: and in every part of such an inquiry he must to some extent go behind money costs to real costs.

d. This footnote was inserted in the 7th ed. (p. 362). In the 4th, 5th and 6th editions there was no mention of quasi-rents throughout Book V, ch. IV. But in the 2nd ed. (p. 417) there was the following paragraph in the text which concluded the chapter:

That part of the receipts of a business which is required to defray the supplementary cost of the things produced in it, may in the long run be regarded as part of its normal profits: because the expectation of getting these gains in the long run was required to induce people to invest their capital and energies in the trade. But on the other hand when once invested the income which they yield is determined by the selling price of the products which they help to produce: it is the excess of this price over the prime cost or immediate outlay required for the production: it is, as has already been hinted, to be regarded as a Producer's Surplus or *Quasi-rent.*

To this paragraph the following marginal summary was attached: "The income that in the long run covers supplementary costs for a normally successful business, may for a short run be regarded as a *Quasi-rent.*"

In the 3rd ed. (p. 435) this paragraph was put at the beginning of a new section (§ 5) in Book V, ch. IV, dealing with supplementary cost and quasi-rent. The marginal summary just quoted was retained in the same form as in the 2nd ed., but in a list of Corrigenda facing p. 1 of the 3rd ed. there is the following correction: "Page 435, the second marginal note should read *The income that covers supplementary costs is a part of normal profits in the long run; but for a short run it may be regarded as a Quasi-rent on investments of capital and energy.*"

The opening paragraph of § 5 in the 3rd ed. was the same as the paragraph just quoted from p. 417 of the 2nd ed., down to the words "the selling price of the products which they help to produce". After that the paragraph ran as follows:

We shall find reason for describing the excess of the price over the prime cost or immediate outlay required for the production as a *Quasi-rent,* because we shall find that it has some analogy to that Producers Surplus, accruing from the ownership of fertile land, which is called Rent.

§5 then continued:

This brings us to the threshold of the main difficulty of the problem of value; and it will be well to pause a little to look at it. What can be said now is not a solution of the difficulty; but a partial statement as to the general nature of the solution which will ultimately be found for it. The statement as it stands will perhaps not be completely intelligible: but it may help to prepare the way for future explanations and to fit them into their place.

Appliances for production are of many different kinds: they include land, factories, machines, business organizations (including even such as a house-letting agency, with a good connection but little or no material capital), business ability and manual skill. The owner of any one of those will not generally apply it to produce anything, unless he expects to gain in return at least enough to compensate him for the immediate and special trouble, sacrifice and outlay involved in this particular operation, and which he could escape by declining to undertake it. Any excess which he gets above this prime cost has obviously some *prima facie* resemblance to that excess value of the produce of land over the direct cost of raising it which is the basis of rent as ordinarily understood; and we are therefore justified in calling it a Quasi-rent.

The question how close this resemblance is involves many subtle considerations, some of which have but little interest for the general reader, and the discussion of them is so arranged that he can omit them. Much of it will turn on the fact that while excess of the gross receipts which a producer gets for any of his commodities over their prime cost (that is, over that extra cost which he incurs in order to

Provisional forecast of the long study of this principle on which we are entering.

375

produce those particular things, and which he could have escaped if he had not produced them) is a temporary surplus (or quasi-rent), yet that in the long run all these temporary surpluses are needed to cover the supplementary costs of the business. They do not therefore, in the long run, yield a true surplus, corresponding to the permanent surplus which the possession of fertile land is commonly supposed to yield, and in some cases does yield, to its owner.

The question how great a part of his expenses he must enter in these prime costs, and how much he must deduct from his selling price before he calculates his surplus, depends on how far he looks ahead; or in other words, on whether he is making his calculations for a long period or only for a short.

The element of time dominates the applications of this principle.

If he is looking only a little way ahead, and is not afraid of spoiling his market; if he has got all his apparatus ready and standing idle; then a new order coming in will give him a surplus over its direct cost to him, consisting of the whole price which he receives after deducting the special outlay for raw material, for extra wages, and for wear and tear of plant involved in filling up the order. But suppose him to be looking far ahead, and proposing to extend his factory so as to do an increased business; he does not then reckon any price as affording him a real surplus, unless, after allowing for all risks, it will yield him, in addition to prime costs, sufficient to give normal profits on all his outlay for material, plant, and for building up his business connection, together with charges for depreciation through the lapse of time, and for office and other general expenses which are not reckoned in the prime, or special and direct, costs of filling up any particular order.

The conditions which govern the amount of this surplus and its relations to value depend not so much on the nature of the industry as on the period of time for which the calculation is made. But a short period for one class of industry may be a long one for another, just as the age of youth for a dog is shorter than for an elephant[1].

---

[1] This and a few other passages are reproduced from an article *On Rent* in the *Economic Journal* for March 1893. See also the remarks on Continuity in the Preface to the first edition of this volume.

To put the same thing in another way, when we are taking a broad view of normal value extending over a very long period of time, when we are investigating the causes which determine normal value "in the long run," when we are tracing the "ultimate" effects of economic causes, then the income that is derived from capital in these forms enters into the payments by which the expenses of production of the commodity in question have to be covered, and it directly controls the action of the producers who are on the margin of doubt as to whether to increase the means of production or not. But, on the other hand, when we are considering the causes which determine normal prices for a period which is short relatively to that required for largely increasing the supply of those appliances for production, then their influence on value is chiefly indirect and more or less similar to that exerted by the free gifts of nature. The shorter the period which we are considering, and the slower the process of production of those appliances, the less part will variations in the income derived from them play in checking or increasing the supply of the commodity produced by them, and in raising or lowering its supply price; and the more nearly true will it be that, for the period under discussion the net income to be derived from them is to be regarded as a producer's surplus or quasi-rent. And thus in passing from the free gifts of nature through the more permanent improvements in the soil to less permanent improvements, to farm and factory buildings, to steam engines, &c., and finally to the less durable and less slowly made implements, we find a continuous series.

From this provisional and incomplete statement it will be obvious that this producer's surplus (or quasi-rent) is of a different character from that which the worker or accumulator of capital derives from the fact that much of his work or waiting involves no sacrifice, while yet the whole of it reaps a reward. For the basis of these surpluses is a psychological peculiarity of the individual: while the quasi-rent of an appliance for production is not generally any surplus at all in the long run; but—under the influence of changing circumstance, varying fashion, innovating invention, fluc-

Caution against a confusion.

377

tuating credit, &c.—sometimes rises above, and sometimes falls below that level which was anticipated when the appliance was brought into existence. Further light will be thrown on this question later on in the present book and in the sixth book.

The whole of §5 in the 3rd ed. was deleted from the 4th ed., with the exception of the penultimate paragraph, which was placed in Book V, ch. IX (pp. 495–6) in the 4th ed., but was deleted from the 5th ed.

The article *On Rent* referred to in the footnote on p. 376 above is reproduced below (pp. 492–512).

BOOK V, CHAPTER V

EQUILIBRIUM OF NORMAL DEMAND AND SUPPLY, CONTINUED, WITH REFERENCE TO LONG AND SHORT PERIODS

PAGE 363

a. The origin of the wording of this chapter is shown throughout in the editorial notes.

b. So since the 4th edition. In the 1st edition (Book V, ch. IV) and in the 2nd and 3rd editions (Book V, ch. V) the title of this chapter was as follows: "Equilibrium of Normal Demand and Supply, continued. The term Normal with reference to Long and Short Periods."

c. This paragraph dates from the 5th ed. (p. 363). In the 1st ed. (Book V, ch. IV, pp. 406–7) the opening paragraphs of §1 ran as follows:

The economic use of the term market is wide as to space and still wider as to time, so that normal conditions may be able to assert themselves.

IT has already been noticed that in economic phrase a *market* is the whole of any district in which trade intercourse is so far free that prices tend to adjust themselves to one level easily and quickly; and that, what is even more important for our immediate purpose, the use of the term is as elastic with regard to time as it is with regard to space. The dealings in a market, in the discussion on which we are now entering, are to be taken as ranging over a sufficiently long period of time for the conditions of normal demand and normal supply freely to act, and freely to react on one another.

The length of the period required for this purpose is different in different cases; but in every case it must be sufficiently long to cover over the effects of minor disturbances and passing fluctuations; it must be long enough to allow the economic forces concerned to work themselves out with some approach to regularity and law. The period may be very short if we are considering the price of some trivial article of dress which comes suddenly into fashion, the production of which requires no specialized machinery or skill, and occupies but a small part of the material and labour that are commonly used by the trades which produce it. A longer period is wanted if we are considering the normal price, say, of wool in London; it being understood that the existing general distribution of sheep-farms all the world over is to be the basis of the calculation; and that such events as drought in Australia, and the raising of wool-freights by combinations among shippers are to be regarded as disturbing causes, the influence of which is to be eliminated in finding the normal price. A still longer period is wanted if we are considering the causes that determine in the long run the wages of shepherds in Australia, or the gradual changes in the rate at which money can be let on good mortgages there: and so on.

There is thus great elasticity in the scope which we assign to a market and in the range of the forces of whose action we take account: and in each separate application of our general reasoning a clear indication has to be given as to what conditions are taken as fixed and what as variable, and as to the length of the period to which the whole inquiry relates. This is indeed done more or less systematically in the ordinary conversation of business life.

The periods required for this purpose are different in different cases.

This elastic use of the term Normal is consistent with ordinary usage.

In the 2nd ed. (p. 418) the sentence in the second of the above paragraphs quoted from the 1st ed. beginning "The period may be very short...etc." was deleted, together with the two succeeding sentences.

In the 3rd ed. (p. 439) the original sentences remaining in the 2nd ed. were deleted and §1 opened as follows:

The present chapter is chiefly occupied with differences of degree between different parts of the problem of value, and especially normal value, resulting from differences in the length of time to which the problem relates.

In the 4th ed. (p. 436) this sentence ran as follows:

The present chapter is chiefly occupied with difficulties in the problem of value, resulting from differences between the immediate and the later effects of the same causes.

d. This paragraph dates from the 4th ed. (p. 436).

e. This paragraph dates substantially from the 1st ed. (p. 407).

f. So since the 6th ed. (p. 363). In the 5th ed. from which it dates, this sentence was inserted at the beginning of the preceding paragraph in the text.

PAGE 364

a. This sentence and the one succeeding it were inserted in the 5th ed. (p. 364).

b. This sentence dates from the 3rd ed. (pp. 439–40). In the 1st ed. (p. 410) the following paragraph was placed at the end of Book V, ch. IV, §3:

The formal language of economics is thus in harmony with the practice of business in leaving the interpretation of the term Normal in relation to demand and supply almost entirely to the context of the passage in which it occurs. By itself the term Normal Supply Price means nothing more than a supply price, the determining causes of which are so far regular in their action that general statements can be made about it, which are at once trustworthy and fairly definite. In ordinary conversation indeed a formal interpretation clause is seldom necessary, because misunderstandings can there be nipped in the bud by question and answer; and though it is more often required in written arguments which have not that safeguard, yet even there it will be found that in the large majority of cases the context explains itself so clearly as to leave no room for doubt. Thus the difficulty arising from the elastic use of the term Normal need not be a serious one, if it is fairly faced: while on the other hand much confusion and fruitless controversy have arisen from ignoring it.

In the 2nd ed. (p. 419) the first two sentences of the paragraph just quoted were deleted, while the last two were placed in a separate paragraph.

In the 3rd ed. (pp. 439–40) the first of the two sentences retained from the 2nd ed. was reworded as in the present edition.

c. The remainder of this section (§ 1) dates substantially from the 1st ed. (pp. 408–10).

d. This reference was inserted in the 2nd ed. (p. 422 n.).

PAGE 365

a. This sentence, which in the earlier editions was in parentheses in the text, was placed in a footnote in the 4th ed. (p. 437 n.).

PAGE 366

a. The whole of this section (§ 2) in its present form dates from the 4th ed. (pp. 438–41) apart from the footnote attached to the end of the first paragraph, which was inserted in the 6th ed. (p. 366 n.).

b. In the 1st ed. there were four references to the notion of a stationary state: (i) in Book IV, ch. VII, §1, p. 287; which will be found on page 223 in vol. I of the present edition; (ii) in a footnote to Book V, ch. IV, §6, p. 416 n., which was retained in the later editions and constituted the first paragraph of the footnote on page 379 in vol. I of the present edition; (iii) in Book VI, ch. III, §7, p. 503, which will be found in the Editorial Appendix to Book V, chapters VIII–X (see pp. 479–80 below); (iv) in Book VII, ch. I, §2, p. 540, where the notion of an "almost stationary state" was adopted as a preliminary to a discussion of the supply prices of labour and capital, in the following terms:

Let us begin by taking a general survey of the causes that govern true Normal value, estimated for a period sufficiently long to enable the economic causes concerned to work out their chief normal effects. The easiest plan for presenting vividly to our minds this uninterrupted action of economic causes is to suppose an almost stationary state, in which there are for a long time no great new inventions nor any other important changes in the methods of production, or in the channels of trade; no great wars and not very much variation in the habits of consumption, or in social and industrial habits and institutions generally. In such a state business

[margin note: Let us suppose an almost stationary state.]

381

will pursue its even tenor from generation to generation, and the experience of the past will enable people to forecast the future with certainty, and to adapt their arrangements closely to it.

In the 2nd ed. (p. 481) and the 3rd ed. (p. 501) the concept of a stationary state was transferred to Book V, ch. XI, §1, where it was used to throw light on the relations between average expenses of production and normal supply price (see Appendix H, §4 in vol. I of the present edition), and was described as follows:

But let us suppose a perfectly stationary state in which the same things are done in the same way and to the same extent for many generations.

In a world of change, such as ours is, the terms "aggregate" or "average" expenses of production have in general no exact and definite meaning; though of course they may be legitimately used, with an artificial interpretation clause, for the special purposes of a particular problem.

One such use is found when we suppose a world in which everything is, and has long been, in a Stationary state; in which the same amounts of the same things have been produced in the same ways by the same classes of people for many generations together; and in which therefore this supply of the appliances for production has had full time to be adjusted to the steady demand.

c.   This footnote was inserted in the 6th ed. (p. 366 n.).

PAGE 367

a.   In the 4th ed. (pp. 439–40) this and the next two paragraphs replaced the following paragraphs dating from the 2nd ed. (Book V, ch. XI, §1, pp. 481–2):

Of course we might assume that in our Stationary state every business remained always of the same size, and with the same trade connection. But we need not go so far as that; it will suffice to suppose that firms rise and fall with the same regular monotony as the trees of a forest; and that, though some firms may turn the economies of production on a large scale to better account than others, yet they will not obtain a preponderating influence in, and change the character of, their own branch of industry. The representative firm would therefore be of a constant size, as the representative tree of a forest is; its internal economies would be constant; and its external also, because the aggregate volume of production would be constant. The marginal price, the expectation of which just induced persons to enter the trade, would be sufficient to cover in the long run the cost of building up a trade connection which was afterwards to decay; these would be the normal expenses governing the normal supply price for long periods.

And in such a state there would be no distinction between long-period and short-period normal value, or between true normal price and sub-normal price, at all events if we supposed that in that monotonous world the harvests themselves were uniform: for the representative firm being always of the same size, and always doing the same class of business to the same extent and in the same way with no slack times, and no specially busy times, its normal expenses by which the normal supply price is governed would be always the same. The demand schedule and the supply schedule would always be the same, and normal price would never vary.

There would be no such things as quasi-rents: for the income earned by every appliance of production being truly anticipated beforehand would represent the normal measure of the efforts and appliances required to call it into existence. But true rents would remain. For that which cannot be increased by man's effort in time however long, would still have no supply price; and its value would still be found by capitalizing the income derived from the differential advantages which it offered for production; and that income would be determined by the expenses of production of that part of the supply which had not the benefit of any permanent differential advantages; i.e. by the marginal expenses of production.

In such a state there would be no quasi-rents; but true rents would remain.

PAGE 368

a. The two paragraphs constituting this section (§ 3) date from the 4th ed. (p. 441).

b. In the 8th edition "V. xi. 6"; emended in vol. i of the present edition to give the correct reference.

PAGE 369

a. The following concluding paragraph of this section in the 4th ed. (p. 441) was deleted from the 6th ed.:

Of the many forces which affect the value of any commodity, some are more important in connection with some questions, and others in connection with others. Problems of value may be classified on many plans: the best plan at starting is to classify them according to the periods to which they refer. Let us do this with reference to a concrete instance.

b. This paragraph dates from the 4th ed. (p. 442). In the 1st ed. (Book V, ch. iv, § 3) and in the 2nd and 3rd editions (Book V, ch. v, § 2), this section began as follows:

But though applications of the term Normal are thus elastic, and capable of being extended gradually from very short to very long periods; yet we shall find, as we go on, that these periods may be divided roughly into two classes according as the problems with which we are dealing do or do not range over very long periods. In the first class there is time for the supply of those things which are used in producing the commodity, (or in other words, its factors of production), to adapt itself to the demand; in the second class there is not. The relation which this first class of normal equilibria bears to the second may be made clearer by observing that it is similar to the relation which this second class bears to the temporary equilibria discussed in chapter II; for in that case the periods over which we were studying the action of the forces of demand and supply were so short, that cost of production could not exercise any direct influence over the supply price.

c. So since the 4th ed. (p. 442). In the 1st ed. (pp. 410–11) this paragraph ran as follows:

For instance, on the day following a large catch of mackerel the price in the market may settle down after a little manœuvring to an equilibrium level at as many pence as it had been at shillings on the previous day; and this change will in no way depend on the normal cost of catching mackerel, it will be governed by the volume of the past catch, with perhaps some slight reference to the chance that a similar catch may be had on the morrow.

In the 2nd ed. (p. 420) the first sentence was the same as the one just quoted from the 1st ed., but the paragraph then continued as follows:

If we suppose the boat owned by a capitalist undertaker who pays the fisherman, the net earnings of his boat for the day will be the excess of the price he gets for his fish over his outlay for wages and stores, together with allowances for injury done to the boat and net by the day's work. This excess will be a Producer's Surplus or quasi-rent, which for that particular day may be either more or less than the normal supply price required to make it worth his while to provide the boat and its equipment and the business organisation needed for managing it and selling its catch. But if, in the long run and on the average, the quasi-rent is more than this normal supply price, capital will drift into the fishing trade; if less it will drift out; that is to say old boats and nets when worn out, will seldom be replaced. And therefore, if the general conditions of the fishing trade are "stationary" the earnings of the boat will oscillate about this normal supply price as a position of stable equilibrium.

In the 3rd ed. (pp. 440–1) this paragraph was only altered by the suppression of the term "quasi-rent"; this involved the following changes in the two sentences affected: "The excess on this particular day may be either more or less than the normal supply price required to make it worth his while...etc."
"But, if in the long run and on the average, the excess is more than this normal supply price, capital will drift...etc."
d.   This sentence dates substantially from the 1st ed. (p. 411).
e.   So since the 4th ed. (pp. 442–3). In the 1st ed. (p. 411) the remainder of this paragraph ran as follows:

The increased demand for fish could be met only by bringing into the fishing trade people from outside, who were not fitted by training to do its work well, and to whom many of its ordinary incidents would prove great hardships. Old and unsuitable boats would be pressed into the service; there would be great waste of labour before the fish were brought to shore. For a year or two the normal price of fish would therefore be much higher than before. Variations in the catch of fish from day to day might make the market price oscillate at least as violently as before about the normal level, but the normal supply price for an increased amount would rise rapidly with every such increase. The normal price we have just been speaking of, is a *short-period* normal supply price; and if we turn to consider the *long-period* normal supply price, we shall find that it is determined by a different set of causes, and with different results.

The following footnote to the second sentence ending with the word "shore" was deleted from the 2nd ed.:

And there would be a further waste before the fish reached the ultimate consumers, because the existing organization of the inland trade in fish would be insufficient for its work. It has already been remarked that there is no reason why we should not include, where it is convenient to do so, as part of the "production" of fish, the work of those who distribute it overland as well as that of the fishermen who take it out of the sea (Book II, ch. III, § 1).

In the 2nd ed. (pp. 420–1) the single paragraph in the text of the 1st ed. was expanded into the two following paragraphs.

But next suppose there to be great increase in the general demand for fish, such for instance as might arise from the spreading of a disease through all kinds of farm stock simultaneously, by which meat was made a dear and dangerous food. The increased demand for fish could not well be met without bringing into the fishing trade some people from outside, who were not fitted by training to do its work well, and to whom many of its ordinary incidents would prove great hardships. Old and unsuitable boats would be pressed into the service; and if seaworthy would earn a surplus, or quasi-rent, above their expenses of working, which they could not earn before: while the better class of boats would earn a quasi-rent that would amount in a single year to fifty per cent. or more of their total cost; and able fishermen, whether paid by shares or by the day, might for a time get twice their ordinary wages; and the (short-period) normal price of fish would be higher than before. Variations in the catch of fish from day to day might make the market price oscillate at least as violently as before about this normal level, but that level for an increased amount would rise rapidly with every such increase of demand.

Of course these high prices would tend to bring capital and labour into the trade: but if it were expected that the disease among live stock would not last very long, and that therefore the unusual demand for fish would die away in a few years, people would be cautious about investing capital and skill in a trade that was in danger of being glutted. And therefore, though when the demand slackened off, the price would fall too, and probably below its old level; yet so long as the demand was fully maintained the price would keep up. And here we see an illustration of the almost universal law that *an increase in the amount demanded raises the short-period normal supply price*.

In the 3rd ed. (p. 441) the only alteration of substance was in the 3rd sentence of the first of the above paragraphs quoted from the 2nd ed., which ran as follows in the 3rd ed.: "Old and unsuitable boats would be pressed into the service; the better class of boats might earn in a year enough to pay fifty per cent. or more on their total cost; and able fishermen...etc."

PAGE 370

a. This paragraph dates, with one small change noted below, from the 1st ed. (pp. 411–12). Apart from the deletion of a footnote there were no changes in the 2nd and 3rd editions. In the 4th ed. the paragraph was almost completely reworded, but in the 5th and later editions (see vol. 1, pages 370–1) the text returned substantially to that of the 1st ed. The following was the text of this paragraph in the 4th ed. (pp. 443–4):

Lastly to study the causes which govern long-period normal supply price, let us suppose that those classes of the people who live largely on a fish diet increase steadily from one generation to another. We now concentrate our chief attention on causes which act slowly but continuously. We put aside fluctuations that come and go in a year or two, very much as in the preceding case we put aside fluctuations from day to day. Our normal supply price now for any amount of fish is the price per unit, which will slowly call into the fishing trade capital and labour enough to obtain that amount of fish in a day's or week's fishing of average good fortune. The governing forces of supply, which we now consider, would not only call sailors back to their fishing homes: they would also induce many farm lads in villages neighbouring on the sea to adopt a seafaring life, and they would cause long-headed men to see that there was a trust-worthy field for the investment of new capital in building fishing boats of the newest and most expensive patterns, and so on. Thus on the assumption that the supply of fish in the sea is inexhaustible, the better organization, which attends on an increasing industry, may bring into play the tendency to increasing return. An increased supply could then be produced at a lower price after a time sufficiently long to enable the normal action of economic causes to work itself out: and, the term Normal being taken to refer to a long period of time, the normal price of fish would *decrease* with an increase in the amount produced.

b. In the 8th edition "V. xi. i."; emended in vol. i of the present edition to give the correct reference.

PAGE 371

a. This sentence was reworded in its present form in the 5th ed. (p. 371). In the first three editions it ran as follows: "In any case the real cost and therefore (the general purchasing power of money being assumed stationary) the normal money cost of equipping a good boat with an efficient crew...etc."

b. The following footnote attached to this sentence in the 1st ed. (p. 412 n.) was deleted from the 2nd ed.:

We are speaking in the text of the price of the fish when brought to land: but the cost of getting fish from the hands of the fisherman to those of the retailer is much greater in proportion than it would be if the traffic were larger, with more special fish trains, more large ice depots and so on; for at present the retailer's profits on his turnover are necessarily at a high rate because as a rule he can sell but few fish in the course of a day. If his neighbours bought more largely, he could sell, and by competition would be compelled to sell at a price much nearer that which he paid. The normal retail price (the term normal having reference to a long period of time), would decrease much more rapidly than the wholesale price with every increase in the aggregate production.

c. This quotation from Tooke dates from the 3rd ed. (p. 444 n.).

d. This sentence dates from the 6th ed. (p. 371 n.) where it replaced the following sentence dating from the 4th ed. (p. 444 n.):

These incidents illustrate well the general principle that an increased demand may raise the supply price of a thing even for several years together where a permanently increased demand would be met by a lower supply price.

PAGE 372

a. This paragraph was inserted in the 4th ed. (p. 444).

b. This paragraph, and the first two sentences of the next, date substantially from the 3rd ed. (p. 445).

388

c. This and the next three sentences were inserted in the 5th ed. (pp. 372–3).

d. So since the 6th ed. (p. 372 n.). This footnote was first inserted in the 4th ed. (p. 444 n.) where the reference in the second sentence was to Book V, ch. XI, §6. The same reference was kept by mistake in the 5th ed., though with the renumbering of that chapter and the transfer of several sections of Appendix H, it should have referred to Book V, ch. XII and Appendix H.

PAGE 373

a. The remainder of this paragraph dates substantially from the 3rd ed. (pp. 445–6).

b. So since the 5th ed. (p. 373) where the following sentences dating from the 3rd ed. (which were slightly modified in the 4th ed.), were deleted:

Their decision exerts some influence on supply and therefore on price. But as a rule they are very few in number; there may be none in this position and anyhow their action is far less important than that of the great body of producers who will produce something whatever be the price (within certain limits), but watch the price to see how far it is worth their while to extend their production.

c. The first four sentences of this paragraph date from the 2nd ed. (p. 424).

PAGE 374

a. The remaining sentences of this paragraph were inserted in the 4th ed. (pp. 445–6).

b. In the 4th ed. (p. 446) this marginal summary replaced the following marginal summary in the 3rd ed. (pp. 446–7):

But for short periods the appliances of production have to be taken for granted and the supply price is that which is just needed to call forth those elements of supply which are on the margin of not being produced with those appliances, account being taken of the fear of spoiling the market.

The first clause of the foregoing summary dates from the 2nd ed. (p. 424).

c. This paragraph and the first two sentences of the next date from the 2nd ed. (pp. 424–5).

d. From the 4th ed. the word "marginal", inserted before the words "supply price" in the 2nd ed. (p. 424) and the 3rd ed. (p. 446), was deleted.

e. The following additional sentence at this point, dating from the 2nd ed. (p. 425), was deleted from the 4th ed.:

This then is the interpretation of marginal supply price for short periods: for which it rises with every increase in the amount that has to be produced.

In the 2nd ed. the following footnote was attached to this sentence, but was deleted from the 4th ed.:

> We shall later study the mutual influences of fluctuations in the purchasing power of money and in the activity of producers; and also the motives and the methods of combinations among employers to restrict their output, and of combinations among employees to restrict their work with the double purpose of extracting better terms for themselves from their employers and of putting pressure on those of their employers who are inclined to sell nearly at prime cost and spoil the common market.

PAGE 375

a. This paragraph dates substantially from the 1st ed. (p. 520) where it was placed in Book VI, ch. VI, §1; in the 2nd ed. in Book V, ch. IV, §4, p. 416; and in the 3rd ed. in Book V, ch. IV, §4, p. 435.

b. So since the 4th ed. (p. 446) where this and the next sentence replaced the following sentences dating from the 1st ed.:

If they pursue this policy constantly and without moderation, they may keep prices so low as to drive capital out of the trade, ruining many of those employed in it, themselves perhaps among the number. During all this time the income derived from their plant will be very low; but after a while the demand for their goods will revive, and the means for meeting it will be inadequate. The prices of the goods will then rise high above their normal level, and the plant that yet remains in working order, will for a time obtain a very high income (or quasi-rent).

In the 2nd ed. the second and third clauses of the last sentence just quoted were deleted.

c. This and the two succeeding paragraphs were inserted in the 4th ed. (p. 447–8).

d. This footnote dates from the 4th ed. (p. 447 n.).

e. The following additional sentences in the 4th ed. were deleted from the 7th ed.:

> But perhaps the public show too much indulgence to those who argue that a trade combination or a trust is the only means available for securing a reasonable steadiness of price. In a later volume we shall study the mutual influences of

fluctuations in the purchasing power of money, in credit, and in the activity of producers; and also the motives and the methods of combinations among employers to restrict their output, and of combinations among employees to restrict their work, with the double purpose of extracting better terms for themselves from their employers and of putting pressure on those of their employers who are inclined to sell nearly at prime cost and spoil the common market.

The first of the sentences just quoted is itself a rewording of a sentence in the 1st ed. (Book VI, ch. VI, §1, p. 520), where it ran as follows: "The public listen with some indulgence to those who argue that a trade combination or a trust is the only means available for securing a reasonable steadiness of price." In its original context this was succeeded by the following sentence: "Questions of this kind are of great and growing importance and will occupy much of our attention later on when we come to consider the causes of commercial fluctuations." Both these sentences were retained in the 2nd ed. (p. 416 n.) and the 3rd ed. (p. 435 n.).

PAGE 376

a. For a more extended treatment of the notion that the marginal unit is a whole process of production, see Book II, ch. 1 of Marshall's *Industry and Trade*, which is reproduced in the Editorial Appendix to Book V, chapters I–VII (pp. 410–26 below).

b. This paragraph dates substantially from the 1st ed. (Book V, ch. IV, §6, p. 416). In the 1st ed. (p. 415) it was preceded by the following paragraph which was deleted from the 2nd ed.:

We may then repeat that the term *long-period* normal supply price indicates the supply price estimated for a period sufficiently long to enable the economic causes concerned to work out their chief normal effects: and the supply-price so estimated has a special right to be regarded as *the* normal supply price. We may contrast with it that *short-period* normal supply price (or more briefly the *subnormal* supply price), which is estimated for periods too brief to enable the broader movements of industrial organization to work themselves out. In the former case there is, and in the latter there is not, time enough to enable the supply of the factors of production of the commodity to be adjusted to the amount of it which has to be produced.

c. So since the 4th ed. (pp. 447–8) where the remaining sentences of this paragraph (apart from the reference to "chapter VIII", inserted in the 5th ed. (p. 377)) replaced the following sentences dating from the 2nd ed. (p. 425):

The particular income derived from them during those times, does not *for the time* affect perceptibly the supply nor therefore the price of the commodities produced by them: but is rather a quasi-rent or surplus of total receipts over prime (money) cost, determined by the more or less accidental relations of demand and supply for that time. But unless that quasi-rent covers in the long run the supplementary costs of the business, production will gradually fall off. In this way the short period supply price is governed in the background by causes ranging over a long period; and the fear of "spoiling the market" often makes those causes act more promptly than they otherwise would.

d. In the 8th edition "chapter xi"; emended in vol. i of the present edition to give the correct reference.

PAGE 377

a. This and the next paragraph date from the 2nd ed. (p. 426).

b. In the 2nd ed. (p. 426) and the 3rd ed. (p. 448) this marginal summary ran as follows: "But for long periods the supply price is that which is just needed to call forth those new investments of capital, material and personal, which are required to make up a certain aggregate volume of production." The summary assumed its present form in the 4th ed. (p. 449).

PAGE 378

a. So since the 4th ed. (p. 450) where this sentence replaced the following sentences dating from the 1st ed. (pp. 414–15):

At any particular moment in any branch of manufacture some businesses will be rising and others falling; some undertakers will be doubting whether to start new factories, others whether to enlarge existing factories, and to provide them with better appliances; while others again feeling themselves behind the age, finding by experience that the equipment and the internal organization of their factories will hardly enable them to sell at current prices and make a profit, will be tending to diminish their average output, or perhaps breaking down altogether.

But when we are taking a broad view of the causes which determine normal supply price, we need not trouble ourselves with these eddies on the surface of the great tide.

392

Such eddies will always exist, and occasionally play an important part in the history of a particular trade; the recent histories of the manufactures of silk, of watches, and of agricultural implements, and again of the shipbuilding, the sugar refining and the chemical industries afford examples of the way in which the energy or the incompetence of a few business men may exert a powerful influence on the development of a great trade in one place and its decadence in another. But significant as such facts are for some purposes, they do not concern us just now; because looking, as we are now, at broad results only, we have no reason to believe that the eddy at any particular time will be moving in one direction rather than another.

b. This sentence dates from the 1st ed. (p. 415). In that edition it had the following footnote attached to the concluding word "business", which was deleted from the 2nd ed.:

> Land on the theoretical margin of cultivation is land that will just pay for the expenses of cultivating it when in the hands of a farmer of normal ability, his normal remuneration being included in the expenses of production. But in fact much land is cultivated which from its position or other cause gives less than this return. We shall return to this subject when discussing agricultural rent and land tenure.

c. So since the 4th ed. (p. 450). This sentence ran as follows in the 1st ed. (p. 415):

Or it may be due to some wealthy firm which by enlarging its premises is enabled to attain new economies altogether out of proportion to the small fraction that the extension of its particular business adds to the aggregate volume of production in its trade.

In the 2nd ed. (p. 427) a new clause was added to this sentence after the word "trade", which ran as follows: "and reap enormous gains or Quasi-rents from its successful adaptation to the environment (Konjunktur), and from the favours of fortune and opportunity".

In the 3rd ed. (p. 449) this clause was reworded as follows: "and reap great gains from its successful adaptation to its surroundings or from the favours of fortune".

d. This sentence dates substantially from the 2nd ed. (p. 428 n.).
e. This paragraph dates from the 1st ed. (p. 416). In the 1st ed. (pp. 416–18) it was succeeded by the following paragraphs:

In those broad inquiries which will occupy the remainder of this and the following Book, we shall be concerned almost

The long period or true normal supply prices are of chief importance here.

exclusively with the true normal equilibria: but when at a later stage we come to consider the quickly moving oscillations of trade and commerce, the subnormal equilibria will claim more of our attention.

Here then we may pause. There are many difficulties relating to supply price yet to be considered. But enough has been said to justify the statement that though the short-period normal supply price almost always increases in consequence of an increase in the amount produced; the long-period or true normal supply price obeys no such simple rule. For in some cases it is diminished, and in others it is increased by an increase in the aggregate scale of production; while in others again it is practically constant in spite of great changes in that scale.

There is no strictly parallel distinction in the case of Demand, but there also the effect may lag behind its cause.

There is nothing in the causes determining normal demand which corresponds exactly to this broad distinction between the causes that determine long-period and short-period normal supply prices respectively. But when discussing the Law of Demand we noticed how long a time may be required to enable an economic cause to produce its full effects; and how a change in demand price often lags much behind the change by which it was really caused. The difficulties to which this fact gives rise, together with the corresponding difficulties relating to supply, make themselves felt in most economic problems: but they are especially troublesome when an attempt is made to represent the theory of equilibrium of demand and supply in its most general form and with quasi-mathematical exactness; and we shall have to consider them carefully in the next chapter.

There are two plans each of which has its own advantages for representing the relations in which quickly passing fluctuations stand to secular changes.

It has already been indicated, and as we go further we shall see more clearly that there are two ways of treating changes in demand and supply, each of which has advantages that make it the more convenient for certain purposes. On the one plan we ignore all disturbances that pass quickly, and consider only the general relations of demand and supply over very long periods; we sacrifice some precision of detail for the sake of being able to take at one glance a broad and comprehensive survey of the ultimate tendencies under discussion. On the other plan we confine our attention in the first instance to those changes which can develop themselves in comparatively short periods, and reason for the while as though those things which move slowly were really stationary. Having then got a compact and definite problem of equilibrium about a centre which does indeed move slowly, but the movements of which we have for the time neglected, we next take account of those movements; and thus gradually get a broader view of oscillations about a centre which is itself moving and perhaps oscillating in a longer period of time about another centre: somewhat as the moon moves round the earth, which itself in a longer period moves round the sun.

But the sun itself is not fixed. It is moving and perhaps with an oscillatory movement about some very distant centre. And so while market prices oscillate about a position of market equilibrium, which perhaps oscillates about a position of short-period normal equilibrium, that position in its turn may not remain stationary, but may move onwards in one direction, or may oscillate more slowly round a position of long-period normal equilibrium; and that again in its turn may itself be liable to slow changes, possibly having an oscillatory movement, the period of which ranges over many generations or even centuries.

In the 2nd ed. (pp. 427–8) and the 3rd ed. (pp. 449–50) the above paragraphs in the 1st ed. were omitted and their place taken by the following sentence:

In those broad inquiries which will occupy the remainder of this Book, we shall be concerned almost exclusively with the true normal equilibria: but when at a later stage we come to consider the quickly moving oscillations of trade and commerce, the short period normal, or as we may conveniently call them, the *sub-normal* equilibria will claim more of our attention.

In the 4th ed. (pp. 450–1) the sentence just quoted was retained at the end of the first paragraph of §8. This sentence was deleted from the 5th ed.

f. This paragraph dates substantially from the 3rd ed. (p. 450 n.) where it formed part of a footnote. It was brought into the text in the 4th ed. (p. 451).

PAGE 379

a. So since the 5th ed. (p. 379). In the 3rd ed. (p. 450 n.) the first clause of this sentence ran as follows: "As regards *short-normal* or *sub-normal* prices, 'Supply' means...etc."

In the 4th ed. (p. 451) this clause ran: "As regards short-period normal prices, 'Supply' means...etc."

b. The word "full" before "*normal*" in the 3rd and 4th editions was deleted from the 5th ed., while the clause succeeding the words "*normal* prices" was inserted in the 5th ed. (p. 379).

c. The words "very gradual or" before "*Secular*" were inserted in the 5th ed. (p. 379).

d. This paragraph dates from the 1st ed. (p. 416 n.) with some change in the last sentence.

e. In the 1st ed. this sentence ran as follows: "Some such assumption is really contained in many popular renderings of Ricardo's doctrines, which give them a sharpness of outline that he had never intended."

The present version of this sentence dates from the 2nd ed. (p. 428 n.).

f. This paragraph and the next were inserted in the 4th ed. (pp. 451 n.–2 n.) except for the reference to Chapter XII and Appendix H at the end of the first paragraph, which dates from the 7th ed. (p. 380 n.).

PAGE 380

a. This paragraph dates from the 7th ed. (p. 380) where it replaced the following paragraphs which were inserted in the 5th ed.:

The remainder of the present volume is chiefly concerned with the third of the above classes. That is, it discusses the normal relations of wages, profits, prices, &c., for long periods of several years. But occasionally account has to be taken of gradual changes; and one chapter, Book VI, ch. XII, is given up to "The Influence of Progress on Value," that is, to the study of very gradual, or secular, changes of value.

On the other hand the first two classes will come into prominence when we discuss, in a later volume, fluctuations of prices and wages arising from quickly passing changes in the state of commercial credit, and other causes; together with the allied problems of trade unions and combinations of employers.

The concluding paragraphs of the corresponding chapter in the 1st ed. (Book V, ch. iv, p. 418) ran as follows:

There are many economic doctrines, the chief practical applications of which are of no great difficulty, in spite of the fact that the doctrines themselves when fully developed are extremely complex and intricate; for many of the subtleties which are necessary to give thorough logical completeness to them in their most general and abstract form, have a very narrow range of practical bearing. An instance of this is to be found in the developments of the theory of demand and supply to which we are about to proceed. Those therefore whose interest in economics is chiefly on the practical side, and who desire as far as possible to avoid theoretical subtleties, are recommended to pass lightly over the next four chapters: a short summary of their chief results is given in the closing chapter of the Book.

The four chapters referred to in the last sentence in the 1st ed. were: ch. v, "The Theory of Stable Equilibrium of Normal Demand and Supply"; ch. vi, "Joint and Composite Demand. Joint and Composite Supply"; ch. vii, "Theory of Changes in Normal Demand and Supply with some of its Bearings on the Doctrine of Maximum Satisfaction"; ch. viii, "The Theory of Monopolies".

In the 2nd ed. (pp. 428–9) the concluding paragraphs of Book V, ch. v, ran as follows:

Such are the broad outlines of the general theory of equilibrium of normal demand and supply; but there remain many important details to be considered. Some of these relate to the several peculiarities, and to the mutual relations of the three great agents of production, Labour, Capital, and Land; and they will be postponed to the following Book. But there are several others which are more general in character and may be taken at once.

The first group is concerned with the relations between the different factors that are required to co-operate for the production of the same goods, and with those between the joint products of the same branch of production, &c.

The second group deals with the relations in which Rent proper, that is the income derived from the free gifts of nature, and quasi-rents of all kinds stand to value. In this

397

group several difficulties, that have been slightly touched on in the present and the last chapter, will be examined at length, with the purpose among others of bringing out the complete continuity between the theory of the income derived from land and from other things which are commonly said to be made by man, but really are only turned to account by him, since man can create only utilities.

This further study of quasi-rents will lead the way to a rather technical discussion of the relations between marginal and average supply price (expenses of production); and of problems in which two or more positions of stable equilibrium between normal demand and normal supply may, theoretically at least, be possible.

The last group relates to the bearings of the theories of demand and supply, and of monopolies on the famous doctrine that free competition tends to make the aggregate satisfaction a maximum.

All of these discussions are integral parts of a complete understanding of the theory of value: but at all events the last two groups are not essential to the discussion of the broad problem of Distribution and Exchange, which will occupy our attention in the following Book. And the summary of their chief results given in the concluding chapters of this Book may suffice for the present purpose of those readers who desire to get as soon as possible to the application of the theory of value to social questions.

In the 3rd ed. (pp. 450–1) these concluding paragraphs in the 2nd ed. were retained with only slight modifications of which the following rewording of the first line of the fourth of the above paragraphs may be noted: "This further study of these incomes from possessions (or quasi-rents) will lead the way...etc." All these concluding paragraphs in the 3rd ed. were deleted from the 4th ed.

b. In the 5th ed. (p. 380 n.) the word "also" replaced the word "not" in the 4th ed., thus correcting an obvious misprint in that edition.

JOINT AND COMPOSITE DEMAND. JOINT AND COMPOSITE SUPPLY

a. Except where otherwise stated, the wording of this chapter dates substantially from the 1st edition.

b. The title of Book V, ch. VI remained unchanged since the 1st edition.

c. In the 1st ed. (p. 430) the opening paragraph of §1 ran as follows:

T H E demand for producers' goods, or goods of the second and higher orders, as we have termed them, is indirect; it is *derived* from the demand for consumers' goods, or goods of the first order, towards the production of which they contribute; or, in other words, the demands for all the various factors of production of a finished commodity are joined together in the *joint demand* for it. Thus the demand for beer is direct, and is a joint demand for hops, malt, brewers' labour, and the other factors of production of beer: and the demand for any one of them is an indirect demand derived from that for beer. Again there is a direct demand for new houses; and from this there arises a joint demand for the labour of all the various building trades, and for bricks, stone, wood, etc., which are factors of production of building work of all kinds, or as we may say for shortness, of new houses. But the demand for any one of these, as for instance the labour of plasterers, is only an indirect demand.

This paragraph was deleted from the 4th ed. in which edition (pp. 453–4) the first four paragraphs of § 1 in the present edition were inserted.

d. This reference, and the first two main clauses of the first sentence of this footnote, date from the 2nd ed. (p. 430 n.); the third main clause of this sentence was inserted in the 3rd ed. (p. 452 n.), and the concluding sentence in the 4th ed. (p. 454 n.). The final reference in the 4th ed. was (correctly) to Book II, ch. IV, § 13, but this was retained erroneously in the 5th and subsequent editions; it has been corrected in the present edition.

PAGE 382

a. The following extract from a letter dated 26 October 1888 from Marshall to John Neville Keynes (when the latter was reading the proofs of the MS. of the first edition of Marshall's *Principles of Economics*) throws light on Marshall's reasons for inserting the warning contained in this paragraph:

And now I want to ask your kind advice on a difficult point.

What I say about *Derived* Demand and Supply, Book V, ch. vi, §§ 1, 2 and 4 is, in my own conceited opinion, new and important: but the exposition gave me a great deal of trouble and is I fear unsatisfactory yet. In particular I have taken an illustration in the text (not in the footnote) about plasterers which I knew at the time was not in perfect logical harmony with the assumption that the curves apply only to periods sufficiently long to allow free action to the normal forces of supply (in this case the growth of plasterers). I took that particular illustration partly because it is a striking one, partly because I shall want it a good deal in Book VI: and I thought that if I apologized for and explained away this logical change of point of view, I should bother the readers: and that if I said nothing about it probably no one would find it out. Also I took care to say nothing of the possibility of the supply curves sloping downwards towards the right. (I have suppressed hundreds of possible queer cases of that sort for fear of overburdening the book by statements of the conditions by which they had to be safeguarded.)

Now the question I want to ask is: Would it be best *a* to explain the change of venue involved by the plasterers' illustration or *b* to destroy it ruthlessly or *c* run the risk of detection by lynx eyed (or minded) readers?

The original of this letter is in the Marshall Library in Cambridge.

b. This clause was inserted in the 2nd ed. (p. 431).

c. In the 3rd ed. (p. 453) the words "lists of supply prices" were substituted for the words "supply schedules" dating from the 1st ed. (p. 431).

d. In the 8th edition "II. iv. 13"; emended in vol. 1 of the present edition to give the correct reference.

PAGE 383

a. So since the 3rd ed. (pp. 453–4). In the first two editions the "general rule" referred to the next paragraph in the present text, which began there: "The demand schedule for any factor of production of a commodity can be derived from... etc.", and carried the following marginal summary "General law of derived demand".

b. This opening paragraph was inserted in the 4th ed. (p. 455 n.).

PAGE 384

a. So since the 7th ed. (p. 384 n.) where this sentence replaced the following clauses in the earlier editions after the words "the equilibrium at *a* also is stable.": "whether the supply curves are positively or negatively inclined; as will be shown in chapter XI." The first of these clauses dated from the 1st ed. (p. 433 n.) and the second from the 4th ed. (p. 456 n.). It may be noted that the reference in the second clause to "chapter XI" should, in the 5th and 6th editions, have been to Appendix H.

b. So since the 3rd ed. (p. 455 n.). In the 1st ed. the reference was to "Mathematical Note XIII", and in the 2nd ed. to "Mathematical Note XIV", though in this latter edition it should have been to "Mathematical Note XIV. *bis*".

PAGE 385

a. So since the 2nd ed. (p. 433) where this "first" condition was explicitly introduced. (See the editorial note **a** to vol. I page 386 for the way in which this aspect was treated in the 1st ed.) The change involved the renumbering of the three conditions which had been laid down in the 1st ed., with the result that the first condition (in the 1st ed.) henceforth became the second condition, and the second and third became the third and fourth conditions; but apart from the renumbering of the conditions the text of the 1st ed. was unchanged, except as noted below.

PAGE 386

a. So since the 7th ed. (p. 386). In the 1st ed. (p. 434) this paragraph ran as follows:

It must be borne in mind that, as above implied, we assume that the factor in question is an essential factor; that it is almost indispensable, no good substitute being available at a moderate price. The rise in plasterers' wages would be checked if it were possible either to avoid the use of plaster, or to get the work done tolerably well and at a moderate price by people outside the plasterers' trade. The law of substitution here as elsewhere exercises a subduing influence on forces which might otherwise lead to startling results. The tyranny which one factor of production of a commodity might in some cases exercise over the other factors through the law of indirect demand is tempered by the law of substitution.

In the 2nd ed. (pp. 434–5) the first sentence in the above paragraph was deleted, since it had become redundant, while the word "derived" was substituted for the word "indirect" before "demand" in the last sentence. In the 5th ed. (p. 386) the words "the action of" were substituted for "the law of" in the last sentence.

b. The words "intensity of the" were inserted before "satisfaction" in the 2nd ed. (p. 435).

PAGE 387

a. This paragraph was inserted in the 2nd ed. (pp. 435–6).
b. In the 1st ed. (pp. 435–6) this section (§ 3) ran as follows:

So far we have spoken as though each factor of production were used in making only one class of goods; but nearly every raw material and nearly every kind of labour is applied in many different branches of industry, and contributes to the production of a great variety of commodities. Each of these commodities has its own direct demand from which the derived demand for any of the factors made in using it can be found. The total demand for the factor may be called a *composite* demand: it is the sum of the derived demands for it, in each of its several uses; and these may be added together, in just the same way as the partial demands of several classes of society for a finished commodity are added together, and thus make up the total *composite* demand for it.[1]

When there is a composite demand for a thing, whether a finished commodity or a factor of production, its distribution between its several uses is of course such that it can be sold for each use at the same price; that is, its marginal utility for each use has the same economic measure. If the last purchasers of it for all the uses were of the same wealth, it follows that its marginal utility was the same in all uses.[2]

[1] See Mathematical Note XV.
[2] Compare Jevons' *Theory*, 2nd ed. pp. 63–6 and 198–200.

c. This paragraph and the first two sentences of the next paragraph date substantially from the 2nd ed. (p. 436).

d. The last two sentences of this paragraph date from the 4th ed. (pp. 459–60), though the footnote attached to the end of the concluding sentence dates from the 1st ed. (pp. 435 n.–6 n.).

PAGE 388

a. This paragraph dates from the 4th ed. (p. 459), where it replaced the following paragraph dating from the 1st ed. (p. 436).

We may now pass to consider the case of things which have a *joint supply*. It corresponds to that of things which have a joint demand, and it may be discussed almost in the same words, by merely substituting "demand" for "supply," and *vice versa*. When two or more things are produced by one and the same process; so that the expenses of producing them all together are not greater than the expenses of producing one of them alone would be; then these things are called *joint products*. Thus wheat and straw are joint products; beef and hides are joint products.

b. This footnote was inserted in the 7th ed. (p. 388 n.).

c. So since the 3rd ed. (p. 459 n.). In the 1st ed. (pp. 436–7) and the 2nd ed. (p. 437) the first paragraph of this footnote was in the text, while the two succeeding paragraphs and the diagram were in a footnote attached to the sentence ending with the words "corresponding amounts".

PAGE 389

a. This paragraph was inserted in the 6th ed. (p. 389) where it began with the following sentences which were deleted from the 7th ed.:

The prices of the gas and the coke that are got from a ton of coal, must together be enough to cover their joint expenses of production. If the demand for gas rises, more coke will be produced, and its price must fall, so that the increased supply may be taken off the market. The rise in the price of gas must be sufficient to cover this fall in the price of coke, and also to cover the increase, if there is any, in the joint expenses of production of gas and coke.

b. In the 1st to the 6th editions the sentence beginning "There are very few cases of joint products...etc." was preceded by the following sentences which were deleted from the 7th ed.:

403

In manufacture and agriculture, in the carrying and distributing trades, it is often a matter of the greatest difficulty to decide what are the real expenses of any one of the many operations that are being done at the same time. The difficulty is greatest with regard to those fixed charges which would run on if little or nothing were being done in the establishment. We shall be much occupied hereafter with the troubles that arise from this source.

PAGE 390

a. In the 4th ed. (p. 462) the words "alter its amount" were substituted for the words "modify their proportions" in the earlier editions.

b. This paragraph and the footnote attached to it were inserted in the 7th ed. (p. 390).

c. In the 1st ed. (p. 438) this sentence was succeeded by the two following sentences:

It is closely connected with the Law of Substitution which has been noticed already. We may consider that two things are *rivals* when they are capable of satisfying the same demand.

In the 3rd ed. (p. 460) the words "or competing commodities" were inserted after "*rivals*", and the footnote referring to Professor Fisher was attached to the word "commodities". In the 4th ed. (p. 462) these sentences were deleted and the paragraph assumed its present form; but the footnote was left unaltered despite the fact that the words "competing commodities" had disappeared from the text.

d. This footnote was inserted in the 7th ed. (p. 390 n.).

PAGE 391

a. This sentence dates from the 4th ed. (pp. 462–3), though the footnote attached to the end of it, and the accompanying diagram, date from the 1st ed. (pp. 438 n.–9 n.), except that the third paragraph was there in the text; it was relegated to the footnote in the 4th ed. (p. 463 n.).

PAGE 392

a. This paragraph was inserted in the 3rd ed. (p. 462) where it replaced the following paragraph dating from the 1st ed. (p. 439):

In real life there are very few things the value of which can be determined without taking some account of all the four chief problems which have been discussed in this chapter. We often find connections between the prices of commodities which at first seem far apart.

b. In the 1st ed. (p. 440 n.) the remainder of this paragraph was in a footnote; it was brought into the text in the 4th ed. (p. 464).

a. This paragraph dates substantially from the 3rd ed. (p. 463).

b. So since the 8th edition (page 393) where these clauses were substituted for the following clauses dating from the 3rd ed. (p. 463): "and these inventions together with the growth of an urban population in the West, are giving a high value to straw that used to be burnt, and are therefore lowering the value of wheat."

c. The first three sentences of this footnote were inserted in the 4th ed. (p. 465 n.). The remainder of the footnote dates from the 3rd ed. (p. 463 n.).

BOOK V, CHAPTER VII

PRIME AND TOTAL COST IN RELATION TO JOINT PRODUCTS. COST OF MARKETING. INSURANCE AGAINST RISK. COST OF REPRODUCTION

a. Except where otherwise stated the wording of this chapter dates from the 1st edition.

b. The title of this chapter dates from the 2nd edition. In the 1st edition where this chapter was Book VI, chapter VI, its title ran as follows: "Cost of Production. Prime Cost and Total Cost. Cost of Marketing. Insurance against Risk. Cost of Reproduction."

c. This section corresponds to §2 of Book VI, ch. VI in the 1st ed.; §1 in that edition contained a discussion of prime and supplementary costs which was later transferred to Book V, ch. IV, §5 and ch. V, §6.

d. This paragraph dates from the 2nd ed. (p. 442), where it replaced the following sentences in the 1st ed. (p. 521), which preceded the sentence beginning with the words "It often happens that ...etc.":

But at present we pass to consider the task of assigning to each branch of a business its proper share of the general expenses, on the supposition that a far-sighted policy is being pursued, and that it is sought to assign to each commodity that price which will enable it, under normal conditions, to be sold permanently and afford a normal profit. We have already discussed the difficulty of assigning to each of several *joint-products* its proper supply price.

PAGE 395

a. The following sentence dating from the 1st ed. (p. 522) was deleted from the 7th ed.: "All such questions are of considerable interest, but we must not pursue them in detail."

In the 1st ed. there was the following footnote to this sentence, which was deleted from the 3rd ed.: "Some interesting particulars are given in Garcke and Fell's *Factory Accounts*."

PAGE 396

a. So since the 2nd ed. (p. 444) where the word "direct" replaced the word "prime" in the 1st ed. (p. 523).

PAGE 397

a. So since the 5th ed. (p. 397) where this clause replaced the following clauses dating from the 1st ed. (p. 524): "that no free play is allowed to the normal action of economic forces, and it can scarcely be said to have a normal supply price."

b. So since the 5th ed. (p. 397) where the words "the cost of making" replaced the words "the prime cost" dating from the 1st ed. (p. 524).

PAGE 398

a. The following footnote to the end of this sentence in the 1st ed. (p. 525 n.) was deleted from the 2nd ed.:

It has already been noticed (Book V, ch. VI, §5) that if an improvement in making a commodity is patented, local producers who cannot avail themselves of the improvement, may make up for this disadvantage by their superior facilities for marketing the commodity in their own neighbourhood; and in such a case two kinds of the same commodity, both of which conform to the law of increasing return, are likely to remain in the market together for a long while.

The reference in this footnote is to footnote 3 on page 391 n. in Book V, ch. VI, § 5 in vol. I of the present edition.

b. So since the 4th ed. (p. 470) from which the following opening sentence of this paragraph dating from the 1st ed. (p. 525) was deleted:

A great part of these expenses of marketing results from the risk that a thing preparing for a certain market will not find the expected sale there.

PAGE 399

a. So since the 3rd ed. (p. 469 n.). In the 1st ed. (p. 526) and the 2nd ed. (p. 447) these sentences were placed in the text; and in the 1st ed. there was the following footnote attached to the word "America", which was deleted from the 2nd ed.: "The plan was originated by the economist Mr Edward Atkinson of Boston."

PAGE 401

a. An earlier version of Marshall's criticism of Carey's doctrine of cost of reproduction is contained in a passage in *The Economics of Industry* by Alfred Marshall and Mary Paley Marshall (1st ed. 1879, pp. 79–80), which ran as follows:

The main outline of the law of normal value was worked out by Adam Smith and Ricardo. They were careful to guard against implying that the price of each individual thing is equal to its expenses of production; but still this mistake has been made. This mistake has indeed led some people to approve a proposal made by Mr Carey, to say that the value of a thing is equal to its expenses (or, as he says, cost) of *reproduction*.

It is quite true, as Mr Carey says, that when a new invention has very much diminished the difficulty of making, say, a steel rail, no one will pay for an old steel rail a price equal to the expenses which were incurred by making it by the old method. He seems to think that they will always pay for it a price equal to the expenses of its reproduction, that is of producing a similar rail by the new method. But this is not the case. If trade has become suddenly bad, and iron-masters have many steel rails on hand, no one will pay for a steel rail a price equal to its expenses of reproduction; because rails are being sold for less. Again, no one will pay

407

for a bell with a flaw in it, or for a dress that has gone out of fashion, the expenses of its reproduction. When fashion is displacing broad ribbons by narrow, broad ribbons sell for less, and narrow ribbons sell for more than their expenses of reproduction. Gunpowder in time of war and quinine in time of fever often fetch more than their expenses of reproduction.

If the phrase "expenses of reproduction" were substituted for the phrase "expenses of production" in our law of normal value, the meaning of the law will not be altered by the change. For the expenses of reproduction of a thing are in the long run the same as its expenses of production. The statement that value must be equal to expenses of production, and that it must be equal to expenses of reproduction, are equally false when they refer to the market value of any thing, and equally true when they refer to the normal value about which the market value oscillates. The advantages of the two phrases are so far about equally balanced; but the phrase "expenses of production" has this very great advantage over its rival, that it calls attention to the way in which the difficulty of producing a thing determines supply in the first instance, and value in the second. Producers debating whether to increase their supply of a commodity do not inquire whether the price they get for it will cover its expenses of reproduction, but whether the price will cover its expenses of production.

b. This clause was inserted in the 7th ed. (p. 401).

c. So since the 7th ed. (p. 401), from which the words "even if it were true", which had been placed between the word "but" and the words "it would not be the same thing...etc." in the earlier editions, were deleted.

PAGE 402

a. This paragraph dates from the 5th ed. (p. 402) where it replaced the following paragraphs which had been inserted in the 4th ed. (pp. 474–5):

Such are the broad outlines of the general theory of equilibrium of normal demand and supply. A study of the several peculiarities, and the mutual relations of the agents of production, labour, capital, organization, and land is post-poned to the following Book. But there are some questions to be considered which are more general in character; and they may be taken at once.

The argument, with regard to the influence of time on value, is continued in the second group. In this group several difficulties, that have been slightly touched on as yet, will be examined at length, with the purpose, among others, of bringing out the complete continuity between the theory of the income derived from land and from other things which are commonly said to be made by Man, but really are only turned to account by him; since man can create only utilities, whether he is working on land or on a movable commodity.

There follows a more detailed study of some difficulties, which have been slightly treated in Chapter v, connected with the relations of demand and supply in industries which have a tendency to increasing return.

The last group discusses the theories of demand and supply, and of monopolies in relation to an abstract form of the famous doctrine that free competition tends to make the aggregate satisfaction a maximum.

These discussions are integral parts of a complete under-standing of the theory of value. But they are not essential to the main discussion of the problem of distribution and exchange, in the following Book; and they may be omitted provisionally by the reader who desires to get at once to that problem. A summary of their chief results is given in chapter xiv.

The reference in the last line to chapter xiv applies to ch. xv in vol. i of the present edition.

b. For convenience of reference I have reproduced as an Appendix to Book V, chapters i–vii, the outline which Marshall gave of his theory of value, from a slightly different perspective, in Book II, ch. i of his *Industry and Trade*.

EDITORIAL APPENDIX TO
BOOK V, CHAPTERS I–VII

In 1920, when he was 78 years of age, Marshall brought out his second main work: a volume of 856 pages entitled *Industry and Trade. A study of industrial technique and business organization; and of their influences on the conditions of various classes and nations.* He furnished it, as a motto, with his favourite dictum—*The many in the one, the one in the many.*

Book II of that volume, dealing with Dominant Tendencies of Business Organization, contained in its first chapter, entitled "The Adjustment of Production to Demand in an Open Market", what Marshall himself described as "a compressed account of the relations among production, consumption, and value; or—to use an alternative phrase—among supply, demand, and price".

The substance of Book II, chapter 1 of *Industry and Trade* (pp. 181–96) ran as follows[a]:

Book II

Chapter I

The Adjustment of Production to Demand in an Open Market. Introductory Summary of the Argument of this Chapter

Production and marketing are parts of the single process of adjustment of supply to demand. The division between them is on lines which are seldom sharply defined: the lines vary from one class of business to another, and each is liable to modification by any large change in the resources of production, transport, or the communication of intelligence.

The term "cost of production," as used in business and in economic literature, generally includes tacitly some portion of the costs of marketing, the extent of which is to be inferred from the context. It can seldom be definitely interpreted without reference (1) to the market for which the

---

[a] Some small portions of the chapter referring to other parts of the volume have been omitted.

production is undertaken; and (2) to a "representative" producing business.

The responsiveness of demand to changes in price (which is sometimes called its "*elasticity*") is a gradual process: and, partly for this reason, the diminution in the costs of manufacture, which corresponds to an enlarged scale of operations, is a gradual, and sometimes an uncertain process.

The cost of producing a single thing can seldom be isolated: for its production is nearly always part of a process, which is concerned with many other things of the same class.

The cost of production of almost every class as a whole is associated with (though it is not strictly speaking a "joint" cost with) that of producing other classes. The "prime," or immediate, costs of producing a thing can often be isolated. But its proper share of the "general" expenses of the business by which it is made, cannot be determined according to any fixed rules.

Thus the tendency of market prices towards cost of production (including normal profits) by a representative firm is much obscured, though not annulled, by the almost ceaseless operation of various disturbing causes.

Ambiguities of the terms Market, and Cost of production

The term *market* is used in many different connections; and in scarcely any two has it exactly the same significance. This difficulty has its origin in the ordinary discourse of life; where the context, or a special explanation, indicates the particular use of the term intended: and economists are compelled to conform, in this as in many similar cases, to general usage. But a short account of the chief groups of these various uses will be proper to our present purpose.

In all its various significations, a "market" refers to a group or groups of people, some of whom desire to obtain certain things, and some of whom are in a position to supply what the others want. A market may consist of all the inhabitants of a town, or of the whole country: or it may consist in effect only of those of them who have a special interest in something, as for instance zinc or leather. In some cases, dealings over the whole Western World may be worked out in such constant unison as to justify the phrase "world-market." Everyone buys, and nearly every producer sells, to some extent in a *"general"* market, in which he is on about the same footing with others around him. But nearly everyone has also some *"particular"* markets; that is, some people or groups of people with whom he is in somewhat close touch: mutual knowledge and trust lead him to approach them, and them to approach him, in preference to strangers. A producer, a wholesale dealer, or a shopkeeper, who has built up a strong connection among purchasers of his goods, has a valuable property. He does not generally expect to get better prices from his clients than from others. But he expects to sell easily to them because they know and trust him; and he does not sell at low prices in order to call attention to his business, as he often does in a market where he is little known.

The demand and the supply of a modern market are not definite stocks on hand at any time, but streams flowing at various rates during a year or some other appropriate period. There are a few exceptions. For instance, in a market for fish on a hot day, with no access to cool storage, the supply is merely the stock in hand; and the demand is a short sharp movement on the part of a compact group of people. But as a rule supply is a gradual process, liable to be influenced at every stage by varying facilities for production, and varying expectations of the terms on which the product can be marketed.

The term *cost of production* is commonly used in two very different senses. Where the affairs of a particular business are under discussion, it always means *money cost*; that is, the aggregate of the outlays in money, that are incurred directly or indirectly in the production of a certain thing. Among these are commonly included a reasonable rate of profit, together with insurance against risks: remuneration of the work of the owner of the business does not appear as a separate item in the accounts; but goes with interest on capital under the head of profits.

But in the discussion of social problems, it is often necessary to inquire whether certain businesses, which may or may not be adequately remunerative to the persons concerned, are worth what they cost to the country or the world: and in this connection the term cost of production refers to real cost. The *real cost of production* of a thing is the aggregate of efforts and sacrifices which are incurred in its production. Thus the work of very young children in factories, even though paid for in money at the full market rate, is seldom worth its real cost: the satisfactions, which are derived from its contributions to production, are not worth the social cost of child life spent in grievous and depressing toil, and without an adequate education to prepare for the duties of after life[1].

A little care in wording will avoid all confusion between real and money costs of production. But there is another difficulty about the term *"cost of production for a market"* which is apt to be overlooked, and calls for careful attention. The manufacturer, or other producer, adjusts his production to his market so as to obtain for himself the greatest net excess of receipts over his "expenses" or "money cost" of production; with due allowance for his own trouble and risk, and for the use of his capital.

Until goods are marketed their production is seldom of much avail in the modern world: and there is no uniformity of practice on the part of manufacturers and other producers as to the extent to which they themselves incur labour and expense on behalf of the marketing of their goods. A manufacturer may sell to wholesale dealers who, after inspecting his goods on his premises, take their own measures for bringing them, together with other goods, to the notice of retailers: but even he must incur trouble and expense in attracting the attention of the merchants: and remuneration for this has to be included in the price received by him; for otherwise he would not earn profits adequate to his outlay. Heavier costs for marketing are incurred by a manufacturer, if he sends round incessant streams of expensively equipped travellers to dealers of various sorts: and much heavier still, if he also advertises largely in order that the general public may demand goods bearing his name or trade-mark from the dealers.

[1] The degree of correspondence between the price paid for any particular industrial work and its real cost, though a matter of vital importance from the social point of view, is not very closely connected with the subject of this Book.

Considerations of this kind will be found to underlie the general reasonings of economists as to the relations between demand, supply, and value; but perhaps they have not been made sufficiently prominent. The rule is simple. When considering the operations of demand and supply in governing price in any general market, we must aggregate the expenses up to one and the same point in regard to every transaction; and take the demand price at that point. The customs of each particular branch of industry and trade indicate the most convenient point for this purpose: it is generally the point of delivery to a wholesale dealer, and less frequently to the retailer. In a few cases, such as that of bread, it is commonly the point of delivery to the ultimate consumer, either at his own house or when fetched by him—a difference in detail of some practical importance[1].

Increased supply, demand being constant, lowers price both immediately and ultimately; though in various degrees for different things. Increased demand for a manufactured product generally sets up forces tending to lower cost, and therefore price, except when increased supplies of raw material can be obtained only at greater cost: but its immediate effect is always to raise price

So far little account has been taken of the time required for the development of the full results of changed conditions, whether on the side of demand or supply. Economic doctrines, when expressed in short and handy form, generally neglect this element of time: they imply that certain results

---

[1] A manufacturer sometimes sells in his own shops to the ultimate consumer goods such as are generally sold to a middleman; and then his point of delivery may be reduced back close to the customary (manufacturer's) point by deducting the expenses, direct and indirect, of his shops together with allowance for his own trouble and risk in regard to them, from the total expenses of his business; and at the same time deducting the *gross* profits of the middlemen, through whose hands similar goods generally pass, from the price which he receives. The results thus reached will correspond to those suggested by an observation of the relations between wholesale demand, supply, and price. They may be faulty in particular instances: but if the profits of manufacturers who retail their own goods were habitually much greater than is indicated on this plan, the practice of the market would change: middlemen would be eliminated; and the point of delivery at which expenses and price would alike be reckoned, would be the ultimate consumer. All this, however, must be taken broadly; and subject to the reflection which will shortly be developed that the production of goods and the marketing of goods are not acts, but processes.

will follow on certain causes, leaving the common sense of the reader to supply the qualification—"provided no great change, working in a different direction, set in before the effects of these causes have time for full development." This qualification being ignored, the doctrines are taken to be unconditional; and thus trouble arises: for, though the causes perhaps begin to produce the effects assigned to them, they have not gone far before their influence is modified or even overborne by other causes with different tendencies. This shows that economic doctrines cannot be stated correctly in a few words.

The growth of demand is in fact gradual. People take some time to learn the uses of a thing which they had regarded as beyond their means. When the price comes within their reach, the more alert may begin to use it, and others in their own class may gradually follow. But there may be hindrances in the way: the thing itself may be of little service without subsidiary appliances that are not yet provided for general use. Thus a fall in the price of gas cannot produce its full effects on consumption till people have had time to experiment with gas-engines and gas-cooking stoves for unaccustomed uses; and perhaps not even till a gradually increasing demand has improved and standardized, and thus cheapened the gas-engines and stoves: and this growing familiarity may of course be checked by a further development of, say, electrical appliances. Again, a fall in the fares charged on a tram line or suburban railway will not have exhausted its effect on increasing the traffic, till new houses have been built near one end to accommodate people whose work lies near the other end.

In this connection it will be well to introduce an academic term, that will be much needed later on. If a given fall in the price at which a thing is offered causes a great increase in the amount demanded, the *elasticity* or *responsiveness of demand* is said to be great; and, if it causes only a small increase, the elasticity is said to be small[1].

---

[1] If the increase in amount for each small fall of price is proportionately equal to the fall, the elasticity is said to be one; if twice as great, it is said to be two; if only three-quarters as great, it is said to be three-quarters; and so on.

It is a general rule that a lowering of the price, at which a thing is offered, increases demand. The increase will be great or small according as the demand is elastic or inelastic: and either a long or short time may be required for developing the extended uses of the commodity, which are rendered possible by the fall in price. But (at all events if exceptional cases, in which a thing is driven out of fashion by a fall in its price, be neglected) the influence of price on demand is similar in character for all commodities. And, further, those demands which show high elasticity in the long run, generally show a high elasticity almost at once: so that it is reasonable to speak of the demand for a commodity as being of high or low elasticity without specifying how far we are looking ahead.

But while the response of demand to increased supply acts on price always in one direction, though with varying degrees of intensity; the response of supply to increased demand acts on costs, and therefore on price, in different directions according to circumstances. Its immediate tendency is to raise price: its later effect, in the case of manufactured and some other goods, is gradually to lower costs and therefore price.

It is, of course, true that an increase in the scale of production of each manufacturing (or other "Increasing Return") industry opens out to it almost invariably opportunities for a gradual increase of the internal economies to be derived from fit coordination of more extensive varieties of specialized ability, skill and plant: as well as for the standardization of products, and for dealing in the most favourable markets. Again an increase in the scale of production of the industry as a whole, or even in that of the industries which supply its needs, tends to open to each business in the industry, whether large or small, access to improved plant, improved methods, and a variety of other "external" economies. But all these tendencies are *gradual*: some move fast: others require several years, and others again several decades for their full development.

Even stronger cases can be found of the importance of the

element of time in regard to the economies of manufacture on a large scale. A large, standing, order for rifles or cartridges of a particular pattern can be filled more cheaply than a small one; because the large order will enable the cost of adapting plant specially to that pattern to be spread very thin over a large surface. In fact, this position is somewhat similar to that of the printing trade, which will take an order for fifty thousand copies of a book at a much lower rate than for five thousand, and at a very much lower rate than for five hundred; because the same expense of setting up type has to be incurred in all three cases. And yet a sudden and unexpected order for a million rifles, *to be delivered promptly*, could not be filled at as low a rate as one for a hundred thousand. For the larger order would require more plant: and much labour skilled and unskilled, not specially adapted to the work, might need to be forced into it. Thus, the tendency to a rise of the price at which increased quantities of anything can be obtained (or their "supply-price") dominates as a rule all industries in regard to short periods. It is therefore even more necessary to make explicit reference to the period of time which is allowed for the adjustment of supply-price to changed conditions of demand, than it is to make reference to the period required for the adjustment of demand-price (that is the price at which any given amount will find purchasers) to changed conditions of supply[1].

It is to be further observed that the effects of a steady increase in demand for a commodity on the economies at the command of the industry, which makes it, cannot be properly studied without some reference to the conditions of industries, which supply it with plant and other things. If its increased demand for their products enables it to fill its requirements at lower costs than before, then an increase in the demand for its products will enable it to lower their

[1] With regard to short periods, and especially to the transactions of a dealer's market there is an "elasticity of supply" which corresponds closely to elasticity of demand: that is, a given rise in price will cause a great or a small increase in the offers which sellers accept, according as they have large or small reserves in the background, and as they have formed low or high estimates of the level of prices at the next market. But in the more fundamental problems of supply our primary concern is with the costs at which a given amount of the commodity can be produced on good notice; and therefore amount cannot here conveniently be regarded as a function of price.

price more than would have been possible otherwise: and therefore yet further to increase its sales, and therefore to obtain yet further economies of production on a large scale and so on. That is to say, the economies of production on a large scale can seldom be allocated exactly to any one industry: they are in great measure attached to groups, often large groups, of correlated industries.

It is not necessary to pursue this matter further here, because so long as competition works freely throughout the industries concerned, the share which each industry in such a group obtains of the aggregate economies and gains resulting from the increased demand, is governed by broad causes; a comparatively small place being left for commercial strategy. But if any of the industries in the group are under some degree of monopolistic control, the matter becomes important.

So far no account has been taken of the dependence of manufacture on supplies of raw material coming from the two "extractive" industries, agriculture and mining. They are commonly classed as "Diminishing Return industries," because in them Nature's resistance to a greatly increased demand generally overbears in the long run the force derived from those resources which man provides: but in fact the constraints which she exerts in the two cases differ fundamentally.

Good cultivation will enable a field to yield the same amount of produce decade after decade in return for the same amount of labour as before: but, no improvement in the arts of cultivation being assumed, it will not, as a rule, enable an increased produce to be raised without the application of labour and capital increased more than in proportion. In other words, what is called "Diminishing Return" in regard to agriculture relates to the difficulty of increasing the *annual* flow of produce, not of maintaining that flow. But what is often called by the same name in regard to mining relates to the difficulty of getting more produce out of a mine, when its accessible and rich supplies of ore have been lessened by a given *aggregate* amount, with but little reference to the period of time over which the operations have extended.

In agriculture improved knowledge and methods are always contending against Nature's resistance to the demands made on her by an increasing population. And no guess can be made as to whether the ratio, which the agriculturist's produce bears to his efforts, direct or indirect, will increase or diminish; until it is known whether the rate of improvement of his methods and appliances is greater or less than the rate of increase of the demands which he makes on his land[1].

Of course this tendency to Diminishing Return in agriculture is of little practical importance in a sparsely peopled country; but it may press heavily on a country, which has a dense and rapidly growing population, unless large supplies of agricultural produce can be obtained on favourable terms from abroad. The pressure may be relieved a little, but only a little, by better adjustments, as for instance better forms of land tenure, or better education of the farmer[2].

---

[1] In regard to the action of an individual farmer, this tendency may be expressed in terms of money: but in regard to broad problems it must be expressed in terms of amounts of appliances and of products, in spite of the inconvenience caused by varieties of labour, of farming plant, and of crops. For the price of staple foods tends to rise more than in proportion to any increase of demand relatively to supply: so that the necessity for a greatly increased production from the land is likely to increase the aggregate money receipts of cultivators more than their aggregate outlays. This difficulty is often overlooked.

[2] It is therefore on a wholly different footing from those tendencies to diminishing return which arise when any producer distributes his resources inappropriately; as when a farmer takes either more land or less land than is appropriate to his capital: or when the number of planing machines in a locomotive factory is either so large that several of them are habitually idle, or so small that work is frequently held up to wait for the planing machine. Such troubles are not very frequent: they are transitional: they do not enter as a primary factor into the conditions of human progress: and some little confusion seems to have been caused by speaking of the permanent tendency to Diminishing Return as though it were merely a particular instance of numerous passing incidents. For they do not, as it does, materially affect the rise and decline of nations; or threaten to offer, ere many centuries have passed, a stern opposition to a further considerable increase of the population of the world.

This is not of great importance in relation to the structure of business; which is the chief matter now in hand. For indeed the reasonings, by which a farmer decides whether his capital will reach out to the profitable cultivation of an additional piece of land that happens to be available for hire, are of the same character as those by which he decides whether it will be better to buy his own steam cultivator, or to hire one on occasion. And again the reasons by which a manufacturer decides whether to put an additional floor on one of his buildings or to take a new piece of land and put a low building on it are similar to those by which he decides whether to instal an electric supply of his own or not. But, from the social point of view, land in an old country is in a class by itself: for however it changes hands from one owner to another, the country's stock of it is fixed: and this is a matter of the first importance in regard to the incidence of taxation and other large issues.

The cost of production which controls value relates to whole processes of production rather than to any particular parcel of products.

The cost of any one thing—a bale of cloth, a lawn-mower, or an engraving—cannot be definitely isolated from that of similar things made in the same process with it; that is, of things made by the aid, in whole or part, of the same business ability and organization, the same labour, and the same machinery and other plant. In other words, the cost of production, which exercises a dominant influence on value, is the cost of a whole process. This elementary but important principle (or chief head) of the doctrine of value has already been to some extent implied in the statement that the immediate influence exerted on cost, and therefore on price, by a great increase in the demand for a manufactured product is generally in the opposite direction to its ultimate effect.

We must go far from the facts of life to get a case, in which the cost of production of a single thing can be exactly deduced from the total cost of the business in which it is made: we must imagine a steady demand without fluctuations for the products of a business, all of which are of the same kind and made under the same conditions. If a hundred things are made by it annually, then the cost of each is a hundredth part of the total annual cost of the business: or, in other words, it is the special cost of that thing together with a hundredth part of the general costs of the business for a year. This imaginary case is commonly taken as the starting-point in discussions of value. But it is not representative; and its suggestions are misleading. It is true that the *prime cost* of a particular thing can frequently be isolated: but its full cost cannot. We must here go a little into detail as to this familiar distinction. Its prime cost, in the narrow use of the term that is common in many industries, consists of those direct expenses for wages, coal, material, wear and tear of plant, etc., which are incurred by making it, and which would have been avoided if the process of production had stopped short of making it. But its full cost includes an appropriate share of the *general charges* of the business.

Thus the taking of an additional order is likely to involve an increase of the wages bill to nearly the full amount of the wages paid to the artisans and labourers who work on it: but foremen and other trusted artisans are seldom dismissed even in slack times; and therefore parts at least of their wages are not prime costs in the strictest use of the term. Again, it is customary not to include any part of the office charges in prime costs; because the salaries paid at any time are but little affected by the amount of work that happens to be in hand at the time. But there are exceptions to this general rule also; for, when work is slack a vacancy in the office may be left unfilled for the time; or occasion may be taken to dismiss someone whose services are no longer desired.

The general charges include interest on capital employed; depreciation of buildings, machinery, etc., otherwise than by actual wear and tear; salaries of officials and others who cannot conveniently be discharged at short notice; and the whole cost of building up the organization of the business both internally and in relation to its customers. And, over all, allowance must be made for the earnings (*i.e.* excess of profits over interest on capital, and insurance) of the heads of the business.

The distinction between special (or prime) and general costs has always the same character: but it differs in detail according to circumstances. In particular a great part of those costs which are properly regarded as "general" when a passing transaction is in view, must be regarded as "special" when reference is made to one which extends over a long period. This consideration is very important in connection with the division of costs between two classes of things, in the production or marketing of which some use is made of the same plant, or the same business organization. If the period in view is short, it will often be impossible to assign approximately to each its proper share of the costs which are common to both; though such an assignment can be made fairly well with reference to a long period of time. The full significance of this contrast between short and long period results is apt to be overlooked: and it will appear to hold the key to many difficulties which we shall encounter later on.

The distribution of the general costs of a business between the various products, to which its resources are devoted: whether they are "joint" in the sense of being practically inseparable, or are produced "in common" for any other reason.

This class of consideration is reinforced if we look at cases of a group of *"joint products"* in that narrow sense of the term in which it is not practicable, or at all events not convenient, to produce any one member of the group without at the same time producing the others. Instances of such groups are the meat, skin, and wool of a sheep; or again wheat and its straw. If the relative proportions of each of these were fixed absolutely by Nature, the cost of each group would need to be set as a single thing against the aggregate of the prices which could be got in the market for the several members of the groups. Cost of production would have no part in determining their relative prices: that would lie wholly in the hands of demand.

In practice, however, there are few, if any, cases of joint products the cost of production of both of which together is exactly the same as that of them alone. So long as any product of a business has a market value, it is almost sure to have devoted to it some special care and expense. If straw were valueless, farmers would exert themselves more than they do to make the ear bear as large a proportion as possible to the stalk. Again, the importation of foreign wool has caused English sheep to be adapted by judicious crossing and selection so as to develop heavy weights of good meat at an early age, even at the expense of some deterioration of their wool. It is only when one of two things produced by the same process is valueless, unsaleable, and yet does not involve any expense for its removal, that there is no inducement to attempt to alter its amount. And it is only in these exceptional cases that we have no means of assigning the separate supply price of each of the joint products. When it is possible to modify the proportions of these products, we can ascertain what part of the whole expense of the process of production would be saved, by so modifying these proportions as slightly to diminish the amount of one of them, without affecting the amounts of the others: and the expense of production of that part of this particular product which would not have been produced, if there had been a lower expectation of demand for it, may in some sense be taken as indicating its cost of production. At all events, it may be said that there is some tendency so to adjust the proportions of the several members of a group even of "joint products" in the narrow use of the term, that the excess of receipts over outlay on the whole group shall be greater than it would have been if Nature had been left to adjust those proportions in her own way. To that limited extent there is some correlation between cost and value even in regard to such products.

When two things, say locomotives and stationary engines, are made in the same works, and in a great measure by the same labour and plant, it is often said that their costs are "joint"; but, this term has a special historical association with groups of things, such as wheat and straw, which cannot be produced separately; and it seems better to speak of such groups as having "common" or "allied" costs.

In cases of such common or allied production, each thing is charged with a share of those expenses which are incurred on account of the general work of the business; it is next charged with a considerably larger share of those expenses for plant, for superintendence, for advertising, etc., which more specially belonged to the particular department by which it is made, in addition to the prime costs incurred directly and specially for it. Simple arithmetic in this case needs to be supplemented by careful analysis and thoughtful study of each problem as a whole: and, as we shall see later on, much systematic and organized effort has been given by accountants and others to the task.

Let us push this a little further. Suppose a manufacturer to be doubting whether to set up some expensive plant, or some addition to the office staff, or some new selling agency, which could not pay its way by the work it did for any one class of his products, but would save a little on each of three classes. If he decided that the aggregate of these savings would make the proposed outlay remunerative, he would adopt it, and regard its cost as part of the costs of those three classes. There would be no direct means of dividing out the cost among them: but he might divide it out roughly in proportion to the savings he made on them. This distribution would have no strict logical basis. But it would be nearly that which competition would have compelled; if each of the three classes had had to meet similar products made by manufacturers, who specialized on them, and found full employment for a machine, or other appliance similar to that which he was contemplating.

General conclusions as to limitations of the tendency towards such an adjustment of supply to demand, as would cause market price to cover expenses of production with normal profits.

This account of the adjustment of supply to demand has aimed only at indicating broad tendencies, which conduce towards the attainment of an equilibrium position; though incessant changes in the conditions, which must be satisfied by a position of equilibrium, prevent them from reaching it. To revert to a familiar illustration, the gravitation, which effects a smooth surface on a pond when the air is still, is making always for an equally restful result on the surface of the ocean: but there the winds build up mighty waves; while tides alternately raise and lower the general surface by amounts, which vary with the positions of the moon and sun: and the explanation of these movements, and their partial prediction are based on a study of elementary physical laws. In like manner business enterprise tends to increase the supply of anything, when the price at which it can be marketed will return its expenses of production with fairly good profits: and this tendency is working at any moment towards an imaginary position of equilibrium, which would be promptly reached if the general conditions then prevailing were rigidly fixed. But in fact it is not reached; any more than is that imaginary position of equilibrium of the sea, which would be reached if the relative positions of the earth, sun and moon were fixed, and the winds were stilled.

Almost every one of the expenses of maintaining any process of production is liable to incessant change. At one time additional machines may have to be bought when the market for them is exceptionally favourable to the seller: while another set may be bought at a time when machine makers were willing to accept a price, which did not go very far beyond covering the mere prime cost of production. The same shop under one manager will turn out more and better work at the same expense than under another. The same manufacturer, using his best energies without stint, will at one time put out a commodity which the market absorbs quickly at a price much beyond its full expenses of production; but at another he will have missed his aim, and be compelled to force his product on the market at a heavy loss. In these and innumerable other ways the return to a whole process of production may be kept for a considerable time a good deal above, or below, the level which might return its whole expenses with normal profits. But yet the tendency to keep expenses and price in close relation to one another is strong and persistent in an open market in regard to whole processes of production; the deviations from normal equilibrium, though ceaseless, are seldom very wide. Thus far-reaching are the various uncertainties of demand on the one side and of supply on the other.

But indeed a perfect adjustment is inconceivable. Perhaps even it is undesirable. For after all man is the end of production and perfectly stable business would be likely to produce men who were little better than machines.

The general position is, then:—Every manufacturer, or other business man, has a plant, an organization, and a business connection, which put him in a position of advantage for his special work. He has no sort of permanent monopoly, because others can easily equip themselves in like manner. But for the time being he and other owners of factories of his class are in possession of a partial monopoly. The prices of the stock, which they put on the market, will be governed by the demand of that market relatively to that stock, nearly in the same way as if they had a true monopoly. Nearly in the same, but not quite: for in the case of a permanent monopoly consumers will seldom gain much by waiting for lower prices; whereas, if prices rise above cost of production in an open trade, those consumers, who can do so conveniently, will wait for the effect of competition in bringing down prices. Combinations for regulating prices aim at consolidating provisionally this partial monopoly, and at putting it in good working order: and this fact goes far towards explaining their gradual, and in some cases almost unconscious, drift towards monopoly in the full sense of the term.

BOOK V, CHAPTER VIII

MARGINAL COSTS IN RELATION TO VALUES. GENERAL PRINCIPLES

PAGE 403

a. The origin of the wording of this chapter is shown throughout in the editorial notes.

In the 5th edition of the *Principles* Marshall made drastic changes in the form of this and the next three chapters. In the Preface to the 5th edition, speaking of Book V, Marshall wrote: "Chapters VIII–X [in the 4th edition] have been rewritten into a group of chapters VIII–XI on Marginal costs in relation to values". The earlier forms of these chapters will be found in the Editorial Appendix to Book V, chapters VIII–X. See also the Tables of Contents of the first four editions.

It may be noted that a large part of §§ 2 and 3 in Book V, chapter VIII in vol. I of the present edition consists of material previously placed in Book VII, chapter I in the 1st edition (Book VI, ch. I in the 2nd to the 4th editions).

b. The title of this chapter remained unchanged since the 5th edition.

c. This sentence dates from the 5th ed. (p. 403).

d. The remainder of this paragraph and the footnote attached to the last sentence thereof were inserted in the 7th ed. (p. 403) in place of the following sentence, which formed the second sentence of the first paragraph of § 1 in the 5th and 6th editions: "They deal with one part of the great problem of value, the general character of which was sketched at the end of Chapter VI." It may be noted that the reference in this sentence to "Chapter VI" should have been to "Chapter V".

e. The remainder of this section (§ 1) dates from the 5th ed. (pp. 403–4).

a. This sentence dates from the 5th ed. (p. 404).

b. So since the 5th ed. (p. 404). In the 3rd ed. (Book VI, ch. 1, §6, p. 576) after a paragraph beginning "We may now leave the imaginary world in which every one owns the capital that aids him in his work...etc." (see the first paragraph of Book VI, ch. 1, §7 in vol. 1 of the present edition) there was the following sentence:

In the world to which we thus return, the action of economic forces is largely directed by a set of men who specialize themselves in the organization of business, and through whose agency the principle to which we have given the name of the law of *substitution* becomes effective.

In the 4th ed. (Book VI, ch. 1, §7, p. 583) this sentence was replaced by the following sentences:

In the world to which we thus return, the greater part of the flow of the national dividend which nature yields to men's efforts, passes through the hands of employers and other business men. They specialize themselves in organizing the economic forces of the people.

c. So since the 7th ed. (p. 404) where this sentence replaced the following sentence dating from the 1st ed. (Book VII, ch. 1, §3, p. 543):

So far as the knowledge and business enterprise of the producers reach, they will in each case choose those factors of production which are best for their purpose.

d. This sentence, itself virtually a repetition of a sentence in Book V, ch. III, §3 (page 341 in vol. 1 of the present edition), dates substantially from the 1st ed. (Book VII, ch. 1, §3, p. 543).

e. The words "arrangement or process" were substituted in the 7th ed. (p. 404) for the word "method" dating from the 1st ed. (p. 543).

f. Apart from the first clause, this sentence dates from the 1st ed. (p. 543). In the 1st ed. this clause ran as follows: "In common language it is said that 'everything tends...etc.'" In the 2nd ed. (Book VI, ch. 1, §2, p. 544) it ran as follows: "And we constantly meet with informal statements to a similar effect in the common sayings of everyday life, that 'everything tends...etc.'" In the 3rd ed. (Book VI, ch. 1, §6, p. 577) it ran as follows: "The principle thus expressed in technical language is in close harmony with such common sayings of everyday life, as that 'everything tends...etc.'" This first clause, in its present form, dates from the 5th ed. (p. 404).

g. The remainder of this paragraph dates from the 3rd ed. (Book VI, ch. 1, §6, pp. 577–8).

h. The following additional sentence inserted in the 5th ed. (p. 404 n.) was deleted from the 7th ed.: "Sections 2 and 3 of this chapter and parts of section 5 were originally in VI, ch. 1; but they properly belong to this place."

PAGE 405

a. The wording of the remainder of this section (§2) dates substantially from the 1st ed. (Book VII, ch. 1, §§3 and 4).

In the 1st ed. (p. 544) there was the following opening sentence to this paragraph which was deleted from the 4th ed.:

Thus in building there are some purposes for which bricks would be used, even if they were much dearer relatively to wood than they are; and others for which wood would be used even if it were much dearer relatively to bricks than it is: but the applications of each material will be carried just so far that it would no longer be cheaper than the other relatively to the advantages gained by using it.

b. The words in parentheses were added in the 2nd ed. (p. 555). In the 1st ed. (p. 544 n.) there was the following footnote, attached to the word "*indifferently*", which was deleted from the 2nd ed.: "The term 'indifference' seems to have been first applied to this use by Jevons."

c. The words "in adding to the money value of the total product" were inserted in the 7th ed. (p. 405).

d. Both footnotes 1 and 2 on this page were inserted in the 3rd ed. (p. 578 n.).

PAGE 406

a. So since the 7th ed. (p. 406), where this clause replaced the following clause dating from the 1st ed. (p. 545): "and thus the law of substitution will have established directly a relation between the wages of labour and the price that has to be paid for horse-power."

b. The following footnote, attached to the word "horse-power" in the 1st ed. (p. 545 n.) was deleted from the 2nd ed.:

It may perhaps not be superfluous to point out that, in speaking of the action of a scientific law, whether it be that of diminishing return, of substitution, or any other, we are adopting, for convenience, a short and elliptical method of speaking. What we mean in not really the action of the law, but the action of those forces the action of which is set forth in the law. When, for instance, we say that the law of substitution is acting strongly, we mean that those forces, the action of which is set forth in the law of substitution, are acting strongly.

c. The wording of this section (§ 3) dates substantially from the 3rd ed. (Book VI, ch. 1, §§ 7–8, pp. 581–2), where it formed part of the general theory of distribution.

d. The following footnote, attached to the end of this sentence in the 4th ed. (Book VI, ch. 1, § 7, p. 545 n.) was deleted from the 5th ed.:

In V, especially chaps. VII–X, the net product of a machine was spoken of as the "net earnings" which it wins for its owner. But we are now entering upon a study of distribution between persons; and we want the phrase "the net earnings" of a carpenter for his personal income; we are inquiring how competition tends to make his personal income equal to the net benefit which his labour earns for society or more directly for his employer; and we had better now describe that net benefit as the net product of his labour.

See also footnote 2 on page 407 in vol. 1 of the present edition.

e. This and the next clause were inserted in the 4th ed. (p. 585).

f. The remainder of this sentence was inserted in the 7th ed. (p. 406).

g. This footnote dates from the 3rd ed. (p. 581 n.) save for the insertion in the 7th ed. (p. 406 n.) of the clause "which he desires" in the first line of the footnote.

PAGE 407

a. Except where otherwise stated the wording of § 4 dates from the 5th ed. (pp. 407–9).

b. So since the 7th ed. (p. 407). In the 5th and 6th editions this marginal summary ran as follows: "The diminishing return from disproportionate use of any agent of production, is akin to, but distinct from, diminishing return of land to good cultivation."

c. The remaining sentences of this paragraph were inserted in the 6th ed. (pp. 406–7).

d. The first two sentences of this footnote date from the 3rd ed. (p. 582 n.).

e. The reference in this footnote to von Thünen was inserted in the 6th ed. (p. 407 n.).

PAGE 409

a. The following paragraph, which concluded § 4 in the 5th ed. (p. 409), was deleted from the 6th ed.:

Again, some parts of a sewing machine may well be made of cast iron; for others a common kind of steel will suffice, and there are yet others for which a special expensive steel-compound is needed; and all parts should be finished off more or less smoothly, so that the machine may work easily. Now if any one devoted a disproportionate care and expense to the selection of materials for the less important uses, it might truly be said that that expenditure was yielding a rapidly diminishing return; and that he would have done better to give some of it to making his machines work smoothly, or even to producing more machines: and the case might be even worse if he devoted an excessive expenditure to mere brilliancy of finish, and put low grade metal to work for which a higher grade was needed.

b. So since the 6th ed. (p. 409 n.), where this sentence replaced the following clauses of the second sentence of this footnote in the 5th ed. (p. 409 n.): "Mr J. A. Hobson, a critic of Ricardian doctrines who is always vigorous and suggestive, but often hasty, argues that if the marginal application...etc."

The following extract from a letter dated 11 July 1901 from Marshall to Professor R. Ely, of the University of Wisconsin, throws some additional light on Marshall's attitude to J. A. Hobson:

Perhaps Dr. Hobson has communicated to you the fact that the particular passages on which he bases what I regard as misinterpretations of my views, in his *"Distribution"* in your series, were mostly expunged from my book; because I had found them to be capable of being taken—with an adequate disregard of the context—in senses in which I had not designed them. I sent him my last edition; and he wrote me a friendly and straightforward answer as to this matter, and similar comments of mine on his *Social Problem*. He is so very busy with other things that he may probably not have thought it necessary to write to you about this. There is an immense deal that is most fascinating about him; and he is certainly very able. But he is in a hurry; and so he disappoints me whenever the only good work is slow work.

But perhaps like some other oldish men, I have an "epidemic" of supposing that younger men polish off difficulties too hastily.

The original of this letter, to which my attention was drawn by Mr A. W. Coats, is in the possession of the Wisconsin State Historical Society.

PAGE 410

a.   Except where otherwise stated, the wording of §5 dates from the 5th ed. (pp. 410–11).

b.   This paragraph embodies a rewording, in the text of the 5th ed. (p. 410), of a footnote to Book VI, ch. 1 in the 3rd ed. (pp. 580 n.– 1 n.) and in the 4th ed. (p. 592 n.):

> An objection raised by some critics that the part played by the marginal use of an agent of production is represented, in modern economics, as governing the whole, is thus seen to rest on a misapprehension. The withdrawal of iron from any of its necessary uses would have just the same influence on its value as its withdrawal from its marginal uses; in the same way as in the case of a boiler for cooking under high pressure, the pressure in the boiler would be affected by the escape of any other steam just as it would by the escape of the steam in one of the safety-valves: but in fact the steam does not escape except through the safety-valves; and iron, or any other agent of production, is not thrown out of use except at points on its marginal use. Compare the illustration taken from the demand for plasterers' labour, in V, VI.

c.   So since the 6th ed. (p. 410), where the words "and costs" were inserted after the words "Marginal uses" in this marginal summary.

d.   So since the 6th ed. (p. 410), where the words "machinery and other appliances of production made by man" replaced "agents of production made by man" in the 5th ed.

e.   So since the 7th ed. (p. 410 n.). In the 5th ed. (p. 409 n.) the last sentence of this footnote ran as follows: "Mr Hobson's illustrations, as Prof. Edgeworth has observed in the *Quarterly Journal of Economics* (Feb. 1904, p. 167), refer to large and not small disturbances; and therefore are irrelevant to the matter at issue." In the 6th ed. (pp. 409 n.–10 n.) the sentence beginning: "The study of changes in complex quantitative relations..." was inserted, but the final sentence there ran as follows: "Professor Edgeworth has commented on this laxity in masterly analysis of the two instances mentioned in this note, see *Quarterly Journal of Economics*, 1904, p. 167; and *Scientia*, 1910, pp. 95–100."

PAGE 411

a.   "Appliances" in the 6th ed., "agents" in the 5th ed.

b.   The wording of §6 with one exception dates from the 5th ed (pp. 411–12).

PAGE 412

a.   In the 7th ed. (p. 412) the words "those which govern" were inserted between the words "degree to" and the word "rents".

MARGINAL COSTS IN RELATION TO VALUES. GENERAL PRINCIPLES, CONTINUED

PAGE 413

a. Except where otherwise stated the wording of Book V, ch. IX dates from the 5th edition.

For the treatment of the subject-matter of this chapter in the earlier editions, the reader should turn to the Editorial Appendix to Book V, chapters VIII–X (pp. 440–512) below. See also editorial note **a** to page 403 of Book V, ch. VIII (p. 410 above).

b. The title of this chapter has been unchanged since the 5th edition.

c. Marshall's answers to questions proposed by the Royal Commission on Local Taxation, together with his Memorandum on the Classification and Incidence of Imperial and Local Taxes, are reprinted in *Official Papers of Alfred Marshall* (pp. 327–64).

PAGE 414

a. So since the 7th ed. (p. 414). In the 5th and 6th editions the first clause of this sentence ran as follows: "Part of the burden,".

b. So since the 7th ed. (p. 414) where the opening word "Finally," replaced the words "In either case," in the 5th and 6th editions.

c. So since the 7th ed. (p. 414) where this clause replaced the following clause in the 5th and 6th editions: "who would meet with diminished custom."

PAGE 415

a. The earlier versions of the meteoric stones illustration will be found in the Editorial Appendix to Book V, chapters VIII–X, pp. 484–92. It will be seen there that part of the wording of this section dates from the earlier editions prior to the 5th ed.

PAGE 419

a. For the earlier versions of the effects of taxes levied on meteoric stones, see the Editorial Appendix to Book V, chapters VIII–X, pp. 487–8 and 490–2.

PAGE 424

a. In the 5th ed. (p. 424) this marginal summary ran as follows: "The existence of inferior agents does not lower but raises the rents of superior." In the 6th ed. (p. 424) this was corrected and the words "lower" and "raises" were transposed so as to be in their proper order.

b. The remainder of this paragraph dates from the 6th ed. (p. 424) where it replaced the following sentences in the 5th ed.:

For the produce raised by the inferior agents tends to lessen the scarcity of the product, and therefore lower the price. This lowering of price acts directly on the rent of the superior agents, as reckoned by the scarcity route. And on the differential route it acts no less clearly, though indirectly: for it increases the amount of service which any marginal use must render in order to be remunerative; and therefore lessens the amount of service which remains as surplus after covering expenses in other uses.

c. The two paragraphs of this footnote were inserted in the 6th ed. (p. 424 n.), where they replaced the following paragraph dating from the 4th ed. (p. 496 n.), in which edition it was placed in a footnote at the end of §5 of Book V, ch. ix; while in the 5th ed. (p. 432 n.) it was placed at the end of §3 of Book V, ch. x:

> Professor Nicholson appears to have overlooked those difficulties connected with the element of time with which the doctrine of quasi-rents is designed to cope; and to have failed to discover the drift of that doctrine. He says (*Political Economy*, vol. I, p. 414):—"In my opinion quasi-rent is a species of *Conjuncture* profits": and (vol. II, pp. 80–2), "The owner of old machinery is supposed to get a rent from it, because it has ceased to yield profit or interest....It seems absurd, because the loss is not total and absolute, to call the partial saving a *quasi*-rent.... Thus quasi-rent is an unforeseen and unstable exceptional profit or loss." A quasi-rent is not any one of these things.

BOOK V, CHAPTER X

MARGINAL COSTS IN RELATION TO AGRICULTURAL VALUES

PAGE 425

a. The origin of the wording of this chapter is indicated throughout in the editorial notes.

b. The title of this chapter has remained unchanged since the 5th edition.

c. This opening paragraph of §1 was inserted in the 5th ed. (p. 425).

d. This paragraph dates in its present form from the 4th ed. (Book V, ch. IX, pp. 489–90). For its earlier form see the Editorial Appendix to Book V, chapters VIII–X (p. 468).

e. This and the following paragraph date (with the exception of one slight change) from the 4th ed. (pp. 490–1).

PAGE 426

a. So since the 5th ed. (p. 426), where the remainder of this paragraph replaced the following concluding clauses of this sentence in the 4th ed. (p. 491):

the incomes derived from them exercise no such direct influence on supply price; and when we are dealing with such periods, these incomes may be regarded as quasi-rents which do not take direct part in determining the price of the produce, but rather depend on them.

The final word "them" in this passage just quoted from the 4th ed. would appear to be a mistake for "it"—i.e. the price of the produce.

b. This footnote dates from the 4th ed. (p. 491 n.).

PAGE 427

a. This paragraph dates mainly from the 4th ed. (Book V, ch. VIII, §1, pp. 478–9), though there were some alterations and additions to conclusions (2) and (4) in the 5th ed. See also the Editorial Appendix to Book V, chapters VIII–X, p. 449. In the 5th ed. (p. 427) the opening words: "We may conclude then:" replaced the following words in the 4th ed. (p. 478): "The classical doctrines may be re-stated thus:" The marginal summary appended to this paragraph also dates from the 5th ed., where it replaced the following marginal summary in the 4th ed.: "Restatement of the classical doctrines."

b. So since the 5th ed. (p. 427) where the present version of conclusion (2) replaced the following version in the 4th ed. (p. 479):

(2) But rent takes no part in controlling the general conditions of demand and supply or their relations to one another. It is governed by the fertility of land, the price of the produce, and the position of the margin: it is the excess of the value of the total returns which capital and labour applied to land do obtain, over those which they would have obtained under circumstances as unfavourable as those on the margin of cultivation.

a.   The words "it does not govern price, but it governs the causes which do govern price" were inserted in the 5th ed. (p. 428).

b.   The following paragraph in the 4th ed. (p. 480), which came immediately after the "Restatement of the classical doctrines" ((1)–(4)), was deleted from the 5th ed.:

Thus differences in the rent (or producer's surplus) of land result from differences in its *net advantages*, account being taken both of its situation and its fertility: but all that is required for the existence of rent is that different parts of the produce should be raised under different advantages, that is at different costs. Rent would exist even if all land were equally advantageous, provided only that the population were just a little more than sufficient to bring it under cultivation. On the outskirts of a new country, where some of the best land still remains uncultivated and free to the first comer, there is no rent.

c.   This paragraph dates from the 4th ed. (p. 480 n.) where it was put into a footnote.

d.   This paragraph dates from the 5th ed. (pp. 428–9).

a.   This, and the succeeding paragraph, date substantially from the 1st ed. See the Editorial Appendix to Book V, chapters VIII–X (pp. 464–6 below).

a.   This paragraph dates (with only slight alterations in one sentence in the 6th ed.) from the 5th ed. (p. 430).

b.   So since the 6th ed. (p. 430). In the 5th ed. this sentence ran as follows: "For similar reasons pioneer farmers require high gains in receipts for the sale of their produce together with the acquisition of valuable title-deeds to remunerate them for their endurance."

c.   In the 2nd ed. (Book VI, ch. IX, §6, pp. 670–1) Marshall inserted a section dealing with the distinction between land and other forms of wealth, which was retained with some rearrangement of sentences and some contraction but no substantial change in the 3rd ed. (pp. 712–13) and the 4th ed. (pp. 717–18), but was deleted from the 5th. This section ran as follows in the 2nd ed.:

§6. Before closing this chapter however it will be well to consider more closely the relations between land, whether agricultural or urban, and other forms of wealth regarded from the point of view of the individual investor.

As argued in Book v, chs. viii, ix, x, the distinction between land and other forms of wealth is slight, but real even in a new country;

The argument of Book V, chs. viii, ix, x, goes to prove that, even from the point of normal value, the distinction, though a real one, is slighter than is often supposed. In a new country, where there is plenty of new land still free to settlers, the whole of the net income derived from land is required to remunerate cultivators for their capital and labour; and is therefore to be regarded as earnings and profits; or at most as quasi-rent and not as rent proper, although even here a far seeing statesman will feel a greater responsibility to future generations when legislating as to land than as to other forms of wealth. Thus it may be admitted that from the economic and from the ethical point of view, land must everywhere and always be classed as a thing by itself.

and in an old country it has very important bearings on the causes that govern normal value

And in an old country, where land is regarded merely as one of the factors of production of material goods, though the only distinction between it and other factors is that they can be increased in quantity and it cannot; yet this distinction is vital in a broad survey of the causes that govern normal value. For the net income derived from the inherent properties of land is a true surplus; which does not directly enter even in the long run into the normal expenses of production, and which are required as rewards for the work and inventive energy of labourers and undertakers. It thus differs from the quasi-rents of buildings, machinery, etc., which are in the long run needed (in the present state of human character and social institutions), to sustain the full force of production, invention and accumulation. The sudden appropriation of rents and quasi-rents by the State would indeed have very similar effects in destroying security and shaking the foundations of society: but if from the first the State had retained true rents in its own hands, the vigour of industry and accumulation need not have been impaired; and nothing at all like this can be said of quasi-rents.

Nevertheless, things being as they are, the distinction between land and other forms of wealth has very little bearing on the detailed transactions of ordinary life. Suppose a cultivator with spare capital to be in doubt whether to buy more land, or to get better buildings and plant for what he already has: he may expect that in either case he would obtain the same increase of net produce (after allowing for depreciation of his perishable plant) by the same total outlay; and, for him as an individual, the question whether to cultivate a large piece of land lightly or a smaller piece intensively, is to be decided by business calculations of just the same character as those that govern other applications of his capital and energy.

But from the point of view of the individual there is no economic distinction between agricultural land and other material agents of production.

d. The first two sentences of this paragraph and the first clause of the third sentence date substantially from the 3rd ed. (Book VI, ch. II, §5, p. 602).

e. The remainder of this paragraph dates from the 4th ed. (Book V, ch. IX, §3, pp. 492–3).

PAGE 431

a. The first three sentences of this paragraph date substantially from the 3rd ed. (Book VI, ch. II, §5, p. 602). A number of other sentences and paragraphs in the 3rd ed. (Book VI, ch. II, §5) were retained in Book VI, ch. II, §5 in the later editions. See the editorial notes to pages 534–6 of vol. I in the present edition.

b. The remainder of this paragraph dates from the 4th ed. (Book VI, ch. IX, §3, p. 493).

c. With the exception of two clauses this paragraph dates substantially from the 4th ed. (pp. 493–4).

d. So since the 5th ed. (p. 431), where this clause in the present text replaced the following clause in the 4th ed. (p. 493): "his investments will leave as good a field as before for an increasing population to improve other land or put buildings on it."

e. So since the 5th ed. (p. 431) where this clause replaced the following clause in the 4th ed. (p. 493): "There is unlikeness because land is a *fixed stock for all time.*"

PAGE 432

a. The whole of this section (§4) was inserted in the 5th ed. (pp. 432–4).

b. The substance of the first paragraph of this footnote dates from the 1st ed. (pp. 492–3). See the Editorial Appendix to Book V, chapters VIII–X, pp. 462–3.

c. This second paragraph dates from the 6th ed. (p. 432 n.) where it replaced a paragraph dating from the 4th ed. (p. 496 n.), referring to

437

Professor Nicholson's failure to discover the drift of the doctrine of quasi-rent. See editorial note **c** to page 424 of Vol. 1 in the present edition.

PAGE 434

a. The first three sentences of this paragraph were inserted in the 5th ed. (p. 434).

b. The substance of the remainder of this paragraph dates from the 1st ed. (pp. 486–7).

PAGE 435

a. This and the next paragraph date substantially from the 4th ed. (pp. 480–1). The marginal summary dates from the 5th ed. (p. 435). For the earlier versions of the treatment of this problem see the Editorial Appendix to Book V, chapters VIII–X, pp. 453–61.

b. The words in inverted commas in the text are quoted from page 356 in vol. 1 of the present edition (Book V, ch. IV, §3).

c. So since the 5th ed. (p. 435 n.) where this paragraph replaced the following paragraph dating from the 4th ed. (p. 481 n.):

> See above III, V, 1, 2, and V, IV, 3; together with Mathematical Note XIV, which emphasizes the fact that distribution of outlay between different enterprises, which will give a maximum aggregate return is fixed by the same set of equations as that distribution under which the marginal return for the outlay in any one direction is equal to that for the outlay in any other direction.

d. This paragraph dates in its present form from the 4th ed. (p. 481 n.). For its earlier form in the first three editions see the Editorial Appendix to Book V, chapters VIII–X, p. 457.

PAGE 436

a. The remainder of §5 (apart from the second and third paragraphs of footnote 1 on page 436) dates from the 5th ed. (p. 436).

b. In the 5th ed. (p. 436), from which this paragraph dates, Marshall used the words "marginal price of oats", and these words were retained down to and including the 8th edition (page 436). These words have been altered in vol. 1 of the present edition to read "marginal price of hops", since the sense clearly requires the substitution here of "hops" for "oats".

c. Apart from changes in two sentences, the wording of this paragraph dates from the 4th ed. (pp. 482 n.–3 n.). See the Editorial Appendix to Book V, chapters VIII–X, p. 460.

The word "needlessly" in the first line, between the words "the ordinary man is" and the word "offended" in the 4th ed. (p. 482 n.) was deleted from the 5th ed.

d. So since the 5th ed. (pp. 436 n.–7 n.) where this and the next sentence replaced the following sentence in the 4th ed. (pp. 482 n.–3 n.):

> Rent does serve as a medium through which the really operative causes raise the price of oats, and it is therefore inexpedient to say that the rent of land does not enter into their price.

PAGE 437

a. This paragraph dates in its present form from the 5th ed. (pp. 437–8). For the earlier versions see the Editorial Appendix to Book V, chapters viii–x, pp. 459–60.

b. The following extract from a letter from Marshall to F. Y. Edgeworth dated 28 April 1902 has a bearing on this statement:

I am not sure that we differ about "rent not entering into cost". The question whether a phrase, which was from the first an indisputably bad one, can be rescued by explanation from misinterpretation, is to be solved only by experience. If I could have foreseen how many people would, in spite of my protests, persist in taking my words as I would have them *not* do, I would have from the first said what I do *now*:—It is *wisest not* to say that "rent does not enter into cost of production": for that will confuse many people. But it is *wicked* to say that "rent *does* enter into cost of production", because that is *sure* to be applied in such a way as to lead to the denial of subtle truths, which, in spite of their being subtle, are of the very highest importance scientifically and also in relation to the practical well-being of the world.

Memorials of Alfred Marshall, p. 436.

c. So since the 4th ed. (p. 483 n.). For the earlier version of this paragraph see pp. 459–60 below.

PAGE 438

a. This paragraph was inserted in the 5th ed. (p. 438).

b. In the first three editions this paragraph began as follows: "Mines, quarries etc., form a class by themselves, as has already been indicated." In the 4th ed. (p. 483) the sentence just quoted was replaced by the following: "It should be added also that a royalty is *not* a rent, though often so called."

c. This sentence dates from the 1st ed. (p. 491).

d. This sentence was inserted in the 5th ed. (p. 438).

PAGE 439

a. This sentence dates from the 1st ed. (p. 491).

b. This paragraph dates from the 1st ed. (p. 484 n.).

c. The first four sentences of this paragraph date from the 4th ed. (p. 484 n.).

d. Apart from a modification in the final part of the last sentence, the rest of this paragraph dates from the 1st ed. (p. 491).

e. So since the 7th ed. (p. 439 n.). In the 1st ed. (p. 491) this clause ran as follows: "the minimum royalty does enter into these marginal expenses." In the 3rd ed. (p. 485) this was altered as follows: "the minimum royalty does enter directly into the expenses paid for any part of the produce, whether it is marginal or not." This form was retained until the 7th ed.

f. In the 1st ed. (p. 491 n.) there was the following footnote to the last sentence of this paragraph (there in the text), which was deleted from the 3rd ed.: "Compare Prof. Sorley's paper on Mining Royalties in the *Statistical Journal* for March 1889."

g. This paragraph was inserted in the 7th ed. (p. 439 n.).

EDITORIAL APPENDIX TO BOOK V, CHAPTERS VIII, IX AND X

RENT AND QUASI-RENT IN RELATION TO COST OF PRODUCTION AND VALUE

In the 5th edition Marshall largely remodelled his treatment of rent and quasi-rent in relation to cost of production. This was substantially the final form and he made very few changes in the later editions.

The alterations made in the 5th edition were so extensive that it has seemed desirable to deal in a separate Appendix with the earlier versions in the 1st to the 4th editions. This Appendix contains all the passages dealing with rent and quasi-rent in the 1st to the 4th editions in Book V, which were wholly or mainly omitted subsequently.

It must remain a question of opinion whether the changes made subsequent to the 4th edition represent any real alterations of doctrine, or whether there was merely a change in presentation, so as to meet misunderstandings and criticisms and to remove ambiguities which experience had shown to have led to misinterpretations of Marshall's fundamental doctrine in this matter. The Editor of this Edition adheres to the latter view.

The reader who is concerned with the structure of the first four editions may find it helpful to consult the Tables of Contents of these editions (pp. 77–130 above) in connexion with the placing of the passages reproduced in this Appendix.

I. GENERAL RELATIONS BETWEEN RENT AND COST OF PRODUCTION

In the 1st edition Book VI, ch. 1 (pp. 481–2), entitled "Cost of Production Introductory", ran as follows:

§ 1. [a] I N the last Book we carried our analysis of cost of production only so far as was strictly necessary for the purposes of the general theory of the equilibrium of demand and supply.

We saw that the term "cost of production" is commonly used in two senses, in one of which it means certain efforts and sacrifices; in the other it means the supply prices or money measures of these efforts and sacrifices. We proposed to call the former the "real cost," the latter the "money cost," or more shortly the "expenses," of production.

We have regarded the expenses of production of a thing as consisting of the supply prices of its several factors of production; and assumed provisionally that these can be analysed, and resolved, at all events theoretically, into earnings of work of many different kinds including that of business management, and the interest obtained by the postponement of present for the sake of future enjoyment. Rent and insurance against risk appear in the first instance as additional elements; but we are now going to inquire how far this is really the case.

We have to examine more closely the connection between the expenses of production of a commodity and those of the things used in making it; and here, as in the preceding Book, it will be the element of Time that will give us most trouble.

[b] Nearly the whole of our inquiry will apply to markets for labour as well as to markets for commodities; to the supply price of skill as well as to the supply price of goods; to the investment of capital in education and industrial training as well as to its investment in the improvement of

---

a. This and the next three paragraphs were deleted from the 2nd ed.

b. In the 2nd and 3rd editions this paragraph was transferred to Book V, ch. VIII, § 1; but it was deleted from the 4th ed.

The argument of the present Book will be generally applicable to Personal as well as to Material Goods: but will be kept for the present in its most general form.

land or the making of machinery; to the income derived from that genius which is, so far as we know, the free and almost arbitrary gift of nature as well as to that derived from a vineyard of unique natural fertility. But the human elements of production have important incidents that are peculiar to themselves; and to introduce them here would add needless complexity to problems which are necessarily intricate. It will be best therefore to keep our argument for the present in its most general form; and to defer to the next Book our application of it to the price of human abilities; although much of its deepest interest lies in this application.[c]

[d] In that Book we are to study the causes by which earnings and interest are normally determined, and to bring together

---

c. In the 2nd ed. (p. 452) the following sentence and paragraph were inserted after the sentence ending with the words "much of its deepest interest lies in this application":

We shall find that much that appears at first sight to be true only of the rent of land is true of many other kinds of income, subject to suitable modifications with regard to the element of Time; and that on the other hand the rent of land in a newly settled country has at first strong points of resemblance to the gains got by "making," that is adapting to human use, other material things.

In this discussion we can hardly avoid treating of some aspects of land which are peculiar to it. But our main concern is with land not as a thing by itself, but as affording the sovereign illustration of a great principle of wide application to other agents of production besides land. And we shall, at present, pursue our inquiry as to land only so far as is necessary for the establishment of general results of which we shall have need when we come to analyse minutely the earnings of the employed and the profits of the employer.

The paragraph beginning: "In this discussion we can hardly avoid...etc." was deleted from the 3rd ed.; while the preceding paragraph beginning: "We shall find that much that appears at first sight ...etc.", was deleted from the 4th ed.

d. This and the next paragraph were deleted, except for one sentence, from the 2nd ed.

into one centre the main issues of the problem of Value, or in other words of Distribution and Exchange.

We shall begin the present Book with the study of the supply price of things, the sources of supply of which are limited by nature, though not monopolized. Ricardo's famous doctrine that "rent does not enter into (money) cost of production" will be found to be true only when the meaning of the terms used is very carefully limited, but when thus interpreted to have a very wide range of application. ^eIt will be found to apply with certain modifications not only to factors of production the supply of which is permanently limited, but also to those the supply of which cannot be increased quickly enough to affect appreciably the production of the commodity in question *during the period which we have in view when speaking of its normal supply price.* This discussion, which will occupy the next two chapters, is technical and difficult. But it has considerable interest from a theoretical point of view, and its bearing on practical problems is more important than at first sight appears.

The argument of the next two chapters

is difficult and technical.

In the 2nd edition, where the six chapters of Book VI in the 1st edition were incorporated in Book V, becoming chapters IV and VII–X, this Introductory Chapter (1st ed. Book VI, ch. 1) disappeared. The opening paragraph of Book V, chapter VIII, in the 2nd edition, which was entitled "On the Value of an Appliance for Production in relation to that of the things produced by it. Rent and Quasi-Rent", ran as follows:

We have already made some study of the broad principle that, on the one hand, the prices of those investments of capital and effort which are incurred for the purpose of producing any thing, enter directly into its price; for the outlay will not be made unless an adequate remuneration for it is expected to be included in this price; and, on the other hand, that the value of those appliances for production which are already in existence at any time, is dependent on the value of the things which they can be used in producing; and

Restatement of the broad principle of which a further study is to be made in this and the following chapter.

---

e.   This sentence, in a slightly modified form, was retained in the 2nd and 3rd editions in Book V, ch. IX (see editorial note i, p. 464 below).

that it affects the value of those things only indirectly, by affecting their supply. The more careful examination of this principle, which will occupy us during the present and the two following chapters, is technical and rather difficult. But it has considerable interest from a purely theoretical point of view, and its bearing on practical problems, though not very broad, is more important than at first sight appears.

In the 3rd edition (p. 473) this opening paragraph of Book V, chapter VIII ran as follows:

We have now to return to the study of the influence of the element of time on the causes which govern value, and mode of operation; taking up the study where it was left in chapters IV and V, with special reference to the (derived) value of an appliance for production which we partially considered in chapter VI.

In the 4th edition (p. 476) the opening paragraphs of Book V, chapter VIII (pp. 476–7) ran as follows:

Drift of this and the following two chapters. In chapter VI the contrast was drawn between the direct demand for such a thing as bread, and the indirect or "derived" demand for the wheat field or flour-mill that play their several parts in producing it. We have now to continue the study of indirect demand, and consider more closely in what ways the value of a piece of land or any other appliance for production is governed by the values of the things which it helps to produce.

This chapter will be occupied with land; and the next with appliances made by man: while some miscellaneous questions allied to the main issue will be discussed in chapter x. Throughout all three chapters the influence of the element of time will be prominent.

General character of the surplus yielded by a differential advantage for production. When a person is in an advantageous position for any branch of production, he is likely to obtain a "producer's surplus", that is, a benefit in excess of what is required to remunerate him for his immediate outlay. This surplus is likely to exist when he produces for his own consumption, as much as when he produces for sale: but such cases are of secondary importance in this modern world: and the easiest as well as most practical course is to go straight to production for sale in a market.[1]

[1] When a person produces for his own consumption, the producer's surplus is apt to be entangled with the consumer's surplus. See below, VI, II, § 13.[f]

In the 3rd edition (pp. 474–6) the concluding paragraphs of Book V, ch. VIII, § 1, ran as follows:

The principle which we have to study is that speaking broadly, the price of anything and the amount of it that is produced are together governed by the general relations of demand and supply: that the price just covers the expenses of production of that part of this amount which is raised at the greatest disadvantage; that every other part yields a surplus above its direct cost; and that this surplus is a result and not a cause of the selling price. For the price is governed by the relation of supply and demand; and while, of course, the surplus does not affect the demand, so neither does it affect the supply, since it is yielded only by a part of the produce which would be produced even at a lower price.

In other words there is a part of the produce which is on the margin of doubt as to whether it will be supplied or not, and the expenses of production of this part of the produce are often said to *determine* the price of the whole. But, more strictly we should say that they take direct part in governing it: that is, that the price of the whole will, other things being equal, be raised or lowered, according as it is decided to produce or not to produce these marginal elements. For those parts which do yield a surplus, will generally be produced whatever the price is, provided only it is not so low as wholly to destroy that surplus; and that surplus is therefore governed by the price and does not govern it: while there is no surplus yielded by that part of the produce the expenses of production of which do take direct part in governing the price. No surplus therefore enters into *that* (money) cost of production which gives the level at which the whole supply is held fixed. This then is what we mean by the phrase "Producer's surplus does not enter into cost of production"; or in Ricardo's words, "Rent

The allied doctrines that marginal expenses of production control value, and that rent does not enter into cost of production are true only in a rather forced sense.

f. This reference is to Appendix K in vol. I of the present edition.

does not enter into cost of production." It is one of those short phrases which do not explain themselves, and are easily misunderstood; but it has an important meaning, and it is applicable to many different trends of income.

The point of the doctrine is to be sought in the fact that the cost of production of the marginal produce can be ascertained (theoretically at least) from the circumstances of the margin, without reasoning in a circle, and that the cost of production of other parts of the produce cannot. For other parts yield a rent or a quasi-rent, or both; which are governed not by the circumstances of production of the parts in question, but by the price of the whole produce. The costs of production of these parts cannot be reckoned up without counting in the corresponding rents and quasi-rents; and therefore the price of the commodity cannot be deduced from them without reasoning in a circle.

Another aspect of the same truth is that the income earned by machinery and other plant already in existence is not any given percentage on their cost of production, but is a quasi-rent determined by the value of what they produce. If they are of obsolete fashion, this quasi-rent is small. But whether it is large or small, this value is found by capitalising their quasi-rent; and if we were to turn round and say that their quasi-rent would return a certain rate of interest on their value, then we should be reasoning in a circle.

The question is of academic rather than general interest.
This then is the principle which we shall have to study in detail. So large a part of the academic controversy of this century, and even of this generation, appears to proceed from a misunderstanding of its general bearings, and in particular of the place which the element of time holds in it, that some fulness of illustration and some persisting of repetition may be advisable; in spite of the fact that it is largely of an academic character, and that the general reader has little interest in some of its intricacies.

The first of the above paragraphs in the 3rd edition was retained with no substantial change in the 4th edition (Book V, ch. IX, §5, p. 495). The remaining paragraphs were deleted from the 4th edition.

In place of the paragraphs just quoted from the 3rd edition there were the following paragraphs in the 4th edition (p. 477):

§2. We start then from the position that when a thing is produced for sale in a free market, its price must in the long run be enough to remunerate the producers for every part of their output. The price must cover the cost of that part of the produce which is raised at the greatest disadvantage; and therefore every other part must yield a surplus above its direct cost. These facts have been indicated in two classical doctrines; viz.:—that the price of the whole produce is *determined by* the expenses, or money cost, of production on the margin of cultivation; and that rent does not *enter into* cost of production. These phrases are true in the senses in which they were meant; but they are frequently misinterpreted.

[margin note:] Classical doctrines as to rent in relation to cost are true but not well expressed.

It is certainly true, for instance, that the expenses of raising agricultural produce are best estimated on the margin of cultivation. That is, they are estimated for a part of the produce which either is raised on land that pays no rent because it is poor or badly situated; or, is raised on land that does pay rent, but by applications of capital and labour which only just pay their way, and therefore can contribute nothing towards the rent. It is these expenses which the demand must just cover: for if it does not, the supply will fall off, and the price will be raised till it does cover them. Those parts of the produce which yield a surplus will generally be produced even if that price is not maintained; their surplus therefore does not govern the price: while there is no surplus yielded by that portion of the produce the expenses of production of which do take direct part in governing the price. No surplus then enters into *that* (money) cost of production which gives the level at which the price of the whole supply is fixed.

In the 1st edition the Introductory Chapter of Book VI (pp. 481–2), which has been reproduced earlier in this Appendix (pp. 441–3), was followed by chapter II, "Cost of Production. Limited Sources of Supply." §1 of this chapter ran as follows:

§1. It will be well at starting to guard against some common errors as to the meaning of Ricardo's doctrine that rent does not enter into cost of production.

[margin note:] Three preliminary cautions.

In the first place, he did not intend to limit it to cases

in which land is cultivated by a tenant who pays rent for it to some one else. Rent is here taken as another name for the *surplus produce* which is in excess of what is required to remunerate the cultivator for his capital and labour; and if the cultivator owns the land himself, he of course retains this surplus.

Next, it may perhaps not be superfluous to repeat that the "marginal" dose, by the return to which we estimate the amount required to remunerate the farmer, is not necessarily applied to land on the margin of cultivation: it is on the *margin of profitable expenditure* on land of any quality.

Lastly, the doctrine does not mean that a tenant farmer need not take his rent into account when making up his year's balance-sheet: when he is doing that, he must count his rent just in the same way as he does any other expense. What it does mean is that when the farmer is calculating whether it is worth his while to apply a certain extra dose of capital to the land, *then* he need not think of his rent; for he will have to pay this same rent whether he applies this extra "marginal" capital or not: and therefore if the "marginal" produce due to this dose seems likely to give him normal profits, he applies the dose; and his rent does not *then* enter into his calculations.

Provisional statement of Ricardo's meaning. Thus Ricardo's contention was that the price of the whole produce was determined by the action of the farmers with regard to their "marginal" produce; and that since this action was not affected by the rent they had to pay, therefore rent did not enter into the price of the marginal produce and therefore did not enter into the price of any part. On the other hand, he continued, this price does play an important part in determining rent. On a closer study this doctrine will be found to be a special case of a very broad scientific principle towards which Ricardo was more or less consciously working his way.

In the 2nd edition (Book V, ch. VIII) the material in chapters I and II of Book VI in the 1st edition was rearranged and expanded, and the statement of the "three preliminary cautions" was preceded by two illustrations, the first of which was drawn from an imaginary shower of meteoric stones (see below pp. 484–92) and the second from the ownership of mineral springs (see below, pp. 450–5). After the latter illustration the text of Book V, chapter VIII, §3 (pp. 457–8) continued as follows:

This brings us to consider the celebrated doctrine that *Rent does not enter into cost of production*. It has had a great place in history; but, it has been much misunderstood. It has often been applied to farm-rents in a sense in which it is not true: and on the other hand its scope has been limited to farm-rent, though in fact we shall find that it is applicable to many other kinds of rents in the same way and to the same extent that it applies to farm-rents.[1]

[1] Ricardo, the original user of this phrase, is himself partly responsible for this error.

§4. Three preliminary cautions may be entered. In the first place, rent is here taken as another name for the *Surplus produce* which is in excess of...etc.

The text of the "three preliminary cautions" was substantially unaltered in the 2nd to the 4th editions, but in the 2nd edition (p. 458) the third "caution" ending with the words "and his rent does not *then* enter into his calculations" was succeeded by the following paragraph:

The doctrine is then, that the price of the whole produce was determined by the action of the farmers with regard to their "marginal" produce; and that since this action was not affected by the rent they had to pay, therefore rent did not enter into the price of the marginal produce and therefore did not enter into the price of any part.

In the 4th edition the paragraph just quoted was deleted, and the three "cautions" were followed (pp. 478–9) by a "Restatement of the classical doctrines", which was transferred in the 5th and later editions, in an expanded form, to Book V, ch. x, §1 (pages 427–8 in vol. 1 of the present edition) under the general heading in the marginal summary—"Summary of relations between marginal costs and value of agricultural produce in general in an old country".

In the 1st edition (pp. 484–6) the general remarks on rent in relation to cost of production and on Ricardo's doctrine were followed by an illustration drawn from mineral springs (see below, pp. 450–5).

In the 2nd edition (pp. 456–7) the mineral springs illustration was placed after the general discussion on rent, and was immediately preceded by an illustration drawn from an imaginary shower of meteoric stones[g].

In the 3rd edition (pp. 476–82) the meteoric stones illustration was followed by the general discussion on rent. After pointing out that the Ricardo doctrine that rent does not enter into cost of production can only be applied with one qualification to "the expenses of production of agricultural produce as a whole", Marshall used the mineral springs illustration in a footnote to emphasize the view that "when the doctrine is applied to any one line of produce taken separately it is misleading".

In the 4th edition (pp. 477–83) after a general "Restatement of the classical doctrines" Marshall placed the mineral springs illustration in two footnotes. The first footnote (p. 479 n.) referred to the general principle that rent does not enter into marginal cost of production, and the second (p. 483 n.) to the modifications which must be introduced when dealing with alternative uses for land. The meteoric stones illustration was put, in the 4th edition, into a separate Note at the end of Book V, ch. IX, §10 (pp. 501–3).

The mineral springs illustration disappeared from the 5th and subsequent editions apart from a single reference in a footnote to Book V, ch. XI, §1 (page 442 n.), in vol. 1 of the present edition

In the 1st edition (Book VI, ch. II, §§2–5 (pp. 484–7) the mineral springs illustration ran as follows:

Neglecting for the present farm rents and the income derived from mines, let us take our first illustration from mineral springs,

§2. [h]In examining the relation which the rent of a natural agent bears to the value of the products that are obtained by its aid, it will be well to avoid, in the first instance, the case of farmer's rent; for that case is encumbered by many

---

g. See pp. 484–92 of the present Appendix.

h. In the 2nd ed. (pp. 455–6) the opening sentences ran as follows:

Our next illustration shall be taken from immovable "Real" property; but not from agricultural land, because that has special incidents of its own, which it is advisable to keep in the background at present. We will take it from the case of perennial springs of natural mineral water.

In the 3rd ed. (p. 481 n.) and the 4th ed. (p. 479 n.) there was the following opening sentence:

This method of treating the rent of land may be supplemented by another, proceeding rather on Cournot's plan of starting with value as determined by a monopoly, and then introducing the competition of many rivals, so as to work towards the circumstances of a free market.

misleading associations arising from the complex incidents of land tenure. Again the case of mines must be avoided; because, as we have already noticed[1], a mine is to be regarded as a store that is being emptied rather than as the source of a steady income. Let us then take an illustration from the case of a perennial spring of natural mineral water.

We may pass by the case in which all the springs of the same kind, if there are more than one, are in the hands of the same owner. For that would be a case of pure monopoly, [i]which we have already discussed: the rent with which we are here concerned is the income derived from one of several sources of supply of the same commodity, these sources being in the hands of persons who are competing with one another[2].

Suppose then that there are in a certain place a number of springs, not all owned by the same person, of a natural mineral water for which there is no available substitute. Suppose also that the supply drawn from each of them [j]can be increased almost indefinitely by the aid of pumping appliances, the expensiveness of which increases more than in

which are not a monopoly, but are limited in number.

[1] Book IV, ch. III, §7.

[2] We have seen (Book V, ch. VIII) that the rental of a single spring would be determined by the "Maximum Monopoly Profit" which it could afford. The lessee would fix the price of the water so that the aggregate (yearly) receipts from the sales would exceed the aggregate (yearly) expenses of working the business by as large a sum as possible: and this excess (his own earnings of management being included in the expenses of working) would be the rent which the owner of the spring could compel him to pay. The fact that these monopoly profits would be determined, other things being equal, by the price of the water, and would not enter directly into that price, is in harmony with the doctrine we are discussing, but is not an illustration of it.

---

i. In the 2nd ed. (p. 456 n.) and the 3rd ed. (p. 481 n.) the reference to monopoly in this sentence was expanded in a footnote as follows:

We shall soon discuss the question of monopoly in some detail, and shall observe more closely the fact that monopoly rent is determined, other things being equal, by the price of the water, and does not enter into that price. This fact is in harmony with the doctrine we are discussing, but is not an illustration of it.

In the 4th ed. (p. 479 n.) the word "governed" replaced the word "determined" in the above sentence.

j. In the 3rd ed. (p. 481 n.) and the 4th ed. (p. 479 n.) this ran as follows: "can be increased by expensive pumping appliances, which yield a constantly diminishing return."

proportion to the additional supplies obtained by their means. Then, [k]it being assumed that there is no combination between the owners of the springs, each will go on increasing his production until the price no longer does more than cover the expenses of an additional supply. The equilibrium price will be such as just to remunerate each producer for his marginal production; that is, for the last gallon of water which his expenditure enables him to raise, when the amounts raised from the several springs are such that they are together equal to the amount which purchasers are willing to buy at that price. The rental value of each spring will be the excess which this price affords over the expenses of working it. Thus the price will be [l]determined by the relations of demand and supply; it will take part directly in determining the rent and will not be determined by the rent: rent will not enter into [m]expenses of production[1].

[1] [n]The plan of starting with value as determined by a monopoly, and then introducing the competition of many rivals so as to work towards the circumstances of a free market was adopted by Cournot as the basis of his mathematical treatment of economics. His work is most fascinating and suggestive: but he seems not to have noticed that if the field of sale of each of the rivals were unlimited, and the commodity which they produced obeyed the law of Increasing Return then the position of equilibrium attained when each produced on the same scale would be unstable. For if any one of the rivals got an advantage, and increased his scale of production, he would thereby gain a further advantage, and soon drive all his rivals out of the field.

[o]Cournot's argument does not introduce the limitations necessary to prevent this result.

---

k. This clause was deleted from the 3rd and 4th editions.

l. In the 4th ed. (p. 480 n.) the words "determined" and "determining" in this sentence were replaced by the words "governed" and "governing".

m. In the 3rd and 4th editions the word "its" was inserted between the words "into" and "expenses".

n. The substance of this footnote, in an expanded form, was placed in the 3rd and subsequent editions in the chapter in Book V dealing with Equilibrium with Reference to Increasing Returns (in the 3rd and 4th editions, Book V, ch. IX, §3; in the 5th and later editions, Book V, ch. XII, §3). See page 459 n. in vol. I of the present edition.

o. In the 2nd ed. (p. 457 n.) this ran as follows:

Cournot ignores the practical limitations which prevent this result from being reached in real life. (See above, Book IV, chs. XI—XIII; we shall return to this subject.)

§ 3.   **p** So far then Ricardo's doctrine might appear to be A latent
true unconditionally: but in fact we have silently introduced assumption must be
the conditions by which it has to be limited.   For we have drawn to
implicitly assumed that every spring will be opened up which the light.
can be worked so as to supply water at an expense less than
the selling price, nothing being allowed in estimating this
expense for the value of the land. That is, we have assumed
that there is no other way of using the land from which a
larger revenue can be derived.   **q**But if one of the smaller
springs happened to be so situated that it could not be
worked without injury to a valuable site, it would probably
not be worked at all; the fact that the site had a high rental
value for other purposes would cut off part of the supply of
mineral water that otherwise would have been forthcoming.
This would cause more water to be obtained from the other
springs at expenses increased more than in proportion**r**: the
expenses of production of that part which determines the
price of the whole would be raised in consequence of the
high rent that could be got by using for other purposes one
of the sites on which machinery for pumping mineral water
might have been erected.**s** Thus the proposition that rent

---

p.   This and the next two sentences were deleted from the 3rd ed.

q.   This and the next sentence, with the modification shown in
r below, were placed in a footnote to Book V, ch. VIII, §4 in the
3rd ed. (p. 481 n.) and in a footnote to Book V, ch. VIII, §3 in the
4th ed. (p. 483 n.). For the latter footnote see below, p. 460.

r.   In the 3rd ed. (p. 481 n.) three new sentences were inserted
after the clause ending with the words "at expenses increased more
than in proportion", which ran as follows:

The expenses of production of that part which is raised at the greatest disadvantage, would be greater than before; and producers would at once raise their
prices. If the price did not rise enough to cover these expenses, the supply would
be curtailed, and the scarcity of supply would compel the price to rise. The price
therefore would be raised in consequence of the high rent that could be got by
using for other purposes one of the sites on which machinery for pumping
mineral water might have been erected.

These sentences were retained in the 4th ed. (p. 483 n.).

s.   In the 2nd ed. (p. 457) this sentence ran as follows:

Thus the proposition that rent does not enter into the
expenses of production when rightly understood is not in-

does not enter into expenses of production is true in its unqualified form only on the assumption that none of the possible sources of supply of the commodity in question have been diverted to purposes that will enable them to render a higher rent.

^tSuch an assumption is generally justifiable with regard to springs of mineral water, and again with regard to agricultural produce taken as a whole; and it was really, though perhaps unconsciously, made by Ricardo, when he contended that the rent of agricultural land does not enter into the price of corn. ^uHe supposed that all kinds of agricultural

It may fairly be made with regard to agricultural produce as a whole.

---

consistent with the fact that if some of the possible sources of supply of the commodity in question have been diverted to purposes that will enable them to render a higher rent, this diminution of supply will raise prices.

This sentence was deleted from the 4th ed.

t. The first two sentences of this paragraph (omitting the reference to mineral springs) were retained substantially in later editions. Their substance is to be found on pages 434–5 in vol. 1 of the present edition.

u. In the 2nd ed. (p. 459) the substance of the remainder of this paragraph was placed, in a different context, after the "three preliminary cautions" referred to above (pp. 447–9), and ran as follows:

If, following Ricardo, we suppose that all kinds of agricultural produce can be regarded as converted into certain quantities of corn; and then take it for granted that all the land will be used for agricultural purposes of some kind or other, with the exception of building sites which are a small and nearly fixed part of the whole; it is then true that the price of agricultural produce taken as a whole is governed, in the long run, and other things being equal, by its marginal expenses of production (or, to use the ordinary metaphor, by the expenses on the margin of cultivation); that these expenses are not in any way affected, directly or indirectly, by the true rent (exclusive of the quasi-rents of improvements) paid for the land; and that therefore this rent does

produce can be regarded as converted into certain quantities of corn; and then took it for granted that all the land will be used for agricultural purposes of some kind or other, with the exception of building sites, which are a small and nearly fixed part of the whole. On the understanding that this assumption is made, his doctrine is valid; it is then true that the price of agricultural produce taken as a whole is governed, in the long run, and other things being equal, by its marginal expenses of production (or, to use the ordinary metaphor, by the expenses on the margin of cultivation); that these expenses are not in any way affected, directly or indirectly, by the rent paid for the land; and that therefore rent does not enter into the expenses of production of agricultural produce taken as a whole.

§ 4. ᵛBut when applied to the case of one kind of agri-

---

not enter into the expenses of production of agricultural produce taken as a whole.

In the 3rd ed. (pp. 479–80) the earliest part of the paragraph just quoted from the 2nd ed. was retained unaltered down to the second semi-colon; while the remainder of the paragraph ran as follows:

it is then true that the price of agricultural produce taken as a whole cannot in the long run be greater, and cannot in the long run be less, than its marginal expenses of production (or, to use the ordinary metaphor, than the expenses on the margin of cultivation). More simply, other things being equal, it is *governed* in the long run by these expenses; these expenses are not in any way affected, directly or indirectly, by the true rent (exclusive of the quasi-rent of improvements) paid for the land; and therefore this rent does not enter into the expenses of production of agricultural produce taken as a whole.

In the 4th ed. (p. 480) the sentences just quoted were deleted, while the substance of the earlier part of the paragraph was retained.

v. This section was retained with minor changes, noted below, in the 2nd and 3rd editions, where it was transferred to Book V, ch. viii. In the 4th ed. (pp. 480–2) the wording underwent considerable change (see pp. 457–9 below).

In the 2nd ed. Marshall also inserted elsewhere (Book V, ch. xiv,

But when the doctrine is applied to any one kind of produce taken separately it is misleading.

cultural produce considered separately, the doctrine is not true as it stands. In order to make it true we must add conditions, the effect of which is almost to explain it away. For instance the production of those oats which only just pay their way is often said to determine the price of all other oats; rent, it is argued, does not enter into their cost of production, and therefore rent does not enter into the supply price of oats. ᵂBut this is not strictly true.

It is true that when we know what are the most unfavourable conditions under which oats are grown, we can calculate the supply price of oats by reckoning up their expenses of production; just as we can discover the temperature by looking at the thermometer. But as it would be misleading to say that the height of the thermometer determines the temperature; so a great deal of confusion has arisen from saying simply that the normal value of oats is determined by their production under the most unfavourable circumstances under which they are grown. This statement needs to be completed by adding that these circumstances are, no less than the normal value itself, ˣdetermined by the general conditions of demand and supply; ʸand that one of the chief of these

---

§ 3, i. 532) a short statement on the relation of rent to cost of production where there are alternative uses of land—a statement which he described in his article entitled "On Rent" (*Economic Journal*, March 1893) as "a more careful version" of his views on this subject. The statement in question will be found in editorial note **d** to page 499 (Book V, ch. xv, § 3) in vol. 1 of the present edition.

Marshall's article "On Rent" is reproduced below (pp. 492–512).

w. In the 2nd ed. (p. 459) and the 3rd ed. (p. 480) this sentence ran as follows: "But this, though true in a sense, is misleading."

x. In the 3rd ed. (p. 480) the word "determined" was replaced by the word "governed".

y. In the 2nd ed. (p. 460) and 3rd ed. (p. 480) this clause ran as follows:

and that one of the chief of these conditions is the amount of land which is capable of growing oats, but for which there is so great a demand for other purposes that it affords a higher rent, when used for them, than when used for growing oats.

conditions is the amount of land capable of growing oats which affords a higher rent when used for other purposes than when used for growing oats. For the expenses of production of those oats which only just pay their way, are greater than they would be, were it not that much of the land which would return the largest crops of oats to the smallest outlay is diverted to growing other crops that will enable it to pay a higher rent than oats would afford; and therefore the rent that land on which oats could be grown, can be made to pay for other purposes, ^zdoes indirectly affect the expenses of production and the normal value of oats[1].

§ 5. The doctrine that rent does not enter into money-cost of production applies then to agriculture only when carefully limited; and if Ricardo had studied its limitations more carefully he would probably have seen that there remained no reason for confining its scope to agriculture. Taken in the natural sense of the words, it is not true of agricultural rent; taken with proper limitations it is equally true of all kinds of rent^{aa}.

Those limitations and conditions which are necessary to make the doctrine true of agricultural rents are sufficient to make it true of urban rents.

In the 4th edition (pp. 480–2) § 3 of Book V, ch. VIII, dealing with the relation of rent to the price of a single product, ran as follows:

§ 3. So far we have treated agricultural produce as a single commodity. In effect we have followed the classical economists in provisionally supposing that all kinds of it can be regarded as converted into certain quantities of corn; and we have taken for granted that all the land will be used for agricultural purposes, with the exception of building sites, which are a small and nearly fixed part of the whole. But now we have to reckon for the competition between the

Relation of rent to the price not of agricultural produce in general, but of one kind of produce.

---

[1] As Mill points out when discussing "some peculiar cases of value," all questions relating to the competition of crops for the possession of particular soils are complicated by the rotation of crops and similar causes (*Principles*, Book III, ch. XVI, § 2). He does not however appear to have noticed the bearing of these remarks on the general problem of "Rent in its relation to Value."

---

z. The remainder of this sentence in the 2nd and 3rd editions ran as follows: "though it does not 'enter into' the expenses of production and the normal value of oats, yet does indirectly affect them."

aa. For urban rents see Book V, ch. XI, §§ 4 and 5 in vol. I of the present edition.

different kinds of agricultural produce for the use of fertile soils.

The conditions which govern the supply of agricultural produce as a whole, at any given price, are the extent and fertility of the whole land and the resources of those who cultivate it. bbBut only a part of the land and of the resources of the cultivators are available for any one crop, say oats or hops. Each crop strives against others for the possession of the land; if any one crop shows signs of being more remunerative than before relatively to others, the cultivators will devote more of their land and resources to it. The change may be retarded by habit, or diffidence, or obstinacy, or limitations of the cultivator's knowledge; or by the terms of his lease. But these obstacles can only hinder the tendency to "substitution": they cannot annul it. It will still be true in the main that each cultivator, "taking account of his own means, will push the investment of capital in his business in each several direction until what appears in his judgment to be the margin of profitableness is reached; that is, until there seems to him no good reason for thinking that the gains resulting from any further investment in that particular direction would compensate him for his outlay."

Thus in equilibrium, oats and hops and every other crop will yield the same net return to that outlay of capital and labour, which the cultivator is only just induced to apply. That "marginal" application which only just repays its expenses, and which therefore contributes nothing to rent, will yield equal returns to the cultivator. For otherwise he would have miscalculated; he would have failed to get the *maximum* reward which his outlay can be made to yield: and it would still be open to him to increase his gains by redistributing his crops, by increasing or diminishing his cultivation of oats or some other crop.

This requires a modification of our amended version of the classical doctrines as to rent and value, in order to adapt

---

bb.   The remainder of this and the whole of the next paragraph were retained substantially in Book V, ch. x, §5, page 435 in vol. 1 of the present edition.

it to the relations between the price of one particular crop, as oats or hops, and the rent of the land on which the crop is grown. The previous phrases hold so far that the amount of oats raised and the position of the margin of cultivation of oats are both governed by the general conditions of demand and supply: and that the price of all the oats must be equal to the cost of those marginal oats which, because they are raised under unfavourable conditions, contribute nothing to rent. But the margin of cultivation has now to be described as the margin of the profitable application of capital and labour to all land which the competition of other crops yields to oats.

The previous doctrines are substantially applicable to a single crop, but must be modified in form.

That is to say, the statement that the normal value of oats is determined by their production under the most unfavourable circumstances under which they are grown, needs to be completed by adding; firstly, that these circumstances are, no less than the normal value itself, governed by the general conditions of demand and supply; and, secondly, that one of the chief of these conditions is the amount of land which is capable of growing oats, but for which there is so great a demand for other purposes that it affords a higher rent, when used for them, than when used for growing oats. For the expenses of production of those oats which only just pay their way, are increased by the diversion to other crops of land which would return large crops of oats: land which would yield a good rent under them, but which yields a better rent under other crops. It is still true that rent is not an element in those expenses of production of marginal oats, to which the price of the whole conforms. But the phrase "rent does not enter into the cost of production" when applied to a particular crop, such as oats, is specially liable to misinterpretation; and it should be avoided.

In the 1st edition (p. 490 n.) there was the following footnote to Book VI, ch. II, § 5, which was concerned with "urban rent in relation to value":

Jevons in the Preface to the Second Edition of his *Theory of Political Economy* argues in the direction of treating agricultural rent on the same footing as ground-rent. But he goes on:—"If land which has been yielding £2 per acre rent, as pasture, be ploughed up and used for raising wheat, must not the £2 per acre be debited against the expenses of production of wheat?" It is true that Mill was inconsistent in answering this question in the negative, while he maintained that when land capable of yielding rent in agriculture is applied to some other purpose, the rent which it would have yielded is an element in the cost of production of the commodity which it is employed to produce. But still the proper answer to Jevons' question is in the negative. For there is no connection between this particular sum of £2 and the expenses of production of that wheat which only just pays its way. The amount of capital applied in cultivation is elastic, and is stretched until the return to it only just repays the outlay: this limit is determined by the general circumstances of supply and demand; and is independent of the particular sum of £2 which the land will afford as rent. Mill ought to have said, "When land capable of being used for producing one commodity (whether agricultural produce or not) is used for producing another, the price of the first is raised by the consequent limitation of its field of production. The price of the second will be the expenses of production (wages and profits) of that part of it which only just pays its way, that which is produced on the margin of cultivation or building. And if for the purposes of any particular argument we take together the whole expenses of the production on that site, and divide these among the whole of the commodity produced, then, the rent which we ought to count in is not that which the site would pay if used for producing the first commodity, but that which it does pay when used for producing the second."

There was no change in the wording of this footnote in the 2nd and 3rd editions, but in the 4th edition (pp. 482 n.–3 n.) it ran as follows.

The ordinary man is needlessly offended by the old phrase that rent does not enter into the price of oats; when he sees that an increase in the demand for land for other uses, manifests itself in a rise of the rental value of land; leaves less land free for growing oats; consequently makes it worth while to force larger crops of oats out of the remaining oat-land, and thus raises the marginal expenses of oats and their price. Rent does serve as a medium through which the really operative causes in the background raise the price of oats, and it is therefore inexpedient to say that the rent of land does not enter into their price. But it is worse than inexpedient to say that the rent of the land does enter into their price: that is false. Jevons asks (Preface to *Theory of Political Economy*, p. liv): "If land which has been yielding £2 per acre rent, as pasture, be ploughed up and used for raising wheat, must not the £2 per acre be debited against the expenses of production of wheat?" The answer is in the negative. For there is no connection between this particular sum of £2 and the expenses of production of that wheat which only just pays its way. What should be said is:—"When land capable of being used for producing one commodity is used for producing another, the price of the first is raised by the consequent limitation of its field of production. The price of the second will be the expenses of production (wages and profits) of that part of it which only just pays its way, that which is produced on the margin of cultivation. And if for the purposes of any particular argument we take together the whole expenses of the production on that land, and divide these among the whole of the commodity produced; then the rent which we ought to count in is not that which the land would pay if used for producing the first commodity, but that which it does pay when used for producing the second."

Reverting to our analogy of the springs of mineral water in a previous note; we may argue that if one of the smaller springs happened to be so situated that it could not be worked without injury to a valuable site, it would probably not be worked at all; the fact that the site had a high rental value for other purposes would cut off part of the supply of mineral water that otherwise would have been forthcoming; and this would cause more water to be obtained from the other springs at expenses increased more than in proportion. The expenses of production of that part which is raised at the greatest disadvantage, would be greater than before; and producers would at once raise their prices: if the price did not rise enough to cover these expenses, the supply would be curtailed, and the scarcity of supply would compel the price to rise. The price therefore would be raised in consequence of the high rent that could be got by using for other purposes one of the sites on which machinery for pumping mineral water might have been erected.

For the later version of this footnote see pages 436 n.–7 n. in vol. 1 of the present edition.

In the 4th edition (p. 485 n.) there was the following paragraph referring to the above footnote on pp. 482 n.–3 n. of the 4th edition:

> Jevons in the passage just quoted argued rightly that Mill is inconsistent in saying that rent does not enter into the price of agricultural produce, but does enter into that of manufactures.

This paragraph was deleted from the 5th edition.

2. THE THEORY OF QUASI-RENT

The following seven sections represent the whole of chapter III of Book VI in the 1st edition where this chapter was entitled "Cost of Production. Limited Sources of Supply Continued." In the 2nd and 3rd editions this became chapter IX in Book V and was entitled "On the Value of an Appliance for Production in Relation to that of the Things produced by it, continued":

§ 1. [a]So far we have supposed that a clear distinction can be drawn between rent and profits[1]. But this cannot always be done; and indeed there is some difficulty in ascertaining the general principles on which the distinction should be based. In the first place, much of what is commonly called the rent of land is properly to be regarded, for some purposes at least, as the profits of capital expended

The question whether the income derived from a factor of production is to be regarded as due to a differential advantage, and therefore as partaking of the nature of rent,

1 [b]Rent is compared with profits rather than with interest, because it commonly includes an element of earnings of management and undertaking: but this is a question of degree; and there are a few exceptional cases in which a net rent emerges that may more fitly be compared with interest. This point will require further discussion at a later stage.

a. In the 2nd and 3rd editions the substance of this paragraph, together with its footnotes, was transferred to Book V, ch. VIII, § 1. In the 4th ed. it was placed in a footnote in Book V, ch. IX, § 5, and in the 5th and later editions in Book V, ch. X, § 3 (page 432 n. in vol. 1 of the present edition).

The first two sentences of the paragraph were deleted from the 2nd ed.

b. The paragraph placed in this footnote was deleted from the 5th ed.

in improving it. And in the second place, as has been observed by a long series of writers, among whom Senior and Mill, Hermann and Mangoldt are conspicuous, much of what is commonly called profits ought rather to be regarded as belonging to a special class of incomes derived from "a differential advantage in producing a commodity;" that is, the possession by one or more persons of facilities for production that are not accessible to all. Since the leading and representative member of this class is the rent of land, the name of rent is sometimes applied to the whole class: though this course is not without danger[1].

As Mill says, "Any difference in favour of certain producers or in favour of production in certain circumstances is the source of a gain, which though not called rent unless paid periodically by one person to another is governed by laws entirely the same with it. c The price paid for a differential advantage in producing a commodity cannot enter into the cost of production of the commodity[2]."

depends not so much on the nature of that factor as on the length of the period for which its influence on production is being estimated.

d But there is yet a difficulty in ascertaining what kinds of advantage are to be regarded as differential. We shall find reason for thinking that in many cases at least the distinction between those advantages which are, and those which are not to be thus regarded, is not absolute, but depends upon the element of Time. It will appear that many advantages which are to be regarded as differential, and as affording a quasi-rent, when we are considering the action of economic causes during short periods of time, are to be regarded as not differential, and as yielding profits, when we are studying the broader effects of economic

---

[1] e Within the last few years this subject has been pursued with great zeal and ability in Austria and America: see for instance Prof. Boehm-Bawerk's *Kapitalzins-Theorien*, Prof. Wieser's *Natürlicher Wert*, General Walker's various writings, Prof. Clark's *Capital and its Earnings*, and Prof. Patten's *Stability of Prices*.

[2] *Political Economy*, Book III, ch. v, §4.

---

c. This sentence was deleted from the 6th ed.

d. The remainder of this section (apart from footnote 1), was deleted from the 2nd ed.

e. The references in this clause to Austrian and American economists were deleted from the 3rd ed.

causes through longer periods[1]. Or to put the case more exactly:—

If the supply of any factor of production is limited, and incapable of much increase by man's effort in any given period of time, then the income to be derived from it is to be regarded as of the nature of rent rather than profits in inquiries as to the action of economic causes during that period; although for longer periods it may rightly be regarded as profits which are required to cover part of the expenses of production and which therefore directly enter into those expenses.

Now the "inherent properties" of land, and other gifts from the bounty of Nature, are incapable of increase by man's effort in any period of time however long; and they may be regarded as the typical instance of this class[2]. But the original gifts of Nature afford no rent when their supply is unlimited[3]; and the relation in which the income derived from land stands to that derived from machinery and other

[1] **f**Senior seems to have had his attention turned somewhat in this direction when he said that "for all useful purposes the distinction of profits from rent ceases as soon as the capital from which a given revenue arises has become, whether by gift or by inheritance, the property of a person to whose abstinence and exertions it did not owe its creation." (*Political Economy*, p. 129.)

[2] Compare Book IV, ch. II, § 1.

[3] **g**This phrase is in common use, and is sufficiently intelligible: but it is not strictly accurate. What we mean is that the amount of them freely available is at all events greater than the amount which the people at the place and time in question care to have even when they can get them freely. (In other words it is greater than the amount represented by the distance from O of the point in which the demand curve cuts Ox.)

---

f. In the 2nd ed. (p. 453 n.) the opening words of this sentence ran as follows:

Again, Senior pointing, though not very clearly, towards the element of time as holding the key of the division between rent and profits, says (*Political Economy*, p. 129)...

In the 4th ed. (p. 496 n.) this was changed to the following:

Senior seemed almost on the point of perceiving that the key of the difficulty was held by the element of time: but here as elsewhere he contented himself with suggestions, he did not work them out. He says (*Political Economy*, p. 129)...

In this form it was retained throughout the subsequent editions (see page 432 n. in vol. I of the present edition).

g. This footnote was deleted from the 2nd ed.

kinds of fixed capital will be made clearer if we follow the former through its successive stages.

§ ʰ2. ⁱA settler who takes up land in a new country exer-

---

h. The substance of this section was retained with little change in all the subsequent editions, and will be found in Book V, ch. x, §2 (pages 429–30) in vol. ɪ of the present edition.

i. In the 2nd ed. (pp. 465–6) where what had been §2 of Book VI, ch. ɪɪɪ, in the 1st ed. became §1 of Book V, ch. ɪx, the illustration of the settler taking up land was preceded by the following paragraph with which the section opened:

§ ɪ. Wᴇ now proceed to consider more closely the application to quasi-rent of the rule that rent does not enter into cost of production, and to inquire what modifications are needed to adapt it to incomes derived from factors of production the supply of which, though not permanently limited, cannot be increased quickly enough to affect appreciably the production of the commodity in question *during the period which we have in view when speaking of its normal supply price*. In order to emphasize this continuity the better we will study the income derived from land in a newly settled country: we shall find that for some purposes they are to be classed as profits, or at most as quasi-rents, rather than rents.

In the 3rd ed. (p. 486) the following additional sentences were inserted at the beginning of this paragraph:

§ ɪ. The illustrations in the last chapter related generally to fixed and stable conditions. Those in the present chapter will bear on the application to less permanent incomes of the rule that rent does not enter into cost of production. We have to inquire what modifications are needed to adapt it…etc.

In the 4th ed. (pp. 499–500) the illustration of a settler taking up land was placed at the end of Book V, ch. ɪx in a separate "Note on Illustrations of the general Principles contained in this Chapter", and was preceded by the following paragraphs:

The following discussion adds little to the statement of general principle already made. And its practical applica-

cises no exclusive privilege, for he only does what any one else is at liberty to do. He undergoes many hardships, if not personal dangers, and perhaps runs some risk that the land may turn out badly, and that he may have to abandon his improvements. On the other hand, his venture may turn out well; the flow of population may trend his way, and the value of his land may soon give as large a surplus over the normal remuneration of his outlay on it as the fisherman's haul does when they come home with their boat full. But in this there is nothing which presents itself to him as rent.

When a new country is first settled land is to be regarded as yielding profits rather than rent.

---

tions are seldom of quite the first order of importance. But they are so obscure, and so full of pitfalls and false tracks, that there may be an advantage in illustrating the principle further by two instances; which will present it in different aspects to those who care to pursue the matter further.

The relation between true rents and quasi-rents may be further illustrated.

The first instance aims at showing that the income yielded by land on the outskirts of a new country has a strong resemblance to that obtained by "making" other material things; that is by adapting matter in other forms to man's service.

We have already noticed that if there be so much free land available in any place that the agricultural population there cannot bring it under cultivation, land will yield no rent[1]. Let us now trace the emergence of rent as population grows in a new country.

[1] Above V, VIII, §2. It is understood that land is not "brought under cultivation" when it is so poorly worked that increasing applications of capital and labour are still giving returns increasing more than in proportion. This general statement is however rather vague: details appropriate to particular instances are needed for definiteness. There are two difficulties to be specially considered. One is that nature's tendency to diminishing return is opposed by a twofold tendency to increasing return arising out of man's economies of production on a large scale: one set being social and "external" to any particular form, and the other being peculiar to it and "internal" (see IV, III, §6 and XII, §2). The second difficulty arises from the possible existence of more than one maximum return to cultivation, as illustrated by the two humps in fig. 15 on p. 236. These subtle issues are however of little practical importance.

The first of the two instances referred to in the first of the three foregoing paragraphs in the 4th ed. was that of the settler in a new country and the second that of the income from meteoric stones.

The references in the footnote to V, VIII, §2, IV, XII, §2, and to fig. 15, apply to V, X, §1, V, XIII, §2, and to fig. 15 on page 159 n. in vol. I of the present edition.

He has engaged in a risky business which was open to all, and his energy and good fortune have given him an exceptionally high reward: others might have taken the same chance as he did; and from a business point of view they ought to have done so, if they thought that, after discounting all the hardships and risks of the venture, it would yield a surplus which could fairly be called the rent of a special privilege or monopoly.

Thus the income which he expects the land to afford in the future enters into the calculations of the settler, and adds to the motives which determine his action when on the margin of doubt as to how far to carry his enterprise. He regards its "discounted value"[1] as profits on his capital, and as earnings of his own labour, in so far as his improvements are made with his own hands.

A settler often takes up land with the expectation that the produce which it affords while in his possession will fall short of an adequate reward for his hardships, his labour and his expenditure. He looks for part of his reward to the value of the land itself, which he proposes after a while to sell to some new-comer who has no turn for the life of a pioneer. Sometimes even, as the British farmer learns to his cost, the new settler regards his wheat almost as a bye-product; the main product for which he works is a farm, the title-deeds to which he will earn by improving the land, and the value of which will steadily rise[2].

[1] Compare Book III, ch. II, §3.

[2] j It has even been maintained that any new country which should refuse to settlers the power of acquiring an absolute right of property in the soil, and should grant long leases only, would see the stream of immigrants into it speedily run away. But there does not seem to be any strong reason for thinking that this effect would be more than temporary: for the more far-seeing class of immigrants might think that what was kept from them as "individual wealth" was more than returned to them as shareholders in the "collective wealth." And even if not, it may be doubtful whether the few people who first arrive on a new shore are justified in assuming that they have the right to dispose of its vast resources in perpetuity. Warned by the experiences of the past our own generation might well pause before entering into new engagements that purport to bind its successors for all time. The gain which the world as a whole can get from turning the stream of migration in this direction rather than that, is not very great; and distant generations may think that the fee simple of the soil was too high a price to pay for such a purpose; and that, since a hundred years, though nothing in the life of the race, is long relatively to individual lives, a free lease for a hundred years would have been a sufficient

j. This footnote was deleted from the 5th ed.

§3. *k*But when the land is all taken up, the desire to obtain its title-deeds no longer acts as a motive to further improvement and to further production. Henceforth that net income which the land affords to its owner in excess of normal profits on his fresh application of capital is a Producer's Surplus standing outside of those gains which are price to pay. But this takes us out beyond the range of our present inquiries: the point with which we are concerned just here is that anything that affects the hopes of a distant gain on the part of the settler exerts a clearly marked, though perhaps slowly acting influence on the amount of produce which will be forthcoming in the country at any given time.

When there are no more title-deeds to be earned in equally favoured situations, rent emerges,

k. The first two paragraphs of this section were deleted from the 4th ed., in which the illustration (in the third paragraph) of "a war which was not expected to last long" was preceded by the following paragraphs:

The farmer pays "rent" to his landlord without troubling himself to distinguish how much of the annual net value of his land is due to the free gift of nature, and how much to the investment of capital by his landlord in the improvement of the land, and in erecting buildings on it. Now the income derived from farm buildings, or houses, is clearly of the same character as the income derived from durable machines; and that income is popularly classed with profits more often than with rent. But yet the farmer's habit of speaking has much justification. For the incomes derived from appliances for production made by man have really something analogous to true rents.

Popular usage recognizes an analogy between incomes derived from land and from farm buildings.

The net incomes derived from appliances for production already made, may be called their *quasi-rents:* partly because we shall find that when we are considering periods of time too short to enable the supply of such appliances to respond to a change in the demand for them the stock of them has to be regarded as *temporarily* fixed. For the time they hold nearly the same relation to the price of the things which they take part in producing, as is held by land, or any other free gift of nature, of which the stock is *permanently* fixed; and whose net income is a true rent. This is the principle to be developed in the present chapter. Let us approach it by an illustration.

Quasi-rents. Preliminary statement of the principle to be established.

required to cover the marginal expenses of production. As population and wealth increase in the neighbourhood this net income also will increase; but except in so far as the improvement may be due to the direct action of individual owners, the whole of it may be regarded as a rent coming under the general argument of the preceding chapter.

and the shorter the period under consideration, the wider are the classes of improvements, the income of which is classed as rent. Its amount therefore will be determined, other things being equal, by the supply price of produce at the margin of cultivation and it will play very little direct part in determining that price. For that price will be governed chiefly by the results which landowners and farmers can get from applying capital and labour in the further development of the resources of the soil, and in cultivating it by more intensive methods than those of the early settler. The results of all kinds of improvements, both those which bear fruit slowly and those which bear fruit quickly, will be watched; and their success or failure will influence those who are thinking of investing more capital in the soil. Local variations of land tenure and custom will affect the issue; but in every case it will be true that the marginal supply price of produce in the near future will not be affected by improvements that bear fruit slowly in the same way that it is by those which act quickly.

An illustrative instance. [1]Suppose, for instance, that a war, which was not expected to last long, were to cut off part of our food supplies. People would set themselves to raise heavier crops by such extra application of capital or labour as was likely to yield a speedy return; they would consider the results of artificial manures, of the use of clod-crushing machines, and so on; and the more favourable these results were, the lower would be the price of produce in the coming year which they regarded as necessary to make it worth their while to incur additional outlay in these directions. But the war would have very little effect on their action as to improvements that would not bear fruit till it was over.

In an inquiry then as to the causes that will determine

---

1. This illustration was retained in subsequent editions (see Book V, ch. x, §1, page 425 in vol. 1 of the present edition).

the prices of corn during a short period, that fertility which the soil derives from slowly made improvements has to be taken for granted as it then exists, almost in the same way as if it had been made by nature; ^mand the income derived from it may be regarded as a quasi-rent. But it is more properly regarded as profits than as rent when we are considering the broader action of economic causes over long periods of time—that action which controls the gradual development of material well being. ⁿFor in the long run the net returns to the investment of capital in the land, taking successful and unsuccessful returns together, do not afford more than an adequate motive to such investment. If poorer returns had been expected than those on which people actually based their calculations, fewer improvements would have been made; and in any case the improvements would depend partly on the conditions of land tenure, and the enterprise and ability and command over capital on the part of landlords and tenants which existed at the time and place in question.

§4. ^oBut this last clause requires some attention. Although we are treating the incomes derived from land as a special instance of the incomes derived from the possession of "any differential advantage in producing a commodity"; and although we are setting aside those aspects of the problem which are peculiar to agricultural land, and especially those which depend upon particular forms of land tenure; yet there have been so many misunderstandings on the subject, that it will be best to say something at once on the difference between the mode of action of competition in agriculture and in manufacture.

Allowance has to be made in its proper place for the influence of different forms of land tenure.

---

m. This clause and the sentence following it were deleted from the 3rd ed.

n. In the 4th ed. (pp. 489–90) the analysis of "the extra income derived from improvements that have been made in the land by its individual owner" was recast in a form which remained substantially unaltered in the later editions (see Book V, ch. x, §1, pages 425–6 in vol. 1 of the present edition).

o. The first four paragraphs of this section were deleted from the 2nd ed.

If one manufacturer is unenterprising, others may be able to step into the opening which he leaves vacant: but when one landowner does not develop the resources of his land in the best way, others cannot make up for the deficiency without calling into play the Law of Diminishing Return; so that his want of wisdom and enterprise makes the marginal supply price a little higher than it otherwise would be. It is true that the difference between the two cases is only one of degree; since the growth of any branch of manufactures may be retarded perceptibly by any falling off in the ability and enterprise of the leading firms engaged in it.

But still it is practically an important difference, whatever be the forms of land tenure and the habits of the agricultural classes: and it rises to the first order of importance where the laws and customs of the country are such that those who own the land take no part in its improvement, and those who cultivate it have no security of reaping a fair share of the fruits of any improvements made by them.

The difference is reduced to a minimum in some parts of America where the land is owned by enterprising and well-to-do "farmers"; and in some parts of England where landlords take a pride in the good condition of their property and those who till it, and are always on the look-out for opportunities of using their capital to aid their tenants in improving the land on terms advantageous to both sides. In such districts any new opening in which capital can get ever so little more than normal profits, allowance being of course made for risks, is almost as sure to be seized on quickly in agriculture as in manufacture.

The results reached with these conditions ᵖWe must then always bear in mind that there are large allowances to be made for the special conditions of land tenure in different places. But on the whole we may conclude that, when the enterprise of landowners is most active, the extra income derived from improvements that have been

---

p.   The remainder of this section, with some rearrangement but no substantial changes, was carried over into the later editions (see Book V, ch. x, § 1, page 426 in vol. 1 of the present edition).

made in the land by its individual owner—this income being so reckoned as not to include any benefit which would have been conferred on the land by the general progress of society independently of his efforts and sacrifices—does not as a rule give a surplus beyond what is required to remunerate him for those efforts and sacrifices. He may have under-estimated the gains which will result from them; but he is about equally likely to have made an overestimate. If he has estimated them rightly, his interest would have led him to make the investment as soon as it showed signs of being profitable: and in the absence of any special reason to the contrary we may suppose him to have done this.

On these suppositions then, when we are considering periods which are long in comparison with the time required to make, and bring into full operation, improvements of any kind, the net incomes derived from them are to be regarded as the price required to be paid for the efforts and sacrifices of those who make them. The expenses of making them thus directly enter into marginal expenses of production, and directly govern long-period supply price. But in short periods, that is in periods short relatively to the time required to make and bring into full bearing improvements of the class in question, the incomes derived from them exercise no such direct influence on supply price; ᵠand when we are dealing with such periods these incomes may be regarded as a quasi-rent which takes little direct part in determining, but is rather dependent on the price of the produce. (It may be noted, however, that rent proper is estimated on the understanding that the original properties of the soil are unimpaired. And when the income derived from im-provements is regarded as a quasi-rent, it is to be understood that they are kept up in full efficiency: if they are being

for long periods

and for short

---

q. In the 4th ed. (p. 491) the following clause was substituted for the above clause in the earlier editions:

and, when we are dealing with such periods, these incomes may be regarded as quasi-rents which do not take direct part in determining the price of the produce, but rather depend on them.

471

deteriorated, the equivalent of the injury done to them must be deducted from the income they are made to yield before we can arrive at that *net* income which is to be regarded as their quasi-rent.)

are
applicable
to all
branches of
industry;

These results do not depend upon the special qualities of land, or on the special conditions of agriculture; they are generally applicable to all branches of industry. ʳThis is perhaps already obvious enough: but as the subject is one of much difficulty, it may be well to take an illustration of the bearing of our results upon manufacturing industries.

as is
further
shown by
an illustra-
tion relating
to
manu-
facture.

§5. ˢLet us suppose that an exceptional demand for a certain kind of textile fabrics is caused by, say, a sudden movement of the fashions. ᵗThe special machinery required for making that fabric will yield for the time an income, which bears no direct relation to the expenses of making the machinery; but is rather a high quasi-rent governed by the price that can be got for the produce, and consisting of the excess of the aggregate price of that produce over the

---

r. In the 2nd ed. (p. 469) and the 3rd ed. (p. 490) this sentence, which was deleted from the 4th ed., ran as follows:

This is perhaps already obvious enough: for the main substance of the argument has already been given in Chapter v. But the subject is one of so much difficulty that the space given in this section to repeating, in another form, what has been said there, may not be wasted.

s. This illustration was deleted from the 5th ed.

t. In the 4th ed. (p. 491) this sentence ran as follows:

The special machinery required for making that fabric will yield for the time a high income, governed by the price that can be got for the produce, and consisting of the excess of the aggregate price of that produce over the direct outlay (including wear-and-tear) incurred in its production.

In the Corrigenda et Addenda placed at the beginning of the 4th ed. there is the following addendum to this sentence:

After *production* add: *and then the net income from the machinery (its quasi-rent) will be for the time greater than normal profits on the original investment.*

472

direct outlay (including wear and tear) incurred in its production.

Next suppose that the tide has turned, and that the demand for a certain class of goods is much less than had been expected. The factories with the most imperfect appliances, and the worst machinery in other factories will be thrown out of work: those machines which it is just worth while to keep in work, will just pay the actual expenses of working them, but will yield no surplus. Their produce will be on the margin of production; and the excess of the price got for the goods made by the better appliances over wear and tear, together with the actual expenses of working them, ^uwill be the surplus or quasi-rent which these appliances yield during the short period of depression. ^vIn this case the quasi-rent will be not more but less than normal profits profits on the original investment.

^wNext, seeking another aspect of the same truth, let us

---

u. In the 3rd ed. (p. 491) this clause ran as follows: "will be the income which these appliances yield during the short period of depression."

v. In the 3rd ed. (p. 491) the word "quasi-rent" in this sentence was replaced by the word "income". In the 4th ed. (p. 492) this sentence ran as follows:

This quasi-rent or net income derived from the machinery will in the first period be greater, but in the second less than normal profits on the original investment.

w. This and the next paragraph were deleted from the 2nd ed., where their place was taken (p. 471) by the following paragraph:

The argument of the last section but one of the preceding chapter applies, so far as short periods are concerned, to quasi-rents very nearly in the same way as to true rents. When existing factories, or machinery which could be applied to producing one commodity are diverted to producing another because the demand for that is such as to enable them to earn a higher quasi-rent by producing it, then *for the time* the supply of the first will be less, and its price higher than if the machinery had not been able to earn a

473

The quasi-rent of old-fashioned machinery.

take the case of a branch of manufacture for the products of which there is a uniform and steady demand; and let us suppose that the machinery required for it is suddenly improved. For a time those who use the new machinery will get exceptionally high profits: but before long its use will have become general and will control the price of the produce. That will in future be equal to the normal expenses of production of those portions of the produce which are made with new machinery, interest being reckoned on the expenses of producing this machinery, together with wear and tear, and "depreciation" at a high rate to allow for the chance that it will in its turn become obsolete. Meanwhile such of the old machinery as is in good repair may perhaps be kept at work; but the income which it earns will bear no direct relation to its own expenses of production; it will be

---

higher quasi-rent by another use. But as in the case of rent, there will be no direct or numerical relation between the increase in the price of the first commodity and the quasi-rent that the machinery can earn by producing the second.

The reference in the first line of this paragraph to "the last section but one of the preceding chapter" should be to the last section but two of the preceding chapter, that is to Book V, ch. viii, §5 in the 2nd ed., where it was argued that the doctrine, that rent does not enter into cost of production, is "misleading" when it is applied to "any one kind of produce taken separately". See above, pp. 456–7. See also editorial note **k** on p. 512 below.

In the 3rd ed. (p. 491) the word "income" replaced the word "quasi-rent" on each of the three occasions on which it was used in the second and third sentences of the paragraph just quoted from the 2nd ed.

In the 4th ed. (pp. 498–9) this paragraph was rewritten and placed in a separate section at the end of Book V, ch. ix where it ran as follows:

Arguments relating to rent extended to quasi-rent of machinery in relation to the value of one kind of thing made by it.

It should be noted that the argument of section 4 of the preceding chapter applies, so far as short periods are concerned, to quasi-rents very nearly in the same way as to true rents. When existing farm-buildings, or other appliances which could be used in producing one commodity are diverted to producing another because the demand for that is such as to enable them to earn a higher income by producing

the small excess of the selling value of the produce made by it, over the wear and tear and other direct outlay involved; this income will be a quasi-rent, the value of which will be determined by the price of the produce, and play no direct part in determining that price.

But it may be noted that the produce made by machinery which is so far obsolete that its owner is in doubt whether to use it at all or to throw it away, gives the means of ascertaining the normal price, equally with that produce which is made under normal conditions by new machinery: save only that in the one case the expenses of production of the machinery do not enter into the account at all, and in the other a full charge is made for them.

§6. Similar illustrations might be taken from any other branch of business. Each branch has special features of its

---

it, then *for the time* the supply of the first will be less, and its price higher than if the appliances had not been able to earn a higher income by another use. But as in the case of rent, there will be no direct or numerical relation between the increase in the price of the first commodity and the income that the appliances can earn by producing the second.

Of course, when machinery is capable of being used in more than one branch of manufacture, the marginal cost in each branch will be affected by the extent to which this machinery is called off for work in other branches. This external demand for the machinery will appear to work through the earnings which it might make elsewhere. This is the true rendering of the plausible statement that the earnings to be got by the machinery in one use enter into the cost of things made by it in another use. Here again the case of quasi-rent is parallel to that of the rent of land.

The reference in the 1st sentence of the first of the foregoing paragraphs to "the argument of §4 of the preceding chapter" was incorrect: the reference should be to Book V, ch. viii, §3 (pp. 480–2) in the 4th ed. See above, pp. 457–9 and Book V, ch. x, §6, pages 437–8 in vol. 1 of the present edition.

The analogy between quasi-rent and rent relates only to short periods, and has no bearing on

own; but with proper modifications in detail, the same general principle applies to all. ˣIn every case the net income derived from the investment of capital, when once that investment has been made, is a quasi-rent. That is to say, when the causes which determine short-period fluctuations of production are under discussion, this quasi-rent may be classed with rent proper, on the ground that it stands outside of the payments which influence producers to take such action as would increase the available supply within a short period. But this resemblance to rent is only partial and in a sense superficial.

the broader problems of economic progress.

ʸFor when land or other free gifts of nature have once become private property, their rent proper does not act as a direct motive to make and save the means of production: though of course a violent appropriation of it might destroy that security on which all such motives depend. It is a true surplus. But the quasi-rent of capital is, speaking generally, no true surplus. If it had been expected to be less than it actually is, the motives to work and to save the product of work would have been less. And if this quasi-rent were to be diminished now, in such a way as to diminish the expectations of the future gain likely to result from the effort and sacrifice involved in working and saving the product of work, the growth of individual capital would at once be checked. The existing plant might indeed be sufficient to prevent the change from considerably affecting the supply of finished commodities, ᶻor *goods of the first order*, for a few years: but the broad course of economic development would be

---

x.   In the 4th ed. (p. 492) the remainder of this paragraph ran as follows:

When the causes which determine short-period fluctuations of production are under discussion, the net income derived from the investment of capital may be classed with rent proper; on the ground that it stands outside of the payments which influence producers to take such action as would increase the available supply within a short period.

y.   This and the next paragraph were deleted from the 4th ed.

z.   This clause was deleted from the 3rd ed.

changed; and, so far as it depends on the supply of individual capital, it would be arrested.

It is true that what was lost in this direction might be counterbalanced by a corresponding growth of collective capital. Whether there would be any considerable chance of this, is a matter on which opinions differ. But when we come to discuss the schemes of modern socialists it will be important to remember that, though there is some real analogy between the quasi-rent of capital and rent proper, yet the analogy does not reach far. It has no validity at all except when short periods only are under discussion: it has no bearing on those broad and slow movements on which the general progress and the ultimate well-being of mankind depend.

§7.   aa bb Thus then, after considering in the last Chapter Ricardo's doctrine as to the relation in which rent proper stands to value, we have now extended that doctrine to the income which man derives from those appliances for production with which he has provided himself, and especially such of them as are durable, and are but slowly made, and the supply of which therefore cannot be rapidly increased. We *Summary of the relations between rent and quasi-rent.*

---

aa.   This and the next paragraph were deleted from the 2nd ed. They were however reinstated in the 4th ed. (pp. 495–6) with the modifications noted below, and finally deleted from the 5th ed.

bb.   In place of the first two sentences of this paragraph there were the following sentences in the 4th ed. (p. 495):

The general principle under discussion may be put thus. The price of anything and the amount that is produced are together governed by the general relations of demand and supply; the price just covers the expenses of production of that part of this amount which is raised at the greatest disadvantage; every other part yields a surplus above its direct cost; and this surplus is a result and not a cause of the selling price. For the price is governed by the relations of supply and demand; and while, of course, the surplus does not affect the demand, so neither does it affect the supply, since it is yielded only by a part of the produce which would be produced even at a lower price. *Statement of the main principles.*

have found that the part which they play in determining normal value, varies with the length of the period which is allowed for their action. When we are taking a broad view of normal value extending over a very long period of time, when we are investigating the causes which determine normal value "in the long run," when we are tracing the "ultimate" effects of economic causes, then the income that is derived from capital in these forms enters into the payments by which the expenses of production of the commodity in question have to be covered, and it directly controls the action of the producers who are on the margin of doubt as to whether to increase the means of production or not. But, on the other hand, when we are considering the causes which determine normal prices for a period which is short relatively to that required for largely increasing the supply of those appliances for production, ^{cc}then their influence on value is chiefly indirect and more or less similar to that exerted by the free gifts of nature. The shorter the period which we are considering, and the slower the process of production of those appliances, the less part will variations in the income derived from them play in checking or increasing the supply of the commodity produced by them, and in raising or lowering its supply price; and the more nearly true will it be that, for the period under discussion, the net income to be derived from them is to be regarded as a producer's surplus or quasi-rent.

In passing from the free gifts of nature through the more permanent improvements in the soil, to less permanent improvements, to farm and factory buildings, to steam-engines, &c., and finally to the less durable and less slowly made implements, we find a continuous series. ^{dd}And parallel to this series of the material agents of production there is a similar series of human abilities; those that are the free gifts of nature, and those that are the result of a more or less

---

cc. In the 4th ed. (p. 495) this clause ran as follows: "then the stock of those appliances has to be taken as fixed, almost as though they were free gifts of nature."

dd. This and the next sentence were deleted from the 4th ed.

long and specialized process of training. Later on we shall find that many of the most interesting applications of the principle which we have just discussed are to human agents of production; but in the present Book we are confining our attention to the material agents of production.

ee We have seen that in the adaptation of demand to sup-ply for short periods, producers have to consider what use to make of their existing appliances for production; but that the long-period supply price of a finished commodity, or a *good of the first order*, is governed by the calculations of producers as to how far it is worth their while to increase their stock of appliances for making it. Thus the supply of factors of production, or *goods of the second order*, is governed by estimates that reach forward over a longer time, and are therefore more liable to error than those which govern the immediate adaptation of supply to demand with regard to *goods of the first order*.

But further the supply of these *goods of the second order* depends partly on the supply of appliances for making them, that is, of things removed by two *orders* from the commodity with which we started: and the adjustment of the supply of these *goods of the third order* to the indirect demand for them, which is derived ultimately from the demand for the finished commodity, is a still more difficult process; it ranges over a still longer period of time, and is still more liable to error: and so on, backwards, without limit. And the case will be stronger still when we come to apply a similar argument to the relations between the supply of labour of any kind and the demand for it.

ff This then points to a limitation of the doctrine that the price at which a thing can be produced represents its real cost of production, that is, the efforts and sacrifices which have been directly and indirectly devoted to its production. That doctrine might indeed represent facts accurately enough

[marginal notes:] The supply of goods of the second and higher orders is governed by estimates that range over long periods and are liable to error.

Looseness of the connection between the supply price of a commodity and its real cost of production.

---

ee. This and the next paragraph were deleted from the 2nd ed.

ff. This paragraph was transferred in the 2nd ed. to Book V, ch. III, §6, where it was retained with some modifications throughout the subsequent editions (see page 347 in vol. I of the present edition).

in a stationary society, in which people's habits of life, and the methods and volume of production remained unchanged from one generation to another; provided that people were tolerably free to choose those occupations for their capital and labour which seemed most advantageous. But in an age of change such as this, the equilibrium of normal demand and supply does not thus correspond to any precise relation

The true significance of a position of normal equilibrium.

between an aggregate of pleasures got from the consumption of the commodity and an aggregate of efforts and sacrifices involved in producing them; and it would not do so even if normal earnings and interest were exact measures of the efforts and sacrifices for which they are severally the money payments. It represents only the equilibrium of the forces working at the margins of demand and supply, tending to increase the amount demanded or to diminish the amount supplied at the equilibrium price.

The following paragraphs dealing with the relations between rent and quasi-rent were inserted in the 4th edition (Book V, ch. ix, §§4, 6 and 7, pp. 494–5 and 496–8) but were deleted from the 5th edition

An illustration.

gg One side of the likeness between rents and quasi-rents may be simply illustrated. The hire of a pony is the excess of its value over that of a pony which is so weak as to have no hiring value at all[1]. The hire of ponies, like that of land, is governed by the value of the services they will render, and the value of those services is governed *for the time* by

[1] This is the Duke of Argyll's argument against the utility of the doctrine of quasi-rents, in his able and suggestive *Unseen Foundations of Society*, pp. 310–11. It is answered in an article "On Rent," in the *Economic Journal*, vol. iii, to which the reader may be referred for further discussion of this and some allied points.

---

gg. This was the second paragraph of §4 of ch. ix, in the 4th ed. The first paragraph, which began "There is likeness amid unlikeness between land and appliances made by man. There is unlikeness because land in an old country...etc.", will be found in the last three sentences of Book V, ch. x, §3, pages 431–2 in vol. i of the present edition

The illustration derived from the hire of a pony was first used by Marshall in the article "On Rent" to which he refers in the footnote to the paragraph just quoted from the 4th edition. This article is reproduced below. See pp. 492–512. The "hire of the pony" illustration will be found on pp. 508–10.

the relations in which the stock of ponies, &c., stands to the demand for such services. But here comes in the unlikeness: for the clause "for the time," which is needed in the case of ponies is not needed in that of land. If nothing unexpected has happened, the stock of ponies will have been so adjusted to the demand that an average (or normal) pony during a life of average length and activity will yield a hire giving normal profits on its cost of production. As a rule it will do this, and yield no 'surplus' above normal profits to the producer. Of course the demand for ponies may have been wrongly estimated, and the hire (or quasi-rent) yielded by an average pony may exceed or fall short of normal profits on its cost of production. But the divergence can be only for short periods in the case of ponies, because they are so quickly reared, and they so quickly die off, that any error in the adjustment of supply to demand can be quickly set right. The unlikeness between the rent of land and the quasi-rents of other things lies in the fact that the hire of other things cannot, under ordinary circumstances, and for a long time, diverge much from normal profits on their cost of production; while the supply of fertile land cannot be adapted quickly to the demand for it, and therefore the income derived from it may diverge permanently much from normal profits on the cost of preparing it for cultivation.

§ hh6. A chief application of this general principle is in the extrusion of a number of circular reasonings, which still linger in a certain class of economic discussions. We have noticed already that, since rent is governed by the price of produce (among other things) it cannot be assumed as already known in a study of the causes which govern that price: and therefore circular reasoning is involved in an attempt to express these causes in terms of the cost of production of any but the marginal produce. To include a charge for rent, and add it to prime cost in order to ascertain that cost of production which plays its part in directly governing

Circular reasonings induced by a neglect of the principle.

---

hh. §5 in the 4th ed. consisted of a statement of the "general principle" underlying the relation of quasi-rent to price, the substance of which will be found on p. 477 of the present Appendix.

supply and value, would be to assume at starting the result to be reached.

We have now to reflect that nearly the same is true with regard to the income yielded by appliances for production made by man, when we are considering periods so short that the supply of the appliances has to be taken practically as a fixed stock: that is, as a stock incapable of being materially affected during such periods by the inflow of new appliances, and the outflow of old appliances. During these periods the income yielded by the appliances is governed by the value of what they produce, and is not any given percentage on their cost of production. Some of them may even be of obsolete fashion, and yield but a very small net income. But whether this income (or quasi-rent) be large or small, the value of the appliances is found by capitalizing their present and prospective income. And therefore to turn round, as is done even by some eminent economists, and speak of their income as deduced from their capital value by means of the current rate of interest is to reason in a circle; just in the same way as is done when the rent of land is deduced from its capital value by means of the current rate of interest.

A similar fallacy of circular reasoning is involved in some attempts to popularize the theory of value and evade the trouble of a special study of marginal costs of production and of the influence of the element of time on value. In such attempts it is suggested that the cost of production of any product is to be ascertained by attributing to it a proportionate share of the cost of production of the appliances used in making it. This method of reasoning is circular, except in those cases, rare in this modern world, in which it is possible to assume that the conditions of the trade have remained without important change, at least so far as the making and use of these appliances are concerned.[1]

§7. When we are taking prime costs narrowly we exclude the salaries of those clerks, porters, etc., which will have

[1] [ii]See V, xi, §6.

---

ii. This reference is to Appendix H, §3 in vol. I of the present edition.

to be paid, whether this particular order in question be taken or not. These salaries which are not quasi-rents have then to be included among supplementary costs; and therefore the statement that the quasi-rents of a business correspond to its supplementary costs, is not strictly correct; though it may be sufficiently near the truth for most purposes. A correct statement is that quasi-rents are equal to that part of its supplementary costs, which corresponds to the charges for the use of appliances, whether material, such as its buildings or machinery, or immaterial such as its organization and trade connections. *Quasi-rents in relation to supplementary costs.*

It may seem at first sight that the importance of all the doctrines connected with marginal costs is diminished by the fact that, in varying degrees, producers pursue the "conservative" policy of refusing new orders; and declining to sell what they have made for stock at prices which only cover the special or prime costs of the goods. This fact does indeed blur the sharpness of outline of the relations between value and marginal cost. But it does no more than that. It does not affect the main body of these relations. And in particular it does not make any new cause for distinction between true rents and quasi-rents. For neither rent nor quasi-rent enter directly into the marginal cost of production. Both are apt to influence it indirectly and in the same way: for both enter in the same way into those general expenses of his business for which the prudent manufacturer, or other trader, makes some allowance, when his plant has little to do, and he has to decide whether to accept a very low price for a new order or for part of what he has made for stock[1]. *Relations between marginal costs, values and quasi-rents are blurred but not substantially altered by practical considerations of marketing.*

[1] This has been indicated in V, III, and the study will be carried further in ʲʲV, XI.

jj. This reference is to Book V, ch. XII in vol. I of the present edition.

3. RENT AND QUASI-RENT—THE METEORIC
STONES ILLUSTRATION IN THE FIRST FOUR
EDITIONS

The first statement of the meteoric stones illustration in the *Principles* is to be found in a footnote on p. 664 in §1 of Book VII, chapter x in the 1st edition. For its development subsequent to the 4th edition, see Book V, ch. IX, §§2–5 in vol. I of the present edition and the editorial notes thereto.

Book VII, chapter x, §1 in the 1st edition ran as follows:

The rent of land is a species of a large genus. For the present we suppose land to be cultivated by its owners.

§1. ᵃWE have seen that the rent of land is no unique fact, but simply the chief species of a large genus of economic phenomena; and that the theory of the rent of land is no isolated economic doctrine, but merely one of the chief applications of a particular corollary from the general theory of demand and supply. ᵇIn the present chapter we have to study those incidents of the rent of land which differentiate it from other species belonging to the same genus: but many of them are connected with special forms of land tenure; and in order to avoid these, we will begin by supposing that the cultivation of the land is undertaken by its owner.

Résumé of the results reached in Book VI with regard to rent and quasi-rent.

ᶜWe have seen that the income expected to be derived from the investment of capital and effort in making any sort of appliances for producing a commodity, affects the action of those who are thinking of investing capital and effort in making similar appliances and thus takes a part in determining the true (or long-period) normal supply price of the commodity. But we saw also that, when that investment has once been effected, whether it be in making a loom, in building a factory, or in draining a field, the income derived from it will for the future be determined by the price of the products in making which it can be used: and therefore, that when we are considering variations in price extending over periods too short to allow for any great change in the total supply of those appliances, we may regard

a. The wording of this sentence was retained in all the later editions; see Book VI, ch. IX, §1, page 629 in vol. I of the present edition.
b. This sentence was deleted from the 4th ed.
c. This paragraph was deleted from the 2nd ed.

the income derived from them as being for that period a producer's surplus or quasi-rent. It will consist, of course, of the excess of the value of the commodities produced by them over that of the direct outlay of new and additional effort and capital required for the work.

[d]Next, assuming that we can theoretically distinguish those productive powers of land which are "natural" or "inherent" in it, from those which have been imparted to it by man's action, we have seen that that part of the income derived from land which results from the former, has an eminent right to be called a producer's surplus in a country the land of which is already occupied. [e]For, although in new countries the inducements to settlers to take up new land depend in a great measure on their prospect of reaping a high income from its natural fertility, and although this income enters for the time into the normal supply price of produce, yet, when all the land has been long taken up, those who are doubting how much capital and effort to apply in cultivating it have to be guided by the experience of those who, like themselves, could look forward only to reaping the fruits of the land and not also to earning title-deeds to fresh soil[1].

Application of these results to land.

---

[1] [f]Comp. [g]Book VI, ch. III, §§2, 3. This eminent claim to be called a producer's surplus is not confined to the income derived from land or other (real) immovable property, such as mineral springs (comp. [h]Book VI, ch. II, §§2, 3), but extends to that derived from all things the supply of which cannot be increased. For instance, suppose that a meteoric shower of a few thousand stones as hard as diamonds, but very large, fell all in one place; so that they were all picked up at once, and no amount of search could find any more. These stones, able to cut the hardest material, would revolutionize many branches of industry; and the owners of them would have a differential advantage in production that would afford a large producer's surplus: this would be a true economic rent, whether they used the stones themselves or loaned them out to manufacturers, though only in the latter case would it be called rent. Its amount would be determined by the marginal services the stones

---

d.   This sentence was deleted from the 3rd ed.

e.   This sentence was deleted from the 2nd ed.

f.   This and the other footnotes to this section, dealing with the illustration of meteoric stones, were transferred to Book V, ch. VIII, §2 in the 2nd ed.

g.   This reference applies to Book V, ch. x, §2 in vol. 1 of the present edition.

h.   See above, pp. 450–5 where the text of these two sections in the 1st ed. is given in full.

The income attributed to the inherent properties of land.

[i]Of the "inherent" properties of land, the chief are its extension and its geographical relations[1]. For it is to these that it owes that income of heat and light and air and rain, which man cannot appreciably affect; and those advantages of situation, many of which are beyond man's control, while but few of the remainder are the direct result of the investment of capital and effort in the land by its individual owners. These are the chief of its properties, the supply of which is not dependent on human effort, and which would therefore not be increased by extra rewards to that effort: and a tax on which would always fall exclusively on the owners[2].

rendered in production; and these would in the main be governed under the law of substitution by the equivalent services of chilled steel and other cutting tools.

Again, if the stones were of exceptional splendour, and useful for ornament rather than for manufacturing purposes, they might be worn by their owners, or let out to be worn by others; and the money value of the satisfactions they rendered would be a true rent, corresponding to the money value of the satisfactions derived from a building site of exceptional beauty, whether its owner lives on it or lets it to others. Similar remarks apply to pictures by a deceased artist. [It has already been noticed that the "rental value" of a country includes rents which the owners of land and houses who keep them in their own occupation are supposed to pay to themselves; and on the same plan, even when a thing is used by its owner, we may speak of the money value of the satisfactions afforded by it, as a producer's surplus, he being supposed to use the thing to produce the satisfactions for himself. This surplus is a different thing from a [j] consumer's surplus, which is the excess of the money value to a person of the satisfactions which he derives from a thing over the price he has to pay for it.]

[1] Comp. Book IV, ch. II ,§ 1, and [k]Book VI, ch. IV, especially § 3, for exceptions to the rule that situation rent does not directly depend on the owner's outlay.

[2] For a like reason, a tax on the stones, in the previous illustration, would fall always and exclusively on their owners: a "leaseholder" of the land or the stones for a given time at a fixed rent being regarded as an owner for that time subject to a mortgage; but to this point we shall return.

---

i. This paragraph was retained substantially in the later editions. See page 629 in vol. 1 of the present edition.

j. It may be noted that this is the only instance in the 1st ed. of the use of the term "consumer's surplus" by itself. Throughout Book III, ch. IV (The Measurement of the Utility of Wealth) the concept was termed "consumers' rent"; and although in one passage in the chapter concerned with the Doctrine of Maximum Satisfaction (1st ed. p. 446) it was termed "consumers' surplus or rent", in all the other numerous passages in which it occurred in the chapters dealing with maximum satisfaction and with the theory of monopolies (1st ed., Book V, chapters VII and VIII) it was termed "consumers' rent". On the other hand the relevant entry in the Index to the 1st ed. reads: "consumers' surplus or rent".

k. This reference applies to Book V, ch. XI, §2, in vol. 1 of the present edition.

[1]On the other hand those chemical or mechanical properties of the soil, on which its fertility largely depends, can be modified, and in extreme cases entirely changed by man's action[1]. But the process is often a slow one; and the income derived from gradual improvements does not affect the supply of them appreciably within short periods; and is of the nature of a quasi-rent; while in extreme cases, such for instance as the drainage of the Lincolnshire fens, which cannot be repeated, and the experience from which does not appreciably affect the enterprise of modern cultivation, it may be regarded for all practical purposes as a true rent. A tax on the income derived from improvements which, though capable of general application are yet slowly made and slowly exhausted, would not appreciably affect the supply of them during a short period, nor therefore the supply of produce due to them; and would consequently fall in the main on the owner. But in a long period it would diminish the supply of them, would raise the normal supply price of produce and fall on the consumer[2].

The income derived from permanent improvements.

[m]Turning lastly to the capital and effort that are directed to preparing a seed bed and sowing crops, to supplying and tending cattle, &c., we find that the gains expected from such investments of capital and labour exercise an immediate influence on the action of producers, and therefore enter into the supply price of produce even for short periods; and that they contain little or nothing of the nature of a quasi-rent. A tax therefore on this part of the income derived from land would immediately act on the supply of produce

The income derived from applications of capital and labour that yield their returns quickly.

[1] See Book IV, ch. II.
[2] So if in our last illustration we had supposed that the stones were scattered over the surface of the earth, and that a long and laborious search might expect to be rewarded by finding one here and there, the income derived from them would be a quasi-rent determined almost entirely by the value of the services they rendered; and a tax on them would at first fall almost exclusively on their owners. But in the long run the tax would diminish the supply, and therefore fall in the main on consumers of the things made by them.

1. With the exception of the second sentence, which was deleted from the 2nd ed., this paragraph was retained in the later editions. (See page 630 in vol. I of the present edition.)

m. This paragraph was deleted from the 2nd ed.

and be transferred at once from the producer to the consumer[1].

In the 2nd edition the meteoric stones illustration was expanded and was placed in the text in Book V, chapter VIII, §2, pp. 453–5, where it ran as follows:

[n] There is however one class of incomes which is not commonly classed as rent, but to which that term may be safely applied. For the eminent claim to be called a true producer's surplus or rent is not confined to the income derived from land or other (real) property, but extends to that derived from all things the supply of which cannot be increased.

An illustration. The income from meteoric stones may be a true rent, if their number cannot be increased;

For instance, suppose that a meteoric shower of a few thousand stones as hard as diamonds, but very large, fell all in one place; so that they were all picked up at once, and

[1] This case resembles that of a tax on the meteoric stones, on the supposition that they were brittle and soon destroyed, and that fresh supplies of them would be found quickly, though at the cost of much labour.

The truth indicated by this illustration may be presented in a more general form thus:—A tax on any set of things that are already produced, falls exclusively on the owners of those things, if it is not accompanied by a tax, or the expectation of a tax, on the production or bringing into use similar or rival things. If it falls also on all rival things, and the supply of them is not absolutely fixed, its incidence will be gradually transferred to the consumer.

---

n. In the 4th ed. (pp. 501–3) the illustration of income from meteoric stones (with very little alteration) was placed in a separate Note at the end of Book V, ch. IX (§§9–10); it was there preceded by the illustration of a settler taking up land in a new country (see pp. 464–6 of the present Appendix).

The opening paragraph of Book V, ch. IX, §10 ran as follows:

Our first illustration went to show how close is the resemblance between land in a new country and other instruments of production. Our second will work towards the same end by another route. It will show that the immoveability of land, though a most important attribute of land for many purposes, is not essential to the eminent claim which the income derived from land in an old country has to be regarded as a true rent. It will start from a perfect form of true rent yielded by a moveable commodity; and show how a change in conditions may modify the character of the income yielded by them; till it loses all special resemblance to rent, and becomes a simple form of ordinary profits.

no amount of search could find any more. These stones, able to cut the hardest material, would revolutionize many branches of industry; and the owners of them would have a differential advantage in production that would afford a large producer's surplus: this would be a true economic rent, whether they used the stones themselves or loaned them out to manufacturers, though only in the latter case would it be called rent. °Its amount would be determined by the value of services the stones rendered in production; and this would in the main be determined by the cost of equivalent services of chilled steel and other cutting tools, which are made by man and have therefore a normal supply price.

Again, if the stones were of exceptional splendour, and useful for ornament rather than for manufacturing purposes, they might be worn by their owners, or let out to be worn by others; and the money value of the satisfactions they rendered would be a true rent, corresponding to the money value of the satisfactions derived from a building site of exceptional beauty, whether its owner lives on it or lets it to others.

Similar remarks apply to pictures by a deceased artist. as may that If these are let out for show, the gratifications which they from pictures of produce are the source of a money income, which, after a deceased deductions for the immediate outlays, is a net producer's artist: surplus or rent; and, if retained by the owners for their own pleasure, yield equally a true rent of real satisfaction.

For it is always understood that the "rental value" of a country includes rents which the owners of land who keep it in their own occupation are supposed to pay to themselves; Pand on the same plan, even when a thing is used by its owner, we may speak of the money value of the satisfactions afforded by it, as a producer's surplus, he being supposed to use the thing to produce the satisfactions for himself. [This surplus is a different thing from a consumer's surplus,

---

o.   In the 3rd ed. (p. 476) the word "determined", in the first and third lines of this sentence, was replaced by the word "governed".

p.   The remainder of this paragraph was deleted from the 3rd ed.

which is the excess of the money value to a person of the satisfactions which he derives from a thing over the price he has to pay for it.]

qA special tax on these stones or pictures would fall entirely on their owners (a lessee being regarded as a part owner); for it would not diminish their supply and therefore would not alter the gross value of the utilities and gratifications which they can be made to afford[1]r.

under certain other circumstances it would be, for long periods, profits,

But next let us suppose that the meteoric stones were not all found at once; but were scattered over the surface of the earth on public ground, and that a long and laborious search might expect to be rewarded by finding one here and there. Then people would hunt for the stones only up to that

---

[1] It should perhaps be noticed in passing, though it is not relevant to the main issue, that in so far as the pictures or the stones, retained for private use, were valued not for their beauty but for the show of wealth which they made, a tax on them would increase their value for display, and therefore would give more to the State than it took from those who paid it.

---

q. In the 3rd ed. (p. 477) the following sentence was inserted at the beginning of this paragraph:

The influence of taxes on value affords excellent illustration of many of the subtlest points in the theory of value. Let us take advantage of this.

r. In the 4th ed. (p. 502) the following additional paragraph was inserted at this point:

But of course the demand for the stones in one trade would lessen the supply of them available for another trade: and no trade could afford to use the stones at all unless it could find some work in which they could be made to yield a net surplus, or rent, at least as good as the lowest which they would yield in any other trade. A special tax falling on their use in any one trade would diminish the demand of that trade for them; and would therefore diminish the net earnings which had to be reaped from them before they could profitably be employed in other trades. And these facts might easily be mistaken for an evidence that the rent of the stones entered into the cost of production of the things which they helped to make.

ˢmargin, at which the probable gain of so doing would in the long run just reward the outlay of labour and capital required for finding it; and the long period normal value of the stones would be kept in equilibrium between demand and supply, the number of the stones gathered annually being in the long run just that for which the normal demand price was equal to the normal supply price. A special tax on these stones would ultimately fall upon the consumers of the utilities produced by them. But, for some time, it would fall chiefly on the owners; for it could not for some time materially diminish the supply of the stones, nor therefore of their services; and accordingly it could not greatly raise the value of their services. This shows that the income derived from the stones may be regarded as a quasi-rent for short periods.

but for short periods it would be quasi-rent;

Next let us suppose that the stones were brittle, and were soon broken and destroyed; but that new supplies could be found quickly. In that case a tax on them would almost at once diminish the supply and raise the price of the services rendered by them; and therefore would be transferred to the consumers.

and in other circumstances again it would be regarded as profits for all except very short periods.

The truths indicated by this illustration may be presented in a more general form thus:—

ᵗA tax on any set of things that are already produced, falls exclusively on the owners of those things, if it is not accompanied by a tax, or the expectation of a tax, on the

General proposition as to the incidence of taxes on rents, quasi-rents and profits.

s. In the 3rd ed. (p. 477) the words "point, or" were inserted between "that" and "margin".

t. This concluding paragraph was deleted from the 4th ed., where the following paragraph was substituted for it:

Thus the influence of time in the problem of value asserts itself. For periods that are long relatively to the life of a stone, the dominant factor in its value is its own cost of production, i.e. the cost of finding it. Its value may fluctuate in consequence of fluctuations in demand, or other causes: but this will be the centre or normal position about which it fluctuates, and its contributions to any processes of production will have their value governed in the main by the fact that they must cover this cost. On the other hand for short periods, there will be no close relation between

production, or bringing into use, of similar or rival things. If it falls also on all rival things, and the supply of them is not absolutely fixed, its incidence will be gradually transferred to the consumers. For any period, for which a tax would fall mainly on the consumers, the income derived from the things may be regarded as of the nature of profits entering directly into supply price. For a shorter period, in which the tax falls mainly on the owners (lessees being regarded as part-owners), the income may be regarded as more or less of the nature of rent.

MARSHALL TO EDGEWORTH ON QUASI-RENT

On 26 April 1892, Marshall wrote a letter to Edgeworth, dealing mainly with Sir Henry Cunynghame's "successive cost curves", but also containing a vehement protest against what he regarded as Edgeworth's misuse of his (Marshall's) concepts of the short period, and quasi-rent.

This letter is reproduced in the Editorial Appendix to Appendix H, (pp. 795–8 below).

4. MARSHALL'S *ECONOMIC JOURNAL* ARTICLE "ON RENT"

In 1893 the Duke of Argyll published a book entitled *The Unseen Foundations of Society* in the course of which he attacked the Ricardian theory of rent and criticized Marshall's treatment of the theory of rent in the first edition of his *Principles of Economics*.

Marshall defended his position in an article "On Rent", which was published in vol. III of the *Economic Journal*, March 1893, and which is reproduced below as follows:

It has been said that man's progress in the knowledge of the world in which he lives may be measured by the extent to which he has been able to see the Many in the One and the One in the Many. Judged by this standard, the modern developments of economic science in relation to rent indicate progress. For we are learning that what is commonly called

---

the value of these services and the cost of production of a stone.

To this paragraph the following marginal summary was attached: "If it (the supply) can be increased quickly the income is an ordinary profit except for very short periods."

the rent of land is really a very complex thing made up of many elements, some of which differ more widely from one another than it, as a whole, differs from profits, or than some elements of it differ from wages. And as the obverse of this movement, those elements in rent, in profits, and in wages, which are similar to one another, are being drawn together, and the particular laws which govern them are being subsumed under more general laws common to all. In many countries simultaneously people of widely different tempers, and of divergent aims in social and political matters, have been developing the same kind of analysis. They sometimes make much of small differences; but they have attained independently broad results which so far agree as to justify the hope that further progress will not destroy, but develop them; just as recent progress has developed Ricardo's work; and has pruned away only the dogmas deduced from it by followers of a different stamp of mind from his.

It is especially difficult for persons, who learnt Ricardian doctrines early in this century, to adjust themselves to the new mode of thought, and to realise how fully the living spirit of Ricardo's work has been freed from the encumbrance of dead dogmas. They think they find inconsistent concessions and naive admissions in work that claims to be a direct development of Ricardo's ideas, but does not harmonise and was not intended to harmonise with Ricardian dogma. The new work seems to them a chaos, and they protest.

The most important of such protests is contained in the Duke of Argyll's *Unseen Foundations of Society.* He writes as a critic of modern as well as classical doctrine; but his own studies seem to have brought him nearer to the newer path than he is aware. He has a remarkable practical knowledge of the modern history of agriculture; he is in the first rank both as a student and as a statesman; he is a vigorous disputant, but he is too keen a thinker to be an unfair or ungenerous one. He undertakes, as his title-page tells us, "an examination of the fallacies and failures of economic science due to neglected elements"; and this calls for some answer from adherents of the new thought, however strongly they may hold that life is too short to allow much time for criticism and controversy.

I propose therefore to attempt to gather together shortly the chief results of modern analysis as applied to that problem of Rent and its relation to Value which lies at the centre of his criticisms. I shall not attempt to break new ground. For brevity, I shall speak only in my own name, without any reference to authority; and shall make no apology for making frequent references to my *Principles of Economics* where I can save space by doing so.

The Duke of Argyll objects to Ricardo's doctrine of rent and its modern developments on the grounds that they treat the rent of land as an isolated thing, instead of as one particular form of hire. But on this, and several minor points his opinions are not inconsistent with modern analysis as I understand it. There are however, other points on which we appear to differ in substance; though it is possible that we misunderstand one another a little, and that even here our differences are really less than they appear. Among these points are the character of what, in spite of the Duke's protests, I must call by the short name of "marginal production"; the relations in which this stands to the price of the whole produce; and lastly, that vague and perhaps misleading sentence—Rent does not enter into cost of production.

I will begin by setting out my own position as to rent: and afterwards consider how it is related to the Duke's position, quoting what I think are the key-passages, in his own words.

The rent of land appears to differ in degree rather than in kind from the net income yielded by other agents of production, the supply of which may be taken as fixed for the time under discussion, whether that be long or short. This keynote is struck in my first Preface:—"The greater part, though not the whole, of the distinction between Rent and Interest on capital, turns on the length of the period which we have in view. That which is rightly regarded as interest on 'free' or 'floating' capital, or on new investments of capital, is more properly treated as a sort of rent—a quasi-rent it is called below—on old investments of capital. And there is no sharp line of division between floating capital and that which has been sunk for a special branch of production, nor between new and old investments of capital; each group shades into the other gradually, and thus even the rent of land is seen, not as a thing by itself, but as the leading species of a large genus, though indeed it has peculiarities of its own which are vital from the point of view of theory as well as practice."

Producer's Surplus is a convenient name for the genus of which the rent of land is the leading species. Producer's Surplus is the excess of the gross receipts which a producer gets for any of his commodities over their prime cost; that is, over that extra cost which he incurs in order to produce those particular things, and which he could have escaped if he had not produced them.

Now the question how great a part of his expenses he must enter in these prime costs, and how much he must deduct from his selling price before he calculates his surplus, depends entirely on how far he looks ahead; or in other words, on whether he is making his calculations for a long period or only for a short.

If he is looking only a little way ahead, and is not afraid of spoiling his market; if he has got all his apparatus ready and standing idle; then a new order coming in will give him a surplus over its direct cost to him, consisting of the whole price which he receives after deducting the special outlay for raw material, for extra wages, and for wear and tear of plant involved in filling up the order. But suppose him to be looking far ahead, and proposing to extend his factory so as to do an increased business; he does not then reckon any price as affording him a real surplus unless, after allowing for all risks, it will yield him, in addition to prime costs, sufficient to give normal profits on all his outlay for material, plant, and for building up his business connection, together with charges for depreciation through the lapse of time, and for office and other general expenses, which are not reckoned in the prime, or special and direct, costs of filling up any particular order.

The conditions which govern the amount of this surplus

and its relations to value, depend not so much on the nature of the industry as on the period of time for which the calculation is made. But a short period for one class of industry may be a long one for another; just as the age of youth for a dog is shorter than for an elephant.

Since human life changes rapidly this difference may give rise to important practical consequences, and in fact it often does so. It is reasonable to suppose that the manufacturing plant existing at any time was made or bought by its owners, or immediate predecessors, in anticipation of economic conditions very much like the present. To interfere with their action, or with the income they derive from the plant, might be for some special reason necessary, just, and wise; but it would certainly be an interference with definite expectations, and would perceptibly diminish the inducements acting on other people to provide similar plant and develop manufacturing industries in general.

Land in a new country, but only there, resembles manufacturing plant from this point of view. The settler engages in a risky occupation open to all; and one of the chief motives to his exertion is the hope of becoming the possessor of title deeds to land that will rapidly rise in value. A tax on any part of his gains, present or in the near future, would instantly discourage the enterprise of himself and others, and make itself felt strongly in the supply and therefore in the price of agricultural produce. Accordingly, the whole of his income is to be regarded as earnings and profits, or at most as a quasi-rent and not as rent proper: although even in a new country a far-seeing statesman will feel a greater responsibility to future generations when legislating as to land than as to other forms of wealth; and even there land must be regarded as a thing by itself from the economic as well as from the ethical point of view.[1]

I admit that the soil of old countries is often as much an artificial product as those pieces of earth which have been arranged into brick walls, and that a great deal of it has yielded but a poor return to the vast capital sunk in it even

---

[1] The argument of this paragraph is developed in some detail in my *Principles*, Book V, ch. IX, of the second, and Book VI, ch. III, of the first edition.

within recent times. And doubtless the returns to new capital applied to the land are for the greater part like the gains of a settler in a new country: a special tax on them would check the supply of produce and be transferred partly to the consumer, in spite of the importation of foreign produce. They are but quasi-rents.

On the other hand the soil receives an income of heat and light, of rain and air, which is independent of man's efforts; most of its advantages of situation—which are especially important in the case of urban land—are independent of the action of its immediate owners; and a special tax on these would not much affect production directly. I regard the income derived from them as true rents for all practical purpose.

This brings me to the Duke's complaint[1] that I underrate the importance of security. That is a large and grave subject on which I have never yet said much. I do not think there is a wide difference between us. But it is true that I care for security for property chiefly as a means to security for liberty, and I might be willing to give up a very little of it, if necessary, in order to increase a great deal the security of well-deserving persons against extreme want. At present we have not got security in the full sense of the term; and we cannot preserve what we have not got. I agree, however, that a violent confiscation even of rent proper would give so great a shock to general security as to be a blunder from every point of view. It would discourage both accumulation and production even more than a moderate special tax on any kind of profits or quasi-rents.

But to return from this semi-ethical question to our analysis. Speaking broadly the price of anything and the amount of it that is produced are determined together by the general relations of demand and supply; the price just covers the expenses of production of that part of this amount which is raised at the greatest disadvantage, and every other part yields a surplus above its direct cost. This surplus is a result and not a cause of the selling price. For the price is determined by the relations of supply and demand; and while,

[1] *Unseen Foundations,* p. 464.

of course, the surplus does not affect the demand, so neither does it affect the supply, since it is yielded only by a part of the produce which would be produced even for a lower price.

In other words, there is a part of the produce which is on the margin of doubt as to whether it will be supplied or not, and the decision to supply it or not will affect price; but this part of the produce yields no surplus. The surplus does not enter into its cost of production; that is to say the surplus does not enter into *that* cost of production that gives the level at which the whole supply is held fixed. And this is what we mean by the phrase "producer's surplus does not enter into cost of production". It is one of those short phrases which do not explain themselves, and are easily misunderstood. But it has an important meaning; and it is applicable to many different kinds of income.

If this surplus is derived from natural advantages which became private property in forgotten ages, there are no practical problems for which it need be regarded as entering into cost of production, or therefore into price. There are not many such problems, if it is derived from any natural advantages, which were brought into use long ago, or again from the improvement of the environment through the growth of population or other causes in which the owners played no direct part.[1]

If the surplus is derived from buildings or other improvements which can be quickly made, but last long, it does not enter into price for short periods, but does enter for moderately long periods; and it is best described as a quasi-rent when there is no special mention of the period under discussion.

But on the other hand, the income derived from such machinery and other plant as is both quickly made and quickly

---

[1] In my *Principles* I have traced in some detail the way in which that part of the rental value of land which is derived from advantages of situation passes by imperceptible gradations from the character of a pure rent, in cases in which the owners of the land have no direct part in improving its environment, to that of a quasi-rent or even profits, when the conditions of the environment were deliberately brought about by and at the expense of the owners of that land in order to raise its value. I have studied this, not so much for its own sake, as because of the strong light which it throws by analogy on the analysis (into rent, profits, and earnings proper) of the total incomes that accrue to business men, to professional men, and even skilled artisans, and are due not solely to their own industry and the capital invested in their education, but also to the accidents of their birth, to advantages of their environment, to opportunity or, in German phrase, to "*Konjunktur*".

destroyed enters into cost for all but very short periods. It is therefore best described generally as profits; though when very short periods come under discussion, it has to be regarded as a quasi-rent.

This account of the relations between rent and value is independent of the incidents of land tenure. For modern analysis regards these incidents as holding but a secondary *rôle* in the fundamental problems of economics. The true nature of the rent of land, the relations in which it stands to the incomes earned by other agents of production, have been disguised by its not being generally worked by its owner as manufacturing plant is. Up to a certain point indeed the progress of the theory of rent in Great Britain was assisted by the fact not wholly accidental that, within recent times at least, the broad line of division between the landlord and the farmer has assigned to the former most of those improvements which bear fruit slowly, and to the latter most of those which bear fruit quickly. The whole of the farmer's net income is therefore as a rule to be regarded as profits except for very short periods; while the greater part of the landlord's income is to be regarded partly as a rent proper for all periods, and partly as a quasi-rent for all except very long periods; and, consequently, Adam Smith and his followers, while discussing the incidents of English land tenure, were impelled towards an analysis of value, the ultimate results of which were quite hidden from them, and have not been fully developed even yet. But we have now got far enough to strip away the accidental from the essential, to see that the central problem of rent is superior to all incidents of land tenure; that these incidents, important as they are, and fascinating as is the interest which attaches to their history, belong to a later chapter of economic analysis.

The producer's surplus, earned by the land and improvements in it, accrues to the landowner if he cultivates it himself; if he does not, then it accrues to him and his tenants, regarded as a firm engaged in the business of cultivation. This holds true whatever be the division which custom or law or contract may have arranged between them with regard to their several shares of the cost of cultivation on the one hand, and the fruits of the cultivation on the other; and from the modern point of view the general analysis of rent proceeds on the assumption "that the cultivation of the land is undertaken by its owner". This includes two facts which the Duke of Argyll seems to think that economists have ignored. One is that when the owner takes a farm into his own hands, it is not considered "to pay", unless it yields as a surplus over the immediate expenses of working it, its rent, that is "the estimated price of the hire of it".[1] And the other is that the landlord who invests his capital in improvements has as much right to be called an "enterprising undertaker" as the tenant farmer has.[2]

The surplus which any piece of land actually yields is governed by the markets, and by the course of cultivation actually followed by landlord and tenant together. That part of this surplus which the tenant is called on to pay as rent is however not that net income which he actually *does earn* (in addition to profits on his own capital, and earnings of his own industry). It is generally that which a farmer of normal ability, enterprise, and command over capital, *may be expected to earn*; but as the result of accidents chiefly of a local and personal character, it is sometimes more and sometimes less than this.[3]

And here something may be said on the law of diminishing return and its application to rent. The returns are always supposed to be such as nature will yield to successive doses of capital and labour, applied not by a cultivator of infinite intelligence, skill, enterprise, and command over capital, but by the ordinary cultivator of the place and time; just as the cost of production of cloth or anything else is estimated on the supposition that it is made not by a person of extraordinary genius, but by the ordinary manufacturer of the place

---

[1] *Unseen Foundations*, pp. 302, 303.

[2] *Ibid.* pp. 373–4. After all the care I have taken to discuss producer's surplus from the point of view of the cultivating owner, and not the tenant farmer, it is a little hard to be told that my interpretation of it is faulty "because the owner is denied his share in 'cultivation'". *Ibid.* p. 322 (footnote).

[3] Something is said of the ethical aspects of this question in my *Principles*, [a]pp. 701–2, of the second, pp. 690–2, of the first edition.

---

a. Pages 656–8 in vol. 1 of the present edition.

and time. In the discussion of the law of diminishing return we cannot go back to pre-historic times and take account of all the capital applied to the land. We go back as far as may be convenient, and reckon the applications of capital and the return to them for long periods or for short, as we like. We can adapt our argument (or our diagrams) to short periods for which the capital invested by the landlord is reckoned with the natural richness of the soil as yielding rent; or to long periods for which a part or the whole of this capital is classed with the tenant's capital as yielding profits. The treatment by Ricardo's method of arithmetical examples, or by the more powerful modern method of diagrams, is elastic and adaptable to almost every kind of problem which is brought to light by commissioners investigating the "Depression of Agriculture", or the need for further "Compensations, for Improvements", amid all the varieties of local customs and economic surroundings.

Some charges which the Duke brings against the forms of modern economic analysis, may here be answered. He objects to such terms as "final utility", "marginal production", &c., as "appropriated to some scrappy conception". Frankly I accept that description, and do not regard it as one of reproach. These terms are used to enable ordinary readers to get the chief advantages which mathematicians derive from their training in the analysis of the laws of continuous growth.[1] And after a little trial and error, at the hands of two generations of workers, they have reached a form which experience shows enables them to render great service to the student. Science, like machinery, must begin with scrappy operations. Analysis is nothing else but break-

---

[1] They correspond to differential co-efficients connecting the rates of growth of two mutually dependent elements. I admit that these terms and the diagrams connected with them repel some readers, and fill others with the vain imagination that they have mastered difficult economic problems, when really they have done little more than learn the language in which parts of those problems can be expressed, and the machinery by which they can be handled. When the actual conditions of particular problems have not been studied, such knowledge is little better than a derrick for sinking oil-wells erected where there are no oil-bearing strata. But the technical language and machinery of every science are liable to a similar misuse; and this evil, though not unimportant, is not to be weighed against the aid which clear-headed and careful students continually derive from them.

ing up a complex conception into scraps, so that they may be easily handled and thoroughly investigated. Afterwards the scraps have to be put together again, and considered in relation to many other complex notions, and the intricately interwoven facts of life.[1]

Science must study facts, ascertain which of them are representative and normal, and then analyse, and reason about normal conditions, at first within a narrow range; and afterwards, as knowledge increases, giving a wider range to these normal conditions, and thus becoming at once more complex and nearer the actual facts of life. But it can never finish off a problem for practical purposes; the finishing touches must always be given by common sense, as the products of even the finest machinery need to be finished off by handicraft. Scientific analyses, like the operations of machinery, are in their first attempts always clumsy and often a little ridiculous. They are, however, changing the face of the world: because their progress is cumulative throughout the whole life of the race, while each man's common sense, like his skill in handicraft, dies with him.

We may now pass to the graver charges which the Duke brings against Ricardo's theory of value and its modern developments. Of course he is able to make some good verbal points against Ricardo; for no one denies that Ricardo's phrases are slovenly, and that they must be interpreted before

---

[1] b The Duke makes a complaint, apparently aimed at myself, as to the use of capital letters for scrappy conceptions. Capital letters are a great disfigurement to a page; and no reasonable writer would use them for his own gratification. Their purpose is solely to assist the reader in bearing in mind that certain terms do correspond to scrappy conceptions, and in finding references to places in which those scrappy conceptions are defined. The Duke suggests that capitals might have been excused in the use of terms already established by authority, but those terms do not need signals to indicate that they are to be taken in an unwonted sense. Perhaps however I should have done better to sacrifice comeliness to the reader's convenience rather less.

---

b.   In his earlier editions Marshall used capital letters extensively for technical terms. In the case of the passages from these editions which have been reproduced in this volume the typography has been standardized in general in accordance with his practice in the later editions, that is from the 4th ed. onwards.

they are defended.[1] In particular, we must supply that allowance for the element of time which a careful reading shows to have scarcely ever been absent from his mind, though he seldom gave signs of it in his words.

The central sentence of the Duke's attack runs[2]:—"With every possible explanation and excuse, the broad and unqualified assertion of Ricardo remains one of the monstrosities of pretended science—that the price of all commodities is regulated by the cost of the worst and most expensive agency employed in its production. The truth of the exact opposite proposition is a matter of continual and familiar experience and observation. We all know, and many of us must have suffered from the fact, that the opening of some cheaper and easier method of production so lowers the exchangeable value, or price, of some given commodity in which we deal, that those who may have before derived a large profit from its production can only thenceforward continue to produce it at a profit comparatively low. In all such cases, and they are numberless in commercial life, the exchangeable value of every article or commodity is always seen to be regulated by the best and cheapest, and not by the worst, or dearest mechanism of production." He gives an instance in which the price of a commodity (nickel) was lowered by the discovery of richer sources of supply. The poorer mines, having to accept the lower price which was forced on them by the richer mines, yielded lower returns to their owners.

He makes a good verbal point as to the phrase "is regulated by"; for no doubt the cost of production at the margin cannot be the sole and ultimate regulator of price; because the margin itself is determined by the general relations of demand and supply. But he seems to hold that "regulated" can mean nothing more here than "ascertained"; and that the marginal cost merely supplies one particular way of calculating the price. I hold that it does more than that.

---

[1] I have urged this repeatedly, but especially in the long ᶜnote on Ricardo's theory of value in my *Principles*, pp. 529–36 of the first and pp. 538–45 of the second edition.

[2] *Unseen Foundations*, p. 348.

---

c. The substance of this Note will be found in Appendix I (pages 813–21) in vol. I of the present edition.

Ricardo's general position appears to be this. Market fluctuations of value are the results of the pressure of temporary (and in some cases local) demand against temporary (and in some cases local) supply. The supply consists mainly of the stocks actually in the market; with more or less reference to "future" supplies, and not without some influence of trade combinations.[1] But the current supply is in itself the result of the action of producers in the past; this action has been mainly determined by their comparing the prices which they expect to get for their goods with the expenses to which they will be put in producing them. The range of expenses of which they take account, will depend on whether they are merely considering the extra expenses of certain extra production with their existing plant, or are considering whether to lay down new plant for the purpose. But in any case it will be the general rule that that portion of the supply, which can be most easily produced, will be produced unless the price is expected to be very low. Every increase in the price expected will, as a rule, induce some people who would not otherwise have produced anything, to produce a little; while those who have produced something for the lower price, probably produce more for the higher price.[2]

[1] Where there is a strong combination, tacit or overt, producers may sometimes regulate the price for a considerable time together with very little reference to cost of production. And if the leaders in that combination were those who had the best facilities for production, it might be said, in apparent though not in real contradiction to Ricardo's doctrines, that the price was governed by that part of the supply which was most easily produced. But as a fact, those producers whose finances are weakest, and who are bound to go on producing to escape failure, often impose their policy on the rest of the combination. And it is a common saying, both in America and England, that the weakest members of a combination are frequently its rulers.

[2] For brevity, I pass by, as the Duke has done, the special conditions of those branches of manufacture which obey the law of increasing return; that is, in which—even after allowing for the difficulties of getting increased supplies of raw material and labour—an increased output can be turned out at a less than proportionate expense. I have always felt that Ricardo's treatment of this case was inadequate; and I do not quite concur in the treatment of it by Cournot, by Auspitz and Lieben, and by the Austrian economists generally. My own attempts to deal with it are given in my *Principles* (second edition), ^dpp. 368–79, 403–4, 426–9, 439–40, 484–97, 535–6. The corresponding discussions in the first edition are less fully and much less carefully written; they are in pp. 371–80, 412–28, 438–9.

d. The corresponding pages in vol. 1 of the present edition are pages 311–22, 342–3, 377–80, 391 n.–2 n., 455–61 and 805–12, 500–2. The editorial notes to these pages show the changes that were made in the successive editions.

The producers who are in doubt whether to produce anything at all, may be said to lie altogether on the margin of production (or, if they are agriculturists, on the margin of cultivation). Their decision exerts some influence on supply and therefore on price. But as a rule they are very few in number; there may be none in this position; and anyhow their action is far less important than that of the great body of producers who will produce something whatever be the price (within certain limits), but watch the price to see how far it is worth their while to extend their production. That part of their production with regard to which such persons are on the margin of doubt as to whether it is worth while for them to produce it at the price, is to be included together with that of the persons who are in doubt whether to produce at all; the two together constitute the marginal production at that price.

Now I hold that the point of Ricardo's doctrine is to be sought in the fact that the cost of production of the marginal produce can be ascertained (theoretically at least)[1] from the circumstances of the margin, without reasoning in a circle, and that the cost of production of other parts of the produce cannot. For other parts yield a rent or a quasi-rent, or both; and these are determined not by the circumstances of production of the parts in question, but by the price of the whole produce. The costs of production of these parts cannot be reckoned up without counting in the corresponding rents and quasi-rents; and therefore the price of the commodity cannot be deduced from them without reasoning in a circle. This is what I take Ricardo's doctrine to mean; and it seems to me fertile in important results.

Another aspect of the same truth is that the income earned by machinery and other plant already in existence is not any given percentage on their cost of production, but is a quasi-rent determined by the value of what they produce. If they

---

[1] The difficulty of getting a case of production free from all quasi-rents is referred to in *Principles*, second edition, [e]pp. 408–9 and 495–7.

---

e. These two references correspond respectively to pages 346–8, and page 460 and pages 809 n.–10 n. in vol. 1 of the present edition.

are of obsolete fashion, this quasi-rent is small. But whether it is large or small, this value is found by capitalising their quasi-rent, and if we were then to turn round, and say that their quasi-rent would return a certain rate of interest on their value we should be reasoning in a circle.[1]

It was then completely in accordance with Ricardo's principles, that when richer supplies of nickel were discovered the price fell to the level of the marginal cost of production under the new relations of demand and supply, and that the net return yielded by the Duke's old mines fell in consequence.[2]

Attention has just been called to the fact that the marginal production is not to be sought only in places and in businesses which have no differential advantages for production. For every producer, whether well-placed or ill-placed, whether cultivating rich land or rentless land, comes to some point at which he is on the margin of doubt whether to go further or not. That shows he thinks any further production would not increase the net surplus, which he gets from his differential advantage; and such production would therefore be marginal. I hold therefore that Ricardo's theory of rent and his deductions from it in no way depend on the existence of rentless land; but the Duke referring[3] to a previous statement of mine to this effect, says:—"Thus we see that the Ricardian argument is defended on the ground that it is

---

[1] See *Principles*, [f]p. 470, p. 622, of the second, p. 500, p. 620 of the first edition.
[2] I do not regard that net yield as income, but partly as the result of the sale of capital. (For I admit that free gifts of nature when appropriated become private capital.) I hold that a royalty is not a rent, any more than is the charge which a grocer makes for sugar. Royalties always do enter into cost of production, because every ton of ore that is raised has to pay its share; there is no marginal produce which pays no royalty. See *Principles*, [g]pp. 463–4 of the second edition, p. 491, of the first.
[3] *Unseen Foundations*, p. 309.

---

f.   There is no passage in the present edition corresponding exactly to p. 470 in the 2nd ed. (p. 500 in the 1st ed.). The passage in question will be found in the Editorial Appendix to Book V, chapters VIII—X (pp. 473–4). The reference to p. 622 in the 2nd ed. corresponds to pages 592–3 in vol. 1 of the present edition.

g.   This reference corresponds to pages 438–9 in Vol. 1 of the present edition.

entirely independent of facts." NO: it is independent only of the accident whether there happens to be any rentless land in the neighbourhood. A statement with regard to the manner in which fish breathe, which claims to apply to all (true) fish, including trout, cannot be described as "independent of facts", on the ground that it is independent of the question whether there happen to be any trout in the stream which is under discussion.[1]

The chief remaining attack by the Duke traverses part of the same ground as the last. He says that rent is only one kind of hire, and therefore must enter into cost of production as other kinds of hire do. I admit that it is a kind of hire, and I say that *relatively to short periods* many kinds of hire do not enter into cost of production. Now, strangely enough, the Duke takes account of the element of time, just as I should, when he is establishing his premiss; but in applying his premiss he ignores it, and then we no longer agree.

He has to meet the argument that the rent of land is marked off from all other kinds of income by the fact that land "is a thing of which the supply is limited, and cannot be increased by man's action". And he contends that the supply of other things also available at any place is also limited *for the time*. He says[2]: "It is true that if I want to hire a farm, and if the owner won't let it to me at a price which I think to be its value, I cannot say to him that I can

---

[1] So far from regarding the existence of rentless land as needed for Ricardo's doctrine of rent, I have urged that new countries, where there is an abundance of rentless land, are just those to which his theory is not applicable without great reservations. He was perfectly aware that marginal produce need not come from rentless land. In his chapter on rent he says: "It commonly happens that before... inferior lands are cultivated, capital can be more productively employed on those lands that are already in cultivation.... In such case, capital will be preferably employed on the old land and will equally create a rent; for rent is always the difference between the produce obtained by the employment of two equal quantities of capital and labour....In this case, as well as the other, the capital last employed yields no rent" (McCulloch's Edition, pp. 36, 37). Ricardo's statement (pp. 38, 39) that "no reduction would take place in the price of corn, though landlords should forego the whole of their rent" is based on the fact that "the value of corn is regulated by the quantity of labour bestowed on its production on that quality of land or with that portion of capital which pays no rent:" and thus it is explicitly independent of the question whether there is any rentless land. The Duke (p. 299) seems to have misconceived his criticism (pp. 34, 35) of Adam Smith's statement that rent is paid for forests in Norway. His point is that the charges made for leave to cut down timber are not rents. He is not, as the Duke thinks, insisting on the existence of rentless land. J. S. Mill's remarks on the subject are a little inconsistent.

[2] *Unseen Foundations*, pp. 292–3.

make another farm at a lower rent. But it is equally true that if I want to hire a boat or a sewing machine, or a steam engine, or a horse or a cow, and if the owner charges for the hire of such articles more than I think they are worth, I cannot practically say to him that I can build a boat for myself, or make a sewing machine, or a steam-engine, or breed for myself a horse or a cow. All of these are things which can be multiplied by man's action. But at any given time and place they are as entirely out of the reach of multiplication by individual men as the acres of a farm. Practically, therefore, everything we can either buy or hire, is strictly limited in quantity by conditions, which are for the time at least, and perhaps for ever, insuperable to every individual buyer or hirer; and in this respect the price we pay for the purchase or for the hire of land cannot be differentiated in principle, or as regards its origin and cause, from the price we pay for the hire of any other article whatever."

So far well. He introduces the limiting words "for the time" always at the critical place, and is so far quite in agreement with Ricardo. But he drops these limiting words when he proceeds to his attack on Ricardo. He says:[1] "The hire of anything which is hired at all is, of course, measured by its excess of value over another thing of the same kind. Thus, the pony or donkey which a costermonger may hire to draw his cart may be either a young and strong pony or donkey capable of much work, which well repays its keep and a considerable hire." As I should say, its work yields a considerable surplus or quasi-rent above the prime cost of that work. He goes on: "Or it may be an old and feeble pony or donkey which just pays for its keep and no more, or so much more as to be a mere nominal amount for hire. In this case the value of the efficient pony or donkey, and the hire the costermonger has to pay for it, may be said to be the excess of the value of that animal over the value of the animal which is so weak as to fetch no hiring value at all. But what is the use of saying this?" And again[2]: "The mere isolation of one particular case of lending and of hiring from all the other innumerable cases of the same transactions,

[1] *Unseen Foundations*, pp. 310–11.   [2] *Ibid.* pp. 370–1.

must of necessity be, in itself, a copious source of fallacy. It essentially consists in, and depends upon the greatest of all failures in science,—the failure to recognise identity of principle and of law, under superficial diversities of form. The fundamental importance attached to the mere half-truth that the rent of land is, in each particular case, predominantly the result or consequence of the price of its produce, and conversely that rent does not directly enter as a cause into the price of produce, is an excellent example of this kind of fallacy. It is true of the price of the hire of the land, only, as we have seen, in the same sense in which it is equally true of the hire of labouring men, or of the hire of horses, or of the hire of implements; so that the isolation of the one particular case of the hire of the land from other cases of hire, which are equally incidents in the same production is essentially a failure to distinguish between the essential and the accidental, which is the worst of scientific errors."

The reader has now the two positions before him. I submit that modern analysis does not "isolate" the rent of land, but says that what is true of the hire or net income earned by ponies for a short time, is true of the hire of or net income earned by houses and permanent improvements in land for a long time; and that it is true of rent proper in an old country, and especially in the towns of an old country for a much longer time. The limiting words "for the time" have disappeared from the later stages of the Duke's discussion of the hire of ponies, and I will not consent to part with them. That is the difference between us.

h In my view, the hire of ponies, like that of land, is governed for a time by the value of the services they will render, and the value of those services is determined by the relations in which the supply of ponies, &c., stands to the demand for such services. If nothing unexpected has happened, that supply will have been so adjusted to the demand that an average (or normal) pony during a life of average

h. This illustration of quasi-rent from the hire of ponies was inserted substantially in the 4th ed. (pp. 494–5) but was deleted from the 5th ed. See the Editorial Appendix to Book V, chapters viii–x, pp. 480–1 above.

length and activity will yield a hire giving normal profits on its cost of production. As a rule it will do this, and yield no "surplus" above normal profits to the producer. Of course the demand for ponies may have been wrongly estimated, and the hire (or quasi-rent) yielded by an average pony may exceed or fall short of normal profits on its cost of production. But the divergence can be only for short periods in the case of ponies, because they are so quickly raised, and they so quickly die off, that any error in the adjustment of supply to demand can be quickly set right. The difference between the rent of land and the quasi-rents of most other things lies in the fact that their hire can never for any long time diverge much from normal profits on their cost of production; while the supply of fertile land cannot be adapted quickly to the demand for it, and therefore the income derived from it may for a long time together, or in some cases even permanently, diverge much from normal profits on the cost of preparing it for cultivation. That is my case on the main issue.

But there is one side issue to which I will refer. The relation in which the rent or quasi-rent of any agent of production stands to the price of the produce which it takes part in raising has been discussed so far without reference to the possibility of diverting that agent from one branch of production to another. We have spoken of the rent of land, for instance, with reference to agricultural produce in general, and without reference to the competition between crops for the occupation of the land. But of course it is true that the marginal cost of production of oats near London is higher than it would be if the land had nothing to do but to grow oats. The high rent which the land can pay for the purposes of market gardeners and others alters the position of the marginal production of oats, and thus alters the price of oats. The Duke quotes [i]a passage from the first edition of

---

i. The passage referred to as having been quoted by the Duke ran as follows in the 1st ed. (p. 487):

For instance the production of those oats which only just pay their way is often said to determine the price of all other

my *Principles* in which I had referred rather clumsily to this fact, and infers[1] that I hold "it would be absurd to say that the cost of producing any one of these crops is determined or caused by the cost of its production on the worst bit of land on which it is actually grown; but it would be perfectly correct to say that the aggregate value of the whole produce of the farm is caused by the cost of production on the poorest bit of it."

I did not intend to say that. But without disputing whether my words really implied it, I will quote a more

[1] *Unseen Foundations*, p. 317. His printer has made the sentence even worse than mine by substituting "agreed" for "argued" in the fourth line of the quotation.

---

oats; rent, it is argued, does not enter into their cost of production, and therefore rent does not enter into the supply price of oats. But this is not strictly true.

It is true that when we know what are the most unfavourable conditions under which oats are grown, we can calculate the supply price of oats by reckoning up their expenses of production; just as we can discover the temperature by looking at the thermometer. But as it would be misleading to say that the height of the thermometer determines the temperature; so a great deal of confusion has arisen from saying simply that the normal value of oats is determined by their production under the most unfavourable circumstances under which they are grown.

The foregoing sentences are reproduced in their context in the Editorial Appendix to Book V, chapters VIII–X (see p. 456).

In the 2nd ed. (pp. 459–60) and the 3rd ed. (p. 480), the latter of which editions appeared in 1895 after the publication of the article "On Rent", Marshall made no substantial alteration in the passage just quoted from the 1st ed.; in the 2nd ed. it was transferred to Book V, ch. VIII as a result of the rearrangement of his material owing to the amalgamation of Books V and VI into the single Book V in the 2nd and later editions.

The "more careful version" mentioned in the text of the article above was embodied in a new paragraph inserted in the 2nd ed. (Book V, ch. XIV, §3, p. 532), which is reproduced in the editorial note to page 499 of Book V, ch. xv in vol. 1 of the present edition.

careful version from my second edition[1]:—"When applied to the cost of production of one particular crop, though still literally true as it stands, experience shows that it [the doctrine that rent does not enter into cost of production] is liable to be interpreted in senses in which it is not true. For if land which had been used for growing hops, is found capable of yielding a higher rent as a market garden, the area under hops will undoubtedly be diminished; and this will raise their marginal cost of production and therefore their price. The rent which land will yield for one kind of produce, though it does not directly enter into those expenses, yet does act as the channel through which a demand for the land for that kind of produce increases the difficulties of supply of other kinds; and thus does indirectly affect their expenses of production." I hold that this can be extended to the ground rents of factories which are applicable to several trades, to the quasi-rents of their machinery;[2] and to the rents of rare natural abilities, and the quasi-rents of trained skill, when they are not limited to a single occupation.[3] There are many other points in the Duke's instructive and suggestive criticisms on which I feel tempted to say a few words. But my article is already too long; and I can only hope that it may lead him to find a little more agreement than before between his own positions and those of the modern followers of Ricardo; and may incline him to the opinion that however untenable may be the so-called "Ricardian dogmas", the analysis of which Ricardo was the chief builder, has firm if often unseen foundations.   ALFRED MARSHALL

1 j Page 532. See also pp. 459–63.
2 k *Principles*, pp. 462–3 and 471 of the second, pp. 490–1, of the first edition.
3 l *Ibid*. pp. 611–13 of the second, pp. 608–9 of the first edition.

j. The first of these references corresponds to pages 499–500 and the second to pages 434–8 in vol. 1 of the present edition.

k. The first of these references to the 2nd ed. corresponds to pages 450–1 in vol. 1 of the present edition. In the case of the second reference there is no corresponding passage in vol. 1. The wording of the passage on p. 471 in the 2nd ed. will be found in the Editorial Appendix to Book V, chapters VIII–X. See pp. 473–4 above.

l. This reference corresponds to pages 577–9 in vol. 1 of the present edition.

BOOK V, CHAPTER XI

MARGINAL COSTS IN RELATION TO URBAN VALUES

a. The origin of the wording of this chapter is shown throughout in the editorial notes.

In the 1st edition the chapter corresponding to Book V, chapter XI in the present edition was Book VI, chapter IV, and in the 2nd to the 4th editions, Book V, chapter X.

Book V, chapter XI assumed its present form in the 5th edition, but most of the material contained in it dates from the 1st and 2nd editions. In the 1st edition the greater part of the substance of §§ 1 and 2 of the present chapter was placed in Book VI, chapter IV; of §§ 4 and 5 in Book VI, chapter II; and of § 7 in Book VII, chapter XI; while § 6 dates mainly from Book VI, chapter IX in the 2nd edition.

b. The title of this chapter dates from the 5th edition In the 1st edition (Book VI, ch. IV) the corresponding chapter was entitled "Cost of Production. The Industrial Environment". In the 2nd and 3rd editions (Book V, ch. X) the title ran: "On the Value of an appliance for Production in Relation to that of the Things produced by it, continued. Situation Rent. Composite Rent." In the 4th edition (Book V, ch. X) it ran: "Influence of the Environment on the Income from an Appliance for Production. Situation Rent. Composite Rent."

c. Except where otherwise stated the wording of this section (§ 1) dates substantially from the 1st ed. (Book VI, ch. IV, § 1, pp. 505–7).

d. So since the 5th ed. (p. 441), where the first line of this sentence replaced the following words dating from the 1st ed. (p. 505): "We have now considered the relation...etc."

e. This sentence dates from the 5th ed. (p. 441).

f. So since the 4th ed. (p. 504) where the words "*the value* of produce" replaced the following words dating from the 1st ed. (p. 505): "the real price which the cultivator can get for every part of his produce."

a. So since the 4th ed. (p. 505). In the first three editions there was a full stop at the end of the word "economies", which concluded the paragraph. This was succeeded by a paragraph which ran as follows:

It is true that situation often counts for little with regard to those economies that result from the gradual growth of knowledge, or from the gradual development of world markets for commodities the value of which is great in proportion to their bulk. Cost of carriage is not a very large element in the budget of a watch-factory wherever it is placed: though near access to markets where specialized skill can be easily got may be very important to it. But in the great majority of industries the success of a business depends chiefly upon the resources and the markets of its own immediate neighbourhood; and the situation value which a site derives...etc.

The foregoing sentences down to the word "neighbourhood" were deleted from the 4th ed.

b. So since the 5th ed. (p. 441), where this clause and the succeeding sentence replaced the following clause and sentence dating from the 1st ed. (p. 507):

and the corresponding difference in the incomes derived from the two businesses is commonly regarded as a difference of *situation rent*. If we suppose the second of the two sites to have less advantages of situation than any other we may regard it as having no special situation rent; and then the income derived from the differential advantage of the former site constitutes the whole of its situation rent.

c. The remainder of this paragraph dates from the 5th ed. (pp. 441–2), though the footnote attached to the end of the last sentence of the paragraph on page 442 dates from the 1st ed. (p. 507 n.).

a. Except where otherwise stated the wording of this section (§2) dates substantially from the 1st ed. (pp. 507–10).

b. So since the 6th ed. (p. 442), where this opening sentence of §2 replaced the following sentence dating from the 5th ed. (p. 442): "It is obvious that the greater part of situation value is 'public value' in the sense in which that term has already been used."

c. So since the 5th ed. (p. 442), where this sentence replaced the following sentence dating from the 1st ed. (p. 507): "There are however some exceptional cases in which this income derived from an advantageous situation is not properly to be regarded as rent but rather as profits."

a. This clause was inserted in the 5th ed. (p. 443 n.).

a. The following footnote attached to the end of this paragraph in the 1st ed. (p. 510 n.) was deleted from the 2nd ed.:

It would delay the main argument too much to discuss here cases in which property is let under a lease, or in which custom or other causes give the tenant a share of any kind temporary or permanent in the ownership of the land. In all such cases the producers' surplus or rent is the same as if the land were held on the English system without a lease; only instead of being the property of one person it is distributed among several.

b. This and the following paragraph were inserted in the 5th ed. (pp. 444–5).

c. The following concluding sentence to this footnote in the 1st ed. (p. 509 n.) was deleted from the 2nd ed.:

But as things are at present, at all events in England, such industries are chiefly those which are devoted to supplying the demands of the army and navy; and it happens that by discouraging private enterprise in these directions Government while avoiding small commercial risks in time of peace, may lay itself open to far more important military risks in times of war.

a. This paragraph dates from the 5th ed. (p. 445).

b. This paragraph and the footnote attached to it date substantially from the 1st ed. (Book VII, ch. xi, § 11, pp. 696–7). They were retained in both the 2nd and 3rd editions (Book VI, ch. ix), were deleted wholly from the 4th ed., but reinserted in their present form in the 5th ed. (Book V, ch. xi, § 3, pp. 445–7).

a. This paragraph, together with its footnote, and the next paragraph, were inserted in the 5th ed. (pp. 446–7).

b. The word "agricultural" was inserted before the word "land" in the 5th ed. (p. 446 n.).

c. So since the 5th ed. (p. 446 n.) where the last sentence of this paragraph was added. In the 1st ed. (p. 697 n.) this paragraph ran as follows:

It may be mentioned that the discounted value of a very distant rise in the value of land is much less than is commonly supposed. For instance if we take interest only at five per cent. (and of course a much higher rate prevailed during the Middle Ages), £1 invested at compound interest would amount to about £130 in 100 years, £17,000 in 200 years and £36,000,000,000 in 500 years: and therefore an expenditure by the State of £1 in securing to itself the reversion of a rise in the value of land which came into operation now for the first time would have been a bad investment, unless the value of that rise now exceeded £130, if the payment was made 100 years ago; if 200 years ago the gain ought now to amount to £17,000, if 500 years ago to £37,000,000,000.

In the 2nd ed. (p. 674 n.) the capital figure for an accumulation of 500 years, in the fifth and tenth lines of the paragraph was changed to £40,000,000,000.

PAGE 447

a. This and the next two paragraphs date substantially from the 1st ed. (Book VI, ch. II, §5, pp. 488–9).

b. In the 5th ed. (p. 477) the word "homesteader" replaced the word "squatter" in the earlier editions.

PAGE 448

a. So since the 5th ed. (p. 448) where this sentence replaced the following sentence dating from the 1st ed. (p. 489):

On the understanding that we do so reckon them, it is true that ground-rent does not enter into the expenses of manufacture and this understanding is exactly parallel to that which has to be supplied in order to make Ricardo's doctrine true, when applied to agriculture.

b. This paragraph dates from the 4th ed. (Book V, ch. VIII, §5, p. 485 n.).

c. The first paragraph of this footnote (except for the last sentence) dates from the 1st ed. (p. 489 n.).

d. This sentence and the next paragraph was inserted in the 5th ed. (p. 448 n.).

PAGE 449

a. In the 5th ed. (p. 449) Marshall wrote "less favourable situation", and these words were retained down to and including the 8th edition (page 449). They have been altered in vol. I of the present edition to read "more favourable situation", as the sense clearly requires the substitution of "more" for "less".

b. This paragraph was inserted in the 5th ed. (p. 449).

c. This paragraph dates from the 1st ed. (p. 490), where the opening sentence in the present text was preceded by the following sentence which was deleted from the 5th ed.:

Reverting to a caution given at the beginning of this chapter against misunderstanding the general bearing of Ricardo's doctrine, we may notice that this argument does not imply that a manufacturer when making up the profit and loss account of his business would not count his rent among his expenses.

a. The words "and rightly" were inserted in the 5th ed. (p. 450). In the earlier editions there was the following additional sentence at this point, which was deleted from the 5th ed.: "But it is no less true that in making up the profit and loss account of the cultivation of land, the farmer's rent must be reckoned among his expenses."

b. This paragraph and the first sentence of the next paragraph were inserted in the 5th ed. (p. 450).

c. This sentence dates from the 1st ed. (pp. 489–90).

d. The remainder of this paragraph dates from the 1st ed. (p. 491).

e. This paragraph was inserted in the 5th ed. (pp. 450–1).

a. The wording of this section (§6) dates substantially from the 2nd ed. (Book VI, ch. IX, §8, pp. 672–4). In the 4th ed. the whole section was transferred to Book V, ch. VIII, §7 (pp. 487–8), as part of a "Note on Rent from Building Land in relation to the Value of Products made on it". The section was brought into its present place in the 5th ed. (pp. 451–2).

b. So since the 5th ed. (p. 451) where the words "the higher the rental values of their sites" replaced the words "the higher their ground-rent" in the earlier editions.

a. So since the 5th ed. (p. 452). In the 2nd and 3rd editions the word "marginal" was inserted before the word "goods". In the 4th ed. the word "marginal" in this place was deleted, but the following clause was inserted in square brackets at the end of this sentence: "[they are marginal goods]."

b. The following sentence dating from the 2nd ed. (p. 673) was deleted from the 5th ed.:

It appears then that rent does not enter into retail price any more than it enters into the price charged by the trader or the manufacturer; intensive demands for land may come from the opportunities it offers either for moderate sales at high prices or for very large sales at lower prices.

PAGE 453

a. Except where otherwise stated the wording of this section (§7) dates substantially from the 1st ed. (pp. 708 n.–9 n.), where it was placed as a footnote to §8 of Book VII, ch. XII. See editorial note **d** to page 625 of vol. I in the present edition. It was transferred in the 2nd ed. to Book V, ch. X, §4, pp. 478–9, where it was placed in the text. In the 5th and later editions this became §7 of Book V, ch. XI.

b. This paragraph dates in its present form from the 6th ed. (p. 453). In the 2nd to the 4th editions its substance was divided into two paragraphs which ran as follows:

The so-called rent of a building is generally composed of two elements, one the quasi-rent of the building itself, and the other the rent—often chiefly a situation rent—of the ground on which it is built. The task of distinguishing between these two elements may be taken here as a special case of a more general problem of composite rents.

At starting there may appear to be some contradiction in the statement that a thing is yielding at the same time two rents: for a rent is in some sense a residual income after deducting the expenses of working it: and it may seem that there cannot be two residues. But really we often find a true producer's surplus or rent, which itself includes two or more minor rents.

In the 5th ed. (p. 453) the two paragraphs were amalgamated into one, and the first two sentences were reworded into three sentences as in the present text, but the wording of the earlier editions was retained for the remainder of the paragraph.

c. This footnote was inserted in the 5th ed. (p. 453 n.).

PAGE 454

a. This footnote dates substantially from the 4th ed. (p. 510 n.).

BOOK V, CHAPTER XII

EQUILIBRIUM OF NORMAL
DEMAND AND SUPPLY,
CONTINUED,
WITH REFERENCE TO THE LAW
OF INCREASING RETURN

PAGE 455

a. The origin of the wording of this chapter is indicated through-out in the editorial notes.

With the exception of two paragraphs in § 1 and two sentences in § 3 none of the material dates from the 1st edition, where Book V, chapter v, entitled "The Theory of Stable Equilibrium of Normal Demand and Supply" dealt with the construction of normal supply and demand curves, with positions of stable and unstable equilibrium and with pro-ducer's surplus. All these sections were subsequently transferred to other chapters, or to a Note which eventually became Appendix H. In the 2nd and 3rd editions (Book V, ch. XI) a good deal of material additional to that previously contained in Book V, chapter v in the 1st edition was inserted, part of which was retained in this chapter in later editions. In the 4th edition (Book V, ch. XI) this chapter was remodelled, a large part of the material being placed in a "Note on the Pure Theory of Stable and Unstable Equilibria" at the end of the chapter. In the 5th edition (Book V, ch. XII) the paragraphs in § 1 on elasticity of supply were inserted, while the Note just referred to was expanded to constitute Appendix H.

b. The title of this chapter dates from the 4th edition (Book V, ch. XI). In the 2nd and 3rd editions (Book V, ch. XI) it was entitled "The Equilibrium of Normal Supply and Demand concluded. Multiple Positions of Equilibrium."

c. The first three paragraphs of this section date in their present from from the 4th ed. (p. 511), though the second and third paragraphs are based on sentences dating from the 1st ed. (p. 413).

d. In the 1st ed. (p. 413) this illustration was placed in Book V, ch. IV and ran as follows:

For instance if a sudden fashion were to set in for wearing watch-shaped aneroid barometers, highly paid labour that had no special training for the work would have to be drawn

519

in from other trades, there would be a good deal of wasted effort and for a time the real and the money cost of production would be increased; the short-period normal supply price would rise with an increase in the amount produced, and the actual selling price might oscillate in the wholesale market for a time about a "normal" level higher than that which had prevailed before. But independently of any new invention in the cost of making aneroids, production on a large scale would quickly develop great economies. For specialized skill in abundance would shortly be forthcoming and properly graduated to the various work to be done: and with a large use of the method of interchangeable parts, specialized machinery would do better and more cheaply much of the work that is now done by hand. We are therefore justified in concluding that a great increase in the annual output of watch-shaped aneroids, will lower very much their supply price provided only time is allowed for that development of industrial organization which normally belongs to a large scale of production; and this conclusion does not involve the assumption that any new substantive invention would be made in the process of manufacture.

In the 2nd ed. (Book V, ch. xi, pp. 490–1) the first three clauses of the first sentence of the foregoing paragraph were made into a separate sentence—that is there was a full stop after the word "increased". The remainder of the paragraph ran as follows:

But it is also true that if the fashion lasted a considerable time, then independently of any new invention in the cost of making aneroids the process of production on a large scale would be economical. For specialized skill in abundance would shortly be forthcoming, and properly graduated to the various work to be cone: with a large use of the method of interchangeable parts, specialized machinery would do better and more cheaply much of the work that is now done by hand; and a steady increase in the annual output of watch-shaped aneroids will lower very much their long-period supply price, as a result of that development of industrial organization which normally belongs to a large scale of production.

There was no change in the foregoing paragraph in the 3rd ed., Book V, ch. xi (pp. 510–11).

e.   The remainder of this section (§1), introducing the concept of elasticity of supply (which did not appear in the first four editions), was inserted in the 5th ed. (pp. 455–7).

PAGE 457

a.   Except where otherwise stated the remainder of this chapter dates substantially from the 4th ed. (pp. 511–15). For the earlier form of the subject-matter of §§2 and 3 see the Editorial Appendix to Book V, chapter XII, pp. 523–9, on "Modes of Action of the Law of Increasing Return".

b.   This footnote was inserted in the 5th ed. (p. 457 n.).

PAGE 458

a.   For the earlier form of this and the following footnote see the Editorial Appendix to Book V, chapter XII, pp. 527 n. and 528 n.

PAGE 459

a.   For the earlier form of this footnote see the Editorial Appendix to Book V, chapter XII, p. 524 n. below.

b.   The following extract from a letter from Marshall to A. W. Flux dated 7 March 1898, throws light on the nature of Marshall's disagreement with Cournot's views on increasing returns:

You say that, à propos of increasing returns, you are inclined to lay stress on the incomplete utilisation of existing production resources. That is of course one of my chief hobbies. My confidence in Cournot as an *economist* was shaken when I found that his mathematics re I.R. led inevitably to things which do not exist and have no near relation to reality. One of the chief purposes of my Wanderjahre among factories was to discover how Cournot's premises were wrong. The chief outcome of my work in this direction, which occupied me a good deal between 1870 and 1890, is in the "Representative Firm" theory, *Principles*, pp. 348–90, the supplementary cost analysis, pp. 435–8 and 464–70; as well as the parts that directly relate to supply price for I.R.

The supplementary cost question can of course only be touched in vol. I. It will give a chief motive to a great part of vol. II, especially as to fluctuations of credit and prices. I still think that my term "process" is the best I have met with for covering in a short space all this group of difficulties.

The first of the references (to the 3rd ed.) in the last sentence of the first of the foregoing paragraphs relates to pages 267–313 in vol. I of the present edition, though it should be extended to cover also pages 314–22. The second references relate to pages 359–62 and 395–400 in vol. I of the present edition. The letter from which the above extracts have been taken is printed in full in *The Memorials of Alfred Marshall* (pp. 406–7).

    c.   The concluding paragraph of this footnote was inserted in the 8th edition (page 459 n.).

PAGE 461

    a.   Although the first two sentences of this paragraph assumed their present form in the 4th ed. (p. 515), they are in fact a rewording of some sentences dating from the 1st ed. (Book V, ch. v, p. 425) where they ran as follows:

It has already been indicated that the theory of stable equilibrium of normal demand and supply in its most abstract form assumes a certain rigidity in the conditions of demand and supply, which does not really exist. This theory however, especially when aided by diagrams, helps to give definiteness to our ideas; and in its elementary stages it does not diverge from the actual facts of life so far as to prevent its giving a fairly trustworthy picture of the chief methods of action of the strongest and most persistent group of economic forces. It is only when pushed to its more remote and intricate logical consequences, especially those connected with multiple positions of equilibrium, that it slips away from the conditions of real life, and soon ceases to be of much service in dealing with practical problems.

    b.   In the 4th ed. (p. 516) this paragraph, except for the last clause, constituted the opening paragraph of the "Note on the Pure Theory of Stable and Unstable Equilibria" which in the 5th ed. became Appendix H.

    c.   This clause was inserted in the 5th ed. (p. 461).

EDITORIAL APPENDIX TO
BOOK V, CHAPTER XII

MODES OF ACTION OF THE LAW OF
INCREASING RETURN

In the 2nd edition (pp. 484–90) and the 3rd edition (pp. 504–10), §2 of Book V, chapter xi contains a lengthy discussion of the modes of action of the law of increasing return, much of which was deleted from the 4th edition, though certain portions were transferred to Book IV, chapter xi, §5 and retained in the later editions. See editorial note to pages 285–7 in vol. 1 of the present edition.

The whole of §2 in the 2nd editions and the first paragraph of §3 (unaltered in the 3rd edition) is reproduced here as follows:

§^a2. The hypothesis of a stationary state is useful to illustrate many points in economics; but it is the nature of such hypotheses to be treacherous guides if pursued far away from their starting point: they soon lead us into a region of unreal abstractions, and, in particular, this one is not suitable for that part of the pure theory of equilibrium of normal demand and supply which remains for us to discuss; and which relates to industries that obey the law of increasing return, a law that belongs essentially to an age of change and progress. *We now pass from this hypothesis and proceed to study further the causes that govern normal supply price in an industry that obeys the law of increasing return.*

It will be recollected that the general view of that theory, given in Chapter iii of this Book, left out of account all cases in which the supply price falls as the amount produced increases; because they present special difficulties which would have obscured those main outlines of the theory of which we were then seeking to obtain a general view. These difficulties arise chiefly from the facts, firstly, that the law of increasing return seldom shows its true character in a *short* period of time; and, secondly, that in the *long* period of time required for its full operation, the general condi-

---

a. § 1 of this chapter in the 2nd and 3rd editions dealt with normal supply price in the stationary state. See Book V, ch. v, §2 and Appendix H in vol. 1 of the present edition.

tions of equilibrium are likely to be modified by external changes[1].

Let us begin with the first of these two difficulties, and, consider further the conditions of production and marketing with regard to short periods in industries that obey the law of increasing return, and inquire what are the reasons which induce any particular producer of a commodity, which obeys the law of increasing return, to produce as much as he does and no more. The fact that the economies of production on a large scale act differently in different trades, makes it difficult to adapt a general theory of equilibrium to the conditions of these industries; and we are compelled to go back a little, and work, partly over old ground, from details to general results.

It may seem that it is the interest of each producer not to limit, but to increase its production.

The question is more difficult to answer with regard to commodities that obey the law of increasing than those that obey the law of diminishing return. With regard to the latter, the producer whose normal marginal expenses of production are just equal to the normal demand price in the market, would generally have no inducement to raise additional produce, even though he could market it on the same terms as the rest. But in the case of a commodity that obeys the law of increasing return, the point at which the producer should stop is not so clearly marked out. It may seem at first sight that by doubling his production, he will increase very much his internal economies, and, marketing his output on nearly the same terms as before, he will more than double his profits. It may be argued that so long as this course is open to him, his production can never be in equilibrium.

---

[1] These difficulties lie rather below the surface and are often concealed in popular discussions of the equilibrium conditions of trade; but they have made themselves felt with great force in the attempts made, from the time of Cournot and von Thünen downwards, to express those conditions by mathematical formulae. Some, among whom Cournot himself is to be counted, have before them what is in effect the supply schedule of an individual firm, representing that an increase in its output gives it command over so great internal economies as much to diminish its expenses of production; and they follow their mathematics boldly, but apparently without noticing that it leads inevitably to the ultimate monopoly of the whole business of its trade in its district by whatever firm first got a good start. While others avoiding this horn of the dilemma maintain that there is no true equilibrium at all for commodities which obey the law of increasing return; and some would appear even to have called in question the validity of any supply schedule which represents prices diminishing as the amount produced increases.

Now it must be admitted fully that in a trade in which there are large internal economies of production still available, an individual firm is seldom in a position of true equilibrium. For a new man working his way with small capital and small trade connection, in a trade in which the economies of production on a large scale tell powerfully on the side of large firms, would probably be able to continue for a time to increase his normal output, to lower his normal expenses per unit, and the price at which he is able to sell. If, as his business increased, his faculties adapted themselves to his larger sphere, as they had done to his smaller; if he retained his originality, and versatility and power of initiation, his perseverance, his tact and his good luck for a hundred years together; he might have absorbed into his own hands the whole volume of production in his branch of trade for his district: and if his goods were not very difficult of transport, he might have extended this district very wide. During all this time there would have been no equilibrium, but only movement; and at the end his price would not be a normal expenses of production price, but that of a limited monopoly; that is, of a monopoly limited by the consideration that a very high price would bring rival producers into the field.

But all that this shows is, that we must be careful not to regard the conditions of supply by an individual producer as typical of those which govern the general supply in a market, without taking account of the fact that very few firms have a long-continued life of active progress; and that while some are growing, others are sure to be decaying, like the older trees of the forest; so that their normal productive power remains nearly constant, though the yield of each one of them is generally either on the rise or on the decline. This argument has been dwelt on so long in this and the preceding Book, that we may take its broad outlines for granted, and consider an objection to applying it to the particular question before us.

The objection is that the decay of human energies is after all a slow process, and that, if a large output would cost much less in proportion than a small one, an able and energetic

It must be admitted that individual businesses whose products obey the law of increasing return are seldom in a state of equilibrium;

but their movements tend to compensate one another,

man could often find the means of increasing his output tenfold or more within a period very short in comparison with the length of his own life. This also must be admitted. It is true that a man who is prospering can often borrow capital so fast and therefore can increase his material appliances so fast, that the expansion of his business might be very rapid, if he could both market his new output easily, and at the same time obtain very important internal economies by every increase of his output. It must be admitted further that there are a few industries, in which these two conditions do coexist; and that such industries are, for that very reason, in so transitional a state that for the time there is nothing to be gained by trying to apply the statical theory of equilibrium of normal demand and supply to them. They must be thought of as in motion, rather than at rest. But, on the other hand, these industries are very few in number. For, though there are many industries in which an individual producer could secure much increased internal economies by a great increase of his output; and there are many in which he could market that output easily; yet there are few in which he could do both. And this is not an accidental but almost a necessary result.

There are not very many industries obeying the law of increasing return in which a producer has equally good access to the whole of a large market. No doubt he may in the case of goods which can be *graded*[1], and which can be sold in a public market. But, most goods that can be graded are raw produce; and of the rest nearly all are simple commodities such as steel rails or calico, the production of which can be reduced to routine, for the same reasons that enable them to be graded. In the industries which produce them no firm can hold its own at all unless equipped with expensive appliances of nearly the latest type; and there remains no very great difference between the economies available by a large and by a very large firm[2]. In these industries,

save in certain exceptional industries.

For in general each producer's market is more or less limited as regards most commodities except those for which the Law of Increasing Return has spent most of its force if it ever had any.

---

[1] See Book V, ch. II.   [2] See above, p. [b]340.

b.   This refers to Book IV, ch. XI, §2, page 281 in vol. I of the present edition.

in short, the tendency of large firms to drive out small ones has already gone so far as to exhaust most of the strength of those forces by which it was originally promoted.

And even in these industries, to produce for an open market, means generally to produce for sale to middlemen who will sell to others: those producers, who can miss out one in the link of middlemen, will often gain by so doing a good deal more than the additional economies to be got by increasing an already large and well found stock of machinery; and when this is so, a large part of the value of any business will consist of its particular trade connections and external organization, in spite of the fact that the commodities which it produces resemble those made by many other firms.

But the majority of commodities with regard to which the law of increasing return acts strongly are, more or less, specialities: many of them aim at creating a new want, or at meeting an old want in a new way. Many of them are adapted to special tastes; some can never have a very large market; and some have merits that are not easily tested, and must win their way to general favour slowly. In all such cases the sales of each business are limited, more or less according to circumstances, to the particular market which it has slowly acquired. There are firms whose business connections have been built up by a gradual investment of capital, and are worth nearly as much as, or possibly even more than, the whole of their material capital. When a business is thus confined more or less to its own particular market, a hasty increase in its production is likely to lower the demand price in that market out of all proportion to the increased internal economies that it will gain, even though its production is but small relatively to the broad market for which in a more general sense it may be said to produce[1]. So generally is this recognized that, when trade is slack, a producer will often try to sell his surplus goods outside of his own particu-

An individual producer can seldom extend his special market quickly.

---

[1] This may be expressed by saying that when we are considering an individual producer, we must couple his supply curve—not with the general demand curve for his commodity in a wide market—but with the particular demand curve of his own special market. And this particular demand curve will generally be very steep, steeper than his own supply curve is likely to be even when an increased output will give him an important increase of internal economies. The whole of this argument lends itself easily to expression in mathematical language.

lar market at prices that do little more than cover their prime costs; while within that market he still tries to sell at prices that nearly cover supplementary costs, a great part of which are the returns expected on capital invested in building up the external organization of his business.

The general conditions of equilibrium for short periods are similar for commodities that obey the laws of increasing and diminishing return;

To conclude then, the supplementary costs are generally, though not always, large relatively to prime costs for commodities that obey the law of increasing return; because their production needs the investment of a large capital in material appliances and in building up trade connections. Each firm has often to acquire a market of its own, partly because of the difficulties of grading; and when this is the case, it seldom sells much at short notice outside this market except at less than total cost price. This does not alter the character, but does increase the intensity of those fears of spoiling his own peculiar market, or incurring odium from other producers for spoiling the common market, which we have already learnt to regard as controlling the short period supply price of goods when the appliances of production are not fully employed[1].

But when they are fully employed, a temporary increase in demand is likely to raise the short-period supply price quite as much for commodities that obey the law of increasing return as for others. For the very fact that their production generally requires much specialized skill and specialized machinery will make a quick increase in the output possible only by working much overtime under great disadvantages; and perhaps calling into use some imperfect skill and some old-fashioned machinery. And therefore the supply schedule for short periods must generally show a price increasing and not diminishing with an increase in the amount produced. There are exceptions to this rule; but their conditions are so peculiar, that each must be treated by itself; there is

---

[1] See pp. 424, 5. It may be noted that the net loss of an omnibus, that is not full and loses a fourpenny fare, is nearer fourpence than threepence, though the omnibus trade conforms perhaps to the law of constant return; and if it were not for the fear of spoiling his market, the Regent Street shoemaker, whose goods are made by hand, but whose expenses of marketing are very heavy, would be tempted to go further below his normal price in order to avoid losing a special order, than a shoe manufacturer who uses much expensive machinery and avails himself generally of the economies of production on a large scale.

nothing to be gained by forcibly moulding our general supply schedules, so as to fit their special conditions.

§3.   It is then only as regards the long-period normal supply price that the true nature of the law of increasing return is shown. If there is a prospect of a permanent large demand for a thing, it will be worth while to invest capital in building up the material appliances, and the external and internal organization of large businesses, which will be able to sell profitably at a low price. The long-period supply price for large amounts will be low, because it is in effect the supply price not of particular things, but of the whole processes of production of those things. The law of increasing return is in truth a law that the supply price of the *processes of production* (and marketing) of large quantities of certain goods falls, when the scale of these processes increases.

but for long periods the conditions are wholly different.

The long-period supply price is really the price of a process.

BOOK V, CHAPTER XIII

THEORY OF CHANGES OF NORMAL DEMAND AND SUPPLY IN RELATION TO THE DOCTRINE OF MAXIMUM SATISFACTION

PAGE 462

a.   Except where otherwise stated the wording of this chapter dates substantially from the 1st edition.

b.   So since the 2nd edition (Book V, ch. XII). In the 1st edition (Book V, ch. VII) this chapter was entitled "Theory of Changes in Normal Demand and Supply, with some of its Bearings on the Doctrine of Maximum Satisfaction".

c.   This sentence was inserted in the 4th ed. (p. 523).

d.   In the 1st ed. this sentence, with only minor verbal changes, was placed in Book V, ch. v, §2, p. 422, where it was succeeded by the following sentence, which was deleted from the 4th ed.:

But so long as there is no substantive change in the conditions of demand or supply; so long as the only important changes in the price at which purchases can be found for the commodity, and the price at which producers can afford to supply it, are those changes which are due to an increase or diminution in the volume of the amount of the commodity produced and sold; so long we may regard the demand schedule and the supply schedule as representing the broad outlines of normal demand and normal supply.

In the 2nd ed. (pp. 496–7) and the 3rd ed. (pp. 516–17) these two sentences (in reverse order) constituted the concluding paragraph of Book V, ch. XI.

In the 1st ed. (p. 441) the opening paragraph of Book V, ch. VII, § 1 (deleted from the 2nd ed.) ran as follows:

WE have watched the oscillations of the price of a commodity about its normal position of equilibrium: we have next to examine the movements of that position of equilibrium itself. The price fluctuates up and down like a cork on the surface of the water in a reservoir. So long as the normal conditions of demand and supply remain unchanged, the equilibrium position about which the price oscillates will be stationary, just as the mean level about which the cork oscillates with every passing wave will remain stationary so long as there is no change in the normal condition of the great body of water. But the mean level of the water changes from time to time, rising after a heavy rain and falling during a long drought; and in consequence the centre about which the cork oscillates moves gradually up or down. So the normal position of equilibrium about which the price oscillates may move gradually up and down, in consequence of a change in the general conditions of demand or in the general conditions of supply.

e. This sentence dates from the 2nd ed. (p. 497).

f. The word "generally" inserted between the word "involves" and the words "an increase" in the 1st ed. (p. 441) was deleted from the 4th ed.

PAGE 463

a. The following footnote attached to the end of this sentence in the 1st ed. (pp. 442 n.–3 n.) was deleted from the 5th ed.:

The theory of the incidence of taxation has been generally treated as a branch of the application of economic science to the practical Art of Government. But really it is an integral part of the general theory of value; and there is a gain of scientific completeness in regarding in the first instance a tax on a thing simply as one of many causes which may raise its normal supply price. It will be best not to trace in detail the incidence of particular taxes until we come to discuss taxation as a whole: but meanwhile a tax may be taken as a representative instance of the changes which may affect supply price.

b. The following paragraph in the 1st ed. (p. 443), which succeeded the paragraph ending with the words "imposition of a tax" was deleted from the 4th ed.:

The typical case of rapid oscillation is that of the current or market price about its normal (or rather its sub-normal) position of equilibrium. But, as has already been explained, the sub-normal (or short-period normal) level moves in a similar manner, though more slowly or less conspicuously about a long period normal level. The longer the periods for which our normal demand and supply schedules are taken the fewer will be the disturbing causes which are so great, and which last so long, as to amount to a distinct change in the general conditions of demand and supply, and to necessitate the making out of a new demand schedule or a new supply schedule, or both. And therefore in the great majority of cases to which the reasonings of this chapter are applicable, the supply schedule will show a supply price increasing with the amount produced. But the exceptions to this rule, though not numerous, are very important.

The only change made in this paragraph in the 2nd ed. (p. 499) and the 3rd ed. (p. 519) was the deletion of the word "very" before the word "important" in the last sentence of the paragraph.

c. In two letters to F. Y. Edgeworth, dated 26 April and 28 April 1892, Marshall expressed some views, *inter alia*, on ideas put forward by H. Cunynghame in the "privately printed" paper referred to in this footnote. For these letters see the Editorial Appendix to Appendix H (pp. 808–13 below).

d. The reference in parentheses dates from the 5th ed. (p. 463 n.). In the 1st ed. (p. 442 n.) the reference ran as follows: "Compare the end of the note on page 429." In the 2nd to the 4th editions the reference continued to be to "the end of the note" on the corresponding pages in those editions—2nd ed. pp. 483 n.–4 n.; 3rd ed., pp. 503 n.–4 n.; 4th ed., pp. 521 n.–2 n. The footnote in question, which was altered in the 2nd ed., but remained substantially the same thereafter, will be found in Appendix H, §4 (pages 810 n.–12 n.) in vol. 1 of the present edition.

PAGE 464

a. This paragraph was inserted in the 5th ed. (pp. 464–5).

b. In the 1st ed. (p. 444 n.) there were the following additional paragraphs and diagram to this footnote which were deleted from the 5th ed.:

[It is interesting to trace the effect of changes of this kind when the curves cut one another several times, as in A, B and C in fig. (29). Suppose the demand curve to rise gradually, then the points of intersection corresponding to A and B will approach one another, until they coalesce. Thus whether price when in equilibrium was actually at A or at C originally (it could not have been at B, because the equilibrium there is unstable) it will by a sufficient rise of demand move away to c.

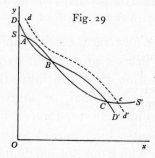

Fig. 29

If the supply curve to the right of A had kept above the original demand curve but only a little above it, so as to have only one point of intersection with it, its point of intersection with the new, and slightly raised demand curve might have been a long way to the right of A; thus representing a simpler instance of the way in which a small increase in the normal demand for a commodity that obeys the law of increasing return may cause a very great fall in its price and a very great increase of its consumption.]

It may be noted that in the 1st to the 4th editions Figs. 24–6 in vol. 1 of the present edition were numbered 26–8. The change in numbering took place in the 5th ed. owing to the transfer of certain diagrams from the text to Appendices.

PAGE 466

a. In connexion with the point to which attention is drawn in this paragraph see the diagram reproduced in editorial note **b** to page 464 of vol. 1 in the present edition.

b. This paragraph was inserted in the 6th ed. (pp. 466 n.–7 n.).

PAGE 467

a. With regard to the use of the term "consumers' surplus or rent" in this paragraph, it may be noted that this dates already from the 1st ed. (p. 446). Throughout the remainder of this chapter Marshall used the term "consumers' rent" in the first three editions, but changed it to "consumers' surplus" in the 4th ed. See also note **j** in the Editorial Appendix to Book V, chapters VIII–X (p. 486 above).

b. This clause was inserted in the 7th ed. (p. 467 n.).

PAGE 469

a. The following concluding clause of this sentence, dating from the 1st ed. (pp. 448–9) was deleted from the 5th ed. "because it diminishes consumers' rent by much more than the total payments which it brings in."

b. This and the next sentence were inserted in the 5th ed. (p. 469), though the footnote attached to the word "exchequer" dates from the 1st ed.

c. This paragraph was inserted in the 5th ed. (p. 469 n.).

PAGE 470

a. So since the 7th ed. (p. 470). In the 1st to the 3rd editions this sentence stopped at the word "*satisfaction*", and was succeeded by the following sentence which concluded the paragraph: "That is a doctrine which needs to be interpreted carefully." This sentence was deleted from the 4th ed. (p. 531) where the end of the paragraph ran as follows:

Much will need to be said at a later stage on that important doctrine, in its more concrete applications. There is however one abstract and trenchant form of it, which has had much vogue, especially since the time of Bastiat's *Economic Harmonics*, and which falls within the narrow range of the theory under discussion here.

From the 4th to the 8th editions Bastiat's *Economic Harmonies* was misspelt *Economic Harmonics*. I have emended the text of vol. 1 in the present edition to give the correct version.

b. In the 8th edition "V. 1. 1", emended in vol. 1 of the present edition to give the correct reference.

PAGE 471

a. This footnote was inserted in the 7th ed. (p. 471 n.).

PAGE 473

a. The reference to Appendix H was inserted in the 5th ed. (p. 473 n.).

PAGE 474

a. The word "generally" was put in italics in the 3rd ed. (p. 530).

b. This paragraph dates from the 2nd ed. (p. 510 n.), and the reference in it to Appendix H, from the 5th ed. (p. 474 n.).

PAGE 476

a. This sentence dates from the 2nd ed. (p. 511 n.), except for the insertion in the 3rd ed. (p. 531 n.) of the word "independently". In the 1st ed. (p. 455 n.) this concluding sentence ran as follows: "And Mr Fleeming Jenkin applied the graphic method in a manner

533

somewhat similar to that adopted in the present Chapter." Among the papers left by Marshall after his death was a page torn out of the 3rd edition of the *Principles of Economics*. On this, the last page of the chapter dealing with the doctrine of Maximum Satisfaction (Book V, ch. xii, §6, p. 531 n. in the 3rd ed.), there is the following note in Marshall's handwriting at the end of the sentence in the footnote referring to the work of Fleeming Jenkin:

Fleeming Jenkin's curves are of a peculiar shape, unlike any with which I am acquainted except those which Rau appended to the earlier editions of his *Volkswirtschaftslehre*. Neither Rau nor Jenkin refer to any predecessor. I saw Rau's work before I saw Jenkin's paper in the Recess Studies published in 1870; but even before that I had learnt from Cournot and von Thünen. The substance of the curves in this chapter was given by me in lectures in or before 1870: the curves relating to monopolies belong to a considerably later stage of my work, and they were described to the Cambridge Philosophical Society in 1873. He however remained as ignorant of my work as I did of the paper he read before the Edinburgh Society for many years. At last he heard of my work and sent me a copy of his own.

BOOK V, CHAPTER XIV

THE THEORY OF MONOPOLIES

PAGE 477

a. Except where otherwise noted the wording of this chapter dates substantially from the 1st edition.

b. The title of this chapter dates from the 1st edition.

c. So since the 4th ed. (p. 537) where the four opening words of this paragraph in the present text replaced the following words dating from the 1st ed. (p. 456): "At a later stage...."

PAGE 482

a. The first three sentences of this paragraph date from the 5th ed. (p. 482) where they replaced the following sentences dating from the 1st ed. (p. 461):

But a change in the total expenses of working a monoply, whether due to a tax, a bounty, or any other cause, is more likely than not to vary in the same direction as the amount of the commodity produced: and then it will affect the monopolist's action. A tax proportional to the amount produced causes a greater total loss of Monopoly Revenue when the amount produced is large than when it is small; and we shall find that it causes the sales which afford the maximum revenue to be somewhat smaller than before, and offers an inducement to the monopolist to raise his price and contract his sales.

b. The following concluding clause of this sentence in the 1st ed. (p. 461), where it was in the text, was deleted from the 7th ed.: "and conversely with regard to a fixed bounty or other fixed diminution of aggregate working expenses."

PAGE 485

a. This paragraph and the footnote attached to it were inserted in the 4th ed. (pp. 545 n.–6 n.).

PAGE 486

a. This sentence was inserted in the 7th ed. (p. 486).

b. Here, and throughout the remainder of this chapter Marshall used the term "consumers' rent" in the first three editions, but changed it to "consumers' surplus" in the 4th ed.

PAGE 493

a. In the 1st ed. (p. 472) the concluding words of this paragraph ran as follows: "...that investigation of the causes which determine distribution and exchange on which we are to enter as soon as we have carried a little further our analysis of cost of production." In the 2nd ed. (p. 527) this was altered to read: "...that investigation of the causes which determine distribution and exchange on which we are about to enter." In the 5th ed. (p. 493) the words "and exchange" after the word "distribution" were deleted.

b. This section (§9) was inserted in the 5th ed. (pp. 493–5).

c. In a letter to Edgeworth dated 28 August 1902 Marshall gave a more critical account of Cournot's theories with regard to monopoly. The relevant extract from this letter ran as follows:

Trusts. I am confirmed in my opinion that Cournot's method of treatment is wholly inapplicable to the real conditions of life. His discoveries were, I think—in so far as they claimed to have a bearing on real problems—rediscoveries of things that had been known in the XVII and better in the XVIII century as the result of the working of the chartered companies. In all the vast talk which I have put into writing on them I have seldom been tempted to refer to the abstract theory of monopolies, except of course in the general introduction. No instance could, I think, be better of the *mischievousness* of an academic education in *abstract* economics not continued into *real* economics (i.e. not continued for at least three years (Hm!)) than the inferences which Cournot's method suggests as to the relative efficiencies and inefficiencies, public usefulnesses and mischiefs of different forms of combination and monopoly. I have in view, e.g., what he says about a monopoly of brass versus a monopoly of zinc and a monopoly of copper (supposing zinc and copper useful only as constituents of brass). I have a notion that that is his illustration. The considerations of which he takes account seem to me to be of very slight importance relatively to those which he ignores: and the conclusion to which he points is, I believe, generally the opposite of the true one.

The text of the letter, of which this is an extract, will be found in *The Memorials of Alfred Marshall*, edited by A. C. Pigou, pp. 435–8.

PAGE 495

a. So since the 7th ed. (p. 495 n.) where this footnote replaced the following footnote dating from the 5th ed. (p. 495 n.):

This and some allied topics are discussed in the forthcoming study of *National Industries and Trade*, to which reference has already been made.

BOOK V, CHAPTER XV

SUMMARY OF THE GENERAL THEORY OF EQUILIBRIUM OF DEMAND AND SUPPLY

PAGE 496

a. The origin of the wording of this chapter is indicated throughout in the editorial notes.

In the 1st edition (Book V, ch. ix) the concluding chapter was short, while there was no summary chapter at the end of Book VI: but there was a summary of the theory of normal value in §§ 1 and 2 of Book VII, chapter xii, which was entitled General View of the Theory of Value, which will be found in the Editorial Appendix to Book V, chapter xv (pp. 545–9 below).

b. The title of this chapter dates from the 1st edition.

c. This paragraph dates from the 4th ed. (p. 554).

d. This paragraph dates substantially from the 2nd ed. (p. 528).

e. This and the next paragraph date substantially from the 1st ed. (p. 473).

PAGE 497

a. The following paragraph, which concluded the summary of Book V, chapters i and ii in the 1st ed. (p. 474) was deleted from the 2nd ed.:

These rapid fluctuations of market or current price, called for our attention chiefly in order that they might be clearly distinguished and set on one side as not bearing directly on the broad and fundamental relations of demand and supply which we were about to study. And yet it was important to notice that the incidents of market bargaining might exert a deep and lasting influence over the general course of economic development, if the advantages in bargaining were not equally divided in the long run between buyers and sellers. They are about equally divided in the chief markets for commodities; but in bargaining for the hire of some kinds of labour, the advantages are habitually on the side of the employer.

b. This sentence was inserted in the 4th ed. (p. 555). The following initial paragraph of the summary of Book V, chapters III and IV in the 1st ed. (p. 474) was deleted from the 2nd ed.:

In passing from these temporary equilibria to the stable equilibria of normal demand and normal supply we came upon a wholly different class of considerations: for here we found that the supply price was determined by cost of production. We analysed therefore cost of production so far as was absolutely necessary to show the general nature of its action, in conjunction with demand, in determining price. But we went no further, and a great part of the analysis of cost of production stands over for Book VI; while the task of investigating the distribution of wealth in its bearing on the normal supply prices of the various agents of production is left for Book VII.

It must be borne in mind that in the 1st edition Book V comprised chapters I–III, V–VI and XII–XV of Book V in vol. 1 of the present edition; while Book VI comprised chapters IV, VII and VIII–XII of Book V in vol. 1 of the present edition; in their original versions Book VII in the 1st edition became Book VI in the 2nd and subsequent editions.

c. This sentence dates substantially from the 1st ed. (p. 474).

d. So since the 4th ed. (p. 555). In the 1st ed. (p. 474) this sentence ran as follows: "Its uses are many and various, some being broad and some narrow; but there is one distinction which, though it has no sharp outlines, is yet fairly well marked." The first main clause of the sentence just quoted was deleted from the 2nd ed.

e. This sentence dates substantially from the 1st ed. (p. 475).

f. In the 1st ed. (p. 475) there was the following additional sentence at this point: "We saw how this true normal supply price may rise or fall with an increase in the amount produced, or may remain approximately stationary, according as the commodity obeys the law of diminishing, increasing or constant return." In the 2nd ed. (p. 529) the sentence just quoted was enlarged and ran as follows: "Whilst postponing to chapter XI the special difficulties connected with the normal supply price of commodities which obey the law of increasing return, we considered generally how this true normal supply price may rise or fall...etc." The whole sentence was deleted from the 3rd ed. In the 1st ed. (p. 475) the sentence ending with the words "the law of diminishing, increasing or constant return" was succeeded by the following paragraphs which were deleted from the 2nd ed.:

In this connection we called to mind the discussions at the end of Book IV of the difficulties which in practice prevent a single powerful firm from driving all rivals out of the field even in the production of a commodity which obeys the law of increasing return. But we concluded that an increase in the aggregate normal production of such a commodity would lower its marginal supply price to some extent, though of course not to as great an extent as if all the production were in the hands of one firm, which had abundant capital, ability and energy, and offered the commodity at the lowest price which they could afford.

Normal demand and supply are in equilibrium when the *equilibrium-amount* of the commodity is being produced; that is when the amount produced is such that its normal supply price is equal to its normal demand price; and this price is called the *equilibrium-price*. When the equilibrium is stable, the price oscillates about its equilibrium level, with more or less regularity: this level is however not necessarily fixed; it may be slowly rising or falling, or perhaps even itself oscillating.

g. This sentence dates substantially from the 2nd ed. (p. 529).

h. This sentence dates from the 1st ed. (p. 474) where it was succeeded by the following sentence which was deleted from the 2nd ed: "This supply price for such intermediate periods, the 'subnormal' supply price as we called it, is almost sure to rise with an increase of the commodity produced."

PAGE 498

a. The remainder of this paragraph dates from the 2nd ed. (p. 530).

b. The following sentences concluding this paragraph in the 2nd ed. (p. 530) were deleted from the 4th ed.:

No doubt this aggregate loss to the trade, may be compensated by a much greater aggregate gain to consumers as a body; and one of the most urgent economic problems of the present day is to inquire in what classes of cases it is desirable that a trade should continue to produce boldly with but little reference to the danger of spoiling the market. Some side lights are thrown on this question by the investigations of consumers' rent in the last two chapters of this Book; but a full study of it is deferred to a later stage.

c. The first two sentences of this paragraph date from the 2nd ed. (pp. 530–1) where they replaced the following sentences in the 1st ed. (p. 476):

We next turned our attention to the *joint demand* for commodities which are used in conjunction with others. The handle of a knife, for instance, which is of no use without its blade, must be regarded as having an indirect or *derived* demand price, which rises, other things being equal, with every increase in the demand for knives, and also with every decrease in the cost of production of blades.

d. This sentence and the next paragraph date substantially from the 1st ed. (p. 476).

a. This paragraph dates from the 2nd ed. (p. 531).
b. So since the 3rd ed. (p. 551).

In the 2nd ed. (p. 531) the second clause of this sentence ran as follows: "we investigated more fully the problem which had already been touched in earlier chapters, of the relation of rents and quasi-rents to cost of production; or in other words of the value of an appliance for production in relation to that of the things produced by it."

In the 2nd ed. (p. 531) the paragraph ended with the following sentence, which was deleted from the 3rd ed.: "It will be convenient to collect here into one view a summary of some parts of chapter v as well as chapters VIII, IX and X."

c. This paragraph dates substantially from the 2nd ed. (pp. 531–2).
d. In the 4th ed. (p. 557) the words "money income" replaced the word "rent" in the 2nd and 3rd eds.

In the 2nd ed. (p. 532) there were the following paragraphs which succeeded the paragraph ending with the words "he can generally get for its use a rent equivalent to this surplus":

Ricardo argued that rent does not enter into cost of production, having in view on the one hand the rent of farming land in general, and on the other the cost of production of agricultural produce in general: and in this connection the doctrine cannot easily be misunderstood. But when applied to the cost of production of one particular crop, though still literally true as it stands, experience shows that it is liable to be interpreted in senses in which it is not true. For if land which had been used for growing hops, is found capable of yielding a higher rent as market garden land, the area under hops will undoubtedly be diminished; and this will raise their marginal cost of production and therefore their price. The rent which land will yield for one kind of produce, though it does not directly enter into those expenses, yet does act as the channel through which a demand for the land for that kind of produce increases the difficulties of supply of other kinds; and thus does indirectly affect their expenses of production.

Ricardo's doctrine requires therefore to be carefully interpreted even with regard to farm rents; but, when so interpreted, it is applicable, though he does not appear to have been aware of the fact himself, to all other classes of rents. A mining royalty however is not a rent.

So important is Ricardo's doctrine as to the relation in which rent proper stands to value, that chapters VIII and IX were given up to considering it further, and extending it to the income yielded by appliances for production which man has made, and especially such of them as are durable, and the supply of which cannot be rapidly increased. It was argued that the part which that income plays in determining the value of the things, in making which the appliances are used, varies with the period of time under consideration.

In the 3rd ed. (pp. 551–2) the first of the three paragraphs just quoted from the 2nd ed. was retained without change, but the second and third paragraphs were reworded as follows:

A mining royalty is not a rent and enters into expenses of production. Ricardo's doctrine requires to be carefully interpreted even with regard to farm rents; but, when so interpreted, it is applicable to other classes of rents, and, subject to some further conditions, to the income yielded by appliances for production which man has made, and especially such of them as are durable, and the supply of which cannot be rapidly increased.

In the 4th ed. (pp. 557–8) the paragraph just quoted from the 3rd ed. was retained unchanged, but the first two sentences of the paragraph from the 2nd ed. were reworded as follows:

Ricardo argued that rent does not enter into cost of production, having in view on the one hand the rent of farming land in general, and on the other the cost of production of agricultural produce in general. He meant that rent is governed by the price of produce and does not govern it: and therefore if cost of production is so estimated as to include a charge for rent and is then treated as one of the causes which govern value, the reasoning is circular. The price of the produce is equal to the cost of production of that part of it, which is raised on the margin, that is under such unfavourable conditions as to yield no rent. The cost of this part can be reckoned up without reasoning in a circle; and the cost of other parts cannot.

Ricardo's phrase is awkwardly expressed; and is apt to be misunderstood even when applied to the price of agricultural produce as a whole. But it is especially confusing when applied to the price of a single crop. For if land which has been used for growing hops...etc.

All these paragraphs were deleted from the 5th ed.

For a fuller discussion of rent in relation to the price of a single crop, in the earlier editions, see the Editorial Appendix to Book V, chapters VIII–X, pp. 453–61.

e. This and the next paragraph were inserted in the 5th ed. (pp. 499–500).

PAGE 500

a. This paragraph dates from the 2nd ed. (p. 533).

b. In the 2nd ed. (pp. 522–3) there was the following additional clause, placed at the end of this sentence, which was deleted from the 4th ed.: "and the more nearly true will it be that, for the period under discussion, the net income to be derived from them is to be regarded as a producer's surplus or quasi-rent."

In the 2nd ed. (pp. 533–4) there were the following additional paragraphs after the sentence just quoted from the 2nd ed.:

In passing from the free gifts of nature through the more permanent improvements in the soil, to less permanent improvements, to farm and factory buildings, to steam-engines, &c., and finally to the less durable and less slowly made implements, we find a continuous series. And even that part of the rental value of land which is derived from advantages of situation—situation rent as it may be called—passes by imperceptible gradations from the character of a pure rent, in cases in which the owners of the land have had no direct part in improving its environment, to that of a quasi-rent or even profits when the conditions of the environment, to which the land owes its situation value, were deliberately brought about by, and at the expense of, the owners of that land in order to raise its value. Thus the situation rent of land presents close analogies to many different classes of income derived from advantages of the environment, from opportunity, or *Konjunktur*. Later on we shall find that many of the most interesting applications of the principle which we have just discussed are to human agents of production; but in the present Book we confine our attention to the material agents of production.

In the course of this inquiry we noted that the supply of factors of production, or goods of the *second order*, is governed by estimates that reach forward over a longer time, and are therefore more liable to error than those which govern the immediate adaptation of supply to demand with regard to goods of the *first order*. But further, the supply of these goods of the *second order* depends partly on the supply of appliances for making them, that is, of things removed by two *orders* from the commodity with which we started: and the adjustment of the supply of these goods of the *third order* to the indirect demand for them, which is derived ultimately from the demand for the finished commodity, is a still more difficult process; it ranges over a still longer period of time, and is still more liable to error: and so on, backwards, without limit.

Both of these paragraphs were deleted from the 4th ed.

c. The text of this section (§4) dates substantially from the 2nd ed. (pp. 535–6).
d. In the 2nd ed. (pp. 534–5) there was the following opening paragraph of this section, which was deleted from the 4th ed.:

In chapter xi, it is argued that the terms "aggregate" and "average" cost of production can have no precise meaning in a world of rapid change such as that in which we live; since the quasi-rents of the appliances of production, both material and personal, are governed for short periods more by the value of the things they produce, than by their own cost of production. For instance machinery of a pattern on which improvements have been made, has its value determined by capitalizing the quasi-rents it can earn; and to count profits on this value as part of the aggregate expenses of production of the commodities it produces, is to reason in a circle. In a rigidly stationary state however in which supply could be perfectly adjusted to demand in every particular, the normal expenses of production, the marginal expenses, and the average expenses (rent being counted in) would be one and the same thing. This point is dwelt on in order to show more clearly what the normal supply schedule does mean and what it does not mean.

PAGE 502

a. In the 2nd ed. (p. 536) there were the following additional sentence and paragraph at the end of this section:

This supply price falls generally with an increase in the amount normally produced; if it falls more rapidly than the demand price in the neighbourhood of the position of equilibrium, the equilibrium is *unstable*, in the opposite case it is stable.

Under certain possible, though rather improbable, conditions there may be two or more positions of equilibrium alternately stable and unstable. But this portion of the theory, though necessary for logical completeness, rests on rigid and artificial assumptions, and has but little practical importance.

The sentence beginning "This supply price falls generally...etc." was deleted from the 3rd ed. and the concluding paragraph (which itself dates from the 1st ed. (pp. 475–6)) was deleted from the 4th ed. where it was replaced by the following paragraph (p. 560): "Under certain improbable conditions there may be two or more conditions of equilibrium alternately stable and unstable." This paragraph was deleted from the 5th ed.

b. The first sentence of this paragraph was inserted in the 3rd ed. (p. 556) where it replaced the following sentences dating from the 1st ed. (pp. 476–7):

We then turned to consider the effects of changes in the general conditions of demand and supply; changes which are due to some new event such as a substantive invention, or the imposition of a tax, or indeed any changes which for any reason we find it best to regard as lying outside, and altering the normal conditions of demand or supply.

After examining their immediate effects on normal value, we proceeded to inquire provisionally, and so far as might be done by reasoning of a general character, how the public well-being would be affected by such changes. And we concluded that, when proper allowance is made for the interests of consumers, in the form of consumers' surplus or rent, there is less *prima facie* cause than the earlier economists supposed, for the general doctrine, that the free pursuit by each individual of his own immediate interest, will lead producers to turn their capital and labour, and consumers to turn their expenditure into such courses as are most conducive to the general interests; or in other words that the free play of demand and supply in an open market leads to the production of just that amount of each commodity and its sale at just that price which affords the Maximum Satisfaction to the community as a whole.

c. The remainder of this paragraph and the next paragraph date substantially from the 1st ed. (pp. 477–8).

PAGE 503

a. This paragraph was inserted here in the 5th ed. (p. 503). In the 2nd to the 4th editions the first two sentences formed the opening sentences of a "Note on Ricardo's Theory of Value" which was placed at the end of this chapter, and which in the 5th ed. became Appendix I.

EDITORIAL APPENDIX TO BOOK V, CHAPTER XV

SUMMARY OF THE THEORY OF NORMAL VALUE

In the 1st edition, Book VII, chapter XII, §§ 1 and 2, Marshall gave a brief résumé of his theory of normal value, which was deleted from the 2nd edition. The sections in question in the 1st edition (pp. 698–701) ran as follows:

§ 1. WE may now collect together the chief threads of our long argument; and may begin on the more abstract side with an endeavour to bring into clear relief the fundamental scientific unity which underlies the whole theory of normal value.

Causes that determine price in markets too short to permit the direct influence of cost of production.

We have seen that many of the apparent differences between the modes of action of the causes that determine value depend on differences in the periods of time required for those forces to work out their full, or normal, or ultimate effects; and that they are not really differences in kind, but only differences in degree, passing into one another by continuous gradations. Thus the equilibrium price in a local fish-market is that at which there will be a demand for last night's catch; it is not appreciably affected by future supplies either from to-morrow's catch, or from other fishing ports. In a market for a durable commodity, such as cotton or wheat, market prices are much influenced by estimates of "futures," that is of stocks expected shortly to arrive, and even crops not yet reaped. But buyers cannot afford to wait for crops not yet sown; and therefore cost of production has no *direct* influence on the market.

That influence beginning to operate.

But it has a direct influence at the next stage when we come to the market price of such a thing as cloth of a particular pattern. For if its price rises even a little relatively to other kinds made of similar material and in the same factories, its supply will be much increased quickly; and therefore its price is directly governed by current (money) cost of production. We say "current" cost because estimates of it take for granted the current price of raw material, the current wages of textile operatives, and so on.

Its scope extending further

Thus the transition from oscillations of price in a fish market to those in a cloth market is similar to the transition from weekly oscillations of price in the latter about its short-period position of equilibrium. And these again resemble the oscillations of this equilibrium position itself about a true (or long-period) normal level. This true normal level must be estimated with regard to periods long enough to allow a change in the habits of dress of the people to work out its chief effects in causing Australian sheep farmers to extend their sheep runs, in causing English capitalists to build new cloth factories, and new factories for making cloth-making machinery, and in causing labour of all grades, from that of the highest business management down to the lowest class required in the production of cloth, to drift towards that trade, and to bring up their children to it.

And these oscillations again resemble those secular oscil- and still further. lations of wages about the customary standard of living, which there is reason for thinking have frequently occurred in the histories of stationary civilizations[1].

§ 2. To look at the same set of facts from another point Another grouping of the same facts. of view:—neither the price at which a thing can be sold, nor the income which can be earned by using it in the production of other things, is directly affected by its own cost of production. For, as Mill said, "Cost of production could have no effect on value, if it could have none on supply."

Thus the price which a sack of wheat already in Liverpool fetches there, is not determined directly by its cost of production, but tends to that equilibrium level at which the amount demanded will be equal to the sum of existing stocks together with those additional stocks which at that price will be brought from elsewhere. The actual price of a building is determined, not by its cost of production, but by the relations between demand on the one side, and on the other the existing stock of such buildings together with the new supplies that current expectations of price are likely to bring shortly into existence. The demand price for it is the capitalized value of all the net incomes that are expected to accrue from its possession.

We have described the income derived from a building or from invested capital in any form, whether material or personal, as a producer's surplus or Quasi-rent: because we have seen that there is a continuous gradation from the income afforded by existing looms, and other machinery,

[1a] In connection with this section compare Book V, ch. II, III, IV and IX, and especially ch. IV, §6: also Book VII, ch. II, §1.

---

a. Book V, chs. II, III, V and XV, "and especially" ch. V, §4: also Book VI, ch. I, §2, in vol. I of the present edition.

The term
quasi-rent
is a symbol
of the
continuous
gradation
from the
income
afforded by
the use of
perishable
implements
to the rent
of the
"inherent"
properties
of land.

through that afforded by factories and by permanent improvements in land, to the rent yielded by the "inherent" and "indestructible" properties of the land. We have seen that this rent itself cannot be distinguished from profits in the case of a new country, where the title-deeds of rich land are waiting to be earned by any one who chooses to settle on it and bring it under cultivation. We have seen that the incomes derived from appliances for production of any kind, are watched by those who are doubting whether to provide similar appliances; and they enter among the causes extending over a long period of time, by which the true normal value of the commodity made by these appliances is determined: for a rise or fall of these incomes above or below the rewards that can be got by investing capital and labour in other ways, increases or diminishes the supply of these appliances and therefore of the goods produced by them: and for the purposes of the theory of normal value they are therefore to be regarded as profits, entering into the money cost of production of the commodities in question.

But so far as current variations in the supply—and therefore the price—of the commodity are concerned, variations in the income derived from these appliances exercise no appreciable effect: and on the other hand variations in the price of the commodity do determine the surplus, which the producers in possession of these appliances receive over and above the fresh outlay of capital and effort required for producing the commodities by the aid of these appliances. And even when we are considering variations in the price of a commodity that range over too long a time to be called "current variations" we find that the shorter that period is, and the slower the process of production of the requisite appliances, the less influence will variations in that income exert on the supply of that commodity, and therefore on its price: and the more closely will the income approach to the nature of a rent which is determined by that price, and does not take a direct part in determining it. This argument applies equally to material appliances for production, such as factories and looms; and to immaterial capital such as business organizations, business connections, and business skill and ability; and if we interpret the term income broadly, the argument applies also to the benefits derived from the direct usance of wealth whether material or immaterial[1].

[1] The main argument of this section is given in Book [b]VI, chs. II and III. The close correspondence of the causes that determine the investment of capital and effort in business plant and in business organization was brought out in Book [c]VI, ch. V; and in the following chapter [d]a similar correspondence was found between supplementary charges which have to be added to the prime cost of a commodity on account of material plant on the one hand and business organization and connection on the other. In Book IV, ch. III and Book [e]VI, ch. II attention was called to the fact that the income derived by taking minerals from nature's storehouses is not a rent: and that therefore the doctrine that "rent does not enter into cost of production" does not apply to mining royalties. But it does apply to the income derived from building ground, and even from fisheries, hunting grounds and woods, provided man does not take away their produce faster than nature replaces it. On the relations between material and immaterial wealth, capital and income, and between money income and that real income which includes the usance of wealth, see Book [f]II, chs. II, V and VI.

---

b. In vol. I of the present edition, Book V, chs. VIII–X.
c. In vol. I of the present edition, Book V, ch. IV.
d. In vol. I of the present edition, Book V, ch. VI.
e. In vol. I of the present edition, Book V, ch. X.
f. In vol. I of the present edition, Book II, chs. II and IV.

BOOK VI

THE DISTRIBUTION OF THE NATIONAL INCOME

CHAPTER I

PRELIMINARY SURVEY OF DISTRIBUTION

PAGE 504

a. In the 1st edition, where the treatment of demand, supply and cost of production, in the determination of value, was divided between Book V and Book VI, the treatment of distribution was placed in Book VII.

After the amalgamation, in the 2nd edition, of the original Books V and VI to form the single Book V, the Book dealing with distribution was renumbered Book VI.

b. The title of this Book dates from the 5th edition, where it replaced the following title dating from the 1st edition: "Value or Distribution and Exchange."

c. The origin of the wording of this chapter is indicated throughout in the editorial notes.

In the 1st edition, the Preliminary Survey of Distribution and Exchange, which in the 2nd and subsequent editions was contained in the first two chapters of Book VI, was spread over the first three chapters of Book VII. A good deal of the subject matter of these chapters was subsequently transferred elsewhere. Apart from §§ 1 and 2 very little of this chapter dates from the 1st edition.

In the 2nd edition (Book VI, ch. 1) the first section was substantially as in the present edition, but most of the remainder of chapter 1 was subsequently either deleted or transferred elsewhere.

It is from the 3rd edition that the bulk of the subject matter of this chapter, in the present edition dates; though considerable changes and additions were made in the later editions.

d. So since the 5th edition (p. 504). In the first four editions the title of chapter 1 ran as follows: "Preliminary Survey of Distribution and Exchange."

e. This paragraph dates from the 4th ed. (pp. 571–2).

a. This paragraph, except for the last clause of the second sentence, dates from the 4th ed. (p. 572).

b. This clause was inserted in the 5th ed. (p. 505), from which the following concluding sentences of this paragraph in the 4th ed. (p. 572) were deleted:

We shall see that, though the methods of "capitalistic" employment do largely affect the character of modern industry and the distribution of wealth; yet many of the most striking features of the modern problem would be found in a world in which everyone owned the implements, raw material, etc., which he used; provided only each class of work required specialized skill. This will lead to a closer study of the "net product" to be ascribed to each man's labour when several different kinds of labour are needed to aid one another in producing a commodity.

c. This paragraph dates substantially from the 4th ed. (p. 572). The following clauses in that edition were deleted from the 5th ed.: "We shall make a preliminary study of the way in which the cost of rearing and training any class of labour affects the supply of it: how the magnitude of the supply affects the demand which others offer for this kind of work;" In the 4th ed. the sentence beginning "We shall make a preliminary study...etc." continued as follows: "and finally how are fixed the broad lines of distribution of the national income...etc."

d. With the exception of the final paragraph, §2 of this chapter dates substantially from the 1st ed. (Book VII, ch. II, §1, pp. 550–5).

e. So since the 4th ed. (p. 573) where this marginal summary replaced the following marginal summary dating from the 1st ed. (p. 550): "The Physiocrats assumed, in accordance with the peculiar circumstances of their time and country, that wages were at their lowest possible level."

f. In the 2nd ed. (p. 549) the word "Economists" replaced the word "Physiocrats" in the 1st ed. (p. 550).

g. So since the 2nd ed. (p. 549). In the 1st ed. (p. 550) the opening words of this sentence ran as follows: "So the Physiocrats assumed for the sake of simplicity...etc."

h. So since the 3rd ed. (p. 566 n.) where this footnote replaced the following footnote dating from the 1st ed. (p. 550 n.):

¹ Comp. Turgot, *Sur la Formation et Distribution des Richesses*, §VI. "In every sort of occupation it must come to pass, and in fact it does come to pass, that the wages of the artisan are limited to that which is necessary to procure him a subsistence....He gains nothing but his life (Il ne gagne que sa vie)."

Marshall was accustomed in conversation to give as an instance of the high quality of the proof readers of the Cambridge University Press the fact that it was one of them who pointed out to him, when he was bringing out his 3rd edition of *The Principles*, that the correct rendering in English of "Il ne gagne que sa vie" is not "He gains nothing but his life", but "He earns no more than his living".

PAGE 506

a. The following footnote attached to the word "luxury" dating from the 1st ed. (p. 551 n.) was deleted from the 3rd ed.:

> Turgot, *ib.* §LXXX. His position was, however, not altogether consistent, as is well shown by Prof. Böhm-Bawerk, *Kapitalzinstheorien*, Vol. I, ch. IV.

PAGE 508

a. The words "Turgot and" were inserted before the word "Physiocrats" in the 4th ed. (p. 575).

b. This and the following sentence were inserted in the 7th ed. (p. 508 n.).

c. So since the 3rd ed. (p. 569 n.) where this footnote replaced the following clauses which, in the first two editions, came at the end of the sentence in the text beginning "This law has been called, especially in Germany,...etc.":

While many German economists, who are not socialists, and who protest that no such law exists, yet maintain that the doctrines of Ricardo and his followers stand or fall with the truth of this law.

PAGE 509

a. This and the next sentence date from the 5th ed. (p. 509 n.). I have emended the original reference to "v. XIV. 5." at the end of the first sentence, so as to make it correct.

b. The remainder of this footnote (except for the reference to Appendix I) dates from the 3rd ed. (p. 570 n.), where it replaced the following footnote dating from 1st ed. (p. 554 n.):

> This habit of Ricardo's has already been discussed in the Note at the end of the last chapter. Prof. Brentano, in his inaugural address at Vienna, gives as a reason for believing that the English classical economists really held the iron law of wages, the fact that they frequently speak of the minimum of wages as depending on the price of corn. But the term "corn", as used by them, was short for "agricultural food products of all kinds." It thus included the product of pasture no less than of arable land; it included meat and milk, fruit and vegetables, just as much as wheat and barley.

c. A reference in the 3rd ed. (p. 570 n.) to the article in which Professor Ashley expressed his views ("Rehabilitation of Ricardo", *Economic Journal*, vol. I) was deleted from the 5th ed.

d. This reference was inserted in the 5th ed. (p. 509 n.).

a. This paragraph dates from the 4th ed. (p. 578), where it replaced the following sentence in the 3rd ed. (p. 571):

Since Mill's time much progress has been made. More careful analysis has shown that no simple solution of the problem of distribution can be valid; and that attempts to make a short cut to the solution must necessarily cause confusion, if they are put forward as anything more than illustrations based on fancied hypotheses, and designed to throw light not on the problem as a whole, but on some particular difficulty in it.

The sentence just quoted from the 3rd ed. had itself replaced the following paragraph in the 2nd ed. (pp. 553–4):

The new views thus obtained during the present generation of the causes that govern the supply of efficient labour, have not attracted much notice, but are really very important and far reaching. But, on the other hand, the new views on the causes that govern the demand for labour, though they have justly claimed and received a great deal of attention, have not really led to any great substantial change in the theory of distribution. They have however given clearness and scientific coherence to the broad outlines of this theory; which by itself is a very real gain, even for practical purposes: and they have filled in important details.

b. The wording of this section (§ 3) dates substantially from the 3rd ed. (pp. 572–3). For the earlier form, in the first two editions, of the illustrations developed in this and subsequent sections, see the Editorial Appendix to Book VI, chapters I and II, pp. 576–91.

c. The following introductory paragraph in the 3rd ed. (pp. 571–2) was deleted from the 4th ed.:

There is a sense in which the agents of production may be regarded as two, nature and man. In return to the labour of men, nature yields resources varying with the diligence and with the advance made by the arts of production; and these resources are divided out among mankind in a manner that is very complex when the problem is obscured by difference in industrial rank and ability, by subdivision into trades, and above all by the ownership of private capital.

PAGE 511

a.   So since the 5th ed. (p. 511). In the 3rd ed. (p. 572) and the 4th ed. (p. 579) the concluding part of this paragraph ran as follows:

In other words, each will have an equal share in the net sum total of things and services produced; or, as we may say, the *National Dividend*. This will constitute the demand for labour; and might be called the common wages-fund, or earnings-fund; or better still earnings-stream, since a fund fails to suggest the constant flow of new goods into the world through supply, which flow out again through demand and consumption.

PAGE 512

a.   With the exception of one clause this section dates from the 3rd ed. (pp. 573–4).

b.   So since the 4th ed. (p. 580) where this clause replaced the following clause in the 3rd ed.: "and that the earnings of everyone vary with the demand for man's work offered by nature, in the then existing state of the arts of production."

c.   This paragraph dates in its present form from the 4th ed. (pp. 580–1). In the 3rd ed. (p. 574) there was the following opening paragraph in the corresponding section:

We have seen how, in some extreme doctrines as to population, it was supposed that the real cost of rearing a family was a fixed quantity; that, if earnings rose above this sum population increased rapidly, pressed against Nature's steady diminishing demand for man, and forced wages down. On this supposition the cost of rearing a family was the absolute governor of wages, subject only to slight disturbances, under an iron or brazen law. It will be of service to balance against this an equally extreme supposition, in which the cost of rearing and training workers exercises no influence on their numbers. This case is one step nearer to reality than the supposition that the numbers of the people are rigidly fixed.

a. In the 4th ed. (p. 580) this sentence replaced the following sentences in the 3rd ed. (p. 574):

Let us conceive then that the growth of population proceeds at a rate, which is either fixed, or governed wholly by other than economic causes. Thus it may be influenced by changes in custom, in moral opinion and in medical knowledge. But we are to suppose that the earnings of parents are always sufficient for the immediate needs of themselves and their children; that no change in their earnings affects either way birth-rate or death-rate; and, a more violent supposition still, that it does not affect either their own willingness to work, or the physical, mental, and moral strength of the rising generation.

b. The remainder of this paragraph dates from the 3rd ed. (p. 574).

c. This and the next paragraph date from the 5th ed. (p. 513) where they replaced the following paragraph and footnote, dating from the 3rd ed. (pp. 574–5):

But, on the other hand, if even a very slow rate of increase is maintained long enough, the growth of population must ultimately outgrow the improvements in the arts of production, and cause the tendency to diminishing return to assert itself; and the value of any kind of produce must equal that of the labour, aided on our supposition by a uniform quantity of capital throughout, which is required to produce it on the margin of cultivation. (The marginal application of labour may be on land that will barely repay any labour at all; or it may be that cultivation of fertile land which is only just remunerative.) The surplus which is returned by nature to the labour applied under advantageous circumstances, and which now generally goes to private persons under the name of rent, may conceivably be appropriated to public uses: or conceivably everyone may have an equal share of land; and in either case there will be a true surplus. But the problem of distribution and exchange will present the simple form of nature's offering for man's labour a demand, which, at all events after some considerable applications of labour have been made, will be at a diminishing rate. The aggregate produce is the national dividend, in which each gets an equal share; each standing to gain equally by any improvement in the arts of production whether in his own trade or any other[1].

[1] This illustrative case will perhaps help to bring out more clearly the parallelism between a man's demand for anything, and nature's demand for man's work; which are represented in outline by the laws of *diminishing utility*, and *diminishing return* respectively: see footnotes on pp. 168, 235.

The references in this footnote relate to pages 93 n. and 156 n. in vol. 1 of the present edition.

d. So since the 4th ed. (p. 581), where this sentence replaced the following sentence in the 3rd ed. (p. 575): "Next suppose that labour is not all of one industrial grade; but of several."

PAGE 514

a. The words "of the people themselves" were inserted after the word "demand" in the 4th ed. (p. 582).

b. This sentence dates from the 4th ed. (p. 582).

c. This sentence dates substantially from the 3rd ed. (p. 575).

d. In the 3rd ed. (p. 576) there was the following additional sentence and paragraph at this point:

Given the abundance of the national dividend, the earnings of artists will be governed simply by the demand for their efforts; under some conditions of demand these earnings might rise very high; under others they might fall very low.

It may so happen that the progress of invention is always finding new openings for one particular grade of labour, and making a little of its work go further relatively to other grades than before. It will then be paid at an ever increasing rate; and as, by hypothesis, this will exercise no influence on the number of people in the grade, their earnings will rise without ceasing. This however is likely to be held in check by the competition of some other grade of labour, which may be made available in substitution for it, the earnings of each being proportional to their (marginal) efficiency. But we must not pursue this further just now.

In the 4th ed. (p. 582) the last sentence in the paragraph just quoted was rewritten as follows:

But this line of inquiry raises incidentally many side issues, which cannot be profitably discussed except in close reference to the actual conditions of life. We shall need to carry it further later on, especially in connection with trade-union problems.

In the 6th ed. (p. 514) the sentence and paragraph just quoted was replaced by the following sentences:

Under some conditions of demand the earnings of artists might rise very high; under others they might fall very low. If, for instance, the progress of invention finds large new openings for any one grade of labour, it will be paid at an ever increasing rate.

Both these sentences were deleted from the 7th ed.

e. This paragraph dates substantially from the 3rd ed. (p. 576).

f. So since the 6th ed. (pp. 515–16), though the substance of this paragraph and footnote dates from the 5th ed. (pp. 515–16) where the footnote was placed in the text.

In the 3rd and 4th editions there was placed here a discussion of the principle of substitution, which was transferred in the 5th ed. to Book V, ch. VIII, §2.

PAGE 515

a. In the 4th ed. (p. 585 n.) there was the following footnote attached to the words "net product" (in a slightly different context) which was deleted from the 5th ed.:

> In V, especially VIII–X, the net product of a machine was spoken of as the "net earnings" which it wins for its owner. But we are now entering upon a study of distribution between persons; and we want the phrase "the net earnings" of a carpenter for his personal income: we are considering how competition tends to make his personal income equal to the net benefit which his labour earns for society or more directly for his employer: and we had better now describe that net benefit as the net product of his labour.

b. This paragraph was inserted in the 6th ed. (p. 515).

c. The first two sentences of this paragraph were inserted in the 6th ed. (p. 515). The remainder of this paragraph and the next paragraph with the footnote attached to it date in their present form from the 6th ed. (pp. 515–17 n.).

For the earlier version of the illustration of the marginal shepherd, see the Editorial Appendix to Book VI, chapters I and II, pp. 582–8 below.

d. This footnote was inserted in the 6th ed. (p. 515 n.).

PAGE 516

a.   This paragraph was inserted in the 7th ed. (p. 516).

b.   This paragraph and also the last paragraph in the footnote, referring to the table, were inserted in the 6th ed. (pp. 516 n.–17 n.). For earlier versions of the intervening paragraphs see the Editorial Appendix to Book VI, chapters I and II, pp. 585–6 below.

PAGE 517

a.   This paragraph dates in its present form from the 5th ed. (pp. 517–18).

PAGE 518

a.   This paragraph dates from the 3rd ed. (pp. 583–4).

b.   This paragraph dates in its present form from the 7th ed. (p. 518). For the earlier versions see the Editorial Appendix to Book VI, chapters I and II, pp. 587–8 below.

c.   This paragraph dates substantially from the 3rd ed. (p. 584).

d.   The first three paragraphs of this section date from the 3rd ed. (p. 585).

e.   This footnote dates in its present form from the 6th ed. (p. 518 n.), apart from the deletion from vol. I of the present edition of a reference to Book V, ch. XI, which was clearly out of place here. For the earlier version of this footnote see the Editorial Appendix to Book VI, chapters I and II, p. 583 below.

PAGE 519

a.   So since the 7th ed. (p. 519). From the 3rd to the 6th editions this ran as follows: "so as to add annually £3 worth...etc." Similarly, in the next sentence "4 per cent" was substituted in the 7th ed. for "3 per cent" in the earlier editions.

b.   In the 1st ed. (Book VII, ch. VII, §8, p. 625), after a discussion of the causes governing the supply of capital, there were the following sentences, which were deleted from the 3rd ed.:

Passing now from the causes which determine the supply of capital to those which determine the demand, we have to move with more caution because interest is but one element of profit: and the chief demand for capital is part of a joint demand for capital and business ability. But we may call to mind the broader aspects of the demand for capital, leaving for the following chapters its relations to the demand for business ability.

It may be noted that in the first two editions the broad theoretical considerations affecting the supply of and demand for capital were mainly placed in the later chapters dealing with Interest (Book VII, ch. vii in the 1st ed., and Book VI, ch. vi in the 2nd ed.). From the 3rd ed. onwards they were placed in Book VI, chs. i and ii.

c. This and the next two paragraphs date substantially from the 2nd ed. (pp. 619–20), where they were placed in Book VI, ch. vi, §2.

From the 2nd to the 6th editions the basic rate of interest adopted for this illustration was 3 per cent. This was changed in the 7th ed. (pp. 519–20) to 4 per cent.

PAGE 520

a. So since the 7th ed. (p. 520). From the 2nd to the 6th editions, where the basic rate (lowest) adopted was 3 per cent, this rate was 4 per cent.

b. This sentence dates from the 2nd ed. (p. 620).

c. This sentence dates substantially from the 1st ed. (Book VII, ch. vii, §8, p. 625).

d. This sentence was inserted in the 7th ed. (p. 520 n.).

e. This footnote was inserted in the 7th ed. (p. 520 n.).

PAGE 521

a. The remainder of this paragraph dates from the 2nd ed. (Book VI, ch. vi, §2, p. 621).

b. This paragraph dates from the 1st ed. (p. 625).

c. This and the next two paragraphs date from the 5th ed. (p. 522), where they replaced the following paragraph in the 4th ed. (p. 592):

To sum up the whole in a comprehensive if somewhat difficult statement:—The limits, or margins, of the applications of each agent of production, including land, are governed by the general conditions of demand in relation to supply: that is, on the one hand by the urgency of all the uses to which the agent can be put, taken together with the means at the command of those who need it; and, on the other hand, by the available stocks of it, whether these are fixed, as in the case of land, or capable of increase, as in the case of labour. The marginal uses of each agent, its marginal net efficiency in each use, and therefore its exchange value in each use, are thus all simultaneously governed by the general relations of demand and supply. Finally, equality is maintained between its values for each use by the constant tendency of competition to shift it from uses in which its

Marginal uses do not govern value, but are governed together with value by the general relations of demand and supply.

559

services are of less value to others in which they are of greater.

The paragraph just quoted, apart from the opening clause, in turn dates substantially from the 3rd ed. (p. 580).

PAGE 522

a. This and the next paragraph with its footnote, date from the 4th ed. (pp. 592–3).

b. This footnote dates in its present form from the 8th edition (page 522 n.). But the substance dates mainly from the 1st ed. (pp. 545 n.–6 n.), where the opening sentences ran as follows:

> [1] *Der isolierte Staat*, II, I, p. 123. He goes on (*ib.* p. 124) to argue that there-fore "the rate of interest is the element by which the relation of the efficiency of capital to that of human labour is expressed"; and finally, in words which have recently become famous, though he has gained but little credit for them, he says (p. 162): "Die Nutzung des zulezt angelegten Kapitalteilchens bestimmt die Höhe des Zinsfusses." He had already established (p. 96) the general law of diminishing return for successive doses of capital in any branch of production. His treatment of these and other great economic principles is independent of those fanciful and unreal assumptions as to the causes that determine the accumula-tion of capital, and...etc.

The rest of the footnote was unchanged from the first to the eighth editions.

In the 2nd ed. (p. 556 n.) the third of the foregoing sentences ran as follows:

> He had already (p. 96) enunciated a general law of diminishing return for successive doses of capital in any branch of production; and what he says on this subject has much historic interest, though it does not show how to reconcile the fact that an increase in the capital employed in an industry may increase the output more than in proportion, with the fact that a continued influx of capital into an industry must ultimately lower the rate of profits earned in it.

In the 4th ed. (p. 593 n.) the only change consisted in the replace-ment, in the second sentence, of the German words of Von Thünen by the English translation as in the present edition.

In the 5th ed. (p. 523 n.) the sentence, beginning: "With charac-teristic breadth of vision...etc." was worded as in the present ed.

In the 8th edition (page 522 n.) the reference to Jevons was inserted in the second sentence.

PAGE 523

a. For the earlier form of definition of the national dividend in the first and second editions see the Editorial Appendix to Book VI, chapters I and II, pp. 588–91 below.

b. This paragraph dates substantially from the 1st ed. (p. 724 n.) where it formed part of a footnote placed in Book VII, ch. XIII, §6.

See editorial note **b** to page 681 of vol. I in the present edition. The words "land, labour, and" were inserted before the word "capital" in the last line, in the 7th ed. (p. 523).

c. This sentence dates from the 1st ed. (p. 560).

d. This and the next sentence were inserted in the 7th ed. (p. 523).

e. The first two main clauses of this sentence date substantially from the 1st ed. (p. 560).

f. So since the 7th ed. (p. 523). In the 3rd to the 6th editions this clause formed a separate sentence which ran as follows:

We may, of course, estimate it for a year or for any other period; the important point is, as already hinted, that it is a continuous stream always flowing, and not a reservoir or store, or in the narrower sense of the word a "fund".[1]

[1] See above, VI, I, §2, also II, IV, especially §6. In Prof. Newcomb's words it is a *Flow* and not a Fund. (See his *Political Economy*, Book IV, ch. I.)

In the 5th ed. (p. 524 n.) the following sentences were added to the footnote just quoted: "But a Fund is not necessarily a stock; "the funds of a charitable trust" is a common phrase for the income at its disposal. See *Economic Journal*, VIII, p. 59."

g. This sentence dates from the 3rd ed. (p. 588).

PAGE 524

a. The following sentences in the 3rd ed. (p. 589) were deleted from the 5th ed.:

We have already noticed that many of the services which a person renders to himself are not in practice counted as part of his income; though if they were performed for him by a valet or hairdresser they would be reckoned among the commodities (or economic goods) on which he spent his means: that is, they would be reckoned as part of his real income. We have noticed also that though the benefits which a man derives from living in his own house are commonly reckoned as part of his real income, and estimated at the net rental value of his house; the same plan is not followed with regard to the benefits which he derives from the use of his furniture and clothes.

b. The remainder of this paragraph dates from the 3rd ed. (p. 589).

c. The following footnote (itself an abbreviation of a longer footnote dating from the 1st ed. (pp. 561 n.–2 n.)) attached to the word "separately" at the end of this paragraph in the 3rd ed. (p. 589 n.) was deleted from the 5th ed.:

> It would be possible, and, for some theoretical purposes, it would be best to include them: but if they are included in the national dividend, the efforts and the material wealth which are their sources must be counted as part of the labour and capital which are agents of production; and the services and the benefits themselves must be counted as earnings of labour or interest on capital as the case may be. It will be recollected that in Book II, ch. IV, the standard delimitations of capital and income were chosen specially with reference to this their most important use.
>
> It is to be understood that the excess of profits over interest is here provisionally reckoned among earnings, subject to a stricter analysis at a later stage. Speaking broadly, taxes may be regarded as those parts of the national dividend which the community elects to devote to the expenses of Government; the share of taxes which the merchant pays may be regarded as coming out of his profits, those which the working-man pays as coming out of his wages; and so on. There are, however, some cases in which it is convenient to regard taxes as a distinct share of the Dividend; and to regard the other shares as modified accordingly.

d. This paragraph was inserted in the 7th ed. (p. 524).

e. In the 8th edition, "V. XIII. 10"; emended in vol. I of the present edition to give the correct reference.

BOOK VI, CHAPTER II

PRELIMINARY SURVEY OF DISTRIBUTION, CONTINUED

PAGE 525

a. Except where otherwise indicated the text of this chapter dates substantially from the 3rd edition (Book VI, ch. II). See also the introductory editorial notes **a** and **c** to Book VI, chapter I, p. 550 above.

b. So since the 5th edition. In the first four editions the corresponding chapter was entitled: "Preliminary Survey of Distribution and Exchange, continued."

c. This paragraph was inserted in the 4th ed. (p. 596).

d. So since the 4th ed. (p. 596). For the earlier versions see the Editorial Appendix to Book VI, chapters I and II, pp. 592–4 below.

e. For the earlier versions of this paragraph in the first and second editions see the Editorial Appendix to Book VI, chapters I and II, p. 593 below.

PAGE 526

a. I have altered the word "nominal" before "value" in this sentence in the 8th edition to read "normal", notwithstanding the (surprising) fact that the use of the word "nominal" in this sentence persists through every edition from the first to the eighth. In making this emendation of the text I have been influenced by the following considerations: (i) In the first ed. (Book VII, ch. 1, §3, p. 546) the sentence in which this word occurred was preceded a few pages earlier (*ibid.* § 2, p. 540) by the following opening sentence of § 2 which clearly applied to the whole of the subsequent discussion in that chapter: "Let us begin by taking a general survey of the causes that govern true normal value, estimated for a period long enough to enable the economic causes concerned to work out their chief normal effect." (ii) Quite apart from this categorical statement, the wording of the rest of the sentence in the text can leave no doubt that Marshall must have had normal value in mind when he wrote it. (iii) The *Oxford English Dictionary* meaning of "nominal", as qualifying price, is "virtually nothing".

b. For the earlier versions, in the 1st and 2nd editions, of these two concluding paragraphs of §1, see the Editorial Appendix to Book VI, chapters 1 and 11, p. 579–80, below.

c. The words in parentheses were inserted in the 7th ed. (p. 526), where they replaced a reference in the last sentence of this paragraph to "any one of the strings that is already stretched", in the earlier editions. See the Editorial Appendix to Book VI, chapters 1 and 11, p. 580 below.

d. In the 3rd ed. (pp. 591–2) this paragraph was succeeded by the following paragraph which was deleted from the 4th ed.:

And though (if we neglect certain elements of prime cost) the earnings of each agent are for the time of the nature of a rent: yet those earnings react on the supply of the agent; and therefore on the amount and therefore on the value of the produce raised by it; and therefore on the demand for the agent itself, and therefore on its earnings, and thus the chain of reciprocal influences is complete. But the doctrine of rent, properly so called, relates to those agents of production of which the supply cannot be increased, and is unaffected by the earnings to be gained by increasing the supply. And those earnings of agents of production which we have called quasi-rents, because they are mainly governed for short periods by the value of the products, are governed ultimately by the laws of supply at least as much as by the laws of demand. To make this clear, it will be well to turn back and recall the substance of our studies of the supply of the agents of production in Books IV and V.

PAGE 527

a. The following footnote in the 3rd ed. (p. 592 n.) attached to the word "misconceptions" was deleted from the 6th ed.: "Especially in view of some recent discussions in Austria and America."

PAGE 528

a. This sentence dates substantially from the 4th ed. (p. 600).

b. The concluding clauses of this sentence were inserted in the 7th ed. (p. 528 n.).

PAGE 530

a. The remainder of this paragraph dates from the 5th ed. (p. 530), where it replaced the following sentence dating from the 3rd ed. (p. 595):

Their extent varies from age to age and place to place; and with its variations there is a corresponding but inverse variation in the extent to which man, himself always the sole end of all production, is also an economical agent of production.

PAGE 531

a. In the 4th ed. (p. 602) the words "and any increase in their earnings" replaced the words "and any increase in the demand for them made by the other agents of production" in the 3rd ed. (p. 596).

PAGE 533

a. This paragraph dates from the 5th ed. (p. 533), where it replaced the following paragraph dating from the 3rd ed. (pp. 598–9):

The case is rather different with regard to capital in general. It is true that some forms of capital are more narrowly specialized than any forms of labour, and that they are even more liable to violent variations of value in consequence of economic changes. But those individuals, who are most affected by such changes, are those whose special rôle it is to bear the brunt of economic vicissitudes and risks and to gain in the long run by doing so; and important as they are for subsequent stages of our inquiry, they may be neglected just now. No social or economic issue, that is vital for our immediate purpose, is confused by ignoring the influence of economic change on the relative values of different kinds of machinery and so on.

In the 3rd ed. (pp. 599–600) the paragraph just quoted was followed by two paragraphs dealing with the rate of interest in relation to old and new investments, which were transferred in the 5th ed. to Book VI, ch. vi, §6. See pages 592–3 in vol. i of the present edition.

b. In the 1st ed. (Book VII, ch. vii, §8, p. 624) there was the following summary (deleted from the 3rd ed.) of the causes governing the supply of capital:

We may now sum up this part of the argument. We have seen that the higher the benefits to be derived from the possession of wealth, whether in the form of trade-capital or any other; the greater, as a rule, are the inducements to work and to wait in order to accumulate wealth. This rule is, as Sir Josiah Child pointed out long ago, not without exceptions[1]; and perhaps these exceptions are increasing in importance. But there is no immediate prospect of their becoming so large as to reverse the rule. The increase of real income above the mere necessaries of life is constantly augmenting the *power* to save, an increased regard for the future is increasing the *will* to save; and under the action of these two causes together the rates of growth of wealth are increasing faster than ever now, in spite of the fact that, as a result of this increase, the rate of interest is falling. But it is still true that other things being equal an increase in the rate of interest tends to accelerate saving, and to increase the aggregate stock of capital.

[1] See Book IV, ch. vii, §9.

c. This reference was inserted in the 5th ed. (p. 533 n.).

PAGE 534

a. This and the next two sentences date substantially from the 1st ed. (pp. 625–6), where they were placed in Book VII, ch. vii, §8.

b. The remainder of this paragraph dates from the 2nd ed. (Book VI, ch. vi, § 3, pp. 621–2).

c. The word "very" before the word "gradually" in the 2nd ed. was deleted from the 3rd ed.

d. In the 1st ed., Book VII, ch. iii, § 1, Marshall gave a brief analysis of "a fundamental difference between earnings and interest on the one hand, and rent on the other". The wording of that section, which was deleted in part from the 2nd ed. and wholly from the 3rd ed., will be found in the Editorial Appendix to Book VI, chapters i and ii, pp. 594–5 below.

e. The following clause after the word "Land" in the 3rd ed. (p. 601) was deleted from the 5th ed.: "by which is here meant all those agents of production which are supplied freely by nature in quantities less than man needs".

f. The following footnote, attached to the word "itself" in the 3rd ed. (p. 601 n.), was deleted from the 5th ed.:

> It is not necessary to repeat here the discussion of the difficulties which surround any attempt to separate practically the "inherent" properties of the land in an old country from those which it has derived from man's action (see Book IV, ch. ii, § 1): nor to dwell on the special circumstances of land in a new country, in which the cultivator may obtain land not from another cultivator, but direct from nature herself, and in which therefore the rent of land has not yet acquired its special features (see Book V, ch. ix, § 1).

The last reference in this footnote relates to Book V, ch. x, § 1 in vol. 1 of the present edition.

g. So since the 5th ed. (p. 535) where this and the next two sentences replaced the following sentence in the 3rd ed. (p. 601):

Thus if the earnings of any class of labour rise, a compensatory action tends to increase its numbers, or efficiency, or both; and, if not to lower again its rate of earnings per head, yet at least to enable them to be paid from an increased national dividend, and not at the expense of other agents of production.

h. This footnote dates from the 4th ed. (p. 607 n.).

a. Although the substance of this and the next paragraph dates from the 3rd ed. (pp. 602–3), the order of the individual sentences was rearranged in the 4th ed. (pp. 607–9). It may be noted also that part of the subject-matter of pp. 602–3 in the 3rd ed. was transferred to Book V, ch. x, § 3 in the 4th ed.

b. The following sentence at this point in the 3rd ed. (pp. 603–4) was deleted from the 7th ed.:

We conclude then that the peculiarity in the earnings from land and other gifts of nature which arises from the fact that their stock cannot be increased by man, is seldom of much importance as regards the affairs of any individual trader, nor even as regards market fluctuations of wages and prices; but that it is of vital importance relatively to the broad central problem of distribution.

The first and third paragraphs of the following footnote, attached to the word "distribution" at the end of the sentence just quoted from the 3rd ed., were deleted from the 4th ed., while the middle paragraph was deleted from the 6th ed.:

> As has been intimated in Book V, ch. VIII–X, part of the argument of which has been reproduced in this section, the difference between rent and the earnings of other agents of production is nowhere more conspicuous nor more important than in the applications of the theory of value to the incidence of taxation: (see especially p. 478); a point to which we shall need frequently to recur in the second volume of this treatise. Some parts of the general argument of this section will be further developed in Book VI, ch. IX. The position that rent of land stands on a similar footing to the hire of a pony for a particular day, but not to the hire of ponies in general, when account is taken of the possibilities of increasing or diminishing their number, is maintained, in opposition to a part of the argument of the Duke of Argyll's *Unseen Foundations of Society*, in an article by the present writer in the *Economic Journal*, vol. III.
>
> The tendency of Austrian economists to minimise the influence which cost of production exerts on value naturally leads them to give little prominence to the differences between land and other agents of production. And a similar position in this respect has been taken by some of those who have applied mathematical expressions to the theory of value. They have laid stress on the fact that the land turned to account by the individual undertaker appears on the same footing with the other agents of production in the general function which expresses his output; (the differential coefficient of this function with regard to that or any other agent corresponding equally to the net product or earnings for him of a unit of that agent, see the foot-note on p. 464); and they have apparently inferred that land and its earnings figure in the general doctrine of distribution on a like footing with other agents of production and their earnings. They have applied a proposition, which is true and important in one class of problems, to a problem which would appear to belong to a different class; (see the review by Mr Flux of Mr Wicksteed's interesting *Co-ordination of the Laws of Distribution* in the *Economic Journal*, vol. IV, especially p. 312).
>
> Mr H. M. Thompson (*Theory of Wages*, Chapter IV) also inclines against a distinctive treatment of the share which land receives of the National Dividend, and he lays stress on the elasticity of man's resources in subjugating to his use new and distant lands and developing old lands. But where we are contrasting the fixity of the supply of land in an old country with the elasticity of the supplies of labour and capital, it would seem that we must not class with the former the results of improvements in agriculture and transport: for they belong to the latter.

The references in the first of the foregoing paragraphs to p. 478, and in the second paragraph to p. 464 relate to pages 413–15 and to page 393 n. respectively, in vol. 1 of the present edition.

Marshall's *Economic Journal* article "On Rent", referred to at the end of the first paragraph will be found in the Editorial Appendix to Book V, chapters VIII–X, pp. 492–512 above.

a. The opening clause of this sentence dates from the 4th ed. (p. 609), where it replaced the following paragraph in the 3rd ed. (p. 604):

This part of the argument may be seen from another side in a study of the relations in which the different kinds of surpluses that we have considered at various stages of our inquiry stand to the national dividend and to one another. The argument of this section is however difficult, and almost exclusively of academic interest; and it should be omitted by the general reader.

b. In the 3rd ed. (pp. 605–8) there followed a discussion of surpluses accruing to consumers, workers, savers, etc., which in the 4th ed. was placed at the end of a "Note on the Doctrine of the Wage Fund", and in the 5th ed. was transferred to Appendix K.

c. The remainder of this paragraph dates from the 5th ed. (p. 537), where it replaced the following paragraph dating from the 3rd ed. (p. 608):

This concludes the main body of our preliminary discussion of distribution and exchange. But there are some points on which a little more should be said here. The first relates to the mutual interactions of various groups of the agents of production; with special reference to the fact that the bond between the earnings of workers in the same grade is generally stronger than that between the earnings of workers in different grades. The second relates to the nature of the influences which the supply of capital exerts on wages in general: and will bring us near to the so-called Wages-Fund theory.

a. This and the next two paragraphs and the footnotes were inserted in the 7th ed. (pp. 538–9) where they replaced the following paragraph and footnote dating from the 3rd ed., pp. 609–10:

Now we know that the wages of any worker, say for instance a shoemaker, tend to be equal to the net product of his labour: and that since the wages of all workers in the same grade tend to be equal to one another, therefore in a state of equilibrium every worker will be able with the earnings of a hundred days' labour to buy the net products of a hundred days' labour of other workers in the same grade with himself: he may select them in whatever way he chooses, so as to make up that aggregate sum[1].

[1] It will be recollected that the net product of an individual agent of production cannot as a rule be separated mechanically from that of other agents which co-operate with it.

The paragraph just quoted from the 3rd ed. in turn dates from the 1st ed. (Book VII, ch. III, p. 564), the only alteration of substance being that, in the 1st ed., the opening words of the third main clause ran as follows: "therefore *in a state of perfect economic equilibrium* every worker will be able...etc." (Marshall's italics). In the 2nd ed. (Book VI, ch. II, p. 568) these words were altered to read as in the above extract from the 3rd ed.; but the footnote was not added till the 3rd ed.

b. In the text of both the 7th and 8th editions Marshall omitted the words "has been carried" from this clause. These words have been inserted here to make this sentence read properly.

PAGE 539

a. The remainder of §7 dates substantially (with certain changes noted below) from the 1st ed. (Book VII, ch. III, pp. 564–5). It may be noted that in the 7th ed. (pp. 539–40) the original word "shoe-maker" was altered throughout to the word "boot-operative".

b. The following footnote attached to the word "wages" in the 1st ed. (p. 564 n.) was deleted from the 3rd ed.:

This neglects the fact that their consumption would probably be increased by a fall in the price of the product. To take account of that we ought to estimate the loss of consumers' rent on the plan adopted in Book V, ch. VII.

The reference in the last line of this footnote relates to Book V, ch. XIII in vol. I of the present edition.

c. This sentence was inserted in the 3rd ed. (p. 610).

PAGE 540

a. This sentence was inserted in the 3rd ed. (p. 610).

b. So since the 3rd ed. (p. 611) where this sentence replaced the following sentence in the 2nd ed. (p. 571).

The process of substitution which we have been discussing is one form of competition; and it may be well to emphasize again here the fact that, when thus discussing the ultimate tendencies of competition, we do not assume that competition is perfect.

c. The remainder of this section (§ 8) dates from the 1st ed. (Book VII, ch. 1, §2, pp. 540–1). The full text of §§ 1 and 2 of Book VII, ch. 1 will be found in the Editorial Appendix to Book VI, chapters 1 and 11, pp. 572–6.

PAGE 541

a. In the 1st ed., Book VII, ch. 111, §§4–5, Marshall dealt at some length with the effects of a fall in the rate of interest on the earnings of shoemakers. This discussion, which was deleted from the 3rd ed., is given in full in the Editorial Appendix to Book VI, chapters 1 and 11, pp. 595–8 below.

b. The following footnote attached to the word "general" in the 3rd ed. (pp. 611 n.–12 n.) was deleted from the 5th ed.:

In Section 4 we noticed that the study of distribution is much more concerned with the causes that govern the earnings of each of many different groups of labour, than with causes that affect them all in approximately the same manner. But yet these latter have some interest even for the modern economist. And the fact that the earlier economists, partly in consequence of the special industrial conditions of their time, gave great prominence to discussions of general wages, makes it important to lay considerable stress on them in the interest of the continuity of the science.

c. This footnote dates from the 4th ed. (p. 613 n.).

PAGE 542

a. So since the 5th ed. (p. 541). In the 3rd and 4th editions this paragraph ran as follows:

For speaking generally, an increase in the power and the willingness to save, will cause the services of waiting to be pushed constantly further, so as to obtain employment at a rate of interest, which will constantly fall unless invention opens new advantageous uses of roundabout methods of production. In either case, but especially in the latter, the growth of capital increases the national dividend; and thus opens out new and rich fields for the employment of labour in other directions, which more than compensate for the partial displacement of the services of labour by those of waiting in particular trades.

b. In the 3rd and 4th editions there followed here a section dealing with "the benefits which wage-earners derive from the increase of wealth not owned by them and not in the form of trade capital". In the 5th ed. this was transferred to form §4 of Appendix J "The Doctrine of the Wage Fund".

c. This footnote dates from the 5th ed. (p. 541 n.).

a. The following footnote attached to the word "capital" in the 3rd ed. (p. 615 n.) was deleted from the 4th ed.: "The details of this doctrine, and the exaggerated importance attached to it by English economists early in this century, are described in the Note at the end of this Chapter." The reference to the "Note at the end of this Chapter" applies to Appendix J in vol. 1 of this edition.

b. The following footnote attached to the word "wages" in the 4th ed. (p. 617 n.) was deleted from the 5th ed.:

> See below, § 12; where also something is said of the notion that the fund from which wages of labour are paid really lies with the consumers who purchase the goods made by the labour.

The reference here to § 12 applies to Appendix J in vol. 1 of this edition.

c. In the 3rd ed. (pp. 616–17) this paragraph was followed by two paragraphs dealing with the argument of "some German economists" that "the resources with which the employer pays wages come from consumers". In the 4th ed. (pp. 623–4) these paragraphs were transferred to a "Note on the Doctrine of the Wages-Fund" which was placed at the end of Book VI, ch. 11; while in the 5th ed. they were transferred to Appendix J.

a. This opening clause dates from the 4th ed. (p. 617).

b. So since the 5th ed. (p. 543) where this sentence replaced the following sentence dating from the 3rd ed. (pp. 617–18): "In the modern world, the employer or undertaker, who may have but little capital as his own, acts as the boss of the great industrial wheel."

c. This paragraph dates from the 5th ed. (p. 544).

a. This paragraph, and the footnote attached to it date substantially from the 6th ed. (p. 544).

b. The following additional sentence at this point in the 6th ed. was deleted from the 7th ed.:

We can study the individual trees in this or that part of a woodland district: but, when we want to take a general view, we must be content to think of the woods, ignoring the trees: and similarly details and their correlations must be left almost out of mind in a broad study of Distribution and Exchange.

EDITORIAL APPENDIX TO
BOOK VI, CHAPTERS I AND II

The extracts which follow represent passages from the earlier editions which were either wholly or in large part deleted from later editions. They have been grouped under a number of general headings:

I. THE TENDENCY TOWARDS NORMAL EQUILIBRIUM IN DISTRIBUTION, ILLUSTRATED FROM AN ALMOST STATIONARY STATE

In the 1st edition, Book VII, chapter 1, §§1 and 2 [a](pp. 539–43) ran as follows:

A position of normal equilibrium is one towards which economic forces are tending. §1.   We have seen how the amount of a thing produced for sale in any market tends constantly to a position of equilibrium; and that this equilibrium amount is determined by the condition that the price at which a steady sale can be reckoned on (or, in other words, the normal demand price) for that amount, is equal to the price at which that amount can be steadily produced (or, in other words, its normal supply price). Time however is required to enable the causes, which determine normal supply price, to work themselves out, and, though in a less degree, those which determine normal demand price; and meanwhile there are constant changes in the general conditions and methods of production, in the course of trade, and in the habits of consumption. Consequently the position of normal equilibrium at any time is rather to be regarded as one towards which the forces of demand and supply at the time are tending, than as one which is ever actually attained.

but like the normal level of the sea it is not actually realized. In the same way the surface of the sea is always tending towards a level, but never attains it. For before the effects of one disturbance have pased away, others have sprung up; the level towards which the surface is tending, changes in less time than is required for the waves and the eddies caused

---

a.   With the exception of portions of two paragraphs in §2 the whole of the subject matter of these two sections was deleted from the 2nd ed.

by the last wind or the last tidal movement to subside. The normal level of the sea is thus an imaginary state which never is attained; but which would be attained if all the external forces acting on it were to cease their restless change, and to remain constant in magnitude and in direction for a long time together.

In the last two Books we have considered the difficulties connected with the element of Time in their more general aspects; and later on we shall have to study them in greater detail; but for the present we may give our chief attention to another class of difficulties. The supply price of a commodity is the price required to cover its money cost or expenses of production. But whereas we have hitherto gone on the supposition that the undertaker of any industrial enterprise takes for granted the prices which he has to pay for any kind of labour and for the hire of capital, we have now to examine the causes which determine the prices paid for labour and the use of capital, and thus to deal with the problem of value as a whole. *In this preliminary survey we may neglect disturbing causes.*

§2. Let us begin by taking a general survey of the causes that govern true normal value, estimated for a period sufficiently long to enable the economic causes concerned to work out their chief normal effects. The easiest plan for presenting vividly to our minds this uninterrupted action of economic causes is to suppose an almost stationary state, in which there are for a long time no great new inventions nor any other important changes in the methods of production, or in the channels of trade; no great wars and not very much variation in the habits of consumption, or in social and industrial habits and institutions generally. In such a state business will pursue its even tenor from generation to generation, and the experience of the past will enable people to forecast the future with certainty, and to adapt their arrangements closely to it. *Let us suppose an almost stationary state.*

In the language of the older economists this would be expressed by saying that the general economic conditions of society remained stationary long enough to enable the effects of free competition to be fully developed. But it will be well to call attention once more to the fact that the phrase free

We do not assume perfect knowledge

competition is apt to mislead. ^bPerfect competition requires a perfect knowledge of the state of the market; and though no great departure from the actual facts of life is involved in assuming this knowledge on the part of dealers when we are considering the course of business in Lombard Street,

and freedom of competition,

the Stock Exchange, or in a wholesale Produce Market; it would be an altogether unreasonable assumption to make when we are examining the causes that govern the supply of labour in any of the lower grades of industry. For if a man had sufficient ability to know everything about the market for his labour, he would have too much to remain long in a low grade. The older economists, in constant contact as they were with the actual facts of business life, must have known this well enough; but partly for brevity and simplicity, partly because the term "free competition" had become almost a catchword, partly because they had not sufficiently classified and conditioned their doctrines, they often seemed

but only the enterprise and business habits which are normal to each several rank of industry.

to imply that they did assume this perfect knowledge. It is therefore specially important to insist that we do not really need to assume the members of any industrial group to be endowed with more ability and forethought, or to be governed by motives other than those which are in fact normal to, and would be attributed by every well-informed person to, the members of that group, account being taken of the general conditions of time and place[1].

We take man as he is, governed by many motives and impulses; but the tendency for each one to adopt that course which he thinks most advantageous will act constantly in one direction,

Thus we have no need to suppose that every one is governed solely by calculations of his own advantage, and is always keen and prompt to turn every opportunity to the best account. There may be a good deal of wayward and impulsive action; sordid and noble motives may mingle their threads together as they do in actual life. But there will be, as in fact there is in modern England, a constant tendency for each man to select such occupations for himself and his

[1c] Compare Book I, ch. VI and ch. VII, § 1; and Book V, ch. IV, §§ 1, 2, and 5.

b. The remainder of this paragraph and the first three sentences of the next paragraph were retained substantially in the later editions. See Book VI, ch. II, pages 540–1 in vol. I of the present edition.

c. These references apply to Book I, ch. II, and ch. III, §4; and Book V, ch. V, §§ 1, 2 and 7, in vol. I of the present edition.

children as seem to him on the whole the most advantageous of those which are within the range of his resources, and of the efforts which he is able and willing to make in order to reach them. The tendency may act slowly, but it will be sure, and it will work constantly in the same direction; for the conditions of life remaining without great change, the same estimates of the relative advantages of different courses will remain valid for long times together: its action may be delayed by the retarding influences of habit and custom, by limitations of knowledge and of enterprise, by casual accident and by the peculiarities of individual temper and character; but it will go on through all. The only forces which could offer it an effective and permanent resistance, would be those of "combinations", themselves the product of firm resolve and deliberate enterprise; and therefore strong for both good and evil. But assuming for the present that there are no such combinations, we may conclude that when a long period has passed under conditions free from great external change, the adaptive power of man will have adjusted fairly well the supply of every commodity, of every appliance for production, and of every kind of skill and training to the demand for it.

The adjustment will not be perfect, any more than the surface of a viscous fluid, which has been left a long time undisturbed, will be absolutely level. But as that surface will have become sufficiently level for all practical purposes, and will have already settled down very nearly in the position which it would have assumed, if it had been left for an unlimited time under the same conditions, so it will be with regard to the adjustment of demand and supply. There may, for instance, be a few persons in one occupation who, if they had their time to go over again, would have chosen another; and those who are in it may be earning a little less than they could have got in another, that seems to be no more difficult and to have equal incidental advantages and disadvantages. But on the whole the earnings of every occupation will have reached about their normal level, account being taken of the conditions, physical and moral, social and industrial, of the district and time under investigation.

and in the absence of disturbances will gradually prevail.

In supposing that the general economic conditions of the district in which the trade is carried on, are almost stationary, we have implicitly assumed that there is no great change in the trade relations between that district and others. It will simplify the case, though it is not strictly necessary for our argument, to consider the district or market to which we refer, as an "isolated" territory; and we may leave for future account the influences that may be brought to bear on it by commerce with other markets, as well as local variations of value due to cost of transport between different parts of it.

2. THE PROBLEM OF DISTRIBUTION ON THE PHYSIOCRATIC ASSUMPTION (WITH SOME MODIFICATIONS) OF "NATURAL" LEVELS OF WAGES AND INTEREST

In the 1st edition Book VII, chapter II, §2 ran as follows[a]:

Let us modify the assumptions of the Physiocrats by supposing that each grade of labour has its own standard of comfort, which is rigidly fixed.

Let us then revert to the position in which the theory of value was left by the Physiocrats. Their argument takes no account of the existence of more than one grade of labour; but it will lose little of its simplicity and clearness of outline if we suppose that society is divided into a number of horizontal grades[1], each of which is recruited from the children of its own members; and each of which has its own standard of comfort, and increases in numbers rapidly when the earnings to be got in it rise above, and shrinks rapidly when they fall below that standard. Let us suppose, then, that parents can bring up their children to any trade in their own grade, but cannot easily raise them above it and will not consent to sink them below it. And let us continue to suppose that changes in the methods of production and in the relative proportions of its various branches are not very rapid; so

---

[1] See Book IV, ch. VI, §§ 7 and 8.

a. With the exception of one paragraph the whole of the subject-matter of this section was retained in the 2nd ed. (Book VI, ch. I, §§ 3 and 4); but it was deleted from the 3rd ed. where it was replaced by the "series of hypothetical illustrations drawn from a society in which the problem of the relations between capital and labour do not exist". See §§ 3–6 in Book VI, ch. I in vol. I of the present edition.

that the supply of the various factors of production required in any trade, whether they be human agents or material appliances, can always be adjusted pretty closely to the demand for them.

On these suppositions the normal wage in any trade is that which is sufficient to enable a labourer, who has normal regularity of employment, to support himself and a family of normal size according to the standard of comfort that is normal in the grade to which his trade belongs; it is not dependent on demand except to this extent, that if there were no demand for the labour of the trade at that wage the trade would not exist. In other words the normal wage represents the expenses of production of the labour according to the ruling standard of comfort, and is a fixed quantity so long as that standard is fixed; the influence of demand is only to determine the number of those who are brought into the trade, and not their rate of wages. *Then the conditions of supply will give the rates of payment for the services of each kind of labour*

Let us retain for the present the assumption made by the Physiocrats that there is a natural rate of interest to which the supply of capital steadily and quickly adjusts itself, increasing rapidly whenever the rate of interest is above this level and shrinking again whenever it falls below this level. *and for the use of capital;*

The tendency of every one to select the best means for attaining his own ends (or, in more technical phrase, the operation of the law of substitution), acting gradually but constantly under almost stationary conditions would then have caused each several kind of labour or machinery, or other agent of production to be used for each several purpose until its further use there was no longer remunerative; each branch of production would have been extended until it so far satiated the wants which it was directed to meet, that no further supply of its products would be sold on such terms as to pay their expenses of production; and meanwhile the employment of each several agent in each branch of production would have been extended until full advantage had been taken of its special fitness for the work; its use would cease only when there remained nothing that could be done by it better or more cheaply than by other means. *while the strength of demand will determine the amounts of these several agents for which there is employment at these rates.*

[b]These three elements, firstly the amount produced, secondly, the marginal utility all along the various uses of the agent, represented by the marginal demand price, and thirdly, the marginal expenses of production, would mutually determine one another[1].

[1c] As we have seen (Book VI, ch. v, §3) producers will not proceed all by the same route. One farmer will use more chemical manures, and another will give more care to his farmyard manures; one manufacturer will apply machinery wherever he can do so with a fair prospect of success, and another only when its use is certain to be advantageous. And therefore the boundary of the profitable application of capital and labour in making a thing is not to be regarded as a point on any one fixed route, but as a line of irregular shape cutting one after another every possible route by which producers can proceed.

3. THE MUTUAL DETERMINATION OF THE AMOUNTS AND PRICES OF THE AGENTS OF PRODUCTION

In the 1st edition Book VII, chapter II, §3 ran as follows[a]:

Next suppose that the supply price is not rigidly fixed, but that there is a definite relation between the amount required of each of these agents and the price at which it will be supplied,

§3. In the last section we assumed that the supply of each of these agents of production conformed itself to the demand by increasing rapidly when the price to be got for it was above a certain fixed level, and shrinking rapidly when the price was below that level. But now let us assume that this level is not fixed, but depends on the amount demanded; (or, in more technical language, that it has a supply schedule of the same character as those for particular commodities, with which we are already familiar). On this assumption, as on those of the last section, the limit or "margin" at which the use of any one of these agents of production terminates, and the aid of another is substituted for it in any

b. This paragraph (but not the footnote attached to it) was deleted from the 2nd ed.

c. The reference in the first line of this footnote applies to Book V, ch. IV, §3, in vol. I of the present edition.

a. With the exception of the deletion of the second sentence of the third of the following paragraphs, the whole of this section was retained in the 2nd ed. (Book VI, ch. II, §4).

In the 3rd ed. Book VI, ch. II, §1, all these paragraphs were deleted with the exception of the two concluding paragraphs, which were retained throughout the later editions. See page 526 in vol. I of the present edition.

branch of production, is found where the relative efficiencies of these two agents are proportionate to their relative costs.

Again, we suppose that we know the whole amount of each agent of production for which there is a demand at each particular price (or, in other words, that there is a demand schedule for it). As before, this amount is the aggregate of the several amounts that are demanded at that price for each trade in which the agent is used. The demand for it in each trade is directly dependent upon, and derived from, the demand for the commodities made by the trade; and this in its turn is determined by the eagerness of purchasers for those commodities and the amount of purchasing power at their disposal. And, as before, the tendency of every one to select the best means of attaining his own ends (or, in other words, the action of the law of substitution), limits the use of each agent to those purposes for which it was at least as efficient as any other, in proportion to the price that had to be paid for it[1].

The production of every commodity is carried forward up to that limit or margin at which there is equilibrium between the forces of demand and supply; that is, the limit at which any further production would bring in less than a remunerative price[2]. The position of the margin is the index of this equilibrium; and taken in conjunction with other *then the amounts and prices of the several agents of production mutually determine one another.*

[1b] The whole of Book V, ch. VI bears closely upon the central problem of distribution and exchange. The attention of mathematicians may also be directed to Note XX in the Appendix, in which all the various cases discussed in that chapter are combined.

[2] We must not forget that every factor is used in each branch of production up to the margin of indifference on each several plan on which the production can with advantage be carried on; and thus this margin is not a point on any one route which that branch of production can follow, but a line intersecting all such routes.

Again, it must be remembered that the margin of profitable production of those goods which obey the law of Increasing Return is liable to be unstable: that in practice it is much dependent on the tendency of firms which have grown large to lose part of the energy and progressiveness by which they first made their way: and that this tendency is liable to great changes in character from one generation to another. See Book IV, chs. XII, XIII, [c] Book V, chs. IV, V.

---

b. The references in the first and third lines of this footnote apply to Book V, ch. VI, and to Note XXI in the Mathematical Appendix in vol. I of the present edition.

c. This reference applies to Book V, chs. V and XII and to Appendix H in vol. I of the present edition.

facts, it indicates, but does not determine, the prices of the commodities made on it, and the prices paid for the labour and the use of the capital employed in making the commodity; just as the finger of the barometer is an index of the position of equilibrium between the pressure of the air and the mercury. The amount of the commodity and its price, the amounts of the several factors or agents of production used in making it, and their prices—all these elements mutually determine one another, and if an external cause should alter any one of them the effect of the disturbance extends to all the others.

Parallel instances from physics.
Just in the same way, when several balls are lying in a bowl, they mutually determine one another's positions; and again when a heavy weight is suspended by several elastic strings of different strengths and lengths attached to different points in the ceiling, the equilibrium positions of all the strings and of the weight mutually determine one another. If any one of the strings that is already stretched is shortened, everything else will change its position, and the length and the tension of every other string will be altered also.

4. [a]THE NET PRODUCT OF LABOUR. THE ILLUSTRATION OF THE MARGINAL SHEPHERD

In the 1st edition Book VII, chapter 1, §5 ran as follows:

§5. [bc]It may however be well, before passing to consider the side of supply, to consider more carefully that

a. For the final version of the net product of labour, as illustrated by the marginal shepherd, see Book VI, chapter 1, §7, in vol. 1 of the present edition, and the editorial notes thereto.

b. The first three paragraphs of this section in the 1st ed. are virtually identical with a passage in the *Economics of Industry* by Alfred Marshall and Mary Paley Marshall (1st ed. 1879, p. 133). The only difference between the two versions to which attention need be drawn is that the term "net product" of Labour in the 1st ed. of the *Principles of Economics* replaced the term "net return" of labour, which was used in the *Economics of Industry*.

c. In the 2nd ed. (Book VI, ch. II, §3, p. 566) this sentence ran as follows:

This two fold action of an increase in the supply of one agent on the demand for others may be seen more clearly,

application of the law of substitution to the theory of distri- The
bution, on which so much stress has been laid by many statement that wages
recent writers. It is that free competition tends to make each tend to
man's wages equal to the *net product* of his own labour, or equal the
Net product
(as is sometimes less accurately said) the *discounted value* of of the
the produce of his labour. worker's labour, is

We may begin with the latter phrase. To interpret it at true,
all, we must take a very simple case. Suppose that a thing
is made by one kind of labour alone; that this labour does
not require any appreciable amount of superintendence, nor
the aid of any capital except that which is advanced in the
payment of wages. Suppose that this capital has been advanced gradually, some of it a short time, some a long time,
but on the average about half-a-year before the thing is
ready for sale. Let the rate of interest for six months, allowing for risk, be three per cent. Then if the thing can be sold
for £103, its discounted value half-a-year beforehand will
be £100. And the competition of employers among themselves will tend to make the wages of those who made it
equal to this discounted value of £100.

But a case as simple as this never occurs in practice. The when
earnings of many different kinds of industry, one of which carefully
interpreted,
is almost always ᵈthat of superintendence and management,
enter into the expenses of production, and therefore into
the price, of almost everything that is sold; and in order
to deduce the earnings of one of these kinds of labour from
the price of the product, we must find out not only the
interest on the capital employed but also the earnings of the
other kinds of industry, and deduct them all from the value
of the produce raised. We cannot therefore speak with perfect accuracy of the discounted value of the work of labour;

---

if we now pass to express in another way that application of
the law of substitution to the theory of distribution which
we have considered in the last chapter, and borrow a phrase
on which much stress has been laid by many recent writers.

d. In the 2nd ed. (p. 566) the words "the (gross) earnings of
management" replaced the words "that of superintendence and
management" in the 1st ed.

but we may still speak of the net product of labour. [e]The net product of a machine is the value of the work that it does, after deductions have been made for expenses of working it, among which are here included the earnings of management. And, in like manner, the net product of a man's labour is the value of the produce which he takes part in producing after deducting all the other expenses of pro-

is useful for some purposes.

ducing it. [f]It is true that this statement is not, as some have thought, an independent theory of wages, but only a particular way of wording the familiar doctrine that the value of everything tends to be equal to its expenses of production. There is, however, no reason why we should not avail ourselves of it as a handy way of stating that doctrine for some purposes[1].

Its meaning illustrated.

There is another method of getting at the net produce of a man's labour. It cannot be applied practically to all cases; but it will help to give us clearer notions. It is to suppose that an employer is in doubt whether he has enough labour to turn his stock, machinery and other trade appliances to good account; and whether he could not, by hiring one more man, increase the production by more than the

[1g] Von Thünen had expressed the fact that wages tend to equal the net produce resulting from the work of the labourer on the margin of employment, by saying (*Der isolierte Staat*, II, I, p. 174) that "wages are equal to the extra produce which is raised by the last of the labourers employed in a large business." The condition that they should be employed in a *large* business is of course introduced in order that their work may be the final *small* increment in the production. He points out (p. 178) that the introduction of each additional labourer introduces some discontinuity into the development of any individual small business; but that on the average these discontinuities correct themselves. His argument is somewhat similar to that given above [h](Book V, ch. IV, §5) on a slightly different point.

---

e. In the 2nd ed. (p. 567) this sentence ran as follows: "In the phrase 'the net product of a machine' the word 'net' is interpreted to mean that from the value of the work that it does, deductions are to be made for the expenses of working it, including (gross) earnings of management."

f. This and the next sentence were deleted from the 2nd ed. at this point, but part of their substance in a varied form was placed elsewhere in the same chapter, immediately after the illustration of the marginal shepherd (see editorial note **1** on p. 584).

g. This footnote was deleted from the 2nd ed.

h. This reference applies to Book V, ch. v, §§6 and 7 in vol. I of the present edition.

equivalent of his wages, without having to supply additional capital in any other way. A sheep farmer, for instance, may be in doubt whether his staff of shepherds is sufficient. He may find that if he hired an additional man, without making any other change, so many more lambs will be kept alive, and the flocks generally so much better cared for, that he may expect to send to market twenty more sheep every year. This will require no extra plant on which interest has to be charged; and the man may be supposed to save the farmer himself just as much trouble in some ways as he gives in others, so that nothing has to be allowed for earnings of management. Then the net produce of that shepherd's labour will be twenty sheep: if the farmer can hire him for the price of twenty sheep, he will decide to do so; otherwise not; the shepherd who is on the margin of not being employed— the *marginal* shepherd, as we may call him—adds to the total produce a net value just equal to his own wages. And though the form may be different, the substance of the problem is the same in every other industry: the wages of every class of labour tend to be equal to the produce due to the additional labour of the marginal labourer of that class [1][i].

In the 1st edition (Book VII, ch. iii, §4, p. 563) there was the following sentence and paragraph referring to the net product of labour in its relation to wages:

[j] We have seen that an important doctrine in the theory of exchange, viz. that the value of a thing tends to equal its

[1][k] Compare Book VI, ch. v, §3.

---

i. In the 2nd ed. (pp. 567 n.–8 n.) there was the following footnote attached to the word "class" at the end of the above paragraph:

This method of estimating the net product of a man's labour is not easily applicable to industries in which a great deal of capital and effort has to be invested in gradually building up a trade connection, and especially if they are such as obey the law of increasing returns. It is hardly worth while to study these difficulties in detail here, for they are technical and intricate. A general account of them has been given in Book V, ch. xi.

The reference in the last line applies to Book V, ch. xii and Appendix H in vol. i of the present edition.

j. This sentence was deleted from the 2nd ed.

k. This reference (deleted from the 2nd ed.) applies to Book V, ch. iv, §3 in vol. i of the present edition.

expenses of production, may be rewritten so as to express a part of the theory of distribution, viz. that the earnings of a worker tend to be equal to the net produce of his work.

The
scientific
use of
partial or
incomplete
statements.

[1]It is true that this phrase by itself has no real meaning; since in order to interpret the term "net produce," we have to take for granted all the expenses of production of the commodity on which he works, other than his own wages. But it is always a difficult task to hold in mind at one and the same time all the actions and reactions of a great number of causes which mutually determine one another. And although the able business man acquires a sort of instinct that enables him to do it as regards his own affairs; while much of the higher training of science is devoted to acquiring a more general power of the kind; yet everyone finds his task lightened, when he is able to break up a difficult problem, and to take one part of it at a time; and the strain necessarily involved by the problem of distribution and exchange, is so great that we should avail ourselves of every aid.

In the 3rd to the 5th editions (Book VI, ch. 1) the illustration of the marginal shepherd ran as follows:

Thus suppose an employer in doubt whether he has enough labour to turn his stock, machinery and other trade appliances to good account; and whether he could not, by hiring one more man, increase the production by more than the equivalent of his wages, without having to supply additional

---

1.   In the 2nd ed. (Book VI, ch. II, § 3, p. 568) where this paragraph was placed immediately after the illustration of the marginal shepherd, the opening sentence ran as follows:

The doctrine that the earnings of a worker tend to be equal to the net produce of his work, is certainly useful in its place, in spite of the fact that by itself it has no real meaning; since in order to estimate "net produce," we have to take for granted all the expenses of production of the commodity on which he works, other than his own wages.

Apart from the changes mentioned in the editorial notes the text of the foregoing passages was identical in the first editions.

capital in any other way. A sheep farmer, for instance, may be in doubt whether his staff of shepherds is sufficient. He may find that if he hired an additional man, without making any other change, and without incurring any extra expenditure for implements, buildings &c., then so many more lambs will be kept alive, and the flocks generally so much better cared for, that he may expect to send to market twenty more sheep every year. [m]This man will require no extra plant on which interest has to be charged; and he may be supposed to save the farmer himself just as much trouble in some ways as he gives in others, so that nothing has to be allowed for earnings of management (even when these are interpreted broadly so as to include insurance against risk &c.). Then the net produce of that shepherd's labour will be twenty sheep: if the farmer can hire him for ever so little less than the price of twenty sheep, he will decide to do so; otherwise not. The shepherd who is on the margin of not being employed—the *marginal* shepherd, as we may call him—adds to the total produce a net value just equal to his own wages[1].

[n] Theoretically a deduction from this has to be made for the fact that by throwing twenty extra sheep on the market, the farmer will lower the price of sheep generally, and therefore lose a little on his other sheep. This correction may

---

m. In the 5th ed. (p. 516) there were the following additional sentences and clause at this point which were deleted from the 6th ed.:

This man is supposed to be representative. If he were exceptionally efficient or exceptionally inefficient, his wages would still tend to be equal to the net product of his labour, at all events if free bargaining were not hindered by custom or trade-union rule or other cause: but his wages would not be representative.

The new shepherd is then to be a man of normal efficiency; he is to require no extra plant on which interest has to be charged; ...etc.

n. In the 5th ed. (p. 517 n.) this and the next note in the 3rd and 4th editions were amalgamated into a single note, to which was brought down (with a slight change) the sentence in the text beginning "It must however be remembered that the price which it is just worth while...etc." This was altered to "It has been argued at length in

It must however be remembered that the price which it is just worth while for the farmer to pay for this labour, merely gauges the outcome of multitudinous causes which between them govern the wages of shepherds; as the movements of a safety valve may gauge the outcome of the multitudinous causes that govern the pressure in a boiler[1].

be of appreciable importance in special cases. But in general discussions such as this, in which we are dealing with a very small addition to the supply thrown by one of many producers on a large market, it becomes very small (mathematically a small quantity of the second order), and may be neglected. In the case of a monopolist who supplied the whole of a market, we had to take account of it; and also when discussing the considerations that induce any producer, or association of producers to abstain from "spoiling" that particular branch of a large market with which they are directly connected, especially in times of depression. This point is discussed at some length in Mathematical Note XIV; the whole of which has a close bearing on this section, and the reader may be asked to reckon it in as part of the present discussion.o

[1] The fact that this marginal shepherd added twenty to the sheep whom the farmer could send to market rested no doubt on physical laws, given the conditions under which he worked. But those conditions include the amount of land at the farmer's disposal which is influenced by the demand for land for raising timber, oats, deer etc. Again the conditions include the number of shepherds that the farmer already has; and that is governed by the general conditions of the broad problem of distribution and exchange, and in particular by the number of those from whom the ranks of shepherds could have been recruited during the current generation, by the demand for mutton and wool and by the area from which supplies of them can be obtained, and by the effectiveness of the shepherds on all other farms.

Further the net product of the shepherd in the exceptional case which we have chosen, plays no greater part in governing the wages of shepherds, than does that of any of the last (marginal) shepherds on farms where they cannot be profitably employed without considerable extra outlay in other directions, as for land, buildings, implements, labour of management, &c. Thus the net product of such shepherds cannot be ascertained simply; but it is a case of derived demand (see Book V, ch. VI), and requires us to take account of the prices which have to be paid for the aid of all these other agents of production. It will be noticed that this holds with regard to all agents of production, however they may differ from one another on the side of supply. It is as true of "land," which is of fixed aggregate quantity, and of which the value is uninfluenced even in the long run by cost of production; as it is of labour and capital, of which the ultimate values are determined by laws of demand and supply co-ordinately.

---

regard to similar cases (see V, VII, 4, 5) that the price which it is just worth while...etc." In the 5th ed. the footnote began with the following sentence:

The importance of the remark that the shepherd is to be one of normal efficiency will appear more clearly in a discussion on labour standardization in ch. XII.

o.   In the 5th ed. (p. 517 n.) there was the following additional paragraph at this point, which was deleted from the 6th ed.:

The supposition that an additional worker can be taken on without a corresponding increase in the supply of capital for plant, raw material, &c., does not alter the substance of the problem of marginal products; but merely simplifies

This illustration has been chosen from a simple industry; but, though the form may be different, the substance of the problem is the same in every industry. Subject to conditions which are indicated in the foot-note, but are not important for our main purpose, the wages of every class of labour tend to be equal to the net product due to the additional labour of the marginal labourer of that class[1].

[1] This method of illustrating the net product of a man's labour is not easily applicable to industries in which a great deal of capital and effort has to be invested in gradually building up a trade connection, and especially if they are such as obey the law of increasing return. In both cases there is a difficulty of accounts, making it almost impossible to decide what part of the gains of the business would have been lost for want of the services of any individual worker. (See V, VII, §§ 1, 2 and PXI, § 2.) But in the latter case there is a second and more fundamental difficulty. For the employer, in taking on an additional worker, may estimate only for the direct good that that man's work will do to his business: whereas to find the total net product of the man's work, even from the employer's point of view, account should also be taken of the part which it plays in enabling the business to avail itself of the economies of production on a large scale. The employer, if of an enterprising temperament, may take account of these also: but there is still something omitted. The increase in the size of that business will tend to increase the demand for subsidiary industries; and in other ways to increase the (external) economies available for other businesses in the same trade: and, since this additional gain to the community will not accrue to the employer himself, it cannot be expected that he should hand it on to the workman. The question why this extra gain, accruing to the undertaker in such an industry from an increase in his business, does not ultimately cause the whole industry to fall into the hands of one large firm, has been discussed in IV, XII. On the whole subject see V, XI or the summary of that chapter on pp. 559, 560.

This is indeed a special application of that general failure of the so-called doctrine of *maximum satisfaction* which we have already noticedq (V, XII). For independently of such considerations as that a great benefit to a poor man will be outweighed in the balance of market exchange by a small benefit to a rich man, that doctrine fails in the case of industries which obey the law of increasing return; because the payment which any particular worker or employer receives in those industries is less than the true equivalent of the net product of his services to the community.

In the 3rd ed. (pp. 584–5) there was an additional concluding paragraph at the end of this section just quoted which ran as follows:

It may be objected that the doctrine that the earnings of a worker tend to be equal to the net produce of his work, has

its form a little. In this exceptional case, we have not to dwell upon the need for the appropriate adjustment of various agents of production, each being used up to the point at which any additional use of it would be less efficient in proportion to its cost than the additional use of some other agent.

p. This and the corresponding reference in the last line of the first paragraph of this footnote apply to Book V, ch. XII in vol. 1 of the present edition, while the page numbers given in the latter sentence apply to pages 500–2 in vol. 1 of the present edition.

q. This reference applies to Book V, ch. XIII in vol. 1 of the present edition.

by itself no real meaning: since in order to estimate "net produce", we have to take for granted all the expenses of production of the commodity on which he works, other than his own wages. The objection is valid against a claim that it contains a theory of wages; but not against a claim that the doctrine throws into clear light the action of one of the causes that govern wages. For indeed it is always a difficult task to hold in mind at one and the same time all the actions and reactions...etc.

The remainder of the paragraph was the same as in the 1st ed. See above, p. 584.

In the 4th to the 6th editions this passage ran as follows:

This doctrine has sometimes been put forward as a theory of wages. In reply to any such pretension, it may be objected that the doctrine that the earnings of a worker tend to be equal to the net product of his work, has by itself no real meaning; since in order to estimate net product, we have to take for granted all the expenses of production of the commodity on which he works, other than his own wages.

But though this objection is valid against a claim that it contains a theory of wages; it is not valid against a claim that the doctrine throws into clear light the action of one of the causes that govern wages.

The final wording of the above paragraphs dating from the 4th ed. (pp. 588–9) was arrived at in the 7th ed. (p. 518).

5. THE DEFINITION OF THE NATIONAL DIVIDEND

In the 1st edition, Book VII, chapter III, §2 ran as follows:

The aggregate Net product of the agents of production is the *National Dividend*.

§2. ᵃThe labour and capital of the country, acting on its natural resources, produce annually a certain net aggre-

a. In the 2nd ed. (Book VI, ch. II, §1) this paragraph was preceded by the following paragraph:

IN the account given in the last chapter of the demand for the several agents of production, it was indicated that the ultimate demand for each depended on the co-operation of the others in raising the joint product of their labour; or to state the case even more broadly, that the demand for

gate of commodities, material and immaterial, including services of all kinds[1]. This is the true net annual revenue of the country, or as we may say the NATIONAL DIVIDEND. It is of course unimportant whether we estimate it for a year or for any other period; the important point is that it is a continuous stream always flowing, and not a reservoir or store, or in the narrower sense of the word a "fund" of capital[2].[b]

[c]The word *net* indicates that the aggregate of commodities produced during the year is estimated so as to allow for the replacement of raw material consumed during the year and for the wear and tear of machinery. But no corresponding reduction is made for the wear and tear of human agents

The significance of the term *Net*.

[1] See Book II, chs. II and [d]VI.
[2] In Prof. Newcomb's words it is a *Flow* and not a Fund. (See his *Political Economy*, Book IV, ch. I.)

---

each is in a great measure governed by the supply of the others. The present chapter will be devoted to examining this dependence more closely, and studying the mutual relations of the two facts, firstly, that the demand for each agent increases generally with the supply of others, and secondly, that the demand for it is lessened when any of those others can profitably be substituted for it.

b. In the 2nd ed. (pp. 562–3) there was the following additional paragraph at this point:

The terms national income and national dividend are convertible; only the latter is the more convenient when we are looking at the national income in the character of the sum of the new sources of enjoyments that are available for distribution.

c. In the 2nd ed. (p. 563) the earlier part of this paragraph ran as follows:

The word *net* has of course no fixed meaning: it merely indicates that certain deductions, specified in the context, have to be made. In this particular case it indicates that the aggregate of commodities produced during the year is estimated...etc.

d. This reference applies to Book II, ch. IV in vol. I of the present edition.

of production; because the earnings of labour are commonly estimated *gross*, that is, without any allowance for the ageing and exhaustion of the worker.

Further explana-tions.

[e] It is not to be understood that the share of the national dividend, which any particular industrial class receives during the year, contains only things that were made during the year. On the contrary, most of the things made, or partly made, during the year are likely to remain in the possession of capitalists and undertakers of industry; while in return they, directly or indirectly, hand over to the working classes some things that had been made in previous years.

The sense in which it is true that the earnings of labour depend on advances made by capital.

The ordinary bargain between labour and capital is that the wage-receiver gets command over commodities in a form ready for immediate consumption, and in exchange carries his employer's goods a stage further towards being ready for immediate consumption. But while this is true of most employees, it is not true of those who finish the processes of production. For instance, those who put together and finish watches, give to their employers far more commodities in a form ready for immediate consumption, than they take from them. And if we take one season of the year with another, so as to allow for seed and harvest time, we find that workmen as a whole hand over to their employers more finished commodities than they receive as wages. But—to say nothing of machinery and factories, of ships and railroads—the houses loaned to workmen, and even the raw materials in various stages which will be worked up into commodities consumed by them, represent a far greater provision of capital for their use than the equivalent of the advances which they make to the capitalist, even when they work for a month for him before getting any wages. And in this sense we are justified

---

e.   In the 2nd ed. (p. 563) the earlier part of this paragraph ran as follows:

It is to be understood that the share of the national dividend, which any particular industrial class receives during the year, consists either of things that were made during the year, or of the equivalents of those things. For many of the things made, or partly made, during the year...etc.

in saying that the earnings of labour depend upon advances made to labour by capital[1].

The net aggregate of all the commodities produced is itself the true source from which flow the demand prices for all these commodities, and therefore for the agents of production used in making them. Or, to put the same thing in another way, this national dividend is at once the aggregate net product of, and the sole source of payment for, all the agents of production within the country: it is divided up into earnings of labour, interest of capital, and lastly the producer's surplus, or rent, of land and of other differential advantages for production. It constitutes the whole of them and the whole of it is distributed among them; and the larger it is, the larger, other things being equal, will be the share of each agent of production[2].

The National Dividend is the sole source of demand for all the agents of production.

---

[1] See the remarks, in the **f**Note at the end of the chapter, on the proposition that "Industry is limited by capital."

[2] It is to be understood that the excess of profits over interest is here provisionally reckoned among earnings, subject to a stricter analysis at a later stage. Also that earnings, interest and rent are interpreted broadly, so as to include all those commodities which a person provides for himself by his own labour or derives from the usance of his own wealth (**g**comp. Book II, ch. VI). It would indeed be more consistent with precedent tacitly to omit these commodities from both sides of the account; but unless that is done thoroughly and consistently—and it is apt not to be—it leads to grave inaccuracies.

Speaking broadly, taxes may be regarded as those parts of the national dividend which the community elects to devote to the expenses of Government; the share of taxes which the merchant pays may be regarded as coming out of his profits, those which the working-man pays as coming out of his wages; and so on. There are, however, some cases in which it is convenient to regard taxes as a distinct share of the Dividend; and to regard the other shares as modified accordingly.

We may suppose that share of the national dividend which goes as rent to be set on one side; and then there remains what would be produced by labour and capital if they were all applied under conditions no more favourable than those under which they are applied at the margin of profitable employment; and a proposal was made in the **h***Economics of Industry* (Book II, ch. IV) that this should be called the

---

f. This refers to Appendix J, § 3 in vol. I of the present edition.

g. The reference applies to Book II, ch. IV in vol. I of the present edition.

Apart from the changes mentioned in the editorial footnotes the subject-matter of the foregoing section was retained unaltered in the 2nd ed. The section was largely reworded in the 3rd and later editions. See § 10 of Book VI, ch. I in vol. I of the present edition.

h. This refers to *The Economics of Industry* by Alfred Marshall and Mary Paley Marshall (1st ed. 1879).

6. RICARDO AND THE INFLUENCE OF DEMAND
ON DISTRIBUTION

In the 1st edition (Book VII, chapter 1, §4) there were the following paragraphs:

Ricardo and his followers were familiar with its action, but did not sufficiently explain it.

Ricardo and the able business men who followed in his wake were perfectly familiar with the practical working of this Law of Substitution. But, perhaps for that very reason, they did not emphasize it, did not make clear the important position which it really holds in their doctrine of wages, and did not even trouble themselves to work out its more remote results. And consequently when the application of mathematical methods of expression to the theory of wages brought into prominence the symmetrical relations between the laws of demand for and those of supply of labour, it seemed to many persons that a great and substantive new discovery had been made. Some recent writers of great ability have even gone so far as to put forward various corollaries of the general law of substitution as new and complete theories of wages destined to supplant the results obtained by the older economists. But all these corollaries are really nothing more than partial explanations of the action of the forces that determine the demand for labour.

i*Wages-and-Profits-Fund*, or the *Earnings-and-Interest-Fund*. These terms were suggested in order to emphasize the opinion that the so-called "Wages-Fund Theory" (see j Note at the end of this chapter), however it might be purified from the vulgar errors which had grown up around it, still erred in suggesting that earnings and interest (or wages and profits) do not stand in the same relation to the national dividend. For although nearly everything that is true and important in the Wages-Fund Theory, *as applied to normal wages*, remains true if throughout profits are written for wages, and wages for profits, yet the title of the theory, as well as the way in which it was applied, appeared to obscure this fundamental symmetry. It seemed therefore worth while to adopt a new catch-word which should emphasize this symmetry.

Experience has however shown that the term "Earnings and Interest Fund" is apt to be misunderstood. For, firstly, a Fund suggests the notion of a reservoir of stored-up wealth, and not a stream, or flow, of new production: and, secondly, the proposal to put rent aside while we are considering how earnings and interest are determined, has been found to suggest that rent is determined first and then takes part in determining earnings and interest; and this is, of course, the opposite of what really occurs.

---

i. An account of the "Wages and Profits Fund, or the Earnings-and-Interest-Fund" will be found in Marshall's paper on "Theories and Facts about Wages", reprinted below (pp. 598–614).

j. This refers to Appendix J in vol. 1 of the present edition.

When we inquire what it is that determines the marginal efficiency of a factor of production, whether it be any kind of labour or material capital, we find that the solution requires a knowledge of the available supply of that factor, and, going a step further, of the causes that determine that supply. The [b]nominal value of everything, whether it be a particular kind of labour or capital or anything else, rests, like the keystone of an arch, balanced in equilibrium between the contending pressures of its two opposing sides. The forces of demand press on the one side, those of supply on the other; and the older economists seem to have been rightly guided by their intuitions, when they silently determined that the forces of supply were those, the study of which was the more urgent and involved the greater difficulty. [c]Nevertheless much harm was done by their undue neglect of the forces of demand. Very much has been gained in clearness, and some substantial additions to our knowledge have been made by the more careful and exact exposition of the action of these forces which is being adopted by the present generation of economists.

[a]It contains a part, but only a small part, of the law of wages.

In the 3rd ed. (Book VI, ch. II, p. 590), the first of the paragraphs just quoted from the 1st ed. was reworded as follows:

Ricardo and the able business men who followed in his wake were familiar with such facts as those which we have been considering. But they took the operation of demand too much for granted as a thing which did not need to be explained: they did not emphasize it, nor did they make clear the important position which it really holds in their doctrine of value, and did not even trouble themselves to

Ricardo and his followers were familiar with the action of the law of substitution, but they laid insufficient stress on the side of demand; and in the reaction too exclusive importance has been assigned to it.

---

a. In the 2nd ed. (Book VI, ch. I, p. 557) this marginal summary ran as follows: "It contains a part, but only a small part, of the explanation of the causes that govern Wages."

b. For reasons that are set out in editorial note **a** to page 526 of vol. I in the present edition (p. 563 above) there can be no doubt the word "nominal" here was a misprint for "normal".

c. This and the next sentence were deleted from the 2nd ed., where they were replaced by the following sentence: "But it must be confessed that their partial neglect of the forces of demand has given occasion to much confusion, and has obscured important truths."

work out its more remote results. And they seem to have been rightly guided by their intuitions, when they silently determined that the forces of supply were those, the study of which was the more urgent and involved the greater difficulty. But it must be confessed that their partial neglect of the forces of demand has given occasion to much confusion, and has obscured important truths. And in the reaction, as we have just seen, too much insistence has been laid on the fact that the earnings of every agent of production come from, and are for the time mainly governed by the value of the product which it takes part in producing; its earnings being so far governed on the same principle as the rent of land. And some have even thought it possible to constitute a complete theory of Distribution out of multifold applications of the law of rent. But they will not reach to that end.

For the subsequent wording of these paragraphs see Book VI, chapter II, §1 in vol. I of the present edition.

7. A FUNDAMENTAL DISTINCTION BETWEEN EARNINGS OF LABOUR AND INTEREST ON CAPITAL AND RENT

In the 1st edition Book VII, chapter III, §1 ran as follows:

But while earnings and interest are among the elements that mutually determine one another, rent is not: it is determined by the others.

§1. WE have seen that the limit or margin of the profitable application of labour and capital in any branch of production, indicates but does not determine the equilibrium rates of the earnings and interest of that labour and capital; the amounts of labour and capital applied, the prices paid for their use, and the price of the commodity produced by them mutually determine one another.

But here we have to call in mind a fundamental difference between earnings and interest on the one hand, and rent on the other. For rent is not one of these mutually determining elements, but is determined by them: the rent or producer's surplus of a differential advantage, not made by man, is the excess value of the return which can be got by its aid where labour and capital are applied with normal ability[1] up to the margin of profitableness over that which the same labour, capital and ability would get if working without the aid of any such advantage.

Thus the central problem of distribution and exchange is concerned with the determination of earnings and interest and the values of commodities. These being known, and the resources of nature and the arts of production being given, the data are supplied from which the producer's surplus afforded by any differential advantage can be calculated by a mere arithmetical process: though it still remains for "particular human institutions," to use Mill's phrase, to determine whether this surplus shall become private property; and if so, whether it shall be held in single or joint ownership, and whether the title to it shall be absolute or subject to special conditions.

[1a] See Book V, ch. IV, §5.

In the 2nd edition (Book VI, ch. 1, §5) the first paragraph in the above section was deleted, but otherwise it was retained unaltered. The remainder of this section was deleted from the 3rd edition; but see §5 of Book VI, ch. II in vol. I of the present edition for the subsequent treatment of the problem discussed here.

8. THE EFFECT OF A FALL IN THE RATE OF INTEREST ON THE EARNINGS OF LABOUR

The following passages represent the last two paragraphs of §4, and the whole of §5 of Book VII, chapter III in the 1st edition:

Again the shoemaker will gain by anything that changes the relative positions of different grades in such a way as to raise his grade relatively to others. In particular, if those grades which are occupied chiefly with the tasks of managing businesses whether manufacturing, trading or any other, should receive so great an influx from other grades, that the earnings of management are lowered permanently relatively to the earnings of manual work, there will be a rise in the net product of every kind of manual labour; and, other

The relations between grades. An increased supply of business ability raises the wages of manual labour

---

a. This reference applies to Book V, ch. V, §5, in vol. I of the present edition.

things being equal, the shoemaker will get more of every commodity on which he spends those wages that represent his own net product.

and so does an increase of capital ultimately. The same is true of an increase in the accumulation of capital, which causes a fall in the rate of interest. It will diminish the amount that has to be deducted from the gross product of the shoemaker's work, in order to find the net product: it will thus increase the net product of his work, and indeed that of workers in all other grades. It will increase the purchasing power of a week's wages to him whether he spends them on the product of his own trade or any other.

But its immediate effect may be to put certain kinds of manual labour at a disadvantage. §5. But it must be noticed that we have just been speaking of the ultimate effect of a fall in the rate of interest and that its immediate effect may be different. For a fall in the rate of interest always gives an advantage to roundabout methods of production over direct methods. If the manufacturer finds that he can borrow money to buy machinery at a low rate of interest, he will substitute machine-work for hand-work in operations for which he would have retained hand-work if he had had to pay a higher rate[1]. In other words more of his outlay will take the form of payments for the work of engineers (as well as for the sacrifices of those who "wait" for the enjoyments over which they have obtained command, and who thus accumulate capital). There will, therefore, be an increased demand for engineers' work, and a diminished demand for shoemakers' work; and for a time engineers' wages are likely to be above, and shoemakers' wages below their normal level. But this inequality will at once bring into action forces tending to redress itself. More parents will bring up their children to the engineers' trade and less to the shoemakers' trade; and when equilibrium has again been reached, the wages of shoemakers will again stand to those of engineers in about the same proportions as the difficulties of their several tasks. The shoemakers, in

[1a] We may again refer to Book VI, ch. v, § 3.

---

a. This reference applies to Book V, chapter IV, §3 in vol. I of the present edition.

common with all others, will then gain the benefit of a diminished rate of charge for the capital that is used in making the shoes and the other things which they consume[1].

Again, an improvement in shoemaking machinery, which makes it more efficient or less costly, will tend to cause it to supplant hand-work, just in the same way as a fall in the rate of interest does. It will benefit all trades, in so far as they are consumers of shoes; and it will benefit engineers for a time by causing an increased demand for their labour, just as a fall in the rate of interest would; but the shoemakers will suffer for a time at least, as we saw they would in the last case. On the other hand, an improvement in the machinery which makes such parts of shoes as are seldom or never made by hand, will lower the supply-price of shoes, and will cause an increased demand for them, and therefore for the work of shoemakers. And they will therefore temporarily gain by the change an even greater increase in the demand for their labour than the engineers do; while as consumers of shoes they will get their small share in the general gain that results from the greater ease with which shoes are produced.

Shoemakers may be temporarily injured by improvements in machinery that can supplant hand work;

A similar effect to this last would be caused by larger and cheaper supplies of leather such as would result from the opening up of improved means of communication with new countries. And this illustrates the general truth that, since England, with her large population and small territory, has to buy much food and raw material from abroad, a very large part of the services on which the English working classes spend their wages, are those of sailors and railwaymen,

but they gain by improvements in machinery that assists hand work, and by a cheapening of leather.

---

[1] This is indeed subject to one correction. It might happen that the task of sewing boots and shoes was specially adapted to the character of a limited number of each generation of workers. Those who had a natural aptitude and liking for such careful monotonous sedentary work, might find that the shoemaking and a few similar trades offered a field of employment in which they were at a greater advantage, or a less disadvantage, relatively to other workers, than in any other trades. In that case the shrinkage of this field of employment, resulting from a large use of shoemaking machinery, might have caused this field to be permanently overcrowded, and might have permanently lowered the normal wages of workers with this particular cast of faculties, relatively to other workers. And, in so far as the grade to which any occupation belongs depends on the rarity of the natural faculties required in it, relatively to the aggregate demand for those faculties, the work of sewing shoes would have been put down to a somewhat lower grade than that in which it would have found its place had there been no machinery.

of shipbuilders and makers of steel rails, and of those who have supplied the capital by which the ships, railways, &c. have been made. Improvements in transport, quite as much as improvements in manufacture, have increased the amount of the necessaries, comforts and luxuries of life which make up that aggregate of the net products of a hundred days' labour of other workers in his own grade (or of workers in other grades in due proportion) which the English shoe-maker or other worker can buy with the wages of a hundred days' of his own labour.

In the 2nd edition (Book VI, ch. II, §§4 and 5) the whole of the above passages were retained unaltered. They were deleted from the 3rd edition; but see §9 of Book VI, chapter II in vol. I of the present edition for the subsequent treatment of this problem.

9. "THEORIES AND FACTS ABOUT WAGES"

In 1885 Marshall read a paper to the Industrial Remuneration Con-ference, which was entitled "How far do remediable causes influence prejudicially (*a*) the continuity of employment, (*b*) the rates of wages?". He attached to this paper four Appendices, of which the fourth (Appen-dix D), entitled "Theories and Facts about Wages"[a] was originally written for and printed in the Annual of the Wholesale Co-operative Society for 1885, and was reprinted in the published *Proceedings of the Industrial Remuneration Conference (1885)*. The text ran as follows:

1. I have been asked to give an account of the doctrines as to wages held by the past and present generations of econo-mists, with some statement of the actual facts of the case. It is difficult to treat such large questions in a short space; but I hope to be able to give the main outlines of them.

We hear a great deal about the supplanting of old-fashioned theories of wages by newer and truer doctrines. But in fact the change in the theory itself has not been very great. Although a good deal of new work has been added, and the old work has been developed, yet but very little has been destroyed. Almost everything that was ever said by the great economists of the first half of the century is true now if properly understood. Much of it will remain true for ever,

---

a. Reference to this article will be found on page 823 n. in vol. I of the present edition.

or at all events till the glorious time comes when people are willing to work as hard from a sense of duty as now they work for pay. There has been a great change; but it has not been in the theory itself, it has been in understanding how it is to be applied, and how it is not to be applied.

At the beginning of the century, when the great economists, Malthus and Ricardo, wrote, the world was in a miserable condition, which, thank God, has passed away. The general principles which they laid down were almost all true; but their way of expressing them was coloured by the peculiar character of the facts among which they lived. It required a great mental effort to grasp the principles of their reasoning; and the effort was made by but few of their followers. But it was easy to take hold of isolated sentences and to repeat them without the conditions implied in the context. And this was done. Political Economy became fashionable. In Parliament and the counting house, in the pulpit and the press, the authority of Political Economy was invoked for all kinds of purposes; but before all and above all, for the purpose of keeping the working-man in his place. Nearly all the greatest economists have been earnest and fearless friends of the working classes; they have been impelled to the study of economics chiefly by a desire to see how far it was possible to diminish the evils of poverty. But Ricardo had very little sympathy one way or the other; and many of those who made themselves a reputation by the confidence with which they misunderstood parts of what he said, were partisans of capital. The reputation of Economic Science has suffered and is suffering for the misdoings of its camp followers.

2. At the beginning of the century the prices of things consumed by the labourer, taken one with another, were nearly double what they are now. And meanwhile the average money wages of manual labour have nearly doubled. There has not indeed been a very great rise in the wages of all occupations; the improvement is chiefly due to the fact that then there were very few skilled workers, while now there are comparatively few who are entirely unskilled. The average income for each man, woman, and child in

the manual labour classes was about £12 then, and is not less than £20 now. These classes have now none too much of the necessaries, comforts, and luxuries of life; but then they had less than a third of what they have now. Starvation and disease ran riot in the land.

Some causes of this misery were seen clearly enough by everyone, without aid from the economists. The great war with France had cost about fifteen hundred million pounds; and that was probably a good deal more than the value of everything that was left in the country, except the land. The imperial taxes were 20 per cent of the total income of the country; the mere interest on the debt was 10 per cent of it. Next an unparalleled series of bad harvests had made wheat terribly dear; it was frequently over £6 a quarter, and once over £10.

But besides all this, the administrators of the Poor Law were raising up new evils by attempting to relieve suffering indiscriminately. What they really did was to discriminate against the industrious and in favour of the dissolute. Farmers sometimes had to turn away hard working men who had saved a little money, and make them live on that, in order to make room for drones forced on them by the parish. The industrious were so much worse provided for than those who went to the parish, that in time independent labourers almost ceased to exist. Wages were lowered all round and eked out by parish pay. He got on best who was the best adept at the arts of imposition. In the South, where the system was carried to the greatest lengths, the labourer has never recovered from the injury thus done to his character and wages. A hundred years ago wages were higher in the South than in the North of England; now they are half as much again in the North as in the South. In these and other ways the Poor Laws did evil. Mischief was done, not by the amount of relief given, but by its being given in the wrong way and to the wrong persons, so as to cause the survival of the worst in place of the best. Probably half of all the lives of extreme misery and want in the country are due to this cause.

The nation at large did not get to see this last cause of

misery till 1834; but the economists saw it earlier. They looked at the history of England, and found that the working population had been well off when it had been increasing slowly in number, and badly off when it had been increasing fast. They studied the history of wages, and found that wages were once really high; it was just after the black death had destroyed a great part of the population. Again, they knew that from 1700 to 1760 population had been almost stationary, and their wages had steadily risen. But from 1760 onwards numbers had increased fast, and misery had increased faster. Trade, indeed, had grown, and there had been a marvellous series of mechanical inventions, but these had been able to do little to diminish the difficulty of getting food. The economists looked abroad, and they saw poverty wherever there was a dense population. If in any happy valley they found everyone well off, they found then, what we find now, a custom that only one son out of each family should marry. They found that in England before 1760 it was not very easy for a man to get a house for himself while he was quite young; he had generally to go on a good while living with other young men in his father's or employer's house before he could see his way to marry. But since then manufacturers had made so many new openings that it had become the habit for everyone to marry when he wanted to, and to trust to luck. And then later on the Poor Law officers made life pretty easy for the father of a large family, if he would only give up all attempts to help himself and cringe enough to them. Meanwhile, as bread grew dearer, cultivation was creeping up the hillsides. Wheat was grown on miserable land that would not give eight bushels an acre, though more labour had been spent on it than was wanted to raise twenty or thirty bushels on fairly good land.

3. The economists saw all this; and they thought rightly, that at that particular time there was no truth more important, none on which the philanthropist should insist with more earnestness, than what they called the law of Diminishing Return. This was:—The natural law of the fertility of the land is that, other things being equal, an increased application of capital and labour to land will not increase in like

proportion the raw produce raised from it. They went on to apply this to the question of wages. If twenty men are employed on a farm and a twenty-first wants to be taken on, he will produce less than the others did, and therefore the farmer cannot afford to pay him so much; and he must therefore take a less quantity of corn as wages. (I say a less quantity of corn so as to avoid all trouble about changes in the price of corn.) The next step will be for the farmer to lower everybody else's wages to his level. The next step will be for the landlord to say to the farmer, "you get your labour for lower wages (at all events when measured in corn), and so you can afford to pay me more rent; if you do not agree to pay it, I will find someone else who will". A rise of rents and a fall of wages is therefore, they argued, the necessary consequence of an excessive growth of population. He who truly loves the people will urge them not to marry early.

Now the first sentence of this reasoning has the clause "other things being equal", and the conclusions may be invalid if other things are not equal. The economists knew of this condition, but they did not pay much attention to it: and this is not so much because they were careless as because it had then no great practical importance. No one, however sagacious, would have anticipated the strange combination of causes which have since then lowered the price of corn: all reasonable expectations were in the other direction. The new machinery was manufacturing things cheaply; but the working-man could not consume many of them himself, and if he wanted to send them abroad and to buy food with them, he had to pay enormous taxes for doing so. The economists were convinced of the advantages of free trade, but they had no hope that the landed interests which then ruled the country could be made to allow it. And even with free trade they did not expect to be able to buy large supplies of corn cheaply, for the wheat lands of America were then chiefly on the poor soil of the Atlantic border. The middle region of America was but little known, and seemed too far off for extensive trade; while the richest wheatland of all, that in the North-Western States and California, was less known than the centre of Africa is now. Since then England has adopted free trade, and railways and steamships have come into existence. So great has been the growth of knowledge, of mechanical invention, and of the aid which capital affords to labour, that the working-man can buy his bread from abroad at the cost of less labour than he could get it with even in 1760, before the rapid growth of population had set in. The old economists made wonderfully good use of their knowledge as far as it went; but we, knowing what they could not even guess, can see the way to improving the first part of their doctrine of wages. But before doing this let us look at the rest of it.

4. Great as was the poverty of the English people then, foreign countries were poorer still. In most of them population was sparse, and therefore food was cheap; but for all that they were underfed, and could not provide themselves with the sinews of war. France, after her first victories, helped herself along by the forced contributions of others. But the countries of Central Europe could not support their own armies without England's aid. Even America, with all her energy and national resources, was not rich; she could not have subsidised Continental armies. The economists looked for the explanation, and found it chiefly in England's accumulated capital, which, though small when judged by our present standard, was very much greater than that of any other country. Other nations were envious of England, and wanted to follow in her steps; but they were unable to do so, partly indeed for other reasons, but chiefly because they had not capital enough. Their annual income was required for immediate consumption. There was not in them a large class of people who had a good store of wealth set by, which they did not need to consume at once, and which they could devote to making machines and other things that would aid labour and enable it to produce a larger store of things for future consumption. A special tone was given to their arguments by the facts that capital was scarce everywhere, even in England; that the efficiency of labour was becoming more and more dependent on the machinery by which it was aided; and lastly, that some foolish followers of Rousseau were

telling the working classes that they would be better off without any capital at all.

In consequence, the economists gave extreme prominence to the statements; first, that labour requires the support of capital, i.e. of good clothes, etc., that have been already produced; and secondly, that labour requires the aid of capital in the form of factories, stores of raw material, etc. Of course the workman might have supplied his own capital, but in fact he seldom had more than a little store of clothes and furniture, and perhaps a few simple tools of his own—he was dependent for everything else on the savings of others. The labourer received clothes ready to wear, bread ready to eat, or the money with which he could purchase them. The capitalist received a spinning of wool into yarn, a weaving of yarn into cloth, or a ploughing of land, and only in a few cases commodities ready for use, coats ready to be worn or bread ready to be eaten. There are, no doubt, important exceptions, but the ordinary bargain between employers and employed is that the latter receives things ready for immediate use and the former receives help towards making things that will be of use hereafter. These facts the economists expressed by saying that all labour requires the support of capital, whether owned by the labourer or by someone else; and that when anyone works for hire, his wages are, as a rule, advanced to him out of his employer's capital— advanced, that is, without waiting till the things which he is engaged in making are ready for use. These simple statements have been a good deal criticised, but they have never been denied by anyone who has taken them in the sense in which they were meant.

The older economists, however, went on to say that the amount of wages was limited by the amount of capital; and this statement cannot be defended; at best it is but a slovenly way of talking. It has suggested to some people the notion that the total amount of wages that could be paid in a country in the course of, say, a year, was a fixed sum. If by the threat of a strike, or in any other way, one body of workmen got an increase of wages, they would be told that in consequence other bodies of workmen must lose an amount exactly equal in the aggregate to what they had gained. Those who have said this, have perhaps thought of agricultural produce, which has but one harvest in the year. If all the wheat raised at one harvest is sure to be eaten before the next, and if none can be imported, then it is true that if anyone's share of the wheat is increased, there will be just so much less for others to have. But this does not justify the statement that the amount of wages payable in a country is fixed by the capital in it, a doctrine which has been called "the vulgar form of the wages fund theory", and which was used for partisan purposes by shallow and dogmatic hangers-on of economic science. Unfortunately isolated sentences can be quoted even from the best of the older economists which seem to support this doctrine. The whole spirit of their reasoning was opposed to it, but those who thought any stick good enough to beat the trades unions with, seized eagerly on these carelessly-worded sentences.

5. Let us, then, look at the doctrine which the economists meant to express by this unfortunate phrase. They saw that if wages rise in one trade without any corresponding increase in efficiency of work, someone or other must lose what that trade gained. They classed all incomes as rent, profits, and wages. Of course, part of the loss might fall on rent; but the economists could prove that that was not very likely unless population diminished. And, therefore, it must fall on profits or wages, or both. If it fell on profits they argued that capital would shrink; there would be less accumulated wealth with which to pay wages to labour, and supply it with the requisite raw material, etc. Therefore there would be less effective demand for labour; and so, by one route or another, other workers would suffer for the extra gain got by the first group. The complete argument has a good deal more detail, and in whatever form it is expressed, it takes up a great many pages in every thorough economic treatise. But what has just been given is its backbone.

Now, when one looks at the argument one finds that there is really nothing in it about a fixed wages fund. There is something in it about there being at any time a definite (not a fixed) wages and profits fund. A world of trouble would have been saved if they had used this phrase from the beginning. The French and German economists, though on the whole they had not done nearly so much good work as the English, have never given any countenance to the doctrine that there is a determinate wages fund.

The great difference between the views of wages taken by English economists in the past and the present generation is then this—they all regard wages as paid out of capital; but while the older economists talked as though wages were limited by the amount of capital that had been already put aside to pay wages with, the younger economists have, for the last ten or fifteen years, put the case in another way. They see that if the efficiency of industry were increased, and more things were produced, higher wages would be paid at once by drawing more rapidly on the stocks already in hand. It might be necessary to be a little careful about the stocks of some kinds of raw produce which could not be replenished very quickly. But with a few exceptions the increased supplies would come in so soon that the stores need never run low. Therefore, the younger economists do not speak of wages as limited by capital. But they say that every increase of capital raises wages, because it increases the productiveness of industry; it increases the competition of the capitalist for the aid of labour, and thus lowers the rate of interest and increases that part of the total produce which capital is compelled to resign to labour.

6. I will now put together the new version of the economic doctrines in my own words, and illustrate it by a reference to facts.

First, as to what determines the produce of capital and labour. With equal capital per head, equal individual efficiency, and equal knowledge of the arts of production, the amount of raw produce raised per head is greatest in a rich new country that is well settled but thinly peopled, and steadily diminishes with every increase in the population. But this abundance of raw produce is not of much use to them unless some of it can be sold at a high price to manufacturing countries. Unless this can be done, life in a thinly-peopled country is very hard, because nothing except raw produce can be got easily. That is verified by history. The early colonists of America got freedom and plenty of plain food; but in almost every other respect they were worse off than the English agricultural labourer on 15s. a week is now. If trade with other places were impossible, the law of the total productiveness of industry, counting in raw and manufactured commodities together, would be generally a law of increasing and not of diminishing return. That is to say, an increase in population (accompanied by a corresponding increase of capital) would increase and not diminish the average material well-being—at all events, until the country had become crowded and raw produce had to be raised in very expensive ways. The railway and steamship have improved the condition of all countries, but most of all, those whose population is very thin and those whose population is very thick. As things are, the total necessaries, comforts, and luxuries that can be got by given capital, labour, and intelligence, is perhaps greatest where the population is ten to the square mile, and diminishes very slowly with every increase in the population. But it must be admitted that the advantage that America and Australia have over the crowded countries of Western Europe is not quite so great as appears. Real as well as money wages are, no doubt, higher there than here; but the work that has to be done to earn them is harder. Even in America itself many of those who can and will work hardest go West, and wages are therefore much higher West than East; but if the Western men came East they would get more than average wages, and some of the Eastern men who go West find it difficult to get employment.

But of course every improvement in knowledge and in the arts of production, as well as every increase in the capital per head, increases the total production per head. So great has been the increase of prosperity in this country, while population has been growing rapidly, that if we could reduce raw and manufactured goods to a common standard of price, we should probably find the average real income of the manual labour classes now higher than was the average income of all, rich and poor together, a century ago.

7. Passing now from the amount of produce per head to the way in which it is distributed, we may first consider the landlord's share. The old economists, writing when the importation of corn on a large scale was out of the question, said that an increase of the population compelled poorer soils to be cultivated, and raised rents; and they expected a rapid and constant rise of rents in England. It has turned out otherwise. Imported food has been so cheap that agricultural rents have sometimes fallen fast. So that agricultural rent proper, i.e. what remains after deducting interest on capital sunk in the land, is now probably not more than it was early in the century. It was then a very important part of the total income of the country—perhaps a sixth part; while now it is certainly less than a twentieth part. But the increase of wealth and population has raised the value of land for purposes of residence, of railways, mining, etc.; so that on the whole the owners of land have probably not lost by free trade.

8. After deducting rent from the total produce of industry, there remains what has just been called the Wages and Profits Fund. But profits are made up of two parts—interest, which goes to the owner of capital, and the earnings got by the employer of the capital. There is a growing tendency to class these earnings, which may be called the Earnings of Management, with other kinds of earnings; so I prefer to speak of this Fund as the Earnings and Interest Fund. Just to fix the ideas, I will give a rough estimate as to this. We may take agricultural rent proper and ground rents at about £75 millions. At least £50 millions more are got from foreign investments, which we do not want to count in here. The rest of the national income, that which constitutes the Earnings and Interest Fund for the labour and capital employed at home, is a little over £1000 millions. Nearly £250 millions are interest on capital, and nearly £800 millions are earnings of labour. This last sum we may again regard as divided up into about £500 millions for the wages of the working-classes, and nearly £300 millions for the earnings of all other classes, including employers. Of course we might go further, dividing up each of these two parts

into the shares of many different grades or classes of labour. Each of these classes of labour has its work in production; we may call it a factor of production.

9. Well, then, the great law of distribution is, that the more useful one factor of production is, and the scarcer it is, the higher will be the rate at which its services are paid. For instance, if two skilled labourers, after allowing for the expense of the machinery they use, can do as much as five unskilled, they will get as much wages as the five unskilled can get should they stay in the trade. Again, supposing an employer can devise such economic arrangements of machinery, etc., as to make the labour of 500 labourers reach as far as ordinary employers would the labour of 600, then his earnings of management will exceed theirs by the wages of a hundred labourers. But he can go on doing this only so long as there are not many employers like him. If there are, they will compete with one another, lower the price of their goods, and distribute the benefit of their skill among the community at large. These illustrations explain the general principle, which we may now state a little more carefully.

The total Earnings and Interest Fund depends on the resources of nature and the efficiency of capital and labour acting on it. The larger this is, the more there will be to be divided up, and the larger, other things being equal, will the share of each be. Thus, in a new and rich country interest can be high, and the earnings of all classes of labour, from the employer down to the lowest unskilled labourer, can be high. But, other things being equal, if any one factor of production increases relatively to the others, it will become in less and less request. If, for instance, capital increases much faster than labour, without there being many inventions to open up new fields for its employment, capital will go a-begging, and the rate of interest will fall. If the number of people who want to do clerk's work increases out of proportion to the population, their wages will fall. If the number of unskilled labourers increases relatively to others, they will find difficulty in getting employment; interest will rise at their expense, and the earnings of employers and of all other kinds of labour will rise at their expense. On the other hand, if the number of unskilled labourers were to diminish sufficiently, then those who did unskilled work would have to be paid good wages. If the total production was not increased, these extra wages would have to be paid out of the shares of capital, and of the higher kinds of labour; but even so, the great aim would have been attained of making the increase of wealth hurry up the diminution of want a little faster. But, if the diminution of unskilled labour is brought about by increasing the efficiency of labour, it will increase production, and there will be a larger fund to be divided up.

10. Now let us apply this general reasoning to the changes in the distribution of wealth in modern England. The leading influence in these changes is, that capital is growing at least twice as fast as population. Population is not quite doubling itself in fifty years, while capital is doubling itself in less than twenty-five. If it had not been for the new uses that are always being found for capital in different forms, it would have been impossible to employ so much with any great advantage.

It must have either migrated, or have competed for occupation until it had forced down its price to perhaps one per cent a year. Even as things are, it has had to submit to a continually decreasing rate of interest; and its loss has been labour's gain.

This change is partly disguised by the fact that when capital is largest its total share of the produce is largest too. For instance, if in California the capital which each workman makes use of is equal in value to his work for one year, while in Lancashire it is equal to his work for ten years, then, though the rate of interest is lower in Lancashire than in California, the fraction of the produce which goes to capital may be six or seven times as large in Lancashire as in California. This accounts for the apparent anomaly, that while the total produce per head is larger in Lancashire, the wages are higher in California. If Lancashire had only as much capital per head as California has, the total produce handed over to capital would of course be less; but that would be no gain to labour. For production could not be carried on efficiently, labour would have to pay a higher rate of interest for whatever capital it did use, and wages would be much lower than they are.

11. The profits of business include the earnings of management got by the employer, as well as the interest got by his capital. But in spite of exceptional cases to the contrary, earnings of management are falling, just as interest is; and for the same reasons. This is a special instance of a great fact that has been noticed in America and on the Continent (especially by M. Leroy Beaulieu) as well as in England. It is that the difference between the earnings in different grades of labour is steadily diminishing. A generation ago so few people got a good education, that for every pound spent on it there might fairly be expected a total return of from perhaps ten to a hundred pounds in after life. But the growth of intelligence has made people more willing to look far ahead; the standard of education has risen in all the ranks of life. So that while the rate of interest on capital invested in material things is about a quarter less than it was, the interest on capital invested in education has perhaps fallen one-half. For each pound invested in education, there is perhaps not more than half as much returned in extra earning in after life as there used to be.

On the other hand, extraordinary natural abilities of every kind find a wider scope and secure higher earnings than ever. If we take as our standard the wages of unskilled labour, there is a steady fall in the earnings that an expensive start in life will secure to people of average ability, whether they be musicians, or painters, or medical men, or lawyers, or, lastly, business men. The fact is much more important, though it attracts much less attention than the fact that in all these occupations people with exceptional ability can make fortunes unheard of till now.

12. Exceptionally favoured men in business get command over vast capitals, and are thus able to do great things. But nearly all very rich men owe a good deal of their wealth to judicious and fortunate speculation. These gains are chiefly at the expense, not of the general public, but of less successful speculators. In old times fortunes were more even, and if a man failed, his story was long remembered

in his neighbourhood; so a fairly true average of gains and losses could be struck. Now, those who fail are quickly lost to sight; their losses heap up the conspicuous gains of successful men. Partly for this reason, few people are aware how great a fall there has been in the real average earnings of men of business with a moderate capital and average ability.

Parallel changes are going on within the ranks of hired labour. Simple writing, simple machine turning, weaving, and similar occupations are sinking in the industrial scale. Almost any one with a sound body and mind, and with a little training, is fit for them. But they used to get high wages, because an insufficient number of people had had the training. Not long ago a clerk who did the simplest work got the wages of two or three agricultural labourers. Now he gets, in England, hardly more than the wages of one; in Australia less than the wages of one. But judgement, self-possession, promptness, and shrewdness, are qualities for which the demand is increasing faster than the supply, though that is increasing very fast. Wages are rising steadily in all occupations in which these qualities are wanted in a high degree; and they are rising most rapidly in occupations which require these together with great powers of physical endurance.

Whenever any new kind of skill is wanted, it is at first rare, and must be paid highly. But if it does not require exceptional natural abilities, there will soon be a good supply of it, and wages are likely to fall. This is, in nine cases out of ten, the explanation of any fall there has been in the wages of particular trades during the last fifty years. But meanwhile new trades are always breaking out that require higher abilities and get higher payment. And in spite of the fact that wages are falling in many trades, the average real wages of manual labour are rising rapidly. It must be remembered that 20s. a week now will buy as much as 25s. would twelve years ago. Thus there is a constant tendency for the lower ranks of industry to gain on the higher; so that a steadily increasing share of the benefits of progress is going to those who have the greatest need to be lifted up.

But to this rule there is one great exception. Those who have a poor physique and a weak character—those who are limp in body and mind—are falling, or if not, it is because they are already as low as they can go. They are found in greatest numbers wherever there is most wealth, but they are not the products of wealth, any more than thrushes are born of gooseberry trees. There are no feeble people in the Prairies. Some feeble people go there, but they either get back quickly to a large town, or else they die. Charity and sanitary regulations are keeping alive, in our large towns, thousands of such persons, who would have died even fifty years ago. Meanwhile economic forces are pressing heavily on them, for they can do nothing but easy monotonous work, most of which can be done as well, or better, by machinery or by children. Public or private charity may palliate their misery, but the only remedy is to prevent such people from coming into existence. It must be remembered that the poorest of the poor are descended from all ranks of society; probably the upper ranks contribute more than their proportionate share to them. Crime and dissoluteness in one generation often engender disease, feebleness, dissoluteness, and crime for many generations to come. The long chains of evils that thus result cannot be cut short without the active aid of all classes; but if all classes help wisely but boldly, tenderly but firmly, they can, I believe, do it.

13. It would be out of place here to discuss the institution of private property. Assuming, as I do, that it is to be kept up without fundamental change, I think I have shown that though there are still great evils, though there is still much needless misery, yet in the main, and on the whole, the changes at present at work are such as to be desired; only they are not going fast enough. Fast as is the increase in the supply in the higher grades of labour, and the diminution in that of the lower, we want them to be faster. An equal increase in all grades would lower earnings a little, but not much if capital grew fast. But an increase of population may go with a rapid rise of average wages, if the children of each grade are brought up with the intelligence, self-command, and vigour that now belong to the grade above

them. Persons in any rank of life who are not in good physical and mental health have no moral right to have children. But in spite of popular Malthusianism, though not in opposition to Malthus' principles, we may affirm that those who bring up a large, healthy family with a thoroughly good physical, mental, and moral training relatively to their own rank of life, do a service to their country. If the children emigrate, they do a still greater service to the world. A good training is not complete if it only makes them efficient producers, it must also make them wise and temperate consumers and good citizens.

It is to be hoped that all these children will save a little capital of their own, and that some of them will rise from lower ranks to be employers of labour. Everyone who so passes upwards benefits labour in two ways—he diminishes the competition of labour for employment, and he increases the competition for labour on the part of employing and directing power.

If small men of business are being pushed out by big men, big men are being pushed out by joint-stock companies and other associations of little men. These are gradually making the great mass of the nation owners of its most important industries and employers of its ablest and most powerful business men. Among these associations the genuine co-operative societies have the noblest work. Besides his wages and interest on his capital, they are giving the workman high mental and moral aspirations; they afford him a real insight into the problems of business, and they help to diminish industrial strife. They are the best of all known means for enabling an increasing share of the income of the country to go into the hands of those who have the greatest need for it and can turn it to the best use.

BOOK VI, CHAPTER III

EARNINGS OF LABOUR

a. Except where otherwise stated the wording of this chapter dates substantially from the 1st edition.

b. So since the 4th edition. In the 1st edition (Book VII, ch. IV) and in the 2nd and 3rd editions (Book VI, ch. III) this chapter was entitled "Demand and Supply in Relation to Labour. Real and Nominal Earnings".

c. This paragraph dates in its present form from the 3rd ed. (p. 624), where it replaced the following paragraph dating from the 2nd ed. (p. 577):

O U R next step must be to supplement the discussion of the general theory of equilibrium of demand and supply given in the last Book. We there left on one side, as far as might be, all considerations turning on the special qualities and incidents of the agents of production. We did not inquire minutely how price and the causes that determine it need to be differently estimated in the case of the hiring price of labour, and the purchase price of commodities. We avoided difficulties connected with the analysis of profits, paying no attention to the many different scopes which the usage of the market place assigns to this term, and even to the more elementary term interest. We took no account of the influence of varieties of tenure on the form of demand for land; and we did not inquire in detail how far the general theories of rent and quasi-rent are applicable to the incomes earned by natural abilities, or by skill and knowledge acquired long ago, whether in the ranks of the employers, the employed, or the professional classes.

d. This paragraph dates substantially from the 3rd ed. (p. 624), where it replaced the following paragraph dating from the 2nd ed. (p. 577):

These deficiencies will be made good in the following three groups of chapters on demand and supply in relation to labour, to capital and business power, and to land, respectively.

615

PAGE 547

a. This paragraph was inserted in the 7th ed. (p. 547).

b. Subject to the change of one word this footnote dates from the 6th ed. (p. 546 n.).

c. In the 8th ed. (p. 547 n.) the words "fifty years" replaced the words "thirty years" dating from the 6th ed.

PAGE 548

a. So since the 6th ed. (p. 547) where these clauses replaced the following clauses dating from the 1st ed. (p. 573).

and we may then regard competition, or to speak more exactly, economic freedom and enterprise, as tending to make *time-earnings* in occupations of equal difficulty and in neighbouring places (not equal, but) proportionate to the efficiency of the workers.

b. In the 7th ed. (p. 548), the word "Lancashire", placed before the words "cotton mills" in the first six editions, was deleted.

PAGE 549

a. So since the 3rd ed. (p. 626) where the wording in the present text replaced the following wording in the earlier editions: "and we may find it in *task-wages*, or what is perhaps better *efficiency wages*, or more broadly *efficiency earnings*."

b. So since the 3rd ed. (pp. 626–7), where the present wording of this clause replaced the following clauses dating from the 1st ed. (p. 574):

but with reference to the severity of the *task* which was imposed on the worker; or to get at the same result by another route, the exertion of ability and *efficiency* required of him.

c. The following footnote attached to the word "worker" in the 3rd ed. (p. 627 n.) was deleted from the 5th ed.

In earlier editions the term *task-wages* was given as an alternative to *efficiency-wages;* but that term is in some trades applied to wages paid by the day on condition that a certain definite *task* be accomplished in it. If as generally is the case the workman is at liberty to exceed the *minimum* task, and to be paid in proportion, the system is really one of piece-work; formal expression being given to the condition latent in all piece-work in which expensive plant is used, that the plant shall be turned to fairly good account. The variations in the conditions of hiring in different trades and places are numerous, but they bear more intimately on labour politics than on normal wages; and what has to be said about them may conveniently be deferred to a later stage. Meanwhile reference may be made to a full discussion of them in Mr Schloss' *Methods of Industrial Remuneration;*

and an article by him in the *Economic Journal*, vol. II. Many interesting facts bearing on the matter are to be found in the *Report of the Labour Commission*, and in Mr Charles Booth's *Life and Labour in London*.

In the 6th ed. (p. 548 n.) the following footnote was inserted, attached to the word "worker", but it was deleted from the 7th ed.:

Prof. Moore (*Economic Journal*, 1907) makes a suggestive comparison between statistical generalizations of Mr Galton and Prof. Pearson as to the proportionate distribution of any particular character (such as efficiency) among a population, and the distribution of high earnings as shown by economic statistics. The data for this purpose are very inadequate; but his line of inquiry seems very promising. He appears however to have misconceived the argument in the text.

PAGE 550

a. So since the 7th ed. (pp. 550 n.–1 n.) where this sentence replaced the following sentence dating from the 1st ed. (p. 576 n.): "As it is, his treatment of wages is less instructive than that of Malthus."

PAGE 552

a. The following footnote was attached to the word "them" in the 1st ed. (p. 577 n.):

Many plans have been suggested for making a special estimate of the purchasing power of money with regard to those things that are chiefly consumed by the working classes, the importance of each thing being taken in such estimate as proportionate to the amount spent on it in an average working class budget. Mr Edward Atkinson has suggested that this measure of purchasing power should be called "a standard ration" (see the Appendix to his *Distribution of Products*). But at best it could only be approximate, partly because the working classes contain within themselves several different grades, with corresponding variations in the percentages of their incomes which they devote to purchasing different things. Working men's budgets have often been collected and compared; as, for instance, by her Majesty's consuls, in the *Reports on the condition of the Industrial Classes*, 1872; and by those of the United States, see Young's *Labour in Europe and America*. See also the reports of various American Labour Bureaux, especially that of the United States Commissioner of Labour for 1886. General Walker's Treatise, *On Wages*, and Roscher's *Political Economy*, contain many suggestive remarks and facts bearing on the subject of this section and indeed of the whole chapter.

In the 2nd to the 4th editions this paragraph was retained subject to the deletion of the fourth and fifth sentences. The whole paragraph was deleted from the 5th ed.

b. The following additional paragraph in the 1st ed. (pp. 578–9) at this point was deleted from the 2nd ed.:

Turning next to the elements of which real earnings are made up, we may call to mind the general remarks made in our discussion of the term income. We saw that there are many elements of real income which do not appear in the form of money, and are in some danger of being overlooked.

The services which people render to themselves or to other members of their families have to be reckoned for, especially when individual, or trade, or local customs differ in this respect; and, when comparing earnings in different places, we must take account of the rights to the use of common property which are enjoyed in them, as for instance toll-free roads and bridges, public parks and museums; and of the services of the State generally, and especially in maintaining security and freedom. In some classes of inquiries we must take careful note on the one hand of the advantages which towns' folk get from the lighting of their streets, and from easy access to varied amusements and social intercourse; and on the other of those which country folk derive from the abundance of fresh air and light, and of open-air play for their children. The greater cheapness of houseroom in the country and of most other things in the towns, is an element of the purchasing power of money referred to in the last section.

c. So since the 4th ed. (p. 635). In the earlier editions this ran as follows:

Next let us take account of the different modes of payment which are adopted in different occupations. We may select for study the case of domestic servants. We have already noticed that when they have to supply themselves at their own cost...etc.

d. This footnote dates from the 3rd ed. (p. 630 n.).

e. So since the 3rd ed. (p. 361 n.) where this footnote replaced the following footnote dating from the first ed. (p. 578 n.):

> This class of questions is of more practical importance than those closely allied questions on which we touched (Book II, ch. v, § 3), and which relate to the lines of division between production and consumption-capital, and between wealth that is and is not capital. The close connection, however, between the two groups of questions illustrates the fact that the earnings of many even of the professional and wage-receiving classes are in a considerable measure dependent on their being in command of some material capital.

Book II, ch. v, § 3 in the 1st ed. is reprinted above. See pp. 224–5.

PAGE 553

a. The following additional sentences, with reference to payment of wages in kind, dating from the 1st ed. (p. 581), were deleted from the 6th ed.:

The most virulent forms of the system have always been those which have lain beneath the surface; and in our own day they still flourish in those industries which retain a semi-mediæval character, while they seldom exist in those in which the modern factory system prevails. The influence of the system for evil in the past has been so great, that it may rank with the old poor law and the unhealthy conditions of juvenile labour early in the century as a chief cause of the degradation of large numbers of the working classes: but its influence is not now great save in a few trades.

b. In the 1st ed. (p. 580) where this paragraph was in the text it was preceded by the following paragraph:

In a new country in which large agricultural, mining and other businesses often spring up at a great distance from any considerable town, the employers are compelled to supply their workpeople with everything they want, either by paying part of their wages in the form of allowances of food, clothing &c., or by opening stores for them. Stores of this kind are generally managed on a straightforward business-like principle, and wholesome customs and traditions thus started are apt to survive even when the employers' shops have ceased to be necessary in consequence of the growth of fairly good independent shops in the neighbourhood. The shops remain an almost unmixed benefit to all concerned so long as dealing at them is voluntary: and even when it becomes compulsory they may be on the whole a benefit to the workpeople, provided they are managed with ability and honesty. For, since the employers ensure themselves prompt sales and secure payments by contracting that a certain part of the wages paid by them shall be taken out in purchases at the stores, they are able to work these stores more cheaply than ordinary retail shops, and thus to pay, with an equal profit to themselves, higher real wages than would otherwise be possible.

[margin note:] The Truck System. In some cases it is almost necessary: and then it is usually worked in a generous spirit for the benefit of all concerned.

In the 2nd to the 4th editions this formed the first paragraph of footnote 1 on this page of vol. I. The fourth sentence of this paragraph was deleted from the 5th ed., and the second and third sentences from the 6th ed., where the first sentence was slightly reworded.

c. So since the 6th ed. (p. 553 n.). In the first four editions there was the following paragraph, which was deleted from the 5th ed.:

The story of the abuses of the *Truck system* in modern England is told in a long series of Parliamentary Reports, which come down to the present time: and while the evil itself has been steadily diminishing, the intensity of the light thrown on what remains has been increasing as steadily. An excellent account of the payments in kind by which the agricultural labourer's wages are supplemented is given by Mr Kebbel (*The Agricultural Labourer*, 2nd ed., ch. II). A table to be found in vol. xx of the United States Census for 1880 shows that of 773 manufacturing firms which answer questions as to the mode of payment adopted by them, 681, or 88 per cent, pay in cash: but in some of the States which are thinly populated the proportion is not much more than one half.

PAGE 555

a. This footnote dates from the 3rd ed. (p. 635 n.).

PAGE 556

a. So since the 2nd ed. (p. 588) where the remainder of this sentence replaced the following clause in the 1st ed. (p. 584): "and the chief influence which the occupation of the head of a family exerts on that of other members comes as a rule from the place in which he works and not directly from the nature of his trade."

b. This footnote dates from the 3rd ed. (p. 635 n.).

PAGE 558

a. The word "sanitary" before the word "science", dating from the 1st ed. (p. 586), was deleted from the 7th ed.

b. The word "therefore" was inserted before the word "dear", in the 7th ed. (p. 558).

BOOK VI, CHAPTER IV

EARNINGS OF LABOUR, CONTINUED

PAGE 559

a. Except where otherwise stated the wording of this chapter dates substantially from the 1st edition.

b. So since the 4th edition. In the 1st edition (Book VII, ch. v) and in the 2nd and 3rd editions (Book VI, ch. iv), this chapter was entitled "Demand and Supply in Relation to Labour, Continued".

PAGE 560

a. The following concluding sentence of this paragraph in the 1st ed. (p. 588) was deleted from the 2nd ed.: "Much of our attention will then be given henceforward to distinguishing those influences which are, from those which are not cumulative."

b. This footnote dates from the 2nd ed. (p. 592 n.).

c. In the 8th edition "I. ii. 1, 2."; emended in vol. 1 of the present edition to give the correct reference.

PAGE 561

a. The following additional sentences and paragraph in the 1st ed. (p. 589 n.), which succeeded the above quotation from Adam Smith, were deleted from the 3rd ed.:

> And hence he argued that though the wages of free men must cover their wear and tear, "the work done by them comes cheaper in the end than that performed by slaves....It is found to be so even at Boston, New York and Philadelphia, where the wages of common labour are so very high." (*Wealth of Nations*, Book I, ch. VIII.) And Cairnes, in his masterly book on the *Slave Power*, brought the evidence on this subject down to more recent times: and demonstrated the inefficiency and extravagance of the modern slave system.
>
> It is true that slavery was not always entirely without advantages. When the dignity of man as man was as yet not understood, and slaves and slaveowners alike regarded their mutual relations as natural, and when, partly in consequence of this, the family life of the slave was respected, the investment of capital in raising him to a fairly high level of industrial and literary and artistic culture, worked almost as smoothly and brought in its returns almost as safely as if the slave had been a machine. But in later times the uneasy consciousness that slavery was wrong made intelligence in the slave a source of fear to his master.

PAGE 563

a. So since the 3rd ed. (p. 642). In the first two editions the first sentence in this paragraph ended with the word "parents". The paragraph then continued as follows:

Thus those government appointments in which a good salary can be earned by but very moderate ability and industry, are even now, though the difference is less than it was, more accessible to the sons of the aristocracy than to those of the middle classes. These in their turn have advantages of their own. Not to speak of those who inherit a share in an existing business, or capital with which to start one of their own, they generally owe some of their success to the business or professional introduction which they receive from relatives and from friends of the family. But the importance of this good start in life is nowhere seen more clearly...etc.

In the first two editions the following marginal summary was attached to the opening sentences of § 3: "In this connection we have to take account not only of the direct investment of capital in the education of children, but also of their access to lucrative careers."

b.   So since the 2nd ed. (p. 596) where this sentence replaced the following sentence in the 1st ed. (p. 592): "The father has indeed special facilities for introducing his son."

PAGE 564

a.   The first clause of this sentence was inserted in the 2nd ed. (p. 597 n.).

PAGE 565

a.   This paragraph dates from the 2nd ed. (p. 597 n.).

b.   The following additional paragraphs at this point, dating from the 2nd ed. (pp. 597 n.–8 n.), were deleted from the 5th ed.:

These estimates include large allowances for parental and other services, that are not actually paid for by money. But it may be noted that, on the alternative plan of capitalizing net productive power, we ought properly to count in all production of real benefits, even though no money passes in exchange for them. But, as Prof. R. Mayo Smith has well pointed out (*Emigration and Immigration*, chapter VI), both of the suggested methods of valuation are open to great objections when used as the basis of a public policy with regard to immigration. For immigrants coming from a country in which the standard of life is low, to one in which it is high, may injure it materially as well as morally even though they carry in their own persons a good deal of invested capital, and produce in the country of their adoption, more than they consume, before they die. But both of these methods are much less misleading when applied to estimate the injury done to a country, such as Ireland, by the loss through emigration of a great many young people, whose bringing up has cost the country much, and who if they had stayed would have produced more than they consumed; while the old and the infirm stay behind to consume more than they produce.

Professor Nicholson (in the first number of the *Economic Journal*) estimates the living capital of the United Kingdom at £47,000 millions, i.e. about £1300 a head; or, say, 33 years' purchase (equal to the value of a permanent annuity) of the gross money income of the country exclusive of rent proper and interest on capital (about £900 millions); together with half as much again added in on account of the real income, consisting of private services and family offices for which no money payment is made. (His own method of arriving at this result is different.) But it seems doubtful whether an estimate of the capital value of the population as a whole can serve any useful purpose; and, if any is made at all, it should perhaps be based on net, rather than on gross earning power. For the outgoings of life, its pains and its efforts, have as good a right to enter into our account as its incomings, its pleasures and enjoyments.

PAGE 568

a.   So since the 3rd ed. (p. 648), where this sentence replaced the following sentence dating from the 1st ed. (p. 597):

The domestic servants of fashionable London got very high wages, and some of them occasionally tyrannized a little over their employers in the last century; and in the present century their total real wages are even higher in comparison with those skilled trades in which equal skill and ability are required.

PAGE 569

a. This sentence was inserted in the 3rd ed. (p. 649 n.).

BOOK VI, CHAPTER V

EARNINGS OF LABOUR, CONTINUED

PAGE 570

a. Except where otherwise stated the wording of this chapter dates substantially from the 1st edition.

b. So since the 4th edition. In the 1st edition (Book VII, ch. vi) this chapter was entitled "Demand and Supply in Relation to Labour, Continued".

In the 2nd edition (Book VI, ch. v) the final word "continued" was replaced by the word "Concluded". In the 3rd edition Marshall reinstated the word "Continued".

c. The first clause of this sentence was inserted in the 4th ed. (p. 654).

PAGE 571

a. The following sentence in the 1st ed. (p. 600) was deleted from the 2nd ed.:

But finished commodities (goods of the *first order*) with scarcely any exceptions, and material appliances for production (goods of *higher orders*) with but few exceptions last only a little while, and the supply of them can be greatly increased in a much shorter time than is required for adding largely to the supplies of efficient labour in the majority of skilled trades.

It is astonishing with what assiduity and sagacity many of them pursue their inquiries not only as to the money wages

623

to be obtained in a trade, but also as to all those incidental advantages and disadvantages which have been discussed in the last chapter but one.

PAGE 572

a. The following sentence in the 1st ed. (p. 601) was deleted from the 2nd ed.: "Thus for instance the rise of miners' wages in the years ending with 1873 was misinterpreted and was the cause of the abnormally low wages that followed it for half a generation."

PAGE 573

a. This paragraph dates in its present form from the 3rd ed. (p. 653). In the 1st ed. (pp. 602–3) the first two paragraphs of §4 ran as follows:

We have so far kept clear of the questions how far the earnings of all those already trained for any industry are to be regarded for the time as a quasi-rent, and how far the earnings of those who have extraordinary natural abilities may be regarded as rent. These questions are not without direct practical bearing: but they are of a highly technical character, and the general reader may prefer to pass over the remainder of the present chapter which will be devoted to them.

The remainder of this chapter is of a technical character.

We have seen that where we are considering the adjustment of a commodity to the demand for it during "short periods," that is, periods too short to enable any great change to be made in the material appliances for its production, we have to take for granted the existing stock of these appliances, almost as though they had been free gifts of nature. The income derived from them will indeed exert a controlling influence in the long run over the supply and the price of these appliances, and therefore over the supply and the price of the commodity itself: and the income that is required to call forth in the long run any given supply of these appliances is the "long period" supply price or (money) cost of production of that supply of them. But within "short periods" there is not time for the exercise of any considerable influence of this kind: whatever supplies of the appliances are available at the beginning of the short

Résumé of the distinction between long and short periods with reference to normal value.

624

period will remain available without much increase or diminution during the whole of it: and the income derived from them may be regarded as a quasi-rent.

The first two sentences of the second of the two paragraphs just quoted were deleted from the 2nd ed.

b. The reference here to Sir H. LL. Smith was inserted in the 2nd ed. (p. 607 n.) and that to Mr Charles Booth in the 3rd ed. (p. 653 n.).

PAGE 574

a. The following sentence dating from the 1st ed. (p. 604) was deleted from the 3rd ed.: "That is to say, they would have to be regarded as including an element of quasi-rent."

b. The following footnote attached to the word "closely" in the 1st ed. (p. 604 n.) was deleted from the 2nd ed.:

> Of course the relations of demand and supply for a commodity cannot be "normal" in the broadest sense in which the term can be used, unless the supply of its factors of production, among which human agents are included, is likewise normally adjusted to the demand for them. And this requires a similar adjustment with regard to their factors of production, and so on backwards *ad infinitum;* and a perfect adjustment of this kind is incapable of being even conceived except with reference to a stationary state. (See Book VI, ch. III, §7, and Book VII, ch. I, §2.) But we do not often want to use the term "normal" in this sense. Speaking generally, a period of time is long enough to permit us to treat the forces of demand and supply with regard to, say, one particular kind of textile fabric as having fairly worked out their normal results, provided that it is long enough to cause the fluctuations from season to season in the supply of the raw material to counterbalance one another; that it is long enough to enable any new factories that may be wanted to be fitted with machinery suitable for making that fabric and that it is long enough to enable any new hands that may be required, to be attracted from the general labour market of the textile districts. It is true, however, that if the producers of any commodity are not a mere branch of a trade, but the whole of the trade; if its production occupies all those who have the skill necessary for producing it, then changes in the supply of the commodity, and changes in the supply of the labour by which it is produced, must correspond closely to one another. And when this is the case, the adjustment of normal demand and supply may have to be reckoned for periods almost as long in the case of the commodity as in the case of labour.

The references at the end of the second sentence of this footnote apply to Book V, ch. III, §§6 and 7; ch. V, §8; and Book VI, ch. II, §8, in vol. I of the present edition.

c. So since the 3rd ed. (p. 654), from which the following concluding clause and footnote to this sentence dating from the 1st ed. (p. 605) were deleted:

and these earnings include for the time a very high quasi-rent of their stock of trained ability[1].

[1] If they have any considerable stock of trade implements, they are to that extent capitalists; and part of their income is quasi-rent on this capital.

In the 3rd and subsequent editions the foregoing footnote was attached to the second paragraph of §6 of this chapter (page 576 n. in vol. 1 of the present edition).

d. The only alterations made in this paragraph since the 1st ed. (p. 605) were the replacement in the 3rd ed. (p. 654) of the original word "quasi-rent" in the second and third sentences of the paragraph by the word "return".

e. The following footnote attached to the word "cost" in the first ed. (p. 605 n.) was deleted from the 3rd ed.:

> See Book VI, ch. vi. That part of the income got by the employers, which is really remuneration of their own labour, ought properly to be analysed further on the method adopted in §6 of this chapter.

The references in this footnote apply to Book V, ch. iv in vol. 1 of the present edition.

PAGE 575

a. In the 3rd ed (p. 655), the words "of the coal trade", which succeeded the word "inflation" in the first two editions, were deleted.

b. In the 3rd ed. the word "governed" replaced the word "determined" dating from the 1st ed. (p. 605).

c. So since the 4th ed. (p. 659). In the 3rd ed. (p. 655) the original words "of the quasi-rent of miners' skill were not narrow", were replaced by the words "of the special earnings of miners' skill were not narrow: (its quasi-rent could become very high)".

d. The following concluding sentence of this paragraph, dating from the 1st ed. (p. 606), was deleted from the 6th ed.: "The miners had therefore to sell their skilled labour in markets which were already over full, and in which their special skill counted for nothing."

PAGE 576

a. So since the 4th ed. (p. 660). In the first two editions the words "a quasi-rent" were used here; and in the 3rd ed. the words "special net earnings (of quasi-rent)".

b. So since the 4th ed. (p. 660) where the words "its net earnings" replaced the words "the quasi-rent earned by it" dating from the 1st ed. (p. 606).

c. So since the 4th ed. (p. 660) where the words "special return of his skill" replaced the words "return of his special skill" in the 3rd ed. In the first two editions the corresponding words were: "quasi-rent of his special skill."

d. The remainder of this sentence was inserted in the 3rd ed. (p. 656).

e. So since the 3rd ed. (p. 656) where this clause replaced the following clause and sentence dating from the 1st ed. (p. 607):

only part of this extra 10*s*. can be regarded as quasi-rent of his skill, for the remainder must be reckoned as the recompense of his additional fatigue (his wear and tear being supposed to be approximately the same in the two weeks). And at the time at which coal miners were earning no more than unskilled labourers could earn for equally fatiguing work, they were really getting no quasi-rent for their skill.

f. This paragraph dates substantially from the 2nd ed. (p. 611), where it replaced the following paragraph in the 1st ed. (p. 607):

To conclude this part of our argument. The market price of everything, i.e. its price for *very* short periods, is determined solely by the relations in which the demand for it stands to the available stocks of it. Passing next to periods that are short relatively to the lives of machinery and other goods of the *second order*, we have found that the income earned by this machinery, &c., is determined by the relation in which the available supply of these appliances stands to the demand for them: and that this demand is "derived" from the demand for those goods of the first order which they are used in making. In these relatively short periods fluctuations in the price of the finished commodity generally precede and are the determining causes of fluctuations in the incomes earned by the material appliances for their production. And what is true of the material agents of production is true also of human agents: for in almost every trade fluctuations in wages follow, and do not precede fluctuations in the selling prices of the goods produced.

Conclusion, and restatement of the argument with regard to the quasi-rent of labour.

The marginal summary was reworded in its present form in the 3rd ed.

a. In the 3rd ed. (p. 657) the words "cost of rearing and training" replaced the words "cost of production" in the first two editions.

b. The remainder of this sentence and the next sentence were inserted in the 3rd ed. (p. 657).

c. In the 1st ed. (p. 608) there was the following sentence, with the footnote attached to it, which concluded this section:

There are indeed constant tendencies towards that point, as surely as, to use an old simile, there is a constant tendency of the surface of the sea towards a position of rest: but the moon and the sun are always shifting their places and always therefore changing the conditions by which the equilibrium of the sea is governed: and meanwhile there are ceaseless currents of the raging winds; the surface is always tending towards a position of normal equilibrium, but never attains it[1].

[1] Attention may again be called to the excellent studies of the theory of value that have been published by Austrian economists of our own generation, especially Professors Menger, Böhm-Bawerk, and Weiser.

Jevons advanced the extreme doctrine that "labour is essentially variable, so that its value must be determined by the value of the produce, not the value of the produce by that of the labour." (*Theory*, 2nd edition, p. 179.) In spite of the prominence which he gave to this doctrine, it seems doubtful whether he held it in the unqualified form in which he stated it. As it stands, it appears to be incompatible with any scientific treatment of the fundamental problem of Distribution: and it is a significant fact that Jevons did not address himself to that problem in his chapter on Labour.

The above sentence and the first paragraph of this footnote were deleted from the 2nd ed., and the second paragraph of the footnote from the 3rd ed.

d. Although with the exception of the final paragraph, the subject matter of this section (§7) dates substantially from the 1st ed., the order of the sentences was rearranged in the later editions.

e. So since the 5th ed. (p. 577) where the words "rent, or" before the words "producer's surplus" were deleted.

f. The following sentence and footnote dating from the 1st ed. (pp. 608–9) were deleted from the 4th ed.:

This analogy has been noticed by a long series of writers:[1] it is instructive and suggestive; but we must be on our guard against the temptation to extend it beyond its proper scope, and to apply it without those conditions which are required to make it true.

[1] See the references given in Book VI, ch. III, §1.

The reference in this footnote applies to Book V, ch. x, §3 in vol. 1 of the present edition.

g. The words "to opportunity, to the conjuncture", were inserted in the 2nd ed. (p. 613) where the last word was written "*Conjunctur*". It was anglicized in the 3rd ed. The modern spelling of the German word is "Konjunktur".

a. The following sentence and paragraph at this point in the 1st ed. (p. 609) were deleted—the sentence from the 7th ed., and the paragraph from the 5th ed.:

They are not, as some writers have urged, a rent which does not enter into that price, and which is rather determined by that price.

It is true that, if we confined our attention to short periods, we might fairly say that the incomes earned by the natural genius already existing among those who had specialized themselves in a certain trade, do not enter directly into the marginal expenses of production of the goods made in it, nor therefore into their price, but are rather to be regarded as a quasi-rent determined by that price. But the same is true, as we have just seen, of the earnings of all others who are already in the trade and specialized to it; even though they seem to have no great ability or success.

b. So since the 2nd ed. (p. 613) where the word "conceded" replaced the word "added" in the 1st ed.

c. In the 3rd ed. (p. 610 n.) this footnote ran as follows:

> Cp. Book VI, ch. III, §2. The argument of the note on p. 490 is applicable to the rent of natural abilities, but also to all quasi-rents. When land capable of being used for producing one commodity is used for another, the supply price of the first is raised (though not by an amount dependent on the rent which the land would yield in this second use). So when existing factories, or persons with trained skill or with great natural ability, who could have been applied to produce one commodity, are applied for another, the supply price of the first is raised *for the time* through the narrowing of its sources of supply.

The reference to "the note on p. 490" applies to the footnote on pages 436–7 in vol. 1 of the present edition.

Except for the reference in the first sentence, this footnote was deleted from the 2nd ed., where the substance was transferred to the text. See page 579 in vol. 1 of the present edition.

a. In the 5th ed. (p. 579) the words "producer's surplus" replaced the word "rent" dating from the 1st ed. (p. 610).

b. This sentence (apart from the specific reference to Book V—in its final form in the 5th ed.) dates in its present form from the 3rd ed. (p. 659). For its form in a footnote in the 1st ed. (p. 610 n.) see editorial note **c** to page 578 of vol. 1 in the present edition. In the

2nd ed., where the substance of the footnote referred to was placed in the text (pp. 613–14) the corresponding passage ran as follows:

Finally it may be observed that the argument of Book V, chapters VIII and IX with regard to the rents and quasi-rents of appliances capable of being used in several branches of production, is applicable to the rent of natural abilities and to the quasi-rents of specialised skill.

c. These two concluding sentences date in their present form from the 2nd ed. (p. 614), subject to the insertion in the 5th ed. (p. 579) of the words "or machinery" after the word "land", in the first sentence, and the replacement in the 5th ed. of the words "rent which the land would yield in this second use" by the words "incomes which those appliances for production would yield in this second use".

BOOK VI, CHAPTER VI

INTEREST OF CAPITAL

PAGE 580

a. Except where otherwise indicated the wording of §1 of this chapter dates substantially from the 3rd edition (Book V, chapter VI) and of the remainder of this chapter (§§2–7) from the 1st edition, Book VII, chapter VII.

In the 1st edition (Book VII, chapter VII, §§1–4 and §8) and in the 2nd edition (Book VI, chapter VI, §§1–3 and §6) this chapter contained a discussion of the general causes governing the rate of interest, of which part was subsequently deleted and part was distributed between Book IV, chapter VII, §§8 and 9, Book VI, chapter I, §8, chapter II, §4, and chapter XII, §4.

See the Editorial Appendix to this Chapter for the text of those sections in the 1st and 2nd editions which were later deleted.

b. So since the 4th edition. In the 1st edition this chapter was entitled "Demand and Supply in Relation to Capital".

In the 2nd edition: "Demand and Supply in Relation to Capital. Gross and Net Interest".

In the 3rd edition: "Demand and Supply in Relation to Capital. A Further Study of Interest".

PAGE 581

a. The words "or, in other words, by their unwillingness to 'wait'", were inserted in the 4th ed. (p. 665).

PAGE 583

a. This paragraph dates mainly from the 2nd ed. (Book VI, ch. vi, §6 pp. 626–7).

b. In the 3rd ed. (p. 664) the words "The scientific doctrine of capital has had...etc." replaced the words "This theory of interest has had...etc.", dating from the 2nd ed. (p. 626).

c. This clause and the next sentence were inserted in the 3rd ed. (p. 664) where they replaced the following sentence in the 2nd ed. (p. 627):

But also scarcely any of them has left the theory exactly where he found it; almost everyone has improved some part, and given it a sharper and clearer outline; or else has helped to explain the complex relations of its different parts.

d. For the earlier forms of this footnote in the 1st and 2nd editions see the Editorial Appendix to Book VI, chapter vi (pp. 643–4 below).

e. So since the 5th ed. (p. 583 n.) where this sentence and the first main clause of the next sentence replaced the following clauses dating from the 3rd ed. (p. 664 n.):

The question has already been raised (p. 152) whether Prof. V. Böhm-Bawerk has not slightly underrated the acumen of his predecessors in their writings on capital and interest; and whether what he regards as mere naïve fragments of theories were not rather the utterances of men well acquainted with the practical workings of business.

The reference in the first line to p. 152 (it should have been to p. 142 n.) applies to page 790 n. in vol. 1 of the present edition.

PAGE 584

a. See editorial note **a** to page 580 above.

b. This paragraph dates from the 2nd ed. (p. 627).

c. So since the 6th ed. (p. 584 n.) where the first two sentences of this footnote replaced the following sentences dating from the 3rd ed. (p. 665 n.):

From St Chrysostom's Fifth Homily, see above, Book I, ch. ii, §8. Compare also Ashley's *Economic History*, VI, 1; and Bentham *On Usury*, Lecky's *Rationalism in Europe*, the economic histories of Kautz, Ingram and Cunningham, the economic treatises of Knies, Roscher and Nicholson, Thorburn's *Musalmans and Money-lenders in the Punjab*, and several recent articles in the *Economic Review*.

In the 1st ed. (p. 617 n.) and the 2nd ed. (p. 628 n.) these sentences ran as follows:

From St Chrysostom's Fifth Homily. On this subject compare Bentham *On Usury*, Mr Lecky's *Rationalism in Europe*, the economic histories of Dr Cunningham, Prof. Ashley and Kautz, the article on "Usury" by Prof. Nicholson in the *Encyclopædia Britannica*, Knies' *Politische Œkonomie*, and Roscher's *Political Economy*, and lastly Mr Thorburn's *Musalmans and Money-lenders in the Punjab*.

It should be noted that I have emended the reference in the 8th edition to "I. II. 8" at the end of the first sentence of the footnote there so as to give the correct reference.

PAGE 585

a. In the 1st ed. (p. 617 n.) there was the following footnote attached to the word "use":

Politics, I, 10. He laid stress on the fact that the Greek word for interest (τόκος) implied that it was the offspring born of money.

In the 2nd ed. (p. 628 n.) this footnote ran as follows:

Politics, I, 10. He laid stress on the fact that the Greek word for interest (τόκος) claimed that it was the offspring born of money; and that, he said, was really barren.

This footnote was deleted from the 3rd ed.

b. The word "fairly" before the word "argued" in the 1st ed. (p. 618) was deleted from the 3rd ed.

PAGE 586

a. So since the 3rd ed. (p. 667).

In the first two editions these concluding clauses of this sentence ran as follows:

that no private person should be allowed to own any of the means of production (goods of the *second* and higher *orders*), nor any direct means of enjoyment (goods of the *first order*) save such as he needs for his own use.

b. In the 1st ed. (p. 619 n.) there was the following footnote attached to the name "Thompson":

Dr Anton Menger, in *Das Recht auf den vollen Arbeitsertrag* has shown well how Rodbertus and Karl Marx have borrowed both their practical conclusions as to the nationalization of the means of production, and the theoretical basis of their arguments, from earlier works, and especially from William Thompson's *Principles of the Distribution of Wealth most conducive to Human Happiness*, 1824.

In the 3rd ed. (p. 668 n.) this footnote ran as follows:

Dr Anton Menger, in *Das Recht auf den vollen Arbeitsertrag*, has shown well how both the practical conclusions as to the nationalization of the means of production and the theoretical basis of the arguments of Rodbertus and Karl Marx had been in a great measure anticipated in earlier works, and especially William Thompson's *Principles of the Distribution of Wealth most conducive to Human Happiness*, 1824.

This footnote was deleted from the 4th ed.

c. So since the 2nd ed. (pp. 630–1).

In the 1st ed. (p. 619) the remainder of this paragraph ran as follows:

They have argued that the value of a thing consists exclusively of the labour that has been spent in making it; and that therefore the payment of interest is a robbery of labour. For their premiss they claim the authority of Ricardo; though it is really as opposed to the general tenor of his theory of value as it is to common sense (see the "Note on Ricardo's doctrine of Cost of Production in relation to Value," at the end of Book VI). But in fact their conclusion is itself silently assumed in their attempt to establish their preliminary proposition; and their argument is thus a complete circle.

The reference to the "Note on Ricardo's doctrine..." applies to Appendix I, §2, in vol. 1 of the present edition.

PAGE 587

a. The words "in general" were italicized in the 2nd ed. (p. 631).
b. The name of Rodbertus was inserted in the 2nd ed. (p. 631).

PAGE 588

a. So since the 3rd ed. (p. 669).

In the 2nd ed. (p. 631) this main clause ran as follows: "though, in the case of Marx, it was shrouded by the mysterious Hegelian phrases with which, to use his own phrase, he 'coquetted'." In the 1st ed. (p. 620) the concluding clause of the above sentence in the text ran as follows: "though shrouded by the mysterious Hegelian phrases in which he delighted."

b. This paragraph dates from the 3rd ed. (p. 669).

In the 2nd ed. (p. 622) the earlier part of the paragraph ran as follows: "The interest of which we have been speaking, and which is the reward of waiting, is true or *Net* interest; but what commonly passes...etc." In the 1st ed. (p. 620) this paragraph ran as follows:

We have spoken of the income derived from capital as Interest. But of course the total income that is derived from any use of capital is Profit: and this is commonly regarded

The line of division between Interest and the other elements of which Profit is composed cannot always be easily drawn.

as consisting of three parts. One is the remuneration of the labour of managing the capital, or earnings of management; another is insurance against the risks involved in that particular use of it; and it is only what remains that is properly to be regarded as *Net* interest. We shall have soon to carry this analysis somewhat further: but first we may pause to notice that much which is commonly called Interest is not interest properly so called, but contains some parts of the other two elements of profit.

c. This paragraph dates from the 2nd ed. (pp. 622–3).

a. This footnote dates from the 2nd ed. (p. 624 n.).

PAGE 592

a. The following sentences at this point in the 1st ed. (p. 624 n.), where the whole of this paragraph was placed in a footnote, were deleted from the 4th ed.:

> He may not be able to obtain a renewal of the loan on moderate, or even on any terms, and may thus be cut short in his most hopeful enterprises. One of the chief symptoms of an impending commercial crisis is a rapid succession of forced sales at a loss by those who have been trading with capital borrowed for short periods.

b. This paragraph dates substantially from the 3rd ed. (p. 599), where it was placed in Book VI, ch. II, §4. In the 3rd ed. the following footnote was attached to the end of the paragraph:

> As Prof. Clark says, the second stream may be regarded from two points of view. First there is something permanent, a body of "pure capital" to use his phrase, like the permanent body of a waterfall; and secondly there are the particular machines, raw materials &c., which are ever coming, passing away and being replaced, like the particular drops of water that pass through the permanent fall.
>
> Among the questions which are here left on one side for future study are the way in which the *net* interest of capital is to be distinguished not only from gross profits but from much that is frequently reckoned under the head of interest, though it really contains elements of earnings of management and insurance against risk: and again how changes in the general purchasing power of money cause the net interest that is really being earned by capital to be sometimes higher than it appears and sometimes lower.

The substance of the first paragraph of this footnote was transferred to Book II, ch. IV, §2, in the 5th ed. (page 73 n. in vol. I of the present edition). The second paragraph was deleted from the 5th ed.

c. The first sentence of this paragraph dates substantially from the 3rd ed. (p. 599), and the second sentence from the 5th ed. (p. 592). In the 1st ed. (Book VII, ch. VII, §9), where this paragraph was placed in a different context, the opening sentences ran as follows:

But here our attention should again be directed to the very limited sense in which alone we can properly speak of the rate of interest on any save new investments of capital. If, as indicated in a previous section, we strip away from gross interest those elements that do not properly belong to interest, the remainder, or net interest, is approximately uniform at three per cent. throughout the whole country; and we may estimate that a trade capital of some seven thousand millions is invested in the different trades of the country at about three per cent. net interest.

But we must recall the relation between the interest on capital and its quasi-rent.

In the 2nd ed. (Book VI, ch. vi, §3) and the 3rd and 4th editions (Book VI, ch. ii, §4) these sentences ran as follows:

But we must recollect that we can properly speak of the rate of interest on any save new investments of capital only in a very limited sense. For instance, we may perhaps estimate that a trade capital of some seven thousand millions is invested in the different trades of the country at about three per cent. net interest.

d. The following marginal summary was attached to this paragraph in the first two editions:

Strictly speaking we can measure the rate of interest only on new investments: because the value of old investments is determined by estimating their probable future quasi-rents and capitalising that.

a. So since the 6th ed. (p. 593), where this sentence replaced the following sentence and footnote dating except for two words from the 1st ed. (p. 626):

For the capital already invested in improving land and erecting buildings, and in making railways and machinery, has its value determined by the net income which it will produce: and if its prospective income-yielding power should diminish, its value would fall accordingly and would be the capitalized value of that smaller income after allowing for depreciation[1].

[1] The same result is of course got by aggregating the discounted values of all its probable future net incomes on the plan discussed in Bk. VI, ch. v, §2.

The only subsequent change made in this sentence prior to the 6th ed. consisted in the insertion in the 2nd ed. (p. 622) of the words "or quasi-rent" after the word "income" in the second clause.

The reference in the footnote applies to Book V, ch. IV, § 2 in vol. I of the present edition.

PAGE 594

a. The first clause of this footnote was inserted in the 5th ed. (p. 594 n.) and the remaining clauses in the 6th ed. (p. 594 n.).

PAGE 595

a. This paragraph dates substantially from the 3rd ed. (p. 674) where it replaced the following paragraph dating from the 1st ed. (p. 628):

Again, a probable change in the purchasing power of money affects the relative values of stock exchange securities which will pay a fixed rate of interest, and of those which represent a direct share in property. The shareholders of a railway are the owners of a property the real value of which is determined in the long run by the services it is capable of rendering; and the excess of the real value of its receipts over that of its working expenses will be very little affected in the long run by changes in the general level of prices. But if there should be a general rise in the purchasing power of money, the real value of the "interest" which it pays on its debentures will rise in the same proportion; and the real value of what remains to be divided among its shareholders will be correspondingly diminished. Hence if we had reason to believe that there would be a continued rise in the purchasing power of money, there would be a double cause for preferring a debenture bond to an ordinary share which would appear of just equal value with it, and if we took no account of changes in the purchasing power of money. Calculations of this kind exercise a direct influence over the actions of only very far seeing persons: but we shall presently find that their indirect influence is considerable, and is clearly perceptible in the prices of land and of some kinds of stock exchange securities. [See an article by Mr de Haas, translated in the London *Statistical Journal* for March, 1889; also an article by the present writer in the *Contemporary*

Review for March, 1877, in which it is argued that fluctuations in prices are caused only to a very slight extent by fluctuations in the supply of the precious metals; and that they would not be much diminished by the adoption of gold and silver instead of gold as the basis of our currency. The evils which they cause are however so great, that it is worth while to do much in order to diminish them a little.]

The article in the *Contemporary Review* for March, 1887 (incorrectly printed "March, 1877") is reprinted in the *Memorials of Alfred Marshall*, edited by A. C. Pigou, pp. 188–211.

b. So since the 8th edition (page 595) where this clause replaced the following words in the earlier editions: "During the last fifty years".

c. This sentence was inserted in the 8th edition (page 595).

EDITORIAL APPENDIX TO
BOOK VI, CH. VI

INTEREST AS THE REWARD OF SAVING

The following passages comprise the whole of §§ 1–4 of Book VII, ch. VII, in the 1st ed.:

§ 1. WE have already discussed some of the peculiarities in the mode of action of demand and supply in relation to capital. ^aBut it is necessary, at the expense of some repeti-

---

a. In the 2nd ed. (p. 615) this opening sentence was replaced by the following sentences and footnote:

WE now pass from the consideration of labour to that of capital. Capital is the result of labour and saving, or rather of labour and waiting, and therefore is not to be regarded as a factor of production altogether independent of labour. But it contains an element that is independent, viz. waiting. Perhaps then we should in strictness say that the three main agents of production are not labour, capital and land, but labour, waiting and land[1]. It is really the demand for and the supply of this waiting which we are

tion, to collect and weave together several rather troublesome threads of reasoning.

Résumé of the history of the motives of saving.

[b] We have seen that the growth of wealth[1] has been governed by many causes, among which custom and unconscious habit played a great part in the early stages of history; while in the later a predominating influence has gradually been acquired by the deliberate intention to sacrifice ease or other enjoyments in the present in order to obtain them in the future. The causes of this change have been of two kinds. [c]In the first place the progress of knowledge has constantly opened up new opportunities of investing present effort in roundabout methods of production which make the total results of that effort in the long run much greater than if it had been devoted to the direct attainment of immediate gratifications: progress has increased the economy of effort which can in the long run be obtained by making machinery and other appliances for use in agriculture, in manufacture, and above all in transport. [d]And secondly the character of man himself has changed: he has obtained a greater "telescopic" faculty; that is, he has acquired an increased

[1] Book IV, ch. VII.

---

to discuss in the present Chapter under the form of a further study of the peculiarities in the mode of action of demand and supply in relation to capital.

[1] Comp. Prof. Böhm-Bawerk, *Kapitalzins,* II, p. 101, where he argues that capital is not an independent factor of production in addition to land and labour. The argument that it is Waiting rather than Abstinence which is rewarded by Interest and is a factor of production was given by Prof. Macvane in the Harvard *Journal of Economics* for July, 1887.

In the 3rd ed. (p. 315 n.) the second sentence of the above footnote in the 2nd ed. was transferred to Book IV, ch. VII, §8. See page 233 n. in vol. 1 of the present edition.

b. This and the next sentence were deleted from the 2nd ed.

c. In the 2nd ed. (p. 619), where this sentence was placed in a different context, it was preceded by the following sentence: "The demand for capital has increased as steadily, and almost as rapidly, as the supply of it; and chiefly as a result of the same causes."

d. Subject to the deletion of the first clause this sentence was retained in the 2nd ed. (p. 617); it was transferred in the 3rd ed. to Book VI, ch. XII, §8. See page 680 in vol. 1 of the present edition.

power of realizing the future and bringing it clearly before his mind's eye: he is more prudent and has more self-control, and is therefore more inclined to estimate future pains and pleasures at a high rate: he is more unselfish, and therefore more inclined to work and save in order to secure a future provision for his family; and there are already faint signs of a brighter time to come in which there will be a general willingness to work and save in order to increase the stores of public wealth and of public opportunities for leading a higher life.

[e] Parallel with these changes there has been a great change in the forms of wealth itself. Not only have the implements of production risen in importance relatively to stored up sources of direct enjoyment, such as houses, furniture, &c., but of these implements of production a constantly increasing proportion has taken the form of trade-capital: that is, it has been applied to produce things that will be sold for money, and not used by those who produce them; and the money income or "interest" which capital can be made to yield has therefore steadily become more important.

§ [f] 2. We have seen[1] that a man who, working on his

Change in the forms of wealth.

---

[1] [g] Comp. Book II, ch. VI, §4, Book IV, ch. I, §1 and ch. VII, §3, and Book VI, ch. V, §1.

---

e. This paragraph was retained in the 2nd ed. (p. 619), where it was succeeded by the following paragraph:

But the demand for capital for trade purposes, which has thus become the typical demand for accumulated wealth, does not depend only on the progress of the state of the arts of production; it is governed also by the rate of interest at which capital can be borrowed.

This paragraph in turn was succeeded in the 2nd ed. by the illustration of the absorption of capital in the hat-making trade, which was placed in Book VI, ch. I in the 3rd and subsequent editions. See pages 519–20 in vol. I of the present edition.

f. The subject-matter of this section was retained substantially in the 2nd ed., pp. 615–16.

g. These references apply to Book II, ch. IV, §§2 and 4, Book IV, ch. I, §2 and ch. VII, §§3 and 8, and Book V, ch. IV, §1, in vol. I of the present edition. These references were deleted from the 2nd ed.

If man chooses as the reward of his labour deferred enjoyments instead of immediate,

own account, makes a thing for himself has the usance of it as the reward for his labour. The amount of his work may be determined in a great measure by custom or habit; but, in so far as his action is deliberate, he will cease his work when the gains of further work do not seem to him worth the trouble of getting them: (i.e. when the marginal disutility of work has caught up the marginal utility of the goods to be gained by it[h]). But the awakening of a new desire will induce him to work on further. He may take out the fruits of this extra work in immediate and passing enjoyment; or in lasting but direct benefits, such as improved house-room; or in implements that will aid him in his work and enable him to obtain in the future greater gains with equal effort, and equal gains with less effort; or lastly in things which he can let out on hire or so invest as to derive an income from them[1].

it is generally because he expects them to show a surplus in the long run.

Man's nature, however, being impatient of delay, he will not, *as a rule*, select any of the three latter methods unless the total benefit which he expects in the long run seems, after allowing for all risks, to show a surplus over the benefit to be derived by taking out the fruits of his labour in immediate enjoyments. [i]That surplus, whether it take the form

1 [i]In an interesting article on the "Theory of Capital" in the Harvard *Journal of Economics* for Jan. 1890, Prof. Giddings argues that goods of the *second order* have a higher cost of production per unit of quantity than luxuries, because their production necessitates working over-time: but to this it may be answered, that so does also the production of extra luxuries.

h. In the 2nd ed. (pp. 615–16) there were the following additional clauses and attached footnote in this parenthesis, after the words "the marginal utility of the goods to be gained by it,":

or, in other words, where there is no further producers' rent to be got by the work.[1]

1 The use of the term rent in this connection is suggested by Prof. J. B. Clark in the *Harvard Journal of Economics* for April, 1891, p. 296.

i. In the 2nd ed. (p. 616) the remainder of this paragraph ran as follows:

It is true that a man may save, though he prefers present pleasure to future, and though he gains no increase of his means by waiting; and some saving might therefore be exof interest on capital, or extra pleasure derived from the direct usance of permanent forms of wealth, is the reward of his *postponing* or *waiting for* the fruits of his labour.

The rate of interest which he can get by investing the fruits of his labour may be taken as a convenient numerical measure of this reward, provided that we are at liberty to assume, firstly that he can secure the return of his capital without additional effort; and secondly that it will on its return afford a gratification equal to that which the immediate consumption of the fruits of his labour would have afforded him at the time when he first obtained control over them. On these ^k suppositions we may say that (the rate of interest being three per cent per annum) the reward which a person can get for postponing his gratification for a year

Conditions under which this surplus can be measured by the rate of interest.

---

pected even if the rate of interest on the loan of capital were negative, that is, if charges had to be paid to those who undertook the safe custody of the capital. But it is equally true that some work would be done even if there were a penalty for it; and yet we speak of wages as the reward of labour, because few people would work hard without that reward. In like manner we are justified in speaking of that surplus benefit which people generally get by waiting for the fruits of their labour (whether it take the form of interest on capital, or extra pleasure derived from the direct usance of permanent forms of wealth) as the reward of postponing or waiting for those fruits because few people would save much without that reward.[1]

[1] See Book III, ch. v, §4 and Book IV, ch. vii, §8. It has to be remembered that a postponement of a pleasurable event is not the same thing as a postponement of a pleasure; since, coming at a later time, the pleasurable event, whether it be spending a certain sum of money or anything else, may give either more or less pleasure than it would have done at the earlier date.

It may be noted that in the 2nd ed. the substance of the last two sentences of the passage just quoted from Book VI, ch. vi in the 2nd ed., was also placed in Book IV, ch. vii, §8, and in that form it was retained in the later editions. See page 232 in vol. i of the present edition.

j. This footnote was deleted from the 2nd ed.

k. In the 2nd ed. (p. 617) the words "somewhat strained" were inserted before the word "suppositions".

is a surplus of pleasure equal to three hundredths of that which he postpones[1].

Accumulated wealth may be regarded as the result of labour and waiting, though not necessarily the labour of its present owners.

§ m 3.   The first accumulations of wealth were made from the fruits of labour acting on natural agents, or more briefly on land; and they were the result of waiting for direct fruits of labour. As time went on some of these accumulations were used to aid and support further production; the fruits of that production were the results of waiting for fruits of labour which this waiting made more effective; they therefore may still be regarded as the result of waiting for the fruits of labour: and the same may be said of all existing accumulations, though much of the labour invested in them is lost sight of in the dim vistas of history. And when we speak of accumulated wealth as the reward of labour and waiting, we do not imply that the labour is necessarily that of the owner of the wealth himself. It is not indeed relevant to remark that much present wealth consists in the ownership of what was originally a free gift of nature: for free gifts of nature may be taken to be excluded from *accumulated* wealth. But we cannot evade the fact that a great part of accumulated wealth was derived from the rent of land or from the profits of business; and that its present owners have obtained their rights to it chiefly by inheritance.

But the surplus offered by deferred enjoyments is always the result of waiting.

There is however no corresponding qualification to the statement that that surplus benefit which a person gets in the long run by postponing enjoyment, and which is measured by the rate of interest (subject as we have seen to certain conditions), is the reward of *waiting*. He may have obtained the *de facto* possession of property by inheritance or by any other means, moral or immoral, legal or illegal. But if, having the power to consume that property in immediate gratifications, he chooses to put it in such a form as

---

1.   In the 2nd ed. (p. 617 n.) there was the following footnote attached to the word "postpones":

> It will be noted that this proposition is so worded as to be applicable to all pleasures, and not merely to "marginal" pleasures, to which some writers have proposed to limit its application.

m.   The whole of the text (as distinct from the footnotes) of this section was deleted from the 2nd ed.

to afford him deferred gratifications, then any superiority there may be in these deferred gratifications over those immediate ones is the reward of his waiting. When he lends out the wealth on a secure loan the net payment which he receives for the use of the wealth may be regarded as affording a numerical measure of that reward[1].

[1] nProf. Böhm-Bawerk (*Kapitalzins*, II, p. 101) raises the question whether capital is an independent factor of production in addition to land (i.e. natural agents of all kinds) and labour; and answers it in the negative. oThe question seems to be to some extent one of words: but on the whole it is perhaps best to say that there are three factors of production, land, labour, and the sacrifice involved in waiting.

Von Thünen (*Der isolierte Staat*, II, I, pp. 127, &c.) dwells instructively on the fact that capital is the result of labour, as well as a possible substitute for it. When discussing the effects of improvements in shoemaking machinery P (Book VII, ch. III, § 5), our attention was called to the fact that the substitution of capital for labour in one trade generally involved an increased use of another kind of labour; and that the substitution really was in part that of one kind of labour for another. The practical importance of this point will appear more clearly later on.

qOpportunity may be taken here of referring the reader to Prof. Böhm-Bawerk's book for a full and able discussion of the history and present position of the economic theory of interest. But perhaps the question may be raised whether he has not somewhat exaggerated the difference between his own position and that of his predecessors; whether the sharp contrasts which he finds between the doctrines of successive schools really existed; and whether those doctrines were generally as fragmentary and one-sided as he thinks. It does not appear certain that there is much of vital importance in the Theory of Interest as it is known now, which was not recognized with more or less distinctness by all the leading economists of the present century. Some have emphasized one side and others another; and Prof. Böhm-Bawerk has perhaps been a little too ready to assume that they ignored altogether those sides which they did not accentuate. They did not however, it must be admitted, make clear the mutual relations of the several sides of the theory. To that difficult and important task much work has been given during the last few years by Profs. Jevons, Menger, Wieser, Pantaleoni, Sidgwick, Walker, Clark, Giddings, and Patten, by Mr Stuart Wood, Mr Sidney Webb and others; and

---

n.   This sentence was retained substantially in the 2nd ed. (p. 615 n.). See above, p. 638.

o.   This sentence and the paragraph following it were deleted from the 2nd ed.

p.   The whole of Book VII, ch. III, §5 in the 1st ed. will be found in the Editorial Appendix to Book VI, chapters I and II (see pp. 595–8 above).

q.   In the 2nd ed. (p. 627 n.) this paragraph ran as follows:

The successive steps of this progress [in the development of the theory of interest] are indicated in Prof. Böhm-Bawerk's learned and able history of the Theories of Interest. But he would appear often to have exaggerated the errors of his predecessors; to have found sharp contrasts between the doctrines of successive schools, where there was really little more than a difference of emphasis; and to have represented their work generally as more fragmentary and one-sided than it really was.

See Book VI, ch. VI, §1, page 583 in vol. I of the present edition for the later versions of the substance of this paragraph.

§4.   ᵣWe have said that a person will not *as a rule* choose deferred in place of present enjoyments, unless he expects them to be greater in the long run. But this rule is not without exceptions. A man of provident and unselfish temper when earning a high income would prefer to put away some of it for the future needs of himself and his family, even if he knew of no safe way of investing it at interest; and had to hoard it at great trouble and risk; or, and this comes to the same thing, if he had to pay some one else for taking care of it for him, or, as we may say, to invest it at a negative rate of interest[1].

All this is true. But a similar statement is true with regard to labour. Some exertion is pleasurable, at least to those who are in sound moral and physical health; political prisoners for instance generally regard it as a favour to be allowed to do a little work; they crave some rest from the wearing strain of enforced idleness. And yet in the ordinary course of business all work has to be paid for, because that part of it which gives more pleasure than pain to the worker, is worth just as much to the purchasers of the labour as that which he does when he has already worked off his superabundant energy, and would no longer work without some special inducement to do so.

And so with regard to the payment for the use of capital. We can perhaps imagine a state of society in which people were so provident and the existing stock of capital so large that roundabout methods of production had been already substituted for direct methods in every case in which they

especially by Prof. Böhm-Bawerk himself. And one more attempt to grapple with it lies before the reader now.

[1] Again some people rate the pleasures of expectation highly; they like to "have something to look forward to"; they resemble the children who take the plums out of their pudding and put them off till the last. On the other hand it must be recollected that *absolute* security exists only with regard to the present. No deferred pleasure is absolutely secure; for life itself is uncertain. Even if there were a bank absolutely certain to return the deposits lent to it on demand, no one who deposited there money that he could have spent today, would be quite certain of living to demand it himself tomorrow.

ᵣ.   In the 2nd ed. the substance of this section, in an abbreviated form, was placed partly in Book IV, ch. VII, §8, see page 232 in vol. I of the present edition; and partly in the sentences quoted above in editorial footnote i to p. 640 of this Appendix.

Marginal notes:

Some people would indeed save something, even if they had to pay for the custody of their wealth.

But as the workman is paid for all his labour, though some of it may be pleasurable,

were more efficient: and then those who wanted to defer their pleasures, might have to pay to others a charge for keeping their wealth in safe custody. But there is no present likelihood of such a state of things: the growth of accumulated wealth, rapid as it is, shows no signs of overtaking the growth of the scope for the employment of human effort in such ways as will yield an increased return of gratification in the long run; the condition of this return being that part of the effort is spent in purchasing the means of gratification a long time beforehand. And the rate of interest cannot therefore fall below that limit at which it offers only just sufficient inducement to those who are on the margin of doubt whether to save or not. For if it did there would be a gradual shrinkage of capital relatively to the growing demand for it: its marginal utility would rise in consequence of this relative scarcity, and therefore the rate of interest which is paid as the price of loans would rise also[1].

so, since the supply of capital is still insufficient for all needs, a reward is required by those least willing to save, and an equal reward is claimed by all others.

[1]On the subject of this section compare the latter part of Book IV, ch. VII, § 1. The suggestion that the rate of interest may conceivably become a negative quantity has been discussed by Prof. Foxwell in a paper on *Some Social Aspects of Banking*, read before the Bankers' Institute in Jan. 1886.

Subject to the exceptions mentioned in the editorial footnotes, the foregoing passages from the 1st and 2nd editions were deleted from the 3rd ed.

BOOK VI, CHAPTER VII

PROFITS OF CAPITAL AND BUSINESS POWER

PAGE 596

a. Except where otherwise stated the wording of this chapter dates substantially from the 1st edition.

b. So since the 4th edition. In the 1st edition (Book VII, ch. VII) and the 2nd and 3rd editions (Book VI, ch. VII) this title ran as follows: "Demand and Supply in Relation to Capital, Business Power and Industrial Organization."

c. This and the next paragraph date in their present form mainly from the 2nd ed. (pp. 634–5), but the first sentence of this paragraph

and the whole of the next paragraph, in turn date with some rearrangement of sentences from the 1st ed. (pp. 629–30). See the Editorial
Appendix to this Chapter (pp. 651–4 below) for the original version of
this part of §1.

d. This and the next sentence were inserted in the 3rd ed. (p. 675).

PAGE 597

a. So since the 2nd ed. (p. 635).

In the 1st ed. (Book VII, ch. VII, §5, p. 635) this paragraph, and
the beginning of the next, ran as follows:

Next we may observe that the services rendered to society
by employers and other undertakers are of two classes, those
who open out new and improved methods of business, and
those who follow beaten tracks. The relation in which these
two classes stand to one another may be best seen by an
illustration.

It is well known that great economies have been introduced
into many branches of iron manufacture by diminishing the
number of times which the metal is heated in passing from
pig iron to its final form. Suppose an iron manufacturer with
a capital of £50,000...etc.

b. This paragraph is substantially identical with part of a paragraph in an article by Marshall entitled "Wages and Profit" in the
Quarterly Journal for Economics, January 1888, which is reprinted in
the Editorial Appendix to Appendix J (p. 826 below).

PAGE 598

a. So since the 2nd ed. (p. 636) where this and the next sentence
replaced the following sentences in the 1st ed. (p. 363):

But as time goes on, his neighbours will copy his plan;
and by so doing they may all of them make more than average profits for a time. This stage however will gradually
come to an end: increased competition on the part of new
men and of those already in the trade will increase the supply,
and lower the price of their wares, unless indeed there is a
combination in the trade to restrict production; and even
that is not likely, as we shall see presently, to do more than
somewhat delay the inevitable tendency. And ultimately
these earnings of management will fall to about their old

646

level; for no one could get extra high wages for making eggs stand on their ends after Columbus' plan had become public property.

b. This paragraph was inserted in the 2nd ed. (p. 636), where it replaced the following paragraphs in the 1st ed. (pp. 636–7):

As soon then as any method of manufacturing is reduced to routine, and no longer requires exceptional ability, those who follow it will be unable to get the earnings of work that is really difficult. And so far competition tends to reward men in proportion to what they have done for society; for those who merely follow the beaten track do not render as important services as they would have done if they had had to think out the method for themselves. Society is indeed just as well off as it would have been if each of these people had found out the path for himself; but less of society's gains would then have had to be credited to knowledge which is the common property of the world, and more to these individual producers. Putting aside the gains of speculation, which requires to some extent a separate treatment, it so far seems true that competition tends to secure to each ordinary employer earnings of management equal to the direct additions which his work makes to the efficiency of production, and no more. *The reward of the latter is seldom very high.*

It must be admitted that occasionally a man will complete improvements which others have nearly worked out, and by patenting the last little link which he has added, get more than his deserts. But if he patents it, and allows others to use it at a moderate premium, he will probably confer on society a total benefit the money equivalent of which, even while his patent lasts, is much greater than the profits which he himself obtains. And if the invention is one that can be easily copied, so that his rivals, making use of it, can compete against him and bring down the price of what he sells, his own profits are likely to be very small, perhaps altogether insignificant, in comparison with the total benefit which he confers. It is, in fact, probable that those business men who have earned large fortunes by striking out new paths for themselves have not, taken all together, reaped a hundredth part of the total benefit that the world has gained from their work; perhaps not a thousandth part. *That of the former sometimes is very high; but is scarcely ever commensurate with their real value to society.*

The reference in the first of the above marginal summaries to "the latter" is to those employers who follow beaten tracks; while the reference in the second summary to "the former" is to those employers who operate new and improved methods of business.

c. The first main clause of this sentence dates from the 3rd ed. (p. 677).

d. This clause was inserted in the 4th ed. (p. 680).

PAGE 599

a. This paragraph dates from the 2nd ed. (p. 637), apart from the replacement in the second line of the words "law of substitution" by the word "competition", in the 4th ed. (p. 681).

PAGE 600

a. The following footnote attached to the word "grade" in the 1st ed. (p. 633 n.) was deleted from the 2nd ed.:

> It should be noted that we assume him to be working chiefly with a good deal of borrowed capital; so that his earnings of management fall short of the profits of a man of normal ability in that grade working with his own capital, by that high rate of interest which the lenders have to charge in some form or other for loans in such cases as his, to compensate them for their risk and trouble (see Book VII, ch. VII, §6). We shall have to return to this point.

The reference in this footnote applies to Book VI, ch. VI, §4 in vol. I of the present ed.

PAGE 601

a. So since the 4th ed. (p. 683) where this paragraph replaced the following paragraph in the earlier editions:

Having watched the law of substitution adjusting the earnings of foremen and of ordinary workmen, and again of employers and foremen, we may now look at its action in adjusting the earnings of employers on a small scale and those on a large scale.

b. "law" in the first three editions; "principle" from the 4th ed.

PAGE 602

a. In connexion with the subject-matter of this section, there is a passage in the *Economics of Industry* by Alfred Marshall and Mary Paley Marshall (1st ed. 1879, pp. 135–8) where the authors pointed out that:

The man who works with his own capital considers that his earnings of management are the whole net profits of his business after deducting the interest that he could obtain by letting out his money on good security. But interest at a much higher rate than this must be paid by a man who borrows capital for his business, at all events unless his own property is sufficient to give good security for it; and interest at this high rate must be deducted from the profits of his business in order to find his earnings of management. The rate of interest which he has to pay is high, because in his case a new set of risks is introduced in addition to those unavoidable risks which exist in every business.

After describing the trade and personal risks borne by the lender who puts capital at the disposal of the borrower, they went on to say:

Thus it appears that a trader who works on borrowed capital has in one form or another to pay a high rate of interest. But though high it is not sufficiently high to prevent him from competing with those who trade with their own capital. On the contrary men trading with borrowed capital seem likely to displace to a great extent those trading with their own.

The reason for this is not far to seek. A man who has a capital of £50,000 can easily obtain a secure income of £2500 by lending it out. And very likely he may not care to undergo the labours and anxieties of a business life unless he can get earnings of management of £2500, or even £5000 a year, exclusive of course of insurance against trade risks. But a man of equal ability who owns little capital, and who therefore cannot live in comfort without working, will be content with lower earnings of management. He may be willing to employ £50,000 of borrowed capital, in addition to his own, even though after allowing for the interest that he actually pays and the indirect risks that he runs through working with borrowed capital, he does not clear more than £1000 a year by the work. He can therefore afford to sell at a price too low to give that rate of profits which a man of independent means requires. Thus those who depend on their business for a livelihood, undersell and drive out of trade those who are not so independent.[1]

[1] This is making English commerce increasingly democratic, and does much harm in preventing "the long duration of great families of merchant princes.... But the propensity to variation in the social as in the animal kingdom is the principle of progress." See Bagehot's *Lombard Street*, Introductory Chapter.

It may be noted that there is a reference to the same passage in Bagehot's *Lombard Street*, on page 604 in vol. 1 of the present edition.

b. This paragraph was inserted in the 6th ed. (p. 602).

c. In the 4th ed. (p. 684) the words "struggle for survival" replaced the word "law of substitution" dating from the 1st ed. (p. 637).

PAGE 603

a. This sentence dates in its present form from the 2nd ed. (p. 641) where this paragraph was brought into the text. In the 1st ed. (p. 638 n.) this opening sentence ran as follows:

> In 1873 twenty years of almost unbroken rise of prices had enriched debtors at the expense of creditors, and had, in ways which we shall have to study in the second volume of this treatise, enriched undertakers of business of all kinds partly at the expense of other members of society. New men found their way...etc.

PAGE 604

a. This section (§ 6) dates in its present form from the 5th ed. (pp. 604–5), but most of the individual sentences date from the 1st ed. (pp. 639–40). See the Editorial Appendix to this chapter for the earlier form of this discussion of joint-stock companies (pp. 654–7 below).

b. This sentence dates from the 4th ed. (p. 686).

PAGE 605

a. The first three clauses of this sentence date from the 5th ed. (p. 605).

b. In the 1st ed. (p. 641) the section on joint-stock companies was concluded by a paragraph dealing with co-operation, the substance of which was transferred in the 2nd ed. to Book IV, ch. XII, § 10. See page 306 in vol. 1 of the present edition.

c. In the 4th ed. the words "under the action of the law of substitution" between the word "extended" and the words "in every direction", dating from the 1st ed. (p. 642) were deleted.

d. The word "normal" was inserted before the word "expenses" in the 3rd ed. (p. 685).

e. In the 4th ed. the word "principle" replaced the word "law" in the earlier editions.

PAGE 606

a. The following paragraph at this point in the 1st ed. (p. 642) was deleted from the 2nd ed.:

We have called the price of the first of these three elements "Net Interest"; we may call the price of the second taken by itself "*Net Earnings of Management*", and that of the second and third taken together "*Gross Earnings of Management*".

b. So since the 3rd ed. (p. 685) where this sentence replaced the following sentence dating from the 1st ed. (p. 643):

The supply of business power is large and elastic, because the area from which it is drawn is large, and its highest qualities are non-specialized and capable of being transferred from one occupation to another.

PAGE 607

a. The following concluding sentences of this footnote in the 1st ed. (p. 644 n.) were deleted from the 3rd ed.:

It is a remarkable instance of the parallelism of the work done by economists in different nations that Bagehot's *Postulates* was first published in the *Fortnightly Review* early in 1876, the very year in which General Walker's *Wages Question* appeared. These two writers have done more than any others to make clear the true characteristics of modern business and modern business men.

PAGE 608

a. This sentence was inserted in the 6th ed. (p. 608 n.).

EDITORIAL APPENDIX TO BOOK VI, CHAPTER VII

The following extracts from Book VII, chapter VIII in the 1st edition were deleted, either wholly or in great part, from the 2nd or later editions:

I. THE OPERATION OF THE PRINCIPLE OF SUBSTITUTION IN RELATION TO BUSINESS UNDERTAKERS

In the 1st ed. (Book VII, ch. VII), §1 ran as follows:

§1. [a]IN the concluding Chapter of Book IV we saw that the supply of business power in command of capital may be regarded as consisting of three elements, the supply of capital, the supply of the business power to manage it, The inquiry of this and the following chapters

---

a. This and the next two paragraphs, and the last sentence of the fifth paragraph, were retained substantially in the later editions. See pages 596–7 in vol. 1 of the present edition.

and the supply of the organization by which the two are brought together and made effective for production. We have now to carry this analysis further; and to study more closely the nature of the services which the business undertaker renders to society, and the rewards of this work.

must be prefaced by a caution.

But we must first pause a little to draw a distinction between the direct and indirect services which the employer renders, for it is with the former only that we are concerned here. The purpose of this preliminary section is to guard against any applications beyond their proper scope of the argument in this and the following chapters that the rewards of every business undertaker tend to be proportionate to the *direct* services he renders to the community.

The immediate efficiency of any form of business management plays

As we have already seen[1] the struggle for survival tends to cause those methods of organization to prevail which are best fitted to *thrive in* their environment; but it is not to be inferred that they are those best fitted to *benefit* their environment, unless it should so happen that all the benefits which they confer, whether direct or indirect, are rewarded in like proportion. And in fact this is not so. For as a general rule the law of substitution—which is nothing more than a special and limited application of the law of survival of the fittest— tends to make one method of industrial organization supplant another when it offers a direct and immediate service at a lower price. The indirect and ultimate services which either will render have, as a general rule, little or no weight in the balance.

the chief part in determining its success in the struggle for survival.

There are some important exceptions to this general rule.

There are indeed some important exceptions to this rule; and they are very instructive. For instance, any business such as that of a railway company, which has a long future before it, may be able to afford a great outlay in the present for the sake of a high income in the distant future; and in that future it may reckon on reaping part of the fruits of those indirect benefits which it confers by developing the resources of its neighbourhood[2].

[1] Book IV, ch. VII.
[2] b Comp. Book III, ch. III, §7, Book V, ch. VII and Book VI, ch. IV.

---

b. These references apply to Book III, ch. IV, §6, Book V, ch. XIII, and Book V, ch. XI in vol. I of the present edition.

So again when any new business is being started, the profits are likely to come in slowly for a time. But meanwhile a good business connection may be acquired; and the expectation of these ultimate gains may keep a good heart in those who are undertaking it; and they may be able to succeed in the long run. They may succeed: but also they may fail. We constantly see promising businesses, which, if they could only have grown past the difficulties of starting, might probably have rendered great services to society, and reaped the reward of those services; but which are stopped short by the overshadowing influences of those who are already strong.

The action of the law of substitution then often enables those who are able to offer immediate and direct services at a low price, to supplant others, whose total services to society if they had prospered at first would have as much exceeded those of the rivals by whom they are kept down, as an oak sapling might have ultimately over-topped the brambles, amidst which it tried in vain to raise its head. Even when the conflict lies between two well-established businesses, and is irreproachable in its methods, a great part of the success of the one may represent not net gain to the world, but a transference of success to itself from its rival. And if this victory is gained by undergoing present sacrifices and selling at a low price, not in order to obtain a great power of doing good work in the future, but in order to drive from the field rivals with smaller capital; and especially if this end is pursued by a trust or other combination, there is no *prima facie* cause for thinking that the result has been beneficial. And yet we must not forget that even in such cases as this, the victors in the struggle for survival being able to produce on a large scale, and so to avail themselves of great economies in manufacture and in marketing, may find that the price which gives them the highest aggregate monopoly profits may be below that previously ruling[1]. But the rule is far-reaching.

[1] ᶜComp. Book V, ch. VIII, §5. Comp. Book VII, ch. v, §4.

---

c. The first of these references applies to Book V, ch. XIV, §5 in vol. I of the present edition; the second appears to have been incorrect in the original, where it should have been "Book VI, ch. VI, §3" (Book V, ch. VII, §2 in vol. I of the present edition).

Again, to say nothing of those cases in which one employer elbows his way on, by means of exceptional skill and tenacity in driving hard bargains with his men, we find in almost every trade cases in which the employer may have to choose between two methods of work, one of which would give him the greater pecuniary gain; while the other would tend the more strongly to develop the higher faculties of his employees and add much in the long run to the productive efficiency, the wealth and the higher well-being of the nation. Unfortunately the tendency of the law of substitution under existing social and economic institutions is frequently to make the former method prevail.

We may then pass from these preliminary explanations, having made it clear that we are not at present dealing with the question whether the existing industrial organization of society is the best conceivable, or even the best attainable; and that the scope of our inquiry is now limited to a study of the action of the law of substitution in determining the earnings of business undertaking and management under existing social institutions.[d]

With the exception of the passages mentioned in the editorial notes the whole of §1 in the 1st edition, just quoted, was deleted from the 2nd edition.

2. JOINT-STOCK COMPANIES

In the 1st edition in Book VII, chapter VIII, §7, there were the following paragraphs:

The officials of joint-stock companies do the work of business management, and their income is almost mere earnings of labour.

In marked contrast with the energy and versatility of the new man are the great joint-stock companies; though they also go beyond the older forms of business association in the facilities which they offer for men without capital to rise to high posts of business management[1]. In such companies it is the shareholders only that are the ultimate undertakers of business risks; and they as a rule know but little of what is being done and what ought to be done.

[1] Comp. Book IV, ch. XII, §8.

---

d. The remainder of the subject matter of this chapter in the 1st ed. (Book VII, ch. VIII) was retained substantially, with some rearrangement, in the later editions (Book VI, ch. VII in vol. 1 of the present edition).

[a]The real work of management is divided between salaried directors (who indeed hold a few shares themselves) and salaried managers and other subordinate officials, most of whom have little or no capital of any kind. Their earnings are almost the pure earnings of labour and are governed in the long run by those general causes which rule the earnings of labour of equal difficulty and disagreeableness in ordinary occupations.

Joint-stock companies are hampered by internal frictions, and conflicts of interest between shareholders and debenture holders, between ordinary and preferred shareholders, and between all these and the directors; and by the need for an elaborate system of checks and counterchecks. They seldom have the enterprise, the energy, the unity of purpose and the quickness of action of a private business. *Disadvantages of public companies,*

But these disadvantages are of relatively small importance in some trades. That publicity, which is one of the chief drawbacks of public companies in many branches of manufacture and of speculative commerce, is a positive advantage in ordinary banking and insurance and kindred businesses; while in these as well as in most of the transport industries (railways, tramways, canals, and the supply of gas, water, and electricity) their unbounded command over capital gives them almost undisputed sway. *and their advantages.*

[b]A peculiar feature of this latter class of industries is that their fixed capital is large relatively to their circulating. And we have already seen[1] that, when this is the case, the prime cost of the goods produced or the services rendered is small relatively to the total or true normal cost which must be defrayed in the long run in order to make the business remunerative. When several companies whose business is *The largest public companies are often found in trades in which prices are naturally unstable.*

[1] [c]Book VI, ch. VI, §1.

---

a. The remainder of this paragraph, and the next two paragraphs were retained substantially in the later editions. See pages 604–5 in vol. 1 of the present edition.

b. This paragraph was retained substantially from the 2nd to the 4th editions, but in the 5th ed. it was much compressed. See page 605 in vol. 1 of the present edition.

c. This reference applies to Book V, ch. v, §6 in vol. 1 of the present edition.

But on the whole they exert a steadying influence on employ-ment.

of this kind are in keen competition, they are under a great temptation to attract custom by selling at much less than normal cost; but probably they do not yield to this temptation more than, or even as much as, private capitalists would under similar circumstances. And on the whole those power-ful joint-stock companies which have great traditions and look forward to a distant future pursue a far-seeing if a sluggish policy; they are seldom willing to sacrifice their reputation for the sake of a temporary gain; they are not inclined to drive such hard bargains with their employees as will make their service unpopular; and they exercise generally a steadying influence on the demand for capital, and on the demand for labour of all kinds, and especially for the services of those who, having business ability but no capital of their own, desire to reap some earnings of management as salaried officials of a great undertaking.

Special features of some classes of public companies.

A somewhat different influence is exercised by those com-panies which are growing up even in trades for which the joint-stock system has no special fitness; this growth being a result of the constant increase on the one hand of people who have business ability but no capital, and on the other of people who have capital but no facilities for employing it themselves or for lending it out safely to be used in private businesses. For the shares in many of these companies are owned by persons who are impatient of delay, and require their directors and managers to pursue an aggressive, pushing policy. A very large proportion of such companies fail; having enriched none but the promoters. But though they lead to much destruction of capital, the opportunities which they offer for the investment of small sums with a promise of a high profit, lead many to save who otherwise would not. Their influence in breaking down partial monopolies and trade combinations, is one of several causes which render them unpopular with some business men; but they probably tend in the long run to increase the wealth of the working and lower middle classes, as well as to develop any business abilities they may have[1].

[1] The Limited Liability Act has to bear the blame of evils that should not properly be charged to it; and the harm really done by it is probably small in comparison with the good; but undoubtedly it does work mischief in several ways,

Apart from the passages mentioned in the editorial notes, all the above paragraphs in the 1st edition were deleted from the 2nd edition.

BOOK VI, CHAPTER VIII

PROFITS OF CAPITAL AND BUSINESS POWER, CONTINUED

PAGE 609

a. Except where otherwise stated in the editorial notes the wording of this chapter dates from the 1st edition.

b. So since the 4th edition.

In the 1st edition (Book VII, ch. IX) and the 2nd and 3rd editions (Book VI, ch. VIII) this title ran as follows: "Demand and Supply in Relation to Capital and Business Power, Continued."

c. So since the 2nd ed. (p. 647) where this paragraph replaced the following paragraph in the 1st ed. (p. 646):

In the last chapter we were chiefly occupied with the modern economic tendencies to adjust to one another capital and the ability required to use it well; and we inquired, more fully than we had done in the Fourth Book, how two sets of forces, the one increasing the capital at the command of able men and the other destroying the capital that is in the hands of weaker men, bring about a close correspondence between the ability of business men and the size of the businesses which they own. Bearing this result with us, we have next to discuss the question whether there is any normal relation between the earnings of management in different businesses and the capital required to carry them on: or, what is nearly the same thing, whether the rate of profits

We have next to inquire whether there is any general tendency of the rate of profits to equality.

two of which may be mentioned here. Firstly, the news of the exceptional profitableness of any business generally takes some time in reaching small investors; and therefore a rush of new companies supported by their capital is likely to continue after the trade is already overstocked, and thus to cause in the long run a great and disastrous reaction. Secondly, when the shareholders borrow, as they frequently do, a great deal of additional capital on debentures, they are apt to divide out nearly the whole surplus of receipts over outgoings, including the interest on that capital. That surplus is in prosperous times large in proportion to their own capital and affords very high dividends: but the company is left without any adequate reserve fund to meet an adverse turn of fortune. Much information on this and similar subjects was collected by the recent Royal Commission on the Depression of Trade.

per annum on capital invested in business has any general tendency to equality.

The marginal summary to the first paragraph of § 1 of this chapter in vol. 1 of the present edition was given its present form in the 4th ed. (p. 691).

PAGE 610

a. This paragraph was inserted in the 3rd ed. (p. 690).

PAGE 611

a. The second and third sentences of this paragraph date, without any substantial change, from a paragraph in the *Economics of Industry* by Alfred Marshall and Mary Paley Marshall (1st ed. 1879, p. 142), which ran as follows:

In some industries large capitals have completely driven their smaller rivals from the field, and afterwards their competition among themselves has reduced the rate of profits very low. In rolling mills for instance there is little detail which cannot be reduced to routine, and a capital of £1,000,000 invested in them can be controlled by one able man. A rate of profits of 20 per cent, which is not a very high average rate for some parts of the iron trade, would give the owner of such works earnings of management amounting to more than £150,000 a year. And since iron-masters can with so little additional effort get the earnings of management on an increased capital, wealthy men remain in the trade longer than in most others; and the competition of the great iron-masters with one another is said to have reduced the average rate of profits in their trade below the ordinary level.

b. This sentence dates from the 5th ed. (p. 611), where it replaced the following sentence dating from the 1st ed. (p. 648):

And since iron-masters can with so little additional effort get the earnings of management on an increased capital, wealthy men remain in the trade longer than in most others; and the competition of the great iron-masters with one another is said to have reduced the average rate of profits in their trade below the ordinary level.

See also the preceding editorial note **a** to this page.

c.   In the *Economics of Industry* by Alfred Marshall and Mary Paley Marshall (1st ed. 1879, pp. 139–42) there was the following account of the relation between the size of businesses and the earnings of management:

A man who has all the rare qualities that are required for managing a large business will, unless he is specially unlucky, make a high rate of profits on his capital. These profits will increase his capital, and will encourage him to devise and carry out bold plans on a broad basis. The confidence that others have in him will enable him to borrow capital easily; and thus because he has the faculties which are one condition of high earnings of management, he will rapidly acquire that control of a large capital which is the other condition.

We see then, firstly, that higher faculties are required for the management of a large than of a small capital; and secondly that there is a process of selection continually going on by which those who have some capital and great business power, soon get control over a large capital; while on the other hand those who have not business power will speedily dissipate a large capital if they happen to get control over it. These facts show that the earnings of management in large businesses must be on the average higher than those in small; and they even give some reason for thinking that the average earnings of management in different businesses in the same trade vary almost in proportion to the capital employed. There is however an independent and stronger reason for believing that there is often the same average rate of profit, on different capitals in the same trade.

Let us suppose for instance that A and B are proprietors of neighbouring cotton factories which are alike in every respect excepting that A's is twice as large as B's. They hire labour and they buy their raw cotton, machinery, building materials, etc., in the same market and at the same price. There may indeed be a few slight economies in A's business of which B cannot avail himself; and on the other hand A may have to pay subordinates for doing some of the work that B with his smaller business finds time for doing himself.

But if these differences be neglected, all the expenses of production, other than profits, of a yard of A's calico, will be the same as those of a yard of B's; and since they sell in the same market at the same price, the profits made on each yard of calico will be the same for A as for B. The rate of A's profits will be the same as that of B's. A's earnings of management will be twice those of B.

The results which theory thus indicates are confirmed by experience. Experience and theory alike tell us that as a general rule there is a constant tendency to equality of the rate of profits not only on equal capitals, but also on unequal capitals in the same trade, and in trades that are equally disagreeable and difficult. But there are three important exceptions to this rule.

The first exception arises from the fact that the head of a large business often pays wages to subordinates to do a great deal of work that the head of a small business does for himself, and the payment for which is reckoned among his profits....

The second exception is closely connected with the first. There are many trades in which small makers and dealers are able to sell at a higher price than the large dealers can, because they get access to a different class of customers. One familiar instance of this is the fact that village shopkeepers generally get a very high price for their goods. Their capital is very small; and their profits, though at a high rate on their capital, are so small in amount as not to attract competition....

The third exception arises from the influence of the law of increasing return. In many industries a large capital can avail itself of great economies that are out of the reach of a small capital; and the large manufacturer can make higher profits than the small manufacturer. These industries would rapidly be concentrated in the hands of a few wealthy firms, if a man whose practical genius has created a large business, could ensure that his successors for several generations should have a like genius. But in the whole course of history we meet with but very few instances of private firms which have been managed with eminent genius for three generations in succession. The sons and grandsons of a successful man of business have seldom that rare combination of ability and assiduity which would enable them to carry on his work. And there are many instances in which a vast inherited business has been quickly destroyed by men who could have managed a small business well.

PAGE 612

a.   The following clause and sentence at this point, dating from the 1st ed. (p. 649), were deleted from the 3rd ed.:

because in fact there seldom are many small businesses in a trade which does not offer them some special advantages in marketing &c. to countervail the economies in production that are available only by large businesses. And these economies are generally turned to account by the large firms not in keeping up their own rate of profits, but in competing with one another by lowered prices for an increased share of custom.

b.   This sentence was inserted in the 3rd ed. (p. 692).

c.   A slightly different explanation for the lower rate of profits in trades where there is much fixed capital was given in the *Economics of Industry* by Alfred Marshall and Mary Paley Marshall (1st ed. 1879, p. 139).

The profits on equal capitals tend continually to equality in trades which involve equal risks, discomforts and exertions; and which require equally rare natural abilities and an equally expensive training.

It has however already been noticed that if £100 has been invested in the production of a thing two years before it is ready for sale, we must allow twice, or rather more than twice as much under the head of interest as if the £100 had been invested only one year before it was ready for sale: but the total amount to be allowed as earnings of management on the £100 will be nearly the same for the long period and for the short: so that the annual rate of profits will be much lower in the former case than in the latter. For this reason the annual rate of profits on the total capital employed is, as a general rule, lower in trades which make great use of fixed capital than in trades in which nearly all the capital is circulating.

d. The following footnote attached to the word "bridges" in the 1st ed. (p. 649 n.) was deleted from the 5th ed.:

> An interesting application of this principle is found in the fact that a manufacturer, who owns the factory he uses, has generally to be contented with a lower rate of profit per annum on his capital, than another who works in a hired factory, and therefore does not count the value of his factory as part of his capital; for the profits on capital invested in buildings are low, because no great trouble is involved by owning them and letting them out. This fact may, however, be regarded from another point of view as an instance of the rule that if a man has borrowed much of the capital he uses in business, his profits even after he has paid a rather high interest on his borrowings, will generally be large in proportion to his own capital.

In connexion with the argument of this footnote, see also Book VI, ch. VII, §5 in vol. I of the present edition, and the editorial notes to that section.

PAGE 613

a. The remaining sentences of this paragraph and the footnote attached to it were inserted in the 3rd ed. (p. 693).

b. The following concluding sentence of this footnote, dating from the 3rd ed. (p. 694 n.), was deleted from the 6th ed.: "The influence of joint-stock companies on the investment of capital in risky trades will be discussed in the second volume."

PAGE 614

a. This and the next paragraph date from the 6th ed. (pp. 614–15).

b. This paragraph dates in its present form from the 6th ed. (p. 614 n.). In the 1st ed. (pp. 650 n.–1 n.) it ran as follows:

> There is great difficulty in ascertaining even approximately the amounts of capital of different kinds invested in different classes of business; for much of it is always shifting from one use to another; much of it is constantly changing in value as the result of new improvements and many other causes; a good deal of it is apt to be overlooked, and a good deal more to be counted twice over (this applies especially to buildings and other capital that is owned by one person and used by another); and finally business men are seldom willing to publish the best guess they can make as to the amount of their capital. In consequence the returns of the American Census are less trustworthy on this subject than on almost any other (see General Walker's remarks in the *Census Report* of 1880, vol. II, p. xxxix). Nevertheless they are the most instructive for our present purpose that we have: they show that the conclusion arrived at in the text gives widely different results from the proposition that profits in different trades tend to be proportionate to the total capital employed. The list includes not only manufactures proper, but all industries such as baking, sugar refining, &c. which make a *slight change* in the form of any material; and in consequence many things are reckoned twice over: for instance, the products of flour mills and bakeries are counted in full, and so are those of tanneries and of boot factories. Comparing firstly Total Product with capital we find that they vary from less

than the capital in watch and cotton factories &c. to four, five, or six times the capital in carpentering and boot factories, as well as in some of the "Slight-change" industries such as sugar refining, and slaughtering and meat packing.

From the 3rd to the 5th editions the first sentence of this paragraph was retained as in the 1st ed., but the remainder was reworded as in vol. 1 of the present edition.

c. In the 2nd ed. (p. 651 n.) there was the following additional paragraph which, in that edition, concluded the footnote: "Much valuable information of the same kind is to be found in the Report of the Massachusetts Bureau of Labor on *Statistics of Manufacture* for 1889; see especially a table on pp. 264, 5." This paragraph was deleted from the 3rd ed.

d. This paragraph was inserted in the 3rd ed. (pp. 694 n.–5 n.).

PAGE 615

a. This sentence dates from the 3rd ed. (p. 695), where it re-placed the following paragraph dating from the 1st ed. (p. 651):

In trades in which the wages-bill and the value of the material consumed are large in proportion to the capital, the aggregate turnover of capital will also be large in proportion. And we are thus brought to consider the causes which deter-mine the rate of profits on the "turnover"; or, which comes to the same thing, the percentage of the supply price of a commodity which has to be classed as profits.

PAGE 617

a. So since the 3rd ed. (p. 697 n.). In the first two editions the word "expert" was placed in inverted commas.

PAGE 618

a. So since the 4th ed. (p. 699), where the opening words of this clause "we have seen how it seeks...etc." replaced the following words dating from the 1st ed. (p. 654): "we have seen how under the action of the law of substitution it seeks...etc."

PAGE 619

a. The first of the two following paragraphs at this point in the 1st ed. (pp. 654–5) was deleted from the 4th ed., and the second paragraph from the 2nd ed.:

But so soon as his skill, his material capital, and his business connection are to any extent specialized to any one branch of business; then to that extent these factors of

But the income derived from capital already invested is generally a quasi-rent determined by price.

Recapitulation of this argument with reference to the investments of capital in acquiring trade skill.

production cease to exert a direct influence on the value of the products due to them: and on the other hand the value of those products (in conjunction with the other circumstances of the case) determines the income which can be derived from these factors; i.e. it determines what we have called their quasi-rent.

This argument was worked out in detail in Book VI and in the last chapter but one of Book VII with regard to material capital; and it was applied to personal or immaterial capital in the sixth chapter of Book VII. We there saw how the earnings which a man expects to obtain from the possession of any kind of industrial skill, supply motives which induce him to acquire that skill; and that therefore in the long run such earnings enter into the supply price of the things in making which that skill is needed. But when once he has acquired that skill, the extra earnings which he gets by it are determined by the relations in which the supply of that skill stands to the demand for it; this being in general an indirect demand derived from the direct demand for those classes of things to the making of which his skill contributes. We saw moreover that industrial skill, being but slowly acquired, is to be compared to those kinds of fixed capital which take a long time in the making: and that when we are contrasting the action of economic forces in long periods and short, we must take the term "long" to indicate a greater duration with regard to labour and slowly produced forms of fixed capital than with regard to ordinary commodities. The whole of that argument, to which the reader is referred, applies generally to the earnings of business power in the same way as to the earnings of industrial skill: though now, continuing from a slightly different point of view the discussion begun at the end of last chapter, we shall find that there are some noteworthy differences between the two cases.

The first of the above references in the second paragraph applies to Book V, chs. VIII–X; the second reference to "the last chapter but one of Book VII" should have been to "Book VI, ch. V" and applies to Book V, ch. IV, in vol. I of the present edition; while the third reference applies to Book VI, ch. V in vol. I of the present edition.

b. So since the 2nd ed. (p. 656), where this clause and the first clause of the next sentence, replaced the following clauses in the 1st ed. (pp. 655–6):

are similar to those which induce an employer or his father to invest capital and labour not only in preparing him for his work, but also in getting together the material plant and the business organization that he will require. In either case the investment is made as a deliberate sacrifice of present ease and present gratifications for the sake of future pleasures and gains: and in either case the investment of sacrifice is (so far as man's action is governed by deliberate motive at all) carried up...etc.

c. A footnote attached to the word "business" in the 1st ed. (p. 656 n.) in explanation of the German word "Konjunktur", was transferred to Book III, ch. VI, §1 in the 3rd ed. (page 125 n. in vol. 1 of the present edition).

PAGE 620

a. The following footnote attached to the word "work" in the 1st ed. (p. 657 n.) was deleted from the 2nd ed.:

> At a later stage we shall have to consider the causes and consequences of the facts that trade unions are strongest, and the proportion of successful to unsuccessful strikes is the largest when trade is prosperous.

b. This clause was inserted in the 3rd ed. (p. 700).
c. The word "even" was inserted before the word "his" in the 3rd ed. (p. 700).

PAGE 622

a. This sentence was inserted in the 5th ed. (p. 621).
b. So since the 5th ed. (p. 621) where the word "income" replaced the word "quasi-rent" dating from the 1st ed. (p. 659). See editorial note **b** to page 664 of vol. 1 in this edition for the other instance where Marshall (in the earlier editions only) coupled the word "negative" with the word "quasi-rent".

PAGE 623

a. See page 578 in vol. 1 of the present edition and editorial note **a** to that page.
b. So since the 2nd ed. (p. 660), where the first two sentences of this paragraph replaced the following sentences in the 1st ed. (p. 660):

But though this is true on the whole, there are very great exceptions. In the case of the humdrum business man, who

665

has inherited a good business and has just sufficient force to keep it together, his income consists chiefly of profits on the investment of capital in the material plant of his business, and in its immaterial internal organization and external connections.

PAGE 624

a. The word "income" in the first sentence, the words "special income" in the second sentence, the words "earning power" occurring twice in the third sentence and once in the fourth sentence of this paragraph, replaced in the 5th ed. (p. 623) the word "quasi-rent" which was used in each instance in the first four editions.

b. The words "producer's surplus" replaced in the 5th ed. (p. 623) the word "rent" dating from the 1st ed. (p. 661).

c. In the first three editions there were two additional sentences (deleted from the 4th ed.) at this point, which concluded the paragraph and the chapter. These sentences (1st ed. p. 661) ran as follows:

Not nearly all these changes in the industrial environment are local in their action: but the chief of them are. And this brings us to consider again situation rent in connection with the general problem of demand and supply in relation to land.

d. The first sentence of this footnote dates in its present form from the 6th ed. (p. 624 n.). In the first five editions the opening sentences ran as follows:

General Walker's excellent services with regard to the causes that determine wages on the one hand and earnings of management on the other, make it all the more to be regretted that instead of developing the old tradition that all earnings of rare natural abilities have in them, from the point of view of the individual, something of the nature of rent, he has worked out only that side of the tradition which relates to earnings of management. And his treatment of that side does not appear altogether satisfactory. He maintains (*Political Economy*, §311) that *profits* do not form...etc.

Marshall wrote a reply in the *Quarterly Journal of Economics*, vol. 1, 1887, to criticisms expressed by General Walker of the treatment of profits in *Economics of Industry* by Alfred and Mary Paley Marshall, 1879. The article in question is reproduced in the Editorial Appendix to this chapter (pp. 670–5 below).

e. This sentence was inserted in the 6th ed. (p. 624 n.) where it replaced the following sentences dating from the 1st ed. (p. 662):

And therefore the argument, in so far as it is valid at all, applies to the "rare ability" part of the earnings of all kinds of labour, as much as of earnings of management. But for the reasons given in the last paragraph of the fifth Chapter of this Book, the analogy between the rent of land and the earnings of rare natural abilities cannot safely be pressed far.

The reference in the second of these sentences applies to page 569 in vol. 1 of the present edition.

666

PAGE 625

a. This section dates substantially from the 2nd ed., where it was placed in Book VI, ch. xi, §8, pp. 712–13. It was transferred to Book VI, ch. viii, §9 in the 4th ed.

In the 1st ed. (Book VII, ch. xii, §8, pp. 707–8), where this same subject was discussed, the corresponding paragraph ran as follows:

The full discussion of market or current wages and profits, belongs to a later stage. But there is one point with regard to them that should be noticed here. It relates to the solidarity of the different industrial classes engaged in the same trade. In some cases and for some purposes nearly the whole income of a business may be regarded as a quasi-rent divisible among the different persons in the business by bargaining, supplemented by custom and by notions of fairness: and, when the several groups are combined among themselves, the same may be said of the aggregate income of all the businesses in a trade. These results are brought about by causes, which though different, bear some analogy to those that, as we saw in the last chapter, have put the producer's surplus from the land, in early forms of civilization, into the hands not of single individuals, but of cultivating firms.

We proceed to consider the quasi-rent of a business in divided ownership between employers and employed.

The reference to "the last chapter" in the final sentence of this paragraph applies to Book VI, ch. x in vol. 1 of the present edition.

b. Except where otherwise indicated the wording of this section dates substantially from Book VII, ch. xii, pp. 708–11, in the 1st ed.

c. In the 3rd ed. (Book VI, ch. xi, p. 753) the word "earnings" in the first and third lines of the first sentence replaced the word "quasi-rent" dating from the 1st ed.

d. The following footnote was attached to the word "diminished" in the 1st ed. (pp. 708 n.–9 n.):

We have not had occasion to discuss the general problem of which this is a particular case; but it has much scientific interest, and some study of it here may throw light on the important special case in the text. At starting, there may appear to be some contradiction in the statement that a thing is yielding at the same time two rents: for its rent is in some sense a residual income after deducting the expenses of working it: and it may seem that there cannot be two residues. But really we often find a true producers' surplus or rent, which itself includes two or more minor rents. For instance, the rent of a flour-mill worked by water includes the rent of the site on which it is built, and the rent of the water power which it uses. Suppose that it is contemplated to build a mill in a place where there is a limited water power, which could be applied equally well on any one of many sites; then the rent of the water power together with the site selected for it is the sum of two rents; which are respectively the equivalent of the differential advantages which possession of the site gives for production of any kind, and which the ownership of the water power gives for working a mill on any of the sites. And these two rents, whether they happen to be owned by the same person or not, can be clearly distinguished, and separately estimated both in theory and in practice. But this cannot be done if there are no other sites on which a mill can be built: and in that case, should the water power and the site belong to different persons, there is nothing but "higgling and bargaining" to settle how much of the excess of the value of the two together over that which the site has for other purposes, shall go to the owner of the latter. And even if there were other sites at which the water power could be applied, but not with equal efficiency, there would still be no means of deciding how the owners of the site and the water power should share the excess of the producer's surplus which they got by acting together, over the sum of that which the site would yield for some other purpose, and of that which the water power would yield if applied elsewhere.

The mill would probably not be put up till an agreement had been made for the supply of water power for a term of years: but at the end of that term similar difficulties would arise as to the division of the aggregate producer's surplus afforded by the water power and the site with the mill on it. Difficulties of this kind are continually arising with regard to attempts by partial monopolists, such as railway, gas, water and electrical companies, to raise their charges on the consumer who has adapted his business arrangements to make use of their services, and perhaps laid down at his own expense a costly plant for the purpose. For instance at Pittsburgh when manufacturers had just put up furnaces to be worked by natural gas instead of coal, the price of the gas was suddenly doubled. (See Mr C. W. Baker's *Monopolies and the People*, ch. III.) The whole history of mines is full of difficulties of this kind with neighbouring landowners (as to rights of way, &c.), neighbouring cottage, railway and dock owners. We shall have to examine these difficulties when we come to the question of combinations, monopolies and collective in relation to private interests. See also Book V, ch. VIII, especially §6.

The subject-matter of this footnote was transferred in the 2nd ed. to Book V, ch. X and there placed in the text as a separate section (§4), under the general heading, "Composite rent". In the 5th and later editions this became Book V, ch. XI, §7. See pages 453–4 in vol. I of the present edition.

The reference in the last sentence of the footnote applies to Book V, ch. XIV, "especially §6" in vol. I of the present edition.

e.   The last three sentences of this paragraph were inserted in the 6th ed. (pp. 625–6).

PAGE 626

a.   In the first two editions the word "quasi-rent" was used in place of the word "gains". In the 3rd ed. (p. 753) this was changed to "gains (or quasi-rents)". In the 5th ed. (p. 625) the words in parentheses "or quasi-rents" were deleted.

b.   This and the next sentence date from the 2nd ed. (p. 713), except for the insertion in the 3rd ed. (p. 753) of the clauses and words beginning with the words "that is an income determined...etc." and ending with the words "*composite quasi-rent*".

c.   In the 8th edition "v. x. 8."; emended in vol. I of the present edition to give the correct reference.

a. The remainder of this paragraph was inserted in the 2nd ed. (p. 715).

b. So since the 5th ed. (p. 627). In the 1st ed. (p. 710) the subject-matter of this sentence ran as follows:

If however employers in any trade act together and so do the employed, the solution of the problem of wages becomes again arbitrary, nearly in the same way as in the last paragraph but one. The trade as a whole may be regarded as receiving a quasi-rent consisting of the excess of the aggregate price which it can get for such wares as it produces over what it has to pay to other trades for the things it buys from them[1]; and there is nothing but bargaining to decide the exact shares in which this should go to employers and employed.

When employers and employed are in combination, the division of the whole income of the trade is in some measure arbitrary.

[1] Regarding the whole trade as a "nation," this becomes the National Dividend: and this analogy is of service when the pure theory of international commerce is applied to the relations between different trades in the same country.

The reference in the first sentence to "the last paragraph but one" applies to lines 5–26 on page 626 in vol. I of the present edition. In the 3rd ed. (p. 755) the first of the sentences just quoted from the 1st ed. was altered to run as follows: "If the employers in any trade act together and so do the employed, the solution of the problem of wages becomes indeterminate." The second sentence and the footnote, and the marginal summary, were retained unaltered.

No alteration was made in the 4th ed.

c. The first clause of this sentence was inserted in the 5th ed. (p. 627).

a. In the 5th ed. (p. 627) the words "the special earnings of skill" replaced the words "the quasi-rent of their special skill" dating from the 1st ed. (p. 711).

b. In the 1st ed. (p. 711 n.) this sentence constituted the first sentence of a footnote which was attached to the end of the preceding sentence in the text. After this sentence the footnote continued as follows:

This point has been argued in Mr L. L. Price's *Industrial Peace* and in a Preface to it by the present writer. In relation to the subject of this section in general see Book V, ch. II, §3; ch. VI, §2 and ch. VIII.

The references in the last sentence of this footnote apply to Book V, ch. II, §3; ch. VI, §2, and ch. XIV, in vol. I of the present edition. The references to Book V were deleted from the 2nd ed., and the reference to Mr Price's *Industrial Peace* and to the "Preface to it by the present writer" were deleted from the 5th ed.

EDITORIAL APPENDIX TO
BOOK VI, CHAPTER VIII

The following pages reproduce an article entitled "The Theory of Business Profits", which Marshall published in the *Quarterly Journal of Economics*, vol. I, 1887 (pp. 477–81) in answer to criticisms made by General F. A. Walker against the treatment of profits in *The Economics of Industry* by Alfred and Mary Paley Marshall (1st ed. 1879):

THE THEORY OF BUSINESS PROFITS

I must respond, on behalf of my wife and myself, to the friendly challenge of General Walker contained in the last number of this journal. In a note to his article on the source of business profits, he quotes from the *Economics of Industry*, "The earnings of management of a manufacturer represent the value of the addition which his work makes to the total produce of capital and industry," and says: "If this remark is to be taken literally and strictly, I do not see why it does not express precisely the same view of the source of profits as is here sought to be set forth. In that case, I gladly yield all claim to priority in its statement." It is certainly to be taken literally. I am very nearly in agreement with General Walker's Theory of Profits; but there is, I think, a real though small difference between us. I do not regard the analogy between rent and the earnings of exceptional ability as confined to the task of business management. I hold that, whatever be a man's occupation, that part of his earnings "which he owes to his education may be regarded as a kind of *profit* on the capital invested in it; that part which he owes to exceptional natural qualities may be regarded as a kind of *rent*,—that is, it is the income derived from an agent of production, the supply of which is determined by natural causes, and not by the deliberate outlay of human effort for the sake of future advantage." (*Economics of Industry*, p. 110.)

As I said in your last number, when asking Professor Laughlin's indulgence, the *Economics of Industry* suffered from not having space to treat properly some of the difficult problems which were raised in it. One of the chief of these relates to the causes that determine earnings of management. But what was said on the subject in that little book was the product of many years' thought; and it claims to contain the outlines of an answer to just that question to which General Walker, if I understand him rightly, addresses himself in your last number. So that I cannot agree with him that there has been a *lacuna* in the theory of economics in that place where the discussion of the causes that determine the earnings of management ought to have been.

No economist in any country has, I think, explained the services which the undertaker renders with such graphic force as he has. Some things that he has said on this point remind me of passages of Adam Smith, which one can read and reread, and every time learn from them something new. The effective demand for the work of business management is based on the value of these services to the community; and, on this side of the question, the *Economics of Industry* is in harmony with General Walker's view, though I am ready to admit that any comparison between the two must be to the disadvantage of the former.

But the value of the undertaker's services conforms to the general law that value is determined by the forces of demand, on the one hand, and the forces to be overcome before supply is forthcoming, on the other; equilibrium being found where these two forces are equal to one another. And, on the side of supply, I cannot entirely accept General Walker's doctrine.

My own position is this. First, suppose that all people were born with equal natural talents, so that the industrial ability of every one depended entirely on the trouble and expense devoted to his education. In that case, the expenses of production of skilled work of any kind, the supply price at which any given amount of it could be obtained, would exceed the wages of ordinary labour by what was sufficient to repay the cost of the education required for it (*Economics of Industry*, Bk. ii, ch. viii, § i); but, in estimating this, we must remember that the expense had generally to be borne by parents who, for various reasons (*Ibid.* §§ 2 ...), could not generally adjust on strict capitalistic methods their outlay to their expectation of the advantage it would bring in extra wages etc., to their children. Among these are difficulties which a lad may find in getting access to the special training and the start in life required for a skilled trade other than his father's.

Next, it is argued (*Ibid.* ch. ix) that the same general reasoning applies to the supply price of business power. Even the difficulties of getting the necessary special training, and of making a start as a business man, resemble in many respects the special difficulties of getting access to the training required by, say, a glass-blower, or of starting with a connection in the profession of law or medicine.

But the business man who has little or no capital of his own must enter into partnership or hire himself out as business manager to a private firm or a public company; or, lastly (and this we may take as the typical case), he must borrow. It is then argued (*Ibid.* ch. xii, § i) that these borrowings, whatever form they take, involve a new set of risks, which may be called *Personal Risks*, and are in addition to the *Trade Risks* that are inseparable from business in his trade. The supply price, therefore, at which business ability, in command of the requisite capital, will be forthcoming, consists of: (*a*) the supply price of the ability itself; together with (*b*) the supply price of the bringing together of that ability with the capital required to give it scope, or, to look at the same thing from another point of view, Insurance against Personal Risks; together with (*c*) the supply price of the capital employed, or interest.

On the supposition, then, that all people have equal natural talents, I should find no scope for a comparison between the Earnings of Management and Rent. I agree with General Walker that the man who had got the best business training and managed his business best would almost inevitably be the one who would cost the least to the community in proportion to the services he rendered it; and that, putting aside cases of fraud, illegitimate combination, monopoly, etc., the cost of production of things would be increased, and not diminished, if the item in them which consists of business earnings were saved, but the services of business men in engineering and superintending production were lost. But this does not seem to me to justify the statement that normal earnings of management do not enter into (cost or) expenses of production. If a man did not paint the outer woodwork of his house, it would decay rapidly; and he would lose more than he would gain. The expense of house room would certainly be greater if paint were not used than it is now. But that does not justify us in saying that the price of painting is not one of the expenses of production of house room.

Next, to take account of the fact that natural talents are not equal. The talents given by nature resemble that part of the fertility of land which is, in common though loose phrase, inherent in the soil. Man cannot produce them at all; and, therefore, they have no expenses of production, they have no supply price. When we want to find the relation between the value of corn and its expenses of production, we are forced to look at that corn which was raised on the margin of cultivation (to use a metaphor, for it is nothing else), so as to just pay its expenses without allowing anything for rent. The rent paid by any corn grown under more favourable conditions is determined by the price—that is, under normal conditions by the expenses of production— of that which is grown on the margin of cultivation. Rent is determined by price: it does not determine price. This, as General Walker has well explained, is what Ricardo meant by saying that rent does not enter into price. This phrase is not very happy because the sense in which it has to be taken in order to make it true is not a very natural one. Most people take it in some other sense; and then they despise Ricardo, unless they are very dull and believe it in spite of not understanding it, and then they make other people despise Ricardo all the more.

I hold that in the same way the expenses of production of calico, in so far as they consist of manufacturer's earnings of management, are the supply price or expense of production of the manager's abilities, together with that of his capital, together with that of the task of getting him and his capital together. The supply price of the business man's abilities must be taken on the assumption that his mind was like land on the margin of cultivation, that is, not that it made *no* return to the capital and labour spent in educating it, but that it made only ordinary profits, i.e. that it made (in addition to interest on the material capital used by him) just enough to pay the expenses of production of his business ability, without allowing anything for rent. Those who have exceptional natural abilities (and average good fortune) get earnings exceeding the earnings of similar manufacturers whose minds are on the margin of cultivation, and this excess I proposed to call rent. The analogy already quoted from the chapter on the Supply of Skilled Labour is continued in the chapter on Earnings of Management (p. 144) thus:

"Business men are chosen by a process of natural selection from among many millions of competitors. For many employers of labour, in some parts of England more than half, have risen from the ranks of hired labour. Every artisan who has exceptional natural abilities has a chance of raising himself to a post of command, and is in fact a candidate for the prizes that may be earned by success in business; and the average of these Earnings of Management is high, partly because the class of employers contains, in addition to the able men that have been born within its ranks, a large share of the best natural abilities that have arisen among the lower ranks of industry. While *Profits* on capital invested in education is a specially important element in the incomes of professional men, *Rent* of rare natural abilities is a specially important element in the incomes of business men."

Thus, while General Walker regards as analogous to rent the whole of the excess of the earnings of the successful business man over those of the man who just gets *no* profits, I apply the analogy only to what may, at a rough guess, be put at a tenth part of this sum. I apply it only to the excess over the earnings of a business man who has average natural abilities and who makes sufficient profits to be a fair return for the trouble of giving a business education and a start in life, and to cover the difficulty of bringing him and his capital together.

I hope this answer, short and imperfect as it must needs be, will tend to clear away some confusions that have arisen in England as well as in America as to the relation in which my theory of business profits stands to that of General Walker. The forthcoming first volume of a work on Economics will contain a full statement of my position as to business earnings, and deal with certain difficulties which are evaded not only here, but in the *Economics of Industry*.

ALFRED MARSHALL

BOOK VI, CHAPTER IX

RENT OF LAND

PAGE 629

a. Except where otherwise stated the wording of this chapter dates substantially from the 1st edition.

It should be noted that the whole of §1 of Book VII, chapter x in he 1st edition is reproduced in the Editorial Appendix to Book V, chapters VIII–X, see above, pp. 484–92.

b. So since the 4th edition. In the 1st edition (Book VII, chapter x) and in the 2nd and 3rd editions (Book VI, ch. IX) the title of this chapter ran as follows: "Demand and Supply in Relation to Land Producer's Surplus."

c. The remainder of this sentence dates from the 2nd ed. (p. 663).

d. The remainder of this paragraph dates from the 4th ed. (p. 709).

e. So since the 3rd ed. (pp. 705–6). This paragraph is substantially the same as the fourth paragraph of §1 in the 1st ed. See the Editorial Appendix to Book V, chapters VIII–X, p. 486 above.

f. This footnote dates from the 5th ed. (p. 630 n.).

In the 2nd to the 4th editions this footnote ran as follows:

> This is a special case of the general principles discussed in Book V, ch. VIII, §2. But compare Book V, ch. x, especially §3, for exceptions to the rule as to situation rent.

The reference in the first sentence of this footnote applies to Book V, ch. x, §4, and that in the second sentence to Book V, ch. XI "especially §2", in vol. I of the present edition.

PAGE 630

a. So since the 2nd ed. (p. 664). For the original form of this paragraph see the Editorial Appendix to Book V, chapters VIII–X, p. 487 above.

b. In the 2nd ed. (p. 664 n.) there was the following footnote attached to the word "consumer":

> The argument is equally applicable to urban land; buildings being of the character of improvements which are slowly made and slowly exhausted.

This footnote was deleted from the 5th ed.

c. In the 1st ed. (pp. 666 n.–7 n.) there was a footnote attached to the word "labour", which in the 2nd ed. was transferred to Book IV, ch. III, §2, pp. 210 n.–11 n. See page 155 n. in vol. I of the present edition and editorial note **a** to that page.

d. The following footnote attached to the word "surplus", dating from the 3rd ed. (p. 706 n.) was deleted from the 5th ed.:

> As Mr Hollander says (*Quarterly Journal of Economics*, January 1895), "marginal expenditure occurs both in extensive and intensive cultivation, and the marginal product is derived in part from no-rent land and in part from no-rent uses of land.

PAGE 632

a. So since the 4th ed. (p. 712).

In the first two editions the opening clauses of this sentence ran as follows:

Next, the "real" producer's surplus, that is, the value of that surplus measured in terms of general purchasing power, will rise relatively to its produce value, in the same ratio as the real value of produce has risen.

In the 3rd ed. (p. 708), these clauses were reworded as follows:

Next, the producer's surplus, that is, measured in terms of general purchasing power, will rise relatively to its produce value, in the same ratio as the value of produce measured in the same way has risen:

b. So since the 3rd ed. (p. 708) where this and the next two sentences replaced the following sentence dating from the 1st ed. (p. 669):

Sometimes it is used to mean the amout of labour (of a given efficiency) that the produce will purchase: but we shall use the term "labour-value" to express that meaning; and by "real value" we shall mean the amount of necessaries, comforts, and luxuries of life that a given amount of produce will purchase.

c. So since the 3rd ed. (p. 708) where the words "may imply" replaced the words "in general implies", dating from the 1st ed. (p. 669).

d. So since the 3rd. ed. (p. 709) where this sentence replaced the following sentence dating from the 1st ed. (p. 669).

But this is not true if the rise in the real value of raw produce has been caused by an improvement of the arts of production, other than agricultural, for that would probably be accompanied by a rise in the purchasing power of wages.

PAGE 634

a. This paragraph dates from the 4th ed. (pp. 714–15).

PAGE 635

a. This sentence, and the footnote attached to it, were inserted in the 3rd ed. (pp. 710–11 n.).

b. This clause was inserted in the 2nd ed. (p. 669).

PAGE 636

a. The remainder of this paragraph dates in its present form from the 4th ed. (p. 716).

In the 1st ed. (p. 671) there was the following sentence which concluded this paragraph:

In other words, that part of the income derived from the land which has to be regarded as a rent or a quasi-rent, that is, as producer's surplus for all periods of moderate length, goes to the landlord; while that part which is to be regarded, even for short periods, as profits entering directly into the normal price of the produce, is the tenant's share.

In the 3rd ed. (p. 711) this sentence was reworded and ran as follows:

In other words the landlord obtains that part of the income derived from the land which has to be regarded as a rent or a quasi-rent; that is, as governed, for all periods of moderate length, mainly by the market for the produce, and with little reference to the cost of providing the various agents employed in raising it; while the tenant retains that part which is to be regarded, even for short periods, as profits entering directly into the normal price of the produce, because the produce would not be produced unless it were expected to yield those profits.

b. In the 2nd ed. (pp. 668–74), the 3rd ed. (pp. 710–16) and the 4th ed. (pp. 717–18), there were a number of additional sections following on §5 of this chapter, which dealt with the distinction between land and other forms of wealth, with the capitalized value of land, and (in the 2nd and 3rd editions only) with urban ground rent. In later editions the subject-matter of these sections was either deleted or else transferred to Book V, ch. xi, §§4 and 6. See the editorial notes to pages 430, 448–9 and 451–2 of vol. i in the present edition.

c. The subject-matter of this footnote was in the text in the first three editions; it was placed here in the 4th ed. (p. 716 n.).

BOOK VI, CHAPTER X

LAND TENURE

PAGE 637

a. Except where otherwise stated the wording of this chapter dates substantially from the 1st edition.

It may be noted that in the later editions there was a considerable rearrangement of the order of the paragraphs in §§8–10 as compared with the 1st edition.

b. So since the 4th edition. In the 1st edition (Book VII, ch. xi), and the 2nd and 3rd editions (Book VI, ch. x) the title of this chapter ran as follows: "Demand and Supply in relation to Land, continued, Land Tenure."

c. Down to, and including the 8th edition (page 637 n.) this sentence, which has here been corrected, ran as follows: "Mention has already been made of the ways in which primitive forms of divided ownership of the land hindered progress, I, ii, 2." From the 5th ed. onwards, where the subject-matter of Book I, ch. ii was relegated to Appendix A, the reference in this sentence ceased to be correct, but Marshall failed to make the appropriate alteration.

PAGE 638

a. So since the 2nd ed. (pp. 681–2), where this sentence replaced the following sentence in the 1st ed. (p. 679):

And the action of our own age in this matter differs from that of earlier ages chiefly in our greater consciousness of the process of change in these customs, and our greater willingness to convert them into legal enactments, and to make them uniform.

b. This footnote dates from the 3rd ed. (p. 723 n.).

PAGE 641

a. This paragraph was inserted in the 2nd ed. (pp. 684–5), though the footnote attached to it dates from the 1st ed. (pp. 681 n.–2 n.) with the exception of its last paragraph, which was inserted in the 3rd ed. (p. 728 n.).

PAGE 643

a. This paragraph was inserted in the 3rd ed. (p. 728 n.).

b. The text of Marshall's article in the *Economic Journal* entitled "A Reply" (he was defending himself against criticisms put forward by William Cunningham) is reprinted in the Editorial Appendix to Appendix A (pp. 735–50 below).

c. The following reference in parentheses at the end of this sentence in the 1st ed. (p. 683 n.) was deleted from the 3rd ed.: " (see the *Report of the Commissioners of Agriculture* for 1887, pp. 585–8)."

PAGE 645

a. So since the 5th ed. (p. 645 n.).

In the 1st ed. (p. 685 n.) this paragraph ran as follows: "See an article on *Rural France* in the *Edinburgh Review* for Oct. 1887; and M. Leroy-Beaulieu *Repartition des Richesses*, ch. IV, especially p. 151." In the 3rd ed. (p. 730 n.) this was expanded to run as follows:

On the elasticity of Metayage in France see an interesting article by Mr Higgs in the *Economic Journal*, Jan. 1894. See also an article on *Rural France* in the *Edinburgh Review* for Oct. 1887; and M. Leroy-Beaulieu, *Répartition des Richesses*, ch. IV, especially p. 151.

PAGE 646

a. In the 1st ed. (p. 686 n.) there were the following concluding sentences and paragraph to this footnote:

Perhaps too great stress has been laid on the fact that the low price of imported food, which in England has benefitted the labourer and weighed heavily only on the landlord and to a less extent on the farmer, has on the Continent depressed the peasant proprietor, and in many cases compelled him to mortgage his land and pay an interest which absorbs the greater part of his little income. For the tide may turn. Some kinds of land in almost all districts, and all kinds of land in some districts have risen in value even during the last fifteen years; and, as the best parts of the New World get taken up, there will probably be a rise in the value of almost all land.

On the wastefulness of consuming less than the necessaries for efficiency compare Book II, ch. IV, §2 and Book VII, ch. V, §2.

The three sentences just quoted were deleted from the 3rd ed. and the final paragraph from the 5th ed.

In vol. I of the present edition the references in the final paragraph apply to Book II, ch. III, §4, and Book VI, ch. IV, §2.

PAGE 648

a. So since the 3rd ed. (p. 733) where this sentence replaced the following sentence dating from the 1st ed. (p. 687):

Let us then turn to that English system of tenure which, faulty and harsh as it has been in many respects, had yet so great a power of stimulating enterprise and economizing energy that it gave to England the leadership of the world in the arts of manufacture and colonization and, though in a less marked degree, in agriculture.

PAGE 649

a. So since the 5th ed. (p. 649), where the concluding clause of this sentence replaced the following concluding sentence of this paragraph dating from the 1st ed. (p. 689):

They seldom go far afield for a new tenant: and until quite recently, they have seldom given facilities for an able working man, similar in character to the American farmer, to make a start on a small farm which he can cultivate with his own hands and those of his family and a few hired men.

In the 1st ed. there was the following footnote appended to the word "men" at the end of the sentence just quoted:

Many landlords are not properly trained for their great positions as the ultimate supervisors of agriculture; and they know little and care little about it. Many have a kindly feeling towards those who have been their neighbours, and in some sense their associates from youth: some valuing land partly for the social or political power which it gives, are unwilling to lessen this power by the unpopular act of importing tenants from a distance, while others again are jealous of their authority in minor matters and would rather have a tenant of submissive demeanour who farmed badly than one of independent habits who farmed well.

This footnote was deleted from the 2nd ed.

b. This footnote was inserted in the 3rd ed. (p. 734 n.).

c. This footnote was inserted in the 5th ed. (p. 649 n.).

PAGE 650

a. In the 1st ed. (pp. 689 n.–90 n.) the following footnote was appended to the word "best":

> It must be recollected that even in modern England a "large" farmer employs men at most by the score, while the manufacturer may employ them by the thousand. But this may ultimately be somewhat changed by the growth of factory farms (Book IV, ch. XI, §7). The chief agricultural improvements have been made by landlords who have themselves been townsmen or at least have associated a good deal with townsmen, and by manufacturers in trades subsidiary to agriculture. Mr R. Prothero (*English Farming*, ch. VI) gives some instances of prolonged resistance to changes, and adds that an act had to be passed in England as late as 1634 "agaynst plowynge by the taile."

The first two sentences of this footnote were deleted from the 2nd ed. The third sentence was placed in the text in the 2nd and subsequent editions, and the fourth sentence was appended to it as a footnote. See page 651 in vol. 1 of the present edition.

b. This clause was inserted in the 2nd ed. (p. 693).

c. This paragraph dates substantially in its present form from the 2nd ed. (pp. 693–4).

d. In the 5th ed. (p. 650) the word "tendency" replaced the word "law" dating from the 2nd ed. (p. 694).

PAGE 651

a. In the 2nd ed. (p. 694) the words "the chief agricultural improvements..." were preceded by the words "It is a significant fact that". These latter words were deleted from the 3rd ed.

b. This paragraph dates from the 3rd ed. (p. 736) where it replaced the following paragraph in the 2nd ed. (p. 694):

This brings us to inquire how far those general tendencies towards production on a large scale, which we studied in Book IV, are applicable to agriculture under modern English conditions.

c. This paragraph and the first sentence of the next paragraph date from the 2nd ed. (p. 694).

d. The rest of this paragraph, and the remaining two paragraphs of this section date substantially from the 1st ed., where they were placed in Book IV, ch. XI, §7, pp. 350–2. These passages were transferred to Book VI, ch. X, §8 in the 2nd ed.

e. So since the 4th ed. (p. 738 n.).

In the 3rd ed. (p. 736 n.) this footnote ran as follows. "See Book VI, ch. XIII, especially p. 397; also Book IV, ch. III, §§5, 6; also the last paragraph of the note on p. 604." The first of these references applies to Book IV, ch. XIII, "especially" pages 317–18 in vol. I of the present edition; and the third reference to the last paragraph in a footnote in the 3rd edition, which will be found in the editorial footnote **b** to page 535 of vol. I in the present edition.

f. So since the 7th ed. (pp. 651 n.–2 n.) in the 1st ed. (p. 350 n.) this footnote ran as follows:

> Horse power is dearer relatively to both steam power and hand power in England than in most other countries. England has taken the lead in the improvement of field steam machinery and America in that of horse machinery and hand improvements.

In the 2nd ed. (p. 695 n.) the word "improvements" in the last line was replaced by the word "implements", and the following additional sentence was inserted:

> The cheapness of horse-power tells generally on the side of moderate sized farms *versus* very small ones; but the cheapness of steam-power tells on the side of very large farms, except in so far as the use of field steam machinery can be hired economically and at convenient times.

The deletion of the words "and America in that of horse machinery and hand implements" from the first of the sentences just quoted, and the insertion of the words "and 'motor' power derived from petrol, etc.", in the second sentence, took place in the 7th ed.

PAGE 652

a. So since the 3rd ed. (p. 737). In the 1st ed. (p. 350) this sentence ran as follows: "Again, agriculture requires ever more and more knowledge: to keep abreast of the changes of the day, the farmer must go beyond the results of his own and his father's experience."

In the 2nd ed. (p. 695) it ran as follows: "Again, the farmer requires ever more and more knowledge, and to go further beyond the results of his own and his father's experience in order to keep abreast of the changes of the day."

b. So since the 5th ed. (p. 652). In the first four editions this marginal summary ran as follows: "It requires a constantly increasing knowledge and this increases the economies to be got by highly organized methods of management."

c. So since the 2nd ed. (p. 695), where the clause "who can do this higher work", replaced the clause "who can do this properly" in the 1st ed. (p. 350).

PAGE 653

a. So since the 5th ed. (p. 653) where the two concluding sentences of this paragraph replaced the following sentences dating from the 1st ed. (p. 352):

Very small holdings however have great advantages wherever so much care has to be given to individual plants, that machinery is out of place. There is reason for hoping that they will continue to hold their own in raising vegetables, flowers and fruit.

PAGE 655

a. In the 1st ed. (pp. 694 n.–5 n.) there was the following footnote attached to the word "diminished":

Many villa gardens are entered in our Agricultural Returns as small holdings. But even allowing for that fact the following table shows that the supply of such holdings is not very small, though indeed it is unevenly distributed.

Classification of Holdings	Percentage of Area of England in each Class	No. of Holdings of each Class			
		England	Wales	Scotland	Ireland
Of ¼ acre but under 1	0·04	21,069	1,083	1,360	49,744
Of 1 not exceeding 5	1·15	103,229	11,044	21,463	61,876
Above 5 „ „ 20	4·89	109,285	17,389	22,132	} 365,113
„ 20 „ „ 50	8·60	61,146	12,326	10,677	
„ 50 „ „ 100	13·19	44,893	10,044	9,778	56,172
„ 100 „ „ 300	41·32	59,180	7,844	12,549	} 30,860
„ 300 „ „ 500	17·39	11,452	389	2,034	
„ 500 „ „ 1,000	10·83	4,131	63	632	} 1,584
„ 1,000	2·95	565	8	90	
Total		414,950	60,190	80,715	565,313

For further statistical information see an excellent paper by Major Craigie *On the Size and Distribution of Agricultural Holdings in England and Abroad* in the *Statistical Journal* for March 1887.

In the 2nd ed. (p. 699 n.) the table was succeeded by the two following paragraphs:

From this table it will be seen that the number of holdings under 50 acres in Great Britain in 1885 was 392,203. A Report of the Board of Agriculture for 1890 shows that this number had risen in 1889 to 409,422, and that at the same ime there were 455,005 ordinary detached allotments under an acre in addition to 262,614 cottage gardens of an eighth of an acre and upwards; and these, together with "potato grounds" and cow-runs, bring up the total number of instances of *petite culture* in Great Britain to 1,300,746.

For further statistical information see an excellent paper by Major Craigie *On the Size and Distribution of Agricultural Holdings in England and Abroad* in the *Statistical Journal* for March, 1887, and a body of Reports *from Her*

Majesty's Representatives abroad on the position of Peasant Proprietors in the Countries in which they reside, published in 1891, from which it appears that the indebtedness of peasant proprietors is increasing in Austria, Belgium, Denmark, Holland and Sweden, but not in France, Germany and Switzerland.

The whole of this footnote was deleted from the 3rd ed., where it was replaced by the following footnote (p. 740 n.): "In 1885 the number of the holdings between one and five acres in England was a quarter of the whole number of holdings; and since then they have rapidly increased." This footnote was deleted from the 5th ed.

b. In the second ed. (p. 699) the word "might" replaced the word "would" in the 1st ed. (p. 694).

c. So since the 5th ed. (p. 655). In the first four editions this marginal summary ran as follows: "Co-operation has great opportunities but also great difficulties in agriculture."

d. So since the 2nd ed. (p. 699), apart from the omission of the word "But" before the words "it requires habits...etc.", which was deleted from the 5th ed.

In the 1st ed. (pp. 694–5) this sentence ran as follows:

It has not so far succeeded well, partly because, while co-operation requires habits of mutual trust and confidence, the bravest and the boldest, and therefore the most trustful, of the countrymen have always moved to the towns, and agriculturists are a suspicious race; partly as a result of a series of unlucky accidents which it may be hoped will not recur in future experiments.

e. The following additional sentence at this point in the 2nd ed. (p. 700) was deleted from the 5th ed.: "Co-operative movements in agriculture therefore must needs be very cautious, until the way has been well prepared for them by the less ambitious but safer system of profit-sharing."

f. The remainder of this paragraph was inserted in the 5th ed. (p. 655).

g. This and the next paragraph were inserted in the 5th ed. (p. 655 n.).

PAGE 656

a. The first three sentences of this paragraph date from the 2nd ed. (p. 700).

b. So since the 2nd ed. (p. 701), where this and the next sentence replaced the following sentences in the 1st ed. (p. 691):

But there is another difficulty which we must study somewhat closely. It lies in the ambiguity which the varying standards of ability among farmers in different parts of the country, introduce into the ending words of the statement that the producer's surplus, or English rent, of a farm is that excess which its produce yields over its expenses of cultivation, including normal profits to the farmer; it being assumed that that farmer's ability and enterprise are such as are normal for farms of that class *in that place.*

PAGE 657

a. The following additional sentences at this point in the 1st ed. (pp. 691–2) were deleted from the 2nd ed.:

This is a type of a large class of ethico-economic problems, which occur in every branch of industry, but are specially prominent in agriculture. And since in it competition must always be relatively feeble and clumsy; and the arts of production must move slowly, we should cherish, as a set off against these disadvantages, the special opportunities which it has for fostering neighbourly relations.

PAGE 658

a. The following footnote was attached to the word "own" in the 1st ed. (p. 692 n.):

The chief of these is that a great change in the industrial environment in its broader sense (Konjunktur), if favourable to the land may enrich the leaseholder without any merit of his own; and if unfavourable may break him in spite of his best efforts. The opening up of the wheat fields of the North-West of America struck some Scotch farmers with long leases almost as heavily as it did many peasant proprietors in the West of Europe. As Sir James Caird points out (*Landed Interest*, ch. XI) the Earl of Leicester's plan of allowing the tenant proper freedom of cropping, till the last four years of his lease, would remove many other evils that have attached to, but are not inherent in the system.

The word "(Konjunktur)" was deleted from the 3rd ed. The whole of the footnote was deleted from the 5th ed.

b. The remainder of this paragraph was inserted in the 5th ed. (p. 658).

c. So since the 5th ed. (p. 658) where this paragraph replaced the following paragraph dating from the 1st ed. (p. 692):

Custom, and, within recent years, legislation, have given the English tenant claims for compensation for improvements made by him which do not alter the character of his holding, and the fruits of which come in quickly. But he cannot claim the compensation till he quits his tenancy: and it is theoretically possible for a hard landlord to exact more than a fair rent from an improving farmer who has an affection for his ancestral home. Such cases are however rare.

d. So since the 2nd ed. (p. 702). In the 1st ed. (p. 695) the opening sentence of this paragraph ran as follows: "Again, private interests collide with those of the public in the matter of open and free spaces in the towns."

e. So since the 5th ed. (p. 658 n.).

f. In the 1st ed. (p. 692 n.) the first three sentences of this footnote were succeeded by the following sentences:

> Partly for the sake of simplicity in working, the law provides that compensation for permanent improvements can be claimed only if they have been made with the consent of the landlord. But Prof. Nicholson argues with great force (*Tenant's Gain not Landlord's Loss*, ch. x) that the tenant should be allowed to claim for all improvements necessary for good husbandry, after giving the landlord notice and time to make them himself, provided only they do not alter the character of the holding.

In the 3rd ed. (p. 743 n.) the sentence ending with the words "with the consent of the landlord" was succeeded by the two following sentences:

> But Prof. Nicholson argues with great force (*Tenant's Gain not Landlord's Loss*, ch. x) that the tenant should be allowed to claim for all improvements necessary for good husbandry, after giving the landlord notice and time to make them himself, provided only they do not alter the character of the holding. New light on all these questions is to be expected from the Report of the Royal Commission on Agriculture.

In the 4th ed. (p. 745 n.) the two sentences just quoted from the 3rd ed. were deleted and replaced by the following sentences:

> The Royal Commission on Agriculture (*Final Report*, 1897, pp. 90–103 and 156) would go a little further than the Act of 1883 in allowing the tenant to make improvements and claim compensation. But more is demanded by some advocates of the farmers' interests, as for instance Mr Channing (see pp. 233 and 301–33). His interesting report takes the extreme position that competition generally acts unfairly to the tenant; and that rents as well as compensation for improvements should be fixed by arbitration. See also Nicholson's *Tenant's Gain not Landlord's Loss*, ch. x.

g. The remainder of this footnote was inserted in the 5th ed. (p. 658 n.).

PAGE 659

a. The following additional sentences and paragraph at this point, dating from the 1st ed. (p. 696) were deleted from the 5th ed.:

It is a difficult question to decide how far the expense of clearing open spaces in land already built on, should fall on the neighbouring owners. But it seems right that for the future every new building erected, save in the open country, should be required to contribute in money or in kind towards the expenses of open places in its neighbourhood.

But we are now trenching on those general relations between collective and private interests, which we shall have to study carefully at a later stage. We shall then have to face several ethico-economic problems as to the limits of perpetual private rights in land "from the centre of the earth to the sky above it"; we shall have to enter on such questions as whether the interests of the mine-owner make him sufficiently careful of Nature's stored-up treasures, especially when they occur in poor seams; and again whether there is a balance of public advantage in allowing the shop-keeper in a town who has given a special value to his premises by the ability with which he has done business in them, a similar claim to compensation for disturbance to that which has been recognized in the case of the improving agricultural tenant.

In the 2nd ed. (p. 703 n.) the following footnote was attached to the word "neighbourhood" at the end of the second of the above sentences:

> It must be borne in mind that a special tax on new building land would however tend to give something of a monopoly value to the land already built on, and thus raise ground-rents of existing buildings.

This footnote also was deleted from the 5th ed.

b. This footnote was inserted in the 5th ed. (p. 659 n.).

BOOK VI, CHAPTER XI

GENERAL VIEW OF DISTRIBUTION

PAGE 660

a. Except where otherwise indicated, the wording of §§1–3 of this chapter dates substantially from the 1st edition, and the wording of §§4 and 5 from the 2nd edition.

b. So since the 2nd edition (Book VI, chapter xi). In the 1st edition (Book VII, ch. xii) this chapter was entitled "General View of the Theory of Value".

c. In the 1st ed. (pp. 698–701) the first two sections of this chapter contained a summary of the influence of cost of production upon value, which was deleted from the 2nd ed. These sections are reproduced in full in the Editorial Appendix to Book V, chapter xv (pp. 545–9) above.

d. The first three sentences of this paragraph date from the 4th ed. (p. 747).

e. The remainder of this paragraph dates substantially from the 2nd ed. (p. 704).

f. This sentence was inserted in the 5th ed. (p. 660).

g. So since the 2nd ed. (p. 704), where this sentence replaced the following sentence in the 1st ed. (p. 701):

We have seen that the chief motives which induce the saving of capital are supplied by the family affections; and that the question whether a man accumulates material capital *for* his son or personal capital *in* that son's education, is from the present point of view a mere matter of detail.

PAGE 661

a. The following footnote attached to the end of this paragraph in the 1st ed. (p. 702 n.) was deleted from the 2nd ed.:

> The analysis in Book VII, ch. IV of the various incidental advantages and disadvantages of a trade, which enter into its real wages, corresponds closely to that in Book VII, ch. XI of the benefits derived from the ownership of land in addition to the money income that it can be made to yield.

The reference in the first line of this footnote applies to Book VI, ch. III, and that in the third line to Book VI, ch. X in vol. I of the present edition.

b. The following additional clause and footnote at this point in the 1st ed. (p. 702) were deleted from the 2nd ed.:

since it is not possible for a comparatively small number of undertakers of great ability to exercise the same controlling influence in agriculture that they can in manufacture or transport.

> Compare Book IV, ch. VI and Book VII, ch. V, §2 with Book IV, ch. XI, §4 and Book VII, ch. XI, §7.

The references in the footnote apply to Book IV, ch. VI and Book VI, ch. IV, §2, and to Book IV, ch. XI, §4 and Book VI, ch. X, §7, in vol. I of the present edition.

c. In the 1st ed. (pp. 702 n.–3 n.) the following footnote was attached to the word "supply":

> To state nearly the same thing in another way, when we are considering periods of moderate length—say of a few years—the average earnings of skill or

688

ability of any kind, have to be regarded more as a quasi-rent determined by the demand for their services, and less as normal profits on the labour and waiting needed for the acquirement of that skill or ability, than is the case with regard to such material appliances for production as are quickly made and quickly worn out (Book VII, ch. v, §§ 1–5). But, on the other hand, a great part of the earnings of a worker are the payment required to induce him to undergo a certain strain or fatigue. And this may be regarded as the Prime cost of his labour, while the remainder is the Supplementary cost required to make up in the long run its total supply price.

The reference at the end of the first sentence of this footnote applies to Book VI, ch. IV, §§ 1–5 in vol. I of the present ed. This footnote was deleted from the 4th ed.

d. This sentence dates from the 7th ed. (p. 661).

PAGE 662

a. The following paragraphs and sentences in the 1st ed. (pp. 703–4), which were deleted from the 2nd ed., preceded the summary, contained in this paragraph, of the function of business men of facilitating the action of the principle of substitution:

The demand for commodities for immediate consumption (goods of the *first order*) presents few theoretical difficulties; though there is no more pressing work for the coming generation of economists than to obtain definite laws of consumption resting on a statistical basis[1]. We may therefore pass to the demand for factors of production, under which head are included raw materials, and the services of human and material agents and of capital in the immaterial form of business organization (or in other words, all goods of the *second* and higher *orders*). The normal demand price for any such factor is equal to the net value of its services; that is, to the value of the things produced by it in conjunction with other factors after deducting their supply prices[2]. The demand for it will be increased by an increase in the demand for those things for which it is used, and by an increase in the facilities of supply of any thing which is used as a joint factor of production with it in the production of any commodity: and this increased demand will raise its normal

(The demand for goods of the first order, and of higher orders.)

---

[1] See Book III, especially ch. III; also Book V, ch. VIII, § 8.

[2] In the more technical but more exact language of Book V, ch. VI, we may say that the demand schedule for any factor of production is *compounded* of its derived demand schedules for all its several uses in producing various commodities; each such schedule being derived by subtracting from the demand price of each separate amount of the commodity the sum of the supply prices for corresponding amounts of the other factors. See also Book VII, ch. III, § 4.

price, if it conforms to the law of diminishing return, but will lower its normal price if it conforms to the law of increasing return.

The law of distribution of a thing in different uses, and the law of substitution.

In equilibrium it will of course be distributed among its several uses, so that equal rewards are earned by its marginal services in each case. And in the struggle between it and rival factors of production, which could render services equivalent to its own, it will hold its ground permanently only when its services are at least as efficient in proportion to their cost as those of any rival that could be substituted for it.

Application to the uses of capital as auxiliary and remuneratory.

We have watched the application of Von Thünen's great law of substitution to the part played by demand in determining the relative proportions of auxiliary and remuneratory or wage-capital.

The references in the first footnote apply to Book III, "especially" ch. IV, and to Book V, ch. XIV, §8; and in the second footnote to Book VI, ch. I, §7, in vol. I of the present edition.

b. So since the 7th ed. (p. 662). In the 1st ed. (p. 704) this sentence ran as follows:

The marginal efficiency of human agents of production supported by wage-capital on the one hand, and that of material agents on the other, are weighed against one another and compared with their marginal costs; and each tends to be applied as far as it is more efficient than the other in proportion to its cost[1].

[1] The growth of wage-capital and the rise of wages do not then stand to one another in the simple relation of cause and effect, as was stated or implied in the cruder forms of the wage-fund theory; but all the chief elements of the problem act and react on one another and mutually determine one another. That is to say, the supply of capital and the supply of labour; the price of the use of capital or the rate of interest, and the price of the use of labour or the rate of earnings; the marginal efficiency of auxiliary capital, and that of the labour supported by wage-capital; and lastly the relative amounts of auxiliary and of wage-capital—all those elements mutually determine one another.

The footnote to this sentence was deleted from the 2nd ed.

In the 3rd ed. (p. 747) the words "supported by wage-capital", in the second line of the above sentence in the text of the 1st ed., were deleted. In the 4th ed. (p. 748) the word "marginal" before the word "efficiency" in the first line, and the word "marginal" before the word "costs" in the fourth line of the above sentence, were deleted.

In the 7th ed. (p. 662) the word "*money*" was inserted before the word "costs" in line 3 of this sentence in vol. I of the present edition and the word "money" before the word "cost" in line 5.

c. So since the 4th ed. (p. 749), where the word "enterprise" replaced the word "undertakers", dating from the 1st ed. (p. 705).

d. Throughout this section, from the 4th ed. onwards, the words "principle of substitution" replaced the words "law of substitution" dating from the 1st ed. (pp. 704–6).

PAGE 663

a. The following footnote attached to the word "another" in the 1st ed. (p. 706 n.) was deleted from the 2nd ed.:

> Some of the most interesting instances of this indirect competition are between different trades in distant places, and especially in different countries. We shall have to discuss them carefully later on when we come to discuss the combined problems of international trade and of local variations of wages and prices.

b. So since the 5th ed. (p. 663) where the word "tendency" replaced the word "law" dating from the 1st ed. (p. 706).

c. The following opening clause of this sentence in the 1st ed. (p. 706) was deleted from the 2nd ed.: "Striking instances of this have been recently shown by American Trusts; but on the other hand there is also...etc."

PAGE 664

a. The following footnote attached to the word "them", dating from the 1st ed. (p. 706 n.) was deleted from the 7th ed.:

> We have postponed a discussion of the contention of the socialists that it would be better for the State to take the work into its own hands and hire business managers to conduct it: and we have postponed also a study of those forms of speculation and commercial competition which are not beneficial to society, and perhaps are even harmful.

b. So since the 4th ed. (p. 751). In the 1st ed. (p. 659) and the 2nd ed. (p. 659) the word "quasi-rent" was used in place of the word "earnings", while in the 3rd ed. (p. 750) the words "earnings at any particular time (or the quasi-rent) of his capital...etc.", were used. See editorial note **b** to page 622 of vol. 1 in the present edition, for the other instance where Marshall (in the earlier editions only) coupled the word "negative" with the word "quasi-rent".

PAGE 665

a. The following sentence and footnote dating from the 1st ed. (p. 703) were deleted from the 4th ed.:

And, just as the wages of skilled cutters enter into the normal supply price of cut diamonds, so the earnings of management of able business men enter into the normal supply price of the goods which they provide[1].

[1] Compare Book VI, ch. III, §§2, 3; Book VII, ch. VI, §8, and ch. IX, §9.

The references in the footnote apply to Book V, ch. x, §§1–3; Book VI, ch. v, §7 and ch. VIII, §9 in vol. I of the present edition.

b. No part of the remainder of this chapter dates from the 1st ed. Except where otherwise stated the text and footnotes of §§4 and 5 date from the 2nd ed. (Book VI, ch. XI, §§5–7). It may be noted that in the first three editions there were a number of sections in the latter part of this chapter which were transferred in the 4th ed. to Book VI, ch. VIII, §§9 and 10. See editorial notes to pages 625–8 of vol. I in the present edition.

c. The following sentence and paragraphs at this point in the 2nd ed. (pp. 709–10) were deleted from the 3rd ed.:

The characteristic feature of a general view of distribution —as distinguished from applications of the theory of value to the prices of particular commodities or the wages of particular trades—is the predominant position taken by this fact.

Thus skilled labour and unskilled labour are often competitors for employment; but an increase in the supply or efficiency of the one will so increase the national dividend, and at the same time so cheapen the rate at which it performs its services that the other will earn a higher reward for their services, and so also will capital and business power.

Or, again, if the supply or efficiency of business ability increases, there is likely to be some displacement of manual labour by new contrivances for economizing effort, and by new inventions of various kinds. But this shrinking in some directions of the field of employment for manual labour will be more than compensated in others. For the increased supply of business ability will both increase the national dividend, and lessen the share of the joint product, which a business man of any given capacity and energy is able to secure, in the face of the competition of other business men for the loan of material capital and the hire of manual labour.

PAGE 666

a. So since the 5th ed. (p. 666) where this clause replaced the following sentence dating from the 2nd ed. (pp. 710–11):

It will, for instance, lead to the making of railways and waterworks in districts which are not very rich, and which would have continued to drag their goods along rough roads, and draw up their water from wells, if people had not been able and willing to support labour while making railway embankments and water conduits, and to wait for the fruits of their investment long and for a relatively low reward.

b. In the 2nd ed. (p. 711 n.) a long footnote was attached to the word "reward", dealing with the relation between capital and interest and with the interpretation of interest as a part of the national dividend.

In the 1st ed. this footnote had been placed in Book VII, ch. xiii, §7 (pp. 723 n.–4 n.).

This footnote was deleted from the 3rd ed. except for three sentences which were transferred to the text of Book VI, ch. i, §10 (page 523 in vol. 1 of the present edition). The footnote is reproduced in editorial note **b** to page 681 of vol. 1 in the present edition.

c. So since the 5th ed. (p. 666) where the present wording of this marginal summary replaced the following wording dating from the 2nd ed. (pp. 711–12): "An increase in the number or the efficiency of any group of workers has similar results on other workers, but very different results on themselves."

d. The following additional paragraph at this point, dating from the 2nd ed. (p. 712) was deleted from the 5th ed.: "We shall have to look at some other aspects of this question in the next chapter while discussing the relative merits of increased leisure and increased material production as aims of progress." The reference in the paragraph just quoted to "the next chapter" applies to Book VI, ch. xiii in vol. 1 of the present edition.

PAGE 667

a. This and the following paragraph, together with the footnote attached to the latter, were inserted in the 5th ed. (p. 667).

BOOK VI, CHAPTER XII

GENERAL INFLUENCES OF ECONOMIC PROGRESS

PAGE 668

a. Except where otherwise stated in the editorial notes the wording of this chapter dates substantially from the 1st edition.

b. In the 1st edition (Book VII, ch. xiii) and in the 2nd to the 4th editions (Book VI, ch. xii) the final chapter of Book VI was entitled "The Influence of Progress on Value". In the 5th edition this was divided into two chapters, Book VI, chapter XII, entitled "General Influences of Economic Progress", and Book VI, chapter XIII, entitled "Progress in Relation to Standards of Life".

PAGE 670

a. This and the next paragraph, together with the footnote attached to the latter, were inserted in the 6th ed. (pp. 670–1 n.), where they replaced the following paragraph and footnote dating substantially from the 1st ed. (p. 714):

There is no reason so far why the rate of (real efficiency) wages should fall. For if, taking one thing with another, the law of production is that of constant return, there will be no change in the reward to be divided between a dose of capital and labour; that is, between capital and labour working together in the same proportions as before. And, since the rate of interest has fallen, the share which capital takes of this stationary joint reward is less than before; and therefore the amount of it remaining for labour is greater[1].

> [1] Of course the aggregate share of capital may have increased. For instance while labour has doubled capital may have quadrupled, and the rate of interest may be two-thirds of what it was; and then, though each dose of capital gets a lower reward by one-third, and leaves for labour a larger share of the joint product of a dose of capital and labour, the aggregate share of capital will have risen in the ratio of 8 to 3. Much of the argument of Mr Henry George's *Progress and Poverty* is vitiated by his having overlooked this distinction.

In the 3rd ed. (p. 759) the wording of the first sentence of this paragraph ran as follows: "There is no reason so far why there should be any fall in the rate of real wages for labour of a given efficiency." In the 3rd ed. also, the first two sentences of the footnote were brought into the text as a separate paragraph immediately after the paragraph ending with the clause "and therefore the amount of it remaining for labour is greater".

PAGE 671

a. So since the 2nd ed. (p. 720), where this sentence replaced the following sentence in the 1st ed. (p. 714): "But though the law of production of commodities may be one of constant return, that of the production of new title-deeds to land is one of rapidly diminishing return."

b. So since the 6th ed. (p. 671). In the first four editions this paragraph opened as follows:

The influence which access to distant markets exerts on the growth of the national dividend has been conspicuous in the history of England also. Her present economic condition is the direct result of those tendencies to production on a large scale, and to wholesale dealings in labour as well as in goods which had long been slowly growing...etc.

PAGE 673

a. The following footnote attached to the word "Europe" in the 1st ed. (p. 717 n.) was deleted from the 2nd ed.:

> In Book I, ch. III, §§6, 7 a caution is entered against treating the new forces of competition as exclusively responsible for those sufferings of the English working classes at the end of the last century and the beginning of this which were partly due to war, bad harvests, and last, but not least, a bad Poor Law. That law was itself antagonistic to free competition, which it set aside in favour of a crude form of socialism, that exercised a degrading influence on character. With reference to the growth of population in England, see Book IV, ch. IV, §§7, 8.

The reference in the first line of this footnote applies to Appendix A, §§16, 17; and the reference in the last line, to Book IV, ch. IV, §§6, 7 in vol. I of the present edition.

PAGE 674

a. The following footnote attached to the word "food" in the 1st ed. (p. 717 n.) was deleted from the 2nd ed.:

> The diminution of England's agricultural population is however somewhat less than at first sight appears. See Book IV, ch. x, §4; and a paper "On the alleged Depopulation of the Rural Districts of England, &c.," by Dr Ogle, in the *Statistical Journal*, Jan. 1889.

b. So since the 5th ed. (p. 674) where this and the next two sentences replaced the following sentences dating from the 1st ed. (p. 718):

But the same is not true of our trade with America, who quickly follows if she does not anticipate, England's improvements. The Bessemer, and other new processes, have enabled England to make steel that will push its way further than it could before in India and China, but not in America. The amount of wheat which can be bought in Illinois with a ton of steel cannot be more than the produce of as much capital and labour as would make a ton of steel in Illinois by the new processes; and therefore it has fallen in the same proportion as these processes have increased the efficiency of English labour in making steel.

c. The words in parentheses "(or dose)" after the word "quantity" in the 1st ed. (p. 718) were deleted from the 2nd ed.

a. So since the 2nd ed. (p. 724), where the word "wealth" replaced the words "real National Dividend" in the 1st ed. (p. 719).

a. The following sentences after the sentence (there part of a footnote) ending with the word "winter" in the 1st ed. (p. 720 n.) were deleted from the 5th ed.:

> It is a significant fact that rabbits, which were probably neither better nor worse than in our own time, were then ten times as dear relatively to an ox as now. (Their furs were highly prized, but only counted for a quarter of their whole value. Rogers' *History*, vol. I, p. 583.)

b. So since the 2nd ed. (p. 725) where this and the next two sentences replaced the following sentences in the 1st ed. (p. 720):

For an increasing part of the population is living in houses on which ground-rents at an urban scale have to be paid, and that scale is rising: though the occupants get in return the excitements and other advantages, such as they are, of modern town life. But house rent proper, that is what remains of the total rent after deducting the full rental value of the ground, is probably little, if at all, higher than at any previous time for similar accommodation. For the labour cost of building materials has not much altered, and the rate of profits on the turnover which is earned by capital engaged in building is generally low.

a. The following sentences in the 1st ed. (p. 720 n.) after the sentence (there part of a footnote) ending with the word "continue" were deleted from the 5th ed.:

> And it is true that in earlier times bad housing was in so far a less evil than now, as those who were badly housed by night had abundant fresh air by day. But a long series of records, ending with the evidence of Lord Shaftesbury and others before the recent Commission on the Housing of the Poor, establishes the fact that all the horrors of the worst dens of modern London had their counterpart in worse horrors of the lairs of the lowest stratum of society in every previous age.

b. This footnote was inserted in the 5th ed. (p. 677 n.).

PAGE 678

a. In the 1st ed. (p. 511) this sentence was placed in Book VI, ch. IV, §4.

b. So since the 5th ed. (p. 678), where the clause "and been carried in ships made of steel and driven by steam turbines", replaced the clause "and been carried in ships made of Bessemer steel and driven by triple expansion engines", dating from the 1st ed. (p. 511). The following footnote, dating from the 1st ed. (p. 511 n.) which was there attached to the word "engines" at the end of this clause, was deleted from the 5th ed.:

> A somewhat similar case is that of many quiet summer resorts. Their humble attractions absorbed the attention of neighbouring residents fifty years ago; but now they are impoverished by those modern facilities of travel which induce people to take longer journeys in search of change of scene, and enrich more fashionable and more distant resorts. As steam carriage favours those soils which are exceptionally fertile but distant from good markets, so it favours those pleasure resorts which have exceptionally beautiful scenery, even though they are far away.

PAGE 679

a. In the 1st ed. (pp. 510–11) this and the next paragraph and the footnote attached to the latter were placed in Book VI, ch. IV, §4.

b. The following clauses in brackets after the word "income" in the 1st ed. (p. 510) were deleted from the 2nd ed.: "which, as we saw in the last chapter, may be regarded as a quasi-rent." The reference in the second of the foregoing clauses to "the last chapter" applies to Book V, ch. X in vol. I of the present edition.

PAGE 680

a. The following concluding paragraph of Book VI, ch. IV (pp. 511–12) in the 1st ed. was deleted from the 2nd ed.:

But, taking one case with another, there is a constant and rapid increase in that part of the aggregate price paid for commodities which does not go to reward the new efforts and sacrifices required for their production, and which does not therefore enter directly into their money cost of production, but goes to the owners of those differential advantages which arise from situation. This is partly due to the increase in the number of sites which derive a high value from their proximity to markets in which the requisites for production can be bought to advantage, and the products can be delivered cheaply and sold well. Partly it is due to the increas-

The importance of the relations in which rent stands to cost of production is being increased by the growing number of valuable sites, and by the increasing scarcity of space.

ing scarcity of space on the earth's surface endowed by Nature with an income of heat and light, air and water; for this income freely given by Nature is the chief of those elements of fertility which man has no power to increase when he engages in agriculture, and the chief also of those elements of a wholesome life, for the want of which man's efficiency suffers in a crowded town. It is these space relations of land, which, as has already been remarked[1], distinguish it most strongly from other material things; and it is they which are the chief source of those differential advantages in production that acquire an increasing scarcity value from the progress of the industrial environment.

[1] Book IV, ch. II, §1.

b. The following footnote attached to the word "population" in the 1st ed. (p. 723 n.) was deleted from the 2nd ed.:

Making use of Mr Giffen's survey of contemporary estimates (*Growth of Capital*, ch. v) we may take the following pairs of figures as giving approximately the number of millions in the population of England, and the number of £ in the property per head:—A.D. 1600, 4½, £22; 1700, 5¾, £60; 1750, 7, £70; 1800, 9, £167; 1850, 18 [£180?]; 1885, 27½, £315. In all these estimates the land is reckoned as part of the national "property" or "capital" and about £30 should be taken from the last estimate of £315, if it is desired to exclude that part of the wealth of Englishmen which consists of property or the right to property in foreign countries. Of course the basis of all valuations of property is income: for the value of any particular thing depends not on the cost of producing it, but on the capitalized value of the future rents or quasi-rents which it is expected to yield; and Mr Giffen has deliberately taken the national income as the basis of his estimates. But it must be recollected that a fall in the rate of interest raises the number of years at which rents and quasi-rents are capitalized; and this raises the nominal estimate of national wealth without making any addition to its real substance. On the other hand, as is explained in the Note at the end of Book VII, ch. VII, borrowers are willing to pay a high rate of interest, if they expect to pay back their loans in a depreciated currency; and therefore a rise in the rate of interest which makes the national wealth appear to grow more slowly than it is doing, is often accompanied by a rise in prices, which has the opposite effect: and vice versa.

The reference to the "Note at the end of Book VII, ch. VII" in the last of the foregoing sentences applies to Book VI, ch. VI, §6 in vol. I of the present edition.

c. The first sentence of this paragraph dates from the 2nd ed. (p. 617), and the two remaining sentences from the 1st ed. (pp. 611–12); while the whole of the next paragraph dates from the 2nd ed. (pp. 617–18).

In the case both of the passages from the 1st ed., and of those from the 2nd ed., these were placed in the chapter dealing with Demand and Supply in relation to Capital (1st ed., Book VII, ch. VII, §1, and 2nd ed., Book VI, ch. VI, §1).

These passages were transferred to their present place in §8 of this chapter in the 3rd ed. See the Editorial Appendix to Book VI, chapter VI, pp. 638–9 above.

d. The two sentences composing this footnote were placed in the text in the 1st ed. (Book VI, ch. IV, §4, p. 511). In the 2nd ed. (p. 729 n.) they were brought down into a footnote in substitution for the following footnote in the 1st ed. (p. 571 n.) which was attached to the same sentence in the text ending with the word "age".

> In such cases as these, it is especially difficult to draw any line of division between rent and profits; nothing more than a rough guess can be made as to how far the high dividends of a successful railroad are due to the advantages of its situation, and how far they are due to good management and organization, and to skill and tact in meeting the wants of customers and in inducing them to make use of it in preference to competing lines.

PAGE 681

a. The following footnote attached to the word "wealth" dating from the 2nd ed. (p. 618 n.) was deleted from the 6th ed.: "Compare two suggestive articles by Prof. Giddings in the *Harvard Journal of Economics* for Jan. 1890 and Jan. 1891."

b. So since the 6th ed. (p. 681), where this paragraph replaced the following paragraph dating from the 1st ed. (p. 723):

This increase of capital per head tended to diminish its marginal utility, and therefore the rate of interest on new investments; but not uniformly, because there were meanwhile great variations in the demand for capital, both for political and military and for industrial purposes. Thus the rate of interest which was vaguely reported to be ten per cent. during a great part of the middle ages, had sunk to three per cent. in the earlier half of the eighteenth century; but the immense industrial and political demand for capital raised it again, and it was relatively high during the great war. It fell again when the political drain ceased; but it again rose in the middle of this century, when railways and the development of the Western States of America and of Australia made a great new demand for capital. These new demands have not slackened; but the rate of interest is again falling fast, in consequence of the great recent accumulations of wealth in England, on the Continent, and above all in America.

In the 1st ed. there was the following footnote attached to the word "America" at the end of the paragraph just quoted:

Attention has already been called to the fact that when the term "capital" is used broadly so as to include all accumulated wealth, the aggregate "interest" on capital (or more strictly its quasi-rent) must be used with corresponding breadth so as to include the "usance" of all accumulated wealth (Book II, ch. I, IV, V; Book VII, ch. III, §2). When we speak of the national dividend, or distributable net income of the whole nation, as divided into the shares of land, labour and capital, we must be clear as to what things we are including and what things we are excluding. It will seldom make very much difference to our argument whether we use all the terms broadly, or all the terms narrowly. But it is essential that our usage should be consistent throughout any one argument; and that whatever is included on one side of the account of the demand for, and supply of, capital should be included also on the other. Thus with the broadest sense of the term (material) capital, those who make direct use of their own property have to be entered on both sides of the account, on the one side among those who demand capital, and on the other among those who supply it. This plan will be found useful sometimes, especially in mathematical versions of economic theory. It closely resembles one that is already in common use with regard to rent. When, for instance, we are comparing the rental value of two counties of England, we do not make out two separate accounts, one for the land that is let out to farmers, and the other for that which is cultivated by the owners, but we suppose the owners of the latter land to pay rent to themselves, and we add into our totals the rents at which that land could probably be let. And we are following this precedent strictly when we add up the benefits derived from houses and furniture and other direct material sources of enjoyment, without separating those which are used by their owners from those which are let out on hire.

The references in the first sentence of this footnote apply to Book II, chs. I, IV; and to Book VI, ch. I, §10; and ch. II, §6 in vol. I of the present edition. In the 2nd ed. (p. 711 n.) this footnote was transferred to Book VI, ch. XI, §6. See editorial note **b** to page 666 of vol. I in the present edition.

This footnote was deleted from the 3rd ed. except for the second, third and fourth sentences which were constituted into a separate paragraph in the text of Book VI, ch. I, §10. See page 523 of vol. I in the present edition.

PAGE 684

a. So since the 6th ed. (p. 684), where the words "But gradually" replaced the words "But later on" in the 5th ed. (p. 584) which latter words in turn had replaced the words "But about a generation ago" dating from the 1st ed. (p. 726).

b. The following sentence dating from the 1st ed. (p. 727) was deleted from the 5th ed.:

In these trades an elderly man finds it difficult to get employment except when trade is brisk, at all events if he is a member of a union which will not allow him to work for less than the full wages of the district.

c. This footnote was inserted in the 5th ed. (p. 684 n.).

PAGE 685

a. The following sentences, which were placed in a footnote attached to the word "shrink" in the 1st ed. (p. 727 n.), and in the text in the 2nd ed. (p. 733), were deleted from the 5th ed.:

Trades-unions are afraid that many abuses might creep in if they allowed men "with grey hairs" to compete for employment at less than full wages. But many of them are coming to see that it is to their own interest, as it certainly is to that of the community, that such men should not be forced to be idle.

b. The words "almost alone" were inserted in the 2nd ed. (p. 734).

PAGE 686

a. This sentence dates from the 2nd ed. (p. 734).

b. So since the 2nd ed. (p. 734) where this sentence replaced the following sentence dating from the 1st ed. (p. 728 n.):

At the beginning of this century a famous singer, Mrs Billington, is said to have earned £10,000 in a season: and so long as the number of persons who can be reached by a human voice is strictly limited, it is not very likely that any singer will make an advance on this to be compared with that which the business leaders of the present generation have made on those of the last; for in their case the second cause cooperates with the first.

c. So since the 2nd ed. (p. 734). In the 1st ed. (p. 728 n.) this sentence ran as follows:

The most conspicuous instances of the power which the modern scale of business may put into the hands of a man of first-rate business genius, are to be found in the recent history of America, where many men who began life poor, have amassed more than £10,000,000 each.

In the 2nd ed. (p. 734) the last clause of the sentence just quoted from the 1st ed. was made into a separate sentence in the text which ran as follows: "This is most conspicuous in America, where several men who began life poor, have amassed more than £10,000,000 each." This latter sentence was deleted from the 5th ed.

d. So since the 5th ed. (p. 686). In the 1st ed. (p. 728 n.) the final clause of this sentence ran as follows: "the late Mr Vanderbilt for instance probably saved to the people of the United States more than he accumulated himself."

PAGE 687

a. So since the 6th ed. (p. 687) where this sentence took the place of the following sentence dating from the 1st ed. (p. 729):

The diffusion of knowledge, the improvement of educa-tion, the growth of prudent habits among the masses of the people, and the opportunities which the new methods of business offer for the safe investment of small capitals:—all these forces are telling on the side of the poorer classes as a whole relatively to the richer.

In the 5th ed. (p. 687) the first sentence of this paragraph ran as follows:

But these fortunes are exceptional: it is even doubtful whether the aggregate of the riches of the very rich are as large a part of the national wealth even in the United States or in England now as they have been in some earlier phases of civilization.

The second clause of this sentence was deleted from the 6th ed.

b. In the 1st ed. (p. 729 n.) the following footnote was attached to the word "artisan":

> A great body of statistics relating to nearly all civilized countries, and uniformly tending in this direction is contained in M. Leroy Beaulieu's *Essai sur la répartition des Richesses, et sur la tendance à une moindre inégalité des conditions*, 1881. Mr Goschen's Address to the Royal Statistical Society in 1887 on *The Increase of Moderate Incomes* points the same way; and so do the careful studies of wage statistics made by Mr Giffen in his private and in his official capacity.

In the 2nd ed. (p. 735 n.) the second clause of the second sentence in this footnote ran as follows: "and above all so do the very careful and instructive studies of wage statistics made by Mr Giffen in his private and in his official capacity."

In the 5th ed. (p. 687 n.) the reference to Giffen was deleted and the footnote there ran as follows: "Statistics relating to many countries, and uniformly tending in this direction, are given in M. Leroy Beaulieu's *Essai sur la répartition des Richesses, et sur la tendance à une moindre inégalité des conditions.*" This footnote was deleted from the 6th ed.

c. The remainder of this paragraph dates from the 6th ed. (p. 687).

d. This paragraph dates from the 2nd ed. (p. 736).

a. So since the 2nd ed. (pp. 736–7), where this and the next sentence replaced the following sentence in the 1st ed. (p. 734 n.):

> It may be noticed that in England the majority of the employees are practically hired by the year in many trades connected with transport; and these, as we have seen, are growing fastest, and are the representative industries of the second half of the nineteenth century, as the manufacturing trades were of the first half.

b. This sentence was inserted in the 6th ed. (p. 688 n.). In the 2nd ed. (p. 736 n.) there was the following concluding paragraph to this footnote: "On the probable instability of industry in the Middle Ages see Dr Cunningham's *Growth of English Industry and Commerce*, vol. I, p. 348." This paragraph was deleted from the 5th ed.

BOOK VI, CHAPTER XIII

PROGRESS IN RELATION TO STANDARDS OF LIFE

PAGE 689

a. The origin of the wording of this chapter is shown throughout in the editorial notes.

This chapter as a whole, in its present form, dates substantially from the 5th edition, though a few minor changes were made in the 6th edition. There was no corresponding chapter in the first four editions. A certain amount of material from Book VII, chapter XIII, in the 1st edition, and a good deal more from Book VI, chapter XII in the 2nd edition, was incorporated in it. See also editorial note **b** to Book V, chapter XII, page 668 of vol. I in the present edition.

b. The title of Book VI, chapter XIII, dates from the 5th edition.

c. Except where otherwise stated the wording of this section dates from the 2nd ed. (Book VI, ch. XII, § 13, pp. 737–9).

d. So since the 5th ed. (p. 689) where this sentence replaced the following opening sentence of § 13 dating from the 2nd ed. (pp. 737–8):

We have not yet reached the stage at which we can profitably examine the general effects of economic progress on human well being. But it will be well, before ending this Book, to pursue a little further the line of thought on which we started in Book III, when considering wants in relation to activities.

The broader influences of progress.

e. So since the 5th ed. where this sentence replaced the following sentence dating from the 2nd ed. (p. 738): "Let us take the term the standard of life to mean the standard of activities and of wants." When this sentence was changed in the 5th ed. a corresponding alteration was made in the wording of the marginal summary which had previously run as follows: "By the *standard of life* we mean the standard of activities as well as of wants."

PAGE 690

a. So since the 5th ed. (p. 690) where this clause replaced the following clauses dating from the 2nd ed. (p. 739): "it can raise wages only by another indirect effect, viz., by diminishing the supply of labour."

b. This sentence dates from the 5th ed. (p. 690). From the 5th ed. were deleted the following paragraphs dating from the 2nd ed. (pp. 739–40), which succeeded there the paragraph ending with the words "by diminishing the supply of labour":

A rise in the standard of wants is consistently regarded as a chief means of raising wages by those who hold the so-called "Malthusian" doctrines in their extreme form.

The doctrine that, merely through its action in diminishing the supply of labour, a rise in the standard of comfort raises wages, and is one of the most effective means for that purpose, has been consistently held by those who believe that population is pressing on the means of subsistence so hardly, that the rate of growth of population exercises a predominating influence on the rate of wages. For if that be true, then it is also true that at least one of the most efficient means of raising wages is to induce people to adopt a higher standard of comfort, in however mean and sordid a sense the term comfort is used: since in order to indulge the new desires rising out of their extended desire for comfort they may probably marry late, or otherwise limit the number of their children.

But it cannot be maintained by those who hold, as most writers of the present generation do, that the new facilities of transport have much diminished for the present the influence which the law of diminishing return exercises on production; and that the countervailing influences of the law of increasing return are so strong that the growth of population is not just now pressing hardly on the means of subsistence.

It is indeed still possible to contend that a mere diminution in the supply of manual labourers as a whole, or of any one class of them in particular, will increase the competition for their aid on the part of the higher grades of labour, and the owners of material capital; and that in consequence their wages will rise. This argument is no doubt valid so far as it goes: but the rise of wages that can be got by any class of labour simply by making itself scarce, and independently of any improvement in its standard of activities is generally not very great, except in the case of the lowest grades. We will consider this problem in some detail with reference to that particular change in the standard of living which takes the form of shortening the hours of labour, and of wise uses of leisure[1].

The influence on wages of a lessened supply of labour of any kind will now be further studied in relation to the hours of work.

[1] Mr Gunton's suggestive writings on the causes that govern wages seem to be somewhat impaired by a lax use of the phrases "standard of comfort" and "cost of production of labour."

In the 3rd ed. (p. 780) the words "has been consistently held by those who believe...etc.", in the first sentence, were replaced by the words "can be held consistently by those who believe...etc.". In the same edition the marginal summary was altered to run as follows: "A rise in the standard of wants can consistently be regarded as a chief means of raising wages only by extreme Malthusians."

c.   The whole of this section (§2) dates from the 5th ed. (pp.690–3).

PAGE 693

a.   The following concluding paragraph of §2 in the 5th ed. (p. 693) was deleted from the 6th ed.: "There are indeed some groups of workers which are free from one of the chief of these dangers. If the numbers of the lowest paid groups shrink, scarcity may tend to raise their wages without attracting many interlopers. But more on that point a little later."

b.   So since the 6th ed. (p. 693) where this paragraph and footnote replaced the following paragraphs dating from the 5th ed. (pp. 693–4):

Let us then look away from standards of comfort or wants; and consider rather standards of life and activities in relation to standards of earnings. Let us inquire how changes in activity affect wages, having in view all the many forms which such a change may assume; but adhering, for the sake of definiteness, throughout the discussion to that particular form of standardizing activity which is simplest and most easily applied, viz. a regulation of the hours of labour.

Standard of activities in relation to hours of work

The influence which the standard hours of work exert on economic activities, is partly obscured by the fact that the earnings of a human being are commonly counted gross; no special reckoning being for his wear-and-tear, of which indeed he is himself often rather careless. Further, very little account is taken of the evil effects of the overwork of men on the well-being of the next generation, although the hours of labour of children are regulated by law in their own interests and those of women in the interests of their families.

The second of the paragraphs just quoted from the 5th ed. was a partial rewording of the following paragraph dating from the 2nd ed. (Book VI, ch. xii, §16, p. 781):

Too little account is often taken of the wear-and-tear of human beings.

The earnings of a human being are commonly counted *gross;* no special reckoning being made for his wear-and-tear, of which indeed he is himself often rather careless; and, on the whole, but little account is taken of the evil effects of the overwork of men...etc.

In the 1st ed. (Book VII, ch. xii, §12, p. 730) there was the following paragraph, which was concerned with labour and leisure:

Progress in relation to leisure.

Finally, in measuring the influence of progress on wages, some account must be taken of changes in the strain and exertion by which they are earned. In warm countries a few hour's work often suffice to earn all the necessaries of life, except the cool fresh air that is needed for the full enjoyment both of work and of leisure. In the middle ages people had plenty of leisure in winter, and took a good many holidays in summer: but England's modern industrial greatness has been achieved by the ability and willingness of her people to work hard and steadily. It is doubtful whether, even in the dark years of the Great War, their hours of labour were

The Anglo-Saxon race works hard though not for long hours.

on the average longer than those of other Western nations, and now their hours are relatively short: but men of the Anglo-Saxon race in all parts of the world work hard while about it, and do more work in the year than any others.

This paragraph was deleted from the 2nd ed.

PAGE 694

a. With the exception of the last sentence, this paragraph dates from the 2nd ed. (p. 740).

b. So since the 6th ed. (p. 694) where this sentence replaced the following sentence dating from the 2nd ed. (p. 740):

706

And, since material wealth exists for the sake of man, and not man for the sake of material wealth, the fact that inefficient and stunted human lives had been replaced by more efficient and fuller lives would be a gain of a higher order than any temporary material loss that might have been occasioned on the way.

c. Subject to certain exceptions, noted below, the remainder of this section (§ 3) dates substantially from the 2nd ed. (pp. 740–3).

d. The following sentences at this point dating from the 2nd ed. (p. 741) were deleted from the 5th ed.:

Moreover they are the one class of workers, whose wages might be raised considerably at the expense of other classes by a mere diminution in the supply of their labour. Some of them indeed are in occupations that are closely pressed by the competition of skilled workers using machinery; and their wages are controlled by the law of substitution. But many of them do work for which no substitute can be found; they might raise the price of their labour considerably by stinting its supply; and they might have been able to raise it a very great deal in this way, were not any rise sure to bring into their occupation other workers of their own grade from occupations in which wages are controlled by the law of substitution.

e. This footnote dates from the 6th ed. (pp. 694 n.–5 n.).

PAGE 695

a. The remainder of this paragraph dates substantially from the 1st ed. (p. 732 n.), where it formed part of a long footnote. See also editorial notes **d** to page 695 and **a** to page 696 of vol. 1 in the present edition. The word "skilled" before the word "labour" in the 6th line of the paragraph was inserted in the 2nd ed. (p. 741).

b. In the 2nd ed. (p. 742) this paragraph replaced the following paragraph in the 1st ed. (pp. 731–2):

It is probable that there are few trades in which a person can with advantage to himself and the community be actually working hard for more than eight hours a day; though he may do light work for longer: and he may be "on duty," ready to act when called on, for much longer. For instance the watchman on a branch line, on which there are only a

The arguments for limiting the hours of labour of human beings do not apply to machinery.

few trains in the day, and who has a cottage close to the gate of which he is in charge, may be on duty all day without hardship. The increasing expensiveness of machinery, however, and the quickness with which it is rendered obsolete, increase every year the wastefulness of keeping the untiring iron and steel resting in idleness during sixteen hours out of the twenty-four. Anglo-Saxon artisans, unsurpassed in accuracy of touch, and surpassing all in sustained energy, would gain more than any others, if they would keep their machinery going at its full speed for sixteen hours a day, even though they themselves worked only eight. Such a change would increase the net produce, and therefore the wages of each worker, because much less than before would have to be deducted from his total output on account of charges for machinery, plant, factory rent, &c.

The economy of working in shifts.

    c.   The first paragraph of this footnote was inserted in the 6th ed. (p. 695 n.).

    d.   Subject to some rearrangement in the 2nd ed. (p. 742 n.) of the order of the sentences, the remainder of this footnote dates from the 1st ed. (p. 732 n.).

PAGE 696

    a.   This paragraph dates substantially from the 1st ed. (p. 732 n.).

    b.   So since the 6th ed. (p. 696). In the 1st ed. (pp. 732–3) the opening paragraph of Book VII, ch. XIII, §13, ran as follows:

A general reduction of the hours of labour would lower wages.

But there is a grave danger that progress may be retarded in consequence of a common belief that a reduction of the hours of labour will raise wages generally by merely making labour scarce; and independently of any effect it might have in keeping machinery longer at work and therefore making it more efficient, or in stopping that premature wearing out of men through overwork which exists in a few trades even now, though it is less common than it was. Some of the arguments offered in support of this notion must stand over for discussion in connection with the theory of credit and commercial fluctuations, and with that of foreign trade. But there are two which should be noticed here.

    In the 2nd ed. (p. 743) the corresponding paragraph (in that edition the last paragraph of Book VI, ch. XII, §16) ran as follows:

708

This leads us to consider the origin of the common belief that a reduction of the hours of labour would raise wages generally by merely making labour scarce, and independently of any effect it might have in keeping machinery longer at work and therefore making it more efficient, or in preventing people from being stunted and prematurely worn out by excessive work. This opinion is an instance of those misunderstandings as to the ways in which a rise in the standard of comfort can raise wages, to which we referred a little while back. Origin of the opinion that a general lessening of the hours of labour would raise wages.

In the 5th ed. (p. 696) this paragraph was replaced by the following paragraph:

It may be well to try to explain the great vitality of the common belief that a reduction of the hours of labour would raise wages generally by merely making labour scarce, and independently of any effect it might have in keeping machinery longer at work and therefore making it more efficient, or in preventing people from being stunted and prematurely worn out by excessive work.

c. So since the 5th ed. (p. 696). In the 1st ed. (p. 733) the paragraph quoted above, ending with the words "to which we referred a little while back", was succeeded by the following sentence: "The first is based on the fallacy that the immediate and permanent effects of a change will be the same."

From the 2nd to the 4th editions this passage ran as follows: "It appears to rest on two fallacies. The first of these is that the immediate and permanent effects of a change will be the same."

It was also in the 5th ed. that the marginal summary at the beginning of this paragraph in the present edition replaced the following summary dating from the 1st ed.: "The fallacy that it [a general lessening of the hours of labour] would cause a permanent increase in the demand for labour."

d. This sentence dates from the 1st ed. (p. 733).

e. This sentence was inserted in the 5th ed. (p. 696 n.).

PAGE 697

a. The following words after the word "wages" in the 1st ed. (p. 733) were deleted from the 3rd ed.: "unless they were prepared to stop work altogether."

b. So since the 3rd ed. (p. 784) where this sentence replaced the following sentences dating from the 1st ed. (p. 733):

It is known that the immediate effect of a reduction of the hours of labour would be to cause those employers who had contracts on hand, and some others, to take on extra men. And it is argued that therefore a reduction of the hours of labour would diminish the number of the unemployed, and raise wages.

c. This sentence dates from the 5th ed. (p. 697).

d. This sentence and the first four main clauses of the next sentence date substantially from the 3rd ed. (p. 784).

e. The remaining clauses of this sentence date from the 5th ed. (p. 697). In the 3rd and 4th editions this sentence ended with the word "suburbs", and was succeeded by the following sentences which were deleted from the 5th ed.:

If it were true that the aggregate amount of wages could be increased by causing every person to work one-fifth less than now, then a diminution of the population by one-fifth would raise aggregate wages, and therefore would increase average wages by more than a fifth—a proposition which goes beyond the doctrine of extreme Malthusians.

f. So since the 5th ed. (p. 697), where this and the next sentence replaced the following sentence dating substantially from the 1st ed. (p. 733): "The source of the error in this argument lies in the assumption that there is a fixed *work-fund*, a certain amount of work which has to be done, whatever the price of labour."

g. The remainder of this paragraph and the first two sentences of the next paragraph date from the 2nd ed. (pp. 743–4).

PAGE 698

a. So since the 5th ed. (p. 698). In the first four editions there was the following additional clause in this sentence after the clause ending with the words "close their works": "and would therefore probably tend, not to lessen, but to increase the inconstancy of employment." In the 5th ed. this clause was replaced by the concluding sentence in the present edition.

b. This paragraph dates from the 5th ed. (p. 698).

c. Apart from the footnote on p. 699, this section (§ 5) dates from the 5th ed. (pp. 698–700) where it replaced the following paragraphs dating from the 1st ed. (pp. 734–5):

The second argument is allied to the first. It rests on the fallacy that all trades will gain by the general adoption of a mode of action which has been proved to enable one trade, under certain conditions, to gain at the expense of others. It is undoubtedly true that, if they could exclude external competition, plasterers or shoemakers would have a fair chance of raising their wages by a mere diminution of the amount of work done by each. But these gains, as we have seen, can be got only at the cost of a greater aggregate loss to other sharers in the national dividend.

The fallacy of arguing that all trades can gain by making their labour scarce.

It is true that some of these will not be members of the working classes; part of the loss will fall on employers and capitalists whose personal and material capital is sunk in building or shoemaking, and part on the well-to-do users or consumers of houses or shoes. But a part of the loss will fall on the working classes as users or consumers of houses or shoes; and part of the loss resulting from the plasterers' gain will fall on bricklayers, carpenters, &c., and a little of it on brickmakers, seamen employed in importing wood for building, and others.

One trade can sometimes do so, but at a more than equal cost to other sharers of the national dividend.

If then all workers reduce their output there will be a great loss of national dividend; capitalists and employers may indeed bear a large share of the burden; but they are sure not to bear all. For—to say nothing of the chance that they may emigrate and take or send their free capital for investment abroad—a great and general diminution of earnings of management, and interest on capital, would lead on the one hand to some substitution of the higher grades of labour for the lower throughout the whole continuous descending scale of employment, and perhaps to some falling off in the energy and assiduity of the leading minds of industry, while on the other hand it would check the saving of capital. And in so far as it had this last result it would diminish that abundance of capital relatively to labour which alone would enable labour to throw on capital a part of its share of the loss of the national dividend.

A general reduction of output would much diminish the national dividend, and the wage-receivers must bear a large part of the loss.

The only alteration of any substance made in these paragraphs in later (2nd to 4th) editions consisted in the rewording in the 2nd ed. (p. 744) of the first sentence in the second paragraph, as follows:

It is a fact—and, so far as it goes, an important fact—that some of these sharers will not belong to the working classes; part of the loss will certainly fall on employers and capitalists whose personal and material capital is sunk in building or shoemaking, and part on the well-to-do users or consumers of houses or shoes.

PAGE 699

a. This footnote dates from the 1st ed. (p. 735 n.). The following additional paragraphs of this footnote in the 1st ed., which succeeded the paragraph retained in the present edition, were deleted from the 5th ed.:

> A small part of the loss might be thrown on rent: but it is not necessary to allow for much under this head. Also our argument assumed, what would be sure to be approximately true, that, taken one with another, the values relatively to shoes of the things that the employer had to buy remain unchanged.
> It may be well to say here dogmatically, and in anticipation of the results of the next volume, that the influence of foreign trade competition in this connection can be proved to be different from what it at first sight appears. An international agreement to diminish simultaneously the hours of labour in all trades would indeed have the important effect of preventing the workers in any one country from having to fear that capital would leave it for others; and further a reduction in the hours of labour whether by a given percentage, or down to a given minimum, would diminish output in unequal proportions in different trades, and would therefore disturb relative values and relative wages; and these disturbances would be aggravated by competition from a foreign country that was not passing through the same changes. If however the hours of labour could be reduced, not on any rigid plan, but in such a way as not to disturb relative values, the change would not directly affect the course of foreign trade, whether other nations adopted the movement or not. For if it just, but only just, paid to export cutlery and import in exchange sewing machines before the change; then after the change, relative values remaining unaltered, it would still pay, and only just pay, to do the same. International agreements are therefore likely to go less far, than at first sight appears, towards lessening the evils of a general diminution of output.

PAGE 700

a. The subject-matter of §6 dates substantially from the 2nd ed., where the first four paragraphs were placed in a footnote (pp. 746 n.–7 n.) and the fifth paragraph in the text (pp. 745–6).

b. So since the 5th ed. (p. 700) where this sentence replaced the following sentence dating from the 2nd ed. (p. 746 n.): "We must distrust all attempts to solve the question, whether a reduction of the hours of labour reduces production and wages, by a simple appeal to facts."

PAGE 701

a. This and the next sentence date from the 5th ed. (p. 701 n.), where they replaced the following concluding sentence of this footnote dating from the 3rd ed. (p. 788 n.): "And it is not certain that the recent commercial troubles in Australia have not been in part caused by over sanguine estimates of the economic efficiency of short hours of labour." This sentence in the 3rd ed. in turn replaced the following sentence in the 2nd ed. (p. 747 n.): "(The history of the *Eight Hour day in Victoria* has been excellently told by Mr Rae in the first Number of the Economic Journal)."

PAGE 702

a. In the 2nd to the 4th editions, where this paragraph closed with the sentence ending with the words "progress of wealth and knowledge", there was the following additional paragraph which was deleted from the 5th ed.:

All this tends to show that a general reduction of the hours of labour is likely to cause a little net material loss and much moral good, that it is not adapted for treatment by a rigid cast-iron system, and that the conditions of each class of trades must be studied separately.

b. This sentence dates from the 5th ed. (p. 702).

c. The whole of §7 dates from the 5th ed. (pp. 702–4).

d. This reference is to the abridgement of Marshall's *Principles of Economics*, which he first published in 1892 under the title: *Elements of Economics of Industry being the First Volume of Elements of Economics*. There was a second edition of this work in 1896, a third in 1899, and a fourth in 1913. It should be noted that this was an entirely different book from the small *Economics of Industry*, by Alfred and Mary Paley Marshall, the first edition of which was published in 1879.

General conclusion as to the hours of labour.

PAGE 704

a. With the exception of two sentences in the footnote on p. 705 the whole of §8 dates from the 5th ed. (pp. 704–6).

PAGE 705

a. So since the 6th ed. (p. 705 n.) where the first two sentences of this footnote replaced the following sentence in the 5th ed. (p. 705 n.):

Misunderstandings on this subject are frequent among trade union leaders: who commonly give as their authority the very weighty and able treatise on *Industrial Democracy* by Mr and Mrs Webb, where it is persistently suggested.

PAGE 706

a. The whole of §9 dates from the 5th ed. (pp. 706–8).

PAGE 709

a. The whole of §10 dates from the 5th ed. (pp. 709–11).

a. As Marshall says, in his footnote to page 710 in vol. 1 of the present edition, the whole of the last three paragraphs of § 10, from the quotation from Mill onwards, is taken without change from the *Economics of Industry* by Alfred and Mary Paley Marshall, 1879 (pp. 154–5). In that book the quotation from Mill was preceded by the following paragraph (p. 154):

After every crisis, in every period of commercial depression, it is said that supply is in excess of demand. Of course, there may easily be an excessive supply of some particular commodities; so much cloth and furniture and cutlery may have been made that they cannot be sold at a remunerative price. But something more than this is meant. For after a crisis the warehouses are overstocked with goods in almost every important trade; scarcely any trade can continue undiminished production so as to afford a good rate of profits to capital and a good rate of wages to labour. And it is thought that this state of things is one of general overproduction. We shall however find that it really is nothing but a state of commercial disorganization; and that the remedy for it is a revival of confidence.

a. In the *Economics of Industry* there was the following footnote attached to the word "rise" at the end of this sentence:

> The most plausible of all the plans that have been suggested by socialists for the artificial organization of industry is one which aims at the "abolition of commercial crises". They propose that in times of depression government should step forward, and, by guaranteeing each separate industry against risk, cause all industries to work, and therefore to earn and therefore to buy each other's products. Government, by running every risk at once, would, they think, run no risk. But they have not yet shown how Government should tell whether a man's distress was really due to causes beyond his own control, nor how its guarantee could be worked without hindering that freedom on which energy and the progress of invention depend.

In the *Economics of Industry* the paragraph ending with the words "prices rise" was succeeded by the following paragraphs dealing with the effects of falling prices upon output and incomes:

The connexion between a fall of prices and a suspension of industry requires to be further worked out.

There is no reason why a depression of trade and a fall

of prices should stop the work of those who can produce without having to pay money on account of any expenses of production. For instance a man who pays no wages, who works with his own hands, and produces what raw material he requires, cannot lose anything by continuing to work. It does not matter to him how low prices have fallen, provided that the prices of his goods have not fallen more in proportion than those of others. When prices are low, he will get a few coins for his goods; but if he can buy as many things with them as he could with the greater number of coins he got when prices were high, he will not be injured by the fall of prices. He would be a little discouraged if he thought that the price of his goods would fall more than the prices of others; but even then he would not be very likely to stop work.

And in the same way a manufacturer, though he has to pay for raw material and wages would not check his production on account of a fall in prices, if the fall affected all things equally, and were not likely to go further. If the price which he got for his goods had fallen by a quarter, and the prices which he had to pay for labour and raw material had also fallen by a quarter, the trade would be as profitable to him as before the fall. Three sovereigns would now do the work of four, he would use fewer counters in measuring off his receipts against his outgoings; but his receipts would stand in the same relation to his outgoings as before. His net profits would be the same percentage of his total business. The counters by which they are reckoned would be less by one quarter, but they would purchase as much of the necessaries, comforts, and luxuries of life as they did before.

It however very seldom happens in fact that the expenses which a manufacturer has to pay out fall as much in proportion as the price which he gets for his goods. For when prices are rising, the rise in the price of the finished commodity is generally more rapid than that in the price of the raw material, always more rapid than that in the price of labour; and when prices are falling, the fall in the price of the finished commodity is generally more rapid than that in the price of the raw material, always more rapid than that in the price

of labour. And therefore when prices are falling the manufacturer's receipts are sometimes scarcely sufficient even to
repay him for his outlay on raw material, wages, and other
forms of circulating capital; they seldom give him in addition enough to pay interest on his fixed capital and earnings
of management for himself.

Even if the prices of labour and raw material fall as
rapidly as those of finished goods, the manufacturer may
lose by continuing production if the fall has not come to an
end. He may pay for raw material and labour at a time when
prices generally have fallen by one-sixth; but if, by the time
he comes to sell, prices have fallen by another sixth, his
receipts may be less than is sufficient to cover his outlay.

We conclude then that manufacturing cannot be carried
on except at a low rate of profit, or at a loss, when the prices
of finished goods are low relatively to those of labour and
raw material; or when prices are falling, even if the prices
of all things are falling equally.

Thus a fall in prices lowers profits and impoverishes the
manufacturer: while it increases the purchasing power of
those who have fixed incomes. So again it enriches creditors
at the expense of debtors. For if the money that is owing to
them is repaid, this money gives them a *great purchasing
power; and if they have lent it at a fixed rate of interest,
each payment is worth more to them than it would be if
prices were high. But for the same reasons that it enriches
creditors and those who receive fixed incomes, it impoverishes
those men of business who have borrowed capital; and it
impoverishes those who have to make, as most business men
have, considerable fixed money payments for rents, salaries
and other matters. When prices are ascending, the improvement is thought to be greater than it really is; because
general opinion with regard to the prosperity of the country
is much influenced by the authority of manufacturers and
merchants. These judge by their own experience, and in
time of ascending prices their fortunes are rapidly increased;

---

* The sense would seem to require that the word "great" should read "greater";
but even down to and including the 8th reprinting of *The Economics of Industry*,
in 1889, the word "great" was retained.

in a time of descending prices their fortunes are stationary or dwindle. But statistics prove that the real income of the country is not very much less in the present time of low prices, than it was in the period of high prices that went before it. The total amount of the necessaries, comforts and luxuries which are enjoyed by Englishmen is but little less in 1879 than it was in 1872.

PAGE 712

a. With the exception of part of the footnote on p. 713 the whole of § 11 dates from the 5th ed. (pp. 712–14).

PAGE 713

a. So since the 8th edition (page 713 n.) where this footnote replaced the following footnote in the 7th ed. (p. 713 n.):

> The annual income of some 49,000,000 in the United Kingdom appears to amount to more than £2,000,000,000. Now many leading artisans earn about £200 a year; and there are a vast number of artisan households in which each of four or five members is earning an income ranging from 18s. to 40s. a week. The expenditure of these households is on as large, if not a larger scale, than would be possible if the total income were divided out equally, so as to yield about £40 annually a head. Several of the suggestions made in the present chapter are further developed in an article on "The Social Possibilities of Economic Chivalry" in the *Economic Journal* for March 1907.

The wording of this footnote in the 7th ed. was identical with that in the 5th and 6th editions, with the exception of the first sentence.

In the 6th ed. (p. 713 n.) the first sentence ran as follows: "The annual income of the 45,000,000 people in the United Kingdom appears to amount to about £1,800,000,000."

In the 5th ed. (p. 713 n.) this sentence ran as follows: "The annual income of the 43,000,000 people in the United Kingdom appears to amount to £17,000,000,000 or a little more." It may be noted that the estimate given in the 5th ed. of the size of the national income —"£17,000,000,000 or a little more"—should have been "£1,700,000,000 or a little more".

Marshall's article on "The Social Possibilities of Economic Chivalry", in the *Economic Journal* for March 1907, is reprinted in *The Memorials of Alfred Marshall*, edited by A. C. Pigou (pp. 323–66).

PAGE 714

a. § 12 dates from the 5th ed. (pp. 714–15).

b. In the 1st ed. (p. 731 n.) the following reference to the problem of the "Residuum" was placed in a footnote:

We have not here to consider the case of the Residuum, many of whom are in so unwholesome a condition that they could not in a long day do the equivalent of two hours' energetic work; nor again of those who have refused to know when old fashioned industries have been beaten by modern appliances, and put out more than all their strength in a vain contest with steam force, as has been done by some branches of hand-weaving and nail-making: nor have we here to deal with those whose want of skill and resource has brought about the evils, of which "the Sweating System" is a product, and to a small extent a cause. The lives of all these people are mistakes, for which some more far-reaching remedy is needed than a mere reduction of their excessive hours of labour.

This footnote was deleted from the 2nd ed., where the problem was discussed in the following paragraph in the text (p. 737):

Progress then has done much: but there still remains a great, and—in consequence of improved sanitation—perhaps a growing Residuum of persons who are physically, mentally or morally incapable of doing a good day's work with which to earn a good day's wage; and some of those who are called artisans, together with many unskilled labourers, work hard for over long hours, and provide for others the means of refinement and luxury, but obtain neither for themselves nor their children the means of living a life that is worthy of man.

This paragraph was retained unaltered in the 3rd and 4th editions.

PAGE 716

a. Except where otherwise stated the wording of § 13 dates from the 5th ed. (pp. 716–19).

PAGE 717

a. The remainder of this paragraph, and the footnote attached to the end of it, date from the 6th ed. (p. 717).

PAGE 719

a. This sentence was inserted in the 6th ed. (p. 719).

b. In the 5th ed. (p. 718) the opening sentence of this paragraph ran as follows: "The lower middle ranks are overcrowded as badly as are the lower ranks of manual labour, both skilled and unskilled. But there is plenty of room in the upper ranks...etc." The foregoing sentence was deleted from the 6th ed.

c. In the 6th ed. there was some rearrangement of the order of the sentences on pp. 718–19.

In the 5th ed. (p. 718) the sentence ending with the words "a sufficiency even of common food" was succeeded by the two following sentences: "There is often a social loss as well as a social gain when the children of any grade press into the grade above them. But it is an almost unmixed gain that children of the lowest class should move upwards. And it is a vast and wholly unmixed gain when...etc."

In the 6th ed. the first of these sentences was transferred to the first paragraph on p. 719, while the second sentence was deleted.

PAGE 720

a. This and the next sentence date from the 5th ed. (p. 719).

b. This sentence dates from the 1st ed. (p. 731). The following marginal summary was attached in the 1st ed. to the paragraph of which this was the opening sentence: "Well spent leisure would be of more real worth than a great part of our material enjoyments. But, as things are, an increase in the incomes of the poor is generally more to be desired than an increase of leisure." The second sentence of this summary was deleted from the 2nd ed.

c. The first clause of this sentence dates from the 5th ed. (p. 719).

d. So since the 5th ed. (p. 719). In the 1st ed. (p. 731) this passage ran as follows:

And it might be well that all should work less, provided that the new leisure be spent well, and the consequent loss of material income be met exclusively by the abandonment by all classes of the least worthy methods of consumption.

In the 2nd to the 4th editions the early part of this sentence ran as follows: "And it would certainly be well that all should work less, if we could secure that the new leisure be spent well, and the consequent loss of material income...etc."

e. This sentence dates substantially from the 1st ed. (p. 731), where it was succeeded by the following sentences most of which were deleted from the 2nd ed.:

And on the whole it seems more urgent to increase the material means of a noble and refined life for all classes, and especially the poorest, than to diminish much the hours of work of those who are not at present over-worked. But children whose education is cut short, and adults, who have not time for their family and social duties, are overworked: and so are those who are exhausted by their work, even though it does not last very long; for there are some exceptional kinds of work, such as that of working in a mine at a very high temperature, which involve so great a strain that they can be performed efficiently only for a few hours a day.

f. The remainder of this paragraph dates substantially from the 2nd ed. (p. 747) where it was succeeded by the following paragraph which was deleted from the 5th ed.:

A person can seldom exert himself to the utmost for more than eight hours a day with advantage to anyone; but he may do light work for longer, and he may be "on duty," ready to act when called on, for much longer. And since adults, whose habits are already formed, are not likely to adapt themselves quickly to long hours of leisure, it would seem more conducive to the well-being of the nation as a whole, to take measures for increasing the material means of a noble and refined life for all classes, and especially the poorest, than to secure a sudden and very great diminution in the hours of labour of those who are not now weighed down by their work.

g. The following footnote attached to the word "life" in the 2nd ed. (p. 747 n.) was deleted from the 5th ed.: "This is well argued by Mr Sidney Webb and Mr Harold Cox in their plea for *An Eight Hours' Day*."

h. This and the next paragraph date from the 2nd ed. (p. 748).

PAGE 721

a. This and the next paragraph date from the 5th ed. (pp. 720–1).

PAGE 722

a. So since the 5th ed. (p. 721) where this marginal summary replaced the following summary dating from the 1st ed.: "The temptation to understate the benefits of progress."

b. This paragraph dates substantially from the 1st ed. (p. 730).

c. This paragraph dates substantially from the 1st ed. (p. 736).

d. The following concluding words of this sentence in the 1st ed. after the word "study" were deleted from the 5th ed.: "of Distribution and Exchange."

e. So since the 4th ed. (p. 788) where this sentence replaced the following sentence dating from the 1st ed. (p. 736):

But the ground which we have already traversed is, in some respects, the most difficult of the whole province of economics; and it commands, and, so to speak, holds the key of, that which lies yet before us.

In the course of a letter to F. Y. Edgeworth, dated 28 August 1902, Marshall cited and developed the statement contained in this final sentence of the text of his *Principles*, as follows:

"The ground traversed in Books V and VI commands and gives access to that which lies yet before us." To that I adhere and I like it better than the old phrase "a kernel". But V and VI rest on III and IV; and VI is often concrete. In that old phrase you would perhaps take the kernel to be the essential part: I take it to be a small part; and, when taken alone, more likely to be misapplied than in the case of other sciences. In my view "Theory" is essential. No one gets any real grip of economic problems unless he will work at it. But I conceive no more calamitous notion than that abstract, or general, or "theoretical" economics was economics "proper". It seems to me an essential but a very small part of economics proper: and by itself sometimes even—well, not a very good occupation of time.

The key-note of my *Plea* is that *the* work of the economist is "to disentangle the interwoven effects of complex causes"; and that for this, general reasoning is essential, but a wide and thorough study of facts is equally essential, and that a combination of the two sides of the work is *alone* economics *proper*. Economic theory is, in my opinion, as mischievous an impostor when it claims to be economics *proper* as is mere crude unanalysed history. Six of ye one, ½ dozen of ye other! (*Memorials of Alfred Marshall*, ed. A. C. Pigou, p. 437.)

The reference to "my *Plea*" in the second paragraph of the foregoing passage relates to Marshall's *Plea for the Creation of a Curriculum in Economics and Associated Branches of Political Science*. (See pp. 160–81 above.)

APPENDIX A

THE GROWTH OF FREE
INDUSTRY AND ENTERPRISE

PAGE 723

a. Except where otherwise stated in the editorial notes, the wording of this Appendix dates substantially from the 1st edition.

In the first four editions the subject-matter of this Appendix was placed in Book I, chapters II and III, entitled "The Growth of Free Industry and Enterprise" and "The Growth of Free Industry and Enterprise, Continued".

In the 5th edition these two chapters were amalgamated to form Appendix A, "The Growth of Free Industry and Enterprise". A Reply by Marshall to criticisms by Dr W. Cunningham of portions of the subject-matter of this Appendix will be found in the Editorial Appendix to Appendix A, see pp. 735–50 below.

b. This paragraph dates from the 5th ed. (p. 723).

c. So since the 2nd ed. (p. 10) where this sentence replaced the following sentences dating from the 1st ed. (p. 10):

The chief events in history are due to the action of individuals. The conditions which have made these events possible are nearly all traceable to the influence of inherited institutions and race qualities and of physical nature.

PAGE 724

a. So since the 3rd ed. (p. 11) where the words "And therefore nearly all early civilization...etc." replaced the words "And therefore, as Buckle has pointed out, all early civilizations...etc." dating from the 1st ed. (p. 11).

PAGE 726

a. In the 1st ed. (p. 14) the footnote now attached to the end of this paragraph was placed in the text immediately after the sentence ending with the words "similar causes in modern times"; and there was the following marginal summary to the whole passage: "Custom is generally a disguised form of slow moving competition."

This summary was deleted from the 2nd ed.

b. The following concluding sentences of this paragraph dating from the 1st ed. (pp. 14–15) were deleted from the 7th ed.:

The affairs of government have always received the careful attention of historians; and prominence has been given to the influence which the forms of government have exerted on the development of industry and commerce. But insufficient attention has been paid to that exerted by the collective ownership of property.

PAGE 727

a. The first two sentences of this footnote date in their present form from the 7th ed. (p. 727 n.).

In the 1st ed. (p. 15 n.) the opening sentences ran as follows:

> Though the matter is not altogether free from controversy, there seems good reason to believe that the Teutonic Three Mark system was a survival of primitive customs that had prevailed, of course with endless variety in detail, among the forefathers of nearly all white races. Traces of such a plan exist even now in India and among some Sclavonic peoples and analogies to it are found among some races of other colours. In the Three Mark system, in its typical form, one small part, the home mark,...etc.

In the 5th and 6th editions (p. 727 n.) the opening sentence ran as follows: "In the Teutonic Mark, in its typical form, one small part, the home mark,...etc."

b. This footnote dates from the 3rd ed. (p. 16 n.).

PAGE 728

a. So since the 3rd ed. (p. 16), where these words replaced the following words dating from the 1st ed. (p. 16): "why modern economic problems were unknown to them."

b. In the 1st ed. (pp. 16–17) there were the following opening paragraph and sentence at the beginning of § 3:

The chief leadership of progress has fallen to the successive waves of Aryans that have spread over Europe and Asia from their early homes in lands of frost and snow[1]. Some went far southwards early: early they became rulers and leaders of other nations, and early they lost their best strength under the influence of luxury and a warm climate. But others went on increasing in strength through long centuries amid the invigorating influences of a bracing climate and constant conflict; and at last a band of them, spreading southwards from the Danube, found itself in a

The Greeks brought Northern energy to bear on Oriental culture.

[1] It matters little for our purposes whether this home was in the lofty plateau that forms the centre of the Asiatic European Continent, or as some now contend, in the north of Europe.

mountainous land whose many harbours opened on the Mediterranean Sea. Each harbour was cut off from its neighbours by the mountains and was united by the sea with the most suggestive thoughts and mysteries of the world. The Greeks were within a few days' sail of nearly all that was best worth knowing about, whether in thought or feeling, in action or in aspiration. Persia, Assyria, Phœnicia, Judæa, and Egypt, were all at the eastern end of that great sea that unites Asia, Africa, and Europe; and India was not far off.

The new impulse towards freedom in thought and action came from the sea.

In the 2nd ed. (p. 16) an additional sentence was added at the beginning of the paragraph just quoted, and the succeeding sentence was also modified. The passage there ran as follows:

Recent studies in biology and in philology have thrown discredit on much that was thought well-established in the early history of civilization. But there seems no reason to doubt that nearly all the chief pioneers of progress have been Aryans who, in successive waves, have spread over Europe and Asia from early homes in lands of frost and snow.

The only other change made in the 2nd ed. consisted in the deletion of the footnote attached to the first sentence of this paragraph in the 1st ed. The whole of this paragraph, and the sentence succeeding it, were deleted from the 7th ed.

c.   In the 2nd ed. (p. 17), the words "and last of all in Hellas proper" replaced the words "and last of all in the Peloponnesus" in the 1st ed. (p. 17). The words "last of all" were deleted from the 5th ed.

PAGE 729

a.   The reference to Grote's *History of Greece* was inserted in the 4th ed. (p. 18 n.).

PAGE 730

a.   The words "at last" were inserted in the 5th ed. (p. 730).

b.   This marginal summary in its present form dates from the 2nd ed. (p. 19) and the summary to the next paragraph from the 3rd ed. (p. 20).

In the 1st ed. (pp. 19–20) there was the following marginal summary: "The strength of character of the Romans fitted them for business, but they preferred to acquire wealth by the sword, and thus exerted little direct influence on economic science."

c. So since the 3rd ed. (p. 20) where this paragraph replaced the following paragraph in the 2nd ed. (p. 20):

They were strong and daring, steady of purpose and abundant in resource: they had in constant use all the faculties that are required for business enterprise; though as a rule they preferred to give themselves to war and politics. Singularly free from the restraints of custom, they shaped their own life for themselves with a deliberate choice that had never been known before[1]: in fact, partly in consequence of the unity of the imperial power and the wide diffusion of the Roman language, there was in some important respects more freedom of commerce and of movement throughout the civilized world in the days of the Roman empire than even now.

[1] Comp. Nasse's *Entwicklung des wirtschaftlichen Individualismus in England* (*Preussische Jahrbücher*, vol. LVII, p. 430).

The paragraph just quoted from the 2nd ed. replaced the following paragraph in the 1st ed. (p. 20):

They were strong and daring, steady of purpose and abundant in resource: they had in constant use all the faculties that are required for business enterprise. Singularly free from the restraints of custom, every one shaped his own life for himself with a deliberate choice that had never been known before: in fact the freedom of trade, of commerce, and of movement throughout the civilized world was in some respects greater in the days of the Roman empire than it is even now[1].

[1] Comp. Nasse's *Entwicklung des wirtschaftlichen Individualismus in England* (*Preussische Jahrbücher*, vol. LVII, p. 430).

In the 1st ed. the paragraph just quoted was succeeded by the following paragraph, which was deleted from the 2nd ed.:

But as soon as Rome obtained dominion, her ablest citizens withdrew themselves from business, and gave their strength to politics, to the arts of government, and to some slight extent to the arts of culture. They respected agriculture; but they allowed large farms worked by slaves to take the place of the small holdings of freemen. They were by no means superior to the lust for wealth; but they acquired it by the sword. So gained it led to a hardness of spirit and a reckless wickedness of luxury amid which Rome fell, having done even less than Greece had done towards investigating the economic conditions of social well-being.

The foregoing paragraphs are referred to by Marshall in his reply to Cunningham's criticisms in the *Economic Journal*, vol. III. See the Editorial Appendix to Appendix A (pp. 744–6 below).

d. This and the next two paragraphs together with the footnotes attached to them, date from the 3rd ed. (pp. 20–1).

e. So since the 3rd ed. (pp. 19 n.–20 n.) where this footnote replaced the following footnote dating from the 1st ed. (p. 19 n.):

> This fundamental opposition between the Greek and Roman tempers was made clear by Hegel in his *Philosophy of History*. He calls the freedom from outward control, whether of thought or action, *objective freedom;* while he gives the name of *subjective freedom* to the freedom from waywardness, "the freedom of spirit which reposes on itself, absolute self-determination." The former belonged to the Greeks, the latter to the Romans; while the Teutonic spirit under the influence of Christianity is uniting the two and working towards complete freedom. Compare also Kautz, *Entwicklung der National Œkonomie*, Bk. I.

PAGE 732

a. In the 2nd ed. (p. 21) the word "universal" replaced the word "essential" in the 1st ed.

PAGE 733

a. The following footnote attached to the word "pleased" in the 1st ed. (p. 21 n.) was deleted from the 2nd ed.: "As regards the whole of this subject, Englishmen owe conspicuous debts to Sir Henry Maine's writings."

b. So since the 3rd ed. (p. 23) where this marginal summary replaced the following summary dating from the 1st ed. (pp. 21–2): "The pride and apathy of the Stoics deprived their lives of inward harmony. The reconciliation of social duties with a striving after perfection was effected by Christianity."

c. The following footnote attached to the word "work" in the 1st ed. (p 22 n.) was deleted from the 2nd ed.: "Hegel's *Philosophy of History*, Part III, iii."

PAGE 735

a. The following concluding paragraph of this section, dating from the 1st ed. (p. 24) was deleted from the 7th ed.:

Switzerland indeed has been free: for its mountains oppose hindrance to the movements of large armies, and render cavalry almost useless; and it has nourished a sturdy race The case of Switzerland is exceptional. which has been strengthened from time to time by refugees from among the bolder spirits of neighbouring lands. But the range of intercourse of those who live in mountains is generally small. Except when enriched by the lavish expenditure of tourists from more favoured lands, they live hard lives, overworked during their short summer, and stagnating in close rooms during their long winter. They have not therefore had that mental activity and enterprise which has characterized the free cities.

b. So since the 2nd ed. (p. 25) where the remainder of this sentence replaced the following sentences in the 1st ed. (p. 25):

And though their self-imposed regulations proved ultimately oppressive, they fitted the conditions of industry for a long time so well that their pressure was not felt. And as they could be altered deliberately when there was any strong occasion for change, there was comparatively little of that dominion of custom which is unrecognized and therefore deadening. The same compactness which rendered it possible for the whole people to meet together for political purposes, enabled them quickly to agree on any changes that their industry might require.

c. This footnote dates from the 3rd ed. (p. 27 n.).

PAGE 736

a. This and the next sentence date from the 2nd ed. (p. 15).

b. The remainder of this sentence, and the next sentence, date from the 2nd ed. (p. 25).

c. So since the 3rd ed. (p. 27) where this marginal summary replaced the following summary dating from the 1st ed. (pp. 25–6): "Chivalry prescribed a high code of honour towards those who were well born, but it used harsh measures to keep the lower classes in their place."

d. So since the 5th ed. (p. 736 n.), where this sentence replaced the following sentence dating from the 3rd ed. (p. 28 n.): "But the treachery that was common in Italian cities was not very rare in northern castles." This sentence in turn had replaced the following sentence dating from the 1st ed. (p. 26 n.): "Treachery was however common."

e. In the 3rd ed. (p. 28 n.) the word "ignoble" replaced the word "disgusting" dating from the 1st ed. (p. 26 n.).

PAGE 737

a. The last sentence of this footnote dates from the 3rd ed. (p. 29 n.).

b. This footnote dates from the 3rd ed. (p. 29 n.).

PAGE 738

a. So since the 3rd ed. (p. 30) where this marginal summary and the summary to the next paragraph replaced the following summaries dating from the 1st ed. (pp. 27–8): "Feudal organization was at first unstable, but at length overthrew the freedom of the cities." "But the hopes of progress were again raised by the invention of printing, the Reformation, and the discovery of the New World."

PAGE 739

a. The following concluding clauses of this sentence, dating from the 1st ed. (p. 29) were deleted from the 7th ed.: "the colonists of England, Holland, and even France demanded and obtained far more freedom than those of Spain and Portugal."

b. So since the 2nd ed. (p. 29) where this sentence replaced the following sentence in the (1st ed. p. 29):

But our Stuart Kings sold their country for French gold; and it was not till 1688 that England awoke from the slumber of a Circean degradation, barely in time to save Holland from destruction; when her bravest and most generous sons had already perished on the battle-field and she was overburdened with debt.

PAGE 740

a. The word "yeoman" before the word "archer", dating from the 1st ed. (p. 32) was deleted from the 7th ed.

PAGE 741

a. The remainder of this sentence dates from the 2nd ed. (p. 33).

PAGE 742

a. This and the next sentence date from the 3rd ed. (p. 36), where they replaced the following sentence dating from the 1st ed. (p. 34). "Thus the English large farm was the forerunner of the English factory, in the same way as English archery was the forerunner of the skill of the English artisan." This was one of the passages criticised by William Cunningham in his article in the *Economic Journal* entitled "The Perversion of History". See the Editorial Appendix to Appendix A, p. 746 below.

b. The following clause dating from the 1st ed. (p. 34), inserted between the clause ending with the word "intermediary" and the clause beginning with the words "and now for the first time...", was deleted from the 7th ed.: "life became intense and full of awe."

c. This footnote dates from the 3rd ed. (p. 36 n.).

PAGE 743

a. So since the 2nd ed. (p. 35), where this sentence replaced the following sentence in the 1st ed. (p. 35): "Their eagerness to give logical definiteness and precision to their religious creed occupied their minds, and disinclined them to lighter thoughts and lighter amusements."

b. The remainder of this sentence dates in its present form from the 7th ed. (p. 743) where it replaced the following sentences dating from the 1st ed. (p. 35):

Individualism had to be purified and softened by much tribulation; it had to become less self-assertive without becoming weaker, before new instincts could grow up around it to revive in a higher form what was most beautiful and most solid in the old collective tendencies. Individualism governed by the temper of the Reformed religion intensified family life, making it deeper and purer, and holier than it had ever been before. It is true that even the highest elements of our nature can be used wrongly, that an exclusive devotion to family cares has evils of its own. Nevertheless the family affections of those races which have adopted the Reformed religion are the richest and fullest of earthly feelings: there never has been before any material of texture at once so strong and so fine, with which to build up a noble fabric of social life.

c. So since the 7th ed. (p. 743), where the opening words of this sentence replaced the following words dating from the 1st ed. (p. 36): "The effects of the Reformation on England's industrial and commercial character were...etc."

d. This marginal summary dates from the 7th ed. (pp. 743–4) where it replaced the following summaries dating from the 1st ed. (p. 36): "The economic influence of the Reformation on England was

729

intensified through her attracting refugee artisans from the Continent."
"It gave a sombre tone to her amusements, and this reacted on her
industries."

PAGE 744

a. The following footnote was attached to the word "commerce"
in the 1st ed. (p. 37 n.):

> Mr Rogers argues with great force (*Six Centuries of Work and Wages*, ch. 1)
> that the early commutation of personal for money dues was the chief cause of what
> is most characteristic in England's political history. And certainly her political
> and industrial institutions not only were common products of the same national
> character, but also have acted and reacted powerfully on one another.

The second of the two sentences just quoted from the 1st ed. was
deleted from the 2nd ed., while the first sentence was deleted from
the 7th ed.

b. This sentence dates from the 2nd ed. (p. 37) where it replaced
the following sentence in the 1st ed. (p. 37):

Freedom of industry and enterprise leads everyone to seek
that employment of his labour and capital in which he can
turn them to best advantage, and the chief advantage which
he has in view is generally, though not always, the increase
of his own income.

c. The following footnote attached to the word "labour" in the
2nd ed. (p. 37 n.) was deleted from the 5th ed.: "This subject is
studied in detail below, Book IV, chs. VII–XII."

PAGE 746

a. The following footnote attached to the word "century" dating
from the 1st ed. (p. 38 n.) was deleted from the 7th ed.: "Comp.
Ochenkowski, *Englands wirtschaftliche Entwicklung*, p. 112."

PAGE 747

a. This sentence dates from the 2nd ed. (p. 41).
b. So since the 4th ed. (p. 43), where the remainder of this paragraph replaced the following sentences dating from the 1st ed. (p. 41):

Up to the eighteenth century manufacturing labour had
been hired, as it were, always retail; in that century it began
to be hired wholesale. Up to that time its price had been in
the main either nominally fixed by custom, or determined
by the incidents of bargaining in very small markets: the
bargaining had been sometimes for the hire of labour, some-

times for the sale of its products, the workman having himself undertaken the risks of production. But since then its price has more and more been determined by the circumstances of supply and demand over a large area—a town, a country, or the whole world.

c. This sentence dates from the 5th ed. (p. 747 n.), where it replaced the following sentences dating from the 1st ed. (p. 40 n.):

> Our own age has seen numberless improvements and new economies in production, prominent among which are those relating to the production of steel, the telephone, the electric light, and the gas-engine; and the social changes arising from material progress are in some respects more rapid now than ever. But the groundwork of the changes that have happened since 1785 was chiefly laid in the inventions of the years 1760 to 1785.

d. The following additional reference in this footnote dating from the 1st ed. (p. 41 n.) was deleted from the 5th ed.: "Compare also Mr Carroll D. Wright's vigorous defence of the Factory system in vol. II of the *U.S. Census for 1880*."

PAGE 748

a. So since the 5th ed. (p. 748), where the words "The first part of last century" replaced the words "The first part of this century", dating from the 1st ed. (p. 42).

b. In the first four editions the word "unfavourable" was used here. When the words "this century" were altered to the words "last century", in the 5th ed., the word "unfavourable" was altered—by an obvious mistake, as is shown by the context—to the word "favourable", and this was retained down to and including the 8th ed.

c. So since the 3rd ed. (p. 44 n.) where this reference replaced the following reference dating from the 1st ed. (p. 42 n.): "See Ochenkowski, l.c. p. 53." The change was made in response to a criticism of Cunningham who pointed out that the reference to Ochenkowski was incorrect. See the Editorial Appendix to Appendix A (pp. 747–8 below).

PAGE 749

a. So since the 2nd ed. (p. 43), where this clause replaced the following sentence in the 1st ed. (p. 43): "But this was prohibited in the interests of the landlords who ruled in Parliament."

b. This clause and the next sentence date in their present form from the 2nd ed. (pp. 43–4) where they replaced the following paragraph in the 1st ed. (p. 43):

It is true, as we shall see presently, that this want did not make a very great difference to his wages directly; for the competition among employers was sufficiently real in manufacture, if not in agriculture, to cause them to bid against one another for any labourer whose wages were less than the net value of what he produced. But the pressure of want caused the workman to consent to excessive hours and unhealthy conditions of work for himself and his wife and children. This kept down the efficiency of the working population, and therefore the net value of their work, and therefore their wages. The moral and physical misery and disease of the factory population in the first quarter of the century is terrible to think of.

PAGE 750

a.　So since the 2nd ed. (p. 44) where this first clause replaced the following clause in the 1st ed. (p. 43): "But after the yearly attempts of the workmen to revive the old rules regulating industry had failed,".

b.　So since the 2nd ed. (p. 44) where this paragraph replaced the following sentences in the 1st ed. (p. 44):

The trades unions, which were rapidly growing in strength and knowledge, were beginning to see the folly of attempting to enforce the old rules by which government had directed the course of industry; and they had as yet got no far reaching views as to the regulation of trade by their own action: their chief anxiety was to increase their own economic freedom by the removal of the laws against combinations of workmen.

c.　In the 1st ed. (p. 45) the subject-matter of this footnote was placed in the text with the following marginal summary: "Loss of national wealth was then equivalent to loss of lives."

PAGE 751

a.　So since the 7th ed. (p. 751), where this sentence replaced the following sentence dating from the 1st ed. (p. 45):

For we are not now struggling for national existence; and our resources have not been exhausted by great wars: on the contrary our powers of production have been immensely increased; and, what is at least as important, the repeal of the Corn Laws and the growth of steam communication have enabled a largely increased population to obtain sufficient supplies of food on easy terms.

The following marginal summary to this paragraph in the 1st ed. (p. 45) was deleted from the 3rd ed.: "As the century wore on the nation became richer, and was no longer compelled to sacrifice everything to increased production."

b. The following footnote was attached to the word "people" in the 1st ed. (pp. 45 n.–6 n.):

> The average income per head in the United Kingdom which was about £15 in 1820 is about £33 now; i.e. it has risen from about £75 to £165 per family of five. There are not a few artisans' families, the total earnings of which exceed £165, so that they would lose by an equal distribution of wealth: but even they have not more than is required to support a healthy and many-sided life.

In the 3rd ed. (p. 48 n.) this footnote ran as follows:

> The average income per head in the United Kingdom, which was about £15 in 1820, is about £37 now; i.e. it has risen from about £75 to £185 per family of five; and its purchasing power is nearly as great as that of £400 in 1820. A few artisans' families earn about £185, and would not gain by an equal distribution of wealth: but they have only enough for a healthy and many-sided life.

In the 5th ed. (p. 751 n.) the figure "£37" in the second line was changed to "£40", and the figure "£185" in the same line to "£200". The words "a few artisans' families earn about £185" was replaced by the words "some artisans' families earn about £200".

The only changes made in the 6th ed. (p. 751 n.) were the insertion of the word "over" before "£200", and a reference back to "page 713". This footnote was deleted from the 7th ed.

c. In the 1st ed. (p. 45) there were the following concluding sentences to this paragraph which was there in the text:

And therefore in judging the action of our forefathers at the beginning of this century we must always remember that in their time every check to the production of wealth was likely to cause a loss of life to English soldiers, and increased the risk of their losing that national liberty which was dearer than life. Even when the war was over, the destruction of wealth which it had caused, though partially disguised by an artificial inflation of prices, rendered it very difficult for them to rate material wealth as low as it should be rated in comparison with the health and happiness and education of human beings.

In the 2nd ed. (p. 45 n.) the foregoing sentences in the 1st ed. were replaced by the following sentence with which the footnote was concluded:

> And at the beginning of this century every check to the production of wealth was likely to cause a loss of life to English soldiers, and increased the risk of their losing that national liberty which was dearer than life.

This sentence was deleted from the 7th ed.

a. So since the 5th ed. (p. 752). In the 1st ed. (p. 47) this paragraph ran as follows:

We have been looking at this movement from the English point of view. But other nations are taking their share in it. In America and other new countries, growth has been so rapid, and migration of the people so unceasing as to hinder the careful thinking out of the problems of social economy. But America faces new practical difficulties with such intrepidity and directness that she is already contesting with England the leadership in economic affairs; and she will probably before long take the chief part in pioneering the way for the rest of the world. Already she supplies many of the most instructive instances of the latest economic tendencies of the age, such as the growing democracy of trade and industry, the development of speculation and trade combination in every form.

In the 2nd ed. (p. 47) it ran as follows:

We have been looking at this movement from the English point of view. But other nations are taking their share in it. America faces new practical difficulties with such intrepidity and directness that she is already contesting with England the leadership in economic affairs; she supplies many of the most instructive instances of the latest economic tendencies of the age, such as the growing democracy of trade and industry, and the development of speculation and trade combination in every form, and she will probably before long take the chief part in pioneering the way for the rest of the world.

It remained in this form until the 5th ed.

b. With the exception of the first clause of the first sentence this paragraph dates from the 2nd ed. (p. 47).

In the 2nd ed. this first clause ran as follows: "Nor is Australia showing less signs of vigour than her elder sister; she has indeed some advantage...etc." The present form of this clause was adopted in the 5th ed. (p. 752).

PAGE 753

a. So since the 5th ed. (p. 753) where the words "They thus differ from the English" replaced the words "They are thus in strong contrast to the English", dating from the 1st ed. (p. 48).

b. So since the 5th ed. (p. 753) where the words "Appendix B" replaced the words "the next chapter", dating from the 1st ed. (p. 49).

EDITORIAL APPENDIX TO
APPENDIX A

MARSHALL'S REPLY TO CRITICISMS BY
WILLIAM CUNNINGHAM

In vol. II of the *Economic Journal* (September 1892) William Cunningham published an article entitled "The Perversion of History", in the course of which he attacked some of Marshall's views on economic history as set out in the opening chapters of the *Principles*—Appendices A and B in the present edition.

In this article Cunningham accused Marshall of making facile generalisations on economic history, which were based, not on a careful and thorough study of the facts, but on the underlying assumption "that the same motives have been at work in all ages, and have produced similar results, and that, therefore, it is possible to formulate economic laws which describe the action of economic causes at all times and in all places".

Marshall defended himself against Cunningham's criticisms in an article entitled "A Reply", which appeared in the same issue of the *Economic Journal* (September 1892).

The text of Marshall's article ran as follows:

A REPLY

DR CUNNINGHAM's suggestions as to the way in which the earlier chapters of my *Principles* were written, are not well founded. I once purposed to write a treatise on economic history, and for many years I collected materials for it. Afterwards I selected such part of these as helped to explain why many of the present conditions and problems of industry are only of recent date[1], and worked it into the chapters in question. But they took up much more space than could be spared for them. So I recast and compressed them; and in the process they lost, no doubt, some sharpness of outline and particularity of statement. Nothing was retained that was not needed for use later on. These two chapters are a mere introduction; they have no claim to be a history: but they were not written without due consideration of those simple and well-known "actual facts", which Dr Cunningham supposes me to have neglected.

Dr Cunningham is mistaken in supposing that my book proceeds on "the underlying assumption...that the same motives have been at work in all ages, and have produced similar results...and that the same laws hold good." On the contrary, the chapter on The Growth of Economic Science insists that modern economists are learning from biology "that if the subject-matter of a science passes through different stages of development, the laws of one stage will seldom apply without modification to others";[2] and my definition of an economic or other social law is "a statement that a certain course of action may be expected under certain conditions from the members of a social group."[3] As an illustration of this, it is urged that "to wrest from history her true teaching on the subject [of land tenure] requires the effects of the common holding of land in the past to be analysed, so as to discover how far each of them is likely to act always in the same way; how far to be modified by

---

[1] The chief of these problems I took to be "whether it is really impossible that all should start in the world with a fair chance of leading a cultured life, free from the pains of poverty and the stagnating influence of excessive mechanical toil" [a] (p. 3).

[2] *Principles*, [b] Book I, ch. IV, §7. See also [c] *Present Position of Economics*, §§3–7.

[3] From the chapter on the Methods of Study, [d] p. 83 of the second edition. I am writing in Switzerland, and am unable to supply the references to the first edition.

---

a. Page 4 in vol. I of the present edition.

b. Appendix B, §7 in vol. I of the present edition.

c. This was Marshall's Inaugural Lecture at Cambridge, which is reprinted in *The Memorials of Alfred Marshall*. Edited by A. C. Pigou (pp. 152–74).

d. Page 33 in vol. I of the present edition.

changes in the habits, the knowledge, the wealth, and the social organization of mankind."[1] The whole volume is indeed occupied mainly in showing how similar causes acting on people under dissimilar conditions produce more or less divergent effects. The leading motive of its argument is the opposite of that which Dr Cunningham ascribes to it.[2]

Dr Cunningham has misread what I have said as to the relation of the classical theory of rent to mediaeval land tenure. He states that I "say that it [Ricardo's theory of rent] will gradually produce a solvent which will explain much that is now unintelligible in mediaeval economic history". But what I really say is (*Present Position*, p. 50), "We are able to cross-examine the facts of modern India; and I believe that our science working on these facts will gradually pro duce a solvent which will explain", etc.; and again (p. 48), "Economic science has done much, and will I believe do a great deal more in applying contemporary observation of the East to explain the economic past".[3] These sentences indicate the drift of the argument in the five pages, at the end of which occur the words quoted by Dr Cunningham. To represent me therefore as holding "that when we possess Ricardo's theory of rent we know the inner working of the determination of rent in all ages", is as though an engineer had urged that coal in gaseous mines should be riven by plugs of quicklime expanded by water, and a critic had represented him as suggesting that it should be done by mere jets of water.[4]

1 e P. 87, footnote.
2 Dr Cunningham refers us to an article in which he maintains that "economics is not a science of 'cause and effect', but a pure science like logic or geometry, where this conception of 'cause' is not appropriate". I hold on the contrary that economics is a science akin to biology, and not to logic; and that the conception of cause and effect is appropriate to it. There is therefore no common ground for the discussion of what the methods of economics *ought* to be, and I confine myself to observing that he is mistaken as to what my method is.
3 See also the latter half of *Principles*, f I, II, §2.
4 In an article on *What did our Forefathers mean by Rent?* in *Lippincott's Magazine* for February 1890, Dr Cunningham bases a similar criticism on a like misquotation, saying "Those who hold that Ricardo's theory can help to supply 'a solvent which will explain much that is unintelligible in mediaeval economic history',

e.   Pages 775–6 in vol. 1 of the present edition.
f.   Appendix A, §2 in vol. 1 of the present edition

I will venture to trespass on the patience of the reader by explaining my position on this subject rather fully. I long held the somewhat extreme views which were once common in historical literature as to the habits of thought and action of the rural classes in primitive times. I thought that the sway of custom was then practically absolute in many relations of life; and I looked on the facts of custom as generally ultimate, and incapable of being analysed and explained. I have not departed very far from this position, and I still think it is in a great measure true. But lately some historians of mediaeval times have assigned to custom a rather narrower scope and a rather greater pliability than before.[1] I believe that such a movement might easily be pushed too far; but that it is proceeding on the right lines, and that, pursued cautiously and with moderation, it may add much to our knowledge. The chief object of what little I have said on the subject was to make one suggestion which I hoped might possibly be of use to those whose knowledge of mediaeval history is greater than mine; and who desire as far as possible to trace to their roots in human nature the causes that have made successive customs grow, change, and decay under the varying circumstances of time and place, and with the ceaseless development of social and political conditions, of trade and the arts of production.

My starting point was in the teaching of Sir Henry Maine and others that, since people brought up under the influence of custom have habits of mind *not* like ours, they are, for that very reason, able to persuade themselves that they are adhering to custom, when they are really modifying it. They adopt different means for attaining their ends from those which we do, and are not nearly as conscious of what they are doing. But I believe that the desire to do what is best for oneself is seldom wholly absent from human nature.

appear to take for granted that mediaeval and modern rents are closely similar." And in his Presidential Address to Section F of the British Association in 1891, he referred his hearers to that article with the suggestions that what I said on this subject was "meant as a sort of scientific witticism", and that I was "making a joke".

[1] Among the most recent instances of this tendency are Prof. Vinogradoff's *Villainage in England* and Prof. Ashley's Introduction to M. Coulanges' *Origin of Property in Land*.

Habit and prescription do indeed prevent many kinds of original individual action from being thought of at all, and they prohibit others: but there always remains a fringe of debatable ground in which a pushing character can assert itself. Those who know best the rural districts of England, or parts of the Continent or of India in which the mediaeval tone lingers most, recognise the most fully how under a very still surface there may be running many keen little pursuits of private gain; and they tell quaint stories of sly devices for getting the best of one's neighbours even in the quietest corners of the world. The very quiet affords time and opportunity for elaborate manœuvring in small matters.

To hold this is quite consistent with the belief that in backward times and places there are many rights and dues which are, for a while at least, as rigidly fixed by custom as they could be by a modern law or a contract made out on stamped parchment. Primitive land tenures "depend on general understandings", and these in so far as they are capable of being expressed in modern business language, are generally to the effect that "the ownership of land is vested not in an individual but in a firm, of which one member or members is the sleeping partner, and another member or group...is the working partner....When the sleeping partner...is restrained by law, or custom which has the force of law, from turning the cultivator out of his holding by an arbitrary increase of the payments exacted from him or by any other means...the payment made by the working partner is not a rent at all, but is that fixed sum or that part of the proceeds which the constitution of the firm binds him to pay."[1]

---

[1] [g]From the first section of my chapter on Land Tenure. The picture of Mediaeval England which I had before my mind when writing this chapter resembled in its broad outlines that which is presented in Professor Vinogradoff's fascinating *Villainage in England*. I had indeed learnt something orally from his broad knowledge and clear insight, just at the time when I was most intent on the bearings of Indian experience on mediaeval tenures. I was then teaching Indian cadets at Oxford, as Richard Jones had done at Haileybury. Jones' book was one of the first on economics that I came across, and his suggestive teaching as to the contrast between Mediaeval and Indian tenures on the one hand and modern English on the other, gave a direction to a good deal of my subsequent reading.

---

g. Pages 637–8 in vol. 1 of the present edition.

If then all the conditions of social life remained stationary and free from external disturbances, the divisions between the partners might long remain as independent of the theory of rent, as the division of the profits between the debenture and the shareholders of a modern railway is of the theory of monopolies. But in fact custom is more or less plastic; and the theory of rent often gives the upper limit to the exactions which can be forced from the actual cultivator by a superior holder, who is in a strong position and is not effectively controlled by the supreme holder, the ruler of the land. When this limit is not nearly reached, an arbitrary increase of dues is indeed simply a tax; while [h] English officials, who exercise full power under a sense of duty towards the people, when they have to fix "rents" in a new district in the North, or at a periodical revision in the South, are consciously governed by such considerations as are discussed in economic textbooks under both the heads of "Rent" and "Taxation".[1] Most of the native landholders, on the other hand, like those in Mediaeval Europe, make no formal analysis: but occasionally it happens to some of them to have to consider whether the necessities of the tenants, with their existing habits, leave a surplus out of which they could (with sufficient pressure) meet increased claims, direct or indirect. And whenever this is the case, they offer unconscious illustrations of the law of rent; just as the expert cricketer fielding at slip, or the sailor bringing up his craft neatly to her buoy, does of the laws of mechanics.

But there is a difficulty. The more primitive the people, the slower and slighter, the less obtrusive and the more "subterranean" are the currents of change; they do not obtrude themselves in the records of distant times, and they cannot

---

[1] Compare a foot-note in the chapter on Land Tenure ([i] p. 685 of 2nd edition of my *Principles*). Some aspects of the question were brought before the readers of this Journal last September in Mr Goodrich's interesting article on *Land Revenue in Madras*.

---

h. The "English officials", of whom Marshall was speaking here, were of course members of the Indian Civil Service serving in India.

i. Pages 641 n.–3 n. in vol. 1 of the present edition.

always easily be brought to light without a clue where to search for them. The geologist studies the subterranean waters of his own country on the spot; he analyses their causes, and finds out the mechanical and chemical conditions by which their paths have been directed. Equipped with this reasoned experience, he comes with a great advantage to the obscure questions suggested by the slender records of travellers in a new country, when they tell of lakes with no exit, and of rivers rising from the ground. Now my only suggestion was that the economic historian should in like manner explore contemporary customs on the spot; and that, aided in like manner by modern analysis, he should use his knowledge to guide him in searching the slender records of mediaeval customs for subterranean channels of change: we can examine and cross-examine the living, but not the dead. Whether the suggestion is a fruitful one, time alone can show. But it is clearly not of the same character as Dr Cunningham supposed it to be, when once and again he omitted as immaterial the middle words of the sentence which he quoted.[1]

This misapprehension of the aim and substance of what I have said on the subject of rent is however only partly to be accounted for by his having read it hastily. Some misunderstanding would have been almost necessarily caused by the fact that Ricardo's teachings on rent do not appear to him to have the same general import as they do to me. For I regard them as containing a living principle applicable, with proper modifications, to the income derived from almost

---

[1] Some of the points on which Indian experience seems to be suggestive are:—
i. the modes in which custom may be evaded without being openly broken; ii. The real vagueness and elasticity of some classes of customary rights, which at first sight appears definite and rigid; iii. The tendency of even well-informed observers to take little account of exceptions to the rule that dues and other payments are fixed by custom; though when asked to enumerate the cases that really conform to the rule, they find that in the aggregate these are less important than those that do not conform; iv. The wide area covered in the course of a few generations by causes that forcibly disturb social and economic conditions; such as famine, pestilence, war, civil commotion, the migration of courts, the rise and fall or change of abode of leading families, the migration of industries, etc. (in India inundations and change of river beds also are important); v. The many various ways in which such changes as these render old customs inapplicable and deprive traditional rights of all exact meaning; and vi. The rapidity with which such disturbances pass from memory and new customs acquire prestige; though of course nature repairs her ravages, whether physical or moral, less rapidly in a Northern than in a tropical climate.

every variety of Differential Advantage for production; and applicable also under almost every variety of rights as to property, dues, and freedom of action, whether those rights be upheld by law or by custom: while he regards them as applicable only to the rents of farms from which "all the corn is taken to one market".[1]

To begin with, though the matter is not of great importance, it seems doubtful whether, as a matter of history, this particular case ever occurred to Ricardo at all: for there was little corresponding to it in the circumstances in which he lived. Even now when modern machinery has centralized the milling trade, the accounts of farmers when they claim to be assessed to the income tax under Schedule D (instead of B), are a good deal complicated by their domestic consumption of farm produce. And in Ricardo's time corn was commonly taken to local mills; and much of what was consumed by the agricultural classes, an appreciable part of the whole crop of the country, never went to market at all: and the same was true, though in a less degree, of mutton, wool, and other things.

But even if this particular case ever did occur to Ricardo, it seems to me quite certain that he did not limit his reasonings in any way to it. What he did (for it is much the simplest and easiest, though not the only possible course) was to reckon the value of the produce *as that which it would have fetched if it had been all sent to the same market.* But this method of reckoning is consistent with a very broad and elastic application of those general principles of which the case referred to by Dr Cunningham is but one special illustration.[2]

The belief that the Classical theory of rent is bound down to that case has I think never been entertained by those who hold that Ricardo's principles of analysis, however incompletely developed at present, and however inadequate as yet

---

[1] In his article in *Lippincott* he says that Ricardo's "law assumes that the produce of the land is taken to market", the word "one" being omitted.

[2] The term "subsistence farming" has several senses: I hold that in some the theory is directly applicable to it, in others hardly at all. Even when so little of the produce is taken to market that there is no true market price, the general principles of Ricardian analysis can often be applied without using the term "market price". But in some cases and especially those in which the terms of partnership between the different holders of the land are "fixed and unalterable, the theory of rent has but little direct application", as I have said before.

for the very difficult tasks with which they have to deal, have done much already and will do more hereafter to help us to understand economic facts. If in my own small way I have on the one hand endeavoured to indicate how the general scope of the theory may be extended, I have striven on the other hand with no less care to show how inapplicable is the rigid letter of the theory even to the case of so-called competition rents in modern England, unless account is taken of a great variety of delicate and intricate side-issues and modifying causes.

In comparison with this difference of opinion as to the general import of Ricardo's teachings as to Rent, it is a matter of small significance that I am unable to follow Dr Cunningham's application of them to particular problems. He says that according to Ricardo the diminished area of corn-growing in the Tudor times ought to have synchronized with a fall, and not a rise, in money rents. I hold on the contrary that Ricardo's teachings show, firstly, that the influx of silver in the Tudor times would have caused a rise in money rents, even though other causes might have been tending slightly to depress real rents: secondly, that a diminution in the area of corn-growing might be due to any of several causes; and that if due to some of these causes, it would result in a rise; if due to others, in a fall of real rents: and thirdly, that the particular cause which was the most prominent at the time, viz. a diversion of land from corn-growing to meet the new demand for wool, would produce a twofold rise in real rents. For it would necessitate more intensive cultivation, and thus diminish the return to the marginal dose of labour and capital and therefore raise the value of each quarter of corn; and this in its turn would enable a smaller quantity of corn to suffice to remunerate the farmer for every other dose of labour and capital; and therefore a larger corn-surplus, or corn-rent, would remain for the landlord.[1] I believe this reasoning to be a well-known

[1] Thus the rise in money rent to be expected under Ricardo's theory, as I hold it, is threefold in all. And I had always supposed that what needs explanation in the history of rents during this period is not the fact that some of them rose much, but the fact that others did not so rise. A good deal has been written to account for this latter fact; but I doubt whether we yet know all the causes of it.

example of that set of doctrines which economists have in their minds when they speak of Ricardo's characteristic teachings as to rent.

I will now pass to Dr Cunningham's minor points and take them in his order.

1. In the great empires and high civilizations of Athens and Rome, the machinery of commerce was of course highly developed; but the sentence which describes how the Greeks failed to anticipate modern economic problems, refers specially to those problems mentioned at the beginning of this paper, which are concerned with the life of the workers rather than the machinery of commerce.[1]

With regard to the business character of the Romans, I say in the second edition:—"They were strong and daring, steady of purpose, and abundant of resource: they had in constant use all the faculties that are required for business enterprise; though as a rule they preferred to give themselves to war and politics. Singularly free from the restraints of custom, they shaped their own life for themselves with a deliberate choice that had never been known before: in fact, partly in consequence of the unity of the imperial power and the wide diffusion of the Roman language, there was in some important respects more freedom of commerce and of movement throughout the civilized world in the days of the Roman Empire than even now."[2] The last lines indicate

---

[1] jIt runs, "The Greeks were more modern in many respects than the peoples of Mediaeval Europe, and in some respects were even in advance of our own time. But they did not attain to the conception of man as man; they regarded slavery as an ordinance of nature; they tolerated agriculture, but they looked on all other industries as involving degradation; and modern economic problems were unknown to them." *Principles*, p. 18. The same phrase however occurred on p. 16, with only a slight indication in the preceding paragraph that there was a special reference to "Methods of Industry".

[2] kP. 20. In the first edition the middle of the passage was slightly different and spoke of the withdrawal of the leading Romans under the Empire from business. I was warned that this might be thought to introduce controversial matter; and, as it was not essential to my purpose, I softened it. But I think it was true as it stood. The wealth of individual Romans has always been notorious; it has only recently

---

j. The references in this footnote to *Principles*, p. 18 and p. 16 apply to page 729 and page 728 in vol. 1 of the present edition.

k. For the final version of the passage quoted by Marshall see page 730 in vol. 1 of the present edition. The earlier versions of this passage are reproduced in full in editorial note c to page 730.

sufficiently for the purpose of this particular chapter the existence of a highly organized machinery of commerce.

The notion that the Greeks and Romans were almost as modern in economic matters as in others is not a new one; a long while ago I studied it with a good deal of interest, and a rather strong hope that I might think it true. But I could not find what I wanted. For, though their economic analysis and theory was often lighted up by flashes of brilliant insight, and elevated by a philosophic perception that wealth is not an end but a means to the higher life of the (full free) citizen; yet it seemed to me not to be free from the same kind of weakness as has been found in their physical science. I thought that it was not really modern, as regards scientific method; and that the tone in which those who bore the brunt of industrial work were spoken of, was very far removed from us.[1]

The power of wealth at Rome was great; the highest education was occasionally given to slaves as a matter of business; and there were some apparent resemblances between the relations of labour and capital there and in modern England; but they seem to me to be generally superficial only and not real. This however belongs to a class of questions on which there will always be some differences of

been surpassed in England and America, and as there were no stock-exchange securities then, a rich man could not easily keep his wealth together without taking some sort of part in its management. But most of it had its origin in the administration of the Provinces; it was dug out with the sword and not the spade. The Senators were "in fact as well as in law" confined in the main to agriculture and allied businesses among which may be reckoned quarrying, brick, lime and pottery making, and so on. The Equites were often pushing and "smart" in financial and other businesses. But even they owed much of their wealth to farming the taxes, and other political work, while—the most significant fact of all—the richest of them were personal favourites of the Emperor. Rome's trade consisted of imports with scarcely any exports; and bore but a partial resemblance as regards mere machinery, and scarcely any real resemblance as regards its influences on the character of the people, to the trade of Venice or Florence or Bruges, based as that was on manufactures in which the leading citizens took a worthy pride. I have not access to Mommsen's *History* just now. But I am sure I should not regard the passages, to which Dr Cunningham refers on p. 495, as inconsistent with my opinions as to Roman business and industry. For when forming those opinions, I knew Mommsen's economic chapters almost by heart; and I read them again when writing the passage now under discussion.

[1] Had this been otherwise classical thoughts might have exerted more influence for good on mediaeval economics, and the condition of the industrial classes might have been much higher than it is. See *Principles*, II, IV, §1.

1.   Appendix B, §1 in vol. 1 of the present edition.

opinion; and perhaps I should have expressed my own with more reserve. I will add that much in Cairnes' *Slave Power* might have been taken with little change from Mommsen; but this seems to prove not that Rome did care, but that the Slave States did not care much for the modern economic problems to which I have specially referred.

2. As regards mediaeval free cities, I do not hold the opinions Dr Cunningham attributes to me, and I cannot guess why he supposes I do.[1]

3. As to his ᵐthird point, his criticism turns mainly on the word "sheep" which he has introduced into his citation of a sentence of mine. The original runs: "Thus the English large farm was the forerunner of the English factory in the same way as the English archer was the forerunner of the skill of the English artisan." The English farm did not "introduce" the factory, any more than archery introduced artisan work: but in each case character and habits formed by success in one occupation lead to a similar success in another.[2]

4. As to his ⁿfourth point, I have not much ground for

---

[1] The sentence which he quotes from my *Elements* (where, by the way, the reference to the mediaeval towns is compressed into a short paragraph) has no meaning by itself. Its first words are, "This modern view"; which is explained in the preceding sentence as the notion that the "well-being of the industrial classes...is an important end in itself and not merely an important condition of political and military strength." His quotation begins with the second word of the sentence.

[2] The sentence quoted in the text is the conclusion of a rather long discussion of the ways in which "the capitalistic organization of agriculture pioneered the way for that of manufacture". The chief of them was the early conversion of labour dues into money payments, and the relaxation of the bonds of custom of which this was partly cause and partly effect; while perhaps the next was the practice of primogeniture. The tenant's practice of borrowing from his landlord not only the land but also the capital invested in improvements began early, continued steadily, and was an important part of the movement. When the time came for a great extension of sheep-farming, the habits already formed developed very large pastoral farms; and these same habits later developed very large arable farms to meet the special needs of a later time.

---

m. Cunningham criticized Marshall for regarding "the large sheep farms of the Tudor times as precursors of the English factory system". For the final and earlier versions of the passage referred to, see page 742 in vol. 1 of the present edition and editorial note **a** to that page.

n. Cunningham objected to the phrase "all writers on money before the sixteenth century" on the ground (i) that it was too wide, (ii) that he doubted whether "the net wealth of a nation" was even

complaint; for I must have omitted some words, or the copy-ist must have made some slip in the sentence, which speaks of all "writers on money before the sixteenth century". I did not intend to make a collective statement with regard to all the writers up to that time from the beginning of the world; I was thinking chiefly of those who supported the policy of the staple towns. But though it may not be easy to discover what that sentence did mean, the preceding sentence seems to express distinctly an opinion inconsistent with, and thus to exclude, the particular meaning Dr Cunningham has suggested.[1]

5. In the footnote on °p. 42 of the *Principles*, I have referred wrongly to Prof. Ochenkowski. He had spoken of "industry showing itself as sensitive (empfindlich) about the full enjoyment of its freedom, and in particular as leaving those places in which encroachments had been made on the privileges granted by the Kings" ("Rechte...welche durch die Könige den Städten gewährt wurden"). His statement is quite explicit; there was no room for a conjecture that he was alluding to the action of Gilds; and there was no need to refer to the Rolls to prove that he was not. But unfor-tunately I made a note of the passage as illustrating the mobility of labour in the Middle Ages, which I believe to have been much greater than is generally supposed; and

[1] The preceding sentence runs:—"On the whole mediaeval opinions as to the relation of money to national wealth...are to be regarded as confused, through want of a clear understanding of the functions of money, rather than as wrong in conse-quence of a deliberate assumption that the increase of the net wealth of a nation can be effected only by an increase of the stores of the precious metals in her." By this I designed to express the fact that early writers did *not* analyse in modern fashion the notions referred to; and the following sentence, which Dr Cunningham quotes, was meant merely to qualify this by saying that assumptions of the kind would be needed for a logical defence of some of their words. I really had in my mind men's action rather than their words; but the sentence does not say so, and I cannot defend it. When writing this chapter I happened to be reading the latter part of Professor Ochenkowski's *Entwicklung*, which contains opinions on the con-trast between mediaeval and mercantile views as to imports and exports of the precious metals similar to those expressed by Dr Cunningham (see especially Ochenkowski, pp. 211–13). I agree with them generally but not entirely.

---

discussed by medieval writers at all. Marshall deleted the criticized passage from the 3rd ed. See editorial note **e** to page 754 of vol. 1 in the present edition.

o. See editorial note **c** to page 748 in vol. 1 of the present edition somehow that note got associated in my mind with another cause of such migration, namely, the excessive regulations of the Gilds. I then entered the reference under this heading without looking at Ochenkowski again. It was a most reprehensible piece of carelessness.

But the Gilds to which I referred were those existing at the time; that is, chiefly Gild Merchants who persistently and with evil results regulated industry, and kept it within narrow and artificial lines.[1] I spoke of the places where industries "were over-regulated by the Gilds"; but Dr Cunningham has converted "Gilds" into "Craft Gilds", though there is no reference in the note or anywhere near it to Craft Gilds; and in this case again his criticism turns mainly on the word which he has himself inserted in my sentence.

On the whole, then, Dr Cunningham has discovered one sentence in which there has been a slip, and which is not defensible, even if it is intelligible; and also one wrong reference. Further he and I differ in opinion as to Roman business, and other matters. But, speaking broadly, his criticisms proceed on assumptions that I hold opinions which in fact I do not hold, and which I believe I have not expressed; while in several cases I think I have definitely expressed opposite opinions. The criticisms in his present papers are part of a series, all with the same general purport, which he has recently published.[2] The first were in a paper read before the British Association in 1889, in which he represented my attitude towards the main body of the historical school of economists as one of antagonism. I think, indeed, that the most urgent need of our age is the investigation of contemporary economic conditions; but my position is, and always has been, one of respect and gratitude to those who, without contemning the good work that has already been done in scientific analysis, have given their lives to the study of economic history.

---

[1] Mr Gross has made the evidence of this clearer than before. See especially the references to vol. II of his *Gild Merchant* given in note 3 on p. 43 of his vol. I. He shows (*ib.* p. 114) that craft gilds did exist in the XIIth as well as the XIIIth centuries.

[2] References to the papers have already been given. They are: British Association 1889 and 1891, *Lippincott*, Feb. 1890, *Economic Review*, Jan. 1892.

Thus his endeavours to interpret me to other people are almost as conspicuous for their industry as for their incorrectness. Some of them may be read by foreign historical economists and others who do not know my views at first hand; and the fact that he is a colleague, and was formerly (as he has just indicated) a pupil of mine might reasonably suggest to such readers that he could not fail to have entered into my point of view, to speak on full information, and to report me accurately. For these reasons I have broken through my rule of not replying to criticisms.

This breach of my rule makes me the more anxious to express my regret for the apparent want of due respect and attention which I have shown to the other criticisms of my *Principles*. Several of them derive such weight from their substance and from the names of those who wrote them, that I certainly ought to have made some reply to them. But in the aggregate they are not very much less bulky than the unwieldy Volume to which they refer: I do not work fast; and if I attempted to reply as I should wish to do, my progress with writing my second Volume, which is now slow, would altogether cease. So any acknowledgments I have been able to make to my critics have been in deeds rather than words. I can only express briefly my thanks for the good will, fairness and generosity of interpretation of those who on the whole condemned the book, as well as of those who on the whole approved it. I have tried to profit by their warnings; and many of the changes made in the second edition are due to their hints. Most of these changes are in wording and in matters of detail; I have modified, and tried to fortify or to make more lucid, the passages to which exception has been taken. But in a few instances the necessary changes have been on a larger scale. In particular the decision to bring back the study of Rent in relation to Cost of Production, to the place that had been originally designed for it in the general Theory of the Equilibrium of Demand and Supply, was caused by my having failed to make myself clear to two such able economists and such careful and generous critics as Professor Pierson and Professor Clark. The next most important change, the further analysis of the notion of Marginal Cost in connection with the Law of Increasing Return, seemed called for by some suggestive remarks of Professor Edgeworth and Mr Henry Cunynghame; and I owe much to the private as well as the printed suggestions of the illustrious Professor Wagner, and of Professor Ashley, Professor Nicholson, Dr Bonar, and others. To all these I would express my thanks, and my regrets that I must have seemed to pass by without due regard many important remarks for the discussion of which I could not find place in the already over-weighted *Principles*, and which I have been unable to acknowledge in the ordinary way in special articles.

ALFRED MARSHALL

APPENDIX B

THE GROWTH OF ECONOMIC SCIENCE

PAGE 754

a. Except where otherwise stated in the editorial notes, the wording of this Appendix dates substantially from the 1st ed.

In the first four editions the subject-matter of this Appendix was placed in Book I, chapter IV, entitled "The Growth of Economic Science". In the 5th edition this chapter was constituted Appendix B with the same title.

b. The following concluding sentences of this paragraph in the 1st ed. (p. 50) were deleted from the 2nd ed.:

Thinkers who had not learnt to break up the problems of physics, and work out one part of them at a time, were not likely to engage in the more difficult and less obvious task of breaking up social questions and dealing first with one order of difficulties and then with another. The Greeks and Romans would not therefore have made very great progress in economics, had they given full attention to the study; but in fact they gave very little. And further, what they have written on economics is not only slight in comparison with their work in other branches of social and political philosophy, but also less applicable to the conditions of modern times.

c. This sentence dates from the 3rd ed. (p. 52).

d. So since the 3rd ed. (p. 52) where this marginal summary replaced the following summary dating from the 1st ed. (p. 51): "The study of economics was stimulated by the discovery of the mines and the trade-routes of the New World."

e. In the 1st ed. (p. 51 n.) the following footnote was attached to the word "nation":

> Much study has been given both in England and Germany to mediaeval opinions as to the relation of money to national wealth. On the whole they are to be regarded as confused through want of a clear understanding of the functions of money, rather than as wrong in consequence of a deliberate assumption that the increase of the net wealth of a nation can be effected only by an increase of the stores of the precious metals in her. But there are perhaps no writers on money before the sixteenth century who did not occasionally use arguments based on this assumption.

In the 2nd ed. (p. 51 n.), after the first two sentences as just quoted, the footnote continued as follows:

> And, though there are perhaps no writers on money before the sixteenth century who did not occasionally use arguments based on this assumption, yet their preference for the precious metals and other durable things had some slight basis in reason, and is to be found even in the writings of the astute Sir W. Petty towards the end of the seventeenth century. He says, *Political Arithmetick*, ch. 1, "The great and ultimate effect of trade is not Wealth at large, but particularly abundance of Silver, Gold and Jewels, which are not perishable nor so mutable as other commodities, but are Wealth at all times and all places: Whereas abundance of Wine, Corn, Fowls, &c. are Riches but *hic et nunc*, so as the raising of such commodities and the following of such Trade which does store the country with Gold, Silver, Jewels, &c. is profitable before others."

The whole footnote was deleted from the 3rd ed. in response to criticisms by Cunningham. See the Editorial Appendix to Appendix A (pp. 746–7 above).

PAGE 755

a. So since the 5th ed. (p. 755), where this sentence replaced the following sentences dating from the 1st ed. (p. 52):

It is not therefore to be wondered at that the Mercantilists are commonly believed to have promoted the state regulation of trade and industry. But they did not. The regulations and restrictions which are found in their systems belonged to the age; the changes which they set themselves to bring about were in the direction of the freedom of enterprise.

b. The following footnote was attached to the word "out" in the 1st ed. (pp. 52 n.–3 n.):

The tendency to exaggerate the importance of gold and silver as elements of national wealth was carried further by their opponents than by them. Much ingenuity had been spent in devising plans for preventing traders from taking gold and silver out of the country and for inducing them to bring gold and silver in; (a graphic account of these plans is given in Richard Jones' collected works). These regulations pressed with special weight on the India Company, which wanted to import goods direct from India, but which could find no market there for English goods; and had therefore to buy with silver or not at all. Its rival, the Levant Company, received the goods in Mediterranean ports after they had borne the expense of a long journey by land, but were able to pay for them by the sale of English goods. Mun writing on behalf of the India Company argued that the superior economy of the sea routes and direct dealing would enable them to supply England's demands for Oriental goods and yet to sell their surplus on the continent for more silver than they had originally exported. He pointed to the farmers burying their seed in the earth in expectation of an increased return in the next harvest. The State which should prohibit them from doing this, on the ground that they lessened the stock of corn in the country, would, he argued, be no more foolish than the State which forbad merchants to export silver, even when the ultimate result of their trade would bring more silver into the country than they had originally taken out. As the farmers enriched the country while engaged in pursuing their own gain, so would the merchants do, at all events if they were compelled to bring back in the long run as much silver as they took out. It is probable that he would have been willing to trust to the silver finding its own way back, but that he did not venture to say so. This is a good instance of the way in which practical needs have constantly suggested the inquiries which have resulted in additions to economic science.

In the 3rd ed. (p. 54 n.) this footnote was replaced by the following footnote: "Some account of the relations between mediaeval and mercantile theories of money and trade will be given in the second volume of this work." This latter footnote was deleted from the 5th ed.

c. The remainder of this paragraph dates in its present form from the 5th ed. (p. 755), where it replaced the following paragraph dating from the 1st ed. (p. 53):

The Mercantilists indeed did not look beyond the immediate purpose for which they were contending; they did not dream of establishing a new principle of social and political life. But by raising the question whether the State would not benefit by allowing the trader to manage his business as he liked in one particular case, they had unwittingly started a new tendency of thought; and this moved on by imperceptible steps in the direction of economic freedom, being assisted on its way by the circumstances of the time, no less than by the tone and temper of men's minds in Western Europe. A little was done here, and a little there in England and Holland, in Italy and France; the steps are difficult to trace. It is not easy to tell how much each writer owes to the suggestions of others, nor how far he himself intended the suggestions which we with our later knowledge read into his passing hints. But we know that the broadening movement did go on till, in the latter half of the eighteenth century, the time was ripe for the doctrine that the well-being of the community almost always suffers when the State attempts to oppose its own artificial regulations to the "natural" liberty of every man to manage his own affairs in his own way.

In the 1st ed. a marginal summary was attached to this paragraph, in continuation of the marginal summary to the preceding paragraph ending with the words "loosen the fetters of trade", which ran as follows: "and started the movement towards economic freedom." This latter part of the summary was deleted from the 3rd ed.

d. This footnote dates from the 7th ed. (p. 755 n.). In the 2nd ed. (p. 53 n.) the following footnote was attached to the paragraph ending with the words "to manage his own affairs in his own way":

> For a sketch of the history the reader may be referred to Kautz's profound, just and suggestive *Die geschichtliche Entwicklung der National-oekonomie*, to Travers Twiss' *View of the Progress of Political Economy*, and to Dr Ingram's *History of Political Economy*.

In the 4th ed. (p. 54 n.) this footnote was expanded, and, after the references to Kautz and Travers Twiss, ran as follows:

> and to the histories of Professors Ashley, Cossa, Cunningham and Ingram, to Dr Bonar's *Philosophy and Political Economy*, and to various articles by Mr Hewins, Dr Stephen Bauer and others in the *Dictionary of Political Economy* and elsewhere.

This latter footnote, as a whole, was deleted from the 5th ed.

PAGE 756

a. In the 1st ed. (p. 53) there was the following additional clause in this summary after the word "natural;": "and that the welfare of the common people should be the first aim of the statesman." This clause was deleted from the 3rd ed.

b. So since the 3rd ed. (p. 56) where this marginal summary replaced the following summary dating from the 1st ed. (p. 55): "They thus gave to economics its modern philanthropic tone, but they also greatly influenced its abstract reasonings."

c. In its present form, the first sentence of this footnote dates from the 4th ed. (p. 55 n.) and the remainder of the footnote from the 3rd ed. (p. 55 n.).

In the 1st ed. (p. 53 n.) this footnote ran as follows:

> I pass by Cantillon, to whom is generally attributed the essay *Sur la Nature de Commerce*. The author of this essay was very acute and in some respects much ahead of his time. But he seems to me wanting in solidity, and I cannot agree with Jevons in regarding him as the true founder of modern Political Economy.

In the 2nd ed. (p. 53 n.) it ran as follows:

> I pass by Cantillon, whose essay *Sur la Nature de Commerce*, written in 1755, does indeed cover a wide range, and has even some claims to be called systematic. It is moreover very acute and in some respects much ahead of his time. But it seems to me wanting in solidity, and I cannot agree with Jevons in regarding its author as the true founder of modern Political Economy.

In the 3rd ed. (p. 55 n.) the first sentence ran as follows: "I pass by Cantillon, whose essay *Sur la Nature de Commerce*, written in 1755, covers a wide range, and has some claims to be called systematic." The remainder of the footnote was reworded as in the present edition.

d. So since the 2nd ed. (p. 53 n.) where the words "writers on economic questions" replaced the words "the Mercantilist writers" in the 1st ed. (p. 53). With the exception of the last two sentences the whole of this footnote was placed in the text in the 1st ed. (pp. 53–4).

e. The following footnote attached to the word "classes" in the 1st ed. (p. 54 n.) was deleted from the 2nd ed.:

> It has been calculated that in 1787, while the clergy paid in taxes but a fourteenth part of their incomes, and the nobility paid a sixth of theirs, the great mass of the people paid two-thirds of theirs.

f. The following reference at this point in the 1st ed. (p. 54) was deleted from the 2nd ed.: "Comp. De Tocqueville's *Ancien Régime* and Maine's Ancient Law."

PAGE 757

a. So since the 3rd ed. (p. 56), where the last two clauses of this sentence replaced the following clause dating from the 1st ed. (p. 55): "the more excellent does his genius become."

b. This sentence dates from the 3rd ed. (p. 57).

c. This sentence dates from the 5th ed. (p. 757 n.).

d. The first two sentences of this footnote date from the 3rd ed. (p. 57 n.), and the third sentence from the 4th ed. (p. 57 n.).

PAGE 758

a. The word "careful" before the word "examination" dating from the 1st ed. (p. 56) was deleted from the 4th ed.

b. So since the 3rd ed. (p. 58) where this marginal summary replaced the following summary dating from the 1st ed. (p. 57): "but his chief work was to show how value by measuring motive affords a basis for applying scientific methods to the study of a large class of social phenomena."

    c. The following extract from Marshall's article "Mr Mill's Theory of Value" in the *Fortnightly Review*, April 1876, contains an expansion of the point made in this sentence:

It has been remarked that, in general, the truths by the discovery of which epochs in history have been made have been simple truths. An epoch has been created not by a new doctrine, but by the acquisition of the point of view from which the doctrine proceeded. A point of view was conquered for us by Adam Smith, from which a commodity is regarded as the embodiment of measurable efforts and sacrifices. Whosoever will put himself at this point of view may, with ease, see through fallacies which clouded the vision of statesmen not only of ancient times, but of an age that had gained the right point of view for the corresponding physical problem of the laws of motion of material masses.

The passage just cited will be found in *The Memorials of Alfred Marshall*, edited by A. C. Pigou, p. 126.

    d. This clause dates from the 3rd ed. (p. 58 n.).

    e. This final sentence dates from the 3rd ed. (p. 58 n.).

PAGE 759

    a. The following sentences at this point in the 1st ed. (p. 57) were deleted from the 2nd ed.

He led us to see how below the surface of a great part of human action there are motives which can be measured; and therefore can be analyzed and subjected to the processes of scientific reasoning. He thus pointed the way to applying powerful and exact methods of study to an important part of social phenomena.

    b. The remainder of this paragraph dates from the 3rd ed. (p. 59).

    c. So since the 3rd ed. where this marginal summary and that on page 760 in vol. 1 of the present edition replaced the following summaries dating from the 1st ed. (pp. 58–9):

The study of facts was carried on by Young, Eden, Malthus and others.

But the great forming mind after Adam Smith was that of Bentham.

755

He was an ardent reformer, but had an extravagant dread of insecurity.

His opposition to customary restrictions on trade for which no valid reason could be given was supported by the course of events, and the economists of the rising generation tended to ignore custom.

d. So since the 3rd ed. (p. 58 n.) where this footnote replaced the following footnote dating from the 2nd ed. (pp. 56 n.–7 n.):

> The relations of Value to Cost of Production had been indicated by the Physiocrats and by many earlier writers, among whom may be specially mentioned Cantillon (*Essai sur la Commerce* I, x, A.D. 1755), Locke (*Essay on Civil Government*, ch. V, A.D. 1689), Sir W. Petty (*Treatise on Taxes and Contributions,* A.D. 1667), who, in words that have often been quoted as containing the germs of much later work, argued that "if 100 men work ten years upon corn and the same number of men the same time upon silver, the net proceed of the silver is the price of the whole net produce of the corn;" to say nothing of some rather vague hints by Hobbes (1642–51) as to how plenty dependeth on labor and abstinence applied by man to working up and accumulating the gifts of nature by land and by sea—*proventus terræ et aquæ, labor et parsimonia.*

e. In the 1st ed. (p. 57) the substance of this sentence was placed in the text.

f. In the 1st ed. (p. 57) this clause, which was there placed in the text as a separate sentence, ran as follows: "And the work which he himself did, though not well arranged, is a perfect model of method so far as its substance goes." The clause in its present form dates substantially from the 2nd ed. (p. 57 n.) though it was there placed at the beginning of the footnote.

g. This sentence dates from the 5th ed. (p. 759 n.).

PAGE 760

a. Although the substance of the remainder of this section (§ 4) dates from the 1st ed. (pp. 58–60) the order and sequence of the sentences date from the 3rd ed. (pp. 60–1).

b. The words "and an ardent reformer" after the word "logician" dating from the 1st ed. (p. 58), were deleted from the 3rd ed.

c. The following sentences after the sentence ending with the words "circumstances of the age", in the 1st ed. (p. 59), were deleted from the 2nd ed.:

As we have seen, gilds and customs and prejudice opposed in vain the tendency to change: if they fortified themselves irresistibly in any town, the wave of progress simply avoided that town. It started rival industries in new districts where new methods could be adopted without opposition; and left the town with its obstructive trade regulations to silent decay.

a.   The following additional sentences and footnote at this point, in the 1st ed. (pp. 60–1), were deleted from the 2nd ed.:

A small party—it is said that at one time there were not more than a score of them—propounded a theory which was opposed to the prejudices of the age and which was received with ridicule. The Directors of the Bank of England passed a resolution opposed to it: but time was on the side of the economists: in a few years the course of events had proved that they were right, and the Bank of England erased its former resolution from the minutes[1].

[1] The doctrine of the economists, embodied in the great Bullion Report of 1810, ascribed the unfavourable Exchanges to an excessive issue of inconvertible bank notes. The Resolution in which the Bank Directors declare that they are "unable to discover any solid foundation for such a sentiment" was passed in 1819 and rescinded in 1827. The principle of the Bullion Report was adopted in 1819 by Parliament, but they had rejected it by a large majority in 1811.

b.   The following concluding sentences of this paragraph in the 1st ed. (p. 61) were deleted from the 2nd ed.:

And though the cause of free trade in other countries has been injured by the narrowness of those of its English advocates, who have refused to take account of any elements of the problem which were not practically important in their own country and their own time, yet this very narrowness has given them precision, lucidity and confidence; and has been of service to them for the immediate purposes of their struggle at home.

c.   So since the 7th ed. (p. 761 n.). In the first six editions there was a full stop after the word "developments.", and the footnote ran on as follows: "there is no truly English economist whose method resembles that of Ricardo; his power of threading his way...etc."

d.   The following sentence after the sentence ending with the word "work" in the 1st ed. (p. 60 n.) was deleted from the 4th ed.: "Even the ablest of them frequently undertake to refute him by establishing propositions which are consistent with his and often even involved in them."

e.   This and the next three sentences were inserted in the 5th ed. (p. 761 n.), where they replaced the following sentence dating from the 3rd ed. (pp. 61 n.–2 n.):

It is to be remembered however that his *Principles* was not originally designed for publication. It consists of terse notes, written for the benefit of himself and perhaps a few friends, on points of special difficulty.

f. This reference was inserted in the 7th ed. (p. 761 n.).

PAGE 762

a. So since the 2nd ed. (p. 61) where this paragraph and the first sentence of the next paragraph replaced the following sentences dating from the 1st ed. (p. 62):

Partly for the sake of simplicity of argument, Ricardo and his followers regarded man as so to speak a constant quantity, and gave themselves little trouble to study his variations. The people whom they knew most intimately were city men; and they sometimes took it for granted that other Englishmen were very much like those whom they knew in the city. They were aware that the inhabitants of other countries had peculiarities of their own; but they regarded such differences, when they thought of them at all, as superficial and sure to be removed as soon as other nations had got to know that better way which Englishmen were ready to teach them.

PAGE 763

a. So since the 2nd ed. (p. 62) where this sentence replaced the following sentence in the 1st ed. (p. 63):

It is therefore not a matter for wonder that the economists, flushed with their victories over a set of much more solid thinkers, did not trouble themselves to examine any of the doctrines of the socialists, and least of all their speculations as to human nature.

b. The first three sentences of this footnote date in their present form, from the 3rd ed. (pp. 63 n.–4 n.); while the remaining sentences were added in the 5th ed. (p. 763 n.).

In the 1st ed. (p. 63 n.) this footnote ran as follows:

As regards wages there were even some logical errors in the conclusions they deduced from their own premises. These errors when traced back to their origin are little more than careless modes of expression. But there were many hangers on of the science, who had no reverence for it, and used it simply as an engine for keeping the working classes in their place. Perhaps no other great school of thinkers has ever suffered so much from the way in which its hangers on and parasites, professing to simplify economic doctrines, really enunciated them without the conditions required to make them true. Miss Martineau for instance,

758

who wrote tales designed to enforce economic doctrines, when describing the course of reading by which she prepared herself, says: "In order to save my nerves from being overwhelmed by the thought of what I had undertaken, I resolved not to look beyond the department on which I was engaged." (*Autobiography*, I, 194). Yet she did not intend to be dishonest, as is proved by her later confession of a "suspicion that economic doctrines might be all wrong."

The last two sentences of the footnote just quoted were deleted from the 2nd ed.

c. So since the 3rd ed. (p. 64 n.) where this sentence replaced the following sentences dating from the 1st ed. (p. 63 n.).

> Half a century later Bastiat published, in opposition to the socialists, an extravagant doctrine to the effect that the natural organization of society under the influence of competition is the best not only that can be practically effected, but even that can be theoretically conceived. The lucidity of his style caused his works to have great vogue; but he really understood economic science, in the name of which he professed to write, scarcely better than did the socialists themselves.

PAGE 764

a. The following sentences in the 1st ed. (pp. 65–6) were deleted from the 2nd ed.:

The predominant position which that book held in England for a long time, and the dogmatism of some of its ardent admirers, have caused an impatient revolt against it. But meanwhile it has gone far towards forming the thoughts of nearly all the older living economists in England; and what is perhaps even more important, it has in a great measure determined the attitude which they take with regard to social questions.

PAGE 765

a. This sentence, in its present form, dates from the 4th ed. (p. 66). In the 1st ed. (p. 66) it ran as follows:

The new temper is shown alike in Jevons' subtle analysis of utility, in Cliffe Leslie's historical inquiries and in other many-sided original work that has been done in England by Bagehot, Cairnes and other writers who are yet living.

In the 3rd ed. (p. 66) it ran as follows:

The new temper is shown in Cliffe Leslie's historical inquiries, and in the many-sided work of Bagehot, Cairnes and other writers yet living; but above all in that of Jevons, which has secured a permanent and notable place in economic history by its rare combination of many various qualities of the highest order.

b.   The following opening sentence of this paragraph in the 1st ed. (p. 66) was deleted from the 3rd ed.: "As we saw at the end of the last chapter, England has recently made great advances in wealth and in knowledge, in temperance and in earnestness." The foregoing reference to "the end of the last chapter" applies to the end of Appendix A in vol. 1 of the present edition.

c.   This marginal summary dates from the 2nd ed. (p. 65).

d.   The words in parentheses in this sentence were inserted in the 3rd ed. (p. 66 n.).

PAGE 766

a.   This sentence dates in its present form from the 3rd ed. (p. 67), where it replaced the following sentence dating substantially from the 1st ed. (p. 67):

It has cleared the ground for newer and stronger machinery, which is being built up with the aid of the manifold experience got in the careful and exact work of modern science in its dealings both with the organic and inorganic world.

b.   This sentence dates from the 3rd ed. (p. 67).

c.   This paragraph dates from the 2nd ed. (p. 65).

d.   The first sentence of this paragraph was inserted in the 4th ed. (p. 68). The remainder of the paragraph dates in its present form from the 3rd ed. (p. 68), except for the insertion of the word "vigorous" before the word "thinkers" and the deletion of the word "many" before the word "signs", in the 4th ed.

In the 1st ed. (pp. 67–8) this paragraph ran as follows:

The American school of economists is sometimes understood to be the group of Protectionists who follow Carey's lead; but Carey owes many of his best thoughts on Protection to the German List: he did however good service in discovering that the early settlers in a new country often avoid, through fear of malaria and other causes, the soils which are ultimately the richest: and on this he based what he thought was a refutation of the chief doctrines of Malthus and Ricardo, but what was in reality only an addition to them. Absorbed in current politics, the older American school did little to extend the boundaries of economic science. But there are growing up in America new schools of thinkers, who are studying the science for its own sake; and there are many signs that America is on the way to take the same leading position in economic thought, that she has already taken in economic practice.

In the 2nd ed. (p. 66) the opening clause of the foregoing sentences ("The American...Carey's lead") was retained. The remaining clauses of the first sentence were deleted, but the last two sentences were retained as in the 1st ed.

e. So since the 3rd ed. (p. 68) where this sentence replaced the following clause dating from the 1st ed. (p. 68): "and the recent work of the Austrian economists is giving them a claim to be regarded apart from the Germans, among whom they have often been classed."

PAGE 767

a. The three last sentences of this footnote date in their present form from the 3rd ed. (p. 69 n.), apart from the insertion in the 7th ed. (p. 767 n.) of the reference to Miss Hirst's *Life of List*. In the first two editions these sentences ran as follows:

His *Outlines of a New System of Political Economy* appeared in Philadelphia in 1827, while Carey's first important work, his *Principles of Political Economy*, was not published till 1837-40. List's *Das nationale System der Politischen Oekonomie* was published in 1840.

PAGE 768

a. So since the 3rd ed. (p. 70), where the remaining clauses of this sentence replaced the following sentence dating from the 1st ed. (p. 69):

It is not therefore to be wondered at that Germans have insisted on and perhaps even exaggerated the fact that altruistic feelings have a much more limited scope in the economic relations between countries than in those between individuals.

b. The second clause of this marginal summary dates from the 3rd ed. (p. 70).

c. This clause, together with the footnote attached to it, was inserted in the 3rd ed. (p. 70).

d. So since the 7th ed. (p. 768) where the remaining clauses of this sentence replaced the following clauses dating from the 1st ed. (p. 70): "and to help us to understand the central plan, as it were, of the Divine Government of the world."

PAGE 769

a. The following marginal summary attached to the last two sentences of this paragraph in the 1st ed. (p. 71) was deleted from the 5th ed.: "Germans and English have much to learn from one another."

APPENDIX C

THE SCOPE AND METHOD OF
ECONOMICS

PAGE 770

a. The origin of the wording of Appendix C is shown throughout in the editorial notes.

In the 1st edition part of the subject-matter of this Appendix was placed in Book I, chapter v, "Methods of Study", and in the 2nd to the 4th editions in Book I, chapter v, "The Scope of Economics" and chapter vi, "Methods of Study. The Nature of Economic Law".

In the 5th and later editions the material, which had been greatly expanded in the 3rd edition, was divided between Book I, chapter ii, "The Substance of Economics" and chapter iii, "Economic Generalizations or Laws", and Appendix C, "The Scope and Method of Economics" and Appendix D, "Uses of Abstract Reasoning in Economics".

b. So since the 5th edition (p. 770). In the 2nd to the 4th editions (Book I, ch. v), the following footnote was attached to the title of the chapter, "The Scope of Economics": "The reader is referred to Mr Keynes' *Scope and Method of Political Economy* for a more full and detailed investigation of the subjects of this and the next chapters."

c. This paragraph dates in its present form from the 2nd ed. (Book I, ch. v, §1, p. 71) where it replaced the following sentences in the 1st ed. (Book I, ch. v, §1, p. 72):

Comte did good service in insisting on the unity that underlies social phenomena, but failed to show that there is no use in making special studies of certain classes of them.

COMTE's doctrine that all the aspects of social life are so closely connected that they ought to be studied together was one side of a great truth. But no serious attempt has yet been made to construct a social science that should do the same work for social life as a whole which has been done for one side of it by economics, young and full of imperfections as that is. Comte and Herbert Spencer have made epochs in thought, by their broad surveys and their suggestive hints: but there is as much reason as ever to fear that the whole world of man's actions is too wide and too various to be analyzed and explained by one intellectual effort.

d. The following footnote attached to the word "science" in the 3rd ed. (p. 73 n.) was deleted from the 5th ed.: "A less ambitious aim has been more nearly attained in the *Bau und Leben des Sozialen Körpers* of the eminent economist Professor Schäffle."

e. This and the next paragraph date substantially from the 1st ed. (pp. 72–3).

f. The words "on the other hand it must be fully conceded to Comte that...", and also the marginal summary to this paragraph, were inserted in the 2nd ed. (p. 72).

PAGE 771

a. So since the 2nd ed. (p. 72) where the words "Mill, conceding this continues:—" replaced the words in the 1st ed. (p. 73) "But, as Mill urges, Comte only proves what no thoughtful person would deny that 'a person...etc.'".

b. The following paragraph dating from the 2nd ed. (p. 73), which succeeded the paragraph ending with the words "social advancement", was deleted from the 5th ed.:

This is a valid answer to Comte's denial of the utility of an independent science of economics. But it does not show that the scope assigned to economics by Mill and his predecessors was exactly the right one. Any widening of that scope must no doubt result in some sacrifice of definiteness and precision, and the resulting loss may be greater than the gain. But it need not necessarily be so; and what is wanted is a general principle which shall determine the point in the widening of the scope of economics, at which the growing loss of scientific precision would begin to outweigh the gain of increasing reality and philosophic completeness. *[margin: On the other hand, the older economists did not show that the limits of their science were fixed in the best possible position.]*

c. The subject-matter of this section dates substantially from the 3rd ed. (Book I, ch. VI, §2, pp. 93–5), but it may be noted that the order of the sentences underwent extensive rearrangement in the 5th ed.

d. The following footnote attached to the word "inductions" in the 3rd ed. (p. 94 n.) was deleted from the 5th ed.:

Long chains of deductive reasoning are indeed directly serviceable in astronomy, in which nature herself has given practically exclusive possession to a few definite forces; and the astronomer's predictions of the movements of the solar system are subject to only one hypothesis, namely that nature will not bring into it any large external body for which he has not reckoned.

e. The first two clauses of this sentence date from the 3rd ed. (p. 94 n.) where they formed part of a footnote which ran as follows:

When the calculations of theoretical mechanics are applied in an engineering problem in which the forces of nature are few and definite, and the materials simple and homogeneous, they correspond roughly to nature—somewhat as does a view seen through a window-pane of inferior glass. The engineer for instance can calculate with fair precision the angle at which an ironclad will lose its stability in still water; but before he predicts how she would behave in a storm, he will avail himself of the observations of experienced sailors who have watched her movements in an ordinary sea. If her lines are new, but specific experience has been had of the speed of ships with nearly similar lines, he may perhaps calculate fairly well what her speed will be. But partly because rushing water lays aside all pretence of being a frictionless fluid, his theory will not enable him to give a good guess under conditions at all far away from specific experience: nor can he even now quite understand why a torpedo is so much more wasteful of propelling force than a fish at an equal distance below the surface. And throughout the whole of his work he has to be guided by specific observation more than by deductive reasoning as to the allowance to be made for flaws of material, and for the fitful action of natural forces.

The last three sentences of this footnote were deleted from the 4th ed.

f. So since the 5th ed. (p. 771 n.). This footnote, in its original version in the 1st ed. (pp. 73–4 n.), was attached to a paragraph in Book I, ch. v, § 1, which was deleted from the 2nd ed. The paragraph and footnote in the 1st ed. ran as follows:

The German school of historical economics

A position independent of Comte's, but in some respects allied to it, has been taken by the historical school of economists in Germany. They have been scarcely less eager than he was to insist on the solidarity of social phenomena; and some of them have spoken disparagingly of economic theory. But, on the other hand, they have carried the division of labour very far in special studies of economic facts, so that their work has thrown light on economic theory, has broadened it, has verified, and has corrected it; but, at the same time, has made use of its aid at almost every step.[1]

[1] Mill's controversy with Comte is still worth studying. Comte's arguments have recently been restated with great force and eloquence by Dr Ingram: but they do not appear to have shaken Mill's position that Comte, though right when he affirmed, was wrong when he denied. A long controversy has been waged in England, Germany and more recently in America, as to the right method of economic study. Perhaps nearly everyone has been right when he has affirmed that a certain method is useful; it has generally been the one best adapted for that part of the many-sided work of economics in which he has had the most interest. But he has been wrong in denying that other methods are useful: they may be applicable for purposes other than those of which he has been chiefly thinking. Reference has already been made (ch. iv, § 8) to the fact that the leaders of the German historical school are careful to avoid the extravagances into which some of their followers have drifted. It may be well to quote Wagner's own words when defending Schönberg's *Handbuch* against Schmoller's attacks: "We all, including I believe the chief representatives, other than Schmoller, of the historical school of National Economy, the founders of this movement, who must understand at least something of the historical conception—we all, Roscher and Knies not excepted, hold that...the identifying of economic history with economic theory (*Wirtschaftsgeschichte und Wirtschaftstheorie*) is not only not right, but is a confusion and an offence against the claims of logic in the systematology and methodology of the sciences." *Zeitschrift für die gesamte Staatswissen-*

schaft for 1883, pp. 265–6. But Schmoller himself, in his controversy with Menger, the able leader of Austrian reaction in favour of the older methods of economic studies, is careful to disclaim some of the extreme pretensions of his followers. A short summary of this controversy is given in an article by Wagner, part of which is reproduced in the first number of the Boston *Quarterly Journal of Economics*.

From the 2nd to the 4th editions (Book I, ch. v, § 1) this footnote ran as follows:

Mill, *On Comte*, p. 82. His controversy with Comte is still worth studying. Comte's arguments have recently been restated with great force and eloquence by Ingram: but they do not appear to have shaken Mill's position that Comte, though right when he affirmed, was wrong when he denied. And this remark may be extended: it would seem that in the long controversy which has been waged in England, Germany, and more recently in America, as to the right method of economic study, nearly every one has been right when he has affirmed that a certain method is useful; it has generally been the one best adapted for that part of the many-sided work of economics in which he has had the most interest. But he has been wrong in denying that other methods are useful: they may be unsuited for those purposes of which he has been chiefly thinking; but they may probably be better suited than his own favourite methods for other and equally important purposes.

In the 3rd ed. (Book I, ch. vi, § 1, pp. 92 n.–3 n.) a footnote dealing with controversies on method was attached to the last paragraph of § 1 of Book I, ch. iii (page 30 in vol. i of the present edition). See editorial note **d** to page 30.
This footnote ran as follows:

The discussions of the last twenty years have gradually proved that those who are doing the most genuine and original work in any part of the large field of economic investigation, are agreed in fundamental principle as to the right use of various scientific methods for various parts of the work: and that what real differences exist between them, are mainly differences of emphasis. It is now generally admitted that the severe criticism which the founders of the German Historical School sometimes made on the older economists if quoted by itself, gives a misleading impression of their true position. Roscher and Knies not only spoke often with generous appreciation of the work of their predecessors; but, especially in their later years, they themselves made habitual use of the analytical methods which had come down to them from the "classical" economists. And on the other hand even those who rate highly the importance of analytical methods are glad to acknowledge the great services which the historical method, in the hands of really able men, renders to economics generally, and even to economic analysis.

The most notable controversy on method of recent times is that between Prof. Carl Menger and Prof. Schmoller. It was conducted with great acumen, but perhaps with some slight exaggeration on either side. Prof. Wagner, who was one of the earliest leaders of the historical movement in economics, and whose unsurpassed learning gives a singular weight to his judgment, took a view of the controversy which seems just and well balanced. (Part of his criticism is accessible to English readers in the first number of the Harvard *Journal of Economics*.) And the account which he has recently published (*Grundlegung*, Ed. III, Book I, ch. II) of the services to be rendered by the historical and analytical methods, and of their mutual interdependence, is a masterpiece of subtle and sound exposition.

But meanwhile it has become apparent that Schmoller's part of the controversy had been somewhat misunderstood. He is now the recognized leader of the specially historical tendencies of German economics; and as his manifesto, in the article already quoted, formally disavows the narrow and contentious doctrines that have been put forward by some of the younger adherents of the school in Germany and elsewhere; it may be hoped that at last the time has come for the cessation of barren controversy and the devotion of all the energies of economists to various forms of constructive work, each supplementing the other. See also Prof. Ashley "On the Study of Economic History" in the Harvard *Journal of Economics*, vol. VII.

In the 4th ed. (p. 92 n.) the footnote just quoted from the 3rd ed. was much abbreviated, only the first sentence of the first paragraph and the whole of the third paragraph being retained. In the final sentence of the third paragraph, after the reference to Ashley, the sentence continued as follows: "and the masterly account of the special provinces, and of the mutual interdependence, of the historical and analytical methods in Wagner's *Grundlegung*, Bk. I, ch. II." This footnote as a whole was deleted from the 5th ed.

PAGE *772*

a.   The following additional sentence at this point in the 3rd ed. (p. 94) was deleted from the 5th ed.: "And further, though unexpected combinations of forces are less likely to produce startling results in economics than in chemistry, yet they are far more difficult to exclude." To this sentence was attached in the 3rd ed. a footnote, of which the first two sentences were deleted from the 5th ed., while the last two sentences were incorporated in that edition into the text of Appendix C as the concluding sentences of this paragraph (lines 10–17). The two sentences in the 3rd ed. (deleted from the 5th ed.) ran as follows:

A knowledge of the actions of an elastic string under tensions of ten and twenty pounds may not tell us how it will act under a tension of thirty: for then it may not stretch further, but break and spring back. And two economic forces acting in the same direction may introduce changes into men's habits and aims in life; and produce results different in kind, perhaps even partly opposed to, those which would result from either alone. For instance a small addition to a man's income...etc.

b.   So since the 5th ed. (p. 772) where the first two clauses of this sentence replaced the following clauses dating from the 3rd ed. (p. 95 n.): "Even the chemist, when he deals not with inanimated matter but with living beings, can seldom sail...etc."

PAGE *773*

a.   The following sentences, dating from the 3rd ed. (p. 96 n.), after the sentence ending with the words "than at first sight appears", was deleted from the 5th ed.:

Compare above, ch. V, §4. For similar reasons the philosophic questions relating to the freedom of the will, do not concern the economist as such: his reasonings do not assume any particular answers to those questions.

The reference to "ch. v, §4", in the first sentence, applies to Book I, ch. II, §2, in vol. I of the present edition.

b. This and the next paragraph date from the 3rd ed. (pp. 97–7).

c. The following footnote attached to the word "reason" in the 3rd ed. (p. 96 n.) was deleted from the 4th ed.:

> It may be well to quote the whole passage, which occurs in Prof. Schmoller's article on *Volkswirtschaft* already mentioned:—"What we call the inductive process starts from the particular, from observation, and seeks the rule which declares to be true of a class what has been found to be true of the observed instances. The more complex a phenomenon, and the even more imperfect our observation of the complex conditions, resulting as they do from a combination of the most various causes, the more difficult is it to discover the true rule, the more often do we get no further than hypotheses, and provisional guesses as to the uniformity of the result. But we apply even these to obtain further conclusions.
>
> Deduction, which rests on the same tendencies, the same beliefs, the same needs of our reason as induction, consists in the wider application of those rules as to causality which have been obtained by induction. What was true in accurately observed cases must be true in all exactly similar cases; the rule is sought for only in order to apply it further. Every rule attributes a predicate, a mode of action, a characteristic to a class of things; an analysis of the notion of the subject and predicate shows what is contained in the rule in question, to what purposes it applies, what cases come under it, what it can account for."

d. The following footnote attached to the word "step" in the 3rd ed. (p. 97 n.) was deleted from the 5th ed.:

> The science of the tides presents many close analogies to economics. In either science one set of leading forces exercises a visible influence over almost every movement, and a predominating influence over some: in the science of the tides, it is the attractions of the moon and sun, in economics it is the desire to obtain comfort at the least cost. In either case a merely deductive study of the action of the leading forces either by themselves, or in conjunction with forces less universal in their action, would give results that might have a scientific interest but would be useless for guidance. But in either case such deductions are useful in giving life to observed facts, in connecting them with one another, and thus helping to build up the secondary laws of the science.
>
> It is true for instance that even now no knowledge of sea-currents and of the action of the wind on the water would enable a man to say exactly what difference there would be between the tides in the ports of Guernsey and Jersey, nor the exact limits of the points on the English coast at which there are four tides every day, nor how strong a gale in the North Sea would be required to make the water at the London Docks fall a couple of feet in the middle of a time of rising tide. And yet a study of general principles has aided in the selection of the right facts for observation, and in connecting them with one another by secondary laws, which aid both in explaining known facts and predicting results of known causes. The same processes, both inductive and deductive, are used in nearly the same way in the explanation of a known fact in the history of the tides, and in the prediction of an unknown fact. (Compare Mill, *Logic*, Book VI, ch. III.)

A paragraph on the science of the tides was inserted into Book I, ch. III, §3 in the 5th ed. (p. 32). See pages 31–2 in vol. I of the present edition.

e. This concluding sentence was inserted in the 5th ed. (pp. 773–4).

a. The subject-matter of this and the remaining paragraphs of § 3 dates substantially from the 1st ed. (pp. 74–6).

b. So since the 3rd ed. (p. 98) where this sentence replaced the following sentences dating from the 1st ed. (p. 76):

To make such inquiries properly with regard to very distant events is often impossible; for we seldom have records of all the facts that are wanted for the purpose. But it can be done with regard to contemporary events in our own country.

c. The following concluding sentence of this paragraph dating from the 1st ed. (p. 76) was deleted from the 3rd ed.:

Controversies of this kind often raise a dust which obscures the truth; but they serve a good purpose in showing us how much knowledge and judgment are required to sift and analyse economic facts, to balance them one against another, to check them and to interpret them by one another.

The first four sentences of the succeeding paragraph in the 1st ed. (Book I, ch. v, § 3) and in the 2nd ed. (Book I, ch. vi, § 4) were also deleted from the 3rd ed.; but the last two sentences were retained (apart from a footnote on the method of scientific inquiry) and transferred to the first paragraph of Book I, ch. vi, § 1 (in vol. 1 of the present edition, Book I, ch. iii, § 1). See editorial note **e** to page 29 in vol. 1 of the present edition. The four sentences just referred to, which were deleted from the 3rd ed., ran as follows:

Induction and deduction mutually depend on one another.

Thus induction and deduction go hand in hand. The progress of economic reasoning depends on the study of economic facts, and on the other hand, that study itself requires to be guided and directed by the scientific knowledge which is the outcome and abstract of a previous study of facts. Every new study of facts adds to our knowledge of the action of economic causes, it enables us to form a better judgment as to the effects which any cause is likely to produce, whether acting singly or in combination with others: and it puts us in a better position to detect the hidden causes of results which come under our notice. But the study to be serviceable must be careful and thorough, and must be so arranged as to isolate the action first of one cause and then of another, and make a careful examination of each.

d.   This sentence dates from the 3rd ed. (p. 98), where it replaced the following opening sentences of this paragraph in the 1st ed. (p. 74):

For indeed facts by themselves are silent, they teach nothing until they are interpreted by reason. In some of the elementary experiments of a physical laboratory the inference may be so palpable, the demand for the exercise of reasoning may be so slight, as almost to justify us in saying that the facts explain themselves, and give us direct information. But without the aid of careful reasoning, there is nothing to be learnt from economic facts, because no economic event or practical problem was ever exactly like any other.

Economic facts require to be carefully interpreted by reason.

In the 2nd ed. (p. 86) the foregoing sentences were preceded by the following paragraph which was also deleted from the 3rd ed.:

The progress of economics as of every other science can be effected only by the reason acting on observed facts; while the ultimate basis of every particular statement, and of every general proposition, or "law", of economics is a study of facts. And in this study nothing can be done by the reason alone, and very little can be done well except by the trained reason.

e.   Except where otherwise stated the wording of this section (§4) dates from the 3rd ed. (Book I, ch. VI, §4, pp. 98–102 n.).

PAGE 775

a.   This paragraph dates from the 1st ed. (Book I, ch. V, §2, p. 75 n.).

PAGE 776

a.   So since the 5th ed. (p. 776) where the first clause of this sentence replaced the following clause dating from the 1st ed. (p. 75 n.): "The whole history of Land Tenure is a most important study."

b.   The following concluding sentence of this paragraph in the 1st ed. (p. 75 n.) was deleted from the 5th ed.:

Historical research of this kind requires all the resources of economic science: and those great men who by doing such work extend the boundaries of economic science, are not reluctant to acknowledge their obligations to its analyses and reasonings.

PAGE 778

a.   In its present form the wording of §5 dates from the 3rd ed. (pp. 102–4 n.) but some parts of it date from the 1st ed.

a. This sentence, and the first three sentences of the next paragraph, date substantially from the 1st ed. (Book I, ch. VII, p. 88).

a. This section (§6) dates from the 5th ed. (p. 780).

APPENDIX D

USES OF ABSTRACT REASONING IN ECONOMICS

a. The origin of the wording of this Appendix is shown throughout in the editorial notes.

This Appendix in its present form dates substantially from the 5th edition; see also editorial note **a** to page 780 of vol. I in this edition.

b. So since the 5th edition (p. 781).

c. §1 dates from the 5th ed. (pp. 781–2), with two exceptions noted below.

d. The first sentence of this paragraph is a rewording of parts of two sentences of a paragraph in the 3rd ed., which was deleted (with this exception) from the 5th ed. The paragraph in question in the 3rd ed. (p. 93) ran as follows:

To begin with, there is no scope in economics for long chains of reasoning; that is for chains in which each link is supported, wholly or mainly, by that which went before, and without obtaining further support and guidance from observation and the direct study of real life. Such chains might indeed afford interesting speculation in the closet: but they could not correspond to nature closely enough to be of use as a guide in action. The classical economists treated economics not as an academic diversion, but as a means towards attaining important public ends; and none of them, not even Ricardo, indulged in long chains of deductive reasoning without reference to direct observation.

e. So since the 6th ed. (pp. 781–2) where this sentence replaced the following sentence and footnote in the 5th ed. (pp. 781–2):

But the direct application of mathematical reasoning to the discovery of economic truths is rarely of much service except in the quest of statistical averages and probabilities and in measuring the degree of consilience between correlated statistical tables.[1]

[1] Compare the last extract from the Preface to the first edition of this volume, printed above. The service, which a mathematical training renders in enabling the mind to comprehend the gradually accumulated effects of complex and mutually dependent changes, is conspicuous in the relations of marginal products to value. See especially V, VIII–XI, VI, I, II, and Note XIV in the Mathematical Appendix.

PAGE 782

a. This paragraph dates from the 5th ed. (p. 782).

b. This sentence dates in its present form from the 5th ed. (p. 782); but the substance of the latter part of this sentence, and the whole of the remainder of §2, date from the 1st ed. (p. 79 n.) where they were placed in a footnote to the third paragraph of Book I, ch. v, §1. In the 1st ed. (p. 79 n.) the matter retained in the present edition (vol. I, page 782) was preceded by a number of sentences which were deleted from the 2nd ed. The paragraph in the text of the 1st ed. and the opening sentences of the footnote, to which reference has just been made, ran as follows:

The chief reason why, though backward relatively to physical science, economics has been able to get in advance of every other branch of social science, is that it deals mainly with just that class of motives which are measurable, and therefore are specially amenable to treatment by scientific machinery. Other branches of social science deal only with the quality of human motive: economics deals with quantity as well as quality. Wide as are the interests of which the economist takes account when applying his doctrines to practice, the centre of his work is a body of systematic reasoning as to the quantities of measurable motives. For the purpose of this or that special illustration he may even neglect all others: but he must never lose sight of the real issues of life; and these are all, with scarcely any important exceptions, affected more or less by motives that are not measurable[1].

[1] Here we look at the individual, not as a "psychological atom" but as a member of a social group: and no method of measurement is of any avail which is not generally applicable to the whole of that group. And, whatever may be the case in the future, there is at present only one such method which avails for this: the method, namely, of reducing to a common measure the things that must be given to people to induce them to perform or abstain from performing certain actions. This then is the sense in which the term measurable motive is used here. As soon as a motive can be measured, so soon a part, at least, of the machinery of economic motives is applicable to it. In the world in which we live, money, as representing general purchasing power, is so much the best measure of motives that no other can compete with it. But this is, so to speak, an accident, and perhaps an accident that is not found in other worlds than ours. When we want to induce a man to do anything for us...etc.

See editorial note **b** to page 22 of vol. 1 in the present edition for the context of the above paragraph in the text of the 1st ed. In the 2nd to the 4th editions the footnote, shorn of the first five of the foregoing sentences quoted from the 1st ed., was attached to a different paragraph in Book I, ch. v and began as follows:

The fact that the predominant position which money holds in economics, results rather from its being a measure of motive than an aim of endeavour, may be illustrated by the reflection that the almost exclusive use of money as a measure of motive is, so to speak, an accident, and perhaps an accident that is not found in other worlds than ours. When we want to induce a man to do anything for us...etc.

In all four editions the footnote continued without alteration as in the text of the present edition, to the end of §2 (vol. 1, pages 782–3). It may be noted that the whole of these last three paragraphs dating from the 1st ed., and now placed in §2 of Appendix D, were taken without any substantial alteration from the Inaugural Lecture entitled *The Present Position of Economics*, which Marshall gave in Cambridge in 1885, after his election to the Professorship of Political Economy in succession to Professor Fawcett. See *Memorials of Alfred Marshall*, edited by A. C. Pigou, pp. 158–9.

PAGE 783

a. This sentence dates from the 5th ed. (p. 783).

b. So since the 5th ed. where this and the next sentence replaced the following sentence dating substantially from the 1st ed. (p. 89 n.):
"German economists have done good service by dwelling on this class of considerations also, but they seem to be mistaken in supposing that it was overlooked by the older English economists."

c. This sentence dates from the 1st ed. (p. 80 n.), except for the word "British" which in the 5th ed. (p. 783) replaced the original word "English".

d. This sentence was inserted in the 5th ed. (p. 783).

e. This sentence dates from the 1st ed. (p. 80 n.).

f. This sentence was inserted in the 3rd ed. (p. 85 n.).

g. The remainder of this paragraph dates substantially from the 1st ed. (pp. 80 n.–1 n.).

h. The word "far" before the word "inferior" in the 1st ed. (p. 80 n.) was deleted from the 2nd ed.

i. This paragraph dates from the 3rd ed. (p. 85 n.).

EDITORIAL APPENDIX TO
APPENDIX D

MARSHALL'S VIEWS AS TO THE USE OF MATHEMATICS IN ECONOMICS AND ECONOMIC STATISTICS

The following extracts bring together a number of Marshall's pronouncements on the use of mathematics in economics and economic statistics:

Statistics organize the collection and arrangement of particular statements as to quantity. Mathematical language enables us to express general statements as to quantity with the utmost brevity, precision and force; and mathematical theory reasons on the basis of these statements. It is true that the results obtained by statistics generally, and in particular the economic branch of statistics, are seldom sufficiently definite and trustworthy to afford much useful material for economic *theory* to work on: but they are sufficiently definite to be able often to gain a great deal by having their general tenor stated in the mathematical *language*.

(The Graphic Method of Statistics, 1885. *Memorials of Alfred Marshall*, p. 180.)

The most helpful applications of mathematics to economics are those which are short and simple, which employ few symbols; and which aim at throwing a bright light on some small part of the great economic movement rather than at representing its endless complexity.

773

(From an article on "Distribution and Exchange", *Economic Journal*, 1898, vol. VIII, reprinted, in part, in *Memorials of Alfred Marshall*, p. 313.

Extracts from letters from Marshall to A. L. Bowley:

3 March 1901

Thus my notion of the use of economic statistics differs widely from that which, on my second view of your [a]book I found implied in it; and which in your last letter you have expressed in the words: "the relation of the mathematics of the subject, which I regard as its furthest scientific development, to actual facts."

In my view every economic fact, whether or not it is of such a nature as to be expressed in numbers, stands in relation as cause and effect to many other facts: and since it *never* happens that all of them can be expressed in numbers, the application of exact mathematical methods to those which can is nearly always a waste of time, while in the large majority of cases it is positively misleading; and the world would have been further on its way forward if the work had never been done at all. It is chiefly when the mathematical method is used not for direct construction, but to train sound instinctive habits (like the practising of scales on the piano) that it seems to me generally helpful. I admit exceptions, and no doubt these are already more than I know of, and yet more will be discovered. For instance, if I were younger I would study the abstract doctrine of correlated curves, which I am ashamed to say I do not fully understand. I think it may occasionally be helpful in determining a controversy as to whether two movements have a casual connection. But at present we are not ripe for that, I think. Look at the Bimetallic controversy.... Surely *the* thing to do is to build the basis of our economic structure soundly and not to put a varnish of mathematical accuracy to many places of decimals on results the premises of which are not established within 20 or 50 per cent: many not even so far as to put

---

a. This refers to *The Elements of Statistics* by A. L. Bowley, the first edition of which was published early in 1901.

beyond dispute the question whether *A* is the cause of *B*, or *B* the cause of *A*, or *A* and *B* are the results of $a + b + c + d + \ldots$ Surely *the* thing to do is to seek the Many in the One, the One in the Many.[b] (*Memorials*, pp. 422–3.)

20 December 1901

There is scarcely any question in economics which might not be advanced by bringing to bear on it (i) a knowledge of what statistics have to say: combined with (ii) a knowledge of what statistics can't be made to tell, but which has to be reckoned for in a realistic solution. (*Memorials*, p. 424.)

27 February 1906

I have not been able to lay my hands on any notes as to Mathematico-economics that would be of any use to you: and I have very indistinct memories of what I used to think on the subject. I never read mathematics now: in fact I have forgotten even how to integrate a good many things.

But I know I had a growing feeling in the later years of my work at the subject that a good mathematical theorem dealing with economic hypotheses was very unlikely to be good economics: and I went more and more on the rules— (1) Use mathematics as a shorthand language, rather than as an engine of inquiry. (2) Keep to them till you have done. (3) Translate into English. (4) Then illustrate by examples that are important in real life. (5) Burn the mathematics. (6) If you can't succeed in (4), burn (3). This last I did often.

I believe in Newton's Principia Methods, because they carry so much of the ordinary mind with them. Mathematics used in a Fellowship thesis by a man who is not a mathematician by nature—and I have come across a good deal of that—seems to me an unmixed evil. And I think you should do all you can to prevent people from using Mathematics in cases in which the English Language is as short as the Mathematical....

---

b. In a letter to Edgeworth, 27 April 1909, Marshall gave the following definition of the phrase used at the end of the above sentence: "...the One in the Many and the Many in the One, i.e. the relations of details to fundamentals" (*Memorials*, p. 442).

I find mathematicians almost invariably follow what I regard as Jevons' one great analytical mistake, his eulogy of the Geometric mean in general: and do not see that, according to his use, erroneous weighting may do far more mischief with the Geometric Mean than with the Arithmetic Mean. I always have to spend some time in convincing them of the danger.

Another trouble is that mathematicians insist on assuming that, if p be the price which may vary to pr or to $\frac{p}{r}$ then the two variations are *prima facie* to be assumed to be equally probable. Whereas, of course, if r is a considerable quantity, that is not true: Jevons has overlooked this also, I think, as a result of not thinking in English. (*Memorials*, pp. 427–8.)

7 October 1906

The longer I live the more convinced am I that except in purely abstract problems—the statistical side must never be separate even for an instant from the non-statistical: on the ground that if economics is to be a guide in life—individual and more especially social—people must be warned off by every possible means from considering the action of any one cause—beyond the most simple generalities—without taking account of the others whose effects are commingled with it. And, since many of the chief of these causes have either no statistical side at all, or no statistical side that is accessible practically for common use, therefore, the statistical element must be kept subordinate to general considerations and included among them....

In the last two years I have given about a sixth of my lectures to almost purely statistical discussions of a general (non-mathematical) character....But my main aim is to help people to read *through* figures, and reach the real values, the true relative proportions represented by them. (*Memorials*, pp. 428–9.)

Attention should further be drawn to the discussion of the use of mathematics in economics at the end of the Preface to the First Edition—see vol. I of the present edition, pages ix–xi; and also in Appendix D, pages 781–2.

APPENDIX E

DEFINITIONS OF CAPITAL

PAGE 785

a. Except where otherwise indicated the wording of this Appendix dates substantially from the 3rd edition, where it formed part of Book II, chapter IV—mostly in footnotes.

In the 4th edition this material was assembled and placed, with some additions, in a "Note on some Definitions of Capital" at the end of Book II, chapter IV.

In the 5th edition this Note was turned into Appendix E, "Definitions of Capital". See editorial note **a** to page 71 of vol. I in the present edition. For Marshall's treatment of capital in the 1st and 2nd editions see the Editorial Appendices to Book II, chapter IV and to Appendix E.

b. So since the 5th ed.

c. The opening sentence of this paragraph dates substantially from the 4th ed. (p. 152) where it replaced the following sentence in the 3rd ed. (p. 145):

The dominant use of the term capital for ordinary purposes is undoubtedly that to which the name of trade capital has been given: and we may look at the causes which have given it this prestige, in spite of its disadvantages.

d. So since the 4th ed. (p. 152) where this sentence replaced the following sentence in the 3rd ed. (p. 145): "But such facts as these are often overlooked; and here lies a part of the explanation of the prestige of this use of the term capital."

PAGE 786

a. This and the next sentence date substantially from the 1st ed. (p. 138). See the Editorial Appendix to Appendix E, p. 788 below.

b. The following sentence in the 3rd ed. (p. 146) at this point was deleted from the 4th ed.: "Loans are indeed made on houses and furniture, on yachts and carriages in private ownership: but they are relatively rare."

c. The remainder of this paragraph is a rewording of a passage in the 1st ed., Book II, ch. VI, p. 139, where, however, as will be seen, the argument was related to income not to capital. This passage in the 1st ed. ran as follows:

But no account is commonly taken of the benefit a man derives from the use of his furniture; so that if he had been in the habit of hiring a piano, and determined to sell a railway share and buy the piano instead of hiring it, his money income would be diminished by the dividend from the share, although it is probable that his total real income would be increased by the change.

d. This and the next sentence date from the 5th ed. (p. 786).

e. For the earlier version of the remainder of this paragraph in the first two editions, see the Editorial Appendix to Appendix E (p. 787 below). In the 3rd ed. (p. 147) the opening clause of the first sentence of this paragraph was preceded by the following paragraph and clause:

But when we try to go further, and to apply clear-cut principles to the line of demarcation of capital, we meet a great divergence of opinion; and that divergence is the result, not of accident but of causes which are not to be removed.

For the notion of social capital enters into many veins of economic thought; and whatever definition a writer takes ...etc.

In the 4th ed. (p. 147) the paragraph just quoted from the 3rd ed. was replaced by the following sentences which were deleted from the 5th ed.:

Later on[1] some account will be given of attempts to mark off social capital from social wealth by formal and exact definitions and of the reasons why they have not succeeded. The fact is that nature has made no hard and fast dividing lines between them; and man must conform to her rule.

[1] Below §§ 11–13. The argument of this section is put somewhat more fully in the *Economic Journal*, vol. VIII, pp. 55–9, together with some account of the steps that have led up to the position that is here maintained.

The reference in this footnote to §§ 11–13 applies to §§ 2–3 in Appendix E. The relevant portions of the article in vol. VIII of the *Economic Journal* referred to are reproduced in the Editorial Appendix to Book II, ch. IV (pp. 229–33 above).

f. The first six sentences of this paragraph date from the 4th ed. (p. 148).

PAGE 787

a. This sentence was inserted in the 5th ed. (p. 787).

b. This paragraph dates from the 4th ed. (p. 153), where it replaced a paragraph and part of a footnote in the 3rd ed. (p. 148), which ran as follows:

For some purposes it is important to insist on the notion of prospectiveness, and to regard capital as a store of things the result of human efforts and sacrifices, devoted mainly to securing benefits in the future rather than in the present. But those who have tried to take their stand definitely on this notion have found themselves on an inclined plane: and have not reached a stable resting-place till they have included all accumulated wealth as capital[1].

Capital regarded mainly as the result of labour and saving.

[1] It may be said that a stone house, which will last many hundred years, is more truly capital than a wooden house, which on the whole gives equal accommodation in the present, but lasts only a short time: and that costly but thoroughly efficient machinery, and other plant of the Western World, are more truly capital than the slight and wasteful appliances of poorer and less prospective countries. But this rather helps to elucidate the notion of capital than to define the term. We shall return to this point in Book III, ch. v and Book IV, ch. vii.

The first line in the paragraph, running: "For some purposes it is important to insist on the...etc.", is that referred to by Marshall in a letter to Cannan. See above, p. 228.

c. The first three sentences of this paragraph date substantially from the 1st ed. (p. 136). See the Editorial Appendix to Appendix E (p. 784 below).

d. The following footnote attached to the end of this sentence in the 5th ed. (pp. 787 n.–8 n.) and dating substantially from the 1st ed. (p. 136) was deleted from the 6th ed.:

The Physiocrats were led in this direction partly for the convenience of representing by a clear-cut mathematical formula the elements of past labours that were devoted to providing for the needs of the future, each multiplied by compound interest for the time during which its fruits were in abeyance. This formula has great attractions, but it does not correspond closely to the conditions of real life. For instance it takes no account of the different rates of depreciation of different products of past labour, according as the purposes for which they were originally intended have retained their ground, or have become obsolete. And when corrections of this class are introduced the formula loses its one great merit of simplicity combined with exactness.

e. The remaining sentences of this paragraph were inserted in the 6th ed. (pp. 787–8).

PAGE 788

a. The following paragraph in a footnote in the "Note on some Definitions of Capital" in the 4th ed. (p. 154 n.) was deleted from the 5th ed.:

Fisher agrees with Cannan that capital is to be regarded as the existing stock of wealth, and contrasted with income which is a flow of wealth. It is, no doubt, essential to distinguish between richness as measured by income and richness as measured by the stock of wealth (see *e.g.* §9 of the present chapter): but custom and convenience seem to require the term wealth by itself to mean a stock of wealth; and therefore if the term capital is to be turned to good account at all, it would seem to need some further connotation. The articles by Fisher and Cannan on the subject in the *Economic Journal*, vols. VII, VIII are, however, full of suggestion.

The reference to "§9 of the present chapter" applies to Book II, ch. IV, §7, in vol. I of the present edition.

b. The clause running: "to the comparative neglect of its productivity", was inserted in the 6th ed. (p. 788).

c. For the earlier version of this and the following paragraph in the 1st ed. (Book II, ch. V, §2, p. 131) see the Editorial Appendix to Book II, ch. IV of vol. I in the present edition (pp. 221–3 above).

d. The words "in the first half of the century" after the word "employed" in the 3rd ed. (p. 150) were deleted from the 4th ed. In the 3rd ed. (p. 150 n.) the following footnote was attached to the word "employed":

> Of course there is a fringe of debateable ground at the margin of each definition. A factory is auxiliary capital simply; a weaver's cottage in which he plies his trade is partly auxiliary and partly consumption capital. The private dwelling-house of a rich man engaged in business is consumption capital to the extent of that accommodation which directly contributes to the health and efficiency of himself and his family: but beyond that, it is not capital at all, in the use of the term which we are adopting.

This footnote, with its contention that a private house occupied by the owner is not capital, dates from the 1st ed. (p. 128 n.). It was deleted from the 4th ed. in response to a criticism from Cannan who pointed out its inconsistency with the definition of capital adopted by Marshall in the 3rd ed. For Marshall's letter to Cannan, see the Editorial Appendix to Book II, ch. IV (p. 228 above).

e. For the earlier versions of these two paragraphs in the first two editions see the Editorial Appendix to Appendix E (pp. 784–6 below).

f. So since the 4th ed. (p. 155 n.) where this sentence replaced the following sentence in the 3rd ed. (p. 149 n.): "But the term 'set aside' does not seem to give a clue to a solution of the difficulties mentioned in the text."

g. For the earlier version of this paragraph in the first two editions see the Editorial Appendix to Appendix E (pp. 781–2 below).

PAGE 789

a. This paragraph dates from the 6th ed. (pp. 789–90).

b. So since the 4th ed. (p. 156 n.) where this clause replaced the following clause in the 3rd ed. (pp. 150 n.–1 n.): "though some of the utterances of the earlier economists seem capable of interpretation quite as obvious as those which Mr Cannan attaches to them, and more consistent with the belief that they were not greatly deficient in common sense."

c. So since the 4th ed. (p. 156 n.) where this footnote replaced the following footnote in the 3rd ed. (p. 151 n.): "An argument to this effect is given by Wagner (*Grundlegung*, Ed. III, pp. 315–16); who includes consumer's capital in his excellent and almost exhaustive discussion of the subject."

PAGE 790

a. This sentence was inserted in the 4th ed. (p. 156 n.).

b. The last two sentences of this footnote date from the 6th ed. (p. 790 n.).

EDITORIAL APPENDIX TO
APPENDIX E

MARSHALL'S SUMMARY OF DEFINITIONS OF CAPITAL BY EARLIER ECONOMISTS

The extracts which follow contain the whole of the "Historical Note on Definitions of the Term 'Capital'", which was attached to Book II, chapter V in the 1st edition, and to Book II, chapter IV in the 2nd edition. Except where otherwise indicated the contents of this Note were deleted from the 3rd edition.

The text here given is that of the 2nd edition (pp. 129–33) but except where otherwise stated in the editorial notes it dates from the 1st edition (pp. 135–8).

HISTORICAL NOTE ON DEFINITIONS OF THE TERM "CAPITAL"

[a]THE following are among the chief definitions of capital in which it is regarded as consisting of those things which relate to future production. It will be found that most of them tacitly assume that capital is to be regarded from the social point of view, even though the wording at first sight seems rather to suggest the individual point of view. Ricardo

---

a. The substance of this paragraph, apart from the second sentence and the last sentence (which were deleted from the 3rd ed.), was retained in the later editions (see pages 788 n.–9 n. in vol. 1 of the present edition).

says (*Principles of Political Economy*, ch. iv):—"Capital is that part of the wealth of a country which is employed in production and consists of food, clothing, tools, raw materials, machinery, etc. necessary to give effect to labour." Malthus in his *Definitions in Political Economy* says:—"Capital is that portion of the stock of a country which is kept or employed with a view to profit in the production and distribution of wealth." Senior in his *Political Economy* says:—"Capital is an article of wealth, the result of human exertion, employed in the production or distribution of wealth." John Stuart Mill in his *Principles of Political Economy*, Book I, ch. iv, § 1, says:—"What capital does for production, is to afford the shelter, protection, tools and materials which the work requires, and to feed and otherwise maintain the labourers during the process. Whatever things are destined for this use are capital." Or to use his own summary:—"Capital is wealth devoted to reproductive employment."

b Rau seems to have been the first to dwell on the distinction between social and individual capital; but he defines capital from both points of view, as "the means of winning a livelihood" (*Erwerbsmittel*). Again Roscher says "Capital we call every product laid by for purposes of further production" (*Political Economy*, §xLII). Wagner says:—(*Volkswirtschaftslehre*, §28) that in regarding capital we must distinguish between the pure economic and the historic-juristic (*geschichtlich-rechtlich*) standpoints. From the former point of view it is a provision of means of production (*Produktionsmittel-Vorrat*). From a second point of view it is regarded as that part of the possessions of an individual which are used

---

b. In the 1st ed. (p. 135) the first sentence of this paragraph ran as follows:

The first great impulse in the direction of insisting on the distinction between social and individual capital seems to have been given by Rau, who defines capital from both points of view, as "the means of obtaining a livelihood" (*Erwerbsmittel*), and makes a suggestive though not completely satisfactory distinction between them, very much in modern fashion (*Volkswirtschaftslehre*, §§51–55, 120–33).

by him as a means of obtaining a livelihood (*Erwerbsmittel*). From this point of view we count in the free gifts of nature which have become private property, but not from the former point of view. Kleinwächter in Schönberg's *Handbuch* remarks with much truth that this definition puts prominently forward, and with the most pregnant brevity, that which is common to all this group of definitions. Somewhat to a similar effect Sidgwick defines social capital as "Wealth employed to bring a surplus or profit not to the individual owner only but to the industrial community of which he is a member," while he holds that "Individual's capital is wealth employed for profit." Böhm-Bawerk (*Geschichte der Kapitalzins-Theorien*) defines capital as "A complex of means of obtaining a livelihood made by man; that is, a complex of goods which had their origin in a previous process of production and are destined not for immediate consumption for the sake of enjoyment (*Genusskonsumption*) but the acquisition (*Erwerbung*) of more goods." The history of the above definitions seems to show a distinct tendency in the direction of those which have been adopted as the standard definitions in the text; and an attempt is made there to carry this movement further in the direction of distinguishing the consumption which is necessary for efficiency on the part of the workers of all grades, from that which is not thus necessary.

ᶜSome writers extend the limits of capital so as to include not only all things which are destined to promote production, but all things which are capable of being so used. Thus for instance they include all the stock of grain in a country without inquiring whether it is to be used in feeding people who work or people who live idly; whether in feeding cart-horses or race-horses. In short they include what is potentially capital according to our definition as well as what is actually capital.

Some go even further; and laying stress almost exclusively on the notion of "prospectiveness" include under capital

---

c. This paragraph and the first sentence of the next paragraph date from the 2nd ed.

all external goods which are made by man and "saved" to become the sources of future enjoyment. ᵈThus nearly all the earlier French Economists have followed in the lines laid down by the Physiocrats before Adam Smith wrote, and used the term "capital" very much in the sense in which he and his immediate followers used the word "stock," to include all accumulated wealth (*valeurs accumulées*); *i.e.* all the result of the excess of production over consumption. And although in recent years they have shown a decided tendency to use the term in the narrower English sense, there is at the same time a considerable movement on the part of some of the profoundest thinkers in Germany and England in the direction of the older and broader French definition. ᵉThe Physiocrats were undoubtedly led in this direction by their bias towards mathematical habits of thought; because it is possible to represent by a clear-cut mathematical formula the elements of past labours that were devoted to providing for the needs of the future, each multiplied by compound interest for the time during which its fruits were in abeyance. This formula has great attractions, but it does not correspond closely to the conditions of real life. For instance it takes no account of the different rates of depreciation of different products of past labour, according as the purposes for which they were originally intended have retained their ground, or have become obsolete. And when corrections of this class are introduced the formula loses its one great merit of simplicity combined with exactness.

ᶠIt was probably Hermann's mathematical bias that inclined him to say (*Staatswirtschaftliche Untersuchungen*, chs. III and v) that capital consists of goods "which are a lasting source of satisfaction that has exchange value." Those which give the satisfaction directly and without changing their form are consumption-capital (*Nutz-Kapital*), and include

---

d. This and the next sentence were retained substantially in the later editions. See page 787 in vol. I of the present edition.

e. This and the next sentence were deleted from the 5th ed.

f. This sentence was retained in the later editions (see page 789 n. in vol. I of the present edition), except for the replacement, as from the

such things as furniture and clothing. He classes under the head of "production capital" nearly all those things which most English writers regard as constituting the whole of capital. But he includes free gifts of nature under each of his heads. ᵍAgain, the same mathematical bias has led Jevons to a very similar conclusion (see in particular his "Quantitative Notions concerning Capital", and his argument that "Articles in the consumer's hands are capital",

---

4th ed. (p. 154 n.), of the words "It was probably Hermann's mathematical bias that inclined him to say" by the words "Hermann says".

g. This sentence was retained in the 3rd ed. (p. 148 n.) where it was succeeded by the following sentences:

His position is thus admirably described by M. Gide:— "Stanley Jevons asserts that stores of food are typical capital, and are its essential and primordial manifestations whence all the other forms have sprung. Indeed his premise is that the true function of capital is to support the worker while waiting for the moment when his labour can give good results. This definition of the function of capital necessarily requires it to exist under the shape of means of subsistence, of *advances*. Of these, all tools, machines, railways, etc. would be only derivative forms, for their production takes some time, perhaps a considerable period; and hence they must have required a previous amount of advances in the shape of stores of food. It is to this primary form, therefore, that we have always to return." (It will be seen that Prof. Böhm-Bawerk has mistaken its drift, when he says (*Positive Capital*, Book I, ch. v) that "if it were correct, every land would be rich in capital in proportion as its wages were high and its means of subsistence cheap.")

In the 4th ed. (p. 154 n.) the sentence beginning with the words "The same mathematical bias has led Jevons...etc." was deleted, and the sentences referring to Jevons began as follows: "And Jevons' position is well described by Gide (*Political Economy* III, iii): 'Stanley Jevons asserts that stores of food...etc.'." The extract from Gide was deleted from the 5th ed. where two short references to Jevons' doctrine of capital were placed in §6 of Book II, chapter IV (pages 77 and 79 n. in vol. I of the present edition).

in ch. VII of his *Theory of Political Economy*). [h] Knies and Cohn have adopted definitions not very dissimilar from Hermann's.

[i] The American Astronomer, Newcomb (*Principles of Political Economy*, Book II, ch. v), defines capital as "wealth desired not for its own sake, but for the sake of the Sustenance [i.e. consumption-wealth] which it will enable us to produce," and proposes that we should debit a person who lives in a hired house with *negative capital* to the amount of the value of that house. He thus carries out to its logical conclusion a proposal that has often been made (as for instance by Mr Macleod) with regard to the loan of capital. This plan simplifies the relation in which social capital stands to individual capital; and it avoids the common difficulty of having to say that when a boat builder hires his carriage from a carriage builder, who meanwhile hires his yacht from the boat builder, the capital of each would be diminished if each were to buy the thing that he had been hiring. But his plan still fails to exhibit clearly the increased provision for the future which is made when a durable stone house is substituted for a perishable wooden one, which gave for the time equal accommodation.

[j] This divergence as to the use of the term capital is due, as has been already remarked, to the fact that economists may not venture to invent for themselves a technical terminology independent of the ordinary language of business. Thinkers who are agreed on all substantial points, continue to differ as to what is the least injurious method of effecting a compromise between scientific consistency and popular usage; and as to what arrangement of the few terms at their disposal will best eke out their resources. The divergence has been a great stumbling-block to many readers of econo-

---

h.   A reference to Knies was retained in the later editions (see page 788 n. in vol. 1 of the present edition), but that to Cohn was deleted from the 3rd ed.

i.   This paragraph was deleted from the 4th ed.

j.   In the 1st ed. this and the next paragraph were in the text of Book II, ch. v (p. 133); they were inserted in this Note in the 2nd ed. (p. 131). The second of these paragraphs was retained substantially in the later editions. See page 786 in vol. 1 of the present edition.

mics; so great a variation in the use of so prominent a term appears necessarily to land the science in confusion. But in fact the difficulty is much less serious than it seems at first sight.

For whether a writer takes a broader or a narrower view of capital, he finds that the various elements of which it is composed differ more or less from one another in the way in which they enter into the different problems with which he has successively to deal. He is compelled therefore to supplement his standard definition by an explanation of the bearing of each several element of capital on the point at issue. These special analyses are substantially the same in the works of all careful writers on economics, however divergent may be their standard definitions of capital; the reader is thus brought to very much the same conclusion by whatever route he travels; though it may sometimes require a little trouble to discern the unity in substance, underlying the differences in the words, which are used by different schools of economists to express their doctrines relating to capital.

kFor instance, whatever definition of capital we take, it will be found to be true that a general increase of capital augments the demand for labour and raises wages: and whatever definition we take it is not true that all kinds of capital act with equal force in this direction, or that it is possible to say how great an effect any given increase in the total amount of capital will have in raising wages, without specially inquiring as to the particular form which the increase has taken. This inquiry is the really important part of the work: it has to be made in very much the same manner and it comes to the same result, whatever be the definition of capital with which we have started. Similar remarks apply to the investigation of the causes which determine the rate of interest.

1Adam Smith's distinction between Fixed and Circulating

---

k. In the 1st ed. this paragraph was placed in a footnote in Book II, ch. v (pp. 133 n.–4 n.); it was inserted in this Note in the 2nd ed. (p. 132), but was deleted from the 4th ed.

1. The substance of this paragraph was retained in the later editions. See Book II, chapter iv, § 3 (page 75 n.) of vol. 1 in the present edition.

capital turned on the question whether the goods "yield a profit without changing masters" or not. Ricardo made it turn on whether they are "of slow consumption or require to be frequently reproduced;" but he truly remarks that this is "a division not essential and in which the line of demarcation cannot be accurately drawn." Mill's modification of Ricardo's definitions of these terms is generally accepted by modern economists.

With slight variation in phraseology productive capital is divided by almost all economists of every country into the raw material, the implements of production and the sustenance of productive labourers; though as we have already seen the limits of this last element have not been properly studied. The plan of including the skill and ability of human beings under the head of capital which was adopted by Adam Smith, has been nearly universal in France, and is now very common in all countries.

[m] Karl Marx and his followers lay down the doctrine that only that is capital, which is a means of production owned by one person (or group of persons) and used to produce things for the benefit of another, generally by means of the hired labour of a third; in such wise that the first has the opportunity of plundering or exploiting the others. This arbitrary doctrine leads them by a different route very nearly to the same result as is reached by those, who neglect all values that do not take a direct money form, and limit capital to what has been called trade-capital in the text. Mr Henry George, though not in general agreement with Marx, seems to have been unconsciously influenced by Marx's followers on this point; and an astonishing number of readers both in America and England have thought that he has overthrown a fundamental doctrine of economic science, when really he has only misunderstood what, when rightly interpreted, is a truism. He objects (*Progress and Poverty*, Book I, ch. 11) to the plan followed by Mill of declaring those things only

---

m. The substance of the first sentence of this paragraph was retained in the 3rd and later editions. See page 786 of vol. 1 in the present edition.

to be capital which are destined to support and aid productive labour. He says that "by remitting the distinction to the mind of the capitalist," Mill makes it "so vague that no power short of omniscience could tell in any given country at any given time what was and what was not capital." And then, with strange a inconsistency, Mr George goes on to give his own definition thus:—"If the articles of actual wealth existing at any time in a given community were presented *in situ* to a dozen intelligent men who had never read a line of political economy, it is doubtful if they would differ in respect to a single item as to whether it should be accounted capital or not. Money which its owner holds for use in business or in speculation would be accounted capital; money set aside for household or personal expenses would not. That part of a farmer's crop held for sale or for seed, or to feed his help in part payment of wages, would be accounted capital; that held for the use of his own family would not be." Thus in his own definition Mr George assumes that any intelligent man will be able to read a distinction that is remitted to the mind of the capitalist: he assumes this not only in the case of corn which the farmer destines to be eaten by his help and not by himself, but also in the case of that impalpable thing, his money, existing perhaps only in the books of his banker, which the farmer destines to be used in his business and not for household expenses. Mr George then applies his definition in an attack on Mill's doctrine that "Industry is limited by Capital." That was an awkward and unfortunate sentence which we shall have to consider later on; but meanwhile it is enough to observe that Mr George's criticisms of it lose their force if we remember that it is deliberately based on a definition which includes under the head of capital, the food of the farmer and of his labourers, even though it be already in their own possession.

APPENDIX F

BARTER

PAGE 791

a. Except where otherwise stated in the editorial notes, the text of this Appendix dates substantially from the 1st edition, but the marginal summaries were inserted in the 3rd edition.

In the first four editions the subject-matter of this Appendix was placed at the end of Book V, chapter 11, and was entitled "A Note on Barter". In the 5th ed. this Note became Appendix F. Barter.

PAGE 793

a. This paragraph dates in its present form from the 5th ed. (p. 793), where it replaced the following paragraph dating from the 1st ed. (p. 397):

This uncertainty of the ultimate position of equilibrium does not depend on the fact that one commodity is being bartered for another instead of being sold for money. It results from our being obliged to regard the marginal utilities of both commodities as varying. And indeed if we had supposed that it was a nut-growing district, and that all the traders on both sides had large stores of nuts, while only the A's had apples, then the exchange of a few handfuls of nuts would not visibly affect their stores, or change appreciably the marginal utility of nuts. In that case the bargaining would resemble in all fundamentals the buying and selling in an ordinary corn market. The real distinction then between the theory of buying and selling and that of barter is that in the former it generally is, and in the latter it generally is not, right to assume that the marginal utility of one of the things dealt with is practically constant.

In the 2nd ed. (p. 397) the words "the ultimate position of equilibrium" in the first line of this paragraph were replaced by the words "the rate at which equilibrium is reached". See p. 794 below. No other change was made in it till the 5th ed. In the 1st ed. (p. 397) the foregoing paragraph was succeeded by the following paragraph:

It may be objected that in a nut country, nuts would per-haps be used almost as money; and that in fact this is almost implied in the case just discussed. No doubt it is so: and here we find an illustration of the general rule that if a commodity is in general use, under such conditions that its final utility to anyone who takes or gives it in exchange is not much affected by small transactions in it, then that commodity is so far well suited to act as a medium of exchange, and dis-charge the simpler functions of money for the small business of a primitive community.

The paragraph just quoted was deleted from the 3rd ed. The only change of any substance which was made in it in the 2nd ed. (p. 397) was the replacement in line 5 of the word "final" by the word "marginal".

b. Except for the last sentence but one, beginning with the words "The real distinction then...", the whole of this paragraph dates from the 2nd ed. (p. 397).

c. This sentence dates in its present form from the 5th ed. (p. 793). The earlier version in the first four editions will be found in the first of the two paragraphs reproduced in editorial note **a** to page 793 of vol. 1 in the present edition.

EDITORIAL APPENDIX TO APPENDIX F

MARSHALL'S CONTROVERSY WITH F. Y. EDGEWORTH OVER THE THEORY OF BARTER

In an article in the *Giornale degli Economisti* for March 1891, entitled "Osservazioni sulla teoria matematica dell' economia politica con riguardo speciale agli Principii di Economia di Alfreda Marshall," Edgeworth had contended that the uncertainty of the ultimate position of equilibrium under barter was due, not as Marshall said in his *Principles*, to the fact that we must regard the marginal utilities of both commodities exchanged as varying, but rather to the absence of competition. He illustrated his article by curves in which quantities (for example of apples) were measured along the OX axis and quan-tities (for example of nuts) along the OY axis; and showed that the ultimate quantities exchanged were indeterminate, though they must lie somewhere along the "contract curve".

He stated incidentally in the course of the article that if one of the articles exchanged (say nuts) had a constant marginal utility, the contract curve would become a straight line parallel to the OY axis, without apparently realizing the significance of this finding, which in fact confirmed Marshall's argument and contradicted his own contention that the constancy of the marginal utility of one of the articles exchanged was immaterial to the argument. He further went on to discuss the possibility that some of those in the market, who had done badly in the earlier stages of bargaining, might be able to improve their position by making further contracts with others whose disadvantage had been of the opposite nature: hence there might be a series of recontracts, and the ultimate equilibrium of the amounts exchanged would not be known until these had all been carried out.

Marshall glanced at the article, without at first apparently realizing its full import, and wrote to Edgeworth in the first instance (the letter is undated, but presumably was written in March 1891) as follows:

BALLIOL CROFT

CAMBRIDGE

(March 1891 ?)

My dear Edgeworth

[a] I have sent all these sheets to be printed off. The copies which I send you of the first three are not quite in their final form. The last sentence of my footnote 1 on [b] p. 179, is my tacit protest against the only thing which you have said on the subject of my $\int \omega R^{-t} \dfrac{dh}{dt}\, dt$, which if I understand you rightly seemed to me a substantial attack on it: and with regard to that I am not sure whether I understood you as I should have done. That was the point with regard to which I was curious especially to see your Giornale article.

Yours very sincerely

ALFRED MARSHALL

---

a. Marshall was engaged at this time on the preparation of the 2nd edition of his *Principles*.

b. This reference applies to footnote 1 on pages 121 n.–2 n. in vol. 1 of the present edition.

I am in no hurry for the return of these papers.

P.S. I think your figure is excellent for itself: and though it would never do for me to substitute your argument for mine—since it is so put as to be of little use for my purpose, I think it so neat in itself that I propose to quote it with the Contract Curve in a Note in the Appendix, referring to my Note on Barter.

I believe I told you that the first chapter of that part of my original MSS (printed by Sidgwick) was given to arguing that the $\left.\begin{array}{l} x = \text{amount} \\ y = \text{amount} \end{array}\right\}$ curves had perhaps more real applications to industrial groups and employer-employé-questions than to Foreign Trade. I have always intended to reproduce that in my vol. II and that is one reason why I have not discussed Trades Unions in vol. I.

At about the same time that Marshall wrote the foregoing letter to Edgeworth he asked Arthur Berry, a mathematical Fellow of King's College, Cambridge, who seems to have had a good knowledge of Italian, to write to Edgeworth on the subject of his article. Berry sent the following letter to Edgeworth:

King's College
Cambridge
Apr. 1st. 1891

Dear Prof. Edgeworth,

Prof. Marshall asked me to read your article in the Italian Economic Review criticising his note on Barter, and at his suggestion I am writing to you now on the subject.

There seems to me to be a misunderstanding on your part of Marshall's position.

There are in your notation three quantities with which we are specially interested, x, y the quantities which change hands, and $\frac{dy}{dx}$ the rate of exchange. In general equilibrium can occur anywhere along a certain part of the contract curve, and all three of these quantities are to that extent indeterminate. But in the case where the final utility of one of the commodities (y) is constant as you point out the contract curve becomes a straight line

$$x = \text{constant}$$

& $\therefore$ one of the quantities x is at once determinate. And as you also point out, since in this case

$$U \equiv f(x) + \alpha y$$
$$V \equiv Q(x) + \beta y$$

where α, β are constants, $\dfrac{dy}{dx}$ is given by $f'(x) + \alpha \dfrac{dy}{dx} = 0$, is $\therefore$ also constant when x is, hence although the position on the contract curve is indeterminate, yet the quantity x, of one commodity, and the rate of exchange $\dfrac{dy}{dx}$ are determinate; the only thing which is indeterminate being y.

I.e. in the case of money, the volume of commodity sold and final price are determinate, but the total amount of money which changes hands is indeterminate.

But this is exactly Marshall's position; he works throughout with two unknowns, amount of commodity and price and when he speaks of determinateness or indeterminateness he refers to these two things only. Amount of money hardly occurs explicitly but it is implicitly stated[c] (pp. 391, 2) that this is indeterminate.

I have suggested that he should alter the last line of [d]p. 396 so as to make the meaning of "uncertainty of—equilibrium" clearer; otherwise the note and chapter seem to me to require no correction.

Your argument as to recontracts which would disturb temporary equilibria, I found very interesting and it seems to me quite true, but I hardly think it bears directly on Marshall's chapter, where recontracts are tacitly excluded.

I venture also to criticize the second of the two special cases which you discuss, the one namely which points out a case in which the labourer has some advantage over the employer. You assume for *simplicity* that there are m A's

---

c. This reference applies to pages 332–4 in vol. 1 of the present edition.

d. For the final and earlier versions of the passage here referred to, see page 793 in vol. 1 of the present edition and editorial note a to that page (p. 790 above).

and m B's; and infer in the end that m employers cannot easily deal with $m-n$ labourers. But this and the argument following is surely only a consequence of your particular assumption of equality of number, which is not true in the actual labour market.

If for instance there were m employers and 10 m workers, we might divide the workers into m groups of 10 each: and then regard each such group as a B: There is now no more difficulty in supposing that $5 m$ workers recontract with m employers than in supposing 10 m workers to recontract with $\frac{1}{2} m$ or $m-n$ employers.

Prof. Marshall is anxious to print off the note on barter as soon as possible, and he would be glad if you would be kind enough to send any answer you may care to make to these criticisms to me under cover to him. I am leaving to-morrow and shall be without an address for two or three days.

Yours faithfully
ARTHUR BERRY

A few days later, on 4 April 1891, Marshall sent the following letter of protest to Edgeworth:

BALLIOL CROFT
CAMBRIDGE
4/4/91

[e]My dear Edgeworth,

I now throw myself on your kind and generous forbearance, and ask you to listen without anger to something I have had it in my mind to say ever since you first misunderstood me about the meaning of R^{-t} and a negatively inclined supply curve. The feeling grew very much when I just saw your Italian article on Barter. At first I said little, because I was unable to translate the Italian properly; and afterwards I felt I should like to get a third person to make sure that I had not misunderstood you.

---

e. The originals of this and the previous letter of Marshall to Edgeworth cited in this Appendix, are in the Marshall Library at Cambridge.

What I want to say is that I do not think you at all appreciate the deadly and enduring injury that A does to B, if he reads rapidly a piece of hard argument on which B has spent an immense deal of work; and then believing that argument to be wrong, writes an article full of the most polite phrases, in which a caricature of that argument is held up to the most refined, but deadly scorn. I fancy you think that the polite phrases diminish the mischief. Really it is they that cause the most harm. Their effect, though *certainly not* their intention, is that of a white flag under which the ship approaches close to another and rams or torpedoes it. It was Cairnes' polite phrases to Mill that caused him in his Leading Principles, to do Mill more harm by his misrepresentations, than all the hostile critics Mill ever had. For readers *did not look behind the returns:* they took it for granted Cairnes' interpretations were correct: and if they had been Mill's whole theory of value would doubtless have been only an inflated wind bag.

As to Barter. My MSS on the subject were of great length. I spent several weeks in boiling down what I had to say, throwing away much, and avoiding complications. I then got these results over and above all the well recognized inferiority of the labourer to the employer in "competitive force" (of which I am to talk at great length in my vol. II when I come to Industrial Groups, Trades Unions, etc., and for which my Foreign Trade curves had at one time much interest to me) I concluded that two markets for corn similar in every respect except that in one the marginal utility of money is variable have different issues thus:

In *both*, the earlier bargainings in which there is a large surplus of utility, are uncertain: but in one only, the ultimate equilibrium (rate of exchange): [the term is used consistently in this sense, *never in any other*, throughout the chapter note] is fixed at 36*s*., in the other it might be anything. Also, but this is a minor point for my purpose, the amount sold is determinate in the one case only. You don't seem to have given yourself the smallest trouble to find out that I had set myself to prove these three points, and only these. But in the politest possible way you imply that my results are absolute nonsense. For whereas my whole point was that certain results did follow on one hypothesis (variable marginal utility of money) and not on another, you professed to have proved that they followed equally in both. You did not even take the trouble to find out that I had proved explicitly every single thing that you had proved with the only problem which I had formulated, or had any desire to discuss at that particular place. You thus got easily the credit of saying something new, whereas it was not new, and also of convicting another of an error of a kind which, if he had made it, would justly shake the credit of a very great part of his book. It would argue a lightness of heart and an absence of a sense of intellectual responsibility, which would justly shake people's credit of those many passages which in a book of this kind are necessarily rather hard to understand.

You supplement my discussion by some of your own on extraneous topics. They may be important. I myself should have preferred to put in some of my own MSS which I suppressed. That is a matter of taste. Very likely they may be really more important than all I have said on that and all other subjects. But that is not to the point. They do not vitiate my argument: but, whatever their truth or value may be, lie wholly outside of it. And they would not have helped me in my special purpose, which was to make people clearly to understand at the outset of a long argument as to demand and supply schedules, what was the exact nature of the danger run by speaking throughout as though the marginal utility of money was constant.

It is now nearly twenty years since I decided that the plan which you and Auspitz follow would, probably if not necessarily, lead to hopeless unreality and unpracticality: and in consequence elected what I thought, and think, the minor evil of making $x =$ amount and $y = ratio$, though in consequence I had to sit upon changes in the marginal utility of money. What you say that is new, however good of its kind, is entirely beyond my purpose. Perhaps I could hardly expect you to have read this into my Book V, ch. ii. But I do complain that you have written a polite article condemning me *for not having proved what I undertook to prove.*

797

There! I feel so much better: I am like a person who has held his mouth full of air under water for a minute. It does feel so nice to have let it out and will you be very good and forgive me. Please, Please do. Yours in great fear and awful dread: but most admiringly and sincerely

ALFRED MARSHALL

In the *Giornale degli Economisti* for June 1891, Berry published an article entitled "Alcuni brevi parole sulla teoria del baratto di Marshall" in which he expanded the points which he had made in his letter to Edgeworth. It was to this article that Marshall made reference in his Mathematical Note XII *bis* (page 845 in vol. 1 of the present edition).

In the *Giornale degli Economisti* for October 1891 Edgeworth wrote a brief note, "Ancora a proposito della teoria del baratto" in which he made a handsome apology to Marshall for having misunderstood him. He conceded the major points which had been made against him; though he did not accept the criticism which Berry put forward on his own account (i.e. without claiming the support of Marshall) with regard to the importance of the assumption of equal numbers of bargainers. (See the two penultimate paragraphs of Berry's letter to Edgeworth.)

Edgeworth concluded his Note by saying, apropos of this last point, "But I make this defence with all modesty, as one who has already burnt his fingers and fears the fire of controversy".

APPENDIX G

THE INCIDENCE OF LOCAL RATES, WITH SOME SUGGESTIONS AS TO POLICY

PAGE 794

a. Except where otherwise stated the wording of Appendix G dates from the 5th edition.

This Appendix, which was first inserted in the 5th edition, was based, as Marshall says, largely on his "Memorandum on The Classification and Incidence of Imperial and Local Taxes" which he wrote in 1897 for the Royal Commission on Local Taxation. The Memorandum has been reprinted in *The Official Papers of Alfred Marshall*, pp. 327–64.

b.   This paragraph dates from the 7th ed. (pp. 794–5).

c.   In the 8th edition "pp. 453 and 659"; emended in vol. 1 of the present edition to give the correct references.

PAGE 795

a.   This sentence was inserted in the 6th ed. (p. 795).

PAGE 801

a.   The remainder of this sentence dates from the 7th ed. (p. 801).

PAGE 802

a.   This paragraph is closely based on a passage in the 2nd ed. (Book VI, ch. IX, §6, pp. 670–1) which was substantially retained in the 3rd and 4th editions. In the 2nd ed. this passage ran as follows:

In a new country, where there is plenty of new land still free to settlers, the whole of the net income derived from land is required to remunerate cultivators for their capital and labour; and is therefore to be regarded as earnings and profits, or at most as quasi-rent and not as rent proper, although even there, a far-seeing statesman will feel a greater responsibility to future generations when legislating as to land than as to other forms of wealth. Thus it may be admitted that from the economic and from the ethical point of view, land must everywhere and always be classed as a thing by itself.

And in an old country, when land is regarded merely as one of the factors of production of material goods, though the only distinction between it and other factors is that they can be increased in quantity and it cannot; yet this distinction is vital in a broad survey of the causes that govern normal value. For the net income derived from the inherent properties of land is a true surplus; which does not directly enter even in the long run into the normal expenses of production, and which are required as rewards for the work and inventive energy of labourers and undertakers. It thus differs from the quasi-rents of buildings, machinery, &c., which are in the long run needed (in the present state of

799

human character and social institutions), to sustain the full force of production, invention, and accumulation. The sudden appropriation of rents and quasi-rents by the State would indeed have very similar effects in destroying security and shaking the foundations of society: but if from the first the State had retained true rents in its own hands, the vigour of industry and accumulation need not have been impaired; and nothing at all like this can be said of quasi-rents.

In the 3rd ed. (p. 713) and the 4th ed. (p. 718) there was the following additional sentence at the end of those just quoted:

The same is true of urban ground rent, which, as we have seen, is governed on the same principle as that of agricultural rent.

APPENDIX H

LIMITATIONS OF THE USE OF STATICAL ASSUMPTIONS IN REGARD TO INCREASING RETURN

PAGE 805

a.   Except where otherwise stated the text, etc. of this Appendix dates substantially from the 4th edition. But see also the editorial notes to Book V, chapter XII and the Editorial Appendix to that chapter.

In the 1st edition the subject-matter of most of this Appendix was placed in Book V, chapter V, entitled "The Theory of Stable Equilibrium of Normal Demand and Supply". In the 2nd and 3rd editions it was placed in Book V, chapter XI, entitled "The Equilibrium of Normal Demand and Supply Concluded. Multiple Positions of Equilibrium". In the 4th edition the more technical parts of the discussion were grouped in a "Note on the Pure Theory of Stable and Unstable Equilibria", which was placed at the end of Book V, chapter XI. In the 5th edition this Note, with a few additions, became Appendix H.

b.   So since the 5th ed.

c.   This paragraph dates from the 5th ed. (p. 805) where it replaced a paragraph dating from the 4th ed. (Book V, ch. XI, §4,

p. 516), which in the 5th ed. became the concluding paragraph of Book V, ch. XII, §3, p. 461. See page 461 in vol. I of the present edition.

d. This paragraph was inserted in the 5th ed. (p. 805).

e. In the 4th ed. (p. 516) the first sentence of this paragraph replaced the following paragraphs dating from the 2nd ed. (pp. 490–1):

It is then only as regards the long-period normal supply price that the true nature of the law of increasing return is shown. If there is a prospect of a permanent large demand for a thing, it will be worth while to invest capital in building up the material appliances, and the external and internal organisation of large businesses, which will be able to sell profitably at a low price. The long period supply price for large amounts will be low, because it is in effect the supply price not of particular things, but of the whole processes of production of those things. The law of increasing returns is in truth a law that the supply price of the *processes of production* (and marketing) of large quantities of certain goods falls, when the scale of those processes increases.

It is true for instance that if a sudden fashion were to set in for wearing watch-shaped aneroid barometers, highly paid labour, that had no special training for the work, would have to be drawn in from other trades, there would be a good deal of wasted effort and for a time the real and the money cost of production would be increased. But it is also true that if the fashion lasted a considerable time, then independently of any new invention in the cost of making aneroids the process of production on a large scale would be economical. For specialized skill in abundance would shortly be forthcoming, and properly graduated to the various work to be done: with a large use of the method of Interchangeable Parts, specialized machinery would do better and more cheaply much of the work that is now done by hand; and a steady increase in the annual output of watch-shaped aneroids, will lower very much their long period supply price, as a result of that development of industrial organization which normally belongs to a large scale of production.

Now their long period supply price when it had been thus lowered, might be either greater or less than the normal demand price for the corresponding scale of production, when at last the force of fashion died away; and the demand for aneroids was again based solely on their real utility. In the former case capital and labour...etc.

The paragraph beginning "It is true for instance that if a sudden fashion...etc." is merely a slight rewording of a passage in the 1st ed. (Book V, ch. IV, p. 413). See editorial note **d** to page 455 of vol. I in the present edition.

PAGE 806

a. The remainder of § 2, apart from the footnote, dates substantially from the 2nd ed. (pp. 491–2).

b. In the 1st ed. (pp. 423–4) the long footnote here placed at the end of this section was preceded by the following discussion in the text:

It sometimes, though rarely, happens that there are two positions of real equilibrium of demand and supply, either of which is equally consistent with the general circumstances of the market, and either of which if once reached would be stable, until some great disturbance occurred.

Take for instance the case of a commodity which has been produced on a small scale and chiefly by hand labour; its high price having prevented its being bought except by the small class of rich persons whose tastes are very liable to change. The method of producing it makes its wholesale price high; and the smallness of the dealings in it makes its retail price much higher than its wholesale price. For if it passes through a middleman's hands on its way to the retailer's he must have high profits on it to compensate him for the risk of its going out of fashion and the smallness of the business done in it; while the retailer himself will certainly add a great deal to the price that he pays for it not only for these reasons, but because the class of customers for whom he lays himself out require him to keep an expensive establishment, and do not much object to being charged high prices. After a time it occurs to someone that it is a thing which the masses would like to have if it were brought within their range; and that if it were produced by machinery on a large scale its wholesale price could be much reduced, that its retail price would fall even more than in proportion, and that consumers would be tempted by the resulting cheapness to purchase largely. Other producers follow suit, and after a time instead of a few hundreds being sold weekly at so many shillings, tens of thousands are sold for an equal number of pence. It is then possible, at all events theoretically, that the price and the amount produced may jump from one position of stable equilibrium to another.

   c.   This footnote dates from the 1st ed. (pp. 424 n.–5 n.).

PAGE 807

   a.   This paragraph in the 4th ed. (p. 518) replaced the following paragraph dating from the 1st ed. (p. 425):

It has already been indicated that the theory of stable equilibrium of normal demand and supply in its most abstract form assumes a certain rigidity in the conditions of demand and supply, which does not really exist. This theory however, especially when aided by diagrams, helps to give definiteness to our ideas; and in its elementary stages it does not diverge from the actual facts of life so far as to prevent its giving a fairly trustworthy picture of the chief methods of action of the strongest and most persistent group of economic forces. It is only when pushed to its more remote and intricate logical consequences, especially those connected with multiple positions of equilibrium, that it slips away from the conditions of real life, and soon ceases to be of much service in dealing with practical problems. The chief cause of this divergence is the fact that, if the normal production of a commodity increases and afterwards again diminishes to its old amount, the demand price and the supply price are not likely to return, as the pure theory assumes that they will, to their old positions for that amount.

   In the 2nd ed. (p. 493) the word "One" replaced the words "The chief" before the word "cause" at the beginning of the last of the foregoing sentences.

   b.   Apart from the first clause of this paragraph, which dates from the 4th ed. (p. 518) the remainder of § 3 dates substantially from the 2nd ed. (pp. 493–6).

803

c. So since the 4th ed. (p. 518) where this sentence replaced the following sentence dating from the 1st ed. (p. 426):

For instance, the prices of cotton during the American war showed that the consumers were bidding for the reduced supply a price higher than that for which an equal amount could have been sold, if its previous low price had not brought it into common use to meet a great variety of wants, many of which indeed it had itself created.

In the 1st ed., the following footnote was attached to this sentence but was deleted from the 2nd ed.:

> Of course the movement of the prices of cotton during the war was the result of many causes; and before deducing statistically the effect of the cause which we are now considering, we should have to isolate it, by allowing for the stock of cotton goods in the hands of consumers, &c. The extreme competition for employment on the part of manufacturers for their machinery, and on the part of artisans for their skill brought the supply price of calico very close to that of the raw material, but of course this did not affect the demand price.

d. The following sentence in the 1st ed. (p. 425 n.), which was placed in brackets after the sentence ending with the words "to the right of that point", was deleted from the 5th ed.:

> (If the curves touch one another at any point, the equilibrium corresponding to it will be stable for displacements in one direction, and unstable for displacements in the other. No practical interest attaches to the investigation of this barely possible case.)

e. The following sentences, which were placed in square brackets as a separate paragraph at the end of this footnote in the 1st ed. (p. 425 n.), were deleted from the 2nd ed.: "[This theory of unstable equilibrium was published independently by M. Walras and the present writer. See Preface.]" See editorial note **b** to page xi of vol. 1 in the present edition (pp. 37–8 above).

a. This footnote dates from the 1st ed. (p. 426 n.).

b. The first three sentences of this footnote date from the 1st ed. (p. 427 n.).

c. The remainder of this footnote dates from the 5th ed. (pp. 808 n.–9 n.).

a. This footnote dates from the 1st ed. (p. 428 n.).

b. This footnote dates from the 4th ed. (pp. 519 n.–20 n.) where it replaced the following footnote dating from the 2nd ed. (p. 496 n.):

> That is to say instead of normal demand and supply curves we should use demand and supply surfaces, price being measured along the axis of z, time along that of y and amount along that of x. Even now there might be some interest in

working out, analytically or geometrically, the curves of intersection of such surfaces drawn on various assumptions as to the influence of time. And though, for many years to come work of this kind must be rather a mathematical diversion, than a solid contribution to economics, yet it may show the way towards such methods of study of social and economic history and statistics, as may enable future generations to impart to such demand and supply surfaces a reality that is altogether beyond our present range.

PAGE 810

a. In the 1st ed. (Book V, ch. v, §5, pp. 428–9) the corresponding section to Appendix H, §4 in the 8th edition ran as follows:

§5. When different producers have different advantages for producing a thing, its supply price is equal to its expenses of production to those producers who have no special and exceptional facilities. When the market is in equilibrium, and the thing is being sold at a price which covers these expenses, there remains a surplus beyond their expenses for those who have the assistance of any exceptional natural advantages; which being free gifts of nature have no cost of production, no supply price. This surplus we may call *producer's surplus* or *producer's rent*. (There is a surplus in any case, and if the owner of the free gift of nature lends it out to another, he can generally get for its use a rent equivalent to this surplus. The term rent has been much used by economists for this purpose; but the more general term surplus seems to be the better adapted for it.) *[margin note: The possession of any rare natural advantages affords to the producers a surplus or rent.]*

The special facilities may be of many different kinds: they may be mental, moral or physical qualities: they may be the possession of rich or conveniently situated fields or mines or building ground. The plan of regarding the expenses of production of a commodity as reckoned for those parts of it which were produced under conditions of no exceptional advantage, and therefore paid no rent, was devised by Ricardo; but applied by him only to the case of agricultural rent. The plan has great difficulties which will be examined carefully in the following Book. Here we are concerned only to notice the place which is left for producer's surplus or rent in the theory of the stable equilibrium of demand and supply in its broadest form[1].

[1] Let DD' and SS' be the demand and supply curves for wheat. Let OH be the equilibrium amount and HA the equilibrium price. Let P be a point on SS', and let QPM be drawn cutting AF a horizontal line through A in Q

and Ox in M. Then the OMth bushel has expenses of production MP: but being sold for price AH, that is, MQ, it affords a Producers' Surplus or Rent equal to PQ. Proceeding as in the case of Consumers' Surplus or Rent (Bk. III, ch. IV, §1), we may regard MQ as a thin parallelogram or as a thick straight line. And as M takes consecutive positions along OH, we get a number of thick straight lines cut in two by the line SA, the lower part of each representing the expenses of production of a bushel of corn, and the upper the contribution which that bushel affords towards rent. The lower set of thick lines taken together fill up the whole space $SOHA$; which therefore represents the aggregate of the expenses of production of OH corn. The upper set of thick lines taken together fill up the space FSA, which therefore represents Producer's Surplus or Rent. Subject to the corrections mentioned in Book III, ch. VI, §2, DFA represents the surplus satisfaction which consumers get from an amount OH over that, the value of which is represented to them by a sum of money equal to $OH \times HA$; and the diagram shows how the name "Consumer's Rent" was suggested for this Surplus.

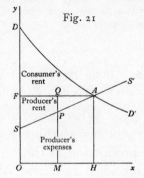

Fig. 21

It must however be remembered that we have tacitly assumed that MP being the expenses of production of that part of the produce which was raised under the most difficult circumstances (so as to pay no rent) when OM was produced, remains also the expenses of production (other than rent) of the OMth unit even when OH is produced, or in other words, that the increase in production from the amount OM to the amount OH did not alter the expenses of production of the OMth bushel. And this assumption is seldom strictly in accordance with facts. The increased production would almost inevitably have improved the organization of production and lowered the expenses of production of the OMth bushel. And it is therefore almost certain that the rent would really be somewhat more than FSA.

[Subject to certain conditions, the rent may be represented by the area lying between FA and a short-period supply curve drawn on the supposition that the economies due to industrial organization are to be taken to be those which properly belong to the amount OH, and which are regarded as attaching to that amount only, when a long-period curve is being drawn. It seems however doubtful whether it is worth while to push the analogy very far; for, as our studies of rent in the next two books will indicate, it could not be made exact without the introduction of intricate and artificial hypotheses. The short-period curve just referred to would be inclined positively and would be steeper than the SS' of our figure; but not necessarily much steeper unless our SS' were drawn for a very long period. If however the diagram had represented the long-period normal supply price of a manufactured commodity, SS' would have been inclined negatively; and the short-period just referred to, being inclined positively, would stand in no close relation to it.]

The footnote which replaced, in the 2nd ed. (pp. 483 n.–4 n.), the foregoing footnote in the 1st ed. was retained without substantial change in the later editions. See pages 810 n.–12 n. in vol. 1 of the present edition.

b.   Although §4 of Appendix H achieved its final form in the 4th ed. (pp. 520–2 n.), its subject-matter dates substantially from the 2nd ed. (Book V, ch. XI, §1, pp. 480–4 n.).

In the 4th ed. the text of Book V, ch. XI, §1 in the 2nd and 3rd editions was divided between Book V, ch. V, §1, and §6 of the "Note on the Pure Theory of Stable and Unstable Equilibria" attached to Book V, ch. xi, which became Appendix H in the 5th ed.

c. The following paragraph (referring to conditions in a stationary state) dating from the 2nd ed. (p. 482), was deleted from the 4th ed.:

There would be no such things as quasi-rents: for the income earned by every appliance of production being truly anticipated beforehand, would represent the normal measure of the efforts and appliances required to call it into existence. But true rents would remain. For that which cannot be increased by man's effort in time however long, would still have no supply price; and its value would still be found by capitalizing the income derived from the differential advantages which it offered for production; and that income would be determined by the expenses of production of that part of the supply which had not the benefit of any permanent differential advantages; i.e. by the marginal expenses of production.

d. In the 2nd and 3rd editions the following marginal summary was attached to this paragraph: "Aggregate expenses of production would then be definite; and, rents being counted in, average expenses would then be equal to marginal and to normal expenses."

e. In the 4th ed. (p. 520) this sentence replaced the following sentence dating from the 2nd ed. (p. 481):

In a world of change, such as ours is, the terms "aggregate" or "average" expenses of production have in general no exact and definite meaning: though of course they may be legitimately used, with an artificial interpretation clause, for the special purpose of a particular problem.

f. So since the 4th ed. (p. 520). In the 2nd ed. (p. 481) this sentence ran as follows: "The present income earned by them will be of the nature of quasi-rents, determined by the general relations of demand for, and the supply of their products; and their values will be arrived at by capitalising these quasi-rents."

In the 3rd ed. (p. 501) the word "incomes" replaced the word "quasi-rents" in the sentence just quoted, but at the end of the sentence, after the last word "incomes" the following words were added in parentheses: "(which will be of the nature of quasi-rents)".

g. This sentence was inserted in the 4th ed. (p. 520).

h. This article was probably similar in substance to that of the "ingenious paper privately printed by Mr H. Cunynghame" to which Marshall referred in a footnote dating from the 1st ed. (see page 463 n. in vol. 1 of the present edition). Cunynghame's *Economic Journal* article contained a section in which he expounded his concept of successive demand and cost curves. Marshall's reaction at the time to this concept is set out in his two letters to Edgeworth, which are printed below in the Editorial Appendix to Appendix H.

i. In the 8th edition "v. 4; and ix. 6"; emended in vol. 1 of the present edition to give the correct reference.

j. This footnote dates in its present form from the 2nd ed. (pp. 483 n.–4n.) apart from the alteration of one sentence, one deletion noted below, and the replacement in the 5th ed. of the original words "consumer's rent" and "producer's rent" in the diagram, by the words "consumer's surplus" and "producer's surplus". For the form of this footnote in the 1st ed. (p. 429 n.) see editorial note **a** to page 810 of vol. 1 in this edition. It will be observed that the term "particular expenses curve" dates from the 2nd ed., and was not used in the 1st ed.

k. So since the 4th ed. (p. 521 n.), where this sentence replaced the following sentence dating from the 2nd ed. (p. 483 n.):

> This case may be illustrated by the adjoining diagram, in which *SS′* is not a true supply curve, but has properties, which are often erroneously attributed to the supply curve; and some study of it may be useful, if for no other purpose, yet as a means of guarding the true supply curve against misunderstandings.

EDITORIAL APPENDIX TO APPENDIX H

MARSHALL'S VIEWS ON SIR HENRY CUNYNGHAME'S
SUCCESSIVE DEMAND AND COST CURVES; AND HIS
PROTEST TO F. Y. EDGEWORTH AGAINST THE
LATTER'S USE OF THE TERM THE "SHORT PERIOD"

In April 1892 Marshall wrote the two following letters to F. Y. Edgeworth, the originals of which are now in the Marshall Library in Cambridge:

26 April, 1892

Cunynghame's "successive $\frac{\text{utility}}{\text{demand}}$ curves" I think I can understand. ("Successive" may imply a regular correlation of sequences, which there is *not*.) I should call them "temporary" demand curves, the term "temporary" being carefully distinguished from "short-period", a technical term used for a special purpose which is quite distinct from that which Cunynghame has in view.

It is a free country. I deliberately decided that temporary demand curves (as contrasted with normal demand curves whose shape could be shifted if need be) would not be of any practical use, and that this would encumber the reader and divert his attention from more important things. [a] I have discussed the notions which they represent in Book III $\dfrac{\text{1st edition, ch. iii, \S 7}}{\text{ch. iv, \S 6, and in Book V}}$, ch. xi, $\S 4$, $\dfrac{\text{ch. v, \S 1}}{\text{ch. xii, \S 1}}$ and $\dfrac{\text{ch. viii, \S 6}}{\text{ch. xiii, \S 6}}$ (all of these except the 2nd are practically unchanged from the original MSS of 17 years ago).

As to his "Successive cost curves", I do not know what they are. I knew others thought highly of them, and put in a note acknowledging them as fully as I could without committing myself to saying I understand them. (Perhaps I implied that I understood more about them than I intended to. I thought the words "seems to come in effect" implied I was not sure whether I understood them: but perhaps I should have used a different phrase.) When I read his article I knew I did not understand them, and thought he did not. I then wrote to him, and I have now no doubt in my own mind that he does not. He is quick, but impetuous; and all through his life has constantly supposed himself to know what he means when he does not. You are graver in charac-

---

a. The upper of the two lines of references in this sentence relates to the 1st edition, while those in the lower line relate to the 2nd edition; the exception made in the words in parentheses relates to Book V, chapter xi, §4 in the 2nd edition.

The corresponding chapters and sections in vol. 1 of the present edition, are as follows:

1st edition, Book III, ch. iii, §7 corresponds to Book III, ch. iv, §6 in vol. 1 of the present edition.

2nd edition, Book V, ch. xi, §4 corresponds to Appendix H, §3 in vol. 1 of the present edition.

1st edition, Book V, ch. v, §1 corresponds to Book V, ch. xiii, §1 in vol. 1 of the present edition.

1st edition, Book V, ch. viii, §6 corresponds to Book V, ch. xiv, §6 in vol. 1 of the present edition.

ter, and write with more responsibility. I think therefore I am justified in asking you, before you lend your great authority in support of what I think a half-thought out notion to answer this simple question. Let $y=f(x)$ be the equation to one of Cunynghame's successive cost curves: What does the y mean, and what does the x mean? There is no answer in Cunynghame's paper, which in itself is an omission that seems to give warning of danger. I really do not know. If you do, please tell me.

You have gone beyond Cunynghame. For he does use a new term; while you utterly wreck my pet phrase "short period", by applying it to a use which seems to me likely to introduce calamitous confusion. The changes which arise from the gradual rise and decline of fashion, and familiarity, the feeling that a thing is select or that it is vulgar, of being unique like an old book or the key of a Bramah lock, or useful like screws in machinery made to Whitworth's gauge which can be easily replaced if lost, these things have nothing in common with the distinction between "short" and "long" period supply prices in my own pet and peculiar use of the term. For they represent casual influences, and it corresponds to a great fundamental difference, common to all branches of work; that namely between periods which are not and those which are long enough to allow the supply of the agents of production (workers, material plant, specialization of skill and machinery, business organization and connection) to be adapted to the demand: For the one Supply price = Total Cost of production at the margin. For the other it means Prime cost mitigated by a fear of spoiling the market. [b]Prime cost itself, being made up in a great measure of

---

b. That Marshall should describe prime cost as "itself being made up in great measure of quasi-rents", might seem at first sight to be in contradiction with his own doctrine of quasi-rent as the surplus (if any) of aggregate receipts over aggregate prime costs in the short period. But he is, of course, not regarding prime costs as quasi-rent from the point of view of the business which incurs them. In 1892, when Marshall wrote this letter, he was still in the habit of applying the notion of quasi-rent to the earnings of the factors or production in general, including labour: it was from the 3rd edition (1895) onwards

quasi-rents. As the parent of this specialised term, I cannot refrain when I see you plunging it into a medium in which it cannot breathe, from calling MURDER! I ask Cunynghame whether "successive" meant "short period", and he said no! He says also that "Successive cost" does not mean the same as my "particular expenses" ^c(p. 483). But I fancy it must be akin to that, more or less.

28 April, 1892

You are good and kind and patient as usual. I am distinctly of opinion that the laws that govern the supply curve have little or nothing in common with those that govern the demand curve; because in demand there is nothing corresponding to the economies of production on a large scale, difference between Prime Cost and Total Cost or which is nearly the same thing between causes that govern the application of Fixed and circulating capital etc., etc., which give rise to the special features of supply. I think Jevons did great harm by talking of supply-price as measuring disutility curve. In picking blackberries, the disutility curve of effort and the supply curve are practically the same thing and they are in *pari materia* with the demand curve or the utility curve. But in the case of aneroid barometers etc., the economic supply curve has but the slightest connection with the laws of disutility; for the greater part they are not in *pari materia* at all. I maintain that Cournot and others knew that: and that Jevons' talk about utility and disutility struck the popular mind merely because it put out in broad clear

---

that he deleted most of the references to quasi-rent in Book VI, dealing with distribution. It seems probable that the sense in which he was regarding prime cost as "made up in great measure of quasi-rents", was in relation to the owners of the capital and labour whose gross earnings are reflected in the prime costs incurred by the business in the process of production. The earnings of the owners of these factors, being determined by the action of short period forces, are liable at any given moment to diverge from what would be their normal long-period level, and therefore can be treated as quasi-rents from the point of view of their recipients.

c. Pages 810 n.–12 n. in vol. 1 of the present edition.

light a very elementary fact, which could be explained even to children. In other directions I think he did good; but in this I think his influence was to obscure the real nature of cost of production. You may repeat any of this that you like to Palgrave.

Cunynghame seems to me hopelessly obscure. He may have made a contribution; but I cannot find out at all what it is. In fact to quote Cummings' striking description of Toynbee Hall work, C's seems to me to be "undergraduate rather than graduate work". He has all a graduate's ability but none of a graduate's patience.

As regards supply the case is this. I have always held and taught in lectures year after year that Producer's rent cannot be represented in the supply curve except in curves in which you can ignore the economies of organization and production on a large scale. In the second Edition I adopted the name *particular expenses* curve for those in which you can do this. Cunynghame claims, as I understand to prove that this is wrong and that you can do it somehow. He may mean something but I cannot after my patient study of this article and his very long letters about it form the smallest notion of what he does mean. And though I cannot prove a negative, I have in my own mind no doubt that he does not himself know, and that if he attempted to say definitely what his *y* and *x* are, some part of his argument would instantly collapse.

That diamonds owe some of their value to their rarity is true but not so novel or striking as most of the remarks to which you commit yourself.

That if straw hats come into fashion, or a new book gets sensational reviews and is the talk of the hour, increased supplies can be sold at a higher price is true. Such facts, I hold, correspond to raising the demand curve; and the analogy to them in supply I find not in the laws that govern the shape of the supply curve but in the fact that substantive inventions such as Bessemers or that of the compound engine may lower the supply curve for steel rails or for 1000 h.p. engines. I myself therefore should not be prepared to imply that Cunynghame's analogy was even *prima facie* a valid one. But there is no reason on earth why you should not, if you think it is *prima facie* valid.

What I mean about diamonds is that the law of Diminishing Utility of a mark of distinction, as a "C.B." or a diamond (in so far as it is desired not for its own sake) is in my opinion of the same kind as the law of Diminishing Utility for Pineapples or Salmon, of which large quantities pall on the palate.

APPENDIX I

RICARDO'S THEORY OF VALUE

PAGE 813

a. Except where otherwise stated the wording of Appendix I dates from the 1st edition (pp. 529–36). The marginal summaries date from the 3rd edition.

In the 1st edition a "Note on Ricardo's Theory of Cost of Production in Relation to Value" was placed at the end of chapter vi of Book VI. From the 2nd to the 4th editions this Note on Ricardo's Theory of Value was placed at the end of chapter xiv of Book V. From the 5th edition onwards it became Appendix I—Ricardo's Theory of Value.

b. The following opening paragraph dating from the 1st ed. (p. 529) was deleted from the 5th ed.:

Ricardo's theory of cost of production in relation to value occupies so important a place in the history of economics that any misunderstanding as to its real character must necessarily be very mischievous; and unfortunately it is so expressed as almost to invite misunderstanding. In consequence there is a widely spread belief that it has needed to be reconstructed by the present generation of economists. The purpose of the present Note is to show cause for not accepting this opinion; and for holding on the contrary that the foundations of the theory as they were left by Ricardo remain intact, that much has been added to them, and that very much has been built upon them, but that little has been taken from them.

c. So since the 2nd ed. (p. 539) where the present sentence replaced the following sentence in the 1st ed. (p. 530): "If we do this with the desire to ascertain what he really meant, we shall find very little to reject in his doctrines, though we may find much that needs to be added to them."

PAGE 815

a. The remainder of this paragraph was inserted in the 3rd ed. (p. 559).

b. The following concluding clause of this sentence after the word "assisted", dating from the 1st ed. (pp. 531–2) was deleted from the 3rd ed.:

that "the principle that the quantity of labour bestowed on the production of commodities regulates their relative value is considerably modified by the employment of machinery or other fixed and durable capital...and by the unequal durability of capital and by the unequal rapidity with which it is returned to its employer."

c. This clause was inserted in the 3rd ed. (p. 559).

d. This and the next paragraph were inserted in the 3rd ed. (pp. 559–60) where they replaced the following paragraph dating from the 1st ed. (p. 532):

He thus insisted that things on which equal amounts of labour had been spent might have very different values, if the labour used on the one was on the average more highly skilled than that used on the other; or if it was assisted by more capital; or, even where the capitals required were equal, if the investment of capital had to be for a longer period in the one case than in the other. But he liked short phrases and he thought that his readers would always supply for themselves the explanations of which he had given them a hint.

PAGE 816

a. The last two sentences of this paragraph date in their present form from the 3rd ed. (p. 561). In the 1st ed. (p. 532) there was a separate paragraph which ran as follows:

Ricardo is more responsible than any one else for the habit of endeavouring to express great economic doctrines in short sentences. But in the problem of normal value the various elements mutually determine one another, as we have already seen in part and shall see more clearly later on; they do not determine one another successively in a long chain of causation.

In the 2nd ed. (p. 541) the word "responsible" was replaced by the word "guilty" and the word "bad" was inserted before the word "habit".

b. This footnote dates from the 3rd ed. (p. 561) where it was inserted in the text in square brackets. It was placed in a footnote in the 4th ed. (pp. 565 n.–6 n.).

PAGE 817

a. So since the 2nd ed. (p. 541) where this sentence replaced the following sentence in the 1st ed. (p. 532): "There is perhaps no writer of modern times who has approached to the brilliant and profound originality of Ricardo more nearly than Jevons."

PAGE 820

a. The following sentences at this point, dating from the 1st ed. (pp. 535–6) were deleted from the 3rd ed.:

In like manner it may be pardonable, but it is not strictly accurate to say that the fluctuations of market values, or the varying prices which the same rare book fetches, when sold and resold at Christie's auction room, are determined exclusively by demand. And in like manner again when Ricardo thought he had made it clear that he had in his mind the "natural" or normal values of those goods the production of which conforms approximately to the law of constant return, and said that value was determined by cost of production, his exposition was grievously at fault, though what he actually meant is true.

b. The following clause at the beginning of this sentence dating from the 2nd ed. (p. 545) was deleted from the 3rd ed.: "[His] statistical work was of the very highest order; and there are few thinkers... etc."

c. Marshall's review of Jevons' *Theory of Political Economy*, in the *Academy*, is reprinted in the *Memorials of Alfred Marshall* (pp. 93–100).

d. The remainder of this footnote was inserted in the 7th ed. (pp. 820 n.–1 n.).

a. This sentence dates from the 3rd ed. (p. 565), though the reference to Professors Walras and Menger dates from the 1st ed. (p. 536).

b. This sentence dates from the 2nd ed. (p. 545). The following clauses after the word "misunderstanding" in the 2nd ed. were deleted from the 4th ed.: "and has done much to sustain that strife which still hinders, and still hides from view, the continuity of the development of economic science."

c. The remainder of this paragraph was inserted in the 3rd ed. (p. 565).

d. This paragraph was inserted in the 5th ed. (p. 821)

APPENDIX J

THE DOCTRINE OF THE WAGES-FUND

PAGE 822

a. Except where otherwise stated the wording of this Appendix dates substantially from the 1st edition. The marginal summaries were inserted in the 3rd edition.

In the 1st edition a "Note on the Wages Fund Theory, and on two of Mill's Fundamental Propositions on Capital" was attached to the end of chapter III of Book VII. In the 2nd edition the Note with the same title was attached to the end of chapter II of Book VI.

In the 3rd and 4th editions the Note was kept in the same place as in the 2nd edition, but was entitled in the 3rd edition "Note on the Doctrine of the Wages-Fund", and in the 4th edition "Notes on the Doctrine of the Wages-Fund and on different Kinds of Surplus" (see editorial note **a** to Appendix K, page 830 of vol. 1 in the present edition).

In the 5th edition the Note became Appendix J, entitled "The Doctrine of the Wages Fund".

b. The whole of §1 dates from the 3rd ed. (pp. 618–19). In the 1st ed. (p. 567) the opening paragraph of this Note ran as follows:

T H E question whether this so-called Wages-fund theory is true or false is in a great measure a question of words.

For it has many forms, some of which are vague and incomplete, rather than untrue statements of those general relations of capital and labour in the problem of distribution, which are discussed in the present Book. But it has also a vulgar form which derives its origin from some careless phrases that Adam Smith and Ricardo used when wishing to lay stress on the importance to the labourer of those stores of wealth by which he is supported while producing further wealth. In this vulgar form it asserts that the amount of wages which could and would be paid in a country in, say, a year, is fixed absolutely by the amount of capital existing there at the time; so that if wages were forced up in any one trade, other wage receivers must lose a sum exactly equal in the aggregate to the gain of that trade. In this form it is inconsistent with the general tenor of Adam Smith's and Ricardo's reasonings; and, though the point is not free from doubt, it seems never to have been unconditionally accepted by any of their chief followers, nor did it find acceptance in Germany or France. But many of the popular expositors of economics gave the theory in this form as the chief teaching of the science on the subject of wages; and unfortunately the position of those popular expositors was strengthened by a passage in the Chapter on Wages in J. S. Mill's *Principles of Political Economy*. This also was the form in which it was used by some capitalists, who were anxious to prevent the working classes from endeavouring to get higher wages by strikes, or otherwise; and who were glad to be able to quote the authority of political economy on their side; and in this form it is certainly false.

In the 2nd ed. (p. 572) the foregoing paragraph was retained with the addition of the following clauses and sentence, which were inserted between the second and third of the above sentences, that is after the clause "discussed in the present Book":

that the growth of wage-capital and the rise of wages do not stand to one another in the simple relation of cause and effect, but that all the chief elements of the problem act and react on one another and mutually determine one another. That is to say, the supply of capital and the supply of labour; the price of the use of capital or the rate of interest, and the price of the use of labour or the rate of earnings; the marginal efficiency of auxiliary capital, and that of the labour supported by wage-capital; and lastly the relative amounts of auxiliary and of wage-capital—all those elements mutually determine one another.

It may be noted that the second sentence in the foregoing paragraph was slightly altered in the 2nd ed., and that the clause beginning with the words "that the growth of wage-capital, etc." succeeded the words "rather than untrue statements of the general doctrines discussed in the present Book".

The whole paragraph was deleted from the 3rd ed.

PAGE 823

a. The paper here referred to is reprinted in the Editorial Appendix to Book VI, chapters I and II, pp. 598–614 above.

PAGE 824

a. The words "economic science" replaced in the 4th ed. (p. 620) the words "political economy" in the earlier editions.

b. The remainder of this sentence and the next paragraph date from the 3rd ed. (pp. 620–1) where they replaced the following clauses and paragraph dating from the 1st ed. (p. 568):

and he would have treated the whole problem from the beginning on those sound lines of reasoning, which he followed when he returned to the subject of distribution after he had discussed the theory of demand and supply. For indeed nearly all of what he says about wages in his fourth Book is thorough and scientific as far as it goes: but it was short and its significance has been overlooked; and the chapter on wages in his second Book has been generally accepted as expressing his deliberate views on the subject.

The doctrine contained in that chapter was attacked by many writers, among whom Longe, Cliffe Leslie and Jevons were conspicuous. But it was the Treatise *On Labour* by Thornton, his old friend and colleague at the India Office, that impressed Mill most, and indeed it seems to have so over-weighted his judgment that when publishing his recantation of his old doctrine (*Dissertations*, vol. IV), he took to himself blame for confusions of thought, of which it is not certain that he had been guilty: and he did not reply, as he might have done, that there is scarcely any trace of those confusions in his discussion of the theory of distribution in the third chapter of the fourth Book of his *Political Economy*.

PAGE 825

a. This paragraph dates substantially from the 3rd ed. (p. 621), but by mistake the words "long periods" and "short periods" were related to the wrong argument; so that line 1 read: "As regards long periods it does not go far enough.", and line 3: "And for short periods, it goes too far." This mistake was not corrected till the 6th ed. (p. 825).

b. The remainder of this paragraph dates mainly from the 3rd ed. (pp. 621–2) where it replaced the following sentences dating from the 1st ed. (p. 569):

He does not call attention to the real differences which there are between markets for labour and markets for goods; while he implies differences which do not exist. He lays stress upon the obvious fact that labour cannot receive as wages things that are only in process of production, and are not yet ready for use; and he goes some little way towards showing how wages are determined by the general economic conditions of the time and place, one of the chief of these conditions being the amount and character of the existing stock of capital. But his constant references to the Wages-fund, while they do not enable him to say anything that could not have been said better in other ways, prevent him from bringing out the fundamental harmony and continuity that exists between the doctrine of wages and the main body of economic theory. (For a further discussion of the Wages-fund theory, the reader may be referred to General Walker's writings, in which may be included his share in a controversy in the second volume of the Harvard *Quarterly Journal of Economics*, to Prof. Sidgwick's *Principles of Political Economy*, Book II, ch. VIII, and to the Article by Prof. Nicholson on *Wages* in the *Encyclopædia Britannica*.)

c. This and the next sentence date from the 8th edition (page 825). In the 3rd to the 7th editions a clause was added to the end of the preceding sentence containing the quotation from Cairnes and was

819

followed by a sentence. This clause and sentence, which were deleted from the 8th edition, ran as follows:

and this seems to point in a wrong direction. For an increase of labour must increase the national dividend, which is one of the causes that govern wages; and therefore if the supply of labour increases, other things cannot be equal.

PAGE 826

a. This sentence was inserted in the 3rd ed. (p. 622).

b. This and the next sentence date from the 3rd ed. (p. 622) where they replaced the following sentences dating from the 1st ed. (pp. 569–70):

Reference has already been made (p. 138) to the first of Mill's Fundamental Propositions relating to capital: viz. that *Industry is limited by capital*. The phrase is an old one, which has been applied for many purposes. Sometimes it has been used to express the obvious fact that labourers cannot exist unless either they or others supply themselves (and their families) with the necessaries for *life;* though it would really be better interpreted to mean that they cannot work efficiently unless they are supplied with the necessaries for *efficiency* (see Book II, ch. IV). Sometimes it is used as a short way of stating the Wages-fund theory in its vulgar form.

The reference to p. 138 in the 1st ed. applies to page 789 n. in vol. 1 of the present edition.

c. This clause dates from the 3rd ed. (p. 622) where it replaced the following clause dating from the 1st ed. (p. 570): "and, the share of it which goes to capital not being diminished, that which goes to labour cannot be increased."

d. This paragraph dates substantially from the 3rd ed. (pp. 622–3).

PAGE 827

a. This and the next paragraph date from the 4th ed. (pp. 623–4).

b. This footnote in the 4th ed. replaced the following concluding paragraph to the "Note on the Doctrine of the Wages Fund" in the 3rd ed. (p. 623):

Some interesting contributions to the history of the Wages-fund theory are to be found in the article by Prof. Taussig in the *Quarterly Journal of Economics* already referred to, and

820

in Mr Cannan's *Production and Distribution*, *1776–1848*. General Walker's writings have thrown much light on the whole subject. The instances of employees rendering their labour in advance of payment, which he has collected, are instructive in many ways; and, though they do not perhaps much affect the main issue, they bear effectively on some turns of the controversy.

PAGE 828

a. This paragraph dates substantially from the 1st ed. (pp. 570–1). The whole paragraph was deleted from the 3rd ed. but was reinstated in the 4th ed. (p. 624) and retained in the later editions.

b. The remainder of this paragraph dates in its present wording from the 4th ed. (p. 624) where it replaced the following sentences in the 1st ed. (pp. 570–1):

Now there is a sense in which this is true. For, of course, the price of the commodities is likely to include a good deal of profits of manufacturer and middleman; and if the purchaser acts as employer, and puts the labour to work in such a way as to require little or no auxiliary capital, it is true that he does slightly diminish the demand for the services of the employing class, and for the loan of capital; and that he does by an equal amount increase the demand for labour, and thus raise wages; but he would have secured very nearly the same result by buying, say, hand-made lace instead of machine-made lace. And this kind of change is not at all what Mill had in his mind; for in his defence of the proposition, he, with seeming unconsciousness, assumes that the wages of labour will be paid, as in practice they commonly are, as the work proceeds; and that the price of the commodities will be paid, as in practice it commonly is, after the commodities are made: and the whole of his argument really hangs on this assumption. It will be found that in every case which he has chosen to illustrate the doctrine, his arguments imply, though he does not seem to be aware of it, that the consumer when passing from purchasing commodities to hiring labour, postpones the date of his own consumption of the fruits of labour. It is this postponement, this waiting, that, in Mill's illustrative instances, really increases the capital ready to aid and support labour; and therefore increases the effective demand for labour. And the same postponement would have resulted in the same benefit to labour if the purchaser had made no change in the mode of his expenditure.

c. This paragraph was inserted in the 5th ed. (p. 828).

d. The remainder of this section (§4) dates substantially from the 3rd ed. (Book V, ch. II, §10, pp. 613–15).

PAGE 829

a. In the 8th edition "Appendix E, 4"; emended in vol. I of the present edition to give the correct reference.

EDITORIAL APPENDIX TO APPENDIX J

MARSHALL'S REPLY TO CRITICISMS BY S. M. MACVANE OF PARTS OF HIS THEORY OF DISTRIBUTION

In October 1887 (volume 2 of the *Quarterly Journal of Economics*, 1888) Professor S. M. Macvane wrote an article entitled "The Theory of Business Profits", in which he criticized certain of Marshall's views on the theory of distribution, as set out in *The Economics of Industry*, by Alfred and Mary Paley Marshall.

In January 1888, in the same volume of the *Quarterly Journal of Economics*, Marshall made the following reply:

WAGES AND PROFITS

Readers of this review will perhaps expect me to say something in answer to Mr Macvane's criticisms, in the last number, on the doctrine of Distribution contained in the *Economics of Industry*.

I have come across most of his objections before, but never, I think, so ably and coherently stated; and I therefore desire to treat them with all respect. They cover, however, so wide a ground that a full answer here is out of the question. I propose, therefore to select what seem to me his two most striking points, and submit my own views with regard to them briefly, and without staying to indicate the respects in which they seem to me to differ from those of General Walker.

I regard the wages fund doctrine not as false, but as pretentious and misleading. As explained by careless writers, it is, I think, false. As explained by Cairnes and others, it is so far explained away that there is very little left in it to justify its title, and nothing at all which cannot be expressed better in other ways. Its form is objectionable, because, while not calling attention to the real differences which there are between markets for labour and markets for goods, it implies differences which do not exist; and, after all, it is but a fragment, isolated, discontinuous with the rest of economics, and a hindrance to a scientific conception of the whole subject.

The theory of Normal Wages given in the *Economics of Industry* is not in contradiction to the wages-fund doctrine as explained by Cairnes, but claims to expand and develop that doctrine, and to fit it into its proper place in the whole body of economic theory. But Cairnes himself could not get free from the misleading associations of that unfortunate phrase. In one case only does he attempt to apply his doctrine so carefully explained to a practical problem. That one case relates not to Normal Wages, but to Market Wages; and on that we join issue.

He argues (*Leading Principles*, pp. 203, 204) that if there is an increase of labour not accompanied by an increase of capital, and if the labour is of such a kind as to be employed in conjunction with fixed capital and raw material, some of the capital in the island will be diverted to this purpose, that therefore the wages fund will "contract as the supply of labour expands". In opposition to this, it is argued in the *Economics of Industry* (p. 205) that the new labour will instantly "increase the net produce of capital and labour, and therefore the Wages-and-profits Fund. It is true that employers will compete less keenly than before for the hire of labour, partly because there is more labour to be hired, and partly because it will answer their purpose to divert some of their means from hiring labourers to providing more auxiliary capital; and therefore the rate of wages will fall. But it is not certain, nor

823

even very probable, that the whole share which labour gets of the Wages-and-profits Fund will amount to less than before." Mr Macvane, as I understand, takes this as the crucial point of difference between us. He says (p. 27, note): "There can be no question that this result will follow in the course of time. But will it—as a matter of physical possibility, *can* it—happen at once? Must not the increase begin at the beginning of production?"

I answer: It can happen at once. The moment the labourer is set to work, more partly finished processes of production are finished than would otherwise have been the case, more processes just begun are carried a little further, more new processes are begun. Though the spinner cannot get as his wages to-day the carpet that will be made of the yarn which he spins to-day, there are pretty sure to be enough carpets in store to meet the increased demand due to the increased aggregate of wages, which in my belief there would be; and manufacturers and dealers, knowing that larger supplies than before are being made, will not hesitate to sell freely from their stocks. Of course, it is true that a sudden and unexpected increase of labour in a place which had no means of importing corn might cause a temporary scarcity of food. But Cairnes, of course, does not assume the increase to take this catastrophic form; and, indeed, if he did, what he says about fixed capital would be irrelevant, for in this extreme case there would be a temporary scarcity of food, whether much fixed capital were used or not. His argument shows that he regards the increase of labour as gradual, so that there is time for producers to divert their energies from the production of wage-capital to that of auxiliary capital.

I admit, however, that "the Wages-and-profits *Fund*" is not a good term. I adopted it as a catch-word, to indicate my opinion that wages and profits have their *normal* values determined by causes of the same general character. For that purpose, I retained the latter half of the old term wages-fund. But really what is meant is not a fund of stored up wealth sufficient to afford wages and profits for a fixed period, say a year: it is rather a flow of income to be distributed.

To avoid misapprehension, I should perhaps say that I

do not speak of wages as "paid out of the products of industry", in a sense in which this may be understood to mean that labour is not supported by capital. On this point I seem to be in entire agreement with Mr Macvane. The bargain between labour and capital is doubtless that the wage-receiver gets command over commodities in a form ready for immediate consumption, and in exchange carries his employer's goods a stage further towards being ready for immediate consumption. But, while this is true of most employees, those who finish the processes—e.g. those who put together and finish watches—give to their employers far more commodities in a form ready for immediate consumption than they take from them; and thus the balance is redressed. Taking one season of the year with another, so as to allow for seed and harvest time, workmen as a whole hand over to their employers more finished commodities than they receive as wages. But—to say nothing of machinery and factories, of ships and railroads—the houses loaned to workmen, and even the raw materials in various stages which will be worked up into commodities consumed by them, represent a far greater advance of capital to them than the equivalent of the advances which they make to the capitalist, even when they work for a month for him before getting any wages.

The other remark of Mr Macvane to which I desire to reply is one the force of which I think must have failed to catch; for, if I have understood him rightly, our difference is here a very real one. He says (p. 9): "If a good manager can create as much wealth as one hundred men when good managers are few, he can do the same when good managers are numerous. If his earnings are to be the addition his work makes to the produce of capital and labour, how can mere increase of the number of men capable of thus adding to the produce of capital and labor diminish his earnings? Mr Marshall, in accounting for the decline, cites as analogous the decline in the wages of skilled labour as the number possessing the skill increases. But there is this fundamental difference between the two cases, which renders analogy between them impossible for the purpose in hand. Skilled labour has specific products of its own, which fall in value as

825

the supply of them is increased. But management has no distinct products of its own. All production needs management, and all products cannot fall in value." Can Mr Macvane mean that every increase in the output of a business must cause a proportionate increase in its exchange value? His words seem to imply this, but I prefer to suppose that I have misunderstood him. So I will merely restate my own position.

[a]It is well known that great economies have been introduced into many branches of iron manufacture by diminishing the number of times which the metal is heated in passing from pig iron to its final form. Suppose an iron manufacturer with a capital of £50,000 to be getting in normal times a net profit of £4000 a year, £1500 of which we may regard as his earnings of management. We assume that so far he has been working in the same way as his neighbours, and showing an amount of ability which, though great, is no more than the normal or average ability of the people who fill such exceptionally difficult posts. That is, we assume that £1500 a year is the normal earnings for the kind of work he has been doing. But, as time goes on, he thinks out a way of dispensing with one of the heatings that have hitherto been customary; and in consequence, without increasing his expenses, he is able to increase his annual output by things which can be sold for £2000 net. And, so long as he can sell his wares at the old price, his earnings of management will be £2000 a year above the average. His neighbours, however, will copy his plan; and perhaps, for a while, they will all make more than average profits. But before long competition will increase the supply and lower the price of their wares, until the profits of the business are such as to give only normal earnings of management as before; for no one could get extra high wages for making eggs stand on their ends after Columbus's plan had become public property. As soon as any plan of manufacturing is so far reduced

---

a. The first eight sentences of this paragraph were incorporated in the *Principles* without substantial change (see Book VI, chapter vii, § 1, pages 597–8 in vol. 1 of the present edition).

to routine that it no longer requires exceptional ability, those who follow the method add much less to the efficiency of production than they would have done if they had had to think out the method themselves. The production is as great as it would have been; but more of it is due to knowledge which is the common property of the world, and less of it is due to the comparatively commonplace men who are able to follow in the now well-beaten track. Putting aside the gains of speculation, which require to some extent a separate treatment, it remains true that competition tends to secure to each ordinary employer earnings of management equal to what his work adds to the efficiency of production, so much and no more. Inventors and pioneers are seldom able to retain for many years, even if they ever get it, the full value of the addition they make to the efficiency of production. It must, however, be admitted that occasionally a man will complete improvements which others have nearly worked out, and by patenting the last little link which he has added, get more than his deserts.

As to the question what part of his profits should be called rent, I wish to say that I do not attach great importance to this method of speaking in spite of the great support which it has from the traditions of Senior and of many foreign economists from the time of Storch and Mangoldt (see, for instance, Mataja's *Unternehmergewinn* chap. 1, §c). I regard it only as an analogy, and, moreover, as one which, if pressed too far, is likely to be misleading. In particular, it is difficult to know how much the success of any business man is to be ascribed to his good fortune in getting on work suited to him, and ought therefore to be balanced against the failures of others, who turn out to have selected a wrong occupation for their faculties. When a fisherman makes a good haul, we do not count it as rent: we set it off against the bad haul, and expect him to get in the long run earnings for his labour and interest on his capital, but nothing more; but this brings us to the fringe of a difficult set of problems, which could not be adequately discussed here.

ALFRED MARSHALL

APPENDIX K

CERTAIN KINDS OF SURPLUS

PAGE 830

a. Except where otherwise stated the wording of this Appendix dates substantially from the 3rd edition.

The subject-matter of Appendix K dates from the 3rd edition (pp. 604–8) where it was placed in §6 of Book VI, chapter II. In the 4th edition the discussion of different kinds of surplus was placed at the end of the Note on the Doctrine of the Wages Fund. (Book VI, chapter II, §13, pp. 624–7.)

In the 5th edition it became Appendix K, "Certain Kinds of Surplus".

b. This paragraph dates from the 4th ed. (p. 624), except that the clause "and it should be avoided by the general reader" coming after the clause "it has little practical bearing" in the 4th ed. was deleted from the 6th ed.

The corresponding paragraph in the 3rd ed. (p. 604) ran as follows:

This part of the argument may be seen from another side in a study of the relations in which the different kinds of surpluses that we have considered at various stages of our inquiry stand to the national dividend and to one another. The argument of this section is however difficult, and almost exclusively of academic interest; and it should be omitted by the general reader.

c. This marginal summary dates from the 4th ed. (pp. 624–5) where it replaced the following summary in the 3rd ed. (p. 604): "The earnings of the several agents of production, according to their marginal services, exhaust the national dividend."

PAGE 831

a. So since the 5th ed. (p. 381 n.) where this footnote replaced the following footnote dating from the 3rd ed.:

This point was emphasized by Gossen and Jevons; and among the many interesting American and Austrian writings on it, special reference may be made to Prof. Clark's *Surplus Gains of Labour*. See also above, Book IV, ch. I.

PAGE 832

a. The reference to "this chapter" here and in the first line of the third paragraph of this section applies to Book VI, chapter II in Vol. I of the present edition.

b. This sentence was inserted in the 4th ed. (pp. 626–7).

c. The following paragraph which preceded the paragraph beginning with the words "All appliances of production", in the 3rd ed. (p. 608 n.) was deleted from the 4th ed.:

> The argument again is given at some length above, Book V, ch. VIII–X, and in the article *On Rent* in reply to the Duke of Argyll already referred to; and some parts of it will be further developed below in ch. IX, X: moreover its substance has much in common with that near the end of the last chapter. But yet it relates to a matter on which misunderstandings are so frequent, that it should perhaps be set out clearly here.

A further reference to the Duke of Argyll is reproduced in editorial note **b** to page 535 in vol. I of the present edition. "Ch. IX & X" apply to Book VI, chapters IX and X, and "the end of the last chapter" to Book VI, chapter I in vol. I of the present edition. Marshall's article "On Rent" is reprinted in the Editorial Appendix to Book V, chapters VIII–X (pp. 492–512 above).

APPENDIX L

RICARDO'S DOCTRINE AS TO TAXES AND IMPROVEMENTS IN AGRICULTURE

PAGE 833

a. Except where otherwise stated the wording of this Appendix dates substantially from the 1st edition, though the marginal summaries were added in the 3rd edition.

In the 1st edition the subject-matter of this Appendix was placed at the end of chapter X of Book VII in a "Note on Ricardo's Doctrines as to the Incidence of Taxes and the Influence of Improvements in Agriculture".

In the 2nd to the 4th editions this Note was placed at the end of chapter IX of Book VI.

In the 5th edition it became Appendix L, "Ricardo's Doctrine as to Taxes and Improvements in Agriculture".

PAGE 835

a. This clause and the reference in parentheses were inserted in the 2nd ed. (p. 676).

b. This footnote was inserted in the 3rd ed. (p. 718 n.).

PAGE 837

a. In the 1st ed. (p. 676) Marshall wrote "qualities" here; but in the 3rd ed. (p. 720), probably as the result of a printer's error, this word was changed to read "quantities", and the word retained this latter form down to and including the 8th edition. The sense, however, clearly requires the word "qualities", and the original word has been reinstated in vol. 1 of the present edition.

b. This paragraph was inserted in the 2nd ed. (p. 679).

MATHEMATICAL APPENDIX

PAGE 838

a. In the first four editions there was an "Appendix of Mathematical Notes", which was placed at the end of the text. In the 5th and subsequent editions this was entitled "Mathematical Appendix", and was placed at the end of the other appendices.

In the 1st edition the Mathematical Notes were numbered I–XXVI; but in the 2nd edition, where there was some rearrangement of the order of the Notes, one new Note was added (the Note dealing with Edgeworth's barter curves—Note XII, *bis* in vol. 1 of the present edition) while two of the previous Notes were each appended to and given the same number as one of the other Notes, with the designation *bis*. Thus from the 2nd edition onwards the Notes were numbered I–XXIV. No new Notes were added after the 2nd edition, though Note XIV in vol. 1 of the present edition (Note XXV in the 1st edition) was expanded, from a single paragraph and two lines of equations, to cover six pages in the 3rd edition.

Note I   **b.** The text of Note I dates in its present form from the 4th edition (p. 789), where the paragraph constituting this Note replaced the following paragraph dating from the 1st edition (p. 737):

The law of diminution of marginal utility may be expressed thus:—If u be the total utility of an amount x of a commodity to a given person at a given time, then $\dfrac{du}{dx}$ measures its marginal utility; and, subject to the qualifications mentioned in the text, $\dfrac{d^2u}{dx^2}$ is always negative.

c. Subject to the exceptions noted below, the text of Note II dates from the 1st edition (pp. 737–8). Note II

d. The words "degree of" before the word "utility" were inserted in the 4th ed. (p. 789).

PAGE 839

a. So since the 4th ed. (p. 790) where the three following opening clauses of this sentence dating from the 1st ed. (p. 738) were omitted: "Treating u as variable, that is to say, allowing for possible variations in the person's liking for the commodity in question, we may regard $\dfrac{dp}{dx}$ ...etc."

b. The text of Note III dates from the 1st edition (pp. 738–40), apart from two changes noted below. Note III

c. So since the 2nd ed. (p. 750) where this expression replaced the following expression in the 1st ed. (p. 738): "$-\dfrac{y}{x}\dfrac{dx}{dy}$".

d. The words "of course", before the words "a rectangular hyperbola" in the 1st ed. (p. 739), were deleted from the 2nd ed.

PAGE 840

a. Subject to certain alterations noted below the text of Note IV dates from the 1st edition (p. 740). Note IV

b. This line was inserted in the 2nd ed. (p. 752).

PAGE 841

a. So since the 5th ed. (p. 841) where this paragraph replaced the following paragraph dating from the 1st ed. (p. 740):

The rate of increase would be constant for all points of the curve if NT were constant and always $= a$, that is, if $-x\dfrac{dy}{dx} = a$ for all values of x; that is, if the equation to the curve were $y = -a \log x$.

b. The first paragraph of Note V dates from the 2nd edition (p. 752) except for the last sentence but one, which is a modification of a sentence dating from the 1st ed.

c. So since the 2nd ed. where this sentence replaced the following sentence in the 1st ed. (p. 737):

Let h be a pleasure of which the probability is p, and which will occur, if at all, at time t; let r be the rate of interest per unit which must be added to present pleasures before comparing them to future, and let $R = 1 + r$; then the present value of the pleasure is phR^{-t}.

d. This paragraph dates substantially from the 1st ed. (p. 737).

e. The text of Note VI dates substantially from the 1st edition (pp. 740–1) except for the last sentence of the fourth paragraph.)

f. From the 1st to the 4th editions this expression read "$f(x)$", but in the 5th ed., by a printer's error this was changed to read "$f(z)$", and so it remained down to and including the 8th edition. The correct reading, "$f(x)$" has been restored in vol. 1 of the present edition.

PAGE 842

a. The first three sentences of this paragraph were inserted here, partly in response to a letter from John Neville Keynes who was reading the proofs of Marshall's 1st edition of the *Principles* and asked him to consider the possible effects on consumer's surplus of a transfer of expenditure to other commodities. Marshall's reply to Keynes (26 November 1889) is reproduced in editorial note **a** to page 128 of vol. 1 in the present edition.

b. So since the 5th ed. (p. 842) where the word "surplus" in this and the next sentence replaced the word "rent" dating from the 1st ed. (p. 740).

c. So since the 3rd ed. (p. 795) where, throughout this paragraph, the word "tea" replaced the earlier word "coals", dating from the 1st ed. (p. 740).

d. It will be observed that Marshall omitted to alter the word "rent" to read "surplus" in this sentence.

e. This concluding sentence was inserted in the 3rd ed. (p. 795).

f. The earlier part of Note VII down to the expression "$\Sigma \int_b^a f(x)dx$." dates substantially from the 1st edition (p. 741), while the latter part of the Note was inserted in the 3rd edition (p. 795).

g. In the 3rd ed. the word "income" replaced the word "wealth" used in the earlier editions.

h. So since the 3rd ed. (p. 795), where the remainder of this Note replaced the following paragraph dating from the 1st ed. (p. 741):

Of course all but a few members of the series b_1, b_2 ... are equal to zero. It must be remembered that this estimate is likely to omit all those elements of wealth which are not habitually sold, and which have therefore no demand-curve. Their utility must be allowed for separately.

i. With the exception of one sentence the text of Note VIII dates Note VIII from the 1st edition (p. 741).

j. So since the 6th ed. (p. 842) where this sentence replaced the following sentence dating from the 1st ed. (p. 741):

Let a be the income sufficient to purchase the necessaries of life, so defined that the total pleasure derived from life with an income less than a is a negative quantity; then

our equation becomes $y = K \log \dfrac{x}{a}$.

PAGE 843

a. With the exception of two lines which were altered in the 3rd Note IX ed. the text of Note IX dates from the 1st edition (pp. 741–2).

b. So since the 3rd ed. (p. 796) where this and the next line replaced the following lines dating from the 1st ed. (p. 742):

$$\phi(x) + \tfrac{1}{2}p(1-p)^2 \, \phi''\{x + \theta(1-p) \, y\} + \tfrac{1}{2}p^2(1-p) \, \phi''(x + \Theta p y);$$

and, since $\phi''(x)$ is negative for all values of x, this is less than $\phi(x)$.

c. The text of Note X dates substantially from the 1st edition Note X (p. 742).

d. The word "always" before the word "positive" in the 1st ed. was deleted from the 2nd ed.

e. The text of Note XI dates mainly from the 1st edition (p. 742), Note XI though certain changes and additions were made in the 3rd and 7th editions.

f. The first two sentences of this Note date in their present form (with one exception) from the 3rd ed. (pp. 796–7), where they replaced the following sentence dating from the 1st ed. (p. 742):

If $f(t)$ be the average length of the giraffe's neck at time t, then the supposition in the passage to which this note refers, is that the rate of increase of the average neck increases (within certain limits) with every increase in the length of the neck, and that therefore $f''(t)$ is positive.

The illustration of the giraffe's neck in the foregoing sentence referred to three sentences in a footnote in the 1st ed. (Book IV, ch. VIII, §5, p. 307 n.), which were deleted from the 3rd ed., in which Marshall mentioned the possibility that "The giraffe whose long neck enables it to survive by feeding on the shoots of trees when the grass is dried up, may possibly lengthen its neck yet further by constantly stretching it, and thus further increase its power of surviving; but this effect is not purposely sought".

See editorial note **f** to page 247 of vol. I in the present edition.

g. The following clause in the 3rd ed. (p. 796) after the clause ending with the word "sport" was deleted from the 6th ed.: "or (as a minority of biologists still think) partly from the inherited effects of use."

PAGE 844

a. The two concluding sentences of this Note were inserted in the 7th ed. (p. 844).

Note XII   **b.** The text of Note XII dates from the 1st edition (p. 743).

Note XII *bis*   **c.** Except for one change made in the 3rd edition the text of Note XII *bis* dates substantially from the 2nd edition (pp. 755–6).

d. In the 8th edition "pp. 414–6"; emended in vol. I of the present edition to give the correct reference.

PAGE 845

a. In the 3rd ed. (p. 798) this first main clause replaced the following clause in the 2nd ed. (p. 756):

If the marginal utility of nuts be constant for A and also for B,

$$\frac{d^2U}{dy^2} = 0 = \frac{d^2V}{dy^2};$$

b. The article by Mr Berry, referred to here, arose out of a controversy between Marshall and Edgeworth over the theory of barter. See the Editorial Appendix to Appendix F—Barter.

c. Except for one change, noted below, the text of Note XIII   Note XIII
dates from the 1st edition (pp. 748–9).

PAGE 846

a. So since the 3rd ed. (p. 759) where the symbol "ω'" replaced
"$\dfrac{\omega'}{1}$", dating from the 1st ed. (p. 749).

b. Except for parts of the first paragraph and the two lines of   Note XIV
equations immediately following it, and two minor changes in latter parts of the Note, the text of Note XIV dates wholly from the 3rd edition (pp. 799–805).

c. So since the 3rd ed. (p. 799) where this opening paragraph with the accompanying equations replaced the following paragraph and equations dating from the 1st ed. (p. 749):

If $\alpha, \alpha', \alpha''\ldots$ be the several amounts of different kinds of labour, as for instance, wood cutting, stone carrying, earth digging, &c., that would be used in building the house on any given plan; and β, β', β'', &c., the several amounts of accommodation of different kinds which the house would afford on these several plans. Then $V, \beta, \beta', \beta''$ are all functions of $\alpha, \alpha', \alpha''\ldots$, and H being a function of $\beta, \beta', \beta''\ldots$ is a function also of $\alpha, \alpha', \alpha''\ldots$. We have then

$$\frac{dV}{d\alpha} = \frac{dH}{d\beta}\frac{d\beta}{d\alpha} = \frac{dH}{d\beta'}\frac{d\beta'}{d\alpha} = \frac{dH}{d\beta''}\frac{d\beta''}{d\alpha} = -$$

$$\frac{dV}{d\alpha'} = \frac{dH}{d\beta}\frac{d\beta}{d\alpha'} = \frac{dH}{d\beta'}\frac{d\beta'}{d\alpha'} = \frac{dH}{d\beta''}\frac{d\beta''}{d\alpha'} = \ldots.$$

In the 1st ed. (p. 749) the foregoing passage constituted the whole of Mathematical Note XXV.

In the 2nd ed. (Note XIV, p. 757) this paragraph with the accompanying equations was retained, but the following second paragraph which was added there was deleted (except for the reference to Prof. Edgeworth) from the 3rd ed.:

These results are in the form most convenient for the general purposes of economics; but they may all be regarded as mathematically contained in the statement that $H - V$ is to be made a maximum. If the series $\alpha, \alpha', \alpha''\ldots$ be extended

835

so as to include investments in land, machinery &c., we obtain general equations representing the causes that govern the investment of capital and effort in any undertaking. Compare Note (f) to Prof. Edgeworth's brilliant Address to the British Association in 1890.

PAGE 847

a. The words "with which we shall be much occupied..." dating from the 3rd ed. (p. 800) have been altered in vol. 1 of the present edition to read: "with which we were much occupied...."

b. The following paragraph, which in the 3rd ed. (p. 800) immediately succeeded the paragraph ending with the words "the theory of distribution" and preceded the paragraph beginning with the words "Let us then suppose a master builder...etc.", was deleted from the 5th ed.:

There will be an advantage in developing it with some fulness here; although to do so will partially anticipate later discussions, especially those in the sixth and seventh chapters of Book V, and in the first two chapters of Book VI: and indeed its full significance will hardly be seen until it is read in connection with the last-named chapters.

It may be observed that the reference in the foregoing paragraph to "later discussions" was out of place here, since the paragraph of which these words formed part was placed in the "Appendix of Mathematical Notes" at the end of the volume.

PAGE 848

a. The words "the money equivalent of" were inserted in the 6th ed. (p. 841), between the the word "represent" and the word "his".

PAGE 849

a. In the 8th edition "V. xi. 1 and VI. i. 8"; emended in vol. 1 of the present edition to give the correct references.

b. So since the 4th ed. (p. 800) where the remaining clauses of this sentence replaced the following clause in the 3rd ed. (p. 802): "but one minor difficulty may be noticed here."

See also the comment at the end of editorial note **b** above, to page 847.

PAGE 850

a. In the 8th edition "p. 417"; emended in vol. 1 of the present edition to give the correct reference.

836

PAGE 852

a. Except for the first paragraph, which was inserted in the 2nd ed., the text of Note XIV *bis* dates, with a few subsequent changes in detail, from the 1st edition (p. 743). Note XIV *bis*

b. This paragraph dates from the 2nd ed. (pp. 757–8), apart from the insertion in the 6th ed. (p. 852) of the word "representative" before the word "business" in the fifth line of the paragraph.

c. So since the 2nd ed. (p. 758) where this equation replaced the following equation in the 1st ed. (p. 743):

$$y = \Phi(x) = \phi_1(m_1 x) + \phi_2(m_2 x) + \ldots \equiv \Sigma\{\phi(mx)\}.$$

d. So since the 2nd ed. where this equation replaced the following equation in the 1st ed.:

$$y = F(x) - \{\Phi(x) - \phi_r(m_r x)\}.$$

e. So since the 2nd ed. where this equation replaced the following equation in the 1st ed.:

$$\eta = f_r(\xi) = \frac{1}{m_r}\left[F\left(\frac{1}{m_r}\xi\right) - \left\{\Phi\left(\frac{1}{m_r}\xi\right) - \phi_r(\xi)\right\}\right].$$

PAGE 853

a. The text of Note XV dates from the 1st edition (pp. 743–4). Notes XV–XXI

b. The text of Note XVI dates from the 1st edition (pp. 744).

PAGE 854

a. The text of Note XVII dates from the 1st edition (p. 744).

b. The text of Note XVIII dates from the 1st edition (p. 745).

c. The text of Note XIX dates from the 1st edition (p. 745).

d. The text of Note XX dates from the 1st edition (p. 745).

PAGE 855

a. The text of Note XXI dates from the 1st edition (pp. 745–6) with one exception noted below.

b. So since the 6th ed. (p. 855) where the concluding clauses of this sentence replaced the following clauses dating from the 1st ed. (p. 745): "so that the total number of factors of production is $\Sigma_1{}^n a_r$: let this $= m$."

PAGE 856

Note XXII   **a.** The text of Note XXII dates from the 1st edition (p. 746).

Note XXIII   **b.** The text of Note XXIII dates substantially from the 1st edition (pp. 746–7).

Note XXIII *bis*   **c.** The text of Note XXIII *bis* dates substantially from the 1st edition (pp. 747–8).

PAGE 857

a. So since the 4th ed. (p. 808) where the word "surplus" replaced the word "rent" in the earlier editions.

PAGE 858

Note XXIV   **a.** The text of Note XXIV dates, with some subsequent modification noted below, from the 1st edition (pp. 749–50).

b. So since the 3rd ed. (p. 811) where the words "cost of his rearing and training" replaced the words "cost of his production" dating from the 1st ed. (p. 749).

c. So since the 2nd ed. (p. 764) where this equation replaced the following equation dating from the 1st ed. (p. 750):

$$\int_T^{-T'} R^{-t}\left(\frac{dx}{dt} - \frac{dy}{dt}\right) dt = 0;$$

In the 5th to the 8th editions the amended integral $\int_{-T'}^{T}$ was incorrectly printed as $\int_{-T}^{T}$. The correct version of this integral, as it stood in the 2nd to the 4th editions has been restored in vol. 1 of the present edition.

d. The following concluding clause of this sentence in the 1st ed. (p. 750) was deleted from the 2nd ed.: "which is in fact the assumption implicitly made by many writers on the subject".

838

e. So since the 4th ed. (p. 809), where this paragraph replaced the following concluding paragraph dating from the 1st ed.:

In saying that Δx is the probable amount of his production in time Δt, we have put shortly what may be more accurately expressed thus:—let p_1, $p_2 \ldots$, be the chances that in time Δt he will produce elements of wealth $\Delta_1 x$, $\Delta_2 x \ldots$, where $p_1 + p_2 + \ldots$ cannot exceed unity: then

$$\Delta x = p_1 \Delta_1 x + p_2 \Delta_2 x + \ldots.$$

Management (*cont.*)

corresponds to amount of work done, I: 613–14; relation between size of business and, II: 659–61; and rent, II: 672–5

gross, I: 313, 343, 596, 602, 607, 620, 621, II: 651; element of insurance against personal risks in, II: 672

net, I: 313, 377, 596, II: 650

Mangoldt, H. von, on rent and profits, I: 432 n., II: 462, 827

Manufacture, present meaning of term, I: 278

"Many in the One and the One in the Many", I: 777, II: 173, 410, 492, 775; meaning of the phrase, II: 775

Margin, notion of, I: xvi, II: 53, 59–60; of cultivation, I: 154–5, 427, 432–4, 468, 630, 633 n., II: 393 n.. 434, 447, 448, 454–5, 459, 468; of building, I: 168, 447–9; of profitableness, I: 356, 359, (for different methods of business organization) I: 605, 630; of indifference, I: 405–6, II: 428, 579; of production, I: 406–7, 805, II: 473, 503, 505, 579 n.; of profitable expenditure, I: 432, II: 448

Marginal, Marshall's adoption of term, I: x, 93 n., II: 8, 37

increment, I: x, 376 n., II: 239

costs, I: xvi, II: 53, 59, 503, and uses, in relation to values, I: 403–12, 413–24, 428, II: 52, 431 n., 433, 445–6, 483; true long-period, as shown by a representative firm, I: 342–3, 396, 460, 497, II: 69–70, 346; in relation to agricultural values, I: 425–39, 447, 534–6, 832, II: 434–7, 445–8, 455–60, 497–8, 505–6, 510–12; in relation to urban values, I: 440–54

demand price, supply price, *see* Demand; Supply

disutility of labour, I: 141, II: 269, 270

dose, I: 154–72, II: 448

production, I: 372–3, 427–8, 805, II: 449, 452, 505, 506

net product, of labour, I: 409 n.–10 n., 515–18, 667, 705 n., 706 n., 849, II: 448, 580–8; marketing of, may cause a fall in the price of the whole product, I: 517 n., 849–50,

II: 585 n.–6 n.; of capital, I: 519–21, II: 446

shepherd, I: 515–18, II: 583–8

utility, *see* Utility; of money, *see* Money

capital, II: 448

Market(s), description of a perfect, I: 112, realistic description of, II: 73 n.; illustration of consumers' surplus in relation to a, I: 128–32; for labour, its peculiarities, I: 141 n., 335–6, 559–79, 709–10, II: 354; large and open (general), I: 286–7, 374, 458–9, 501, 849–50, II: 412, 526–7; special (particular), I: 287, 458–9, 501, 849, II: 412, 527–8; scope of, I: 323–30; definitions of a, I: 324–5, II: 411–12; illustration of extent of various, I: 325–6; highly organized, I: 326–7; wholesale and retail, I: 328; narrowly confined, I: 329; in relation to time and space, I: 330, II: 329, 378–9; for rare or unique things, I: 332, II: 353 n.; bargaining in a local, as illustration of temporary equilibrium of demand and supply, I: 332–4, 496, II: 353–4, 537; certain assumptions regarding the foregoing illustration, I: 334–6; in times of depression, a producer will sell surplus goods outside his own, I: 458; for short loans, I: 593; distant, production of goods for, has influenced industrial development, I: 671–2; uncertainties of bargaining in, when barter is used, I: 791–3; curves, II: 64–5, 364, 809

values, I: vii, 332–5, 349, 369, 372, 378, 496–7, II: 364, 384, 385–6, 627; and cost of production and of reproduction, I: 401–2, II: 364–5

"spoiling the market", manufacturers' aversion from, resembles labourers' unwillingness to sell their labour cheaply, I: 141 n.; producers' fear of (in time of depression), I: 374, 498, 849, II: 389, 495, 539; attitude to, of trade morality, I: 375; fear of, accelerates causes affecting movements of short-period supply price, I: 377, II: 392, 528; specialist manufacturers' fear of, I: